MW01672219

# THE BEATLES

## ANTHOLOGY

CHRONICLE BOOKS
San Francisco

Copyright © Apple Corps Ltd. 2000
All rights reserved. No part of this publication may be reproduced in any form
without written permission from the publisher.

"Apple", the Apple logo, "Beatles" and "The Beatles" (in both cases with and without
the stylised letter "T") are all trademarks of Apple Corps Ltd.
The Chronicle Books logo and "Chronicle Books" are trademarks of Chronicle Books LLC.

Portions of the text originally appeared in 'The Playboy Interview: John Lennon and Yoko Ono'
*Playboy* Magazine (January 1981). Copyright © 1980 by *Playboy*. Reprinted by permission.
All rights reserved. Interview by David Sheff.

Printed in Hong Kong

Library of Congress Cataloging-in-Publication Data available.

ISBN 0-8118-2684-8

Distributed in Canada by Raincoast Books,
9050 Shaughnessy Street, Vancouver, BC V6P 6E5

1 3 5 7 9 10 8 6 4 2

Chronicle Books LLC
85 Second Street, San Francisco, CA 94105
www.chroniclebooks.com

First Edition published 2000.

Cover Painting: Klaus Voormann and Alfons Kiefer

*Editorial Direction:*
GENESIS PUBLICATIONS, GUILDFORD

*Editorial Team:*
BRIAN ROYLANCE
JULIAN QUANCE
OLIVER CRASKE
ROMAN MILISIC

*Consulting Editor:*
DEREK TAYLOR

*Art Direction:*
DAVID COSTA, *Wherefore* ART?, LONDON

*Design:*
NICKY PAGE
DAN EINZIG
FIONA ANDREANELLI
SIAN RANCE
RACHEL GODFREY

*Clearances:*
BRYONY CRANSTOUN
JEREMY NEECH

*Executive Producer:*
NEIL ASPINALL

# EDITORIAL NOTE

Many books have been written about The Beatles, but this is their own permanent written record of events up until 1970.

The text attributed to Paul McCartney, George Harrison and Ringo Starr, and the supplementary text by Neil Aspinall, Sir George Martin and Derek Taylor, comes in part from the interviews from which the television and video programmes *The Beatles Anthology* were made, and includes substantial material which was not included in either. Further major interviews were conducted with Paul, George and Ringo specifically for this book.

The text attributed to John Lennon comes from an enormous wealth of worldwide sources researched over several years (again, specifically for this book), including print and broadcast media, and public and private archives. These sources are credited at the back of this volume. The text has been arranged to follow the book's chronological structure and to maintain the pace of the narrative. To allow the reader to place John's quotes in their correct historical perspective, each quotation is suffixed by the date it was spoken, written or first published. The year of the quotation is represented by the last two digits only, such that, for example, 1970 is represented by $^{70}$. The date generally applies to all text preceding it until another date is reached.

In a very small number of cases it has not been possible to date a quotation accurately (even though it contains John's words); in this event, the words, but no date, are included.

For additional historical context, a small number of original quotations by Paul, George, Ringo and others from the period up to 1970 have also been included. These have also been dated using the two-digit year suffix, as with John's words.

The photographs, documents and memorabilia reproduced come from a wide variety of sources. George Harrison, Paul McCartney and Ringo Starr have each granted access to their private archives during the compilation of this volume. Furthermore, unrestricted access was granted to the photographic and documentary archives of Apple, as well as the archives of EMI. This is in addition to the work of the other photographers and agencies represented, who are also credited at the back of this volume, where the reader will find, too, selected captions which clarify the content of certain photographs and other illustrations.

This book has been prepared for publication by the editorial team at Genesis Publications for Apple, with the co-operation of the late Derek Taylor who consulted on the book up until his death in 1997.

# A TREASURY OF ART and POETRY

This book contains only the work of J.W. Lennon, with additional work by J.W. Lennon, and a helping hand given by J.W. Lennon, not forgetting J.W. Lennon.
Who is this J.W. Lennon?
Here are some remark by a few famous News papers.

"A good book better" — J.W. Lennon of the Daily Howl
"This book has many good uses and should go down well" — The Sanitory Journal
"Yes" — FRED Emney Fan Club Magazine
"(Belch!)" — Garston Herald.

"And then there's the one about the Bishop and the actress....."

# JOHN LENNON

## WHAT CAN I TELL YOU ABOUT MYSELF WHICH YOU HAVE NOT ALREADY FOUND OUT FROM THOSE WHO DO NOT LIE?

I wear glasses. Being born on 9th October 1940, I wasn't the first Beatle to happen. Ringo, being born on 7th July 1940, was. Although he didn't happen as a Beatle until much later than the rest of us, having played with his beard at Butlins and things before realising where his awful destiny lay.

Ninety per cent of the people on this planet, especially in the West, were born out of a bottle of whisky on a Saturday night, and there was no intent to have children. Ninety per cent of us were accidents – I don't know anybody who has planned a child. All of us were Saturday-night specials.[80]

My mother was a housewife, I suppose. She was a comedienne and a singer. Not professional, but she used to get up in pubs and things like that. She had a good voice. She could do Kay Starr. She used to do this little tune when I was just a one- or two-year-old. The tune was from the Disney movie – 'Want to know a secret? Promise not to tell. You are standing by a wishing well.'[80]

My mother and father split when I was four and I lived with an auntie, Mimi.[71]

Mimi told me my parents had fallen out of love. She never said anything directly against my father and mother. I soon forgot my father. It was like he was dead. But I did see my mother now and again and my feeling never died off for her. I often thought about her, though I'd never realised for a long time that she was living no more than five or ten miles away.[67]

There were five women that were my family. Five strong, intelligent, beautiful women; five sisters. One happened to be my mother. My mother just couldn't deal with life. She was the youngest and she couldn't cope with me and I ended up living with her elder sister.

Those women were fantastic. One day I might do a kind of *Forsyte Saga* about them, because they dominated the situation in the family.[80]

The men were invisible. I was always with the women. I always heard them talk about men and talk about life, and they always knew what was going on. The men never ever knew. That was my first feminist education.[80]

The worst pain is that of not being wanted, of realising your parents do not need you in the way you need them. When I was a child I experienced moments of not wanting to see the ugliness, not wanting to see not being wanted. This lack of love went into my eyes and into my mind.

I was never really wanted. The only reason I am a star is because of my repression. Nothing would have driven me through all that if I was 'normal'.[71]

Sometimes I was relieved to have no parents. Most of my friends' relations bore little resemblance to humanity. Their heads were filled with petty-cash bourgeois fears. Mine was full of my own ideas! Life was spent entertaining myself, whilst secretly waiting to find someone to communicate with. Most people were dead. A few were half-dead. It didn't take much to amuse them.[78]

Most people never get out of it. Some people cannot see that their parents are still torturing them, even when they are in their forties and fifties. They still have that stranglehold over them, their thoughts and their minds. I never had that fear of, and adulation for, parents.[80]

Penny Lane is a suburban district where I lived with my mother and father (although my father was a sailor, always at sea), and my grandfather. I lived on a street called Newcastle Road.[80]

That's the first *place* I remember. It's a good way to start – red brick; front room never used, always curtains drawn, picture of a horse and carriage on the wall. There were only three bedrooms upstairs, one on the front of the street, one in the back, and one teeny little room in the middle.[79]

After I left Penny Lane, I moved in with my auntie, who lived in the suburbs in a nice semi-detached place [251 Menlove Avenue, Woolton] with a small garden and doctors and lawyers and that ilk living around, not the poor, slummy image that was projected. I was a nice clean-cut suburban boy, and in the class system that was about a half a niche higher-class than Paul, George and Ringo who lived in council houses. We owned our own house, had our own garden; they didn't have anything like that. So I was a bit of a fruit compared to them, in a way. Ringo was the only real city kid.[80] I think he came out of the lousiest area. He doesn't care, he probably had more fun there.[64]

The first *thing* I remember is a nightmare.[79]

I dream in colour, and it's always very surreal. My dream world is complete Hieronymus Bosch and Dali. I love it, I look forward to it every night.[74]

One recurrent dream, all through my life, was the flying bit. I'd always fly in time of danger. I remember it as a child, flying around, like swimming in the air. I'd be swimming round where I lived or somewhere I knew very well usually. The other times in dreams I remember are nightmarish, where there'd be a giant horse or something and whenever it would get near to a danger point I would fly away. I used to translate it to myself, when I used to dream it in Liverpool, that it was that I wanted to get away from the place.[71]

Some of my most vivid dreams were about me being in a plane, flying over a certain part of Liverpool. It was when I was at school. The plane used to fly over time and time again, going higher and higher.

One really big one was about thousands of half-crowns all around me. And finding lots of money in old houses – as much of the stuff as I could carry. I used to put it in my pockets and in my hands and in sacks, and I could still never carry as much as I wanted. I must have had ambition without realising it – a subconscious urge to get above people or out of a rut.[66]

You dream your way out until you actually, physically get out of it. I got out.[68]

I have exactly the same feeling anybody does about their home town. I have met people who don't like their home town. Probably because they've had a lousy time. I had a happy, healthy childhood in Liverpool and I like it. It doesn't stop you living somewhere else or going somewhere else, it's still my home town.[64]

Liverpool is where the Irish came when they ran out of potatoes, and it's where black people were left or worked as slaves or whatever. We were a great amount of Irish descent and blacks and Chinamen, all sorts.

It was going poor, a very poor city, and tough. But people have a sense of humour because they are in so much pain, so they are always cracking jokes. They are very witty.[70] And we talk through our noses. I suppose it's adenoids.[64]

We were a port, the second biggest in England. The North is where the money was made in the 1800s. That was where all the brass and heavy people were, and that's where the despised people were. We were the ones that were looked down upon as animals by the Southerners, the Londoners.[70]

There were two famous houses [in Woolton]. One was owned by Gladstone – a reformatory for boys, which I could see out my window. And Strawberry Field, just around the corner from that, an old Victorian house converted for Salvation Army orphans. (Apparently, it used to be a farm that made strawberries.) As a kid I used to go to their garden parties with my friends Ivan, Nigel and Pete. We'd all go up there and hang out and sell lemonade bottles. We always had fun at Strawberry Field.[80]

John and Julia

I was hip in kindergarten. I was different from others. I was different all my life. It's not a case of 'then he took acid and woke up', or 'then he had a marijuana joint and woke up'. Everything is as important as everything else. My influences are tremendous, from Lewis Carroll to Oscar Wilde to tough little kids that used to live near me who ended up in prison. It's that same problem I had when I was five: 'There is something wrong with me because I seem to see things other people don't see.'[80]

I was always a homebody; I think that a lot of musicians are – you write and you play in the house. When I was wanting to be a painter when I was younger, or write poetry, it was always in the house.[80]

I spent a lot of time reading. Hanging around the home never bothered me. I enjoy it. I love it.[80] I thought it was because I was an only child. Although I had half-sisters, I lived alone. I always tripped out on my own or in books.[71]

I always had this dream of being the artist in a little cottage in a little road. My real thing is just to write a little poetry and do a few oils. It seemed like such a dream, living in a cottage and wandering in the trees.[69]

I was passionate about *Alice in Wonderland* and drew all the characters. I did poems in the style of 'Jabberwocky'. I used to love Alice, and *Just William*. I wrote my own William stories, with me doing all the things. *Wind in the Willows*, I loved. After I'd read a book, I'd re-live it all. That was one reason why I wanted to be the gang leader at school. I'd want them all to play games that I wanted to play, the ones I'd just been reading.[67]

I did fight all the way through Dovedale [primary school], winning by psychological means if ever anyone looked bigger than me. I threatened them in a strong enough way that I would beat them, so they thought I could.[67]

With the fact that I wasn't tied to parents I would infiltrate the other boys' minds. That was the gift I got, of not having parents. I cried a lot about not having them, but I also had the gift of awareness of not being something.[80]

I was shot at once for stealing apples. I used to go thieving with this kid. We used to ride on the bumpers of tram cars in Penny Lane and ride miles without paying. I'd be shitting myself all the time. I was so scared. I nearly fell off while riding on the bumpers.[67]

I was the kingpin of my age group. I learnt lots of dirty jokes very young; there was a girl who lived near who told me them.[67]

I wasn't taught anything about sex. I learnt it all from the bog walls. I knew everything when I was about eight. Everything had been shown, everybody had seen dirty pictures, everybody knew all the perversities and the naughty things that there were – you just found out. When we are free of our guilt and hypocrisy about it, sex will take its rightful place in society – just part of living.

Edinburgh is one of my favourite dreams. The Edinburgh Festival and the Tattoo in the castle. All the bands of the world's armies would come and march and play. The favourites were the Americans, because they swung like shit – apart from the Scots, who were really the favourites. I always remember feeling very emotional about it, especially at the end where they put all the lights out and there's just one guy playing the bagpipes, lit by a lone spotlight. Och aye.[79]

I was obviously musical from very early, and I wonder why nobody ever did anything about it – maybe because they couldn't afford it.[65]

[When I was young] I was travelling to Edinburgh on my own to see my auntie, and I played the mouth organ all the way up on the bus. The driver liked it and told me to meet him at a place in Edinburgh the next morning and he'd give me a fantastic one. It really got me going. I also had a little accordion which I used to play – only the right hand – and I played the same things on this that I played on mouth organ, things like 'Swedish Rhapsody', 'Moulin Rouge' and 'Greensleeves'.[71]

I can't remember why I took it [harmonica] up in the first place – I must have picked one up very cheap. I know we used to take in students and one of them had a mouth organ and said he'd buy me one if I could learn a tune by the next morning. So I learnt two. I was somewhere between eight and twelve at the time; in short pants, anyway.

There's an exam in England that they hang over your head from age five, called the Eleven Plus: 'If you don't pass the Eleven Plus, you're finished in life.' So that was the only exam that I ever passed, because I was terrified.

(After that exam's over, the teacher says you can do whatever you want. So I just painted.)[74]

I looked at all the hundreds of new kids [at Quarry Bank grammar school] and thought, 'Christ, I'll have to fight all my way through this lot,' having just made it at Dovedale. There was some real heavies there. The first fight I got in, I lost. I lost my nerve when I got really hurt. Not that there was much real fighting; I did a lot of swearing and shouting, then got a quick punch. If there was a bit of blood, then you packed in. After that, if I thought someone could punch harder than me, I said, 'OK, we'll have wrestling instead.'

I was aggressive because I wanted to be popular. I wanted to be the leader. It seemed more attractive than just being one of the toffees. I wanted everybody to do what I told them to do, to laugh at my jokes and let me be the boss. I suppose I did try to do a bit of school work at first, as I often did at Dovedale. I'd been honest at Dovedale, if nothing else, always owning up. But I began to realise that was foolish; they just got you. So I started lying about everything.

I only got one beating from Mimi – for taking money from her handbag. I was always taking a little, for soft things like Dinky's, but this day I must have taken too much.[67]

When I was about twelve, I used to think I must be a genius but nobody'd noticed. I thought, 'I'm a genius or I'm mad. Which is it? I can't be mad because nobody's put me away – therefore I'm a genius.' I mean, a genius is a form of mad person. We're all that way, but I used to be a bit coy about it – like my guitar-playing. If there's such a thing as genius, I am one. And if there isn't, I don't care. I used to think it when I was a kid writing my poetry and doing my paintings. I didn't become something when The Beatles made it; I've been like this all my life. Genius is pain, too. It's *just* pain.[70]

John, right, outside 251 Menlove Avenue

I always wondered, 'Why has no one discovered me?' In school, didn't they see that I'm cleverer than anybody in this school?[70]

If I look through my report card, it's the same thing: 'Too content to get a cheap laugh hiding behind this,' or, 'Daydreaming his life away.'[80]

I daydreamed my way through the whole school. I absolutely was in a trance for twenty years because it was absolutely boring. If I wasn't in a trance, I wasn't there – I was at the movies, or running around.[80]

I used to embarrass authority by chanting out a weird version of 'The Happy Wanderer' at inappropriate moments. I was suspended for a spell. I think it was for eating chocolate in prayers or ducking a swimming instructor; something daft like that.[63]

One maths master wrote, 'He's on the road to failure if he carries on this way.' Most of them disliked me, so I'm always glad to remind them of the incredible awareness they had.

But there was always one teacher in each school, usually an art teacher or English language or literature. If it was anything to do with art or writing, I was OK, but if it was anything to do with science or maths, I couldn't get it in.[71]

When I was fifteen I was thinking, 'If only I can get out of Liverpool and be famous and rich, wouldn't it be great?'[75]

I wanted to write *Alice in Wonderland*, but when you think, 'Whatever I do I'm never going to topple Leonardo,' you get to thinking, 'What's the use?' A lot of people had more pain than me and they've done better things.[71]

I wouldn't say I was a born writer; I'm a born thinker. I'd always been able at school – when they want you to imagine something instead of giving you a subject; I could do that.[64]

At school we used to draw a lot and pass it round. We had blind dogs leading ordinary people around.[65]

I suppose I did have a cruel humour. It was at school that it first started. We were once coming home from a school speech day and we'd had a few bevvies. Liverpool is full of deformed people, three-foot-high men selling newspapers. I'd never really noticed them before, but all the way home that day they seemed to be everywhere. It got funnier and funnier and we couldn't stop laughing. I suppose it's a way of hiding your emotions, or covering it up. I would never hurt a cripple. It was just part of our jokes, our way of life.[67]

All kids draw and write poetry and everything, and some of us last until we're about eighteen, but most drop off at about twelve when some guy comes up and says, 'You're no good.' That's all we get told all our lives: 'You haven't got the ability. You're a cobbler.' It happened to all of us, but if somebody had told me all my life, 'Yeah, you're a great artist,' I would have been a more secure person.[69]

They should give you time to develop, encourage what you're interested in. I was always interested in art and came top for many years, yet no one took any interest.[67]

It's like when they ask you, 'What do you want to be?' I would say, 'Well, a journalist.' I never would dare to say, 'An artist,' because in the social background that I came from – as I used to say to my auntie – you read about artists and you worship them in museums, but you don't want them living around the house. So the teachers said, 'No, something real.' And I'd say, 'Well, present me with some alternative.' They'd suggest veterinarian, doctor, dentist, lawyer. And I knew there was no hope in hell of me ever becoming that. So there was never anywhere for me to go.[80]

They only wanted scientists in the Fifties. Any artsy-fartsy people were spies. They still are, in society.[80]

Even at art school they tried to turn me into a teacher – they try to discourage you from painting – and said, 'Why not be a teacher? Then you can paint on Sunday?' I decided against it.[71]

At school I saw a lot wrong with society. I revolted the same way as all my colleagues. Anyone who had anything didn't fit in with the school curriculum, and all my reports from Quarry Bank were on the line: 'He is clever, but doesn't try.' I was a particularly offensive schoolboy. I am one of your typical working-class heroes. Mine was the same sort of revolution as D. H. Lawrence's – I didn't believe in class and the whole fight was against class structure.[69]

I always was a rebel because of whatever sociological thing gave me a chip on the shoulder. But on the other hand, I want to be loved and accepted. That's why I'm on stage, like a performing flea. Because I would like to belong. Part of me would like to be accepted by all facets of society and not be this loudmouth, lunatic, poet/musician. But I cannot be what I'm not. What the hell do you do? You want to belong, but you don't because you cannot belong.[80]

I was fairly tough at school, but I could organise it so it seemed like I *was* tough. It used to get me into trouble. I used to dress tough like a Teddy boy, but if I went into the tough districts and came across other Teddy boys, I was in danger. At school it was easier because I could control it with my head so they thought I was tougher than I was. It was a game. I mean, we used to shoplift and all those things, but nothing really heavy. Liverpool's quite a tough city. A lot of the real Teddy boys were actually in their early twenties. They were dockers. We were only fifteen, we were only kids – they had hatchets, belts, bicycle chains and real weapons. We never really got into that, and if somebody came in front of us we ran, me and my gang.[75]

The sort of gang I led went in for things like shoplifting and pulling girls' knickers down. When the bomb fell and everyone got caught, I was always the one they missed. I was scared at the time, but Mimi was the only parent who never found out. Most of the masters hated me like shit. As I got older, we'd go on from just stuffing rubbish like sweets in our pockets from shops, and progressed to getting enough to sell to others, like ciggies.[67]

Aunt Mimi

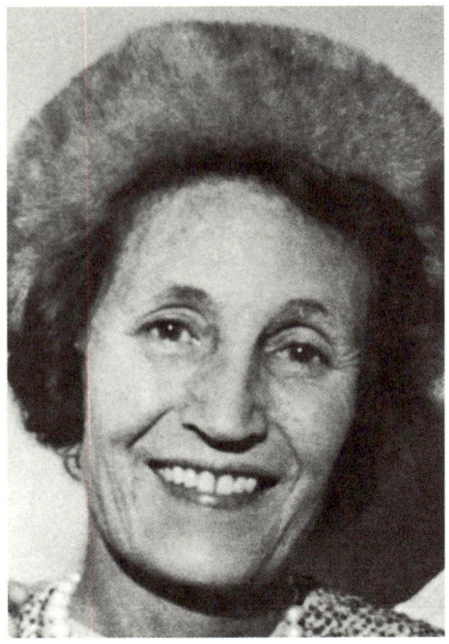

I'm not a tough guy. I've always had to have a façade of being tough to protect myself from other people's neuroses. But really, I'm a very sensitive weak guy.[71]

I'd say I had a happy childhood. I came out aggressive, but I was never miserable. I was always having a laugh.[67]

We [Mimi's husband and I] got on fine. He was nice and kind. [When] he died, I didn't know how to be sad publicly – what you did or said – so I went upstairs. Then my cousin arrived and she came upstairs as well. We both had hysterics. We just laughed and laughed. I felt very guilty afterwards.[67]

Mimi was looking after me on her own and she wanted to keep up this semi-detached house and not go down, and so we took students in at one time.

She always wanted me to be a rugby type or a chemist. I was writing poetry and singing since she had me. All the time I used to fight and say, 'Look, I'm an artist, don't bug me with all this maths. Don't try and make me into a chemist or a vet, I can't do it.'

I used to say, 'Don't you destroy my papers.' I'd come home when I was fourteen and she'd rooted all my things and thrown all my poetry out. I was saying, 'One day I'll be famous and you're going to regret it.'[72]

I'd seen these poems around, the sort you read to give you a hard-on. I'd wondered who wrote them and thought I'd try one myself. Mimi found it under my pillow. I said I'd been made to write it out for another lad who couldn't write very well. I'd written it myself, of course.[67]

When I did any serious poems, like emotional stuff later on, I did it in secret handwriting, all scribbles, so that Mimi couldn't read it.[67]

My mother [Julia] came to see us one day in a black coat with her face bleeding. She'd had some sort of accident. I couldn't face it. I thought, 'That's my mother in there, bleeding.' I went out into the garden. I loved her, but I didn't want to get involved. I suppose I was a moral coward. I wanted to hide all feelings.[67]

Julia gave me my first coloured shirt. I started going to visit her at her house. I met her new bloke and didn't think much of him. I called him Twitchy. Julia became a sort of young aunt to me, or a big sister. As I got bigger and had more rows with Mimi, I used to go and live with Julia for a weekend.[67]

[Twitchy was] otherwise known as Robert Dykins or Bobbie Dykins. Her second husband – I don't know if she married him or not; little waiter with a nervous cough and the thinning, margarine-coated hair. He always used to push his hand in the margarine or the butter, usually the margarine, and grease his hair with it before he left. He used to keep his tips in a big tin on top of a cupboard in the kitchen, and I used to always steal them. I believe Mother got the blame. That's the least they could do for me.[79]

I'd always had a fantasy about a woman who would be a beautiful, intelligent, dark-haired, high-cheekboned, free-spirited artist (*à la* Juliette Greco). My soul mate. Someone that I had already known, but somehow had lost. Of course, as a teenager, my sexual fantasies were full of Anita Ekberg and the usual giant Nordic goddesses. That is, until Brigitte Bardot became the love of my life in the late Fifties. (All my girlfriends who weren't dark-haired suffered my constant pressure to become Brigitte. By the time I married my first wife – who was a natural auburn – she too had become a long-haired blonde with the obligatory bangs. I met the real Brigitte a few years later. I was on acid and she was on her way out.)[78]

I read some guy saying about the sexual fantasies and urges that he had all his life. When he was twenty, and then when he was thirty, he thought they'd cool down a bit. Then when he got in his forties he thought they'd cool down, but they didn't, they went on: sixty, seventy… until he was still dribbling in his mind when he couldn't possibly do anything about it. I thought, 'Shit!' because I was always waiting for them to lessen, but I suppose it's going to go on forever. 'Forever' is a bit too strong a word – let's say you go on until you leave this body, anyway. Let's hope. Maybe the game is to conquer it before you leave, otherwise you come back for more (and who wants to come back just to come?).[79]

I remember a night, or should I say day, in my teens when I was fucking my girlfriend on a gravestone and my arse got covered in greenfly. This was a good lesson in karma and/or gardening. Barbara, where are you now? Fat and ugly? Fifteen kids? Years of hell with me should have made you ready for anything. What's so sad about the past is it's passed. I wonder who's kissing her now.[78]

America used to be the big youth place in everybody's imagination. America had teenagers and everywhere else just had people.[66]

We all knew America, all of us. All those movies: every movie we ever saw as children, whether it was Disneyland or Doris Day, Rock Hudson, James Dean or Marilyn. Everything was American: Coca-Cola, Heinz ketchup – I thought Heinz ketchup was English until I went to America.

The music was mainly American before rock'n'roll. We still had our own artists, but the big artists were American. It was the Americans coming to the London Palladium. They wouldn't even make an English movie without an American in it, even a B movie, because nobody would go to the movie. They'd have a Canadian if they couldn't get an American.[75]

There was no such thing as an English record. I think the first English record that was anywhere near anything was 'Move It' by Cliff Richard, and before that there'd been nothing.[73]

Liverpool is cosmopolitan. It's where the sailors would come home on the ships with the blues records from America.[70] We were hearing old funky blues records in Liverpool that people across Britain or Europe had never heard about or knew about, only the port areas.

There is the biggest country-and-western following in England in Liverpool, besides London. I heard country-and-western music in Liverpool before I heard rock'n'roll. The people there – the Irish in Ireland are the same – they take their music very seriously. There were established folk, blues and country-and-western clubs in Liverpool before rock'n'roll.[70]

As kids we were all opposed to folk songs because they were so middle-class. It was all college students with big scarfs and a pint of beer in their hands singing in la-di-da voices, 'I worked in a mine in Newcastle,' and all that shit. There were very few *real* folk singers, though I liked Dominic Behan a bit and there was some good stuff to be heard in Liverpool. Occasionally you hear very old records on the radio or TV of real workers in Ireland singing, and the power is fantastic. But mostly folk music is people with fruity voices trying to keep alive something old and dead. It's all a bit boring, like ballet: a minority thing kept going by a minority group. Today's folk music is rock'n'roll.[71]

Folk music isn't an acoustic guitar with a singer who talks about mines and railways, because we don't sing like that any more. We sing about karma, peace, anything.[70]

In our family the radio was hardly ever on, so I got to pop later: not like Paul and George who'd been groomed in pop music coming over the radio all the time. I only heard it at other people's homes.[71]

In the garden at Menlove Avenue

The Bill Haley era passed me by, in a way. When his records came on the wireless my mother would start dancing around, she thought they were so good. I used to hear them, but they didn't do anything for me.[63]

This fella I knew called Don Beatty showed me the name Elvis Presley in the *New Musical Express* and said he was great. It was 'Heartbreak Hotel'. I thought it sounded a bit phoney: 'Heart-break Hotel'.

The music papers were saying that Presley was fantastic, and at first I expected someone like Perry Como or Sinatra. 'Heartbreak Hotel' seemed a corny title and his name seemed strange in those days. But then, when I heard it, it was the end for me. I first heard it on Radio Luxembourg. He turned out to be fantastic. I remember rushing home with the record and saying, 'He sounds like Frankie Laine *and* Johnnie Ray *and* Tennessee Ernie Ford!'[71]

I'm an Elvis fan because it was Elvis who really got me out of Liverpool. Once I heard it and got into it, that was life, there was no other thing. I thought of nothing else but rock'n'roll; apart from sex and food and money – but that's all the same thing, really.[75]

John with Uncle George

People have been trying to stamp out rock'n'roll since it started. It was mainly parents who were against rock'n'roll. The words had a lot of double entendre in the early days.

They cleaned it up for the white audience, a lot of it. That black stuff was very sexual. They made Little Richard re-record 'Tutti Frutti'. Whatever was going on, they had to clean up a lot of words. Elvis did 'One Night With You'. The original was 'One Night Of Sin' – 'One night of sin is what I'm praying for.' The words were pretty good; they were street words or black words.[75]

They've been saying it will never last ever since I heard about it, and it's always written in the papers that it's dying. It'll never die. It's been apparent in all the music since it began. It came out of its roots of blues and rhythm-and-blues and jazz and country. It was really a combination of black and white music. That's what finally made it.[75]

There have only been two great albums that I listened to all the way through when I was about sixteen. One was Carl Perkins's first or second, I can't remember which. And one was Elvis's first. Those are the only ones on which I really enjoyed every track.[80]

On things like 'Ready Teddy' and 'Rip It Up' I have visions of listening to the record when I was younger. I remember how the London-American label looked. I remember playing it to my auntie and she was saying, 'What is it?' Or I remember dance-hall scenes where we were all dancing.[75]

Buddy Holly was great and he wore glasses, which I liked, although I didn't wear them in public for years and years. But Buddy Holly was the first one that we were really aware of in England who could play and sing at the same time – not just strum, but actually play the licks. I never met him, I was too young. I never saw him live either. I saw Eddie Cochran. I saw Gene Vincent and Little Richard, but I met them later. Eddie Cochran was the only one I saw as a fan, just sitting in an audience.[75]

Little Richard was one of the all-time greats. The first time I heard him a friend of mine had been to Holland and brought back a 78 with 'Long Tall Sally' on one side, and 'Slippin' And Slidin'' on the other. It blew our heads – we'd never heard anybody sing like that in our lives, and all those saxes playing like crazy.

The most exciting thing about early Little Richard was when he screamed just before the solo; that was *howling*. It used to make your hair stand on end when he did that long, long scream into the solo.[69]

I still love Little Richard, and Jerry Lee Lewis. They're like primitive painters. Chuck Berry is one of the all-time great poets; a rock poet, you could call him. He was well advanced of his time, lyric-wise. We all owe a lot to him, including Dylan. I've loved everything he's done, ever. He was in a different class from the other performers. He was in the tradition of the great blues artists but he really wrote his own stuff – I know Richard did, but Berry *really* wrote stuff. The lyrics were fantastic, even though we didn't know what he was saying half the time.[70]

In the Fifties, when people were virtually singing about nothing, Chuck Berry was writing social-comment songs, with incredible metre to the lyrics. When I hear rock, good rock, of the calibre of Chuck Berry, I just fall apart and I have no other interest in life. The world could be ending if rock'n'roll is playing. It's a disease of mine.[72]

That's the music that brought me from the provinces of England to the world. That's what made me what I am, whatever it is I am. I don't know where we'd have been without rock'n'roll and I really love it.[75]

Rock'n'roll was *real*, everything else was unreal. It was the only thing to get through to me out of all the things that were happening when I was fifteen.[70]

I had no idea about doing music as a way of life until rock'n'roll hit me. That's the music that inspired me to play music.[80]

When I was sixteen my mother taught me music. She first taught me how to play banjo chords – that's why in very early photos of the group I'm playing funny chords – and from that I progressed to guitar.[72]

I remember the first guitar I ever saw. It belonged to a guy in a cowboy suit in a province of Liverpool, with stars and a cowboy hat and a big Dobro. They were real cowboys, and they took it seriously. There had been cowboys long before there was rock'n'roll.[70]

I used to borrow a guitar at first. I couldn't play, but my mother bought me one from one of those mail-order firms. It was a bit crummy, but I played it all the time and got a lot of practice.[63]

I played the guitar like a banjo, with the sixth string hanging loose. My first guitar cost £10. All I ever wanted to do was to vamp; I only learnt to play to back myself.[64]

When I got the guitar I'd play it for a bit then give it up, then take it up again. It took me about two years, on and off, to be able to strum tunes without thinking. I think I had one lesson, but it was so much like school I gave up. I learnt mostly by picking up bits here and there. One of the first things I learnt was 'Ain't That A Shame' and it has a lot of memories for me. Then I learnt 'That'll Be The Day'. I learned the solos on 'Johnny B. Goode' and 'Carol', but I couldn't play the one on 'Blue Suede Shoes'. In those days I was very much influenced by Chuck Berry, Scotty Moore and Carl Perkins.[71]

The best quote Mimi ever said was: 'The guitar's all right for a hobby, John, but you'll never make a living at it.' (Fans in America had that framed on steel and sent it to her, and she has it in the house I bought her; she has it looking at her the whole time.)[72]

About the time of rock'n'roll in Britain – I think I was about fifteen so it would be about 1955 – there was a big thing called 'skiffle', which was a kind of folk music; American folk music with washboards, and all the kids from fifteen onwards had these groups.[64]

I listen to country music. I started imitating Hank Williams when I was fifteen, before I could play the guitar – although a friend had one. I used to go round to his house, because he had the record-player, and we sang all that Lonnie Donegan stuff and Hank Williams. He had all the

Below: John's copy of 'Rock Island Line'

records. 'Honky Tonk Blues' is the one I used to do. Presley was country, country-rock. Carl Perkins was really country, just with more backbeat.[73]

We eventually formed ourselves into a group from school. I think the bloke whose idea it was didn't get in the group. We met in his house the first time. There was Eric Griffiths on guitar, Pete Shotton on washboard, Len Garry, Colin Hanton on drums and Rod [Davis] on banjo – and somebody named Ivan [Vaughan]. Ivan went to the same school as Paul.

Our first appearance was in Rosebery Street – it was their Empire Day celebrations. They had this party out in the street. We played from the back of a lorry. We didn't get paid. We played at blokes' parties after that; perhaps got a few bob, but mostly we just played for fun. We didn't mind about not being paid.[67]

The Quarry Men is the name of the group before it turned into The Beatles. The original group was named after my school, which was Quarry Bank and had a Latin motto which meant 'out of this rock' – that's symbolic – 'you will find truth'.

Anyway, we always failed the exams and never did any work and Pete was always worried about his future. I would say, 'Don't worry, it'll work out,' to him and the gang that was around me then. I always had a group of three or four or five guys around with me who would play various roles in my life, supportive and subservient. In general, me being the bully boy. The Beatles became my new gang.

I always believed that something would turn up. I didn't make plans for the future. I didn't study for the exam. I didn't put a little bit on the side, I wasn't capable. Therefore I was the one that all the other boys' parents would say, 'Keep away from him.' Because they knew what I was. The parents instinctively recognised I was a troublemaker, meaning I did not conform and I would influence their children, which I did. I did my best to disrupt every friend's home. Partly out of envy that I didn't have this so-called home. (But I did. I had an auntie and an uncle and a nice suburban home. This image of me being the orphan is garbage because I was well protected by my auntie and my uncle, and they looked after me very well.)[80]

I think I went a bit wild. I was just drifting. I wouldn't study at school, and when I was put in for nine GCEs I was a hopeless failure. Even in the mock I got English and art, but in the real one I didn't even get art.[65]

I was disappointed at not getting art at GCE, but I'd given up. All they were interested in was neatness. I was never neat. I used to mix all the colours together. We had one question which said do a picture of 'travel'. I drew a picture of a hunchback with warts all over him. They obviously didn't dig that.[67]

We knew that the GCE wasn't the opening to anything. We could have ground through all that and gone further, but not me. I believed something was going to happen which I'd have to get through – and I knew it wasn't GCE.

Up to the age of fifteen I was no different to any other little cunt of fifteen. Then I decided I'd write a little song, and I did. But it didn't make me any different. That's a load of crap that I discovered a talent. I just did it. I've no talent, except for being happy, or a talent for skiving.[67]

I was always thinking I was going to be a famous artist and possibly I'd have to marry a very rich old lady, or man, to look after me while I did my art. But then rock'n'roll came along, and I thought, 'Ah-ha, this is the one.' So I didn't have to marry anybody or live with them.[75]

I didn't really know what I wanted to be, apart from ending up an eccentric millionaire. I had to be a millionaire. If I couldn't do it without being crooked, then I'd have to be crooked. I was quite prepared to do that – nobody obviously was going to give me money for my paintings – but I was too much of a coward. I'd never have made it. I did plan to knock off a shop with another bloke, do it properly for a change, not just shoplifting. We used to look at shops at night, but we never got round to doing it.[67]

Mimi had said to me that I'd done it at last: I was now a real Teddy boy. I seemed to digust everybody, not just Mimi. That was the day that I met Paul.[67]

It was through Ivan that I first met Paul. Seems that he knew Paul was always dickering around in music and thought he would be a good lad to have in the group. So one day, when we were playing at Woolton, he brought him along. We can both remember it quite well. The Quarry Men were playing on a raised platform and there was a good crowd because it was a warm, sunny day.[63]

[It was] the first day I did 'Be Bop A Lula' live on stage.[80] 'Be Bop A Lula' has always been one of my all-time favourites. It was at a church-hall garden fête, and I was performing with a mutual friend of Paul's and mine. Another mutual friend who lived next door brought Paul along and said, 'I think you two will get along.'[75] We talked after the show and I saw he had talent. He was playing guitar backstage, doing 'Twenty Flight Rock' by Eddie Cochran.[80]

Paul could play guitar, trumpet and piano. That doesn't mean to say he has a greater talent, but his musical education was better. I could only play the mouth organ and two chords on a guitar when we met. I tuned the guitar like a banjo, so my guitar only had five strings on it. (Paul taught me how to play properly – but I had to learn the chords left-handed, because Paul is left-handed. So I learnt them upside down, and I'd go home and reverse them.) That's what I was doing – playing on stage with a group, playing a five-string guitar like a banjo – when he was brought around from the audience to meet me.[80]

Paul told me the chords I had been playing weren't real chords – and his dad said that they weren't even banjo chords, though I think they were. He had a good guitar at the time, it cost about £14. He'd got it in exchange for a trumpet his dad had given him.[71]

I was very impressed by Paul playing 'Twenty Flight Rock'. He could obviously play the guitar. I half thought to myself, 'He's as good as me.' I'd been kingpin up to then. Now, I thought, 'If I take him on, what will happen?' It went through my head that I'd have to keep him in line if I let him join. But he was good, so he was worth having. He also looked like Elvis. I dug him.[67]

Was it better to have a guy who was better than the people I had in? To make the group stronger, or to let me be stronger? Instead of going for an individual thing we went for the strongest format – equals.[70]

I turned round to him right then on first meeting and said, 'Do you want to join the group?' And he said 'yes' the next day as I recall it.[80]

Paul had a trumpet and had this wild theory that he'd actually learnt how to play the oldie 'When The Saints Go Marching In'. He just blew away as hard as he could, drowning out everything we were trying to do. He thought he was doing a great job on the tune, but we didn't recognise any of it![63]

Now George came through Paul.[80]

Paul introduced me to George and I had to make the decision whether to let George in. I listened to him play and said, 'Play "Raunchy".' I let him in and that was the three of us then, and the rest of the group was thrown out, practically.[70]

We asked George to join us because he knew more chords, a lot more than we knew. We got a lot from him. Paul had a friend at school who would discover chords, and these would be passed round Liverpool. Every time we learnt a new chord, we'd write a song round it.

We used to sag off school and go to George's house for the afternoon. George looked even younger than Paul – and Paul looked about ten, with his baby face.

It was too much. George was just too young. I didn't want to know at first. He was doing a delivery round and seemed a kid. He came round once and asked me to go to the pictures with him, but I pretended I was busy. I didn't dig him until I got to know him. Mimi always said he had a low Liverpool voice, a real whacker. She said, 'You always seem to like lower-class types, don't you, John?' [67]

Paul and I hit it off right away. I was just a bit worried because my old mates were going and new people like Paul and George were joining, but we soon got used to each other. We started to do big beat numbers like 'Twenty Flight Rock' – funny, really, because we were still meant to be a skiffle group. 'Let's Have A Party' used to be my big number.[63]

There was no point in rehearsing for non-existent dates. But we went on playing together just for kicks. Usually in each other's homes. We kept the record-player going a lot of the time, playing the latest American hits. We'd try and get the same effects.[63]

You'd go and play at the dance hall, and the real Teddy boys didn't like you, because all the girls would be watching the group – you had the sideboards and the hair and you're on stage. Afterwards the guys would try and kill you, so most of fifteen, sixteen and seventeen was spent running away from people with a guitar under your arm. They'd always catch the drummer; he had all the equipment. We'd run like crazy and get the bus because we didn't have a car. I'd get on the bus with the guitar, but the bass player – who only had a string bass with a tea chest – used to get caught. What we used to do was throw them the bass or a hat and they'd kick and kill *it*, so you could escape.[75]

When I left Quarry Bank I went to Liverpool College of Art with an idea that I might finish up drawing gorgeous girls for toothpaste posters.[63]

I think they asked me years ago rather vaguely if I would like to go back and look, but I saw enough of it when I was there. I have fond memories, not *too* fond though.

The headmaster [of Quarry Bank], Pobjoy, recommended me to go to art school. He said, 'If he doesn't go there he may as well just pack up life.' So he arranged for me to go. I developed a great sense of humour and met some great people and had a laugh and played rock'n'roll. (Of course, I was playing rock'n'roll during all this time at grammar school, developing the basic form of the music.)[64]

I wasn't really keen. I thought it would be a crowd of old men, but I should make the effort to try and make something of myself. I stayed for five years doing commercial art.[63]

I went because there didn't seem to be any hope for me in any other field and it was about the only thing I could do, possibly. But I didn't do very well there either, because I'm lazy.[64]

College life was so free I went potty.

I was an art student when Paul and George were still in grammar school. There is a vast difference between being in high school and being in college. I already had sexual relationships, already drank, and did a lot of things like that.[80]

They all thought I was a Ted at art college when I arrived. Then I became a bit artier, as they all do, but I still dressed like a Ted, in black with tight drainies.[67] I imitated Teddy boys, but I was always torn between being a Teddy boy and an art student. One week I'd go to art school with my art-school scarf on and my hair down and the next week I'd go for the leather jacket and tight jeans.[73]

Arthur Ballard, one of the lecturers, said I should change a bit, not wear them as tight. He was good, Arthur Ballard; he helped me, kept me on when others wanted to chuck me out. But I wasn't really a Ted, just a rocker. I was only pretending to be one.

I never liked the work. I should have been an illustrator, or in the painting school because it seemed groovy. But I found myself in lettering. I didn't turn up for something, so they had just put me in that. They were all neat fuckers in lettering. They might as well have put me in sky-diving for the use I was at lettering. I failed all the exams. I stayed on because it was better than working.[67]

I maintained abstract art was easy, and chucked paint everywhere, and they all said it was rubbish. I said, 'Prove it,' and they did.[64]

I went in for painting. Really I wasn't a painter, I was a book illustrator. But I wasn't interested in illustrating. I liked the painting at school because they were more fun. All my friends were in that mob and they had more parties. So I wanted to be a painter, but I'd never have made one. I had no career that would have done me any good lined up.[65]

I always felt I'd make it, though. There were some moments of doubt, but I knew something would eventually happen.[67]

When I was seventeen I used to think, 'I wish a fucking earthquake would happen, or a revolution.' Just to go out and steal. If I was seventeen I'd be all for it, because what have I got to lose? And now I've got nothing to lose. I don't want to die and I don't want to be hurt physically; but if they blow the world up, we're all out of our pain then. Forget it – no more problems.[70]

I was staying with Julia and Twitchy this weekend. The copper came to the door, to tell us about the accident. It was just like it's supposed to be, the way it is in the films, asking if I was her son and all that. Then he told us, and we both went white.[67]

She got killed by an off-duty cop who was drunk, after visiting my auntie's house where I lived. I wasn't there at the time. She was at the bus stop and he ran her down in a car.[80]

It was the worst thing that ever happened to me. We'd caught up so much, me and Julia, in just a few years. We could communicate. We got on. She was great. I thought, 'Fuck it, fuck it, fuck it. That's really fucked everything. I've no responsibilities to anyone now.' Twitchy took it worse than me. Then he said, 'Who's going to look after the kids?' And I hated him. Bloody selfishness.

We got a taxi over to Sefton General where she was lying dead. I didn't want to see her. I talked hysterically to the taxi driver all the way, ranted on and on, the way you do. The taxi driver just grunted now and again. I refused to go in, but Twitchy did. He broke down.[67]

That was another big trauma for me. I lost her twice. Once when I was moved in with my auntie. And once again at seventeen when she actually, physically died. That was very traumatic for me. That was really a hard time for me. It made me very, very bitter. The underlying chip on my shoulder that I had got really big then. Being a teenager and a rock'n'roller and an art student and my mother being killed just when I was re-establishing a relationship with her.[80]

It helps to say, 'My mummy's dead,' rather than, 'My mother died,' or, 'My mother wasn't very good to me.' (A lot of us have images of parents that we never get from them.) It doesn't exorcise it – bang, gone – but it helps. First of all you have to allow yourself to realise it. I never allowed myself to realise that my mother had gone. It's the same if you don't allow yourself to cry, or feel anything. Some things are too painful to feel, so you stop. We have the ability to block feelings and that's what we do most of the time. These feelings are now coming out of me, feelings that have been there all my life. And they continue to come out. I don't know if every time I pick up a guitar I'm going to sing about my mother. I presume it'll come out some other way now.[70]

All art is pain expressing itself. I think all life is, everything we do, but particularly artists – that's why they're always vilified. They're always persecuted because they show pain; they can't help it. They express it in art and the way they live, and people don't like to see that reality that they're suffering.

When you're a child you can only take so much pain. It literally blocks off part of your body. It's like not wanting to know about going to the toilet or having a bath. If you don't do it for a long time, it accumulates. And emotions are the same, you accumulate them over the years and they come out in other forms: violence or baldness or short-sightedness.[71]

I even got confirmed at about seventeen, for very materialistic reasons. I thought I had better do something in case I didn't make it.[69]

I'd always suspected that there was a God, even when I thought I was an atheist. Just in case. I believe it, so I am full of compassion, but you can still dislike things. I just hate things less strenuously than I did. I haven't got as big a chip about it because maybe I've escaped it a bit. I think all our society is run by insane people for insane objectives.

I think that's what I sussed when I was sixteen and twelve, way down the line, but I expressed it differently all through my life. It's the same thing I'm expressing all the time, but now I can put it into that sentence, that I think we're being run by maniacs for maniacal ends. But I'm likely to be put away as insane for expressing that. That's what's insane about it.[68]

I'm not afraid of dying. I'm prepared for death because I don't believe in it. I think it's just getting out of one car and getting into another.[69]

I was pretty self-destructive at college.[80] I was a drunk and smashed phone boxes. On the street in Liverpool, unless you were in the suburbs, you had to walk close to the wall. And to get to the Cavern it was no easy matter, even at lunchtime sometimes. It's a tense place.[75]

It was mainly one long drinking session, but when you're eighteen or nineteen you can put away a lot of drink and not hurt your body so much. At college I always got a little violent on drink, but I used to have a friend called Geoff Mohammed, God rest his soul, who died. He was a half-Indian Arab and he would be like a bodyguard for me. So whenever I'd get into some controversy he would ease me out of it.[80]

Everybody hung round in this club called the Jacaranda, which is near the art school in the centre of Liverpool. And we started hanging round there before we really formed a band – when there was just me, Paul and George.[74]

The first thing we ever recorded was 'That'll Be The Day', a Buddy Holly song, and one of Paul's called 'In Spite Of All The Danger'.[74]

I got more confidence and used to ignore Mimi. I went away for longer spells; wore what clothes I wanted. I had to borrow or pinch, as I had no money at college. I was always on at Paul to ignore his dad and just wear what he wanted.[67]

He wouldn't go against his dad and wear drainpipe trousers. And his dad was always trying to get me out of the group behind my back, I found out later. He'd say, 'Why don't you get rid of John, he's just a lot of trouble. Cut your hair nice and wear baggy trousers.' Like I was the bad influence because I was the eldest, so I had all the gear first usually.[72]

I lived rough all right. It was a dirty old flat [in Gambier Terrace]. I think we spent about four months there, practising and painting. It was just like a rubbish dump. There must have been seven of us in the same place. It was in a terrible condition. There was no furniture, just beds. And as we were just loafing about, we didn't really think of it as a home. The others tried to tidy it up a bit but we didn't bother – except I think I bought a piece of old carpet or something. I left all my gear there when I went to Hamburg.[63]

I had a friend who was a blues freak; he turned me on to blues. He was the same age as me and he understood rock'n'roll – he knew what Elvis, Fats Domino and Little Richard were all about, but he said, 'How about this?' It didn't take my love of rock'n'roll away and it added the real blues to my consciousness.[80] The blues is real. It's not perverted, it's not thought about, it's not a concept – it's a chair. Not a design for a chair, or a better chair, or a bigger chair, or a chair with leather or with design – it's the first chair; chairs for sitting on, not chairs for looking at or being appreciated. You sit on that music.[70]

We used to play blues at college. We were allowed to play rock'n'roll by infiltrating, by playing blues. They'd only let you play trad jazz on the art-school record-player, so I got myself voted onto the committee so we could play rock'n'roll. We could get the snobs by playing blues, anyway; Leadbelly and whatever it was in those days.[69]

I met Cynthia at art school.

Cynthia was a right Hoylake runt. Dead snobby. We used to poke fun at her and mock her, me and Geoff Mohammed. 'Quiet please,' we'd shout, 'No dirty jokes. It's Cynthia.'

We had a class dance. I was pissed and asked her to dance. Geoff had been having me on, saying, 'Cynthia likes you, you know.' As we danced I asked her to come to a party the next day. She said she couldn't. She was engaged.

I was triumphant at having picked her up. We had a drink and then went back to Stu's [Stuart Sutcliffe's] flat, buying fish and chips on the way.

I was hysterical. That was the trouble. I was jealous of anyone she had anything to do with. I demanded absolute trust from her, because I wasn't trustworthy myself. I was neurotic, taking out all my frustrations on her. She did leave me once. That was terrible. I couldn't stand being without her.

I was in a blind rage for two years. I was either drunk or fighting. It had been the same with other girlfriends I'd had. There was something the matter with me.[67]

My education was sorely lacking; the only thing we did learn was fear and hatred, especially of the opposite sex.[78]

As a teenager, all I saw were films where men beat up women. That was tough, that was the thing to do, slap them in the face, treat them rough – Humphrey Bogart and all that jazz. So that's the attitude we're brought up with. It took me a long time to get that out. That isn't reality.

The way I started understanding it was thinking, 'What would happen if I said to Ringo or Paul or George: "Go fetch that. Put the kettle on. Somebody's at the door..."' If you treated your best male friend the way you treat your woman, he'd give you a punch in the face.[72]

My childhood was not all suffering. We saw these articles in the American fan mags that said, 'Those boys struggled up from the slums.' I was always well dressed, well fed and well schooled, and brought up to be a nice lower-middle-class English boy. That's what made The Beatles different, the fact that George, Paul and John were grammar-school boys. Up until then all rock'n'rollers, basically, had been black and poor: rural South, city slums. And the white had been truckers, like Elvis. Buddy Holly was apparently more of our ilk, a suburban boy who had learnt to read and write and knew a little more. But the thing of The Beatles was that we were pretty well educated and not truckers. Paul could have gone to university. He was always a good boy. He passed his exams. He could have become, I don't know – Dr McCartney. I could have done it myself if I had worked. I never worked.[80]

I think sometimes of the friends who left school at the same time as me, when I made up my mind to go to art school. Some of them went straight to nine-to-five jobs and within three months they looked like old men. Fat chance of that ever happening to me. The great thing is never having to be in an office – or anywhere. I like to live on the spur of the moment; I hate to make forward plans.

Who knows why The Beatles happened?

It's like the constant search for why you go down one road and why you go down another. It has as much to do with being from Liverpool, or being from Quarry Bank grammar school or being in a household where the library was full of Oscar Wilde and Whistler and Fitzgerald and all the Book of the Month Club.[80]

## PROGRAMME

STALLS — SIDESHOWS — ICE CREAM — LEMONADE

*Teas and Refreshments in large Marquee situated behind the hut.*

2-00 p.m. PROCESSION leaves Church Road, via Allerton Road, Kings Drive, Hunt's Cross Avenue; returning to the Church Field.
Led by the Band of the Cheshire Yeomanry.
Street Collection by the Youth Club during the procession.

3-00 p.m. CROWNING OF THE ROSE QUEEN (Miss Sally Wright) by Mrs. THELWALL JONES.

3-10 p.m. FANCY DRESS PARADE.
Class 1. Under 7 years.
Class 2. 7 to 12 years.
Class 3. Over 12 years.
Entrants to report to Miss P. Fuller at the Church Hall before the procession.

3-30 p.m. to 5-00 p.m. MUSICAL SELECTIONS by the Band of the Cheshire (Earl of Chester) Yeomanry. Band-master: H. Abraham.
(By permission of Lt.-Col. G. C. V. Churton, M.C., M.B.E.).

4-15 p.m. THE QUARRY MEN SKIFFLE GROUP.

5-15 p.m. DISPLAY by the City of Liverpool Police Dogs. By kind permission of the Chief Constable and Watch Committee.

5-45 p.m. THE QUARRY MEN SKIFFLE GROUP.

**8-0 p.m. GRAND DANCE in the CHURCH HALL**

GEORGE EDWARDS BAND also *The Quarry Men Skiffle Group*

**TICKETS 2/-**

REFRESHMENTS AT MODERATE PRICES.

GARDEN FETE

ST. PETER'S CHURCH FIELD

WOOLTON PARISH CHURCH    Rector: M. Pryce Jones

Saturday, 6th July, 1957

at 3 p.m.

ADMISSION BY PROGRAMME:

CHILDREN 3d.

PROCEEDS IN AID OF CHURCH FUNDS.

Top: St Peter's Church garden fête, 6 July 1957
Left to right: Eric Griffiths, Colin Hanton, Rod Davis, John, Pete Shotton, Len Garry

Right: Rosebery Street, 22 June 1957

When I get older losing my hair,
Many years from now
Will you still be sending me a Valentine
Birthday greetings bottle of wine,
Middle.
You'll be older too,
And if you say the word, I could stay with you
I could be handy, mending a fuse
When your lights have gone.
You can knit a sweater by the fireside
Sunday mornings: go for a ride
Doing the garden, digging the weeds
Who could ask for more!
Will you still need me etc.....
Mid. Every summer we can rent a cottage,
in the Isle of Wight, if it's not too dear.
We shall scrimp and save
...Grandchildren on your knee
Vera, Chuck and Dave
Send me a postcard, drop me a line,
Stating point of view
Indicate precisely what you mean to say
wasting away
your answer fill in a form
mine for evermore...
etc...

# I WAS BORN IN WALTON HOSPITAL ON 18TH JUNE 1942.

My mother was a nurse and came from Fazakerley, Liverpool. My dad was born in Everton and was a cotton salesman who'd left school when he was fourteen.

# PAUL McCARTNEY

Mum was a Catholic, Dad was a Protestant. They got married quite late, and had me when they were around forty. My mother was a midwife and we were always given the midwife's house wherever she worked. We always felt like a pioneer family in a wagon train. No sooner would we be established in one house than we would be moved to a new one, on the outskirts of Speke, say, where they hadn't built the roads yet. We'd live there for a while and then it would be 'whipcrack away', and we were moving again. It was all right; we adjusted. They were frontiers, the outskirts of Liverpool, where we were sent. I had a very secure childhood, though. I have one brother, one and a half years younger than me, Michael.

Liverpool has its own identity. It's even got its own accent within about a ten mile radius. Once you go outside that ten miles it's 'deep Lancashire, lad'. I think you do feel that apartness, growing up there.

As a child, Liverpool was trams. You'd get to the end of the tram route and the driver would go to the controls at the other end to drive back. Reminders of the war were all around. We played on bomb-sites a lot and I grew up thinking the word 'bomb-site' almost meant 'playground'. I never connected it with bombing. 'Where are you going to play?' – 'I'm going down the bombie.' We said words like 'shell-shock', never realising their true significance. There used to be a guy in a demob suit who walked along twitching. People would ask, 'What's wrong with him?' – 'Oh, shell-shock.'

I remember winters. They were like being in Siberia, getting chapped knees in short trousers. The insides of my knees and thighs always had red chap-marks from the wet and the cold, and the wind whipping them. I was a boy scout, but I didn't get many badges – I got a bivouac badge for camping out. And I remember there were always millions and millions of car tyres down on the dock, which we'd play amongst.

I used to go down to the docks a lot. I had very romantic feelings about them. I had a mate whose father was the dockmaster of Herculaneum Dock, and I stayed there one night. A Spanish boat came in and we wanted to practise our Spanish, since we'd just started learning it at school. The only phrase I practised was *'non rapidamente'*, because they kept talking too fast and we didn't know the word for 'slowly'. I remember one Spanish guy on deck having his hair cut.

There was a market called St John's until we were teenagers, and then it got turned into a car park or something. I have good memories of the market. You'd hear a guy shouting, 'What am I bid for this crockery?' He'd start off saying, 'That lot's worth fifty quid, and I'm not even asking twenty. I'm not even asking ten. 'Ere you are, lady, three quid the lot.' He'd stack it all up precariously – all the plates would be amazingly balanced – and then bang them down, proving what great crockery it was. There was always someone in the audience, a plant, who would say, 'I'll have them,' and then everyone would rush in. You'd be tempted to buy them even if you didn't have three quid and didn't need a lot of plates, because he was such a good salesman. I loved that.

We used to go down Dungeon Lane to the beach where the lighthouse was, on the Mersey shoreline. Two lads who were tougher than me robbed me of my watch there one time. I was ten. They lived in the next street – their garden backed onto ours – so all I had to say was, 'It's him, Dad. He got me watch.' We reported them to the police, and they went to court and got put away, silly guys. I had to go and give evidence against them. It was my first time in court.

Jim Mac's Band – Ballroom, Liverpool (Jim McCartney sits third to right of drum)

roasting hot day near the swimming pool, when out of the Calypso Ballroom came five guys from Gateshead. And they all looked alike. They each had on a little tartan flat cap, with a grey crewneck sweater, tartan shorts, pumps, and carried white towels under their arms. They walked in a line across to the pool to have a good old swim and I noticed everyone's heads turn and go: 'WHO'S THAT?' In that second a penny dropped for me and I realised the power of *looking something*. They won the talent contest at Butlins that week for whatever they did – and you just *knew* that they would win.

My dad was an instinctive musician. He'd played trumpet in a little jazz band when he was younger. I unearthed a photo in the Sixties which someone in the family had given me, and there he is in front of a big bass drum. That gave us the idea for *Sgt Pepper*: The Jimmy Mac Jazz Band. My dad is sitting there as a 24-year-old in his tux with my Uncle Jack next to him. Uncle Jack played trombone. It was all very 'family'.

Dad played the trumpet until his teeth gave out. Later he tried the clarinet, but that was a disaster and we'd laugh at him. He would play piano at home. We always had a piano. (It's a great-sounding piano, which I still have. It was bought, incidentally, from North End Music Stores, NEMS. Brian Epstein was the son of Harry Epstein, the owner, and my dad bought his first piano from Harry. It is all like that in Liverpool, pretty intertwined.) I have some lovely childhood memories of lying on the floor and listening to my dad play 'Lullaby Of The Leaves' (still a big favourite of mine), and music from the Paul Whiteman era (Paul Whiteman was one of his favourites), old songs like 'Stairway To Paradise'.

The school I went to was an old ex-public school, the Liverpool Institute. It was very dark, dank and gloomy – it seems almost Dickensian, looking back on it. You started aged eleven and were immediately in the third year. It was a hangover, because years before you would have gone there aged nine. There were all these little crazies: 'Why am I in the third year when this is my first year?'

A lot of people don't like school. I didn't like it very much, but I didn't dislike it; and I quite enjoyed bits of it. I enjoyed English literature because we had a good master. What I didn't like was being told what to do.

If I tried to get the bus at school it was always full, but if I walked for a quarter of an hour down to the pierhead where they started I could get on an empty bus and pick a prime seat (which was upstairs at the front, or back, depending on what the mood was). There was a little period later in my life when I would take a pipe up onto the top deck of a bus and sit there feeling like Dylan Thomas or someone, reading Beckett plays or Tennessee Williams.

As kids we went to Sunday school. My mum liked to see us go. We didn't do much else in the way of religion. Of course, everyone did the usual things, like sing the hymn at school assembly in the morning. I grew to like a lot of hymns that way. (When I started writing, I remember asking people, 'What does this sound like? How do you like this song?' And they'd say, 'Well, it sounds a bit like a hymn.' It was one of the damning things people said about some of my early numbers.)

Dad plus pipe with the boys on Welsh hill (Paul is on the left)

But I developed my religious philosophy at the pierhead. It was like Speakers' Corner. You always had the Catholics arguing with the Protestants. The Protestant would say, 'What my friend over there is telling you is all wrong. There is no such thing as mortal sin, you're not born a sinner.' And then the Catholic guy would start up: 'My friend over there doesn't know that there *is* such a thing as mortal sin, and if you don't get rid of your guilt you will burn in hell and damnation.' They couldn't get it together, even though they were both Christians. The Irish problem, the Middle-Eastern problem – it's all down to that.

I was exposed to many religious arguments on the pierhead, and I came to the conclusion that 'God' is just the word 'good' with the 'o' taken out, and 'Devil' is the word 'evil' with a 'D' added. Really, all that people have done throughout history is to personify the two forces of Good and Evil. And although they've given them many names – like Jehovah or Allah – I've got a feeling that it's all the same.

One memorable thing of importance happened when I was about eleven. My mum and dad and my brother and I went to Butlins holiday camp. I have a photograph of me there in short trousers and school blazer – a chubby little kid. (You would never wear your school uniform going on holiday, but I think it was all I had – my posh gear.) My brother took the picture. I'm in front of a hot-dog corner, which we thought was dead hip: an American hot-dog stand!

So I was standing there in my school cap and everything, on a

To this day, I have a deep love for the piano, maybe from my dad: it must be in the genes. He played the piano from when I was born through until I was well into The Beatles. And you can start to see where I'm coming from when you hear an old number like 'Stumbling', which is a very clever tune. Dad told me what was clever about it; he was my musical education. There was none in school; we never got music lessons. He would always point out things like the chord changes at the beginning of 'Stairway To Paradise'. Later, he'd tell us we should do that one with The Beatles. We'd say, 'Dad, Dad... "Build a stairway to paradise"? Please!'

We were listening recently to 'Like Dreamers Do', one of my early songs – and George and I looked at each other and he said, 'That's your old man, that's "Stairway To Paradise".' So a lot of my musicality came from my dad.

I remember my dad would often have a mate round and he would say, 'Now, he can *really* play.' There was one fellow called Freddie Rimmer, a pianist. I did talk to him later, and he didn't think he was *that* great, but to me as a child he was playing rich, juicy chords – the like of which I had never heard. He played the same things as my dad, 'Chicago' and all the old jazz songs. They were interested in funny time signatures without knowing it.

Dad was a pretty good self-taught pianist, but because he hadn't had training himself, he always refused to teach me. I would say, 'Teach us a bit,' and he would reply, 'If you want to learn, you've got to learn properly.' It was the old ethic that to learn, you should get a teacher. It *would* have been OK for him to teach me, but I respect the reason why he wouldn't. In the end, I learnt to play by ear, just like him, making it all up. I did then take lessons, but I always had a problem; mainly that I didn't know my tutor, and I wasn't very good at going into an old lady's house – it smelt of old people – so I was uncomfortable. I was just a kid. I quite liked what she was showing me, but then she started setting homework: 'By next week I want you to have learnt this.' I thought it was bad enough coming for lessons, but homework! That was sheer torture. I stuck it for four or five weeks, and then the homework really got difficult so I gave up. To this day I have never learnt to write or read music; I have a vague suspicion now that it would change how I'd do things.

My father did write a song – only the one, to my knowledge – and many years later I said, 'Dad, you know that song you wrote: "Walking In The Park With Eloise"?' He said, 'I didn't *write* it – I just made it up.' Anyway, I told him that I'd recorded it with some friends of mine in Nashville. One of the friends was Chet Atkins, and he'd brought along Floyd Cramer. We got together and made a little recording of the song specially to play to my dad.

Dad had told me: 'Learn the piano, because you'll get invited to parties.' He'd always play on New Year's Eve. Our family always had big New Year's Eve parties. They were some of the best parties I ever remember, because everyone got together.

Cousin Bett and son Ted, with Paul on Ted's pushchair

We kids were allowed to help behind the bar, which was a few crates and a bit of table. We were taught that if someone asked for a 'gin and it', it was gin and Italian, and that 'rum and black' was rum and blackcurrant. We learnt how to do it all: 'If they want beer, get it from that barrel there, and if they want mild, that's there.' It was wonderful, because everybody would get pissed out of their arses. Old Uncle Jack, a wheezy old man, would say, 'All right, son. Have you heard this one?' and tell the best jokes ever. A really good joke is a great acquisition for me, it's like gold bullion. I don't remember Uncle Jack ever coming up with a bad one, they were always killers. There'd be him and my Uncle Harry, drunk out of their minds. And at midnight on New Year's Eve at Uncle Joe's house in Aintree, a piper would come in – just a neighbour – and it was lovely; very, very warm.

When I used to talk to John about his childhood, I realised that mine was so much warmer. I think that's why I grew up to be so open about sentimentality in particular. I really don't mind being sentimental. I know a lot of people look on it as uncool. I see it as a pretty valuable asset.

The New Year's party would traditionally be my dad's night. I only took over as the New Year's Eve pianist from him because he had arthritis and he couldn't do it any more. There was an older man called Jack Ollie, married to a cousin of mine, who'd come up with a pint for me and plonk it on the top of the piano. He'd stand and listen to me, and as he sipped his pint he'd say, 'I like it, I like it – *I like it*.' That's all he'd say, and just buy me drinks.

I haven't done it for a while, but part of my repertoire was 'Red Red Robin', and 'Carolina Moon'. I had a lovely uncle, Ron, who would come up and say, 'All right, son. Now, you know "Carolina Moon"?' and I'd say, 'Yeah.' He'd say, 'Well, don't play it yet, wait till I tell you. I'll give you the OK.' I'd wait and everyone would get steamed up, you could feel the party rise and the atmosphere building, and at about eleven he'd come up to me and tap me on the shoulder – 'All right, son, go for it.' That would be it: 'Carolina Moon…' and everyone would cheer. He was always right, the timing was always spot on. I used to keep going for hours and hours, and it was good practice. It was a lot of my training. Later on, people wanted me to do 'Let It Be' and other songs of mine at these do's. But I never wanted to. It didn't seem kosher.

My dad was also a great crossword-puzzle man, and used to tell us kids to practise crossword puzzles – it would improve our word power. Having left school very early, he'd had to educate himself. He taught me words that no one else knew and I was the only kid in my class who could spell 'phlegm'. He had met a lot of people at his workplace whom he looked up to, so he and my mum believed in education and in furthering yourself. I think a lot of my ambition comes from them.

Dad could also be quite shy. My parents didn't tell me about sex, they were too embarrassed. Dad used to try to tell me, but it came out all wrong. He'd say, 'See those two dogs over there?' and I'd say, 'Well, throw some cold water over them.' – 'No, no, what I'm trying to tell you is…' He'd try to tackle the subject like that; but I found out from the other kids, anyway, when I was about eleven: 'Don't you know?' they'd say. 'Where have you been?'

But he was great; very well meaning, and always upwardly mobile. He didn't actually move very far up himself, but he aspired heavily and so did my mum. Because she was a nurse, my brother and I were always going to be doctors, which we could never have achieved because we were too lazy. That was the kind of environment I was in.

My mum dying when I was fourteen was the big shock in my teenage years. She died of cancer, I learnt later. I didn't know then why she had died.

My mum wanted us to speak properly and aspired to speak the Queen's English. One of my most guilty feelings is about picking her up once on how she spoke. She pronounced 'ask' with a long 'a' sound. And I said, 'Oh – "aarsk"! That's "ask", mum,' and I really took the piss out of her. When she died, I remember thinking, 'You asshole, why did you do that? Why did you have to put your mum down?' I think I've just about got over it now, doctor.

My mother's death broke my dad up. That was the worst thing for me, hearing my dad cry. I'd never heard him cry before. It was a terrible blow to the family. You grow up real quick, because you never expect to hear your parents crying. You expect to see women crying, or kids in the playground, or even yourself crying – and you can explain all that. But when it's your dad, then you know something's *really* wrong and it shakes your faith in everything. But I was determined not to let it affect me. I carried on. I learnt to put a shell around me at that age. There was none of this sitting at home crying – that would be recommended now, but not then.

That became a very big bond between John and me, because he lost his mum early on, too. We both had this emotional turmoil which we had to deal with and, being teenagers, we had to deal with it very quickly. We both understood that something had happened that you couldn't talk about – but we could laugh about it, because each of us had gone through it. It was OK for him to laugh at it and OK for me to laugh at it. It wasn't OK for anyone else. We could both laugh at death – but only on the surface. John went through hell, but young people don't show grief – they'd rather not. Occasionally, once or twice in later years, it would hit in. We'd be sitting around and we'd have a cry together; not often, but it was good.

Now Mum was gone there were chores to be done: I had to do the fire and a bit of cleaning. But we also made a point of playing out, too. We did have a couple of aunties, which was a blessing. Auntie Milly and Auntie Jinny came on Tuesdays, and that was a golden day in my week because I could come home and not have to do anything. They'd have a dinner waiting for me and I could just flop in a chair and go to sleep.

Sketches from Paul's schoolbook

I learnt to cook some things. I'm a reasonable cook. I used to take a tin of tomatoes and boil them down to make a very good tomato purée. Even when we started getting known, playing the clubs in Liverpool, my dad would show up at the Cavern with half a pound of sausages and throw them at me – and that would be dinner. I would be expected to go home, stick them under the grill and make some mashed potatoes – I'm a good mashed-potato maker to this day.

I went occasionally to watch football. My family team was Everton and I went to Goodison Park a couple of times with my uncles Harry and Ron. They were nice memories for me, but I wasn't that keen on football. (The Beatles weren't very sporty at all.) When I went to the match it was the witticisms that I liked. You'd always get the comedians in the crowd; they must be the people who invent jokes. I remember being at one game and a guy had a trumpet and was commenting on the game musically. Someone would have a shot at goal which would go way, way over the top and he'd play: 'Over the mountains, over the sea.' Very skilful.

My dad bought me a trumpet for my birthday, at Rushworth & Draper's (the *other* music store in town), and I loved it. There was a big hero-thing at the time. There had been Harry James – The Man With The Golden Trumpet – and now, in the Fifties, it was Eddie Calvert, a big British star who played 'Cherry Pink And Apple Blossom White' – all those gimmicky trumpet records. There were a lot of them around back then, so we all wanted to be trumpeters.

I persevered with the trumpet for a while. I learnt 'The Saints', which I can still play in C. I learnt my C scale, and a couple of things. Then I realised that I wasn't going to be able to sing with this thing stuck in my mouth, so I asked my dad if he'd mind if I swapped it for a guitar, which also fascinated me. He didn't, and I traded my trumpet in for an acoustic guitar, a Zenith, which I still have.

It was OK as a first guitar. Being left handed, I would play it upside down. Everyone else had right-handed guitars, but I learnt some chords my way up: A, D and E – which was all you needed in those days. I started writing songs, because now I could play *and* sing at the same time. I wrote my first when I was fourteen. It was called 'I Lost My Little Girl' – 'I woke up this morning, my head was in a whirl, only then I realised, lost my little girl, uh, huh, huh.' It's a funny, corny little song based on three chords – G, G7 and C. I liked the way one melody line went down and the other went up, which I think is called contrary motion. It was a very innocent little song. All my first songs, including that one, were written on the Zenith; songs like 'Michelle' and 'I Saw Her Standing There'. It was on this guitar that I learnt 'Twenty Flight Rock', the song that later got me into the group The Quarry Men.

Eventually, it got the worse for wear. My cousin Ian was quite a good carpenter (he and his dad were builders), and he repaired it for me with a brace unit and two-inch screws, the sort used for holding up shelves. It's actually been properly restored now, and looking better than it ever looked.

John was the local Ted. You saw him rather than met him. I know John's story, and as I got older I realised it was his childhood that made John what he was. His father left home when he was four. I don't think John ever got over that. I talked to him about it. He would wonder, 'Could he have left because of me?' Of course he couldn't, but I don't think John ever shook off that feeling.

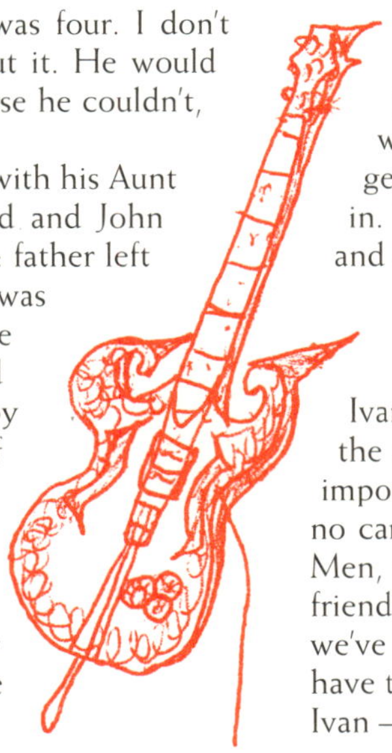

Instead of living with his mother, he went to live with his Aunt Mimi and Uncle George. Then Uncle George died and John began to think that there was a jinx on the male side: father left home, uncle dead. He loved his Uncle George; he was always quite open about loving people. All those losses would really have got to him. His mother lived in what was called 'sin' – just living with a guy by whom she had a couple of daughters, John's half sisters, Julia and Jacqui; very nice people. John really loved his mother, idol-worshipped her. I loved her, too. She was great: gorgeous and funny, with beautiful long red hair. She played the ukulele, and to this day, if I ever meet grown-ups who play ukuleles, I love them. She was killed, so John's life was tragedy after tragedy.

It was this tragedy that led John to be a wild guy, a Ted. There was a lot of aggression around Liverpool; there were lots of Teddy boys, and you had to try to avoid them if you saw them in alleyways. If, like John, you were a guy who had lived on his own, you had to put up some kind of a front. So he grew long sideburns, he had a long drape jacket, he had the drain-pipe trousers and the crepe-soled shoes. He was always quite defensive because of that. I would see him from afar, from the bus. This Ted would get on the bus, and I wouldn't look at him too hard in case he hit me, because he was just that much older. That was before I got to know him.

Ivan Vaughan was a friend of mine born on exactly the same day as me. (He was a smashing fellow, who unfortunately got Parkinson's disease and has died.) Ivan was also mates with John. Ivan said to me one day, 'The Woolton Village Fête is on Saturday' – he lived near John in Woolton – 'Do you want to come?' I said, 'Yeah, I'm not doing anything.'

It was 6th July 1957. We were fifteen years old. I remember coming into the fête; there was the coconut shy over here and the hoopla over there, all the usual things – and there was a band playing on a platform with a small audience in front of them.

We headed for the stage first, because as teenagers we were interested in music. There was a guy up on the platform with curly, blondish hair, wearing a checked shirt – looking pretty good and quite fashionable – singing a song that I loved: the Del-Vikings' 'Come Go With Me'. He didn't know the words, but it didn't matter because none of us knew the words either. There's a little refrain which goes, 'Come little darlin', come and go with me, I love you darling.' John was singing, 'Down, down, down to the penitentiary.' He was filling in with blues lines, I thought that was good, and he was singing well. There was a skiffle group around him: tea-chest bass, drums, banjo, quite a higgledy-piggledy lot. They were called The Quarry Men because John went to the Quarry Bank school, and I quite liked them.

I wandered around the fair and then Ivan and I went backstage. The band were getting ready to move indoors, into the church hall for the evening show. There was some beer being drunk. Really, I was too young for that then, but, 'Sure, I'll have a sip.' I was trying to be in with the big lads who, being sixteen, were into pre-pub drinking. We went to the evening show and that was good, although a fight almost broke out; we'd heard that the gang from Garston was coming over. I was wondering what I had got myself into. I had only come over for the afternoon and now I was in Mafia land. But it all worked out fine, and I got on the piano.

John was a little afternoon-pissed, leaning over my shoulder, breathing boozily. We were all a little sloshed. I thought, 'Bloody hell, who's this?' But he was enjoying what I was playing, 'Whole Lotta Shakin' Goin' On' in C; and I knew 'Tutti Frutti' and 'Long Tall Sally'. Then I played guitar – upside down. I did 'Twenty Flight Rock', *and* knew all the words. The Quarry Men were so knocked out that I actually knew *and* could sing 'Twenty Flight Rock'. That's what got me into The Beatles.

I knew all the words because me and my mate Ian James had just got them. He and I used to get into all these records and write down the words. 'Twenty Flight Rock' was a hard record to get; I remember ordering it and having to wait weeks for it to come in. We'd buy from Curry's or NEMS. We used to go around shops and ask to hear a record, and then not buy it. They used to get very annoyed but we didn't care – now we knew the words. I never had a very big record collection.

I often pedalled around Woolton at that time, going to see Ivan. I lived a bike ride away, in Allerton. (You could walk through the golf links, so it was quite handily placed for me and John. It was important then whether you lived near each other or not. There were no cars for kids in those days.) Pete Shotton, who was in The Quarry Men, was cycling around too, and we met by chance. Pete was a close friend of John's. He said, 'Hey, Paul, it was good the other day, and we've been having a talk. Would you like to join the group?' I said, 'I'll have to think about it.' But I was quite excited by the offer, so – through Ivan – I agreed to join.

A great thing about Liverpool, Newcastle, Glasgow and the provinces, is that they all have places with famous names, and the first gig with The Quarry Men was on Broadway – in Liverpool. (We made our first record in a little demo studio in Kensington, Liverpool.) For my first gig, I was given a guitar solo on 'Guitar Boogie'. I could play it easily in rehearsal so they elected that I should do it as my solo. Things were going fine, but when the moment came in the performance I got sticky fingers; I thought, 'What am I doing here?' I was just too frightened; it was too big a moment with everyone looking at the guitar player. I couldn't do it. (I never played a solo again until a few years ago.) That's why George was brought in.

I knew George from the bus. Before I went to live in Allerton, I lived in Speke. We lived on an estate which they used to call the Trading Estate. (I understand now that they were trying to move industry there to provide jobs, but then we didn't ever consider why it was called a trading estate.) George was a bus stop away. I would get on the bus for school and he would get on the stop after. So, being close to each other in age, we talked – although I tended to talk down to him, because he was a year younger. (I know now that that was a failing I had all the way through the Beatle years. If you've known a guy when he's thirteen and you're fourteen, it's hard to think of him as grown-up. I still think of George as a young kid. I still think of Ringo as a very old person because he is two years older. He was the grown-up in the group: when he came to us he had a beard, he had a car and he had a suit. What more proof do you need of grown-upmanship?)

I told John and the other Quarry Men about this guy at school called George: 'He is a real good guitar player, so if you're thinking of guitar – this is your boy.' They said, 'OK, let's hear him, then.'

George could play 'Raunchy' so well it really sounded like the record. We were all on the top of an empty bus one night and I said, 'Go on, George.' He got his guitar out and sure enough he *could* play it, and everyone agreed, 'You're in. You've done it.' It was rather like me knowing the words to 'Twenty Flight Rock'. With George it was: 'He's a bit young, but by God he can play "Raunchy" well.' George was like our professional guitarist from then. Later, John did play some Chuck Berry-style solos, but he gave over the solo chair to George and became known as rhythm guitarist.

Dad and 'the smalls' – 20 Forthlin, Liverpool

John was at art school by now. I was fifteen, John was almost seventeen. It seemed an awful lot at the time. If we wanted to do anything grown-up we worried about George looking young. We thought, 'He doesn't shave... can't we get him to look like a grown-up?'

Once, George and I had gone to see the film *The Blackboard Jungle*. It starred Vic Morrow, which was good, but more importantly it had Bill Haley's 'Rock Around The Clock' as its theme tune. The first time I heard that, shivers went up my spine, so we *had* to go and see the film, just for the title song. I could just about scrape through the sixteen barrier. Even though I was baby-faced, I was just able to bluff it in the grown-up world; but George couldn't. He had all the attitude, but he really was young-looking. I remember going out into his back garden and getting a bit of soil and putting it on his lip as a moustache. It was ridiculous, but I thought, 'He looks the part – we'll get in.' And we did. It was a teenage juvenile-delinquent film, and we were quite disappointed: all acting and talking!

I actually went to see Bill Haley at the Odeon. I think it was twenty-four shillings. Consequently, I was the only one who could go, because no one else could save that amount. I didn't have any source of income; I had to save for quite a long time. I was very single-minded about it: once I'd had that tingle, I had to go. I remember I was in short trousers – for a rock'n'roll concert! It was great, although Vic Lewis and his orchestra had the first half of the show. I thought that was a bit of a swizz – I wanted Bill all the way.

I had film heroes. Fred Astaire was always one of my big heroes, he was just so suave and debonair. I liked his voice a lot. Marlon Brando we were all very keen on. Robb Wilton, a comedian, whose autograph I got once. One of my relatives was a stage-door keeper at the Liverpool Empire, and he'd get autographs for me. I'm generally quite good natured about giving autographs (not always, but generally) and it's all because I used to collect them myself at the Empire stage door, from the Crew Cuts, people like that. And the fact that they treated me well never left me.

I once wrote to Craven Cottage, Fulham Football Club, for Johnny Haynes's autograph and it's a special little tingly memory for me of it coming back in the post. Sir Peter Scott I wrote to. (I was a skiving bastard when you think about it, but I always thought nothing ventured nothing gained.) Peter Scott had a TV show and he used to draw various birds every week. I wrote to him, 'Can I have the drawings of them ducks if you're not doing anything with them?' I got a polite reply.

The telly showed us most of what was going on then. I'd first heard about 'Rock Around The Clock' on telly, and even Maharishi. Granada, the local television station, saw to it that anyone wandering through the region was nabbed and interviewed. So we would hear about all those things; rock'n'roll films – *The Blackboard Jungle*, Marlon Brando in *The Wild One* (I was a bit disappointed with *The Wild One*).

But it was music that I loved. There have been times when I've been feeling down, and then I've heard a particular song and it has lifted me. Me and my teenage mate Ian James both had fleck jackets with a little flap on the breast pocket, and we'd knock around the fairgrounds and places. If we were feeling lousy, we'd go back and play an Elvis 78 – 'Don't Be Cruel' – and we'd be right up there again. It could cure any blues.

I remember being in the assembly hall at school one day – it was a free period and all us kids were hanging out together. Somebody pulled out a music paper, and there was an advert for 'Heartbreak Hotel'. Elvis looked so great: 'That's him, that's him – the Messiah has arrived!' Then when we heard the song, there was the proof. That was followed by his first album, which I still love the best of all his records. It was so fantastic we played it endlessly and tried to learn it all. Everything we did was based on that album.

I went off Elvis after he left the army. I felt they tamed him too much. It was all wrong – *GI Blues* and *Blue Hawaii*. I know they have kitsch value to a lot of people now, and I have also heard people say that they liked Elvis best when he was fat and bloated in Vegas, because there was an edge, a fear that something was going wrong, which they could be voyeuristic about.

But I like him best around 1956, when he was young and gorgeous and had a twinkle in his eye; when he had a sense of humour, plus that great voice. He was an incredible vocalist. Try and do it sometime – we all have – and he is still the guv'nor. The video *Elvis Live in '56* is great, but it was just one year later that he went to Hollywood and the light had gone out of his eye. In that video he performs like he's playing to an audience of screaming girls, but by his actions he is saying, 'I don't believe in this screaming.' Every line, he is reacting. It is an incredible performance, which I love still. Elvis made a huge impression on us.

Chuck Berry was another massive influence with 'Johnny B. Goode'. We'd go up to John's bedroom with his little record-player and listen to Chuck Berry records, trying to learn them. I remember learning 'Memphis, Tennessee' up there.

I saw Eddie Cochran on television, too: *Oh Boy!*, I think it was. Most of the other guys like Cliff Richard and Marty Wilde were good singers, but Eddie was suddenly the first one who played guitar. He was playing 'Milk Cow Blues' and had a Gretsch guitar with a Bigsby vibrator, and it looked very glamorous.

*The Girl Can't Help It* is still *the* great music film. They had always treated music films as B pictures up till then, or used music just as a theme tune, as in *The Blackboard Jungle*. Or those little black-and-white productions with an Alan Freed as the personality, and lots of what they thought were 'black acts'. To us it was not just *a* black act, it was Clyde McPhatter! We idolised these people and we always thought they were given crummy treatment – until *The Girl Can't Help It*. There is a famous moment at the beginning when Tom Ewell takes the screen. He says, 'Wait a minute,' and pushes the picture out so it becomes a wide screen. Then he clicks his fingers and it changes from black-and-white to colour: the big epic, exactly what we wanted! Then Jayne Mansfield comes on and the game's over, and the guy's glasses break. At the same time, Little Richard is singing 'The Girl Can't Help It', and then Eddie Cochran does 'Twenty Flight Rock'. And Gene Vincent sings 'Be Bop A Lula', which was the first record I ever bought. I still love that film.

There were lots of people coming up then. Buddy Holly was completely different; he was out of Nashville, so that introduced us to the country-music scene. I still like Buddy's vocal style. And his writing. One of the main things about The Beatles is that we started out writing our own material. People these days take it for granted that you do, but nobody used to then. John and I started to write because of Buddy Holly. It was like, 'Wow! He writes and is a musician.'

We'd always watched the Elvis films checking to see if he could play guitar, and he *could* – a little bit. He wasn't bad; he held the shapes. Some 'guitarists' held like wallyville. We'd think: 'That's not a shape, that is not a chord,' so it would be: 'Goodbye – we don't like you any more. You mustn't strum the guitar if you can't play. Put it down and dance.' But you could tell that Buddy played the solo on 'Peggy Sue'. We were very attracted to him for that reason, and the fact that there was always 'Holly/Petty' or 'Petty/Holly' on the records, so we knew he was one of the writers. We tried for ages to learn the intro to 'That'll Be The Day', and finally John found it. Buddy did it in F with a capo, but we didn't know that so we did it in A.

John was very short-sighted. He wore glasses, but he would only wear them in private. Until Buddy Holly arrived on the scene he would never get them out because he felt like an idiot, with his big horn-rimmed glasses. So he was constantly banging into things; he used to make a joke out of it. Another friend of his at college, Geoff, was even more short-sighted. John and Geoff used to have very funny moments going around town: two blind guys who wouldn't put their glasses on. But when Buddy came out, the glasses came out too. John could go on stage and see who he was playing to. In our imaginations back then, John was Buddy and I was Little Richard or Elvis. You're always someone when you start.

Rock'n'roll wasn't all I liked in music. Kids these days must find it hard to imagine a time when rock'n'roll was only one of 'the musics'. Now it is *the* music. There is a huge spectrum, from pop to serious blues players. Back then I wasn't necessarily looking to be a rock'n'roller. When I wrote 'When I'm Sixty-Four' I thought I was writing a song for Sinatra. There were records other than rock'n'roll that were important to me. And that would come out in The Beatles doing songs like 'Till There Was You'.

I had an elder cousin, Elizabeth Danher (now Robbins). She was quite an influence on me. She had a fairly grown-up record collection, and she would say, 'Have you heard this?' She was the first person ever to play me 'My Funny Valentine' – 'Don't change a hair for me, not if you care for me.' The words were good. For the same reason I've always liked Chuck Berry, who writes great lyrics.

Betty would play me records like Peggy Lee's 'Fever'. Peggy Lee did 'Till There Was You' as well. I didn't know that was from the musical *The Music Man* until many years later. (Funnily enough, my company now publishes the music from that show.) This led me to songs like 'A Taste Of Honey' and things which were slightly to the left and the right of rock'n'roll.

The original 1958 shellac disc featuring 'That'll Be The Day' and 'In Spite Of All The Danger'

John's, George's and my tastes were all pretty much in common. We shared our influences like mad. And when John would show another side to his musical taste, it would be similar to what I'd been brought up on, like my dad's music. One of John's favourite songs was 'Don't Blame Me'. It is a really nice song that I believe his mother had shown him; another one was 'Little White Lies'. We would learn the chords to some of these. But the main feeling was for the rock'n'roll and that was what we started to devour.

When we weren't playing parties or talent contests we would listen to other guys on guitar, and it became a quest to find chords and records. It was like looking for the Holy Grail. We would hear of some guy in Fazakerley – was *that* a long way away! It was, of course, in Liverpool but it was like going across the world for us: this guy knows B7! We must all go on a journey. So a little crowd of us would get on the bus there. It would be enough that he knew B7. We'd sit down: 'Oh guru, we hearest thou knowest B7. *Please* show it to us.' – 'Certainly, kids.' Then we'd go home: 'Wey-hey, we know E, A and D – now let's get B7.' We didn't know exactly how to do the last part of B7 for a while.

A rumour reached town one day that there was a man over the hills who had the record 'Searchin'' by The Coasters. Colin, the drummer with John's skiffle group, knew him and so there was a great trek to find the man, and indeed we found him. And relieved him of it. It was too big a responsibility for him to keep. We couldn't return it. We just had to have it; it was like gold dust. 'Searchin'' became a big number with The Beatles; we always used to do it at the Cavern. (There were little groups of fans there who gave themselves names. One group was called The Woodentops and there were two girls, Chris and Val, who would shout in their Scouse accents, 'Sing "Searchin'", Paul. Sing "Searchin'".')

That was how we found things out – going on a bus somewhere to see a man with a record, or to teenage parties. Kids would come with a handful of 45s – a little shopping bag full of them. And great villainy went on then, of course. As people got more and more drunk we used to nick their records.

I'd started fiddling around on my dad's piano again. I wrote 'When I'm Sixty-Four' on that when I was still sixteen (it was all rather tongue in cheek) and I never forgot it. I wrote that tune vaguely thinking it could come in handy in a musical comedy or something. Like I say, I didn't know what kind of career I was going to take back then.

I remember standing at the bus stop, thinking, 'If only I could win £75,000 on the pools and have the bare essentials of life – a guitar, a car and a house.' I couldn't even think of anything else. My dad gave me ten shillings once and, as far as I can recall, that's the only person in my whole life who's ever given me anything for free.

I would often sag off school for the afternoon and John would get off art college, and we would sit down with our two guitars and plonk away. We'd go to my house because there wasn't really anywhere else. Dad was at work. We'd get a pipe out and smoke some Typhoo tea to feel like adults. (It didn't taste too good.) We'd both have acoustic guitars and we'd sit opposite each other and play. It was great, because instead of looking into my own mind for a song I could see John playing – as if he was holding a mirror to what I was doing. It was a good way to write.

We wrote songs together. I wrote them down in an exercise book and above them it always said, 'Another Lennon/McCartney original.' Next page, 'Another Lennon/McCartney original.' It was just the lyrics and indications of the chords. We would have to remember the melodies, with indications of the 'oh's that would be the back-up vocals; I had no way of writing them down. There were no cassettes and you could hardly go to the expense of getting hold of a Grundig tape-recorder. You had to know somebody who had one. We did know one person, but we didn't record much on it – we weren't *that* interested in our own material early on. The whole deal was to remember the songs we'd written. John and I had an unwritten law, which was that if *we* couldn't remember them, then how could we expect people who hadn't written them to remember them?

We did 'Love Me Do' and 'I Saw Her Standing There', and got the basis of a partnership going. One of us would come up with an idea and then it would see-saw. So there was a mild competitiveness in that we were ricocheting our ideas. 'Love Me Do' was very much G and G7, C and D – not too hard. The harmonica is a great bit. John was a good harmonica player. He had a chromatic one, which is more like Stevie Wonder's – it was a little square, so he had to learn how to get the blues sounds out of it.

We were learning our skill. John would like some of my lines and not others. He liked most of what I did, but there would sometimes be a cringe line, such as, 'She was just seventeen, she'd never been a beauty queen.' John thought, 'Beauty queen? Ugh.' We were thinking of Butlins so we asked ourselves, what should it be? We came up with, 'You know what I mean.' Which was good, because you *don't* know what I mean.

We were learning together and gradually the songs got better and most of what we called our 'first hundred' (which was probably about five – we would lie our faces off then to get anyone to notice us) were written in my house in Forthlin Road. Then we had to waft all the tea-tobacco smell away and get out before my dad came home and caught us.

In those early days, you could go to the local studios and, as long as you could get the money together – five pounds, which was a lot for kids to find – you could cut a record. You would show up with all your equipment and wait; it was a bit like a doctor's waiting room. When the group or the performer before you had made their record, you would go into the studio and a guy would come in, adjust a few microphones and you would sing. Then it was back out to the waiting room for fifteen minutes while he processed the tape (I think it was tape, though it went straight onto shellac), and off you went. It was a very primitive recording.

We made a shellac disc like that in 1958. There were five of us: George, John, Colin Hanton, 'Duff' Lowe and me. Duff was a friend of mine from school who could play the piano. He could play the arpeggio at the beginning of Jerry Lee's 'Mean Woman Blues'. That was the reason he was in. No one else we knew could play arpeggios right up the piano keyboard; we could do one broken chord and pause, and then do another and pause again – he could go right through with the correct fingering.

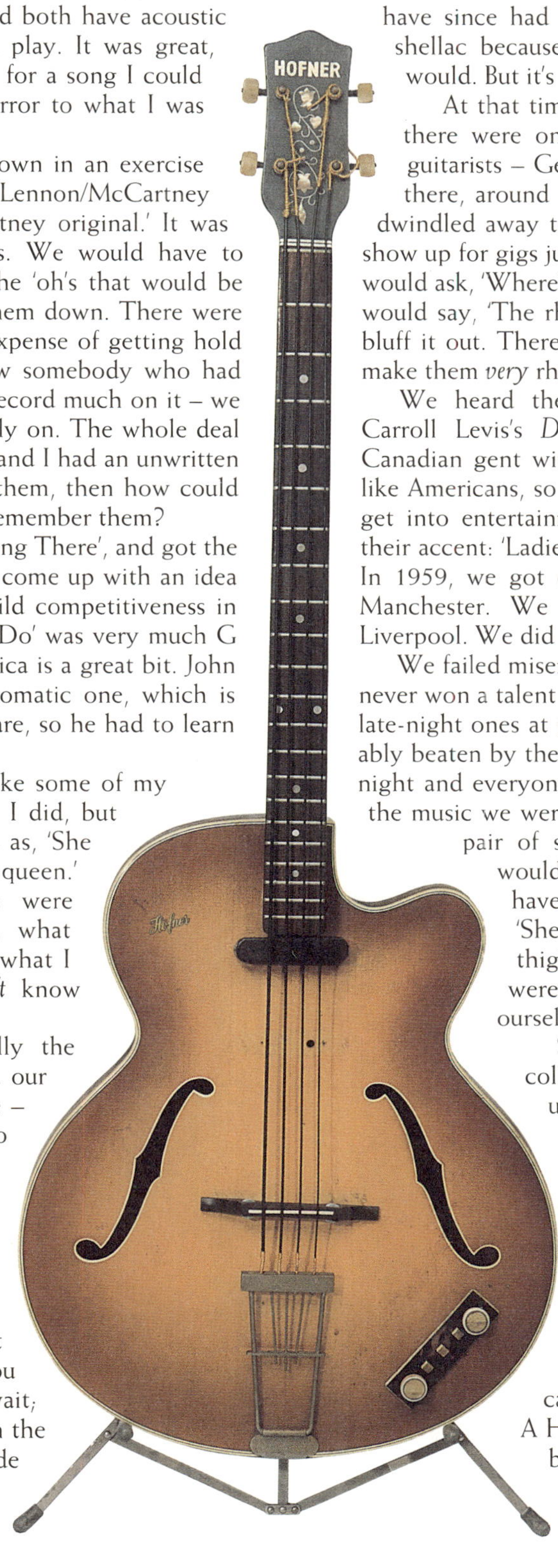


We went to Phillips in Kensington, which sounded very posh. John sang 'That'll Be The Day', and the B side was 'In Spite Of All The Danger'; a self-penned little song very influenced by Elvis. John and I sang it and George played the solo.

When we got the record, the agreement was that we would have it for a week each. John had it a week and passed it on to me. I had it for a week and passed it on to George, who had it for a week. Then Colin had it for a week and passed it to Duff Lowe – who kept it for twenty-three years. Later, when we were famous, he said, 'Hey, I've got that first record.' I ended up buying it back for a very inflated price. I have since had some replicas made. I don't want to play the shellac because it would wear out, as demos in those days would. But it's great to have.

At that time I was playing guitar too. In fact, at one time there were only three of us in the band, and we were all guitarists – George, John and me. We were playing here and there, around Liverpool, and after a while everyone else had dwindled away to get jobs, go to college, whatever. We would show up for gigs just with three guitars, and the person booking us would ask, 'Where's the drums, then?' To cover this eventuality we would say, 'The rhythm's in the guitars,' stand there, smile a lot, bluff it out. There was not a lot you could say to that, and we'd make them *very* rhythmic to prove our point.

We heard there were opportunities on talent shows like Carroll Levis's *Discoveries*. Carroll Levis was a rather portly Canadian gent with blondish hair. We thought Canadians were like Americans, so they were very special to us. They could easily get into entertainment, as Hughie Green did – just because of their accent: 'Ladies and gennelmen...' Oh wow, he's professional! In 1959, we got on Levis's *Discoveries* and went to Ardwick in Manchester. We rehearsed our set on the train over from Liverpool. We did 'Think It Over' and 'Rave On'.

We failed miserably in the contest – we always got beaten. We never won a talent show in our lives. We were always playing little late-night ones at pubs and working-men's clubs. We were inevitably beaten by the woman on the spoons, because it was eleven at night and everyone was well tanked up, they didn't want to hear the music we were playing. It was always the fat old lady with a pair of spoons who would beat us hands down. We would come back on the bus saying, 'We shouldn't have lost to her, you know, she wasn't that good.' – 'She had a certain something about her, on the thighs, you know?' – 'No, we were better, we really were: they were all pissed.' We had to buoy ourselves up after every failure.

Stuart Sutcliffe was a friend of John's from art college. Stuart had sold a painting for £65. (He used to paint in the style of Nicolas de Staël, his favourite artist. The paintings were basically abstract – to us it looked like throwing on a bit of paint and wiggling it about a bit.) So what do you do with £65? We all reminded him over a coffee: 'Funny you should have got that amount, Stuart – it is very near the cost of a Hofner bass.' He said, 'No, I can't just spend all that.' It was a fortune in those days, like an inheritance. He said he had to buy canvases or paint. We said, 'Stu, see reason, love. A Hofner, a big ace group... fame!' He gave in and bought this big Hofner bass that dwarfed him. The trouble was he couldn't play well. This was a bit of a drawback, but it looked good, so it wasn't too much of a problem.

When he came into the band, around Christmas of 1959, we were a little jealous of him; it was something I didn't deal with very well. We were always slightly jealous of John's other friendships. He was the older fellow; it was just the way it was. When Stuart came in, it felt as if he was taking the position away from George and me. We had to take a bit of a back seat. Stuart was John's age, went to art college, was a very good painter and had all the cred that we didn't. We were a bit younger, went to a grammar school and weren't quite serious enough.

So, with whatever occasional drummer we had – and there were a few – that made five of us.

# I WAS BORN IN 12 ARNOLD GROVE, LIVERPOOL, IN FEBRUARY 1943.

My dad had been a seaman, but by then he was driving a bus. My mother was from an Irish family called French, and she had lots of brothers and sisters. My mother was Catholic. My father wasn't and, although they always say people who weren't Catholics were Church of England, he didn't appear to be anything.

# GEORGE HARRISON

I had two brothers and one sister. My sister was twelve when I was born; she'd just taken her Eleven Plus. I don't really remember much of her from my childhood because she left home when she was about seventeen. She went to teacher training college and didn't come back after that.

My grandmother – my mother's mother – used to live in Albert Grove, next to Arnold Grove; so when I was small I could go out of our back door and around the back entries (they called them 'jiggers' in Liverpool) to her house. I would be there when my mother and father were at work.

My father's father, whom I never knew, was a builder, and he built a lot of the great Edwardian houses in Princes Road, Liverpool. That was where all the doctors and other professionals lived. They knew how to build in those days: good masonry, bricks and timber. Perhaps my interest in architecture comes from my grandfather. I like to see nice buildings, whether it be a little cottage with a thatched roof or St Pancras Station. I always felt that life was to go through and grow and make opportunities, make things happen. I never felt that because I was from Liverpool I shouldn't live in a big mansion house myself one day.

Our house was very small. Two up and two down – step straight in off the pavement, step right out of the back room. The front room was never used. It had the posh lino and a three-piece suite, was freezing cold and nobody ever went in it. We'd all be huddled together in the kitchen, where the fire was, with the kettle on, and a little iron cooking stove.

A lot of the garden was paved over (except one bit where there was a one-foot-wide flowerbed), with a toilet at the back and, for a period of time, a little hen-house where we kept cockerels. There was a zinc bathtub hanging on the backyard wall which we'd bring in and fill with hot water from pans and boiling kettles. That would be how we had a bath. We didn't have a bathroom: no jacuzzis.

My earliest recollection is of sitting on a pot at the top of the stairs, having a poop – shouting, 'Finished!' Another very early memory is as a baby, of a party in the street. There were air-raid shelters and people were sitting around tables and benches. I must have been no more than two. We used to have a photograph of me there, so it's probably only because I could relive the scene when I was younger, through the photograph, that I remember it.

Arnold Grove was a bit like Coronation Street, though I don't remember any of the neighbours now. It was behind the Lamb Hotel in Wavertree. There was a big art-deco cinema there called the Abbey, and the Picton clock tower. Down a little cobbled lane was the slaughterhouse, where they used to shoot horses.

In the early days, the city of Liverpool was really busy. The Mersey was very prominent with all the ferry boats, and the big steamers coming in from America or Ireland. There were many old buildings and monuments; slightly dirty, but basically nice. And amongst all the fine buildings were big bombed-out areas that had never been cleared. (Even until the day in 1963 when I left Liverpool there were still many patches full of rubble from direct hits.) Going shopping, there would be crowds of people on one or other bomb-site, watching a bloke in handcuffs and chains inside a sack, trying to escape. There were always people doing that kind of thing – the Houdini syndrome.

Tramlines ran through cobbled granite streets, and overhead, the tram cables. We went everywhere on the tram, and we'd go on the underground train across to the Wirral. By the time I had a bike, buses had replaced the trams, and they ripped out all the tramlines and asphalted over the cobbles.

George, his mother and his sister Louise

GEORGE: Me and my mum, with guitars and bottles of Drambuie.

I have memories of being taken around by my mother when she went shopping on Saturdays. I used to be dragged around, seeing old ladies whom she always seemed to know and had to visit. They probably weren't that old, but when you are a child anyone over twenty seems old.

And there were news theatres – cinemas in little period buildings – that would show cartoons and the Pathé Pictorial News. They wouldn't have any main features and a show would be about fifty minutes long. So you could do your shopping and when you got tired go and have a coffee, go to the news theatre, watch a few cartoons, then go and continue shopping.

When I was very small I joined the Cubs, which was at a Catholic church called St Anthony's of Padua – a hell of a long way to go to Cubs! (I had to fly there Alitalia – the only airline with hair under its wings.) And when we got home Akela would thrash us to sleep with her woggle. My mother used to go to church occasionally, at the usual times – Easter, Christmas and that – and as a kid I would get taken with her. I went to Communion aged eleven. But I avoided the rest because by then we'd moved out to Speke.

I didn't really like school. I remember going to the infant school for a while. That didn't please me too much. I have three recollections of Dovedale Road Infant School: the smell of boiled cabbage, a little girl who had blond curly hair and a Peter Pan house in the corner of the room, made by all the kids.

Then I went to Dovedale juniors. That was quite good because there was a lot of sport. There was football and messing about. I used to think I was able to run pretty quick, and I liked playing football. I think all kids think they are good, but really they are useless. John was at Dovedale when I was there. We were both in the same schoolyard but I didn't know him – probably because when I was in my first year, he was in his last.

I was still at Dovedale when we moved to Speke. I now lived in Upton Green, No. 25. They'd been building new council houses out there with bathrooms and kitchens. We'd been waiting for a new house for years and eventually we got to the top of the list and moved there.

Speke is on the outskirts of Liverpool going away from the docks. It was quite a way out, about a forty-minute bus ride. As the Mersey river winds upwards, it becomes narrower at Widnes and Runcorn. Out there were all the factories built in the Forties – Bryant and May (who made matches) and Evans Medical Supplies. Dunlop had a place right on the edge of Speke airport. On the airport perimeter was a great place, Speke Hall, an old Tudor building.

We were just a stone's throw from Widnes. I used to go all the time down to Oglet, the shoreline of the river. The tide would go out miles and the riverbed would be all mud. People would go up and down it on motorbikes. I would walk for hours along the mud cliffs of the Mersey and through farm fields and woods. I liked the outdoors.

I remember some nasty moments after we'd moved to Speke. There were women whose husbands were running away and other women who were having kids every ten minutes. And men were always wandering round, going into houses – shagging, I suppose. I remember my mother having to deal with someone who'd come around cursing and swearing about something or other. She got a bucket of water and threw it from the front step and closed the door and went in. She had to do that on a couple of occasions.

Priests used to come round to all the houses in the neighbourhood collecting money. We weren't particularly bad, but there were some really awful families in some houses. They'd switch all the lights off, turn the radio down and pretend they were out. My dad was making probably £7 10s a week, so a donation of five shillings, which he would give, was quite a lot of money. I never saw people out of work at that time. I was probably too small to notice. When you're young you're just dealing with day-to-day things, as opposed to following world politics or anything else outside your life.

They built a large church out of all the donations. Before that, there was a temporary church in a big wooden hut. It had the stations of the cross around it, and that's my earliest remembrance of wondering, 'What is all this about?' OK, I could see Christ dragging his cross down the street with everybody spitting on him, and I got the gist of that; but it didn't seem to make any sense.

I felt then that there was some hypocrisy going on, even though I was only about eleven years old. It seemed to be the same on every housing estate in English cities: on one corner they'd have a church and on the other corner a pub. Everybody's out there getting pissed and then just goes in the church, says three Hail Marys and one Our Father and sticks a fiver in the plate. It felt so alien to me. Not the stained-glass window or the pictures of Christ; I liked that a lot, and the smell of the incense and the candles. I just didn't like the bullshit. After Communion, I was supposed to have Confirmation, but I thought, 'I'm not going to bother with that, I'll just confirm it later myself.'

From then on, I avoided the church, but every Thursday a kid would come round to herald the arrival of the priest. They'd go round all the streets, knock on the door and shout, 'The priest's coming!' And we'd all go, 'Oh shit,' and run like hell up the stairs and hide. My mother would have to open the door and he'd say, 'Ah, hello Mrs Harrison, it's nice to see you again, so it is. Eh be Jesus...' She'd stuff two half-crowns in his sweaty little hand and off he'd go to build another church or pub.

I had a happy childhood, with lots of relatives around – relatives and absolutes. I was always waking up in the night, coming out of the bedroom, looking down the stairs and seeing lots of people having a party. It was probably only my parents and an uncle or two (I had quite a few uncles with bald heads; they'd say they got them by using them to knock pub doors open), but it always seemed that they were partying without telling me. I don't remember too much about the music. I don't know whether they had music at the parties at all. There was probably a radio on.

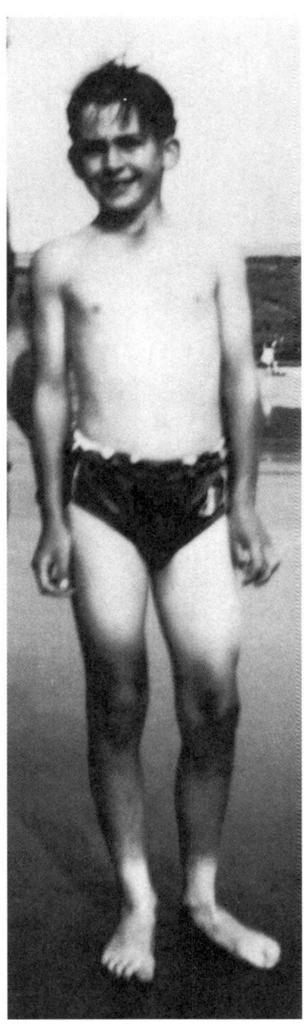

In those days the radios were like crystal sets. Well, not quite. The radios had batteries: funny batteries with acid in them. You had to take the battery down to a shop on the corner and leave it with them for about three days to charge up.

We'd listen to anything that was played on the radio: Irish tenors like Josef Locke, dance-band music, Bing Crosby, people like that. My mother would always be turning the dial on the radio until she'd found a station broadcasting in Arabic or something, and we'd leave it there until it became so crackly that you couldn't hear it any more. Then she'd tune in to something else.

I remember as a child listening to the records my parents had – all the old English music-hall music. We had one record called 'Shenanaggy Da': 'Old Shenanaggy Da, he plays his guitar...' but the hole in the middle was off centre so it sounded weird. Brilliant. There was another called 'Fire, Fire, Fire, Fire, Fire'. It went: 'Why do all the engines chuff-chuff? It's a fire, fire, fire, fire, fire.' It had loads of verses, with sound effects of fire engines and crowds gasping and people trapped up some building. It was a double-sided 78. When it ran out on one side, it said, 'Eh, turn me over lads and I'll play you some more.' And when you turned it over it went back into the refrain and another twenty verses.

I don't understand people who say, 'I only like rock'n'roll,' or, 'I only like the blues' or whatever. Even Eric Clapton says he was influenced by 'The Runaway Train Went Over The Hill'. As I said in my own book, *I Me Mine*, my earliest musical memories are things like 'One Meatball' by Josh White, and those Hoagy Carmichael songs and others like it. I would say that even the crap music that we hated – that late Forties, early Fifties American schmaltz records like 'The Railroad Runs Through The Middle Of The House' or the British 'I'm A Pink Toothbrush, You're A Blue Toothbrush' – even that has had some kind of influence on us, whether we like it or not. All that is in me somehow, and is capable of coming out at any point. It shows in the comic aspect of some of our songs, like the middle of 'Yellow Submarine'.

Aintree racecourse, Liverpool, 1955

You can hear something and think that you don't like it, and think that it's not influencing you. But you are what you eat, you are what you see, what you touch, what you smell and what you hear. Music has always had a transcendental quality inasmuch as it reaches parts of you that you don't expect it to reach. And it can touch you in a way that you can't express. You can think that it hasn't reached you, and years later you'll find it coming out. I think, as Beatles, we were fortunate that we were open to all kinds of music. We just listened to whatever happened to be on the radio. That was the main thing in those days.

My eldest brother, Harry, had a little portable record-player that played 45s and 33s. It could play a stack of ten records, though he only owned three. He kept them neatly in their sleeves; one of them was by Glenn Miller. When he was out everything was always left tidy; the wires, the lead and plugs were all wrapped around, and nobody was supposed to use it. But as soon as he'd go out my brother Pete and I would put them on.

We'd play anything. My dad had bought a wind-up gramophone in New York when he was a seaman and had brought it back on the ship. It was a wooden one, where you opened the doors; the top doors had a speaker behind and the records were stored in the bottom. And there were the needles in little tin boxes.

He'd also brought some records from America, including one by Jimmie Rodgers, 'the Singing Brakeman'. He was Hank Williams's favourite singer and the first country singer that I ever heard. He had a lot of tunes such as 'Waiting For A Train', 'Blue Yodel 94' and 'Blue Yodel 13'. The one that my dad had was 'Waiting For A Train'; that led me to the guitar.

Later there were people like Big Bill Broonzy and a Florida country-and-western singer called Slim Whitman. He made big hits out of the tunes from the film *Rose Marie*. The first person I ever saw playing a guitar was Slim Whitman, either a photo of him in a magazine or live on television. Guitars were obviously coming in.

I'd just left Dovedale Junior School and gone to the big school, the Liverpool Institute, when I went into hospital. I got sick when I was twelve or thirteen with kidney trouble. I always used to get tonsilitis; childhood illnesses. I had a really sore throat, and this one year the infection spread and gave me nephritis, an inflammation of the kidneys.

I was in Alder Hey Hospital for six weeks on a non-protein diet: I had to eat spinach and horrible food. It was during this time that I first wanted to get a guitar. I heard that Raymond Hughes, who used to go to Dovedale – I was now at the Institute and hadn't seen him for a year – had a guitar he wanted to sell. £3 10s, it cost. It was a lot of money then, but my mum gave me the money and I went to Raymond's house and bought it.

It was a real cheapo horrible little guitar, but it was OK at the time. I saw that it had a bolt in the back of the neck. Being inquisitive, I got a screwdriver and unscrewed it and the whole neck fell off. I couldn't get it back on properly, so I put it in the cupboard in two pieces and left it there. Finally – it seemed like a year later – my brother Pete fixed it back together for me. Now it had a concave neck, so the most you could get out of it was a couple of chords. All the frets buzzed and the strings hit the frets.

My dad had played a guitar when he was in the Merchant Navy. But when there was no work, he gave up being a seaman and sold it. When I started playing, he said, 'I had a friend who plays,' and somehow he still knew him, and he phoned him up. His name was Len Houghton and he had an off-licence that he lived above. On Thursdays he would be closed, so my dad arranged for me to go down there each week on that night for two or three hours. He'd show me new chords and play songs to me like 'Dinah' and 'Sweet Sue', and Django Reinhardt or Stéphane Grappelli sort of tunes. Songs of the Twenties or Thirties, like 'Whispering'. It was very good of him.

With Arthur Kelly

By this time I'd met Paul McCartney on the bus, coming back from school. In those days they hadn't brought the buses into the housing development where I lived, so I had to get off the bus and walk for twenty minutes to get home. Paul lived close by where the buses then stopped, on Western Avenue. Just nearby was Halewood, where I used to play in the fields. There were ponds with sticklebacks in. Now there's a sodding great Ford factory there that goes on for acres and acres.

So Paul and I used to be on the same bus, in the same school uniform, travelling home from the Liverpool Institute. I discovered that he had a trumpet and he found out that I had a guitar, and we got together. I was about thirteen. He was probably late thirteen or fourteen. (He was always nine months older than me. Even now, after all these years, he is still nine months older!)

As I became a teenager, I first heard Fats Domino's 'I'm In Love Again'. That was what I would call the first rock'n'roll record I ever heard. Another record from when I was still a schoolboy was The Del-Vikings' 'Whispering Bells' – I still remember the sound of the guitars on that. And then, of course, 'Heartbreak Hotel'. That just came out of somebody's radio one day and lodged itself permanently in the back of my brain. Elvis, Little Richard and Buddy Holly influenced us very much, and to this day theirs is my favourite rock'n'roll music.

The pop scene then was mixed. There were the big stars – the Fats Dominos, The Coasters and Elvis – and then artists that you heard records by, but never really saw much of; maybe a photo in a fan magazine. Then there were the British artists, such as Tommy Steele (the first pop or rock star in England) and later Cliff Richard. And the Larry Parnes lot: Billy Fury and Marty Wilde, and others. It was exciting, because it was the first time you ever saw a pink jacket or a black shirt, or a Fender Stratocaster or any electric guitar.

When you started seeing a performer come to the Liverpool Empire and they'd got an amplifier, it was so exciting. It was not like these days, when you've got so much to select from that you can have your own taste, a different taste from somebody else. In those days it was a case of beggars can't be choosers. We were just desperate to get anything. Whatever film came out, we'd try to see it. Whatever record was being played, we'd try to listen to, because there was very little of anything. It was only a few years after rationing. You couldn't even get a cup of sugar, let alone a rock'n'roll record.

I remember once how I'd got the money and I wanted 'Rock Around The Clock' by Bill Haley and I'd asked somebody in the family to get it for me. I couldn't wait to get that record. They came home, and they gave me a record and said, 'Oh, they sold out of Bill Haley, so I got you this one.' It was The Deep River Boys. I thought, 'Oh no, fuckin' hell.' It was such a disappointment. That was the first record I didn't get. I've learnt in my life that you mustn't disappoint people who are counting on you.

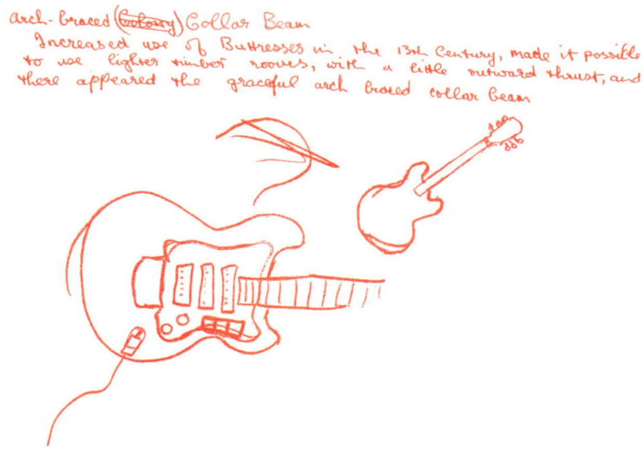


I wasn't able to see Buddy Holly when he came over, other than on the London Palladium TV show. When Bill Haley came to Liverpool, I couldn't afford a ticket. It was fifteen shillings – which was a lot of money for a schoolboy. I always wondered where Paul got his fifteen shillings from, because he got to see him. But I went to the Liverpool Empire in 1956 to see Lonnie Donegan, and people like Danny and the Juniors, and The Crew Cuts (they did 'Earth Angel' and 'Sh-Boom', which was a cover version of The Penguins' original).

I saw quite a few shows, the best being the Eddie Cochran one. This was a couple of years later. He was backed up by an English band. I remember Eddie Cochran well: he had his black leather waistcoat, black leather trousers and a raspberry-coloured shirt. He came on doing 'What'd I Say', and as the curtains opened he had his back to the audience, playing the riff. I was watching his fingers, to see how he played. He had his Gretsch guitar, the one in all the pictures, with a black Gibson pick-up and a Bigsby tremolo. It was the orange Chet Atkins 6120, like the one I later used on the Carl Perkins TV special, with the 'G' branded in the wood. He was a very good guitar player and that's what I remember most. I was very impressed by not only his songs (because he had a lot of very good songs including 'Summertime Blues', 'C'mon Everybody' and 'Twenty Flight Rock'), but by his cover numbers, like Ray Charles's 'Hallelujah, I Love Her So'.

There was a funny break in-between songs. He was standing at the microphone and as he started to talk he put his two hands through his hair, pushing it back. And a girl, one lone voice, screamed out, 'Oh, Eddie!' and he coolly murmured into the mike, 'Hi honey.' I thought, 'Yes! That's it – rock'n'roll!'

And, of course, he brought with him the great secret from America – the unwound third string. Years later, I became friendly with Joe Brown, who had toured with Eddie, and learnt about the unwound third string. When I listen to early Beatles recordings, one thing that's very apparent to me is a little piece that I play on the third string which is like three notes. It goes 'de diddle dum', which if I'd had an unwound, lighter-gauge third string, I could have done it in one bend. In those days I wasn't smart enough to think, 'I'll put another second string on in place of the third, so I can bend it.' But Eddie Cochran had that all sussed out.

First guitar, a £3 10s Egmond

The skiffle boom had started in my early teens. Lonnie Donegan had a much bigger influence on British rock bands than he was ever given credit for. In the late Fifties, he was virtually the only guitar player that you could see. He was the most successful person, and had the highest profile. He had a great voice, a lot of energy and sang great songs – catchy versions of Leadbelly tunes and things.

I loved him. He was a big hero of mine. Everyone got guitars and formed skiffle bands because of him. Skiffle came out of the blues, but the way it was performed made it accessible to us white Liverpudlians. It was dead cheap – just a washboard, a tea chest, a bit of string, a broom handle and a £3 10s guitar. And it was a simple way into music because a lot of the songs had just two chords, and the maximum was three. There were so many great songs; train songs like 'Midnight Special', 'Wabash Cannonball' and 'Rock Island Line' – hundreds of really good tunes that had their origins in black slave culture.

So everyone was in a skiffle group, and whilst most of them faded away the ones that were left became the rock bands of the Sixties. There was a folklore about those bands. I remember there was a band called Eddie Clayton (that Ringo was in for a while) and we thought, 'Hey, these are good.' A little later I formed a skiffle group called The Rebels, with Arthur Kelly and my brother, who had a guitar that he'd found in somebody's garage. We only played one gig, at the British Legion Club.

When I was thirteen or fourteen, I would sit at the back of the class and try to draw guitars: big cello guitars with 'f' holes, and little solid ones with cutaways. I was totally into all that. I even tried making a guitar, which was very bold. In ignorance you can do virtually anything. I only took woodwork for one year in school; I wasn't that good at it, but I wasn't that bad either. The things we did were very simple: a dovetail joint and a chamfered edge. I must have read somewhere about how to make a guitar, because there's no way I could have come up with the concept on my own.

I got some three-ply wood. I first drew the shape that I wanted, then cut it out. (It was like a Les Paul shape, but it had 'f' holes.) It had a hollow body, and on the inside of the back and the front I cut out little squares. I fitted dowelling into the holes to hold the front in place. Then I soaked and bent the wood that went around the edge. It was very rough and a bit lumpy where it was glued on. The big mistake I made was with the neck, which I couldn't make in one piece because I didn't have a piece of wood big enough. I made it go to just beyond the nut, with the head as a separate piece. I dug out the back of each and screwed in an aluminium plate to hold them together. I filled it all over with wood filler, bought the tail-piece, the bridge, the machine heads, the nut, and put the strings on. I put the 'f' holes in and even varnished it in sunburst colours. It must have taken me ages. Then, as I tightened up the strings, it just ripped itself apart. In frustration, I threw it in the shed and never spoke to it again.

The Hofner President was the first decent guitar that I had. It had big cutaway cello 'f' holes, based on the big Super Gibson guitars. I would sit around for hours, playing and trying to figure things out. I used to sit up late at night. I didn't look on it as practising, more learning. It was the only thing I really liked. When I had a new set of strings I'd take all the old ones off, and I'd polish the guitar and clean it and make it really impeccable.

In the very early days I'd bought a guitar manual, which showed the finger positions for some chords. After I met Paul I showed him the manual. He still had the trumpet at that point. We looked and worked out some chords, like C, F and G7. But it only showed the first two fingers of the C chord and the same with F; so I had to re-learn them later. I remember feeling a bit annoyed about that: 'Why didn't they show the full chord in the first place?'

I remember discovering inversions, when you learn all the chords around the bottom of the neck. Suddenly I realised how all the shapes transform up the neck – all the same chords inverted higher and higher. It was great, just working that out. Then when I was a bit older someone gave me a Chet Atkins album and I started to try and figure out tunes with different chords.

Left: Upton Green, Speke Centre: Hitchhiking with Paul Right: *South Liverpool Weekly News*, 4th May 1957

**Intense excitement is shown above by the clenched fists of George Harrison and Jim Kelly, who were watching the Cup Final on the projection television in the Speke Congregational Church Hall on Saturday last.**

**Spectators in church hall saw cup final**

I was never a technical guitar player; there was always a better player around. There was a bloke who went to school with Paul and me who ended up in The Remo Four – Colin Manley; he was one of those guys who could copy Chet Atkins when he'd been playing two tunes at the same time. Somehow I never had the patience. God knows how I ever made anything of myself. I used to sit there and practise as a kid, but I couldn't sit there forever; I wasn't that keen.

My first girlfriend was Rory Storm's sister, Iris Caldwell. She was really nice and had cotton wool in her bra. (She probably didn't ever think she was my girlfriend. You never know when you're young; you just fancy somebody, or someone's in the same room as you, and you end up thinking they're your girlfriend.) So I knew Rory before I knew The Beatles. I'd met Iris a couple of times and went round to her house and hung out. They had a little basement that they were trying to turn into a coffee club. That seemed to be the craze in the Fifties. Rory was an athlete. I remember a couple of times I came to have a date with Iris, and Rory would come running up to his front door sweating and panting, and checking his stop-watch, because he'd been training.

Rory's real name was Alan Caldwell. Ernie was their dad. They were a great family and were very friendly to all of us. Later – after we'd come back from Hamburg and were doing loads of gigs in Liverpool and the North of England – we used Rory's house as a place to hang out when we got back to town after shows. His mother Vi would make endless pots of tea and toast for us all.

Ernie was a porter in his spare time in the local hospital, Broad Green Hospital. He used to sing songs to the patients. He was a really nice fella, and a window cleaner by occupation. After we'd arrived late at night, he'd go to bed and they'd all make jokes about him, but in a nice way. He was a simple, quiet, mild-mannered bloke. By the time he died, we'd already made our records and left Liverpool. The sorry story I heard was that after Ernie died, Vi and Rory both committed suicide. Iris later married Shane Fenton, who became Alvin Stardust.

One year, Paul and I decided to go hitchhiking. It's something nobody would ever dream of these days. Firstly, you'd probably be mugged before you got through the Mersey Tunnel, and secondly everybody's got cars and is already stuck in a traffic jam. I'd often gone with my family down South to Devon, to Exmouth, so Paul and I decided to go there first.

We didn't have much money. We found bed-and-breakfast places to stay. We got to one town, and we were walking down a street and it was getting dark. We saw a woman and said, 'Excuse me, do you know if there's somewhere we could stay?' She felt sorry for us and said, 'My boy's away, come and stay at my house.' So she took us to hers – where we beat her, tied her up and robbed her of all her money! Only joking; she let us stay in her boy's room and the next morning cooked us breakfast. She was really nice. I don't know who she was – the Lone Ranger?

We continued along the South Coast, towards Exmouth. Along the way we talked to a drunk in a pub who told us his name was Oxo Whitney. (He later appears in *A Spaniard in the Works*. After we'd told John that story, he used the name. So much of John's books is from funny things people told him.) Then we went along to Paignton. We still had hardly any money. We had a little stove, virtually just a tin with a lid. You poured a little meths into the bottom of it and it just about burned, not with any velocity. We had that, and little backpacks, and we'd stop at grocery shops. We'd buy Smedley's spaghetti bolognese or spaghetti milanese. They were in striped tins: milanese was red stripes, bolognese was dark blue stripes. And Ambrosia creamed rice. We'd open a can, bend back the lid and hold the can over the stove to warm it up. That was what we lived on.

We got to Paignton with no money to spare so we slept on the beach for the night. Somewhere we'd met two Salvation Army girls and they stayed with us and kept us warm for a while. But later it became cold and damp, and I remember being thankful when we decided that was enough and got up in the morning and started walking again. We went up through North Devon and got a ferry boat across to South Wales, because Paul had a relative who was a redcoat in Butlins at Pwllheli, so we thought we'd go there.

At Chepstow, we went to the police station and asked to stay in a cell. They said, 'No, bugger off. You can go in the football grandstand, and tell the cocky watchman that we said it was OK.' So we went and slept on a hard board bench. Bloody cold. We left there and hitchhiked on. Going north through Wales we got a ride on a truck. The trucks didn't have a passenger seat in those days so I sat on the engine cover. Paul was sitting on the battery. He had on jeans with zippers on the back pockets and after a while he suddenly leapt up screaming. His zipper had connected the positive and negative on the battery, got red hot, and burnt a big zipper mark across his arse.

When we eventually got to Butlins, we couldn't get in. It was like a German prisoner-of-war camp – Stalag 17 or something. They had barbed-wire fences to keep the holiday-makers in, and us out. So we had to break in. (Ringo started off playing there.)

Paul moved from Speke to Forthlin Road in Allerton, which was very close to where John lived on Menlove Avenue. Paul had realised by then that he couldn't sing and play the trumpet at the same time, so he'd decided to get a guitar. We had started playing and were hanging out in school at that time, and when he moved we kept in touch. He lived close enough for me to go on my bike. It would take me twenty minutes or so. (I'm amazed when I go back now by car: what seemed like miles then is really only a three-minute car ride.)

There was a guy at the Liverpool Institute, Ivan Vaughan, that lived by John, who introduced Paul to him. John already had a reputation, he was the character of his school and he knew it. I met John a little later (I don't recall where) and they asked me to join the group, The Quarry Men. John was in the art college by this time. I don't know what I felt about him when I first met him; I just thought he was OK. At that age I only wanted to get into music. I think that with anybody you meet who sings or is into music like that, you just buddy with them instantly.

John's mother had taught him some chords. His guitar was cheap, with a little round sound-hole. It only had four strings. John didn't even know that guitars should have six strings. He was playing banjo chords: big extended finger chords. I said, 'What are you doing?' He thought that that was how it should be. So we showed him some proper chords – E and A and all those – and got him to put six strings on his guitar.

The Quarry Men had other members, who didn't seem to be doing anything, so I said, 'Let's get rid of them, then I'll join.' Nigel Whalley had a tea-chest bass and he was in the group for a week, and Ivan was there and a couple of others – one called Griff (Eric Griffiths), the guitar player. They came and went, and after a while there was only John, Paul and me left. That seemed to go on for a while. We played a few weddings and parties. John, Paul and I played at my brother Harry's wedding – drunk. We played the Cavern once. It was still a jazz place and they tried to kick us off, because we were rock'n'roll.

I would see quite a lot of John; he used to come round to my house. My mother was a big fan of music, and she was really pleased about me being interested in it. She'd been the one who'd bought me the guitar and she was really happy about having the guys around. And John was keen to get out of his house because of his Aunt Mimi, who was very stern and strict. He was always embarrassed by Mimi and he'd swear at her.

Above: John, Paul, George and… Dennis – Dinahs Lane, Liverpool. Right: After brother Harry's wedding

GEORGE: Upper 5E, my homework. I was fifteen. Paul drew the figure of the woman.

I remember going to John's house once, soon after we met. I was still at the Institute and I looked a bit young. We were trying to look like Teddy boys – and I must have looked pretty good, because Mimi didn't like me at all. She was really shocked and said, 'Look at him! Why have you brought this boy round to my house? He looks dreadful, like a Teddy boy.' And he'd say, 'Shut up, Mary, shut up.' So he would come round to my house a lot and my mother would give us little glasses of whisky.

I'd started to develop my own version of the school uniform. I had some cast-offs from my brother. One was a dog-toothed check-patterned sports coat, which I'd had dyed black to use as my school blazer. The colour hadn't quite taken, so it still had a slight check design to it. I had a shirt I'd bought in Lime Street, that I thought was so cool. It was white with pleats down the front, and it had black embroidery along the corners of the pleats. I had a waistcoat that John had given me, which he'd got from his 'uncle' Dykins (his mother's boyfriend), Mr Twitchy Dykins. It was like an evening-suit waistcoat – black, double-breasted, with lapels. The trousers John also gave me, soon after we first met – powder-blue drainpipes with turn-ups. I dyed them black as well. And I had black suede shoes from my brother.

Aunt Mimi's husband was George Smith, and his brother was our English teacher at the Institute. He was a little effeminate, to say the least, and always had a silk hankie out of his top pocket. His mannerisms and the way he talked were to us early-teen boys pretty hysterical, and all the boys called him Cissie Smith. He was always saying, 'They're not school shoes, Harrison. Come and stand in the Chewers' Corner.'

That outfit of mine was very risky, and it felt like all day, every day, for the last couple of years I was going to get busted. In those days we used Vaseline on our hair to get the rock'n'roll greased-back hairstyle. Also, you were supposed to wear a cap and a tie, and a badge on your blazer. I didn't have my badge stitched on, I had it loose. It was held in place by a pen clipped over it in my top pocket, so I could remove it easily, and the tie.

Paul and I used to skive out of school and try our best to pretend not to be grammar-school boys. We would hang out with John in the evenings. But in the school days we'd also go out at lunchtime – even though you weren't allowed out without a special dispensation from the Pope. We'd have to leg it out of school, go around the corner, dispose of as much of our school uniform as possible and then go into the art school. (The building was connected onto the Liverpool Institute.)

It was unbelievably relaxed there. Everybody was smoking, or eating egg and chips, while we still had school cabbage and boiled grasshoppers. And there'd be chicks and arty types, everything. It was probably very simple, but from where we came from it looked fun. We could go in there and smoke without anyone giving us a bollocking. John would be friendly to us – but at the same time you could tell that he was always a bit on edge because I looked a bit too young, and so did Paul. I must have only been fifteen then.

I remember that the first time I gained some respect from John was when I fancied a chick in the art college. She was cute in a Brigitte Bardot sense, blonde, with little pigtails. I was playing in Les Stewart's band. (I was in two bands at the same time – there weren't many gigs, one in every blue moon. He lived on Queen's Drive by Muirhead Avenue, so I was hanging out with him as well and learning music in the hope of making a couple of quid.) Anyway, Les had a party at his house and the Brigitte Bardot girl was there, and I pulled her and snogged her. Somehow John found out, and after that he was a bit more impressed with me.

Les played banjo, mandolin and guitar. I met him through a fella who worked in a butcher's shop. I'd got a job there as a delivery boy on a Saturday; the guy there had a Dobro guitar (the first one I ever saw) and knew Les. Les was a good player: Leadbelly tunes and Big

Below: George with early girlfriend, Jennifer Brewer, at Binfield Heath

Bill Broonzy and Woody Guthrie – more like rural blues and bluegrass, not rock'n'roll. I'd play along with his band – I don't even remember its name – and we did a few parties. It was there at a gig in a club in Hayman's Green in West Derby that I heard about another club being built at No. 8 Hayman's Green. I was taken down there and I looked into the cellar that was to become the Casbah. That's when I first met Pete Best. It was some months later that I remembered Pete and the fact that he had his own drum kit, and got him to join us so we could go to Hamburg.

Paul and I got to know Stuart Sutcliffe through going into the art college. Stuart was a thin, arty guy with glasses and a little Van Gogh beard; a good painter. John really liked Stuart as an artist. Stuart obviously liked John because he played the guitar and was a big Ted. Stuart was cool. He was great-looking and had a great vibe about him, and was a very friendly bloke. I liked Stuart a lot; he was always very gentle. John had a slight superiority complex at times, but Stuart didn't discriminate against Paul and me because we weren't from the art school. He started to come and watch us when we played at parties and he became a fan of ours. He actually got some parties for John, Paul and me to play at. It was just the three of us, mostly. And John was always trying to con his Students' Union into buying equipment for our group. He did eventually get an amplifier, so we had to play there occasionally. I can't even remember if we had an act; we must have learnt a few tunes together.

One art-school party in Liverpool, in a flat in the students' accommodation, was the first all-night party I ever went to. It was even designated an all-nighter: the rules were that you had to bring a bottle of wine, and an egg for your breakfast. So we bought a cheap bottle of plonk from Yates's Wine Lodge and put our eggs in the fridge when we arrived. The great thing about the party (and I'm sure John and Paul would agree) was that somebody had a copy of 'What'd I Say' by Ray Charles, a 45rpm with Part Two on the B side. That record was played all night, probably eight or ten hours non-stop. It was one of the best records I ever heard. I puked up next morning. Cynthia was there, and I remember saying drunkenly to her, 'I wish I had a nice girl like you.'

Panto Day in Liverpool was when students from Liverpool University and the art college collected money for local causes. It was a Rag day. Everyone dressed up weirdly with make-up and could do just about anything they liked: jump onto buses without paying, with tins for collecting money; go into shops, and generally go around the city having a laugh. Paul and I weren't students, but we decided it was a lark; so we met at John's place in Gambier Terrace, the flat he was sharing with Stuart, dressed up and joined in. John and Stuart had more collecting boxes than they should have so they gave a couple to us. After a few hours collecting we went back to Gambier Terrace and broke open the tins and took all the money. There was probably about four shillings in pennies.

I left school and was out of work for ages. Months elapsed after school had finished; the school holidays were over, everybody had gone back and I was still not getting a job, and not going back to school. I used to borrow money from my dad. I didn't want a job – I wanted to be in the band. But it got a bit embarrassing when my father kept saying, 'Don't you think you'd better get a job?'

My dad never had a trade, but he had the idea that all his three sons would have different trades. My eldest brother was a mechanic, my second brother did panel-beating and welding. So Dad thought, 'George can be an electrician, and then we can have our own garage.' For Christmas Dad bought me a little kit that opened up and inside were screwdrivers and tools, and I thought, 'Oh God, he really does want me to be an electrician.' That was depressing, because I had no chance of being one.

My dad got me into an exam to get a job with the Liverpool Corporation, and I failed it miserably. It wasn't deliberate – I just didn't pass. I was no good at maths. It was very embarrassing, because the people who went to work for the Corporation weren't exactly the sharpest people around. I went down to the Labour Exchange and they said: 'Go down to Blackler's, the shop in town. Somebody is required as a window-dresser.' The head of window-dressing at Blackler's said, 'Sorry, that job's gone. But go up and see Mr Peet.' Mr Peet was the head of the maintenance department. He gave me a job as an apprentice electrician, which is what my dad really wanted me to be.

I wanted to be a musician and, though there was no justification for it and no qualifications, when the group got together we all had an amazing, positive feeling about being in the band full-time. I don't know why – we were just cocky. It was felt that something good was going to happen. But then, in those days, something good would be getting to do a tour of Mecca Ballrooms. That was a big deal!

My father had something to do with the Liverpool Transport Club in Finch Lane and he got The Quarry Men a gig there once, on a Saturday night. It was a dance hall with a stage and tables and people dancing and drinking. My dad was pleased and proud that he'd got us to appear there. We had to play two sets.

We played the first set of fifteen or twenty minutes and then, in our break, we got really drunk on black velvet, the craze at the time – a bottle of Guinness mixed with half a pint of cider (not champagne). I was sixteen, John was eighteen, Paul seventeen, and we had about five pints of it. By the time we had to go on again, we were totally out of it. We embarrassed ourselves and everybody else, and my father was very pissed off: 'You've made a show of me...' and all that. That was the club where Ken Dodd got his big break.

In December 1959, we had an audition for Carroll Levis, who hosted a *Discoveries* TV programme. I don't know that anybody was ever discovered on that programme, and nobody ever won anything. You keep going on and on and on, whilst he sold tickets to the theatres with lots of free artists performing. At the end of the show the clapometer would tell you who had won, and the next week there'd be another show.

We were doing the show in Manchester, under the name of Johnny and the Moondogs. This was a period when John didn't have any guitar. I think his 'guaranteed not to split' guitar must have done so. We performed 'Think It Over' with John standing in the middle with no guitar, just singing with a hand on each of our shoulders. Paul and I were on our guitars – one pointing this way, one that way – doing the back-up voices. We thought we were really good, but because we had to catch the last train back to Liverpool we didn't have time to hang around and wait to see if the clapometer registered anything for us.

THE UNITED LIVERPOOL HOSPITALS
ROYAL LIVERPOOL CHILDREN'S HOSPITAL
TELEGRAPH ROAD HESWALL

**ADMIT ONE VISITOR**

Patients Name Richard Starkey

Ward Hugh Owen Thomas

Date of Issue 16-8-'54

THIS CARD MUST BE PRODUCED EACH VISITING DAY

# RINGO STARR

# I WAS BORN ON 7TH JULY 1940 AT NO. 9 MADRYN STREET, LIVERPOOL 8.

I don't remember the war and all the bombs, although they did actually break Liverpool up a lot. Our neighbourhood was really bombed. We had to hide a lot, I've been told since; we used to hide in the coal cellar (it was more like a cupboard). I remember big gaps in the streets where houses had stood. We used to play on the rubble when I was older, and in the air-raid shelters.

My very first memory is of being pushed in a pram. I was out with my mother, my grandma and my grandad. I don't know where we were, but it must have been countrified in some way, because we were chased by a goat. Everybody was so frightened, including me. People were screaming and running because an animal was chasing us. I can't imagine it was in Toxteth or Dingle!

We've always been ordinary, poor, working-class on both sides of the family. My mother's mother really was very poor. She had fourteen kids. There's a rumour that my great-grandmother was fairly well off – she had chromium railings round her house. Well, they were very shiny anyway. Perhaps I just made that up. You know what it's like: you dream things, or your mother tells you things, so you come to believe you actually saw them.

There was a light at the end of a tunnel that I had to get to, and I came out like that, and then I was born. There was lots of cheering. In fact my mother used to say that because I was born, the Second World War started. I don't know what that meant, really; I never understood it, but that's what she used to say. I suppose it was the only way they could celebrate, and it could be true – you never can tell.

My real name is Parkin, not Starkey. My grandad was named Johnny Parkin. When my grandfather's mother remarried, which was pretty shocking in those days, she married a Starkey, so my grandfather changed his name to Starkey, too. (I went to have my family tree done in the Sixties, but I could only trace back two generations – and they couldn't find me! I had to go to my family to find out, and even they hadn't wanted to say anything in case the press found out.)

Dad was a baker; I think that's how my parents met. He worked making cakes, so we always had sugar through the war. When I was three he decided that was enough of that, and he left us. I was an only child, so from then it was just me and my mother, until she remarried when I was thirteen.

I have no real memories of my dad. I only saw him probably five times after he left, and I never really got on with him because I'd been brainwashed by my mother about what a pig he was. I felt angry that he left. And I felt really angry later on, going through therapy in rehab, when I came to look at myself and get to know my feelings, instead of blocking them all out. For me, I felt I'd dealt with it when I was little. I didn't understand that really I had been blocking my anger out. You get on with it; that's how we were brought up. We were the last generation to be told, 'Just get on with it.' You didn't let your feelings out much.

Mum didn't do too much for a while. She was in a bit of pain after my dad left, and she ended up doing any down-home job she could get to feed and clothe me. She did everything: she was a barmaid, she scrubbed steps, worked in a food shop.

We lived at first in a huge, palatial house with three bedrooms. It was too big and we couldn't afford it now my dad had stopped supporting my mother. We were working-class, and in Liverpool when your dad left you suddenly became lower working-class. So we moved to a smaller, two-bedroom place. (They were both rented – houses always were.) It had been condemned as derelict ten years before we moved in, but we lived in it for twenty years.

The move was from one street to the next, from Madryn Street to Admiral Grove – people around us didn't move very far. We went on a van and they didn't even put the back up, because it was only 300 yards. I remember sitting on the back of the van. It's such a heavy memory as a kid; you get used to being where you are. (Although, with *my* poor kids we seemed to move every other week.)

I don't remember the inside of our house in Madryn Street – I know we never had a garden – but a lot of my pals grew up on the same street and I went into their houses. I remember the Admiral Grove house, and that didn't have a garden either. It had a toilet down the yard; we never had a bathroom. But it was home, and it was fine. We had two bedrooms: one for my mum, and one for me.

In Admiral Grove there were the Poveys next door, and the Connors up the road. My grandparents lived on Madryn Street. You all moved in around the grandparents in Liverpool. My mother's best friend, Annie Maguire, also lived on Madryn Street.

Now my dad had gone, I was brought up by my grandparents and my mother. It was strange because the grandparents were the parents of my father; they weren't my mother's parents. They really loved me and looked after me. They were great. They'd take me on holiday, too.

My grandmother was a big woman, Annie (*I* never called her Annie, of course), and my grandad was a little guy. He'd maybe have a drink or whatever and get into things, and she would roll her sleeves up, clench her fists, take up a boxing pose and say, 'Come on, Johnny! Don't talk to me like that – get over here, you little bastard.' A big girl, she was, scrubbing steps and all, surviving.

She was also the voodoo queen of Liverpool. If I was ever ill, my mother would wrap me up in a blanket and take me down to my nan's, and she would fix me. She had two cures for everything: a bread poultice and a hot toddy – I loved those hot toddies! They were warm, and everyone would be fussing over me – the centre of attention. Being an only child, I was always pretty much the centre of attention anyway.

Grandad loved the horses: 'the gee-gees'. He'd come in and, if the horses had lost, he'd be swearing and throwing the paper around – 'Those bastard nags, blah, blah…' just like any other gambler. Grandma would say, 'Johnny, not in front of the child!' and he'd be saying, 'The bastards!' It was all pretty exciting for me.

He had his chair which he always sat in. He sat in his chair right through the war. He never went and hid anywhere, even though bricks were blowing out of his house; he just sat in his chair. So as a kid I always wanted to sit in that chair. He'd come in, and he would only point and I'd have to move. But, of course, because it was his, it was the only thing I wanted.

When my grandad died, it was one of the saddest moments of my life. I was nineteen or twenty. They put him in the ground and that was just the saddest day. From that moment I knew I'd be cremated – I'm not putting anyone through that terrible thing of digging a big hole and putting me in. It wasn't until that moment that I broke down. I couldn't cry until they put him in, and then that was it.

School is a big event in my memory. St Silas's School. I'm not sure if I actually remember my first day, or if it's because my mother has told me so many times. She took me to the gate that first morning – it was just up the road, a couple of minutes' walk. In those days your parents took you to the gate and then just said, 'Well, on your way.' (There was no sitting with you in class, getting you settled, like we did with our kids.) And I have a vision to this day of a huge building – the biggest building on the planet – with about a million kids in the playground, and me. I was pretty fearful.

I walked home for lunch – as kids we could walk anywhere we liked back then; there was no danger. Supposedly, I came home and said, 'We've got a holiday.' In my little way I said, 'That's it for today, mum.' She believed me until she saw all the other kids walking by the window going back to school after lunch and said, 'Get out of here.' I don't remember ever enjoying school. I was always sagging off; I was only in school for about five years in all.

At six and a half I was very ill with peritonitis. My appendix burst; it was a huge drama. We were all at home and I was dying with pain, so there were quite a few of the family around. The doctor came and suddenly these people were lifting me up, putting me on a stretcher and carrying me out of the house. I was put in an ambulance and whisked away. When we got to the hospital, a woman doctor examined me, pressing on my side, and it was the worst pain I've ever felt.

As they went to put me to sleep for my operation, they said, 'Is there anything you want?' I said, 'Can I have a cup of tea?' They said, 'You can have a cup of tea when you come out of the theatre.' It was ten weeks later that they gave me the cup of tea, because that's how long it took for me to come round. They'd gone in and found I had peritonitis. That was a heavy operation, especially then. They told my mother three times that I'd be dead in the morning. That was hard for her, and I realised later why she was so possessive. I was very lucky to survive. Even after coming round, I was barely conscious for long periods.

Hospital was a boring place. It becomes your world when you're in for a long time – and I spent *two years* in there (the second year was when I was thirteen). Suddenly that's your life. You get in a routine. You have all these friends who are ill as well, and then you start getting on your feet and you lose touch with them. My mum would come in practically every day, and my grandparents. I'll never forget my dad coming in: he stood there with a notebook, because my birthday was coming up (I was six years old, going on seven), and he asked me, 'What do you want, son? and he wrote it all down in this notebook! I never saw him for years – he never bought me a damn thing. He wasn't in my good books.

I was put in a cot, so I got very good at picking things up with my feet: pennies, bits of paper, anything that fell out of the cot. When I'd been in the hospital about six months, I was really getting better and could have come home in a couple of weeks. I'd got a little toy bus for my birthday. The cot had sides on, and the kid in the next bed wanted to see the bus so I leaned over to get it. It was about four feet off the ground and I leaned too far, fell right out and ripped open all the surgery scars. That was a dangerous time. They kept me in for another six months for that.

I was in hospital for about a year and after that I was convalescing, so I didn't go back to school for two years. There was no catching up at school in those days. I was always behind at least a year. No teacher put his arm round me, saying, 'Well, let me deal with you, son.' I was just stuck in a class, always behind. I was the joker, and would make friends with the biggest boy in the class for protection. I started to hate school even more, and it became easier to stay off. My mother would pack me off to school, but I'd just walk around the park with a couple of school friends. We'd write little excuse notes, but always get caught because we couldn't spell.

I didn't learn to read until I was nine. My mother couldn't take much interest in that because she had to go to work, but I was taught by a girl who used to look after me, Marie Maguire. She was the daughter of my mother's friend Annie, and she used to mind me when my mum went to the pub or the pictures. Marie taught me to read with *Dobbin the Horse*. (I can read, but I can't spell – I spell phonetically.) I regret not learning earlier: it means that your knowledge is so limited. I never took Latin. John took the Latin and the painting.

The Dingle was one of the roughest areas in Liverpool, and Toxteth still has quite a reputation. It was really rough. In those days there were still gangs and fights and madness and robberies. But kids were fine, women were fine and old people were fine. Nobody messed with those three groups of people. Nowadays – I'm disgusted – they're dragging people off wheelchairs and beating 90-year-old ladies. What absolute cowards. If someone beat up an old lady back then, all the gangs in the neighbourhood would come and find him and beat the fuck out of him. They would not let that go down.

Liverpool was dark and dreary, but it was great fun to a kid. Davy Patterson, Brian Briscoe and me: we were the Three Musketeers, we were the Skull Gang, and the Black Hand Gang – this little gang of three. We were going to do everything together. We were detectives, we were cowboys and we went to the same school; we were really close. Up to ten or eleven it was my world, and all those bomb-sites were paradise. You didn't feel anything about the people who were bombed in them; it was just a big playground. 'I'll see you on the bombie,' we used to say.

We used to walk everywhere as kids. My big ambition was to be a tramp, because they just walk to places. The three of us couldn't afford to get the bus. We were eight or nine years old, and we would walk five or eight miles to Speke, to the park, to the woods that were out of town. We used to follow the buses – 'Oh, it went left!' – and we'd run down that street and wait for the next bus to come along so we'd know where it went. I didn't have a bike until much later on. My mother got me a second-hand bike, and we cycled to Wales and back. I was so sore afterwards that I lost a lot of interest in the bike. North Wales was only twenty or thirty miles away.

I had many plans besides being a tramp, when I was a kid. I always wanted to be a merchant seaman. It was like an automatic thing for me, going away to sea: 'I want to go and see those places, and I want to buy those camel saddles.' Everyone in Liverpool had a camel saddle in the corner; because in every other house someone went to sea and would bring all this crap back. The good thing about it was they were bringing records and styles of clothes back. My first musical memory was when I was about eight: Gene Autry singing 'South Of The Border'. That was the first time I really got shivers down my backbone, as they say. He had his three compadres singing, 'Ai, ai, ai, ai,' and it was just a thrill to me. Gene Autry has been my hero ever since.

You could always tell the sailors: they were the best dressed. That was my plan – going away to sea. I was in the Sea Scouts. We'd go to a hall and drill, and play with rifles – that was the big thing. I was thrown out because I ran away with a rifle. I never saw a boat. I was never in anything too long; I always did something that annoyed people.

I did have some toys: Christmas came, and I got an orange and an old cardboard box… That's not true – I got presents as much as my mother or my aunties and uncles could afford. I always received a pack of sweets or some little toy. I was always swapping my toys anyway. I always wanted something else. So somebody would give me a nice present like a chemistry set, and I'd be swapping it for something else, and some of the family would be a little disappointed. I was never satisfied. I did a little stamp collecting, and collected Dinky cars, but swapping was my hobby. Me and my friends used to steal bits and pieces from Woolworths. Just silly plastic things you could slip in your pocket.

All my collections I ended up giving away. My collection of 78s I gave to my cousin, who sat on it. (When I left Liverpool I took the rest of my record collection with me, but my mother wouldn't let me take my Patsy Cline or Little Richard records – she laid claim to them.)

My grandad would bring bits of metal home, cogs and wheels from the docks where he worked, for me to play with. He was a boilermaker and one time he made me a train with a real fire in the engine. That was probably the most fabulous toy I ever had. You could sit on it; it was quite big. I was always an entrepreneur, and I decided I would charge people to have a ride. Or I would put on little plays, and have zoos in the backyard. We'd have a spider in a jam jar – just local stuff, no lions or tigers. Once we had a dead cheetah's skin, again from a guy in the navy. It would cost you a halfpenny to come in. On one occasion it cost you nothing to come in but a penny to go out – or you had to jump off the wall with an umbrella as a parachute! So we were always trying to make a penny.

With Geraldine McGovern at H. Hunt & Son's Christmas dance

I had a great scheme once, later on – I wasn't even that young by this time. I was going to call all these millionaires, including Frank Sinatra. Somehow I was going to get in touch to ask them to lend me a million dollars. I wasn't going to touch it; I'd just have the interest. They wouldn't realise this, and one year later I'd give back their million dollars, thinking they wouldn't know about this scam! I never did anything about it, of course.

I moved to Dingle Vale Secondary Modern School when I was twelve, but I didn't go there much either. The biggest memory I have of Dingle Vale is buying lunch, which was a small Hovis loaf. We'd take out the middle of the Hovis and stuff it with chips. That was the best meal, because I hated the school dinners. We'd buy it outside, and then go and sit on the swings and eat it.

It was a hell of a walk to Dingle Vale – a good half an hour. We could either walk through Princes Park or down Park Road. I remember one time Brian Briscoe and I were walking through the park after it had snowed, and ours were the first footprints in the snow, so we didn't go to school; we just walked round the park all day making footprints.

There were always lots of little fights going on. If you had a fight with a kid and you hurt him, the next day there'd be a huge guy waiting for you at the school gate, and he'd either punch you out, or shake you or really frighten you by grabbing you: 'Don't you touch our Frank again!' I was always on the losing end. In my head I really wanted a big brother who could beat up the bastards who used to beat me up. I didn't have a father or a big brother, but my mother had many a fight for me. If anybody bigger picked on me, she'd be down knocking on the door and would deal with them. She was very, very loving. I was an only child and quite ill, so I was the apple of her eye.

Harry, my stepfather, came into the picture when I was eleven. He worked as a painter and decorator up at Burtonwood, which was an American army base. He made me laugh, he bought me DC comics; and he was great with music. He used to lay music on me, but would never force any of it. He was into big bands and jazz and Sarah Vaughan, while I'd be listening to stupid people. He'd say, 'Have you heard this?' That was always his line: 'Have you heard this?' He was a really sweet guy; all animals and children loved him. I learnt gentleness from Harry.

I loved Harry, and my mum loved him – and then she said they were going to get married. She asked me, 'What do you think?' I was pretty angry for a while, because I was thirteen; but I knew if I said 'no', she wouldn't have got married. It was a terrible position to be put in as a kid. But I said, 'Sure, great,' because he was a good guy.

The guy who owned the local sweet shop, Len, became a good friend of my stepfather. I got a bit of work with him, marking the newspapers. I never actually went out and did a round – I avoided the cold – but I would do odd jobs for him, so I'd get the occasional sweet. That was quite lucky, because we still had ration books then.

It was a big day when the rationing ended, but it wasn't as though we could suddenly go out and buy sweets or butter or eggs, because we had no money. In fact wartime rationing didn't make any difference to poor people, because we were always rationed by economics anyway. I got lucky the first time I was in hospital because they wanted me to eat anything, so I lived on new potatoes and butter. A dollop of butter was big news in those days.

From about thirteen, things came into focus a little. I felt Liverpool was dark and dirty; I wanted to get out, to live somewhere there was a little garden. I wanted to escape Admiral Grove. I didn't need to move very far – just somewhere like Aigburth where there was some green. I used to love the park; we'd sag off school and go to Sefton Park and Princes Park. I have an affinity with green, the sea and space. In my life I have had houses with lots of land, but it's the view that I need. In Monte Carlo the view is to the end of the Earth. It's the space; I need to be able just to look. It doesn't have to be mine, as long as I can see it. If I had a little house with half an acre on a hill I'd be OK, because I could see. I remember when Maureen (my first wife) and I and the kids moved to Hampstead. It was very nice, but I hated the garden – everywhere you sat there was a bloody fence. So we got out; I just couldn't deal with it. I think that's all down to Liverpool being so closed in.

I'm still a bit of a mover, a tramp. I'm trying to stop, but it's something in me. Barbara (my wife now) and I laugh about it: we have a home, get it finished, decorate it, do everything – and then I feel, 'Shouldn't we move now?'

At thirteen I got pleurisy. Liverpool was a breeding ground for tuberculosis, especially where I lived. I had lots of time off with bad lungs, and it turned into tuberculosis: I was put in a greenhouse for a whole year.

That second time I went into hospital, there was Sister Clark and Nurse Edgington. Being thirteen or fourteen, it was puberty for me, and when the nurses would kiss us goodnight it was all quite frisky: 'Will you kiss me goodnight, nurse?' – and I'd get a really good kiss off a lot of them. They were all young (they weren't old, anyway): eighteen to twenty. We'd never ask the sister to kiss us goodnight!

We had two wards separated by a partition, with girls in one ward and boys in the other. There was a lot of hot passion going on. We'd sneak in at night to the girls' ward and fumble around. I'd stand there for hours trying to get a touch of tit. We all had tuberculosis, of course, spreading those damn germs to each other. You had your girlfriends, but it never lasted because once you got better you were out on the town. It was part of growing up, and it was so slow in those days.

Outside the Calypso Ballroom, Butlins, 1960. Left to right: Johnny Guitar, Ty Brian, Rory Storm, Lou Walters and Ringo

You'd go to the movies and try to get your arm round a girl so you could stretch it down a little and get a feel.

I'd found out about sex at a very early age, twice. Two girls told their mother that I'd had their knickers off and was looking at them and feeling them. This was when I was eight. We were all kids; we were just looking and touching – the natural way of growing up. It was like living on a farm. We had a friend whose sister we could all feel. We wouldn't do anything else; we'd just look at it and feel it, and all laugh.

I actually lost my virginity in Sefton Park at about sixteen. It was very weird: two girls and a friend of mine on the grass at the back of a fairground, and there was all the fairground music and Frankie Laine and millions of people around – and this was it, us in the grass and 'Ghost Riders In The Sky'! It was really exciting. And at that age, once in and you want to live there. It was always on my mind for a long time.

Before I went to hospital the second time, walking to school I used to pass a little music store on Park Road. It had guitars, banjos, accordions and mandolins in the window, but I used to look at the drums. There was one, a tom-tom, that used to freak me out and every morning walking to school I would go and look at it, and walking back I'd look at it again. It cost £26, which was a fortune.

Playing drums for me started in hospital in 1954, where, to keep us entertained, they gave us some schooling. A teacher would come in with a huge easel, with symbols for instruments shown on a big piece of board. She gave us percussion instruments: triangles, tambourines and drums. She would point at the yellow and the triangle would sound, and she would point at the red and the drum would sound. I'd only play if they gave me a drum.

I was in the hospital band. I started using cotton bobbins to hit on the cabinet next to the bed. I was in bed for ten months: it's a long time, so you keep yourself entertained; it was that and knitting. That's where I really started playing. I never wanted anything else from then on. Drums were the only thing I wanted and when I came out I used to look in music shops and see drums; that's all I'd look at. My grandparents gave me a mandolin and a banjo, but I didn't want them. My grandfather gave me a harmonica when I was seven – nothing; we had a piano – nothing. Only the drums.

I was listening to music at this time. At fourteen I bought three records: The Four Aces' 'Love Is A Many Splendoured Thing', Eddie Calvert's 'Oh Mein Papa' and David Whitfield's 'Mama'. The Four Aces lasted, and still holds up. I don't play the others too often now.

I was never really into drummers. I loved seeing Gene Krupa in the movies, but I didn't go out and buy his records. The one drum record I bought was 'Topsy Part Two' by Cozy Cole. I always loved country-and-western; a lot of it was around from the guys in the navy. I'd go to parties and they'd be putting on Hank Williams, Hank Snow and all those country acts. I still love country music. Skiffle was also coming through, and I was a big fan of Johnnie Ray. Frankie Laine was probably my biggest hero around 1956 – and I also liked Bill Haley. I went to see *Rock Around the Clock* in the Isle of Man. My grandparents took me there after I came out of hospital. The film was sensational because the audience ripped up the cinema, which was great to watch. I didn't join in, because I was a sickly child; I was just so excited that they were doing it for me.

My first kit came on the scene about this time. I bought a drum for thirty shillings. It was a huge, one-sided bass drum. There used to be lots and lots of parties then. An uncle would play banjo or harmonica, my grandparents played mandolin and banjo; there was always someone playing something. So I would bang my big drum with two pieces of firewood and drive them mad, but because I was a kid they would let me do it. They would say, 'Oh, yeah,' and then just move me out.

They would have played songs like 'Stardust', 'That Old Black Magic', 'You'll Never Know' or 'They're Building Flats Where The Arches Used To Be' (that was Uncle Jim and Auntie Evy's big number) – all those old-time records, the sort of songs I had on my *Sentimental Journey* album. Everybody had their party-piece in Liverpool – you had to sing a song! My mother's was 'Little Drummer Boy'; she would sing it to me, and I would sing 'Nobody's Child' to her and she would always cry. 'I am nobody's child, mum.' She'd say, 'Oh, don't!' 'Climb Upon My Knee' was another one they all loved.

When I was about fifteen, I used to sing in the choir – for the money. I'd been to Sunday school a little when I was younger. I was a Protestant – my mother had been a member of the Orange Lodge for a while, although not for long. On 17th March, St Patrick's Day, all the Protestants beat up the Catholics because they were marching, and on 12th July, Orangeman's Day, all the Catholics beat up the Protestants. That's how it was, Liverpool being the capital of Ireland, as everybody always says.

I never went back to school after thirteen. I had to collect my sign-off papers one time so that I could pick up the dole until they found me a job. I went to the school and said, 'Excuse me, can I have the piece of paper to say that I'm actually fifteen and that I was at this school?' And they went through all their files, everything, and said, 'You never came to this school.' I said, 'Honestly, I came here.' They found me in the end, but the fact is they had no recollection of me ever being there. Then, seven or eight years later when we'd made it in The Beatles, they had 'my' desk at the school garden party and were charging people to sit in it. They wouldn't know my desk from anyone else's.

It was easy then for school-leavers to get jobs. I started work as a messenger boy on the railways, and was there for five weeks. I'd gone to the railways because they used to give you suits – it was a good way to get warm clothes. But they only gave me the hat before I had to leave: I was very disappointed. During my fifth week they'd sent me for the medical, said, 'Are you kidding?' and discharged me. My sickliness left me when I was about sixteen, so I was OK from then on.

Then I worked on the *St Tudno*, a pleasure steamer that went from Liverpool to Menai in North Wales. I wanted to go deep sea, and this was an easy way to get my ticket. If you did three months on the local boats, it was easier to get on the big liners. I got as far as the day boats, but that was it. It was great for picking up chicks in the pub, because I pretended I was in the Merchant Navy. I'd say 'Yeah, just got back from Menai.' They would say, 'Oh yeah, when did you leave?' and I would say, 'Ten o'clock this morning.' And then they would tell me to piss off.

I was terrified about conscription and the thought of being called up to the army. That's why I became an apprentice engineer, because the army weren't taking apprentices in 1956 or '57. It got down to, 'If you've got a real job, we won't take you.' It seemed the best way out for me. The last place I wanted to go was in the army. My dad knew someone in the pub who knew of a job at a firm called H. Hunt & Son. I went there to be a joiner, but they put me on the delivery bike for about six weeks. I got fed up and I went to complain: 'Come on, I'm here to be a joiner, not on the bike.' The man said, 'Well, there's no places for joiners – would you like to be an engineer?' So I became an apprentice engineer, going to school one day a week and working with the guys the rest.

It was at this place – my last proper job – that I met Roy Trafford. We became great friends. We still are; although we don't see a lot of each other, I still love the guy. He and I would go to the pubs (I was introduced to pubs at a young age, sixteen) and then to the Cavern. At the Cavern we'd get a pass-out, go to the pub – and then go back in and pass out!

Roy and I loved the same sort of music – we loved rock'n'roll. I listened to Radio Luxembourg all the time. The reception was bad, but it was great whatever you got, because at least they were playing different music. Alan Freed used to have a show on Sunday, and we'd always be at Roy's house listening to it. We'd hear rock'n'roll, and it was great. Roy and I would dress alike, and go and have our suits made together, because we were Teddy boys. I'd have it in black and he'd have it in blue. We did everything together.

We were by the docks in Liverpool and each and every area had its own gang. It was like New York or Hamburg. I was a Teddy boy; you had to be. Where I lived, you had to associate with some gang, otherwise you were 'open city' for anybody. The choices were: you could either be beaten up by anybody in your neighbourhood, or by people in other neighbourhoods (which I was, several times).

There was a terrible thing in Liverpool where you'd walk past somebody and they'd say, 'Are you looking at me?' If you said 'no' they'd say, 'Why not?' and if you said 'yes' they'd get you anyway. So you couldn't win. There was no answer to that question. If you were in a gang, you were safe. It must have been difficult for John, Paul and George because they were never in gangs. None of them were Teddy boys, really.

One time, Roy and I decided to go to the Gaumont cinema. When we came out, we walked up Park Road and saw the gang who used to meet on the corner. We knew them, but they said: 'Come here.' So we did, and they said, 'We're going to Garston to have fights, so just hang out till we go.' You knew immediately that you could either say 'no', and the whole gang would beat you up there and then, or you could go to where the fight was going to happen and take your chances. You could mingle with the crowd, rip your belt off, just look OK and hope to God that the big guy in the other gang didn't pick on you. There were a lot of really angry people around: Liverpool working-class, tough-gang shit.

I had a Teddy-boy suit. My cousin who went to sea – it all revolves around sailors – would give me his old clothes, and he was a Teddy boy; so I had a big long jacket with very tight trousers and crepe-soled shoes. But he was much bigger than me, so I had to strap the pants up with a big heavy belt, which I'd put washers on. I started to dress like that when I was sixteen. Then I began getting some money and buying my own clothes. Besides the money I made at the factory, we were bartering and 'borrowing and selling' – quite a bit of that went on.

The washers and the buckle on the belt would be filed down sharp, and a whack from that would really hurt – all that Teddy-boy madness. People would have razor blades behind their lapels, so whoever grabbed them would get their fingers chopped off. It was deadly serious, because that's what life was about.

We were into area fights. I wasn't a great fighter, but I was a good runner, a good sprinter – as I still am – because if you were suddenly on your own with five guys coming towards you, you soon learnt to be. There was no messing about; it was, 'You! Come here!' – bang, bang. I didn't knife or kill anyone, but I got beaten up a few times – mainly by the people I was with. It's that terrible gang situation where if you're not fighting an outsider you get crazy and start fighting among yourselves, like mad dogs. It was quite vicious. I have seen people lose their eyes; I have seen people stabbed; I have seen people beaten up with hammers.

The gangs didn't have names, but there were leaders. We were the Dingle gang. There were several gangs in the area and you'd walk en masse to try to cause trouble; 'walking with the lads', it was called. But all you'd do was walk up and down roads, stand on corners, beat someone up, get beaten up, go to the pictures… It gets boring after a while. I wanted to leave all that, and I started moving out of walking with the lads when I started playing. Roy and I wanted to be musicians, and we started leaving the gang life. Music possessed me and I got out. I was nineteen when I finally made it out, thank God.

From 1957 the big craze was skiffle. It was based on American blues; bottle parties or rent parties, where it would be open house and people would pay a quarter or a dime towards the rent. You'd have someone with a jug, someone with a washboard, a tea-chest bass and a guitar – made-up instruments.

I thought about emigrating to the USA with a friend called Johnny (I don't want to give his second name because he may still be in hiding – he had some difficulties a few years later!). I wanted to go to Texas to live with Lightnin' Hopkins – *the* blues man, my hero. I actually went to the Embassy and got the forms. This was in 1958. We filled these in and, God, they were hard, but when we got the second lot of forms it was just too daunting: questions like, 'Was your mother's grandmother's Great Dane a communist?' Like teenagers, we gave in. But we'd got lists of jobs to go to in Houston – factories that would take us. We were pretty serious about it.

In England there was Lonnie Donegan and The Vipers skiffle group. It was traditional jazz and skiffle then at the Cavern (that's why we started playing skiffle). Eddie Miles, Roy and I started a skiffle band together: the first band I was in – the Eddie Clayton Skiffle Group. (There wasn't really an Eddie Clayton.) We all worked in the same place. Eddie was a lathe operator, I was an apprentice engineer and Roy was a joiner.

When someone in Harry's family died, he'd gone down to Romford and there was a drum kit for sale for £12. The whole family collected together and he brought this drum set to Liverpool. I was given it for Christmas. Up till then I'd been playing drums at home – just something I'd made myself from biscuit tins and pieces of firewood. This kit was amazing. It wasn't *a* drum but *drums*: a snare, a bass drum, a hi-hat, one little tom-tom, a top cymbal and a bass-drum pedal (I didn't have to kick it any more).

I had about three lessons once I got interested. I thought, 'Every night I'll read music and learn how to play.' I went to the house of a little man who played drums, and he told me to get some manuscript paper. He wrote it all down and I never went back! I couldn't be bothered; it was too routine for me, I couldn't stand it.

Once I'd got my drum kit, I set it all up in my bedroom, the back room, and off I went, banging away. And then I heard from the bottom of the stairs, 'Keep the noise down, the neighbours are complaining!' I only ever did it twice and got shouted at both times, so I stopped and never practised at home. The only way I could practise was to join a group. I got the drum kit on Boxing Day and I was in a group by February, so there wasn't a chance in hell that I could play by then. But neither could anyone else except the guitarist, who knew a couple of chords. The rest of us were making it up. We had no sense of time – though Eddie was a great player, one of those guys who, if you gave him any instrument, could play it. Very musical.

I was working in the factory and we played for our fellow workmen at lunchtime in a cellar. With a few of the other guys from the factory we built up the band. And then we started playing all the freebies we could get, playing clubs or weddings.

We did a few weddings. Someone we knew would get married and we'd fetch the gear along and play for a few hours. Once a guy at work said, 'You've got to come and play at this wedding,' and then, cheeky git, 'Can I join the group if I get you the booking?' We said, 'OK,' and he joined and said, 'We're going to be all right here, it's a big fur-coat wedding. It's all shorts, there'll be none of that beer.' They were all out at the pub when we arrived to set up. When they came back it was with medicine bottles full of brown ale – it was the roughest wedding I'd ever been to! 'It's a real fur-coat do…'

I became semi-professional: I was an engineer during the day and I'd play drums at night. I would go and play at dances in other neighbourhoods with Eddie Clayton or some other band, and later with Rory. We would play, and the girls would always be looking at the musicians, which would piss the other guys off. So we'd be lucky to get out of those clubs without being beaten up, because we were in strange neighbourhoods without our local mates.

My career started there. Then I began going through bands in Liverpool: The Darktown Skiffle Group – that was the biggest band at the time – then it was Rory Storm, then with Tony Sheridan, then with The Beatles. I played with a lot of groups. I practised with every group in Liverpool. We were all intermingling in those days. We all got to know each other, so if someone was sick or didn't turn up you'd sit in with another group.

The drum kit I was using had a really cool snare and everything, but it was old. So in the summer of 1958 I went to my grandfather and borrowed £46 and took it down to Frank Hessy's music shop in town, where I bought an Ajax single-headed kit, which looked similar to the Ludwig Silver Pearl one.

I thought Rory Storm and the Hurricanes were great. They were the first ones in Liverpool who really wanted to get into rock'n'roll. We were all playing skiffle before that, but they had a rock'n'roll blond hair attitude – Rory liked to be the big cheese, to be Mr Rock'n'Roll, and Johnny 'Guitar' Byrne was Liverpool's Jimi Hendrix.

I'd left Roy and Eddie behind by now and was playing with The Darktown Skiffle Group. They decided they wanted to stay as they were – they didn't want to make it their careers. They stayed as engineers and joiners, got married, and did that, while I auditioned for Rory and the Hurricanes. It was good; I knew all their songs – every band was playing the same songs. I don't even know if Rory auditioned anyone else, but I passed the test, they said 'yes', and I joined. It's interesting because Rory and, later, The Beatles both had the same first impression about me. When I went for the audition I looked a bit rough: I was still in my black drape jacket with my hair back, looking like a Ted, so they were a bit insecure about me.

When trad jazz was the big thing, a skiffle group would play in the intermission, because they were cheap. You had to get a lot of gigs to make any money. In Liverpool, the Cavern was *the* place to play with any band. There was a lot of screaming in there. When I played there with Rory, we were thrown off because we were meant to be a skiffle group but Johnny Guitar brought a radio with him, and he plugged his guitar into it and it suddenly became electric. So we were a bit more rock'n'roll. We were thrown off for being traitors: 'Get that damn noise off!' They wanted 'Hi Lili Hi Lo' – that stuff. There were a lot of people in big sweaters. I was in black corduroy in those days – we were all like beatniks.

With Rory and the Hurricanes, we played loads of places, up and down the country, and even abroad. When we came down to London for a gig, I remember that we went to the Lyceum and no girl would dance with us. As a group, the five of us would line up and pick on one girl and we'd say, 'Excuse me, do you want to dance?' She'd say, 'Huh? Crazy.' And the next one would get the same, and I would say, 'Excuse me, do you want to dance?' – 'Piss off.' The only dance I had that night was with a French girl who didn't know any better. That's how it happens.

I was earning a bit of money, working and drumming, and I got my first car at eighteen. It was a big thing, because before that I was dumped all the time. I'd have to go to gigs on the bus, so most of the time I could only take a snare drum, a cymbal and the sticks. I'd have to beg to borrow the bass drum and the toms from the other bands who were playing that night. Sometimes I didn't get them. And on the occasions we did take my equipment, going to the gig everyone was so helpful, but after it they just split – so I'd be dumped with the lot. I remember one miserable night when the rest of the band had helped me get my kit on the bus. I got off at my stop, and it was half a mile to the house, and I had four cases. I had to run twenty yards with two cases, keeping my eye on the other two left behind, then go back, pick them up and run forty yards with those, drop those, go back, and so on. It was the most miserable thing and all I thought was, 'Shit, I need a car.'

Johnny Hutch, another drummer, was making cars out of spare parts – and from him I got a Standard Vanguard. I loved that car. It gave me a terrible time: the tyres were always puncturing and it wouldn't go into second gear, but I used to be so proud of it. It was hand-painted red and white, like a big ice-cream car. 'Hand-painted' just meant he couldn't afford to have it sprayed, but I would always say, 'Oh, it's hand-painted, you know?'

In 1959, the army decided that anyone born later than (I think) September 1939 would not be conscripted. I'd made it by ten months. That's when I thought, 'Great, now we can play,' and I left the factory and decided to go professional with Rory. We had a big family meeting when I asked to go with Rory and the band to Butlins, to play in the Rock and Calypso Ballroom for £16 a week. Up to then I had been playing just at night, or some afternoons.

I come from a long line of labourers and soldiers, and I would have been the first in our line to get a piece of paper to say he was actually *something* – an engineer. I remember my uncles, my aunties and the boss of the factory saying, 'You'll come back in three months, and you'll only be semi-skilled when you do.' I said, 'I don't care. Drums are my life, I want to be a musician and I'm going away with Rory to Butlins to fulfil this dream.' Which I did. I stopped work at twenty. I've always believed I'd be playing drums. That was my dream, although through my life I've forgotten that dream occasionally and let substances take over.

We were down at the Jacaranda club in Liverpool one afternoon, shortly before we were to go to Butlins. They usually had a steel band downstairs at night, but this afternoon there were three guys down there messing around on their guitars. Rory, Johnny Guitar and I wandered down to see what was happening there. I didn't know them: it was John and Paul teaching Stuart Sutcliffe to play bass. We were the

Far Left: 'Hand-painted' Standard Vanguard

professionals and they were the boys, the struggling artists. They didn't have a big image in my head. They meant nothing in those days – they were just a group of scruffs. We were ready to go to Butlins: we had the suits and shoes that matched – black and white shoes, red suits, red ties and a hankie – so we felt we were big time. (The reason Rory Storm and the Hurricanes were the biggest band in Liverpool at one time was the matching suits. Later on Brian Epstein started doing that to The Beatles.)

We were away at Butlins for three months, and it was fabulous. When we first arrived there, we all picked names. That was when Johnny Guitar picked his; and for me, it started because in Liverpool I was still wearing a lot of rings, and people were starting to say, 'Hey, Rings!' My name was Richard, hence Ritchie… and Rings. When we changed our names, I called myself Ringo. It was going to be Ringo Starkey, but that didn't really work, so I cut the name in half and added an 'r'. I had it put on the bass drum, and it's been that ever since. We were working steadily, with a new audience every week. It was the best place we could have been. It was the summer months, and we weren't missing anything back in Liverpool. Winter was always the club time there. Rory was a real athlete. There was a piano behind the drums, and the finale of Rory's act was that he would climb on top of it, shake, and then jump over my head. This was fabulous! My favourite number was 'Whole Lotta Shakin' Goin' On'.

A new coachload of girls would arrive every week at Butlins, and we'd be like, 'Hi, I'm with the band, you know.' It was paradise for that.

There'd be tears at the end of the week, and then a new coach. In a way it was part of the attraction of rock'n'roll. My main reason, of course, was to play, but you couldn't help but enjoy yourself at Butlins every week! I ended up living with a hairdresser in a caravan at Butlins. It was growing up. Everyone was on holiday. It's the same as goes on now, except that they go to Benidorm.

I got engaged to one girl, but it didn't last because she started to put the pressure on: it was her or the drums. That was a very poignant moment in my life. I left her one night, and I got on the bus and thought, 'Well, what happens if I don't go back?' And I never went back. I just wanted to play; it was more important to me. But I *was* engaged and I did love her, and she loved me, and we'd got our bottom drawer started and made all the preparations that go into marriage.

I sold the Standard Vanguard to another drummer in Liverpool, and after the first three months at Butlins I bought myself a Zephyr Zodiac, which I adored. I was The King in that car. I was The Big Guy With The Car, driving people around. I drove to the factory in it, parked it outside and went to see the guys still working there: 'Hey, I'm really doing well!' – because my wages had gone right up. I'd been getting £6 a week in the factory and £20 a week at Butlins. I was loaded.

It wasn't all rosy; I was on the dole a lot, too, and I still have a piece of paper from the DHSS saying, 'He left the factory to join a dance band.' There wasn't that much unemployment then, and I could always work. But I had to join the dole queue. There were a lot of old winos in the queue, shaking – that was the first time I saw that happen. There were a lot of us queuing up, but it wasn't like it is now.

When I was a kid, we'd never really been on holiday. We'd go up the coast to Seaforth now and then, or across to New Brighton. For my big holiday I went to London with my mum and Harry when I was fifteen. Actually we went to Romford, because that's where Harry's folks were from. But I recall we went to London for the day, and there's a photo of me with the Horse Guards and my hand patting the horse. We did all those things: Buckingham Palace, the British Museum, the Tower of London. That was the big day out. I went to the Isle of Man a couple of times with my grandparents, so that was like going abroad, but we never went to Europe.

I went abroad in 1962 with Rory and the Hurricanes, when we got a job playing American army bases in France. The problem was we needed a girl singer, because the army didn't want to look at us guys. So we found a blonde girl in Liverpool (whose name I can't remember) and we went out there and played in all those bases in the wilderness.

On the way there, when we got off the boat, we got on a train which was supposed to go right through to Lyons – but once it pulled into Paris, we were all thrown off. It was frightening. The French were fighting the Algerians at the time, and there were cops with machine guns right in my face because I had the big drum cases. Clutching my passport, all I could think of was to scream, '*Anglais!* Don't shoot!'

The rooms we were in were very cheap, but the French food cost a fortune. We had no money, and we were in doss houses. But we didn't care because the audiences were great and the personal expenses were great. We could go and buy hamburgers in the American canteen store and eat like kings for nothing, because we were getting food for the same rates as the soldiers. We weren't really allowed in the mess, because we weren't American – and they kept trying to throw us out – but we would go in anyway, and stock up with Hershey bars and hamburgers.

My apprenticeship was with Rory – we were real professional. We'd go away to play and come back to Liverpool. That's what I was doing while John, Paul and George were still getting it together. We were doing so well that when the first offer came to go to Hamburg, we turned it down. But in the autumn of 1960 we eventually went to play in Germany and that's where I met The Beatles. Whatever happened to those guys?

# 1960-62

nineteen sixty to nineteen sixty-two

JOHN: *Once upon a time there were three little boys called John, George and Paul, by name christened. They decided to get together because they were the getting together type. When they were together, they all wondered what for after all, what for? So all of a sudden they all grew guitars and formed a noise. Funnily enough, no one was interested, least of all the three little men. Sooo… on discovering a fourth little even littler man called Stuart Sutcliffe running about them, they said, quote: 'Sonny, get a bass guitar and you will be all right,' and he did – but he wasn't all right because he couldn't play it. So they sat on him with comfort till he could play. Still there was no beat, and a kindly old aged man said, quote: 'Thou hast not drums!' We had no drums! they coffed. So a series of drums came and went and came. Suddenly, in Scotland, touring with Johnny Gentle, the group (called The Beatles called) discovered they had not a very nice sound – because they had no amplifiers. They got some. Many people ask what are Beatles? Why Beatles? Ugh, Beatles, how did the name arrive? So we will tell you. It came in a vision – a man appeared on a flaming pie and said to unto them, 'From this day on you are Beatles with an A.' – 'Thank you, Mister Man,' they said, thanking him.*[61]

PAUL: It was John and Stuart who thought of the name. They were art students and while George's and my parents would make us go to bed, Stuart and John could live the little dream that we all dream: to stay up all night. And it was then they thought up the name.

One April evening in 1960, walking along Gambier Terrace by Liverpool Cathedral, John and Stuart announced: 'Hey, we want to call the band "The Beatles".' We thought, 'Hmm, bit creepy, isn't it?' – 'It's all right though; a double meaning.' One of our favourite groups, The Crickets, had got a dual-meaning name: cricket the game, and crickets the little grasshoppers. We were thrilled with that – we thought it was true literature. (We've spoken to The Crickets since, and found that they hadn't realised that we had a game called cricket. They never knew they had a second meaning.)

GEORGE: It *is* debatable where the name came from. John used to say that he invented it, but I remember Stuart being with him the night before.

There was The Crickets, who backed Buddy Holly, that similarity; but Stuart was really into Marlon Brando, and in the movie *The Wild One* there is a scene where Lee Marvin says: 'Johnny, we've been looking for you, the Beetles have missed you, all the Beetles have missed you.' Maybe John and Stu were both thinking about it at the time; so we'll leave that one. We'll give it fifty/fifty to Sutcliffe/Lennon.

PAUL: In *The Wild One*, when he says, 'Even the Beetles missed ya!' he points to the motorcycle chicks. A friend has since looked it up in a dictionary of American slang and found that it's slang for 'motorcycle girls'. So work that one out!

JOHN: We had one or two names. Then we began to change the name for different bookings, and we finally hit upon 'The Beatles'.

I was looking for a name like The Crickets that meant two things, and from crickets I got to beetles. And I changed the BEA, because 'beetles' didn't mean two things on its own. When you said it, people thought of crawly things; and when you read it, it was beat music.[64]

GEORGE: Stuart was in the band now. He wasn't really a very good musician. In fact, he wasn't a musician at all until we talked him into buying a bass. We taught him to play twelve-bars, like 'Thirty Days' by Chuck Berry. That was the first thing he ever learnt. He picked up a few things and he practised a bit until he could get through a couple of other tunes as well. It was a bit ropey, but it didn't matter at that time because he looked so cool. We never had many gigs in Liverpool before we went to Hamburg, anyway.

PAUL: That spring of 1960, John and I went down to a pub in Reading, The Fox and Hounds, run by my cousin Betty Robbins and her husband. We worked behind the bar. It was a lovely experience that came from John and I just hitching off down there. At the end of the week we played in the pub as The Nerk Twins. We even made our own posters.

Betty's husband turned me on to showbusiness in a big way, and the talk we had with him about how we should do the show was very formative. He'd been an entertainments manager hosting talent contests at Butlins, and been on radio. He asked what we were going to open with, and we said 'Be Bop A Lula'. He told us: 'No good. You need to open with something fast and instrumental. This is a pub, a Saturday night, what else have you got?' We said, 'Well, we do "The World Is Waiting For The Sunrise".' (I played the melody and John did the rhythm.) He said, 'Perfect, start with that, *then* do "Be Bop A Lula".' He was good like that, and I would remember his advice years later when we were organising our shows.

GEORGE: A lot was happening at the beginning of 1960. I remember there was a show at the Liverpool Stadium in which Eddie Cochran was due to appear, but he got killed a couple of days before so Gene Vincent topped the bill.

RINGO: I never forgave Eddie for that. I was so looking forward to seeing him.

GEORGE: It was held in a stadium where Pete Best's dad, Johnny, used to promote boxing. Ringo was in that show with Rory Storm and the Hurricanes. We weren't big enough to play (we didn't even have a drummer) and I remember thinking how we'd got to get our band together because the Hurricanes all had suits and dance steps – a proper routine. It was semi-professional; it looked impressive from where we were sitting.

Brian Cass had a band called Cass and the Cassanovas that also played. (He disappeared a year or so later, and those left became The Big Three.) Somehow Cass had the ability to get gigs, and one night he put us in a show in a little club cellar, which was the first time we played as 'The Silver Beetles'. He'd actually wanted us to be Long John and the Pieces of Silver.

PAUL: He said, 'What's your name?' We had just thought of 'The Beatles' so we thought we would try this out at the audition. Cass said, 'Beatles – what's that? It doesn't mean anything.' (Everyone hated the name, fans and promoters alike.) He asked John's name. John, who at that time was pretty much the lead singer, said, 'John Lennon.' – 'Right, Big John… Long John… OK, Long John Silver.' So we compromised and had Long John and the Silver Beetles. We would do anything for a job, so that's what we became.

GEORGE: He perceived John as being the leader because he was the biggest, the pushy one. He was the leader when it was The Quarry Men, and he was certainly the leader at this point. I think he is still the leader now, probably.

PAUL: In May, Larry Parnes came to town, auditioning. He was the big London agent. His acts nearly always had a violent surname. There was Ronnie Wycherley who became Billy Fury; and a less furious guy you have yet to meet. A sweet Liverpool guy – the first local man who made it, in our eyes. Marty Wilde was also in Larry's stable; he had another tempestuous surname. But Larry Parnes had some new singers and was looking for backing groups, and someone had told him there were a few groups around in Liverpool. So he came up to the Blue Angel. Billy Fury came with him.

Allan Williams ran the Blue Angel and the Jacaranda. He was the little local manager (little in height, that is – a little Welshman with a little high voice – a smashing bloke and a great motivator, though we used to take the mickey out of him). He held the auditions in conjunction with Larry Parnes. All the groups in Liverpool were there and we were one of the bands.

GEORGE: They were going to use the Blue Angel, which in those days was called the Wyvern Social Club, to audition back-up bands for Larry Parnes's acts. Beforehand we went out and bought some string shoes with little white bits on top. We were very poor and never had any matching clothes, but we tried to put together a uniform – black shirts and these shoes.

When we arrived at the club our drummer hadn't shown up, so Johnny Hutchinson, the drummer with Cass and the Cassanovas, sat in with us. I don't think we played particularly well or particularly badly.

JOHN: We just had a stand-in drummer for the day. And Stu couldn't play bass, so he had to turn his back.[72]

PAUL: We had to tell Stuart to turn the other way: 'Do a moody – do a big Elvis pose.' If anyone had been taking notice they would have seen that when we were all in A, Stu would be in another key. But he soon caught up and we passed that audition to go on tour – not with a furious name at all like the other acts, but with a guy called Johnny Gentle.

GEORGE: It was a bit of a shambles. Larry Parnes didn't stand up saying that we were great or anything like that. It felt pretty dismal. But a few days later we got the call to go out with Johnny Gentle. They were probably thinking, 'Oh well, they're mugs. We'll send a band that doesn't need paying.'

PAUL: Now we were truly professional, we could do something we had been toying with for a long time, which was to change our names to real showbiz names. I became Paul Ramon, which I thought was suitably exotic. I remember the Scottish girls saying, 'Is that his real name? That's great.' It's French, Ramon. Ra-*mon*, that's how you pronounce it. Stuart became Stuart de Staël after the painter. George became Carl Harrison after Carl Perkins (our big idol, who had written 'Blue Suede Shoes'). John was Long John. People have since said, 'Ah, John didn't change his name, that was very suave.' Let me tell you: he was Long John. There was none of that 'he didn't change his name': we all changed our names.

So here we were, suddenly with the first of Larry's untempestuous acts and a tour of Scotland, when I should have been doing my GCE exams. A lot of my parents' hopes were going up the spout because I was off with these naughty boys who weren't doing GCEs at all.

JOHN: During my whole time at art school I used to disappear from time to time. When my first exam came up I was with The Beatles in Scotland, backing Johnny Gentle. For the second, I was away with the group in Hamburg. Eventually I decided to leave whether I ever passed an exam or not, but when I got back there was a note saying, 'Don't bother to come back.' Believe it or not, I actually got annoyed.[63]

GEORGE: I remember asking my big brother, 'Would you pack in work and have a go at this if you were me?' He said, 'You might as well – you never know what might happen. And if it doesn't work out you're not going to lose anything.' So I packed in my job, and joined the band full time and from then, nine-to-five never came back into my thinking. John was still at art college and Paul was doing an extra year at school.

That was our first professional gig: on a tour of dance halls miles up in the North of Scotland, around Inverness. We felt, 'Yippee, we've got a gig!' Then we realised that we were playing to nobody in little halls, until the pubs cleared out when about five Scottish Teds would come in and look at us. That was all. Nothing happened. We didn't really know anything. It was sad, because we were like orphans. Our shoes were full of holes and our trousers were a mess, while Johnny Gentle had a posh suit. I remember trying to play to 'Won't you wear my ring around your neck?' – he was doing Elvis's 'Teddy Bear' – and we were crummy. The band was horrible, an embarrassment. We didn't have amplifiers or anything.

What little pay we did get was used to take care of the hotels. And we all slept in the van. We would argue about space. There weren't enough seats in the van, and somebody had to sit on the inside of the mudguard on the back wheel. Usually Stu.

JOHN: We were terrible. We'd tell Stu he couldn't sit with us, or eat with us. We'd tell him to go away, and he did – that was how he learnt to be with us. It was all stupid, but that was what we were like.[67]

PAUL: We did OK on that tour, playing church halls all over Scotland, places like Fraserburgh. It was great – we felt very professional. But we were endlessly on the phone to Larry Parnes's office, complaining that the money hadn't arrived. (Years later I said this on a radio programme and Larry threatened to sue me, because his aunties had got onto him: 'Larry, you didn't pay those nice Beatle boys.' That was a true shame in his book.)

For a while, when we returned, we became a backing group. We were still going around as The Silver Beetles – I think there's a few posters of us with a double 'e' – but soon we started to drop the 'silver'; because we didn't really want it. John didn't wish to be known as 'Long John Silver' any longer and I didn't wish to be known as Paul Ramon – it was just an exotic moment in my life.

We backed all sorts of people. It was a good little period and we felt professional learning other people's songs. Sometimes it was quite hard, because we weren't that good at chords. They'd throw us sheets of music and we'd ask: 'Have you got the words, have you got the chords?' We were very naive – one time we thought that the girl with one of the artists was his wife. We kept calling her Mrs Whatever, and it took us ages to realise she was a girlfriend.

JOHN: We had all sorts of different drummers all the time, because people who owned drum kits were few and far between; it was an expensive item.[70]

GEORGE: We had a drummer, Tommy Moore, who had come with us to Scotland. He was a funny kind of guy who played with a lot of different bands. He used to show up for a while and then not show up again, and so we'd get someone else.

We had a stream of drummers coming through. After about three of these guys, we ended up with almost a full kit of drums from the bits that they'd left behind, so Paul decided he'd be the drummer. He was quite good at it. At least he seemed OK; probably we were all pretty crap at that point. It only lasted for one gig, but I remember it very well. It was in Upper Parliament Street where a guy called Lord Woodbine owned a strip club. It was in the afternoon, with a few perverts (five or so men in overcoats) and a local stripper. We were brought on as the band to accompany the stripper; Paul on drums, John and me on guitar and Stuart on bass.

She came out and gave us her sheet music: 'Now here are the parts for my act.' We said, 'What's that? We can't read it.' She told us it was 'The Gypsy Fire Dance'. We said, 'Well, how does that go? What's the tempo?' We decided to do 'Ramrod' instead, because we knew it, and then 'Moonglow'.

PAUL: The Grosvenor Ballroom in Wallasey was one of the worst places; there would be a hundred Wallasey lads squaring up to a hundred lads from Seacombe and all hell would break loose. I remember one night a rumble had started before I realised what was happening. I ran to the stage to save my Elpico amp, my pride and joy at the time. There were fists flying everywhere. One Ted grabbed me and said, 'Don't move, or you're bloody dead!' I was scared for my life, but I *had* to get that amp.

JOHN: We'd been playing round in Liverpool for a bit without getting anywhere, trying to get work, and the other groups kept telling us, 'You'll do all right, you'll get work some day.' And then we went to Hamburg.

# JOHN: I GREW UP IN HAMBURG, NOT LIVERPOOL.'[71]

GEORGE: We'd heard about musicians getting gigs in Stuttgart, where there were American army bases. We knew that those kinds of gigs were available around Germany, so it was an exciting thought.

The story behind *our* going there was that another Liverpool group, Derry and the Seniors, had given up their jobs to do a gig for Larry Parnes. And when they didn't get it, they were all really annoyed so they decided to go to London to beat Larry up. Allan Williams said to them: 'If you are going to London you should take your instruments.' He drove them down and got them into the 2I's (the club where Tommy Steele had been discovered). They didn't beat up Larry Parnes, but they did go down well at the club.

Bruno Koschmider, a German promoter, saw them there and hired them for his own club, the Kaiserkeller in Hamburg, and they were there for a couple of months. He must have really liked them, because he then got in touch with Allan Williams and said, 'We want another Liverpool band, to play at the Indra.'

Allan Williams offered the gig to us, 'But,' he said, 'the fellow wants a five-piece.' We needed another person, since there were only the three of us and Stuart. We were excited, but we thought, 'Paul isn't really the drummer. Where do we get one from?' Then I remembered a guy I'd met who'd been given a drum kit for Christmas. His name was Pete Best; the Casbah club was in his basement.

PAUL: Pete Best's mother, Mona – a very nice woman, an Anglo-Indian – ran the Casbah in a part of Liverpool, West Derby. We'd started to go round there and we'd ended up painting the place.

It was great to be involved in the birth of a coffee bar – they were such important places then. The concrete and wood in the basement had been stripped and we painted each part a different colour. All of us lent a hand – John and George and all the others. And after we'd painted it up, it was *our* club – The Beatles used to play there. Pete had a drum kit so he would sometimes sit in with us. He was a good drummer, and when Hamburg came up he joined us. He was a very good-looking guy, and out of all the people in our group, the girls used to go for Pete.

JOHN: We knew of a guy and he had a drum kit, so we just grabbed him, auditioned him, and he could keep one beat going for long enough, so we took him.[70]

PAUL: I was still at school at the time of the Hamburg offer; hanging on, trying to take exams. I didn't want to leave because I didn't want to put my life in a pigeonhole quite yet. I thought I might become a teacher – it was about all I could qualify for with a decent salary – but I was scared to solidify my life in a block of cement.

There was a guy at art college who was twenty-four, and that seemed very old when we were seventeen. I thought that if he could keep going until that age without getting a job, then so could I. So I had my eye set on blagging around the sixth form, doing anything that would protect me until I was twenty-four when I would have to decide what to do. Then Hamburg came up.

Someone must have realised that there were a lot of good groups in Liverpool, and how we were cheaper than the London groups, and didn't know that much so we would work long hours. We were a promoter's dream. We were told, 'You can go to Hamburg and get £15 a week.' Now, £15 a week was more than my dad earned. In fact the teachers at school didn't earn more than that. So Hamburg was a real offer. It was as if we had found a profession, and the money was there too. I remember writing to my headmaster very proudly that summer: 'I am sure you will understand why I will not be coming back in September, and the pay is – wait for it – £15 a week.' It was a 'that's more than you earn' kind of a letter.

But first of all my dad had to decide whether to even let me go. I pleaded. I knew he might not, because although my dad was not strict, he was a fairly sensible kind of bloke. This was letting his kid go off to the famous stripper land, to the Reeperbahn – it was known to be a dodgy place – with gangsters, where sailors were murdered. I remember Dad giving me lots of advice, but there was an agreement that he had to sign. But this was The Big Thing.

JOHN: Allan Williams took us over in a van. We went through Holland, and did a bit of shoplifting there.[72]

GEORGE: We probably met with the van outside Allan Williams's club, the Jacaranda. There were the five of us and then Allan, his wife Beryl and Lord Woodbine.

It was cramped. The van didn't even have seats; we had to sit on our amplifiers. We drove down to Harwich and got the boat to the Hook of Holland. Driving through Holland, I remember we stopped at Arnhem where all the people had parachuted out to their deaths (another little Winston Churchill trick). There were thousands of white crosses in the cemetery.

PAUL: The strangest memory for me is being asked at the borders if we had any coffee. I couldn't understand it. Drugs, yes, guns, yes – we could understand booze or something like that; but a roaring trade in contraband coffee?

Anyway, we ended up in Hamburg very late one night. We got the timing wrong; there was no one there to meet us. We could find Hamburg from the map but then we had to find the St Pauli district, and then the Reeperbahn. By the time we found the street and the club it was all closed. There we were, with no hotel or anything, and it was now bedtime.

We managed to shake up someone from a neighbouring club who found our guy, and he opened up the club and we stayed the first night in the little alcoves, on red leather seats.

GEORGE: Of course, on the first night we got there there weren't arrangements for anything. The club owner, Bruno Koschmider, drove us round to his house, and we ended up staying, all in the one bed. Bruno wasn't with us, fortunately, he left us to stay in his flat for the first night and went somewhere else. Eventually he put us in the back of a little cinema, the Bambi Kino, at the very end of a street called the Grosse Freiheit.

Bruno wasn't some young rock'n'roll entrepreneur; he was an old guy who had been crippled in the war. He had a limp and didn't seem to know much about music or anything. We only ever saw him once a week, when we'd try to get into his office for our wages.

The city of Hamburg was brilliant; a big lake, and then the dirty part. The Reeperbahn and Grosse Freiheit were the best thing we'd ever seen, clubs and neon lights everywhere and lots of restaurants and entertainment. It looked really good. There were seedy things about it, obviously, including some of the conditions we had to live in when we first got there.

Telephone No.
ROYAL 6544

JACARANDA ENTERPRISES

PAUL: I had been reading Shakespeare, Dylan Thomas and Steinbeck, so that when we came to this Hamburg experience it was as students, a little bit as artists, in a way: 'This will be good for the memoirs one day.' We saw it differently from the other groups. I think we saw it as if we were Dylan Thomas and this was his time in Germany. It was a very rich period for experience because we were kids let off the leash.

The club we were to play was called the Indra, and it had a big elephant over the street to signify India. Later, with our Indian influence, it seemed funny that that should have been our first place.

GEORGE: The Indra was at the far end of Grosse Freiheit, off the Reeperbahn, the main club zone. Bruno had just opened up the club and put us on there.

The whole area was full of transvestites and prostitutes and gangsters, but I couldn't say that they were the audience. I don't recall there being many people at all at first. It took a little while before word of mouth built up, by which time the church across the street had made Bruno close down because of all the noise we were making.

PAUL: We lived backstage in the Bambi Kino, next to the toilets, and you could always smell them. The room had been an old storeroom, and there were just concrete walls and nothing else. No heat, no wallpaper, not a lick of paint; and two sets of bunk beds, like little camp beds, with not very many covers. We were frozen.

JOHN: We were put in this pigsty, like a toilet it was, in a cinema, a rundown sort of fleapit. *We were living in a toilet*, like right next to the ladies' toilet.[72] We would go to bed late and be woken up the next day by the sound of the cinema show. We'd try to get into the ladies' first, which was the cleanest of the cinema's lavatories, but fat old German women would push past us.[67]

We'd wake up in the morning and there would be old German fraus pissing next door. That was where we washed. That was our bathroom. It was a bit of a shock in a way.[72]

PAUL: People would be coming in from the cinema to the toilets, and they would find these little Liverpool lads going, 'Morning,' all shaving. *'Ah, guten morgen, alles ist gut?'*

GEORGE: I never used to shower. There was a washbasin in the lavatory at the Bambi Kino, but there was a limit as to how much of yourself you could wash in it. We could clean our teeth or have a shave, but not much else. I remember once going up to the public baths, but that was quite a long way from the Bambi Kino. Later on, maybe the third time we visited Hamburg, we'd go to Astrid Kirchherr's to wash. I don't think we bathed or showered at all when we were first there, probably not even the second time.

ADDITIONAL CLAUSES.

A PROMPT START IS REQUIRED
10% COMMISSION TO BE DEDUCTED
FROM FEE OF £100 WEEKLY WAGE
TO BE PAID TO MR A.R. WILLIAMS
RETURN PASSAGE TO ENGLAND TO BE PAID BY BAND
PASSAGE FROM LIVERPOOL TO HAMBURG TO BE PAID BY MR KOSCHMIDER

Signature

Address

"KAISERKELLER"
Inh. Bruno Koschmider
HAMBURG-ST. PAULI
Große Freiheit 36 - Tel. 31 07 63

GEORGE: This was taken when we first played at the Indra. I remember the outfits: a neighbour of Paul's made these lilac jackets and after a few weeks at the Indra they melted, just dropped apart. PAUL: The neighbour was Mr Richards, a tailor. He lived next door to me at Forthlin Road. We picked out some material ourselves and took it to him to make these jackets. The others came to my house for fittings. Eventually, the sweat got to them.

JOHN: We'd done the Johnny Gentle tour, but we'd only been on stage for a bit, for twenty minutes or so, because he'd be on most of the time.[72] In Liverpool we just used to do our best numbers, the same ones at every gig. In Hamburg we would play for eight hours, so we really had to find new ways of playing.[67] It was still rather thrilling when you went on stage. It was a little nightclub and it was a bit frightening because it wasn't a dance hall, and all these people were sitting down, expecting something.

At first we got a pretty cool reception. The second night the manager told us: 'You were terrible, you have to make a show – "mach shau",' like the group down the road were doing.[67] And of course whenever there was any pressure point I had to get us out of it. The guys said, 'Well, OK John, you're the leader.' When nothing was going on, they'd say, 'Uh-uh, no leader, fuck it,' but if anything happened, it was like, 'You're the leader, you get up and do a show.'[72]

We were scared by it all at first, being in the middle of the tough clubland. But we felt cocky, being from Liverpool, at least believing the myth about Liverpool producing cocky people.[67] So I put my guitar down and I did Gene Vincent all night: banging and lying on the floor and throwing the mike about and pretending I had a bad leg. That was some experience.[72] We all did 'mach shauing' all the time from then on.[67]

PAUL: We had to actually invite the audience in, because we would be playing to a completely dark and empty club. The minute we saw someone we'd kick into 'Dance In The Street' and rock out, pretending we hadn't seen them. And we'd perhaps get a few of them in. We were like fairground barkers: see four people – have to get them!

It was good training because, at first, the main thing they were looking at was the price of the beer. We would see them (usually a couple) come in and look at us: 'Yeah… pretty good.' Then she'd nudge him and say, 'One mark fifty. We can't afford this place,' and they'd leave. We were saying to Bruno, 'Bring the price down, man. It's doing us in. You will get 'em in if you bring it down a bit.' Eventually, out of this, we built a little audience. We would grab two people and do anything they wanted – our whole repertoire: 'You want a request?' (There was only one table filled.) 'Yes.' We would do all the jokes and try to be marvellous and make them want to come back.

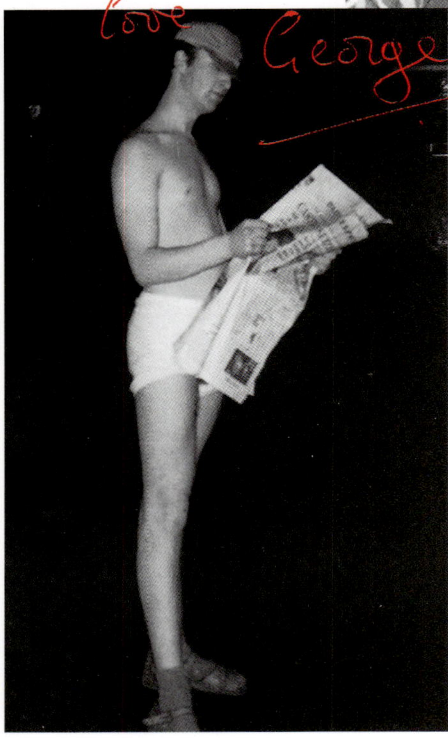

GEORGE: Inside the Bambi Kino. Our room was midway between the cinema and the ladies' lavatory, on an old dark corridor that led up to the fire escape. We used to sleep there in a bare concrete room with little cots and no windows.

Left: John in his undies outside the Bambi Kino. Just in this door is our concrete passageway, where Paul and Pete burned the condom.

JOHN: Me sightseeing. Hamburg, November 1960.

GEORGE: We were at the Indra for about a month, and then the club shut down and we moved into the Kaiserkeller, where Derry and the Seniors were. It was right at the time they were leaving. They'd finished their two months and Rory Storm and the Hurricanes were coming out.

The Kaiserkeller was great – at least it had a dance floor. And all the tables and chairs were located inside pieces of ship. The tables were barrels and there were ropes and nautical things around.

JOHN: There was beer and tables. And there was another group.

They had brought Howie Casey over, with the Seniors – or maybe they were even there when we got there – anyway, they were playing here, at Bruno's other club. They were pretty competent. They had saxes; they were really a together group. They had a black singer [Derry Wilkie] who couldn't really sing, but was a real showman. So we had to compete with them at first, and we had to start putting on this show to get enough people into *our* club, even though they were owned by the same person. Then they moved us in – with Rory Storm and Ringo. They were professionals; we were still amateurs. They'd been going for years, and they'd been to Butlins, and God knows what, and they really knew how to put on a show.[72]

RINGO: Hamburg was great. I went with Rory Storm and the Hurricanes. No van for us – we had the suits – we went by plane, which was a thrill. But when we got there Koschmider wanted us to sleep in the back of the Kaiserkeller, because The Beatles were in the back of the cinema.

Before us, Howie Casey and the others had been sleeping in the back of the club. I'll never forget when we arrived and they said: 'Yes, this is where you live now.' There were a couple of old settees with Union Jack flags, which were our sheets. We said, 'Are you kidding? We've got the suits!' So Rory and I and the band all stayed in one room in the German Seaman's Mission, and that was luxury – absolute bloody luxury.

I MET THE BEATLES WHILE WE WERE PLAYING IN GERMANY. WE'D SEEN THEM IN LIVERPOOL, BUT THEY WERE A NOTHING LITTLE BAND THEN, JUST PUTTING IT TOGETHER. IN FACT, THEY WEREN'T REALLY A BAND AT ALL.

GEORGE: In the Kaiserkeller we had to start earlier and finish later. They'd double us up with the other band, so we were alternating – first with Derry and the Seniors and then Rory Storm and the Hurricanes. In the contract we had to play for six hours and the other band had to play six hours, so it made it into a twelve-hour set. We'd do an hour, they'd do an hour and it seemed to rotate like that, day in and day out, for tuppence a month. But when you are a kid you don't care, really.

We started hanging out with them. I think we'd met Ringo once before, in England. I know we all had the same impression about him: 'You'd better be careful of him, he looks like trouble.'

Ringo seemed to us to be cocky. Relative to what we were like at the time, the band he was with were very professional. Maybe they wouldn't seem all that good now, but then they all had good instruments, they had a full drum kit and they had uniforms, matching ties and handkerchiefs. All their tunes were put into a routine, in a running order, and they did it as a show. And Rory was out at the front, always trying to leap around and 'mach shau'. Out of all the amateur bands in Liverpool, they were the most professional. So when they came to Hamburg Allan Williams told us: 'You'd better pull your socks up because Rory Storm and the Hurricanes are coming in, and you know how good they are. They're going to knock you for six.'

They would do their show and Ringo was the cocky one at the back; and with the way he looked, with that grey streak in his hair and half a grey eyebrow and a big nose, he looked a real tough guy. But it probably only took half an hour to realise it was actually... Ringo!

RINGO: By the time we all got together in Germany, with them playing one club and us playing another, they were already great. Then we ended up in the same club and The Beatles had the last set. I'd be semi-drunk, demanding they play slow songs.

PAUL: Ringo used to come in very late at night. He liked the bluesy sessions, when there weren't very many people there. I can see what he liked, too. We were getting down by then, pulling out all the B sides. We used to do a number called 'Three-Thirty Blues'. I remember Ringo would always come in, order a drink, settle back and request 'Three-Thirty Blues'.

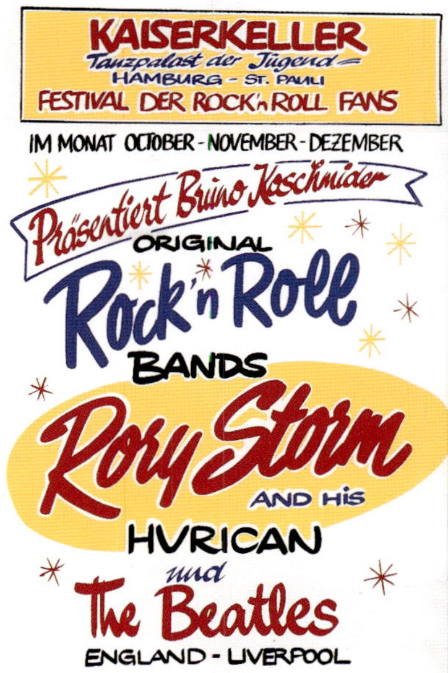

RINGO: I was still a Teddy boy and I only found out later from John that they were a bit scared of me. John told me, 'We used to be a bit frightened of you – this drunk, demanding slow songs, dressed like a Teddy boy.'

They were great in Hamburg. Really good – great rock. I knew I was better than the drummer they had at the time, and we all started hanging out some (not a lot); and then we moved to the same club, and that's when the battle started. We played twelve hours on a weekend night between two bands. That's a hell of a long time, especially when in each set we were trying to top them and they were trying to top us.

GEORGE: There was another thing: Pete would never hang out with us. When we finished doing the gig, Pete would go off on his own and we three would hang out together, and then when Ringo was around it was like a full unit, both on and off the stage. When there were the four of us with Ringo, it felt rocking.

JOHN: In Hamburg we had to play for hours and hours on end. Every song lasted twenty minutes and had twenty solos in it. We'd be playing eight or ten hours a night. That's what improved the playing. And the Germans like heavy rock, so you have to keep rocking all the time; that's how we got stomping.[72]

STUART SUTCLIFFE: *We have improved a thousand fold since our arrival and Allan Williams, who is here at the moment, tells us that there is no band in Liverpool to touch us.*[60]

GEORGE: We had to learn millions of songs. We had to play so long we just played everything. So it was all the Gene Vincent – we'd do everything on the album; not just a lazy 'Blue-Jean Bop', whatever. We'd get a Chuck Berry record, and learn it all, same with Little Richard, the Everly Brothers, Buddy Holly, Fats Domino – everything. But we'd also do things like 'Moonglow', which we used to play as an instrumental. Anything, because we'd be on for hours – we'd make up stuff.

Hamburg was really like our apprenticeship, learning how to play in front of people.

JOHN: We once tried a German number, playing to the crowd.

We got better and got more confidence. We couldn't help it, with all the experience, playing all night long. It was handy, them being foreign. We had to try even harder, put our heart and soul into it, to get ourselves over.[67] Our performance was good then. We worked and played long hours – good at that age, when you could get work.[76] And we'd all end up jumping around on the floor. Paul would be doing 'What'd I Say?' for an hour and a half.[72]

PAUL: 'What'd I Say' was always the one that really got them. That was one of our big numbers. It became like trying to get into the *Guinness Book of Records* – who could make it last the longest. It is the perfect song; it has the greatest opening riff ever. And if you had a Wurlitzer (which we didn't) you could keep that riff going for hours. Then it went, 'Tell your MAMA, tell your PAW. Gonna take you back to ArkanSAW. See the girl with the red dress on…' We could string that out. Then the chorus: 'Tell me, what'd I say?' and you could keep that going for hours. Then it had the killer, 'Oh yeah!' – audience participation.

JOHN: As far as I know, that was the first electric piano on record that I ever heard. 'What'd I Say' seemed to be the start of all the guitar-lick records. None of us had electric pianos so we did it on guitar to try and get that low sound. Before that, everything was mainly licks like on Little Richard rock'n'roll records, like 'Lucille' where the sax section and the guitar played it. 'What'd I Say' started a whole new ball game which is still going now.[74]

PAUL: We never thought to write our own songs over there. There was so much other stuff. I had written a couple of little things but I didn't dare show them to anyone because they *were* little. There was always a Chuck Berry song instead. 'A Taste Of Honey' was one of my big numbers in Hamburg – a bit of a ballad. It was different, but it used to get requested a lot. We sang close harmonies on the little echo mikes, and we made a fairly good job of it. It used to sound pretty good, actually.

We got better and better and other groups started coming to watch us. The accolade of accolades was when Tony Sheridan would come in from the Top Ten (the big club where we aspired to go) or when Rory Storm or Ringo would hang around to watch us.

GEORGE: Saturday would start at three or four in the afternoon and go on until five or six in the morning. We'd have breakfast when we finished. Everyone would be drunk – not just the band but the audience and all the people in St Pauli. They'd all go and eat something and perhaps drink more, then go to the fish market on Sunday morning (I never did figure out why). We'd just wander around in the broad sunlight, pissed as newts, with no sleep. Eventually we'd go to bed. Then the Sunday show would start early, but not finish too late.

For the early period the audience would be much younger, around fifteen, sixteen, seventeen. At eight or nine o'clock they'd start to get a bit older and after ten o'clock it would be eighteens and over only. By two in the morning it would be the hardened drunks and other club owners, who'd all come around and hang out with our club owner. They'd all be sitting at a big table getting thrashed, chucking around crates and bottles of Sekt, all kinds of schnapps – that's not to count what we were drinking by buying our own drinks, because at this point we discovered whisky and Coke.

RINGO: The Germans were fabulous, because if they liked you they would send up crates of beer. And if there were people with money, out-of-towners or the snobs of Hamburg, they would send champagne. We didn't give a damn, we'd drink it all.

Gangsters would also come into the clubs, and they had guns, which we'd never seen before. People would come in and sit at the bar and drink until they fell off the stool, or they had no money left. They wouldn't be shown to the door, they'd actually be kicked out of it to say, 'Don't do that again.'

JOHN: All these gangsters would come in – the local Mafia. They'd send a crate of champagne on stage, imitation German champagne, and we had to drink it or they'd kill us. They'd say, 'Drink, and then do "What'd I Say".' We'd have to do this show, whatever time of night. If they came in at five in the morning and we'd been playing seven hours, they'd give us a crate of champagne and we were supposed to carry on.

My voice began to hurt with the pain of singing. But we learnt from the Germans that you could stay awake by eating slimming pills, so we did that.[67] I used to be so pissed I'd be lying on the floor behind the piano, drunk, while the rest of the group was playing. I'd be on stage, fast asleep. And we always ate on stage, too, because we never had time to eat. So it was a real scene… It would be a far-out show now: eating and smoking and swearing and going to sleep on stage when you were tired.[72]

RINGO: This was the point of our lives when we found pills, uppers. That's the only way we could continue playing for so long. They were called Preludin, and you could buy them over the counter. We never thought we were doing anything wrong, but we'd get really wired and go on for days. So with beer and Preludin, that's how we survived.

JOHN: The first drugs I ever took, I was still at art school, with the group (we all took it together), was Benzedrine from the inside of an inhaler...[74]

GEORGE: There was a bearded guy from a suburb of London, a Beat Poet named Royston Ellis. He came up to Liverpool to read his poetry and we were used to back him. Ellis had discovered that if you open a Vick's inhaler you find Benzedrine in it, impregnated into the cardboard inside. (He later exposed this fact to the *News of the World*.)

JOHN: The beatnik, a sort of English version of Allen Ginsberg, was turning everybody onto this inside of an inhaler, and everybody thought, 'Wow! What's this?' and talked their mouths off for a night.

In Hamburg the waiters always had Preludin (and various other pills, but I remember Preludin because it was a big trip) and they were all taking these pills to keep themselves awake, to work these incredible hours in this all-night place. And so the waiters, when they'd see the musicians falling over with tiredness or with drink, they'd give you the pill. You'd take the pill, you'd be talking, you'd sober up, you could work almost endlessly – until the pill wore off, then you'd have to have another.[74]

GEORGE: We were frothing at the mouth. Because we had all these hours to play and the club owners were giving us Preludins, which were slimming tablets. I don't think they were amphetamine, but they were uppers. So we used to be up there foaming, stomping away.

We went berserk inasmuch as we got drunk a lot and we played wildly and then they gave us these pills. I remember lying in bed, sweating from Preludin, thinking, 'Why aren't I sleeping?'

PAUL: My dad was a very wise working-class guy, so he saw it all coming. As a lad going out to Hamburg on my own, I'd been forewarned: 'Drugs and pills: WATCH OUT, right?' So in Hamburg, when the Preludin came around I was probably the last one to have it. It was: 'Oh, I'll stick to the beer, thanks.'

They'd all get high, and I'd come up just on the buzz. I remember John turning to me, 'Blah, blah, blah,' saying, 'What are you on?' and I said, 'Nothing, blah, blah.' I'd be talking just as fast as them; their high would do it for me.

I really was frightened of that stuff, because you're taught when you're young to 'watch out for those devil drugs'. I actually saw the dangers and tried to keep away from it at first. Looking back, I realise it was only peer pressure; and to resist seems cooler now than it did at the time. It would have been rather wise and mature of me to say, 'Hey guys, I don't have to do everything you do,' but at the time it just felt like I was being a cissie. And that was the attitude that prevailed.

JOHN: The things we used to do! We used to break the stage down – that was long before The Who came out and broke things; we used to leave guitars playing on stage with no people there. We'd be so drunk, we used to smash the machinery. And this was all through frustration, not as an intellectual thought: 'We will break the stage, we will wear a toilet seat round our neck, we will go on naked.' We just did it, through being drunk.

Paul was telling me that he and I used to have rows about who was the leader. I can't remember them. It had stopped mattering by then. I wasn't so determined to be leader at all costs. If I did argue, it was just out of pride.

All the arguments became trivial, mainly because we were fucked and irritable with working so hard. We were just kids. George threw some food at me once on stage. The row was over something stupid. I said I would smash his face in for him. We had a shouting match, but that was all; I never did anything.[67] And I once threw a plate of food over George. That's the only violence we ever had between us.[69]

GEORGE: John threw all kinds of stuff over everybody, over the years. I can't remember that happening, but if he said it it must have happened. There were times when he did throw stuff. He got pretty wired. The down, adverse effects of drink and Preludins, where you'd be up for days, were that you'd start hallucinating and getting a bit weird. John would sometimes get on the edge. He'd come in in the early hours of the morning and be ranting, and I'd be lying there pretending to be asleep, hoping he wouldn't notice me.

One time Paul had a chick in bed and John came in and got a pair of scissors and cut all her clothes into pieces and then wrecked the wardrobe. He got like that occasionally; it was because of the pills and being up too long. But we threw things at the *Germans*; all the bands did.

JOHN: We used to shout in English at the Germans, call them Nazis and tell them to fuck off.[70]

PAUL: One of those days we were doing our stuff and some slightly strange-looking people arrived who didn't look like anyone else. Immediately we felt, 'Wey-hey... kindred spirits... something's going on here.' They came in and sat down and they were Astrid, Jürgen and Klaus. Klaus Voormann later played bass with Manfred Mann. Jürgen was Jürgen Vollmer, who is still a good photographer. So was Astrid Kirchherr, who was to be Stuart's girlfriend – they were the big love. Anyway, they arrived, sat down, and we could see they had something different. And we were also what *they* were looking for.

GEORGE: Astrid was the girlfriend of Klaus at first and they'd had a row one night, so he'd gone off in a huff. He was pissed off with her and he came down to this very bad area of Hamburg, where he would never have gone otherwise. He was walking around and he heard this noise coming out of a cellar so he came into the Kaiserkeller, saw us and thought we were really interesting. He went back and told Astrid and brought her and some of their friends – there were ballet dancers with them – and they started coming in on a regular basis to see us. Astrid and Klaus would come in most frequently. They liked our band and she wanted to photograph us.

PAUL: They all liked the rock'n'roll and the quiffed-back hairdos, but they were different; they all wore black. In fact, we got a lot of our look from them. They called themselves 'Exis' – Existentialists. They were not rockers or mods, but 'Exis'.

We were still in rocker mode but, as I say, a little bit different from the other groups: different material, different sense of humour. Stuart had got himself looking like James Dean. He would put his shades on and stand there with his bass – it was all a big pose. At first, they were blown away by Stuart: they evidently weren't looking for musicianship – it was image. And when Stuart turned out to be a painter, and as John was an art student and *they* were art students, there was this great connection. So we had drinks with them and chatted, and soon really got to know them well.

STUART SUTCLIFFE: *Just recently I have found the most wonderful friends, the most beautiful looking trio I have ever seen. I was completely captivated by their charm. The girl thought that I was the most handsome of the lot. Here was I, feeling the most insipid working member of the group, being told how much superior I looked – this alongside the great Romeo John Lennon and his two stalwarts Paul and George: the Casanovas of Hamburg!*

GEORGE: They were all very nice people. It was really good for us to meet them, too, because they were more cultured than the locals. They had a great appreciation for us, but they were very artistic and interesting in themselves. They were the arty crowd around Hamburg.

We started hanging out with them. We learnt more from them at that point than they learnt from us, including style. Klaus, Astrid and Jürgen became real friends. Klaus later became a bass-player himself and played on many of my records and other people's. And Astrid was so loving; she'd take us home and feed us. She helped us a lot, even just to let us have a bath. Astrid was twenty-two at that time, and I was seventeen; she seemed so much older than me, and so grown up.

Eventually Stuart and Astrid got off with each other; Astrid was really cute – so was Stuart; you can see from their pictures that they were.

PAUL: We got in with these people very tight. Jürgen and Astrid took some early photos of us. We would go to their studio, as they had one (or they knew a man who did). We had never had this kind of treatment before.

JOHN:

IT WAS HAMBURG THAT DID IT. THAT'S WHERE WE REALLY DEVELOPED. TO GET THE GERMANS GOING AND KEEP IT UP FOR TWELVE HOURS AT A TIME WE REALLY HAD TO HAMMER. WE WOULD NEVER HAVE DEVELOPED AS MUCH IF WE'D STAYED AT HOME. WE HAD TO TRY ANYTHING THAT CAME INTO OUR HEADS IN HAMBURG. THERE WAS NOBODY TO COPY FROM. WE PLAYED WHAT WE LIKED BEST AND THE GERMANS LIKED IT AS LONG AS IT WAS LOUD.'[67]

REELIN + ROCKIN.
LONG TALL SALLY.
STICKS + STONES.
BOBBY VEE. MORE THAN I CAN SAY.
JAMBALAYA.
I KNOW.
HI HEEL SNEAKERS.

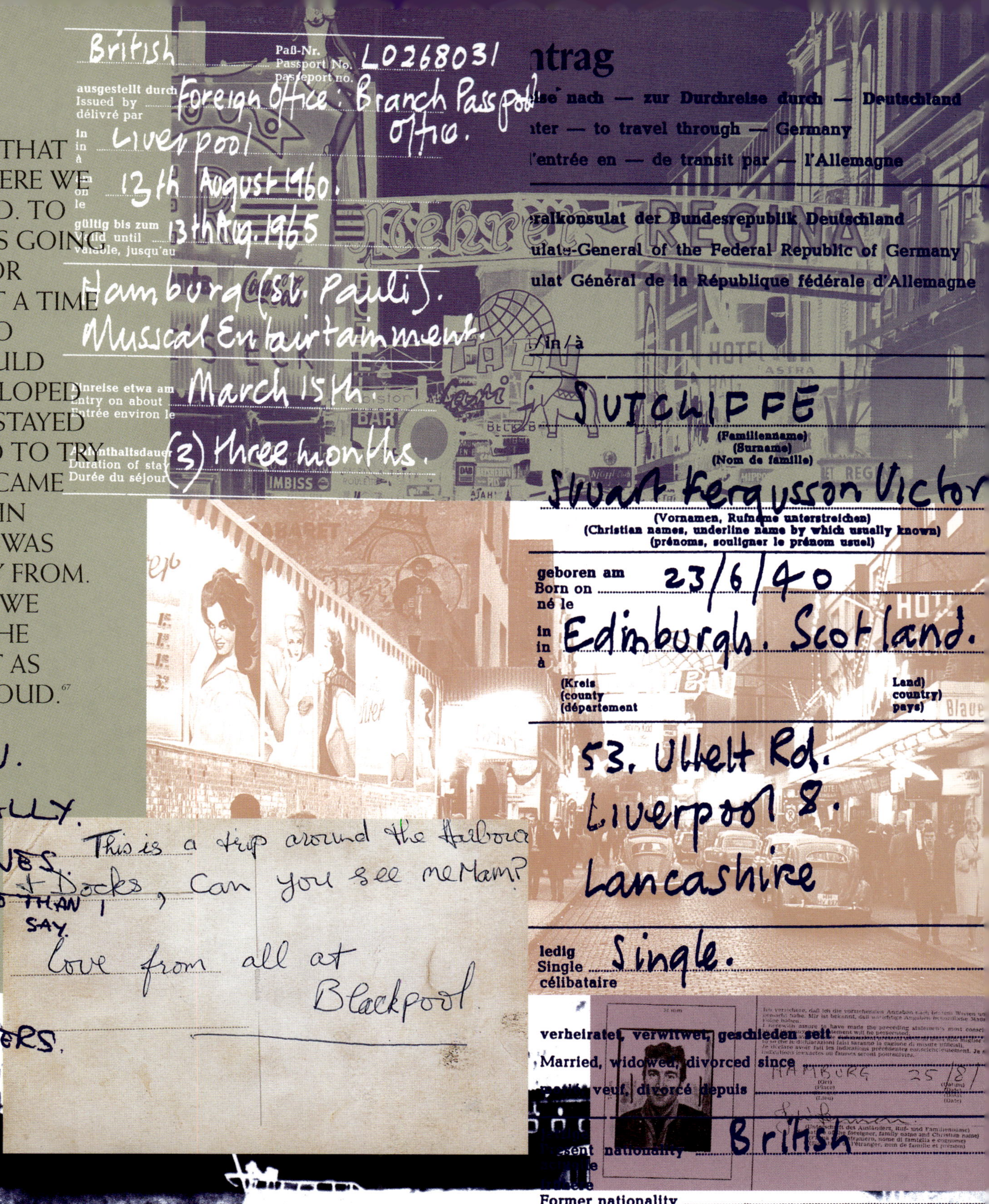

PAUL: Jürgen and Astrid would take us to a seedy place like a fairground and photograph us against it, so we started to see how that side of things was done. For a lot of our early hand-out photographs we would ask the photographer, 'Can we go out on site?' We liked that sort of image – it looks great. Glitter we always hated.

We found a shop with leather jackets, which we knew no one in Liverpool would have, and it was really cool. So that was going to be great for when we got back home.

GEORGE: It was everybody's idea to wear leather as soon as we saw it. Leather jackets were always the thing – Marlon Brando – and jeans. In Germany they had great leather, and our friends wore it. Astrid was dressing like that when we were still just Liverpool scruffs. She was the one who had the leather kecks and the Beatle haircut.

We got friendly with a few other local people; the waiters and the managers of the clubs. They really got to like us because we went back to Hamburg again and again.

GEORGE: These early Beatles photographs are fantastic. They were taken by Astrid at the funfair in Hamburg (the truck we are sitting on carried pieces of the rollercoaster). The Beatles look great. Astrid was the one, really, who influenced our image more than anybody. She made us look good.

PAUL: It was still very close to the war and all the people in Liverpool and on our estate hadn't forgotten, so it was good that we could meet young Germans. All these kids coming in had forgotten about the war, and this was very good for our relationships with those people.

It was strange for us. It was all very different, the whole ambience of Germany. Going to the *Postamt* to get stamps. It was like being at scout camp as a kid, where the post becomes very important: when they were handing out the post you prayed that there'd be two or three letters for you. If there weren't any you'd be gutted.

Here, the club managers would hand them to us and when we got one it was great – we'd go off in a corner reading these long letters.

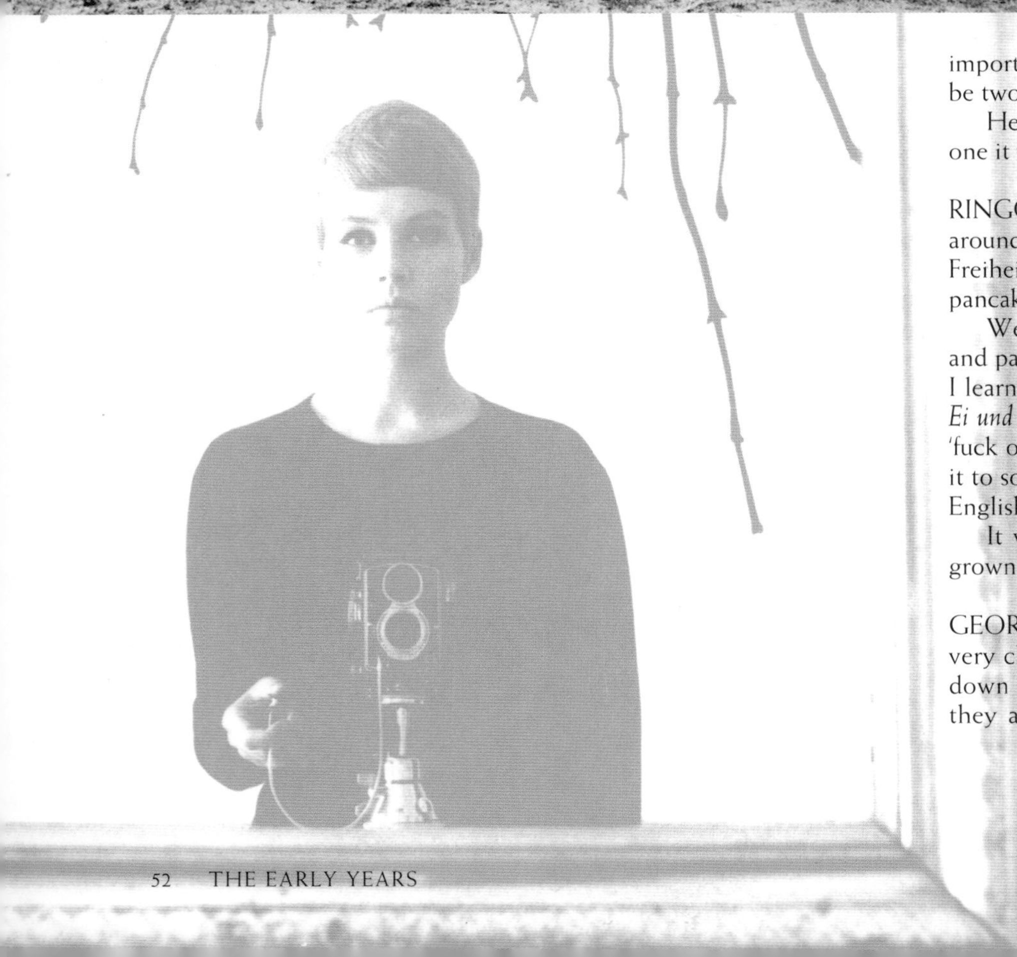

RINGO: One morning, when I first got to Germany, I was wandering around, wondering where to go, and I bumped into Stuart in Grosse Freiheit. I didn't really know him at all, but he took me to a café that sold pancakes and got me my first meal.

We all hung around together in the Reeperbahn and ate cornflakes and pancakes together – that's how I learnt some German. The first word I learnt was for cornflakes, and then I learnt *Pfannkuchen* (pancakes) and *Ei und Kartoffeln* (egg and potatoes). The waiters would teach you to say 'fuck off' or 'kiss my arse' and pretend it was something else. So we'd say it to someone, and they'd grab you by the throat and we'd say, 'No, we're English! *He* told me to say it!'

It was very rough in that area. So was Liverpool, but because we'd grown up there we knew how to deal with it.

GEORGE: There were a couple of places we'd go to eat. There was a very cheap, horrible place just around the corner from the Kaiserkeller, down a little side street on the right. The customers were locals but they all seemed to be war veterans – people with no legs or eyes or arms – and cats. We'd go there and have a horrible slap-up meal for very little money.

Much better than that, though, was Harald's. He used to give us cornflakes, and egg and chips. And milk; that probably saved us – there was lots of fresh milk in that street. We'd wake up in the morning and buy a litre of cold milk at a little dairy place opposite the Bambi Kino. A couple of times we got buttermilk and didn't know what it was. We thought, 'Phew! What's going on?' It tasted curdled.

PAUL: Harald's was on the Grosse Freiheit. They would serve hamburgers called *Frikadellen*. (We could never understand why they didn't call them 'hamburgers' in Hamburg.) Harald's was right near the clubs, but if you went round the back there was Chug-ou. That's the place George was thinking of. It was a Chinese place just three hundred yards up the road, slightly off the Reeperbahn. Its great attraction was pancakes – *'Pfannkuchen mit Zitrone bitte, und Zucker'* – pancakes with lemon and sugar. It was the only place that sold them; everywhere else was 'foreign food' to us. My main memory of that place is that you could tell we'd been in there, because ours were the only plates that were empty except for the gherkins – we didn't understand miniature pickles. So there'd always be two little gherkins left in our otherwise meticulously scrubbed plates.

It was great to have pancakes; it was like Shrove Tuesday every day. The down side of it was that there were quite a few limbless old people sitting around; old guys with black berets who'd obviously been in the war. And if you think about it, the war was only fifteen years before. We would see millions of veterans. And Germans all had uniforms – be it for the dustman, the binman, or for the man who lays the tarmac. These were war veterans so they would have a uniform or an armband, but no arm or no leg. It was a very clear reminder of what had recently happened. Our reaction as Liverpool lads was, 'Ah well, we won the war – don't worry.' There was always that 'don't mention the war'; but when it came to it we felt quite nationalistic, slightly gung ho about it.

STUART SUTCLIFFE: *One thing I'm sure about since I've been here, I hate brutality. There is so much in this area…*[60]

GEORGE: The problem with the nightclubs in Hamburg was that most of the waiters and the barmen were gangsters. They were tough guys, anyway; they were fighters, and there would always be fights.

The most popular tune to fight to, not only in Hamburg but in Liverpool too, was 'Hully Gully'. Every time we did 'Hully Gully' there would be a fight. In Liverpool they would be hitting each other with fire extinguishers. On Saturday night they would all be back from the pub and you could guarantee 'Hully Gully'!

I remember there were many nights in Hamburg when they pulled tear-gas guns out. But on one particular night you could smell the Players and Capstan cigarettes and we thought, 'Oh, eh up, the British are here.' Soldiers were in, and I remember telling one not to mess around with the barmaid, that she belonged to the club manager – one of the tough guys. But this soldier was getting drunk, trying to make it with the barmaid, and the next minute 'Hully Gully' was playing and all hell broke loose. By the end of the song we had to stop playing because of the tear gas.

JOHN: Gangs of fucking British servicemen [would] try to stir things up. When we could smell Senior Service in the audience we knew there would be trouble before the night was out. After a few drinks, they'd start shouting, 'Up Liverpool' or 'Up Pompey'. [But later] they'd all be lying there half dead after they'd tried to pick a fight with the waiters over the bill, or just over nothing. The waiters would get their flick-knives out, or their truncheons, and that would be it. I've never seen such killers.[67]

GEORGE: They had truncheons, coshes, knuckle-dusters. There was a shop just around the corner from where we lived where you could buy all this stuff. They would have fights and beat the hell out of each other and then the bad guy would get thrown out of the back door, and so an hour later he'd come back with reinforcements and then it was really wicked – blood everywhere. It happened a lot, especially when the troops came in. The seamen and the soldiers would come into town; they'd all get drunk and inevitably it ended in blood and tears. And tears for the band, too, with the gas in our faces.

PAUL: There were sailors everywhere. The waiters were all violent – they had to be because fights would always break out; so it was a crazy time. But we loved it.

JOHN: We chose to roll a British sailor. I thought I could chat him up in English, kid him on we could get him some birds. We got him drinking and drinking and he kept on asking, 'Where's the girls?' We kept chatting him up, trying to find out where he kept his money. We never made it. We just hit him twice in the end, then gave up. We didn't want to hurt him.[67]

PAUL: I used to get on Pete's case a bit. He'd often stay out all night. He got to know a stripper and they were boyfriend and girlfriend. She didn't finish work until four in the morning, so he'd stay up with her and roll back at about ten in the morning and be going to bed when we were starting work. I think that had something to do with a rift starting.

Round about this time, Stuart and I got a little fraught, too. I claim that I was making sure that we were musically very good, in case anyone was watching. I felt we had to be good for any talent-spotters. People would now call that the perfectionist in me. I see it as trying to get it right, but not obsessively so. This did create a couple of rifts and I could have been more sensitive about it. But who is sensitive at that age? Certainly not me.

Stuart and I once actually had a fight on stage. I thought I'd beat him hands down because he was littler than me. But he was strong and we got locked in a sort of death-grip, on stage during the set. It was terrible. We must have called each other something one too many times: 'Oh, you…' – 'You calling me that?' Then we were locked and neither of us wanted to go any further and all the others were shouting, 'Stop it, you two!' – 'I'll stop it if he will.'

JOHN: Paul was saying something about Stu's girl – he was jealous because she was a great girl, and Stu hit him, on stage. And Stu wasn't a violent guy at all.[72]

PAUL: Of course, all the big gangsters round there were all laughing at us because they were used to killing people. Here were me and Stu – neither of us big fighters. None of this helped my relationship with Stuart *or* Pete.

RINGO: It was pretty vicious, but on the other hand the hookers loved us. They'd do my laundry – and the girls behind the bar were always good to us.

PAUL: Hamburg was quite an eye-opener. We went as kids and came back as… old kids!

It was a sex shock. There were the Reeperbahn girls, and then there was a nicer class of girl who came in on weekends who had to go by ten o'clock because the German police would make an *Ausweiskontrolle* (an identity check). There were a few others who were a little more 'Reeperbahn' and then there were the striptease artists, and suddenly, you'd have a girlfriend who was a stripper. If you had hardly ever had sex in your life before, this was fairly formidable. Here was somebody who obviously knew something about it, and you didn't. So we got a fairly swift baptism of fire into the sex scene. There was a lot of it about and we were off the leash.

We were just Liverpool guys who, as far as we were concerned, could not get arrested back home. In Liverpool all the girls wore very rigid girdles; it was medieval. Here, in Hamburg, they were almost flashing it. And seemed to know what the score was. That was the proof of the pudding, that we could pull them. They were great-looking girls, too, so it really was pulling the birds time. They were all barmaids; it wasn't your average sweet virgin that you were mixing with, but we were quite happy to be educated. We all got our education in Hamburg. It was quite something.

GEORGE: In the late Fifties in England it wasn't that easy to get it. The girls would all wear brassieres and corsets which seemed like reinforced steel. You could never actually get in anywhere. You'd always be breaking your hand trying to undo everything. I can remember parties at Pete Best's house, or wherever; there'd be these all-night parties and I'd be snogging with some girl and having a hard-on for eight hours till my groin was aching – and not getting any relief. That was how it always was. Those *weren't* the days.

There's that side of it which will always be there, with the different sexes and their desires and all that Testa Rossa-terone bubbling up. And there's the other side of it – the peer-group pressure: 'What, haven't you had it yet?' It becomes, 'Oh, I've got to get it,' and everyone would be lying: 'Yeah, I got it.' – 'Did you get some tit?' – 'I got some tit.' – 'Well, I got some finger pie!'

I certainly didn't have a stripper in Hamburg. I know Pete met one. There were young girls in the clubs and we knew a few, but for me it wasn't some big orgy. My first shag was in Hamburg – with Paul and John and Pete Best all watching. We were in bunkbeds. They couldn't really see anything because I was under the covers, but after I'd finished they all applauded and cheered. At least they kept quiet whilst I was doing it.

PAUL: We kept quiet, kept our faces to the wall and pretended to be asleep. The rest of us were a little more experienced by then. George was a late starter.

That was the intimacy we had. We would always be walking in on each other and things. I'd walked in on John and seen a little bottom bobbing up and down with a girl underneath him. It was perfectly normal: you'd go, 'Oh shit, sorry,' and back out the room. It was very teenage: 'Are you using this room? I want to have a shag.' And you'd pull a girl in there.

That's why I've always found very strange the theory that John was gay. Because over the fifteen years of sharing rooms, sharing our lives, not one of us has an incident to relate of catching John with a boy. I would have thought that kind of thing would be more prevalent, and John's inhibitions were certainly free when he was drunk.

RINGO: We were twenty (at least, I was) and were going to all the strip clubs and it was exciting. The closest I'd been to anything like that in Liverpool was watching *Nudes on Ice* – those perspex boxes with naked women in who couldn't move – and suddenly, in Germany, it was in your face. I was around all the clubs and we learnt to stay up day and night.

JOHN: What with playing, drinking and birds, how could we find time to sleep?

GEORGE: One time our friend Bernie came out from Liverpool to visit us. One day we were in a club and Bernie walked in and said, 'I've just had a wank off this great-looking bird in the lav.' We all said, 'That's not a bird, Bernie!'

PAUL: We set Bernie up. There was a club called the Roxy we all knew about. There were some cracking-looking birds there; they had deepish voices and they'd call you 'my little schnoodel poodel', which was like 'little sweetie'. We didn't realise at first, but after being there a few weeks someone put us straight – they were all guys. There were a few who fancied us because we were good-looking young boys. And so Bernie came out and he was a Liverpool kid: 'Eh, all right lads – whoa, look at her, she's great!' We all knew the score by then and we said, 'Yeah. I've had her, she's fantastic.' The next day he came up and said, 'Ooh, I put me hand down there and she's got a fuckin' knob.' We all collapsed in a heap.

We grew up by experiencing this kind of thing, and got quite used to it. We spent all our money on drinking and generally having a good time.

GEORGE: The whole area, the Reeperbahn and St Pauli, was like Soho. So if you had a few beers and were feeling merry and talking loudly with a few friends, you wouldn't stand out. We were in an area where the whole place was raving. There were places where there were donkeys shagging women or whatever – allegedly, I never saw it – and mud-wrestling women and transvestites and all that. All we were doing was getting a bit pissed and playing rock'n'roll, and maybe getting a bit noisy occasionally. Not like the folklore; the history books have glorified and exaggerated it.

PAUL: There was a curfew at ten o'clock every night. The German police would come up on stage and announce: 'It is twenty-two hours and all young people under eighteen years must leave this club. We are making an *Ausweiskontrolle*.' Eventually we got so used to it that we started saying it ourselves. We would do joke announcements. I knew a bit of German; George and I had learnt it in school. (Everyone else had learnt French, but they taught us German and Spanish.) So it was very handy and we could do all the silly stuff. We eventually got a really big steaming club full and they loved us.

GEORGE: We would be sitting up on the bandstand, waiting, while all this went on. The *Kontrolle* would turn on all the club lights and the band would have to stop playing. Men would go around the tables, checking IDs.

PAUL: We used to call them 'the Gestapo' – guys in very convincing German uniforms, going around looking at all the kids' passports. We had never seen the like of it. In Liverpool you could go anywhere as long as you didn't get caught in a pub, and certainly nobody came round and asked you for your pass. I suppose it was all leftovers from the war.

GEORGE: It went on for two months before the penny dropped as to what they were actually saying: 'Everybody under eighteen years old get out.' I was only seventeen and I was sitting with the band and getting worried, and eventually somebody did find out; I don't know how. We didn't have any work permits or visas, and with me under-age they started closing in on us; then one day the police came and booted me out.

On 1:30 approx. on Saturday morning the entire group gave notice to H.K. He was annoyed when we refused to sign an agreement stating that we would not play in Hamburg in December, and then he refused to give us our fare to England, which we would have used in 2 wks. time. Our interview with K. ended when he said he refused to talk any more and told us to leave his office. We were not angry, and we left thinking only of our new job at the Top Ten club. We then went to eat, and then returned to our rooms in the Bambi Kino, owned by K.

Whilst packing my belongings, I found a box of damp matches. I went out into the dark, bare corridor and began to test some matches there. I was followed by Best, who took some of my matches and lit them. We noticed a piece of cord nailed to the wall, and somehow the dry old cording and the matches suggested the burning of the cording. We burnt it in several places (5? or 6?) and then seeing the smoke around us we realised that we had gone too far, and extinguished the small flames immediately. When we were certain that the fire was completely out, we went to bed and slept.

We both swear that we had no intention whatsoever of burning the cinema, or maliciously damaging its property. The whole incident had no motive to prompt it, in fact there was no reason at all behind the burning. It was just a stupid trick, which we feel we ought to have been punished for in a far less drastic manner.

Neither of us drink alchohol, and so we were not under the influence of drink. We committed the offence but failed to think that it could

PAUL: Extracts from a letter I drafted to the German police in 1961, found in the back of an old school exercise book of mine. I sent the final version and eventually we were allowed to go back to Hamburg.

ever be called gross misconduct. We believe that H.K. knew that our moving to the Top Ten club would not be good for his business, + so he

I had to go back home and that was right at a critical time, because we'd just been offered a job at another club down the road, the Top Ten, which was a much cooler club. In our hour off from the Kaiserkeller we'd go there to watch Sheridan or whoever was playing. The manager had poached us from Bruno Koschmider and we'd already played a couple of times there. There was a really good atmosphere in that club. It had a great sound-system, it looked much better and they paid a bit more money.

Here we were, leaving the Kaiserkeller to go to the Top Ten, really eager to go there – and right at that point they came and kicked me out of town. So I was moving out to go home and they were moving out to go to this great club.

Astrid, and probably Stuart, dropped me at Hamburg station. It was a long journey on my own on the train to the Hook of Holland. From there I got the day boat. It seemed to take ages and I didn't have much money – I was praying I'd have enough. I had to get from Harwich to Liverpool Street Station and then a taxi across to Euston. From there I got a train to Liverpool. I can remember it now: I had an amplifier that I'd bought in Hamburg and a crappy suitcase and things in boxes, paper bags with my clothes in, and a guitar. I had too many things to carry and was standing in the corridor of the train with my belongings around me, and lots of soldiers on the train, drinking. I finally got to Liverpool and took a taxi home – I just about made it. I got home penniless. It took everything I had to get me back.

I had returned to England, on my own and all forlorn, but as it turned out, Paul and Pete were booted out at the same time and were already back ahead of me. It seems Bruno didn't want The Beatles to leave his club and, as there had been an accidental fire, he had got the police in.

Bruno said that they were burning his cinema down and they took Pete and Paul and put them in the police station on the Reeperbahn for a few hours and then flew them back to England. Deported them. Then John came back a few days after them, because there was no point in him staying and Stuart stayed for a bit because he'd decided to get together with Astrid. It was great, a reprieve, otherwise I had visions of our band staying on there with me stuck in Liverpool, and that would be it.

STUART SUTCLIFFE: *We finished at the Kaiserkeller last week. The police intervened because we had no work permits. Paul and Peter the drummer were deported yesterday and sent in handcuffs to the airport. I was innocent this time; accused of arson – that is, setting fire to the Kino where we sleep. I arrive at the club and am informed that the whole of the Hamburg police are looking for me. The rest of the band are already locked up, so smiling and on the arm of Astrid, I proceed to give myself up. At this time, I'm not aware of the charges. All of my belongings, including spectacles, are taken away and I'm led to a cell, where, without food or drink I sat for six hours on a very wooden bench, and the door shut very tight. I signed a confession in Deutsch that I knew nothing about a fire, and they let me go. The next day Paul and Pete were deported and sent home by plane, John and I were without money and job. The police had forbidden us to work as already we were liable to deportation for working three months in the country illegally. The next day John went home. I stay till January at Astrid's house. At the moment she's washing all my muck and filth collected over the last few months. God I love her so much.*[60]

JOHN: They were all deported and I was left in Hamburg, playing alone with another group of musicians. It was quite a shattering experience to be in a foreign country, pretty young, left there all on my own.[76] We'd spent our money as we went along. I didn't have any to spare and being stuck in Hamburg with no food money was no joke, especially just around Christmas.

It was terrible, setting off home.[67] I was feeling really sorry for myself and it was a pretty hungry business working my way back to Liverpool.[63] I had my amp on my back, scared stiff I was going to get it pinched. I hadn't paid for it. I was convinced I'd never find England.[67]

When I did get home, I was so fed up I didn't bother to contact the others for a few weeks. A month is a long time at eighteen or nineteen; I didn't know what they were doing. I just withdrew to think whether it was worth going on with.[80] I thought, 'Is this what I want to do?' I was always a sort of poet or painter and I thought, 'Is this it? Nightclubs and seedy scenes, being deported, and weird people in clubs?' Nowadays they call it decadence but those days it was just in Hamburg, in clubs that groups played at, strip clubs. I thought hard about whether I should continue.[76] Now, when George and Paul found out, they were mad at me, because they thought, 'We could have been working now.' But I just withdrew. You see, part of me is a monk and part of me is a performing flea. Knowing when to stop is survival for me.[80]

Anyway, after a while I got to thinking that we ought to cash in on the Liverpool beat scene. Things were really thriving and it seemed a pity to waste the experience we'd got, playing all those hours every night in Hamburg.[63]

PAUL: After Hamburg it wasn't too good. Everyone needed a rest. I expected everyone to be ringing me to discuss what we were doing, but it was all quiet on the Western front. None of us called each other, so I wasn't so much dejected as puzzled, wondering whether it was going to carry on or if that was the last of it.

I started working at a coil-winding factory called Massey and Coggins. My dad had told me to go out and get a job. I'd said, 'I've got a job, I'm in a band.' But after a couple of weeks of doing nothing with the band it was, 'No, you have got to get a proper job.' He virtually chucked me out of the house: 'Get a job or don't come back.' So I went to the employment office and said, 'Can I have a job? Just give me anything.' I said, 'I'll have whatever is on the top of that little pile there.' And the first job was sweeping the yard at Massey and Coggins. I took it.

I went there and the personnel officer said, 'We can't have you sweeping the yard, you're management material.' And they started to train me from the shop floor up with that in mind. Of course, I wasn't very good on the shop floor – I wasn't a very good coilwinder.

One day John and George showed up in the yard that I should have been sweeping and told me we had a gig at the Cavern. I said, 'No. I've got a steady job here and it pays £7 14s a week. They are training me here. That's pretty good, I can't expect more.' And I was quite serious about this. But then – and with my dad's warning still in my mind – I thought, 'Sod it. I can't stick this lot.' I bunked over the wall and was never seen again by Massey and Coggins. Pretty shrewd move really, as things turned out.

JOHN: I was always saying, 'Face up to your dad, tell him to "fuck off". He can't hit you. You can kill him, he's an old man.' He treated Paul like a child, cutting his hair and telling him what to wear at seventeen, eighteen. But Paul would always give in. His dad told him to get a job; he dropped the group and started working on the lorries, saying, 'I need a steady career.' We couldn't believe it. I told him on the phone, 'Either come or you're out.' So he had to make a decision between me and his dad then, and in the end he chose me.[72]

GEORGE: We got a gig. Allan Williams put us in touch with a guy called Bob Wooler, a compere on the dance-hall circuit. He tried us out one night and put an ad in the paper: 'Direct from Hamburg: The Beatles'. And we probably looked German, too; very different from all the other groups, with our leather jackets. We looked funny and we played differently. We went down a bomb.

PAUL: We all wore black that we had picked up in Hamburg. All the Liverpool girls were saying, 'Are you from Germany?' or, 'I saw in the paper you are from Hamburg.'

JOHN: Suddenly we were a wow. Mind you, 70% of the audience thought we were a *German* wow, but we didn't care about that. Even in Liverpool, people didn't know we were from Liverpool. They thought we were from Hamburg. They said, 'Christ, they speak good English!' which we did, of course, being English.

It was that evening that we really came out of our shell and let go. We stood there being cheered for the first time. This was when we began to think that we were good. Up to Hamburg we'd thought we were OK, but not good enough. It was only back in Liverpool that we realised the difference and saw what had happened to us while everyone else was playing Cliff Richard shit.[67]

PAUL: HAMBURG TOTALLY WRECKED US. I REMEMBER GETTING HOME TO ENGLAND AND MY DAD THOUGHT I WAS HALF-DEAD. I LOOKED LIKE A SKELETON. I HADN'T NOTICED THE CHANGE, I'D BEEN HAVING SUCH A BALL.

JOHN: WE WERE ALWAYS ANTI-JAZZ. I THINK IT IS SHIT MUSIC – MORE STUPID THAN ROCK'N'ROLL – FOLLOWED BY STUDENTS IN MARKS AND SPENCER PULLOVERS.[67]

PAUL: We started getting gigs down the Cavern. The Cavern was sweaty, damp, dark, loud and exciting. As usual we didn't start out with much of an audience, but then people began to hear about us. We could always entertain them. It became our strength later, whether playing live or making records – we always had something up our sleeve.

GEORGE: We used to play lunchtime dates. We'd get up and go down to the Cavern and play from noon till about two. It was very casual; we'd have our tea and sandwiches and cigarettes on stage, sing a couple of tunes and tell a few jokes. There was something that even Brian Epstein liked about all that, although he pushed us away from that to a bigger audience.

JOHN: In those old Cavern days, half the thing was just ad lib; what you'd call comedy. We just used to mess about, jump into the audience, do anything.[64]

PAUL: We'd go on stage with a cheese roll and a cigarette and we felt we really had something going in that place. The amps used to fuse and we'd stop and sing a Sunblest bread commercial while they were being repaired. We used to do skits – I'd do an impersonation of Jet Harris from The Shadows, because he'd played there. He fell off the stage once and I'd fall off it, too – you couldn't beat it.

JOHN: Neil's our personal road manager. He was in from the start – he went to school with Paul and George.[64]

NEIL ASPINALL: *It was when they came back from Hamburg that The Beatles needed transport to get them to the Cavern and other places. They were using cabs at the time and all the money they were earning was going to the cab drivers. I had a van and needed the money, so Pete (I was a friend of his and living at his house at the time) told the others that I would drive them round. I did that for £1 a night, which wasn't bad: I'd make £7 a week, which was better than the £2.50 I was getting as a trainee accountant.*

*I used to drop them off in the van, go home and do my correspondence course, then pick them up later; and it developed from there. Soon, I wasn't doing the accountancy any more – I just didn't bother turning up – and was with the band on a permanent basis. It was great, because it was the start of the whole rock'n'roll era in Liverpool and it was very exciting.*

*I first met Paul when we were about eleven, though I didn't get to know him as a friend until a number of years later. I had gone to grammar school with him. We were both in the same class in the first year, then we went off into different streams. George was in the same school, but a year younger – we used to smoke together, behind the air-raid shelter in the playground.*

*My first memory of John is in Penny Lane in Liverpool. I think we were going to Paul's house. I was fifteen. People were into the skiffle then, and would go to each other's houses and play instruments – there were no bands formed, as I recall. I remember this: getting off the bus at Penny Lane and we're all waiting there and I ask, 'Who are we waiting for?' A bus stops and a guy gets off with his arm around an old man that he is talking to – and walks off down the road.*

*He was back in a few moments and somebody asked him, 'Who was that?' – 'I don't know, never seen him before.' That was my first impression of John: 'What's he doing with his arm round some old guy he's never met before?' That was John Lennon.*

GEORGE: Behind the air-raid shelters at school there used to be this smoking club; that's where I met Neil – smoking cigarettes in playtime. I'd see him throughout our school years and by the time we left school he was living in Pete Best's house, the one that had the Casbah club in the basement. Neil had a job as an accountant, and he had a little van, so when we needed somebody to drive us around it occurred to us that Neil might want to make some extra money – probably only about five shillings at the time. We put all our equipment into his van and he drove us to a gig, and he kept on with it. That became the makings of the road manager.

NEIL ASPINALL: *They were doing a lot of gigs in and around Liverpool at the time. There were a lot of ballrooms and town halls and clubs like the Cavern and the Iron Door and the Blue Angel that bands could play in, but they were mainly jazz clubs. They'd never let The Beatles play. You had to try and force your way in. It was Kenny Ball/Acker Bilk sort of stuff at the Cavern. They might let a rock'n'roll group play in the break, before the main band came on, a jazz band.*

JOHN: Jazz never gets anywhere, never does anything; it's always the same, and all they do is drink pints of beer. We hated it because they wouldn't let us play at those sort of clubs.[67]

NEIL ASPINALL: *Often, after a gig, we'd go to a drinking club – maybe the Blue Angel – and see what was happening and just hang out. Everybody knew everybody else. A lot of people in the different bands had gone to school with each other so there was quite a bit of camaraderie, and plenty of rivalry as well.*

*People used to say to me then, 'What do you do?' I'd stopped being an accountant or pretending to be one by this time and I said, 'I drive the band around,' and they'd say, 'Yeah, I know that – but what do you do for a living?' Two years later, the same people were saying, 'You lucky git, Neil.'*

RINGO: Our band all came home to Liverpool, too. It was pretty hard, trying to find jobs, and we couldn't make a lot of money. I was still playing with Rory, and The Beatles were on their own. We would do some gigs at the same venue and I started to go and watch them. I just loved the way they played; I loved the songs, the attitude was great, and I knew they were a better band than the one I was in.

GEORGE: We began to get other gigs at dance halls. There would always be a bunch of groups on, maybe five, and we'd follow somebody and do our bit and it became more and more popular. They liked us because we were kind of rough, and we'd had a lot of practice in Germany. They couldn't believe it. There were all these acts going 'dum de dum' and suddenly we'd come on, jumping and stomping. Wild men in leather suits. It took us a while to realise how much better we'd become than the other groups. But we began to see that we were getting big crowds everywhere. People were following us round, coming to see *us* personally, not just coming to dance.

In those days, when we were rocking on, becoming popular in the little clubs where there was no big deal about The Beatles, it was fun. A lot of those old nightclubs were just real fun. I think we were a good, tight, little band.

JOHN: One of the main reasons to get on stage is it's the quickest way of making contact. We went to see those movies with Elvis or somebody in, when we were still in Liverpool, and everybody'd be waiting to see them (and I'd be waiting there, too), and they'd all scream when he came on the screen. We thought, 'That's a good job.' That's why most musicians are on stage, actually. It is a good incentive for all performers.

In the very early days, when we were playing dance halls, there were a certain type you'd call groupies now, available for 'functions' at the end of the night. Most kids would go home with their boyfriends or whatever, but there was a small group that went for any performer. They didn't care if it was a comedian or a man who ate glass, as long as he was on stage.[75]

PAUL: It certainly wasn't all pleasure. We did a lot of hard slog. We'd play places and people would throw pennies at us. To disarm them we'd stop playing and pick up all the coins. We thought, 'That'll teach 'em, they won't keep throwing now.' We had pockets full of pennies.

JOHN: I remember one hall we were at. There were so many people that we told each other that there must be other managers around and we'd get a lot of work out of it. What we didn't know was that the management had laid on lots of bouncers to stop the other promoters getting near. So nobody came to us, except this bloke from the management who said he liked us and would give us a long series of dates at £8 a night. It was a couple of quid more than we were getting anyway, so we were pleased.[67]

GEORGE: There were a lot of fights in clubs in Liverpool; that was after Hamburg, when we started touring dance halls.

PAUL: The Hambleton Hall was a place with a reputation for fights. One gig there, we were playing 'Hully Gully', and they turned fire-extinguishers on each other. By the end of the song, everyone was soaking wet and bleeding.

GEORGE: We came back from Hamburg in November 1960 and went back out again in April 1961. I'd become eighteen when we went the second time so I was able to go back, and whatever the problem was of Paul and Pete's deportation we managed to get round it. Peter Eckhorn sorted it out. He was the owner of the Top Ten Club, where we were going to play; and the fact he'd made that effort meant that he was keen to get The Beatles, so we were happy to work there.

When we went back we were playing at the Top Ten and living above the club; a really grubby little room with five bunk beds. In the next room was a little old lady known as Mutti. She was pretty stinky. She used to keep the toilets clean – they were really bad up there.

PAUL: German toilets always have a lady to look after them and we formed a friendship with our one, Mutti. Every time you went to the toilet you were supposed to leave ten pfennigs in the saucer. And if anyone was ever sick in there Mutti would come roaring out of the toilet with a bucket and demand that the drunk clean it up. You wouldn't see so many people being sick there.

Mutti found a houseboat for me and my then girlfriend to stay in. The girls were coming over one time, Cynthia and Dot Rhone, and we needed a place. We found a rather nice little houseboat through her.

RINGO: At the Top Ten Club there were just bunk beds – and you could have Mutti look after you! It was tough, but we were twenty years old, we didn't give a damn; it was fabulous. This was opening your eyes, this was leaving home, this was leaving the country. Hamburg was fabulous; I think when you are twenty everywhere's wild. To me Hamburg felt like Soho.

PAUL: We tried our 'Beatle' hairstyle in Hamburg this time. It was all part of trying to pull people in: 'Come in. We are very good rock'n'roll!'

GEORGE: Astrid and Klaus were very influential. I remember we went to the swimming baths once and my hair was down from the water and they said, 'No, leave it, it's good.' I didn't have my Vaseline anyway, and I was thinking, 'Well, these people are cool – if *they* think it's good, I'll leave it like this.' They gave me that confidence and when it dried off it dried naturally down, which later became 'the look'.

Before that, as a rocker, I wore my hair back; though it would never go back without a fight – it goes forward when I wash it. (It just grows into a Beatle cut!) I used to have to put thick Vaseline on my hair to hold it back.

I remember cutting John's hair one time, and I tried to get him to cut mine. We did it just as a joke, only the once, but I don't think he cut mine as professionally as I cut his...

JOHN: That was the last time I cut anybody's hair.[65]

GEORGE: And then we saw those leather pants and we thought: 'Wow! We've got to get some of them!' So Astrid took us to a tailor who made us some *Nappaleders* – those great pants. And we had found a shop in Hamburg that sold genuine Texas cowboy boots. It was just a matter of trying to get some money. We may have even paid for them 'on the weekly'. We all had little pink caps we used to call 'twat hats' that we'd bought in Liverpool. So that became our band uniform: cowboy boots, twat hats and black leather suits.

JOHN: We had a bit more money the second time, so we bought leather pants and we looked like four Gene Vincents – only a bit younger.[63]

GEORGE: The Top Ten Club had a mike system called the Binson Echo. It was a silver and golden unit which had a small Grundig tape machine with a little green light, that would twitch with the volume. That had a great echo – on it you'd sound like Gene Vincent doing 'Be Bop A Lula'.

We were backing up lots of people at the Top Ten. The singer Tony Sheridan was there – he had been there the first time as well, now he was the resident. He'd managed to get himself a job working the club permanently and we used to back him.

RINGO: It was great being out there with Tony Sheridan. I was there in 1962 backing him with Roy Young, and Lou Walters on bass. It was all very exciting. Tony was really volatile. If anyone in the club was talking to his girl he'd be punching and kicking all over the place, while we'd just keep on jamming. Then he'd come back and join us, covered in blood if he'd lost. But he was a really good player.

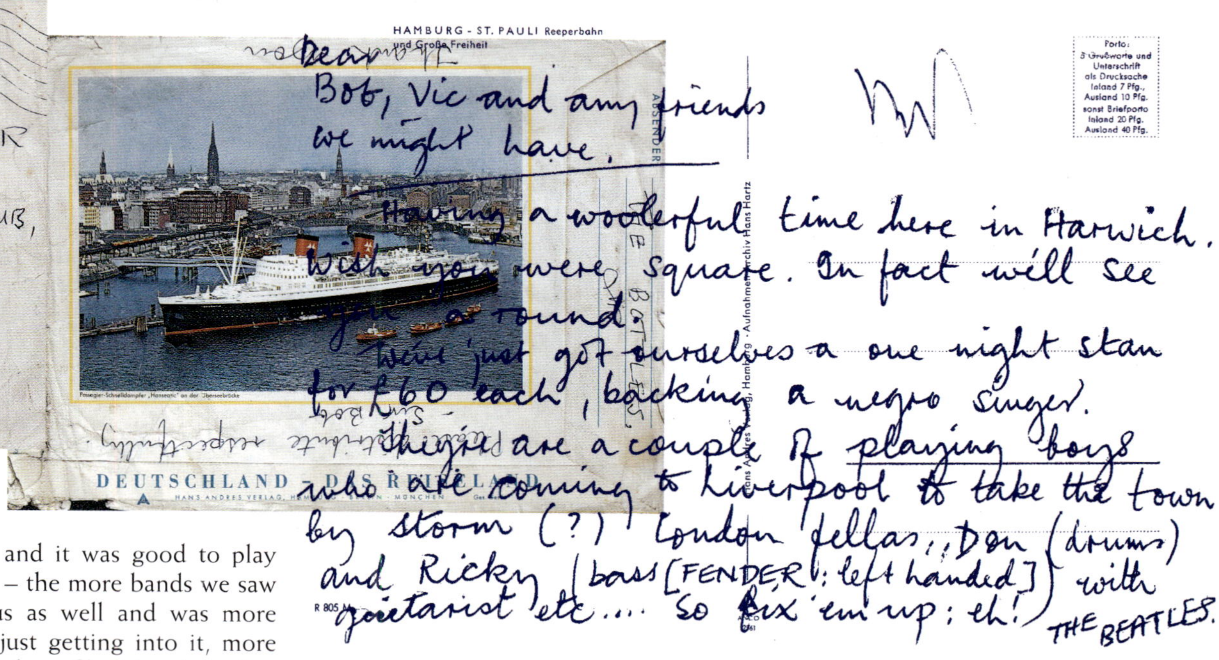
HAMBURG - ST. PAULI Reeperbahn und Große Freiheit

Dear Bob, Vic and any friends we might have.

Having a wooderful time here in Harwich. Wish you were square. In fact will see you around.

We've just got ourselves a one night stan for £60 each, backing a negro singer. They are a couple of playing boys who are coming to Liverpool to take the town by storm (?) London fellas,, Don (drums) and Ricky (bass [FENDER: left handed]) with guitarist etc... So fix 'em up; eh!

THE BEATLES

DEUTSCHLAND - DAS REISELAND

GEORGE: Tony Sheridan had an up-side and a down-side. The up-side was that he was a pretty good singer and guitar player, and it was good to play along with him because we were still learning – the more bands we saw and heard the better. He was older than us as well and was more hardened to the business, whereas we were just getting into it, more bouncy and naive. On that basis it was good to have Sheridan there; but at the same time he was such a downer. He'd fled from England – some kind of trouble – and was always getting into fights. I remember he managed to cut the tendon in his finger on a broken bottle in a fight – fortunately, not on his guitar-playing hand. When he used his guitar pick after that, his injured finger stuck right out.

They used to have a talent night at the Top Ten Club, a Tuesday evening. People from the audience would come up and sing and we'd have to back them up. We did this for a while and we would really wind people up, take the piss out of them.

I remember one bloke who came up, a sax player. At that time, we didn't know that much about music; all we knew were the names of each key. This guy started playing his sax and we were playing along with him when we decided to play a joke. We began to say among ourselves another key, say D; someone gave the nod and we all suddenly changed into that key, pretending nothing had happened. The guy didn't know what was going on, but he tried to follow. And then we whispered, 'B flat,' to each other and we all changed key again. We were really stretching this guy and he was trying desperately to find out what key we were in and keep up with us.

There were other Germans who'd come on stage and try to sing Little Richard and Chuck Berry songs without knowing the words. They knew the sounds of the words but they couldn't really get them, especially if it was something like 'Tutti Frutti'. And the German accent doesn't really lend itself to rock'n'roll so it could be quite hysterical. The funniest noteworthy story is how, back then, when we were still performing the latest records, one was Johnny Kidd and the Pirates' 'Shakin' All Over' and it went, 'Shivers down my backbone, shaking all over…' but the Germans thought we were singing *'Schick ihn nach Hannover'* – 'Send him to Hanover' – the German equivalent of 'send him to Coventry'.

We were learning how to gel as a band, we learnt a lot of songs and we learnt a lot of improvising within all the songs we knew. We gained a bit of confidence, but we were always looking for the next thing, thinking *if only we could get a recording*. That was the big thing when we were in the Top Ten Club: you'd hear, 'Bert Kaempfert's here.' – 'Who the fuck is he?' – 'Bert Kaempfert; you know, "Wonderland By Night", he's a record producer and he's looking for talent.' – 'Oh shit, we'd better play good then.'

PAUL: We did a recording with Tony Sheridan, 'My Bonnie', for Bert Kaempfert, a band leader and producer. It was actually 'Tony Sheridan und die Beat Brothers'. They didn't like our name and said, 'Change to The Beat Brothers; this is more understandable for the German audience.' We went along with it – it was a record.

JOHN: When that offer came we thought it would be easy. The Germans had such shitty records. Ours were bound to be better. We did five of our own numbers, but they didn't like them. They preferred things like 'My Bonnie'.[67] It's just Tony Sheridan singing, with us banging in the background. It's terrible. It could be anybody.[63]

GEORGE: We recorded 'Ain't She Sweet', too. It was a bit disappointing because we'd been hoping to get a record deal as ourselves. Although we did 'Ain't She Sweet' and the instrumental 'Cry For A Shadow' without Sheridan, they didn't even put our name on the record. That's why it's so pathetic that later, when we'd become famous, they put the record out as 'The Beatles with Tony Sheridan'. But when it first came out they'd called us 'The Beat Brothers'.

We also recorded with Lou Walters. He was Rory Storm's bass player. He was a guy who thought he was a singer. He paid to have the record made himself, as we had done in Liverpool with 'That'll Be The Day'.

JOHN: Gene Vincent's recording of 'Ain't She Sweet' is very mellow and high-pitched and I used to do it like that, but the Germans said, 'Harder, harder' – they all wanted it a bit more like a march – so we ended up doing a harder version.[74]

RINGO: I recorded with Rory over in Hamburg. Somewhere out there is an amazing acetate which I'd like a copy of. We did 'Fever' and another track.

Würzburger Hofbräu
TOP TEN CLUB
MCC
JAM
(Christian
geboren am
Born on
né le
in
in
à
LAN
(Kreis
(county
(département
20
LI

LENNON
(Familienname)
(Surname)
(Nom de famille)
JOHN WINSTON
(Vornamen, Rufname unterstreichen)
(Christian names, underline name by which usually known)
(prénoms, souligner le prénom usuel)
geboren am
Born on
né le
9th october 1940
in
in
à
ENGLAND
(Kreis
(county
(département
Land)
country)
pays)
136 REEPERBAHN
'TOP TEN CLUB'
HAMBURG
RTNEY
(Familienname)
(Surname)
(Nom de famille)
PAUL
amen, Rufname unterstreichen)
underline name by which usually known)
ns, souligner le prénom usuel)
8 / 6 / 42
ASHIRE, ENGLAND
Land)
country)
pays)
ORTHLIN Road
RPOOL 18
NCASHIRE

JOHN: We were a good live band and, in general, it's pretty pleasant memories of struggling along to Lord knows where. But at the time it didn't seem any more fun than that. It was just you had a job or you didn't have a job. When you look back on it, you realise how good things were, even though at the time you might have thought, 'Gor, we've got to play six hours a night and all we get is two dollars and you've got to take these pills to keep awake, man; it's not right.'[76]

We repeated the shows many, many times, but never the same. Sometimes we'd go on with fifteen or twenty musicians and play together and we'd create something that had never been done on stage by a group before. I'm talking about before we were famous, about the natural things that happened, before we were turned into robots that played on stage. We would, naturally, express ourselves in any way that we deemed suitable. And then a manager came and said, 'Do this, do that, do this, do that,' and that way we became famous by compromise.

GEORGE: Stuart was engaged to Astrid and after that trip decided that he was going to leave the band and live in Germany because Eduardo Paolozzi was coming to be the lecturer at Hamburg Art College. Stu had never really been that single-minded about music. We liked him in the band: he looked great and he'd learnt enough to get by, but he was never totally convinced that he was going to be a musician.

He said, 'I'm out of the band, lads, I'm going to stay in Hamburg with Astrid.' At that point I said, 'We're not going to get a fifth person in the band. One of us three is going to be the bass player, and it's not going to be me.' And John said, 'It's not going to be me,' and Paul didn't seem to mind the idea.

Colin Milander, the bass player in Tony Sheridan's trio, had a Hofner violin bass, which was really a rip-off of the Gibson bass. So when Paul decided he was going to be the bass player he went out and bought one like Colin's.

PAUL: I really got lumbered with bass. Nobody actually wanted to play bass, that's why Stuart was playing it. We all wanted really to be guitarists, and we were three guitar players to start off with.

There's something I'd like to get straight because it is kind of historical – someone a few years ago said how it was my relentless ambition that pushed Stu out of the group. We did have some arguments, me and Stu, but actually I just wanted us to be a really cracking band, and Stu – being a cracking artist – held us back a little bit, not too much. If ever it came to the push, when there was someone in there watching us I'd feel, 'Oh, I hope Stu doesn't blow it.' I could trust the rest of us; that was it. Stuart would tend to turn away a little so as not to be too obvious about what key he was in, in case it wasn't our key.

When it became clear that Stu was leaving because of Astrid, I asked him in the transition period to lend me his bass, which, for me, was upside down – although I couldn't change the strings around in case he ever wanted to play it. By then I had learnt to play guitar upside down, anyway, because John would never let me turn the strings around on his guitar, neither would George – it was just too inconvenient for them to have to turn them all back again.

NEIL ASPINALL: *They went to Aldershot in December; their first gig down South. I don't know that they were that popular down there yet – only eighteen people turned up!*

GEORGE: Bill Harry started the *Mersey Beat* newspaper in Liverpool in the summer of 1961, soon after we'd come back from Germany. John, who was at art college with him, would do funny things for the paper.

John had a gift for writing and drawing and speaking – particularly funny stuff. He had a book which he wrote when he was at Quarry Bank called the *Daily Howl*. It was quite big, the size of the *Beano* annual. It was a kind of newspaper with little jokes and cartoons – schoolboy humour, but really good and nicely illustrated. He was good at all that.

JOHN: I wrote for *Mersey Beat*. Some things went into *In His Own Write*, and I used to write a thing called 'Beatcomber', because I admired the column 'Beachcomber' in the *Daily Express*. That's when I wrote with George, 'A man came on a flaming pie...' because even back then they were asking: 'How did you get the name, "The Beatles"?'[72]

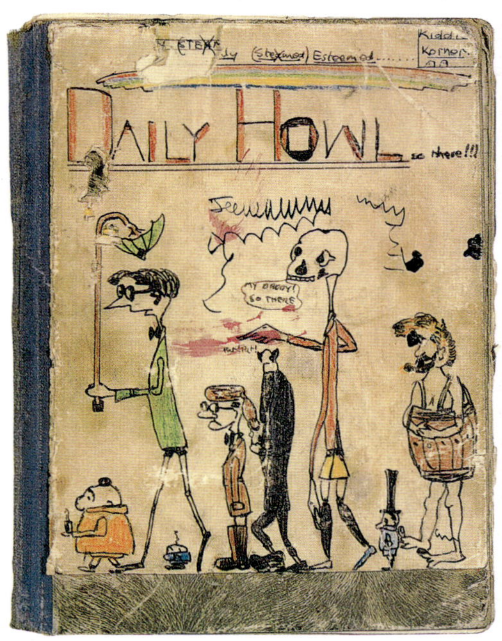

PAUL: We used to go back to Vi Caldwell's. I went out for a short time with Rory's sister Iris, a dancer. Their house was the only one open at that time of night. Vi was a night owl. It was our late-night hang-out, really, just cups of tea and card games and chatting. A lot of us would go back there. I remember playing a Ouija board with Cilla (Black, as she is now) and her friend Pat. •

JOHN: 'GEAR' IS A LIVERPOOL EXPRESSION FROM THE FRENCH *DE RIGUEUR*, MEANING SOMETHING LIKE 'VERY COOL'.

JOHN: I was twenty-one/twenty-two before The Beatles ever made it in any way. And even then that voice in me was saying, 'Look, you're too old.' Before we'd even made a record I was thinking, 'You're too old,' that I'd missed the boat, that you'd got to be seventeen – a lot of stars in America were kids. They were much younger than I was, or Ringo.[74]

STUART SUTCLIFFE: *Last night I heard that John and Paul have gone to Paris to play together – in other words, the band has broken up! It sounds mad to me, I don't believe it...*[61]

PAUL: John and I went on a trip for his twenty-first birthday. John was from a very middle-class family, which really impressed me because everyone else was from working-class families. To us John was *upper* class. His relatives were teachers, dentists, even someone up in Edinburgh in the BBC. It's ironic, he was always very 'fuck you!' and he wrote the song 'Working Class Hero' – in fact, he wasn't at all working class. Anyway, one of John's relatives gave him £100 for his birthday. A hundred smackers in your hand! Then it was a real windfall. None of us could believe it. To this day if you gave me £100 I would be impressed. And I was his mate, enough said? 'Let's go on holiday.' – 'You mean me too? With the hundred quid? Great! I'm part of this windfall.'

JOHN: Paul bought me a hamburger to celebrate.

I wasn't too keen on reaching twenty-one. I remember one relative saying to me, 'From now on, it's all downhill,' and I really got a shock. She told me how my skin would be getting older and that kind of jazz.

Paul and I set off on a hitchhike to Paris. Well, it was going to be a hitchhike but we ended up taking the train all the way – sheer laziness.[63] We'd got fed up. We did have bookings, but we just broke them and went off.[67]

PAUL: We planned to hitchhike to Spain. I had done a spot of hitchhiking with George and we knew you had to have a gimmick; we had been turned down so often and we'd seen that guys that had a gimmick (like a Union Jack round them) had always got the lifts. So I said to John, 'Let's get a couple of bowler hats.' It was showbiz creeping in. We still had our leather jackets and drainpipes – we were too proud of them not to wear them, in case we met a girl; and if we did meet a girl, off would come the bowlers. But for lifts we would put the bowlers on. Two guys in bowler hats – a lorry would stop! Sense of Humour. This, and the train, is how we got to Paris.

We'd never been there before. We were a bit tired so we checked into a little hotel for the night, intending to go off hitchhiking the next morning. Of course, it was too nice a bed after having hitched so we said, 'We'll stay a little longer,' then we thought, 'God, Spain is a long way, and we'd have to work to get down there.' We ended up staying the week in Paris – John was funding it all with his hundred quid.

We would walk miles from our hotel; you do in Paris. We'd go to a place near the Avenue des Anglais and we'd sit in the bars, looking good. I still have some classic photos from there. Linda loves one where I am sitting in a gendarme's mac as a cape and John has got his glasses on askew and his trousers down revealing a bit of Y-front. The photographs are so beautiful, we're really hamming it up. We're looking at the camera like, 'Hey, we are artsy guys, in a café: this is us in Paris,' and we felt like that.

We went up to Montmartre because of all the artists, and the Folies Bergères, and we saw guys walking around in short leather jackets and very wide pantaloons. Talk about fashion! This was going to kill them when we got back. This was totally happening. They were tight to the knee and then they flared out; they must have been about fifty inches around the bottom and our drainpipe trousers were something like fifteen or sixteen inches. (Fifteen were the best, but you couldn't really get your foot through at fifteen, so sixteen was acceptable.) We saw these trousers and said, '*Excusez-moi, Monsieur, où* did you get them?' It was a cheap little rack down the street so we bought a pair each, went back to the hotel, put them on, went out on the street – and we couldn't handle it: 'Do your feet feel like they are flapping? Feel more comfortable in me drainies, don't you?' So it was back to the hotel at a run, needle and cotton out and we took them in to a nice sixteen with which we were quite happy. And then we met Jürgen Vollmer on the street. He was still taking pictures.

JOHN: Jürgen also had bell-bottom trousers, but we thought that would be considered too queer back in Liverpool. We didn't want to appear feminine or anything like that, because our audience in Liverpool still had a lot of fellas. (We were playing rock, dressed in leather, though Paul's ballads were bringing in more and more girls.)[67] Anyway, Jürgen had a flattened-down hairstyle with a fringe in the front, which we rather took to. We went over to his place and there and then he cut – hacked would be a better word – our hair into the same style.[63]

PAUL: He had his hair Mod-style. We said, 'Would you do our hair like yours?' We're on holiday – what the hell! We're buying capes and pantaloons, throwing caution to the wind. He said, 'No, boys, no. I like you as Rocker; you look great.' But we begged him enough so he said 'all right'. He didn't do it quite the same as his.

His was actually more coming over to one side. A kind of long-haired Hitler thing, and we'd wanted that, so it was really a bit of an accident. We sat down in his hotel and he just got it – the 'Beatle' cut!

For the rest of that week we were like Paris Existentialists. Jean Paul Sartre had nothing on us. This was it. 'Sod them all – I could write a novel from what I learnt this week.' It was all inside me. I could do anything now.

RINGO: What a sight they looked when they arrived back!

PAUL: When we got back to Liverpool it was all, 'Eh, your hair's gone funny.' – 'No, this is the new style.'

We nearly tried to change it back but it wouldn't go, it kept flapping forward. And that just caught on. We weren't really into the coiffure. It was like Mo's out of the Three Stooges. It fell forward in a fringe. But it was great for us because we never had to style it or anything – wash it, towel it, turn upside down and give it a shake, and that was it. Everyone thought we had started it, so it became 'the Beatle hairdo'.

JOHN: We go along with the trends, we always have done. To a degree we can make a trend popular – we don't usually invent clothes, we wear something we like and then maybe people follow us. Our original style was continental, because English people wore English kinds of clothes. Then continental styles caught on in England, too.[65]

I was ashamed to go on the Continent and say I was British before we made it. The Beatles have tried to change Britain's image. We changed the hairstyles and clothes of the world, including America – they were a very square and sorry lot when we went over.[69]

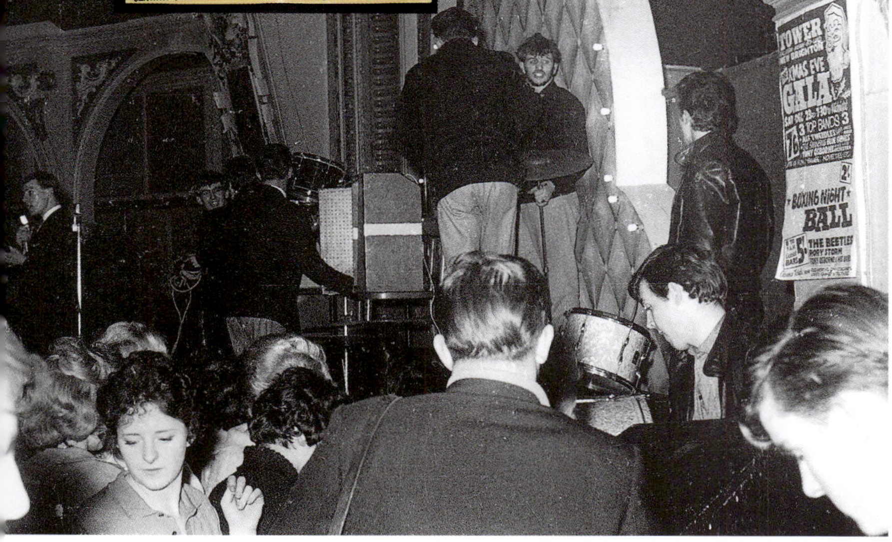

PAUL: Brian Epstein had a shop called NEMS. He was the son of the owner, Harry Epstein. NEMS stood for North End Music Stores and we bought our records there. It was quite a gathering place; one of the shops where you could find the records you wanted.

We did well at the Cavern, attracted some big audiences and word got around. What had happened was a kid had gone into Brian's record store and asked for 'My Bonnie' by The Beatles. Brian had said, 'No it's not, it's by Tony Sheridan,' and he ordered it. Then Brian heard that we were playing 200 yards away. So he came to the Cavern and the news got to us: 'Brian Epstein is in the audience – he might be a manager or a promoter. He is a grown-up, anyway.' It was Us and Grown-ups then.

GEORGE: Brian came down the street and checked us out. I remember Bob Wooler, the disc jockey, announcing, 'We have with us a Mr Epstein, who owns NEMS,' and everybody going, 'Oh wow. Big, big deal.'

He stood at the back listening and afterwards came round to the band room. We thought he was some very posh rich fellow: that's my earliest memory of Brian. He had wanted us to sign up, but I believe he came a number of times before he actually decided to be our manager.

JOHN: He looked efficient and rich, that's all I remember.[67]

He tried to manage us, but he couldn't get through to us. It lasted about a week: we said, 'We're not having you.' He didn't take over as though he just walked in and said, 'Right, cut your hair like that, put this suit on,' any of that.[69]

Paul wasn't that keen, but he's more conservative in the way he approaches things. He even says that himself – and that's all well and good. Maybe he'll end up with more yachts.[75]

PAUL: At that age we were very impressed by anyone in a suit or with a car. And Brian was impressed with us; he liked our sense of humour and our music and he liked our look – black leather.

So one evening we went down to the NEMS shop. It was very awe-inspiring, being let into this big record shop after hours with no one there. It felt like a cathedral. We went upstairs to Brian's office to make the deal. I was talking to him, trying to beat him down, knowing the game: try to get the manager to take a low percentage. And the others tried as well, but he stuck at a figure of 25%. He told us, 'That'll do, now I'll be your manager,' and we agreed.

With my dad's advice – I remember Dad had said to get a Jewish manager – it all fitted and Brian Epstein became our manager.

BRIAN EPSTEIN: *On Saturday 28th October 1961, I was asked by a young boy for a record by a group called The Beatles. It had always been our policy in records to look after whatever request was made. I wrote on a pad: '"My Bonnie". The Beatles. Check on Monday.'*

*I had never given a thought to any of the Liverpool beat groups then up and coming in cellar clubs. They were not part of my life, because I was out of the age group, and also because I had been too busy. The name 'Beatle' meant nothing to me, though I vaguely recalled seeing it on a poster advertising a dance at New Brighton Tower and I remembered thinking it was an odd and purposeless spelling.*

*Before I had had time to check on Monday, two girls came in the store and they too asked for a disc by this group. This, contrary to legend, was the sum total of demand for The Beatles' disc at this time in Liverpool. But I was sure there was something very significant in three queries for one unknown disc in two days.*

*I talked to contacts and found what I hadn't realised, that The Beatles were in fact a Liverpool group, that they had just returned from playing clubs in the steamy, seedy end of Hamburg. A girl I know said: 'The Beatles? They're the greatest. They're at the Cavern this week…'*

PAUL: I LOVED THE CAVERN. IT WAS A CLAUSTROPHOBIC HELL, BUT IT WAS A GREAT ONE.

The Beatles Fan Club presents
**An Evening with John, George, Paul & Pete**

**the Beatles for their fans**

**At The Cavern**
7-30 pm Thursday
**5th April 1962**

Tickets 6s 6d

Purchasers of tick[ets] will receive a FREE photograph and may apply f[or] free membership [of] the Fan Club

Guest Artists will include
**The Four Jays**
and the Beatles' favourite Compere
**Bob Wooler**

Tickets available from NEMS Whitechapel or Gt Charlotte St and at The Cave[rn] Club

Printed by Swale (Widnes) Ltd

Photo: Harrison Layout: Swerdlow

JOHN: Epstein was serving in a record shop and he had nothing to do, and saw these rockers, greasers, playing loud music and *a lot* of kids paying attention to it. And he thought, 'This is a business to be in,' and he liked it – he liked the look of it. He wanted to manage us, and he told us that he thought he could, and we had nobody better so we said, 'All right, you can do it.'[75]

We were in a daydream till he came along. We'd no idea what we were doing. Seeing our marching orders on paper made it all official.[67]

NEIL ASPINALL: *It was impressive to us. Till then, the guy who was running a particular venue would book you up for the next four Tuesday nights and it would be written in somebody's diary – in Paul's diary or Pete's, or somewhere. They'd book it up but it was all ad hoc, done as we went along. When Brian came along, the first thing he did was double the money at the Cavern from £7 10s to £15.*

PAUL: The gigs went up in stature and though the pay went up only a little bit, it did go up. We were now playing better places. We would still do our rock act, though we wouldn't get decent money for any gig apart from cabaret. I could pull out 'Till There Was You' or 'A Taste Of Honey' – the more cabaret things – and John would sing 'Over The Rainbow' and 'Ain't She Sweet'. These did have cred for us because they were on a Gene Vincent album and we didn't realise 'Rainbow' was a Judy Garland number; we thought it was Gene Vincent, so we were happy to do it.

NEIL ASPINALL: *It was Brian's theatrical training – that's where the clothes and bowing to the audience after each number came from, and cutting off the end of the guitar strings. In those days guitar strings cost money, so when one snapped you undid the end of it, pulled it through and tied a knot, then wound it up and got on with playing. All those wires hanging at the end of the guitar didn't look very tidy, so Brian's advice was, 'Cut off the end of that and tidy this act up – get it more presentable for the general public.'*

*These suggestions were resisted at first. With the guitar strings, it meant taking the whole thing off and putting a new one in: that took longer to do. And the bowing – John would do it, but under protest. He would flick his hands about and he'd always add a little quip just for us in the crowd – we knew what he was doing and we'd be laughing about it, but I don't think the audience ever caught on.*

JOHN: Brian Epstein said, 'Look, if you really want to get in these bigger places, you're going to have to change – stop eating on stage, stop swearing, stop smoking...'[75]

He wasn't trying to clean our image up: he said our look wasn't right, we'd never get past the door at a good place. We used to dress how we liked, on and off stage.[67] He'd tell us that jeans were not particularly smart and could we possibly manage to wear proper trousers, but he didn't want us suddenly looking square. He let us have our own sense of individuality.[75]

To us, Brian was the expert. I mean, originally he had the shop. Anybody who's got a shop must be all right. And a car, and a big house... Fuckin' hell, you don't care if it's all his dad's or not, we thought he was it.[72]

It was a choice of making it or still eating chicken on stage. We respected his views. We stopped champing at cheese rolls and jam butties; we paid a lot more attention to what we were doing, did our best to be on time and we smartened up.[75]

GEORGE: Brian put in a lot of time getting us off the ground. He believed in us from the start.

JOHN: He went around, smarming and charming everybody, the newspaper people – and they all thought highly of him.[72]

Trying to get publicity was just a game. We used to traipse round the offices of the local papers and musical papers asking them to write about us, because that's what you had to do. It was natural we should put on our best show. We had to appear nice for the reporters, even the very snooty ones who were letting us know they were doing us a favour. We would play them along, agreeing how kind they were to talk to us. We were very two-faced about it.[67]

Brian would go from Liverpool to London. And he came back and said, 'I've got you an audition.' We were all excited: it was Decca. He'd met this Mike Smith guy and we were to go down there. So we went down and we did all these numbers; terrified and nervous, you can hear it. It starts off terrified and gradually we settle down.[72] We recorded 'To Know Her Is To Love Her', the Phil Spector song, and a couple of our own; we virtually recorded our Cavern stage show, with a few omissions – around twenty songs.[74]

We made tapes for Decca and Pye, but we didn't actually go to Pye.[64]

NEIL ASPINALL: *I remember we had to drive down to London on New Year's Eve 1961, because of The Beatles' audition for Decca Records. (We got lost somewhere in the Midlands.) That New Year's Eve was our first in London.*

GEORGE: It was snowing and I remember going into the Decca studios. We just went in, set up our amps and played.

In those days a lot of the rock'n'roll songs were actually old tunes from the Forties, Fifties or whenever, which people had rocked up. That was the thing to do if you didn't have a tune: just rock up an oldie. Joe Brown had recorded a rock'n'roll version of 'The Sheik Of Araby'. He was really popular on the Saturday TV show *Six-Five Special* and *Oh Boy!*. I did the Joe Brown records, so I sang 'Sheik Of Araby'. Paul sang 'September In The Rain'. We each chose a number we wanted to do.

It was unusual at that time to have a group where everybody did the singing. In those days it was all Cliff and The Shadows, a lead guy out the front; the whole band in suits, matching ties and handkerchiefs, all with regular movements, and one guy at the front who sang.

The audition lasted for a couple of hours and that was it. We left and went back to our hotel.

NEIL ASPINALL: *All of us were broke and it was snowing and very cold. We went down Shaftesbury Avenue and around there; amazing things to buy. The bootshop Anello & Davide was on one corner, then Cecil Gee, the clothes store. We went into a club up by St Giles Circus. We didn't stay long because it was boring. Some of the women had an after-eight shadow. We were starving and we went into a restaurant. All that we could afford was the soup so they threw us out and we went into Soho and got something there. London was all very exciting and new.*

GEORGE: We had met a London group who had what later became known as 'Beatle boots'. The first pair of those boots I ever saw was on that trip. They had elastic in the edges and I found out that they were made in a shop on Charing Cross Road called Anello & Davide.

As for Decca's response, we didn't hear anything for ages, though Brian kept bugging them to find out; and in the end they turned us down. The funny thing is that it was by someone from one of those 'dum de dum' bands, Tony Meehan, a drummer who had become big-time as the A&R man for Decca. There's a famous story that Brian Epstein was trying to get him to say whether he liked us, whether we'd got the job or not. He replied, 'I'm a busy man, Mr Epstein,' and he was just a kid!

JOHN: We went back and we waited and waited, and then we found out that they hadn't accepted it; we really thought that was it then, that was the end.

'It's too bluesy,' or, 'It's too much like rock'n'roll and that's all over now,' they used to keep telling us. Even in Hamburg when we auditioned for those German companies they would tell us to stop playing the rock and the blues and concentrate on the other stuff, because they all thought rock was dead; but they were wrong.[72]

PAUL: Listening to the tapes I can understand why we failed the Decca audition. We weren't that good; though there were some quite interesting and original things.

JOHN: I listened to it. I wouldn't have turned us down on that. I think it sounded OK. Especially the last half of it, for the period it was. There weren't many people playing music like that then.[72] I think Decca expected us to be all polished; we were just doing a demo. They should have seen our potential.[67]

GEORGE: Years later, I found out they'd signed Brian Poole and the Tremeloes instead. The head of Decca, Dick Rowe, made a canny prediction: 'Guitar groups are on the way out, Mr Epstein.'

PAUL: HE MUST BE KICKING HIMSELF NOW.

JOHN: I HOPE HE KICKS HIMSELF TO DEATH![63]

PAUL: There were millions of groups around at that time – The Blue Angels, The Running Scareds – but they were mostly lookalike groups; The Shadows and Roy Orbison had a lot of followers. Then there were groups like us, more into the blues and slightly obscure material. And because we had the unusual songs, we became the act you had to see, to copy.

We started to get a lot of respect. Guys would ask where we'd got a song like 'If You Gotta Make A Fool Of Somebody' from – we'd explain it was on a James Ray album. The Hollies came to see us once and came back two weeks later looking like us! We were in black turtleneck sweaters and John had his harmonica and we were doing our R&B material. The next week, The Hollies had turtleneck sweaters and a harmonica in their act. This is what had started to happen. We would come back to Liverpool and Freddie and the Dreamers would be doing 'If You Gotta Make A Fool Of Somebody' as *their* hit number. (Freddie Garrity saw us playing that song in the Oasis Club in Manchester and took it.)

So we were a big influence on these people. We had too much material anyway. We couldn't record it all when we did get a deal, so other groups took songs from our act and made hits out of them – like The Swinging Blue Jeans with 'The Hippy Hippy Shake', which was one of my big numbers.

NEIL ASPINALL: *There wasn't much pop radio. You had Radio Luxembourg on a Sunday night; that was it. Through the merchant seamen you could get a lot of American records that weren't being played in England. And whichever of the bands heard a record first got to do it. So if Gerry Marsden found a number before everybody else, then it became his; and whoever else played it, it was as if they were copying Gerry.*

PAUL: I think we sussed early on that we weren't going to get anywhere unless we were different; because if you weren't original you could get stranded. An example: I used to sing 'I Remember You' by Frank Ifield. It went amazingly well anywhere I played it; but if the group on before us did 'I Remember You', that was our big number up the spout. We'd ask bands, 'What numbers do *you* do, then?' If they ever mentioned 'I Remember You', it was, 'Oh dear.' So we had to play numbers no one else had or, if we'd both got the big number, trade off with the other band.

This grew into writing songs ourselves and daring to introduce them. At first we'd only do that at the Cavern. I think the first original song we ever did was a really bad one of mine called 'Like Dreamers Do' (which was also covered later). It was enough. We rehearsed it and played it and the kids liked it because they had never heard it before. It was something they could only hear when they came to see our show.

Looking back, we were putting it all together very cleverly, albeit instinctively: we were making ourselves into a group that was different.

JOHN: Introducing our own numbers started round Liverpool and Hamburg. 'Love Me Do', one of the first ones we wrote, Paul started when he must have been about fifteen. It was the first one we dared do of our own. This was a quite traumatic thing because we were doing such great numbers of other people's, of Ray Charles and Richard and all of them.[72] (I used to do an old Olympics number called 'Well' at the Cavern, a twelve-bar thing.)[80]

It was quite hard to come in singing 'Love Me Do'. We thought our numbers were a bit wet. But we gradually broke that down and decided to try them.[72]

JOHN: WHEN THE BEATLES WERE DEPRESSED, THINKING, 'THE GROUP IS GOING NOWHERE, AND THIS IS A SHITTY DEAL, AND WE'RE IN A SHITTY DRESSING ROOM...' I'D SAY, 'WHERE ARE WE GOING, FELLAS?' THEY'D GO, 'TO THE TOP, JOHNNY!' AND I'D SAY, 'WHERE'S THAT, FELLAS?' AND THEY'D SAY, 'TO THE TOPPERMOST OF THE POPPERMOST!' AND I'D SAY, 'RIGHT!' THEN WE'D ALL CHEER UP.

PAUL: A lot of our tracks may not have been 'cool'. (I think if we'd just been cool, we wouldn't have made it how we did.) But that *was* a great aspect of us. John would do 'A Shot Of Rhythm And Blues' or 'You Really Got A Hold On Me' – you could call that cool. But then we'd have something like 'If You Gotta Make A Fool Of Somebody' – which was actually *more* cool because it was probably the first R&B waltz that anyone did.

I could never see the difference between a beautiful melody and a cool rock'n'roll song. I learnt to love all the ballady stuff through my dad and relatives – 'Till There Was You', 'My Funny Valentine' – I thought these were good tunes. The fact that we weren't ashamed of those leanings meant that the band *could* be a bit more varied. And there was a need for that, because we played cabaret a lot. Songs like 'Till There Was You' and 'Ain't She Sweet' would be the late-night cabaret material. They showed that we weren't just another rock'n'roll group.

The Lennon/McCartney song-writing collaboration was forming during that period. We went on from 'Love Me Do' to writing deeper, much more intense things. So it was just as well someone didn't come up and tell us how uncool 'Till There Was You' was.

NEIL ASPINALL: *The touring pattern was steadily evolving. They were spreading out farther and farther from Liverpool. They would play, say, Swindon. Wow! That was miles away from anywhere. And Southport and Crewe, then Manchester; ballrooms, mainly. They wanted publicity, and a recording contract; but it took a long time to get one and there were lots of disappointments.*

*Brian had a tape of the recording they'd done at Decca, which he took round.*

JOHN: We paid £15 or something to make the tape, in a Decca studio. Brian Epstein hawked it round. He would go down on his own, on the train, to London with this tape and he'd come back with a blank face and we'd know we'd bombed out again.

When you hear the tape, it's pretty good. It's not great, but it's good and it's certainly good for then, when you consider that all that was going on was The Shadows – especially in England. But they were so dumb, when they listened to these audition tapes they were listening for The Shadows. So they were not listening to it at all – they're listening like they do now – you know how these people are – for what's already gone down. They can't hear anything new.

It was pretty shaky then, because there's nowhere else to go if you don't get the records.[74] We didn't think we were going to make it at all. It was only Brian telling us we were going to make it, and George. Brian Epstein and George Harrison.

Brian used to come back from London and he couldn't face us because he'd been down about twenty times. He'd come back to say, 'Well, I'm afraid they didn't accept it again.' And by then we were close to him, and he'd be really hurt. He'd be terrified to tell us that we hadn't made it again.[72]

We did have a few little fights with Brian. We used to say he was doing nothing and we were doing all the work. We were just saying it, really – we knew how hard he was working. It was Us against Them.[67] He got us to EMI, it was his walking round. If he hadn't gone round London, on foot, with the tapes under his arm, and gone from place to place, and place to place, and finally to George Martin, we would never have made it. We didn't have the push to do it on our own. Paul was more aggressive in that way: 'Let's think up publicity stunts, or jump in the Mersey' – something like that, in those kind of terms, to make it.[72]

GEORGE: In April 1962, Stuart Sutcliffe died. He had already left the band. Not long before he died, he showed up in Liverpool (in the Pierre Cardin jacket with no collar; he had one before we did) and he went round and hung out with us – almost as if he'd had a premonition that he wasn't going to see us again. He came to visit me at my house quite apart from when I saw him with the others and it was a very good feeling I got from him.

I didn't know Stuart was ill, but he was trying to give up smoking. He'd cut his cigarettes up into little bits and every time he fancied a cigarette he'd smoke a little piece, like a dog-end. All the stories make out that somebody kicked him in the head and he died of a haemorrhage, and I do remember him getting beaten up after a gig once in Liverpool (just because he was in a band), but that was a couple of years before.

There was something really warm about his return, and in retrospect I believe he was finishing something; because he went back to Hamburg and suffered a brain haemorrhage and died soon after, only a day before we were due to fly back there. I had German measles so I went a day later than the other guys, on a plane with Brian Epstein. That was the first time I'd been in an aeroplane.

We didn't go to the funeral. That was it: as the man said, 'He not busy being born is busy dying.' But we all felt really sad and I remember feeling worst for Astrid. She was still coming to the shows and sitting there. I think it made her feel a bit better, at least, to hang out with us.

JOHN: I looked up to Stu. I depended on him to tell me the truth. Stu would tell me if something was good and I'd believe him. We were awful to him sometimes. Especially Paul, always picking on him. I used to explain afterwards that we didn't dislike him, really.[67]

JOHN: I WAS ALWAYS SLIGHTLY DISAPPOINTED WITH ALL THE PERFORMERS I SAW, FROM LITTLE RICHARD TO JERRY LEE. THEY NEVER SOUND EXACTLY LIKE THEIR RECORDS. I LIKE 'WHOLE LOTTA SHAKIN'', THE 1956 TAKE ON THE RECORD, BUT I'M NOT INTERESTED IN A VARIATION ON THE THEME. WHEN GENE VINCENT DID 'BE BOP A LULA' IN HAMBURG, HE DIDN'T DO IT THE SAME. IT WAS A THRILL TO MEET GENE VINCENT AND SEE HIM, BUT IT WAS NOT 'BE BOP A LULA'. I'M A RECORD FAN.[80]

GEORGE: Sometimes in the van, with all the stress we were under, a little bitching went on and Paul and he used to punch each other out a bit. I remember the two of them wrestling one time – Paul thought he'd win easily because Stuart was such a little bloke, but Stuart suddenly got this amazing strength that Paul hadn't bargained for.

I once had a bit of a fight with Stuart as well, but we were very friendly other than that – certainly by the end.

PAUL: Not many of our contemporaries had died; we were all too young. It was older people that died, so Stuart's dying was a real shock. And for me there was a little guilt tinged with it, because I'd not been his best friend at times. We ended up good friends, but we'd had a few ding-dongs, partly out of jealousy for John's friendship. We all rather competed for John's friendship, and Stuart, being his mate from art school, had a lot of his time and we were jealous of that. Also, I was keen to see the group be as good as it could be, so I would make the odd remark: 'Oh, you didn't play that right.' But Stuart's death was terrible, because if nothing else he should have been a great painter – you can see that from his sketchbooks.

The rest of us weren't as close to Stu as John was – they'd been to college together and shared a flat – but we were still close. Everyone was very sad, though the blow was softened by the fact that he'd stayed in Hamburg and we'd got used to not being with him.

John didn't laugh when he heard Stuart died, as people have made out; but being so young, we didn't go on about it. The kind of questions we'd ask were, 'I wonder if he'll come back?' Among ourselves we'd had a pact that if one of us were to die, he'd come back and let the others know if there was another side. So as Stuart was the first one to go, we did half expect him to show up. Any pans that rattled in the night could be him.

GEORGE: We came back to play the Star-Club, a big place and fantastic because it had a great sound system. This time we had a hotel. I remember it was quite a long walk from the club, at the top of the Reeperbahn going back towards the city. We were there for a couple of months.

PAUL: The Star-Club was great. Manfred Weissleder, owner of the Star-Club, and Horst Fascher had Mercedes convertibles, which were pretty swish. Horst had been in jail for killing a guy. He'd been a boxer and he killed a sailor in a bar-room brawl. But they were very protective towards us; we were sort of like their pets. We were safe around these people, paradoxically.

JOHN: We were in Hamburg with Gene Vincent and [later] Little Richard and there's still many a story going round about the escapades, especially with Gene Vincent, who was a rather wild guy. We met Gene backstage. 'Backstage' – I mean, it was a 'toilet' and we were thrilled.[75]

PAUL: Gene had been a marine and he was always offering to knock me out; he knew two pressure points. I said, 'Get out of it. Sod off!' He'd say, 'Oh come on, you'll only be out for a minute.'

GEORGE: I met Gene Vincent in the Star-Club bar one day, in a break. He said, 'Quick, come with me.' We jumped in a taxi and went up the Reeperbahn to the apartment where he was staying. I began to notice that he was all uptight – he thought the tour manager was bonking his girlfriend!

WE RAN INSIDE, UP TO THE FRONT DOOR AND GENE OPENED HIS COAT AND PULLED OUT A GUN. HE HANDED IT TO ME SAYING, 'HOLD THIS,' AND STARTED KNOCKING ON THE DOOR AND SHOUTING, 'HENRY, HENRY, YOU BASTARD!' I THOUGHT TO MYSELF, 'I'M OUT OF HERE,' GAVE HIM THE GUN BACK AND CLEARED OFF QUICK.

PAUL: We used to drive up to Lubeck, on the Ost See. Astrid was the connection. Her family had a bathing hut or something down there. We went out on various day excursions. I went certainly once I remember, with Roy Young, a pianist, and was very impressed with the *Autobahn*; we didn't really have motorways in Britain at that time. It was very fast and we were driving a Mercedes so it all seemed ultra-wonderful to me.

*NEIL ASPINALL: They had been rejected by almost every record label. Finally, Brian sent the guys a telegram to Hamburg: 'EMI request recording session. Please rehearse new material.' Brian told them it was a record contract. It wasn't really; it was just an audition with a producer, George Martin.*

GEORGE: The Parlophone audition was in June 1962. It went not too badly. I think George Martin felt we were raw and rough but that we had some quality that was interesting. We did 'Love Me Do', 'PS I Love You', 'Ask Me Why', 'Besame Mucho' and 'Your Feet's Too Big', among others. ('Your Feet's Too Big' was Fats Waller. That was Paul's dad's influence.)

What I recall about George Martin the first time we met him was his accent. He didn't speak in a Cockney or a Liverpool or Birmingham accent, and anyone who didn't speak like that we thought was very posh. He was friendly, but schoolteacherly: we had to respect him, but at the same time he gave us the impression that he wasn't stiff – that you could joke with him. There is a well-known story about when we'd finished playing and we were walking up the stairs to the control room in Studio Two. He was explaining things and he said, 'Is there anything that you're not happy about?' We shuffled about silently, then I said, 'Well... I don't like your tie!' There was a moment of 'Ohhhhh', but then we laughed, and he did too. Being born in Liverpool you have to be a comedian.

PAUL: George Martin had been known at EMI for producing the lesser acts – people who weren't serious recording artists, such as The Goons. The big acts like Shirley Bassey would go to other producers. George was thrown the 'scrag ends', and we were 'scrag ends'. He agreed to audition us, and we had a not-very-powerful audition in which he was not very pleased with Pete Best.

George Martin was used to drummers being very 'in time', because all the big-band session drummers he used had a great sense of time. Now, our Liverpool drummers had a sense of spirit, emotion, economy even, but not a deadly sense of time. This would bother producers making a record. George took us to one side and said, 'I'm really unhappy with the drummer. Would you consider changing him?' We said, 'No, we can't!' It was one of those terrible things you go through as kids. Can we betray him? No. But our career was on the line. Maybe they were going to cancel our contract.

It was a big issue at the time, how we 'dumped' Pete. And I do feel sorry for him, because of what he could have been on to; but as far as we were concerned, it was strictly a professional decision. If he wasn't up to the mark (*slightly* in our eyes, and *definitely* in the producer's eyes) then there was no choice. But it was still very difficult. It is one of the most difficult things we ever had to do.

JOHN: This myth built up over the years that he was great and Paul was jealous of him because he was pretty and all that crap. They didn't get on that much together, but it was partly because Pete was a bit slow. He was a harmless guy, but he was not quick. All of us had quick minds, but he never picked that up.

The reason he got into the group in the first place was because we had to have a drummer to get to Hamburg. We were always going to dump him when we could find a decent drummer, but by the time we were back from Germany we'd trained him to keep a stick going up and down (four-in-the-bar, he couldn't do much else) and he looked nice and the girls liked him, so it was all right.[74] We were cowards when we sacked him. We made Brian do it. But if we'd told him to his face, that would have been much nastier. It would probably have ended in a fight.[67]

PAUL: It was a personality thing. We knew that he wasn't that good a player. He was slightly different to the rest of us; not quite as studenty. Pete was a straight-up kind of guy and so the girls liked him a bit. He was mean, moody and magnificent.

JOHN: There were two top groups in Liverpool – The Big Three and Rory Storm and the Hurricanes – and Ringo was in the Hurricanes. The two best drummers in Liverpool were in those two groups and they were established before we'd even got going.

We knew of Ringo. Ringo was a star in his own right before we even met.[74] Ringo was a professional drummer who sang and performed, so his talents would have come out one way or the other. I don't know what he would have ended up as – whatever that spark is in Ringo, we all know it but we can't put our finger on it. There's something in him that's projectable and he would have surfaced as an individual.[80]

GEORGE: Top: Us in cloth caps at Hamburg airport, 1962.
Above: In a lay-by on the road between Hamburg and the Ost See. Me, Paul and John with Gerry and the Pacemakers (left to right: Freddie Marsden, Gerry, Les Chadwick and Les Maguire). Pete must have taken this one.

PAUL: WE REALLY STARTED TO THINK WE NEEDED 'THE GREATEST DRUMMER IN LIVERPOOL', AND THE GREATEST DRUMMER IN OUR EYES WAS A GUY, RINGO STARR, WHO HAD CHANGED HIS NAME BEFORE ANY OF US, WHO HAD A BEARD AND WAS GROWN UP AND WAS KNOWN TO HAVE A ZEPHYR ZODIAC.

So we made Ringo an offer to join us, and Pete had to have the dreadful talking-to.

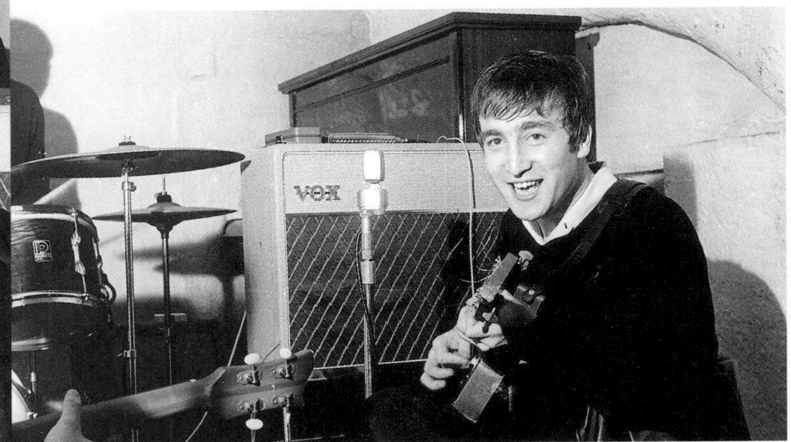

GEORGE: To me it was apparent: Pete kept being sick and not showing up for gigs so we would get Ringo to sit in with the band instead, and every time Ringo sat in, it seemed like 'this is it'. Eventually we realised, 'We should get Ringo in the band full time.'

I was quite responsible for stirring things up. I conspired to get Ringo in for good; I talked to Paul and John until they came round to the idea. I remember going to his house. He wasn't in so I sat and had some tea with his mother and I said, 'We'd like Ringo to be in our band.' She said, 'Well, he's in Butlins holiday camp with Rory at the moment, but when he rings me I'll get him to phone you,' and I gave her our number.

We weren't very good at telling Pete he had to go. But when it comes down to it, how do you tell somebody? Although Pete had not been with us all that long – two years in terms of a lifetime isn't very long – when you're young it's not a nice thing to be kicked out of a band and there's no nice way of doing it. Brian Epstein was the manager so it was his job, and I don't think he could do it very well either. But that's the way it was and the way it is.

RINGO: At the same time that I got the offer from The Beatles, I got one from King Size Taylor and the Dominoes, and from Gerry and the Pacemakers. (Gerry wanted me to be his bass player! I hadn't played bass then or to this day, but the idea of being up front was appealing. That you'd never played a particular instrument before wasn't important back then!)

I used to go and watch The Beatles a lot and there are photos around showing them playing, with me sitting on the side of the stage: 'Hello, lads.' Then one morning, I'm in bed, it's about noon, and my mother knocks on the bedroom door and says, 'Brian Epstein is outside.' I didn't know much about him, except how strange it was that The Beatles had a manager, because none of us had a real manager. He said, 'Would you play the lunchtime session in the Cavern for us?' I said, 'Give us a minute to get a cup of tea and get me trousers on, and I'll come on down.' He drove me to the Cavern in his posh car, and I played the session.

All bands played a lot of the same numbers at that time. One gig I did in Crosby, there were three bands on. Each band had two sets, half an hour each; and as the other two drummers hadn't turned up I sat in with all three bands – I never got off the kit. As the curtain closed I would change jackets and the next band would come on and I'd still be there. It would close and then it would open and – me again! This happened six times. It was OK because I had a lot of stamina in those days and we all knew what we were doing.

After the Cavern gig we all went to another club for a drink. It was, 'Thanks a lot, lads' – we'd had a good time and I was off. But I was asked again later: 'Would you play with the boys? Pete can't make it.' I got good money playing with them, I loved playing with them, so I said, 'Sure.' This went on three or four times – we were pals and we'd have a drink after the show and then I'd be back with Rory.

Then one day, a Wednesday – we were doing Butlins again, our third season: three months' work, sixteen quid a week; fabulous – Brian called and said, 'Would you join the band for good?' I wasn't aware that it had been on the cards for a while, because I was busy playing. In fact, the guys had been talking to Brian, and George had been hustling for me.

The Beatles had a piece of tape for record companies, they had done some tracks, they were going to EMI and were getting a recording deal! A piece of plastic was like gold, was more than gold. You'd sell your soul to get on a little record. So I said, 'OK. But I've got four other guys here. We've got a gig for months. I can't pull out now and have it all end for them.'

I said I would join on Saturday. We used to have Saturdays off at Butlins; that was when they changed the campers. That gave Rory Thursday, Friday and Saturday to bring someone in to open again on Sunday, which was a lot of time.

And that was it. John said, 'Get rid of your beard, Ring, and change your hairstyle.' I cut my hair, as the saying goes, and joined the band. I never felt sorry for Pete Best. I was not involved. Besides, I felt I was a much better drummer than he was.

The first gig in the Cavern after I'd joined was pretty violent. There was a lot of fighting and shouting; half of them hated me, half of them loved me. George got a black eye, and I haven't looked back.

GEORGE: Some of the fans – a couple of them – were shouting 'Pete is best!' and 'Ringo never, Pete Best forever!', but it was a small group and we ignored it. However, after about half an hour it was getting a bit tiring so I shouted to the audience. When we stepped out of the band room into the dark tunnel, some guy nodded me one, giving me a black eye. The things we have to do for Ringo!

JOHN: Nothing happened to Pete Best. At one time he went touring America with The Pete Best Band and I suppose he was hyped and hustled. And then he married and settled down and was working in a bakery. I read something about him. He was writing that he was glad about the way things turned out; he was glad he missed it all.[71]

RINGO: A light-hearted side note: Neil Aspinall was really friendly with Pete Best and his family and so for a while he wouldn't set my kit up. This lasted for a few weeks, but he got over it. He was all we had; he was driving the van, setting up the gear and everything, and he was a little miffed.

PAUL: Pete Best was good, but a bit limited. You can hear the difference on the *Anthology* tapes. When Ringo joins us we get a bit more kick, a few more imaginative breaks, and the band settles. So the new combination was perfect: Ringo with his very solid beat, laconic wit and Buster Keaton-like charm; John with his sharp wit and his rock'n'rolliness, but also his other, quite soft side; George, with his great instrumental ability and who could sing some good rock'n'roll. And then I could do a bit of singing and playing, some rock'n'roll and some softer numbers.

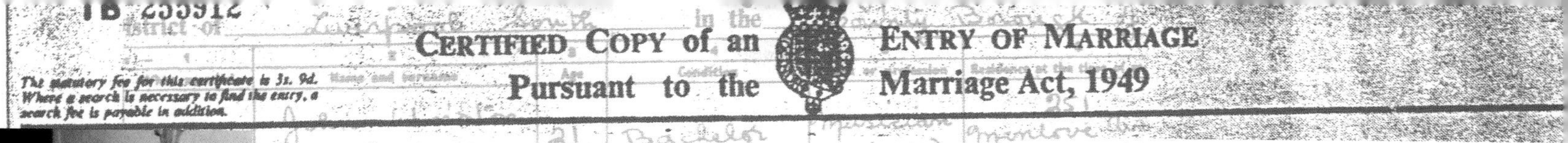

JOHN: I GOT MARRIED BEFORE I EVEN KNEW WHAT RELIGION MY WIFE WAS, I NEVER ASKED HER. SHE COULD HAVE BEEN ANYTHING, AN ARAB.[64]

GEORGE: I don't remember much about John's wedding. It took place in August 1962. He just went in some office in Liverpool one afternoon, and in the evening we got in Brian's car, went to the gig (we actually did a gig that night) and it was, 'Well, we got married.' It wasn't hushed up, it just wasn't mentioned to the press. There *was* no wedding – it was a five-minute thing in a Registry Office. It was different in those days. No time to lose.

JOHN: Cynthia's grown up with it, with me.

We got married just before we made the first record. I was a bit shocked when Cynthia told me [she was pregnant], but I said, 'Yes, we'll have to get married.' I didn't fight it.[67] I went the day before to tell Mimi. I said Cyn was having a baby, we were getting married tomorrow, did she want to come? She just let out a groan. There was a drill going on all the time outside the Registry Office. I couldn't hear a word that bloke was saying. Then we went across the road and had a chicken dinner. It was all a laugh.

I thought it would be goodbye to the group, getting married. None of us ever took girls to the Cavern as we thought we would lose fans (which turned out to be a farce in the end). But I did feel embarrassed, walking about, married. It was like walking about with odd socks on or your flies open.[65]

RINGO: I didn't go to the wedding – John never even told me he'd got married. John and Cynthia were keeping it a secret from everyone. If something got mentioned it was, 'Shh, Ring's in the room.'

It was kept from me because I wasn't considered a real member at the beginning. I was in the band, but emotionally I had to earn my way in. John didn't tell me anything until we went on tour and got to know each other in all the doss houses where we camped.

JOHN: We didn't keep it secret, it's just that when we first came on the scene nobody really asked us. They weren't interested whether we were married or not. The question they used to ask was, 'What kind of girls do you like?' And if you get our early news sheets it says 'blondes'. I wasn't going to say, 'I'm married,' but I never said, 'I'm not.' I always disliked reading about people's families.

BRIAN EPSTEIN: *I first encouraged them to get out of leather jackets and I wouldn't allow them to appear in jeans after a short time. After that I got them to wear sweaters on stage and eventually, very reluctantly, suits. I'm not sure that they didn't wear their first suits for a BBC broadcast for a live audience.*

PAUL: When we met Brian Epstein we were still into the leather. But when we had photos taken people started saying, 'Maybe the leather is too hard an image.' And agents would agree. Even Astrid began to take pictures of us wearing suits in Germany. Somehow Brian persuaded us to get suits. He quite wisely said, 'If I get a huge offer, they won't take you in leather,' and I didn't think it was a bad idea because it fitted with my 'Gateshead group' philosophy that you should look similar, and because we got *mohair* suits it was a bit like the black acts.

It was later put around that I had betrayed our leather image but, as I recall, I didn't actually have to drag anyone to the tailors. We all went quite happily over the water to Wirral, to Beno Dorn, a little tailor who made mohair suits. That started to change the image and, though we would still wear leather occasionally, for the posh do's we'd put on suits. It was suits for a cabaret gig. We were still on the edge of breaking in a big way and cabaret was well paid. So that was something of an end to the Hamburg era.

JOHN: Outside of Liverpool, when we went down South in our leather outfits the dance-hall promoters didn't really like us. They thought we looked like a gang of thugs. So it got to be Epstein saying, 'Look, if you wear a suit you'll get this much money...' And everybody wanted a good, sharp, black suit. We liked the leather and the jeans, but we wanted a good suit, even to wear off stage. 'Yeah man, all right, I'll wear a suit – I'll wear a bloody *balloon* if somebody's going to pay me; I'm not in love with leather *that* much!'[75]

GEORGE: People thought we looked undesirable, I suppose. Even nowadays kids with leather jackets and long hair are seen as apprentice hooligans, but they are just kids; that's the fashion they like – leathers. And it was like that with us. With black T-shirts, black leather gear and sweaty, we did look like hooligans.

Brian Epstein was from an upper middle-class background and he wanted us to appeal to the producers of radio, television and record companies. We gladly switched into suits to get some more money and some more gigs.

RINGO: HE CHANGED OUR IMAGE ONLY IN MAKING US A BIT SMARTER. THEY *ALL* CHANGED MY IMAGE. I USED TO HAVE MY HAIR RIGHT BACK, LIKE A TEDDY BOY, WITH A TONY CURTIS CUT AND SIDEBOARDS AND SUDDENLY IT WAS, 'SHAVE THEM OFF AND PUT YOUR HAIR DOWN,' WHICH I DID.

Details of engagements w/e 16.11.62

| | | | |
|---|---|---|---|
| Friday | November | 16th | 11.30 a.m. interview with 'Disc'<br>3.0 p.m. George Martin at EMI House. |
| Saturday | " | 17th | MATRIX BALLROOM, COVENTRY<br>You must have a good programme for this date as this is for a new London Agent (also for our best fee yet) - One hour spot. |
| Sunday | " | 18th | CAVERN (Specially advertised welcome home show) |
| Monday | " | 19th | Midday CAVERN |
| " | " | " | This is a double in the BIRMINGHAM area. First at the Baths Ballroom SMETHWICK and then at the Adelphi Ballroom WEST BROMWICH. There will be a ¾ hour spot at each ballroom. Group and equipment to arrive at the first ballroom no later than 7.0 p.m. A good performance here to impress new territory. |

be a ¾ hour spot at each ballroom. Group and equipment to arrive at the first ballroom no later than 7.0 p.m. A good performance here to impress new territory.

Tuesday " FLORAL HALL, SOUTHPORT<br>This is for Lewis Buckley and should be a good night. It's in the form of a stage show and you must have a good programme. You will probably be doing two 45 minute spots.

Wednesday " Midday CAVERN<br>CAVERN

Thursday " MAJESTIC BALLROOM, BIRKENHEAD<br>One hour spot.

Friday " Audition for BBC TELEVISION at St. James Hall, Gloucester Terrace London W. 2 at 12.20 p.m.

- Engagements for November/December, 1962.

| | | |
|---|---|---|
| November | 17th. | Coventry. |
| " | 18th. | Cavern. |
| " | 19th. | Midday Cavern. |
| " | " | Smethwick ) Birmingham area.<br>West Bromwich) |
| " | 20th. | Southport. |
| " | 21st. | Midday Cavern. |
| " | " | Evening Cavern. |
| " | 22nd. | Birkenhead. |
| " | 23rd. | New Brighton. |
| " | 24th. | Prestatyn. |
| " | 25th. | Cavern. |
| " | 26th. | EMI (Recording) |
| " | 27th. | BBC London. |
| " | 28th. | Cavern. |
| " | 28th. | Lewis's Liverpool. |
| " | 29th. | Birkenhead. |
| " | 30th. | Earlstown (Nr. Newton-le-Willows) |
| December | 1st. | Northwich. |
| " | 2nd. | Peterborough (Embassy Theatre with |
| " | 3rd. | Friday Spectactular at EMI London. |
| " | 5th. | Cavern |
| " | 6th. | Southport. |
| " | 7th. | New Brighton. |
| " | 8th. | Manchester. |
| " | 9th. | Cavern. |
| " | 10th. | Midday Cavern. |
| " | 11th. | Runcorn. |
| " | 12th. | Cavern. |
| " | 13th. | Bedford. |
| " | 14th. | Shrewsbury. |
| " | 15th. | Birkenhead. |
| " | 16th. | Cavern. |
| " | 17th. | Departure for Hamburg. |
| " | 18th. | Opening night Star Club, Hamburg. |
| January | 1st. | Return from Hamburg. |
| " | 2nd. | Frist night Scottish Tour. |

PAUL: I think John in later years liked to feel that he was the rebel and I somehow tried to straighten him up – but that's bullshit. We all changed to the straight image. I didn't cut his hair for him; I didn't care if his tie was straight or his button done up. Check the pictures – John's not scowling in *all* of them!

NEIL ASPINALL: *By 1962 they were pretty big in the Northwest, in Liverpool and Manchester. Granada had got the regional TV franchise in 1956.* Know The North *was a local show and, having heard of The Beatles, they came down to the Cavern and filmed a performance. Ringo had just then come into the band, as you can hear from the heckling in the crowd.*

GEORGE: I remember Granada TV cameras coming to the Cavern that August. It was really hot and we were asked to dress up properly. We had shirts, and ties and little black pullovers. So we looked quite smart. It was our first television appearance. It was big-time, a-TV-company-coming-to-film-us excitement – and John *was* into it.

PAUL: In September we went down to London with Ringo and played for EMI again. By this time we did have a contract.

This was our intro to that world. We came in the tradesman's entrance and set up our own gear. We were there at 10.00, ready to work at 10.30 sharp, expected to have done two songs by 1.30. Then we had an hour's break for lunch (which we paid for). We would go round the corner to the Alma pub, at the back of St John's Wood. We were young and pubs were still grown-up places, so we'd have a ciggy to look older and order half a pint with a cheese roll. Inevitably, the chat would be about the session. Then it was back to the studio from 2.30 to 5.30. Those were the main sessions: two daytime sessions in which you were expected to have completed four songs.

If we'd done a particularly good take they might say, 'Would you like to listen to it in the control room?' We'd think, 'What, us? Up those stairs, in heaven?' We'd never properly heard what we sounded like until then. We'd heard ourselves doing it 'live' in the headphones, but through speakers it was very exciting: 'Oh, that sounds just like a record! Let's do this again and again and again!' From then we were hooked on the recording drug, and when John and I sat down to write the next batch of songs it was with this in mind: 'Remember how exciting it was? Let's see if we can come up with something better.'

JOHN: It was a constant fight between Brian and Paul on one side and me and George on the other.[70] Brian and Paul used to always be at me to cut my hair.[69] At that time it was longer than in any of the photographs – it was generally trimmed for the photographs, but there were some private pictures that show it was pretty long, greased back, hanging around. There was a lot of hair on the Teddy boys; the Tony Curtises that grew larger and larger because they never went to the hairdresser. We were pretty greasy.[75]

So Brian put us in neat suits and shirts and Paul was right behind him. My little rebellion was to have my tie loose, with the top button of my shirt undone, but Paul'd come up to me and put it straight. I used to try and get George to rebel with me. I'd say to him: 'Look, we don't need these fucking little suits. Let's chuck them out of the window.'

I saw a film, the first television film we ever did. The Granada people came down to film us, and there we were in suits and it just wasn't us. Watching that film, I knew that that was where we started to sell out.[70]

GEORGE:
I DON'T THINK JOHN PARTICULARLY LIKED WEARING A SUIT – NOR DID I – BUT WE WANTED MORE WORK, AND WE REALISED THAT'S WHAT WE HAD TO DO. BACK THEN EVERYONE WAS MORE STRAIGHT, THE WHOLE BUSINESS WAS.

ents w/c 16.11.62.

16th. 11.30 a.m. Interview with "Disc".
3.0 p.m. George Martin at EMI

17th. MATRIX BALLROOM, COVENTRY.

18th. CAVERN.

19th. Midday CAVERN.
" First at Baths Ballroom Smethwick,BIRMINGHAM.
Second at Adelphi Ballroom, WEST BROMWICH.

20th. FLORAL HALL, SOUTHPORT.

21st. Midday CAVERN.
" CAVERN.

22nd. MAJESTIC BALLROOM, BIRKENHE

23rd. Audition for BBC TELEVISION
Hall, Gloucester Terrace

23rd.(contd) After audition le
arriving approxim
proceed to THE N
one hour spot so

24th. ROYAL LIDO, PREST

-2-

THE BEATLES

**Details of engagements w/c 16.11.62 ..cont.**

**Friday November 23rd...** **"This audition will not be held under full television studio conditions but costume and makeup are obviously desirable. Dressing room accommodation will be available and Artistes should arrive no less than 30 minutes earlier than the time stated. Yo performance should be designed to present you to the best advantage but in any case no longer than 10 minutes in length." Reservations will be made on the plane which leaves London airport at 6.30 arriving at Liverpool air at approximately 7.45 from where you will have to proceed to THE BRIGHTON TOWER for a one hour sometime after 8.30 p.m.**

**Sat... 24th ... ROYAL LIDO, PRESTATYN understand this venue is an extremely pleasant one and the Manager a 'particular type'. ... not do anything to upset ... Two 45 minute spots.**

NEMS ENTERPRISES LTD
DIRECTORS ... AND C. J. EPSTEIN
12-14 WHITECHAPEL, LIVERPOOL 1 TELEPHONE ROYAL 7895

BE/BA:

8th December 1962

Dear Mr. Lockwood,

In connection with your enquiry for THE BEATLES for January 18th I regret to advise you that I still cannot obtain any clearance on this date. In the circumstances possibly we had better settle for Friday April 5th. I am willing to issue a contract for this date at a fee of £75 with the following proviso: 'that it is agreed that if THE BEATLES' disc "Please, Please Me" reaches the top five in the chart of the Record Retailer/ New Record Mirror prior to the date of this engagement then the fee for same will be increased to £100'.

I will look forward to hearing from you in due course.

Yours sincerely,
Brian Epstein.

P.S. So that I can issue a contract would you please let me have the name of the venue concerned.

LIVERPOOL'S top beat group The Beatles make disc debut today (Friday) with "Love me do" (Parlophone)

RINGO: The response to us at EMI was OK, because we'd done the auditions and George Martin was willing to take a chance. (Though the reaction from people because we were from the North was a bit weird.)

On my first visit in September we just ran through some tracks for George Martin. We even did 'Please Please Me'. I remember that, because while we were recording it I was playing the bass drum with a maraca in one hand and a tambourine in the other. I think it's because of that that George Martin used Andy White, the 'professional', when we went down a week later to record 'Love Me Do'. The guy was previously booked, anyway, because of Pete Best. George didn't want to take any more chances and I was caught in the middle.

I was devastated that George Martin had his doubts about me. I came down ready to roll and heard, 'We've got a professional drummer.' He has apologised several times since, has old George, but it was devastating – I hated the bugger for years; I still don't let him off the hook!

So Andy plays on the 'Love Me Do' single – but I play later on the album version; Andy wasn't doing anything so great that I couldn't copy it when we did the album. And I've played on everything since then. (Well, bar 'Back In The USSR' and a few other things.)

PAUL: Horror of horrors! George Martin didn't like Ringo. Ringo at that point was not *that* steady on time. Now he is rock steady; it's always been his greatest attribute and that was why we wanted him. But to George he was not as pinpoint as a session guy would be. So Ringo got blown off the first record. George did the, 'Can I see you for a moment, boys?' – 'Yeah?' – 'Um... without Ringo.' He said, 'I would like to bring in another drummer for this record.'

It was very hard for us to accept that decision. We said, 'Ringo has to be the drummer; we wouldn't want to lose *him* as the drummer.' But George got his way and Ringo didn't drum on the first single. He only played tambourine.

I don't think Ringo ever got over that. He had to go back up to Liverpool and everyone asked, 'How did it go in the Smoke?' We'd say, 'B side's good,' but Ringo couldn't admit to liking the A side, not being on it.

NEIL ASPINALL: *The Beatles were asked in those sessions, on 4th and 11th September, to record a song by Mitch Murray, 'How Do You Do It'. That is the way things were done: the songwriter is with the publisher, the publisher knows the record producer, who gives it to the band to record. But The Beatles came along and said they'd prefer to do their own songs.*

PAUL: George Martin told us that the music-business network was made up of songwriters and groups. Normally, you would be offered a couple of songs by a publisher, like Dick James, in cahoots with your producer. But we were starting as a group that had its own material.

Mitch Murray was writing songs. He came up with, 'How do you do it? How do you do what you do to me?' We listened to the demo and said, 'It's a hit, George, but we've got a song, "Love Me Do".' George said, 'I don't think yours is such a big hit.' We said, 'Yes, but it is *us*, and it is what we're about. We're trying to be blues, we're not trying to be "la de da de da". We're students and artsy guys – we can't take *that* song home to Liverpool, we'll get laughed at. We can take "Love Me Do": people in the groups we respect, people like The Big Three, will go for it.' We didn't want to be laughed at by other bands. But George insisted that his song was still a hit. So we said, 'OK, we'll learn it up.'

We went home and did a reasonable arrangement and recorded 'How Do You Do It', and George Martin said, 'It's still a Number One.' We insisted that we hated it, so George gave it to Gerry and the Pacemakers; and Gerry did it faithful to our demo and had his first big hit.

GEORGE: We had played 'Love Me Do' on stage and it felt quite good and it was one of Paul's and John's. We wanted that; the other song we were being offered was really corny.

George Martin listened to both songs and I think he decided 'How Do You Do It' could still be our second single. But then we speeded up 'Please Please Me' and that was it.

GEORGE MARTIN: *It was common in those days to find material for artists by going to Tin Pan Alley and listening to the publishers' wares. That was a regular part of my life: I spent a long time looking for songs, and what I wanted for The Beatles was a hit. I was convinced that 'How Do You Do It' was a hit song. Not a great piece of songwriting, not the most marvellous song I had ever heard in my life, but I thought it had that essential ingredient which would appeal to a lot of people – and we did record it. John took the lead. They didn't like doing it, but we made a good record and I was very close to issuing it as their first single.*

*In the end I went with 'Love Me Do' but would still have issued 'How Do You Do It' had they not persuaded me to listen to another version of 'Please Please Me'.*

PAUL:
IT WAS SYMPTOMATIC OF OUR GROUP THAT WE TURNED 'HOW DO YOU DO IT' DOWN. THE OTHER HUGE STAND IN OUR LIFE, A LITTLE LATER ON, WAS SAYING TO BRIAN EPSTEIN, 'WE'RE NOT GOING TO AMERICA UNTIL WE'VE GOT A NUMBER ONE THERE.' WE WAITED, AND I THINK THAT WAS ONE OF THE BEST MOVES WE EVER MADE. WE WERE VERY CHEEKY. IT WAS ALL BASED ON CLIFF RICHARD, WHO HAD BEEN TO AMERICA AND BEEN THIRD ON THE BILL TO FRANKIE AVALON. WE THOUGHT, 'OH DEAR, CLIFF IS A BIGGER STAR THAN AVALON! HOW COULD HE DO THAT?' AND ADAM FAITH – ALL THE EARLY STARS WE LOOKED UP TO HAD GONE WITH TERRIBLE BILLING. SO WE SAID, 'WE'RE NOT GOING UNTIL WE GET A NUMBER ONE AND WE'RE HEADLINING.'

RINGO: At EMI, besides my being distraught that I wasn't even on the drums, I remember us all being ready to stand up for the principle of, 'We have written these songs and we want to do them.' We had to make a really big stand on that, and the others made it more than I did because I was the new boy. I just said, 'Go on, lads, go get 'em.'

I was still trying to find my place, but they were adamant, thank God, about not wanting this song we'd been given. On reflection, this was a huge stance because, as I say, for that bit of plastic you would sell your soul. I don't think Cliff Richard would have refused. Cliff was never a writer. Dickie Pride and Billy Fury, all that crowd, were just given songs, and sang them.

GEORGE: We released 'Love Me Do' and it did very well. It got to Number Seventeen in the charts. That was based mainly on local sales; there were enough fans of The Beatles around because we were playing all over the Wirral, Cheshire, Manchester and Liverpool. We were quite popular, so the sales *were* real.

First hearing 'Love Me Do' on the radio sent me shivery all over. It was the best buzz of all time. We knew it was going to be on Radio Luxembourg at something like 7.30 on Thursday night. I was in my house in Speke and we all listened in. That was great, but after having got to Seventeen, I don't recall what happened to it. It probably went away and died, but what it meant was that the next time we went to EMI, they were more friendly: 'Oh, hello lads. Come in.'

RINGO: When 'Love Me Do' came out, Brian would get the playlist and tell us we were on at, say, 6.45 or 6.26, and we'd stop the car to listen (because we were always doing something – travelling, working) and it was a thrill.

NEIL ASPINALL: *They were doing a gig somewhere in the Wirral, or Birkenhead, when we learnt that 'Love Me Do' had sold 5,000 copies. I remember John saying, 'Well, there you go – what more do they want?'*

JOHN: The best thing was it came into the charts in two days and everybody thought it was a fiddle, because our manager's stores sent in these returns and everybody down South thought, 'Ah-ha, he's buying them himself or he's just fiddling the charts.' But he wasn't.[63]

RINGO: Even though 'Love Me Do' didn't make Number One, it was exciting. All we had wanted was a piece of vinyl – my God, a record that you hadn't made in some booth somewhere! And now we wanted to be Number One. They were both as important.

By the end of 1962, 'Love Me Do' had sold 100,000 copies, most of them in Liverpool. We've still got a bunch of them in our house. (Joke.)

PAUL: Ted Taylor first told us how to use make-up. We were playing the Embassy Cinema at Peterborough late that year, very low on the bill to Frank Ifield and below The Ted Taylor Four as well. Ted had a funny little synth on the end of his piano on which he could play tunes like 'Sooty'. He would use it for 'Telstar' – the audience went wild to hear his synth sound. It was Ted that said, 'You looked a little pale out there, lads. You should use make-up.' We asked him how. He said, 'There's this pancake stuff, Leichner 27. You can get it from the chemist. Take a little pad and rub it on; it gives you a tan. And put a black line around your eyes and lips.' We said, 'That's a bit dodgy, isn't it?' He said, 'Believe me, they will never see it, and you'll look good.'

GEORGE: The Ted Taylor Four had a record called 'Son Of Honky Tonk'. We were in their dressing room and found their stage make-up called 'pancake'. We thought we'd better put some on because the lights were bright and we supposed that's what people did on stage. So we put it on and we looked like Outspan oranges. There were photos taken of us, and John is also wearing eye shadow and black eye-liner. Big orange faces and black eyes.

PAUL: Right afterwards we were being photographed for a poster for Blackpool. They had been bootlegging posters (which meant we were obviously getting quite popular), and the poster company said we should do an official one. So they did four squares – one of us in each square. And you can see the black line around our eyes. We never lived it down!

NEIL ASPINALL: *Brian started to promote shows himself so he could put on his own bands. He'd hire the Tower Ballroom in New Brighton and get a star like Little Richard, who was touring England anyway. He'd call the agent in London and do a deal for him to play the Tower Ballroom as top of the bill. On the same bill – this was 12th October 1962 – there were The Beatles and Gerry and the Pacemakers and The Undertakers – a whole pile of Liverpool bands. But The Beatles would always be second on the bill to the big visiting star.*

JOHN: Brian used to bring the rock stars who were not making it any more, like Gene Vincent, Little Richard. No reflection on them, but they were coming over for that reason and he put us on the bill with them, second billing; so we'd use them to draw the crowd.

It's hard for people to imagine just how thrilled we, the four of us, were to even *see* any great rock'n'roller in the flesh, and we were almost paralysed with adoration with both of them, and the side note was Little Richard's organist was Billy Preston. He looked about ten then.[75]

GEORGE: Little Richard was also on the bill with us for our fourth trip to Hamburg in November. By then things were better for us there. They had new Fender amplifiers for all the bands and we had a hotel room each; just in a little hotel on the Reeperbahn, but our own rooms nevertheless. Brian Epstein had hired Little Richard to play on the same bill as us at the Liverpool Empire and at the Tower Ballroom in New Brighton so we'd met him briefly.

Hamburg was really happening then and they were coining quite a bit of money in those clubs, with all the drinks and the admission fees: they'd have four shows so they could get four different audiences in a night.

JOHN: We used to stand backstage at Hamburg's Star-Club and watch Little Richard play. Or he used to sit and talk. He used to read from the Bible backstage and just to hear him talk we'd sit round and listen. It was Brian Epstein that brought *him* to Hamburg. I still love him and he's one of the greatest.[75]

RINGO: We went in November and in December. I don't know where we stayed that final time. It's hazy, to say the least. The staying wasn't important, the living was cool. It was fairly crazy; I'd been there with Rory Storm, and I'd been separately to play with Tony Sheridan (I'd played with him for a month) and I was back this time with The Beatles, and it really felt good. It was becoming like home.

Little Richard played the Star-Club with Billy Preston. Billy was sixteen and he was fabulous; still is. I watched Little Richard twice a night for six days: it was so great. He did show off a bit in front of us – he'd want to know we were in the wings; he'd heard of us by that time.

We were only twenty-two and we still loved the Preludins and we still liked to drink and we could get away with anything as long as we went on and played. The only thing that the Germans wouldn't tolerate was your not going on stage, and you could go on (and we did) in several states of mind.

JOHN: We had great happenings on stage. We used to eat on stage, we'd smoke, we swore. Some shows I went on just in my underpants – this was at the larger club, the Star-Club, when Gerry and the Pacemakers and the whole of Liverpool was over there. We really got them going then. I'd go on in underpants with a toilet seat round me neck, and all sorts of gear on. *And out of my fucking mind!* And I'd do a drum solo – which I couldn't do, because I can't play drums – while Gerry Marsden was playing.[72]

RINGO: It was par for the course to swear at the audience by then. They knew what we were saying and they swore back, but they loved us. I don't know about all the Germans, but the ones from Hamburg, the ones who were really around us like Horst Fascher, Rudi and a few of the other guys, were really rough – I don't know how many of them are still alive.

You had to go on, however bad you felt. I'd heard musicians saying, 'Knock me out, I don't want to go on.' Because *they* would knock you down, they would kick you on stage. But every time we left they'd all cry – that's what blew me away; that the people of Hamburg were so sensitive. While we were there they'd put on a show of being tough guys, but when the time came for us to leave, here were these big tearful Germans saying, 'I don't want you to go.' Horst Fascher would cry at the drop of a hat. All this sadness, when the night before it had been, 'Mach shau, you mach fuckin' shau.' They'd get right on your brain.

PAUL: There was a guy called Harry in a group called The Strangers. He'd got a little pissed and was in the wings at the Star-Club, obviously not as ambitious or as keen as we were. He didn't want to go on so he kept asking people to knock him out. I remember not understanding that, thinking, 'It's all very well being pissed, but not wanting to go on stage when you're in a group – that's a serious problem you've got, maybe we *should* knock you out!'

JOHN: You would only have two hours' sleep, and then you'd have to wake up and take a pill, and it would be going on and on and on, since you didn't get a day off; you'd just begin to go out of your mind with tiredness and you'd think you'd be glad to get out of there. But then you'd go back to Liverpool, and only remember the good fun you had in Hamburg, so you wouldn't mind going back. But after the last time we didn't want to go back.[72] We were beginning to feel stale and cramped. We were always getting the pack-ups. We'd get tired of one stage and be deciding to pack up when another stage would come along.

We'd outlived the Hamburg stage and wanted to pack that up. We hated going back to Hamburg those last two times. We'd had that scene.[67] Brian made us go back to fulfil the contract – if we'd had our way, we'd have copped out on the engagement, because we didn't feel we owed them fuck all – we made all those clubs into international clubs.[72]

GEORGE: That's one thing I'll say for The Beatles, we always honoured our agreements. For years, every time we had a record that went to Number One we still had six months' work already booked at little ballrooms for fifty quid a night when we could have been earning maybe £5,000. But we always honoured them, because we, or rather Brian Epstein, was a gentleman. He didn't want to say, 'Well, screw them, let's do the London Palladium instead.'

RINGO: Brian was really a cool guy. We played every gig. We'd play some daft club in Birmingham because we'd been booked. I'm glad now we did that and not drop the little clubs for the Palladium and say 'fuck you'. We were an upright band, and Brian was really upright.

JOHN: There's big exaggerated stories about us in Hamburg, about us pissing on nuns and things like that, but there was a lot of things that went on. What actually happened with that was – we had a balcony in these flats – one Sunday morning we were just pissing in the street as all the people were going to church, and there were some nuns over the road going into the church. It was just a Sunday morning in the club district, with everyone walking about and three or four people peeing in the street.[72]

GEORGE: I think that Hamburg and the early years between Hamburg trips, becoming established in the Merseyside area, were great. But Hamburg was the more exciting because they had Mercedes Benz taxis and the nightclubs. There was a lot going on. It seems in my memory like one of those black-and-white jazz movies of the Fifties.

I'd have to say with hindsight that Hamburg bordered on the best of Beatles times. We didn't have any luxury, we didn't have any bathrooms or any clothes, we were pretty grubby, we couldn't afford anything; but on the other hand we weren't yet famous, so we didn't have to contend with the bullshit that comes with fame. We could be ourselves and do whatever we wanted to do without people writing about it in the newspapers. We were free to piss on anyone we wanted to, if we wanted, although we never actually did. (John didn't piss on the nuns – we peed over a balcony into a deserted street at about 4.30 in the morning.) We were just like everybody else and we could have a great time and just rock on.

PAUL: In Hamburg we used to think, 'We'll have to save money here, in case it all finishes.' But we never did and it used to worry me that we'd have no money to show for it and we'd have to get jobs and do what we didn't want to do and still have no money.[65]

Hamburg was certainly a great childhood memory. But I think all things are enhanced by time. It was very exciting, though I think it felt better to me a little later in our career, once we'd started to get a bit of success with the records.

JOHN: We always talk about Hamburg and the Cavern and the dance halls in Liverpool because that's when we were really hot musically.[72] We were performers then and what we generated was fantastic when we played straight rock – there was nobody to touch us in Britain.

[By the time we were playing theatres] we had to reduce an hour or two of playing to twenty minutes, and repeat the same twenty minutes every night.[70] Suddenly everything had to be done in twenty minutes and you had to do all your hits, and you'd only do two shows a night because the live theatre only held a few thousand people.[72]

So we always miss the club days. Later on we became technically efficient recording artists, which was another thing, because we were confident people, and whatever media you put us in we can produce something worthwhile.[70]

# 1963

nineteen sixty-three

PAUL: I started out with just an acoustic guitar. I'd been brought up not to borrow (an ethic my dad instilled in me), so when I first moved to an electric I had to buy a Rosetti Lucky Seven; a terrible guitar but cheap, and it was electric. I had a little Elpico amp for it (which I've still got), of a very Fifties design in bakelite. This Elpico wasn't really a guitar amp. It only had microphone and gramophone inputs; but I got a reasonable sound from the mike input. I took that and the little electric to Hamburg and they stood me in good stead for a month or so, until the sweat got to the guitar. It looked OK, pretty-ish for three days, and then the paint started to wear and it fell apart. One day someone just broke it, sort of over my head. It was never going to last, it was just a crappy piece of show. I think it was designed to fall apart, actually. Built-in obsolescence in an early form.

Stuck out in Hamburg with no instrument, I was forced onto piano as they had one on stage at the Kaiserkeller. I was used to facing the audience so this was an excuse to turn my back on the audience and just get into the music, which was good. I started to get into numbers like 'Don't Let The Sun Catch You Crying', a Ray Charles B side. That was a good little period for me, and I think I developed my piano-playing quite a bit. I ended up being slightly better than the other guys on piano from that period by pure default: having no guitar.

So acoustic guitar is really my instrument, inasmuch as that's what I started on. But I went through to the Rosetti Lucky Seven, then the piano. And then, when it became clear that Stuart was leaving the band, I went on to Stu's bass. This got me back in the front line, which I wasn't too keen on since I'd been having quite a good time at the back. At that time I could just about get by on bass, putting in a very simple bassline now and again.

We used to actually cut strings out of the piano for the bass (which I hear is impossible, but we managed to do it). If we needed an A string, say, we'd just get on the piano and go dink, dink, dink – A! And then it was out with the pliers, thinking, 'They'll never notice the odd string,' and then try to fix it onto the bass. It worked occasionally but it's hardly the thing to do and probably puts a huge strain on the guitar. But back then it was very different from today where you have a roadie with a trunk full of strings. One packet was as much as anyone ever had. It just wasn't a priority to have strings. If a string went you just worked on the other three (or, if it was a guitar, the other five). You would ignore the one that had gone and think, 'One of these days I'll get one.'

GEORGE: These days, you amplify the kit and have proper bass amplifiers – *we* had some little Mickey Mouse amplifiers. Now there are fifty-nine gauges of guitar string; for us it was, 'Can I have some of your strings, please?' I don't think we even knew the difference between electric and acoustic strings: they were all like telegraph wires, really thick so you couldn't even bend them. I don't expect it sounded very good.

PAUL: Anyway, after a bit I decided that I wanted to get my own guitar. In the centre of Hamburg there was a little music shop. I recall passing now and again and seeing a violin-shaped bass, which in itself was intriguing. And it appealed to me, being left-handed, that it was symmetrical; so when I turned it upside down it wouldn't look too bad. I got one; a little Hofner. I paid for it outright. It was the equivalent of about thirty quid, which was pretty cheap even back then.

That was it; that was the start of what became a kind of trademark. It is a lovely instrument. And because it's so lightweight, I didn't even feel as if I had a bass on – that had quite a liberating effect. It actually does something to you; because it's so light you treat it more like a guitar. I found I became more melodic on bass than other bass-players because I could do lots of high stuff on the twelfth fret. Being melodic in my writing, it was good not always to have to play the root notes. *And* you need a few more muscles on a big bass! So, being melodic anyway, and the combination of the instrument being very light yet with a very bassy sound, things just came together to make a certain sound; luck, really. And when I was given a Rickenbacker, during the *Sgt Pepper* years (though it was slightly heavier and slightly more electric), I had firmly developed this melodious style, which gave songs like 'With A Little Help From My Friends' and 'Lucy In The Sky With Diamonds' fairly interesting basslines.

After some years I put my Hofner in a case and consigned it to history, but I was watching the film of us on the rooftop in *Let It Be*, years afterwards, and I noticed how lightly I was playing the bass and it brought it all back: 'Wow, that was what I used to love about it.'

RINGO: The drummer always sets the feel and I think that was the way that I played, and then with Paul on bass – he is an amazing bass-player; to this day he is *the* most melodic bass-player – we would work at putting the bass and bass-drum together. As long as *they're* together, you can put anything on top.

I only have one rule and that is to play with the singer. If the singer's singing, you don't really have to do anything, just hold it together. If you listen to my playing, I try to become an instrument; play the mood of the song. For example, 'Four thousand holes in Blackburn, Lancashire,' – boom ba bom. I try to *show* that; the disenchanting mood. The drum fills are part of it.

The other thing is, I couldn't do the same drum sequence twice. Whatever beat I would put down, I could never repeat identically, because I play with my soul more than my head. My head knows to play the rhythms –. rock'n'roll, swing, whatever – but it comes out as whatever the feeling is at that moment. The interesting thing about The Beatles was that we seemed to have telepathy. Without thinking, we'd all be up or bringing it down – together. It was magic, and that was one of the forces of The Beatles, the telepathy. (And, of course, the love of music, the great songs…) I've never had anything like that before or since.

When I first was around I was always being put down, like it was: 'JOHN, PAUL, GEORGE… and Ringo.' Particularly in Britain it was, 'There's them and there's him.' And to this day, there are music critics who don't really appreciate the drums. But when we went to America it was great because there are drummers like Jim Keltner (who's still my finest drummer), who would say 'Wow!' So, in the end, being appreciated by other musicians was a lot more important to me than the press's opinion.

My two favourite drummers in the world are Jim Keltner and Charlie Watts. Buddy Rich and Ginger Baker and all those great drummers are very fast, but they just don't get me off at all because they're too busy being complicated. I like drumming to be solid instead of busy.

JOHN: Ringo's a damn good drummer. He was always a good drummer. He's not technically good, but I think Ringo's drumming is underrated the same way as Paul's bass-playing is underrated. Paul was one of the most innovative bass-players that ever played, and half the stuff that's going on now is directly ripped off from his Beatles period. He was coy about his bass-playing. He's an egomaniac about everything else, but his bass-playing he was always a bit coy about. He is a great musician who plays the bass like few other people could play it. If you compare his bass-playing with The Rolling Stones's bass-playing, and you compare Ringo's drumming with Charlie Watts's drumming, they are equal to them, if not better. I always objected to the fact that because Charlie came on a little more 'arty' than Ringo and knew jazz and did cartoons, that he got credit. I think that Charlie's a damn good drummer, and the other guy a good bass-player, but I think Paul and Ringo stand up anywhere, with *any* of the rock musicians. Not technically great. None of us were technical musicians. None of us could read music. None of us can write it. But as pure musicians, as humans inspired to make noise, they're as good as anybody.[80]

I'm what I call a primitive musician. Meaning no schooling. I didn't ever take the instrument that far. I just took it enough to enable me to do what I wanted to do, which was express myself.[74]

I played a lot of harmonica and mouth organ when I was a child. 'Love Me Do' is rock'n'roll, pretty funky: the gimmick was the harmonica. (There had been 'Hey! Baby' and then there was a terrible thing called 'I Remember You'; and we did those numbers, so we started using it on 'Love Me Do' just for arrangements.) And then we stuck it on 'Please Please Me' and then we stuck it on 'From Me To You', and then we dropped it; it got embarrassing.[70]

And I've always loved guitars. I still have my black Rickenbacker, which used to be blond, which is the first good guitar I ever had. It's a bit hammered now. I just keep it for kicks, really. I bought it in Germany, on HP. I remember that whatever it cost, it was a hell of a lot of money to me at the time.[66]

GEORGE: When we were first in Hamburg, we'd gone to Steinways because we didn't have very good equipment. That's where John bought his Rickenbacker and at the same hire-purchase session I bought a Gibson amplifier. I've no idea what happened to that amp. It was beautiful looking, but it didn't have any balls.

My sequence of guitars was: first; my crummy little £3 10s number. Second; a Hofner President. Non-electric, but you could buy a pick-up for a few pounds that would screw on to the bottom of the finger board – which I did – which made the guitar semi-electric. (Alternatively, put the head of the guitar to some sort of cavity, a wardrobe or a cupboard or a door, anything that will vibrate, and – because sound resonates that way – it will amplify slightly. I used to play my guitar against the wardrobe.) The Hofner guitars were quite nice (especially after the little £3 10s one). They had a good range and each one came either blond or sunburst. Mine was the straight one.

I didn't have an amp to start with. The first thing I ever plugged into was John's stepfather's radiogram. It only amplified the sound a little, but it was great; except for the fact that we kept blowing out the amp or the speakers. John knew how to get into Twitchy's house when he was out, so we'd plug in and play and mess about and then blow his amp, and then we'd sneak off and have to wait a few weeks until he got it fixed.

I swapped the Hofner President with one of the Swinging Blue Jeans for my third guitar, a Hofner Club 40. Next came the Futurama, which I got at Frank Hessy's. A very bad copy of a Fender Stratocaster.

PAUL: In passing, I've never felt like I could afford a Fender. Even now there's a strange thing at the back of my mind that makes me think I can't afford a Fender. (Amazing how these things form and stay with you.) A Fender is still a bit of an exotic instrument to me and, even though I could probably afford the factory, it seems out of reach.

GEORGE: Paul came with me when I bought the Futurama. It was on the wall with all the other guitars and Paul plugged it into the amp but couldn't get any sound out of it, so he turned the amp right up. The guitar had three rocker switches and I just hit one and there was an almighty 'boom' through the amplifier and all the other guitars fell off the wall. My mother signed the hire-purchase agreement for me. That is, one pound down and the rest when they catch you.

My fifth guitar was the Gretsch I bought in 1962 from a sailor in Liverpool for £75. A black Duo-Jet. (Chet Atkins used Gretsch guitars. He always had a different Gretsch in photos on his album covers.) That was my first American guitar. It was advertised in the *Liverpool Echo*. God knows how I managed to get seventy-five quid together. It seemed like a fortune. I remember having it in my inside pocket, thinking, 'I hope nobody mugs me.'

Next, in 1964, while we were staying at the Plaza in New York for *The Ed Sullivan Show*, the Rickenbacker people came and gave me one of their twelve-string guitars. After that trip I used it a lot. It was a great sound, and in those days the only other type of twelve-string available had a great big fat neck (it would have a high action, be a bugger to get in tune and impossible to mash the strings down). The Rickenbacker had a slim neck and low action. The twelve machine heads were fitted very tidily, and in a way which made it simple to recognise which string you were tuning. The pegs for the six regular strings were positioned sideways while the pegs for the octave-extra six were placed backwards as on old Spanish guitars.

John already had a little six-string Rickenbacker, the famous blond one with the short-scaled neck that he later had painted black; so after I was given the twelve-string at the Plaza, John and I both had Rickenbackers and they became synonymous with The Beatles.

JOHN: The arm on the old one wasn't bad, but we had the Rickenbacker people to see us in New York. They gave me a new one and the neck is great. I'd like to play this make of guitar all the time. George only got his because he didn't want me to be the only one in the group with a Rickenbacker.[64]

GEORGE: I used a Stratocaster around *Rubber Soul* time, on 'Drive My Car' and those kind of things. I used it quite a lot later when I got into playing slide in the late Sixties and early Seventies. I painted it before we did the 'All You Need Is Love' TV satellite show. It was powder blue originally. The paint started flaking off immediately. We were painting everything at that time; we were painting our houses, our clothes, our cars, our shop! Everything. In those days day-glo orange and lime paints were very rare, but I discovered where to buy them – very thick rubbery stuff. I got a few different colours and painted the Strat, not very artistically because the paint was just too thick. I had also found out about cellulose paint, which came in a tube with a ball tip, so I filled in the scratch plate with that and drew on the head of the guitar with Pattie's sparkly green nail varnish.

PAUL: IT WAS NEVER AN OVERNIGHT SUCCESS.

It started in pubs; we went on to talent contests and then to working men's clubs. We played Hamburg clubs, and then we started to play town halls and night clubs, and then ballrooms. There could be as many as 2,000 people in a ballroom, so if you did a gig there the word really got round. Next up from that was theatres, and Brian took us through all these steps.

When we began to headline bills on theatres, we felt we had really arrived. The next ladder to climb was radio. It was a gentle thing; we had conquered the clubs – we'd conquered the Indra, we'd conquered the Cavern – and we had gradually became quite known, so it was, 'Well, what's left? Radio!'

We wanted to be on Brian Matthew's *Saturday Club*. This was a huge radio show, and the thing I loved about listening to it was that I could wake up after a week of school and have a lie-in. I had a radio by my bed and I would lie there until about eleven. The most delicious lie-ins of your life are those teenage lie-ins: wake up feeling great, turn the radio on and *Saturday Club* is still on for an hour. So we really wanted to be on that, and we knew that it had a huge audience.

NEIL ASPINALL: *They'd sold a lot of records for 'Love Me Do' to get to Number Seventeen, which was great for a Liverpool band – they'd made the charts! Now that The Beatles were known nationally, not just in the Northwest and Liverpool, they were being played on the radio and people everywhere were hearing them. In 1963 they started doing BBC radio shows, playing live. They did about five numbers on each show, all through 1963–1965.*

JOHN: We did a lot of tracks for *Saturday Club*, a lot of stuff we'd been doing in the Cavern or Hamburg. 'Three Cool Cats' I think we did. There's some good stuff and they were well recorded.[80]

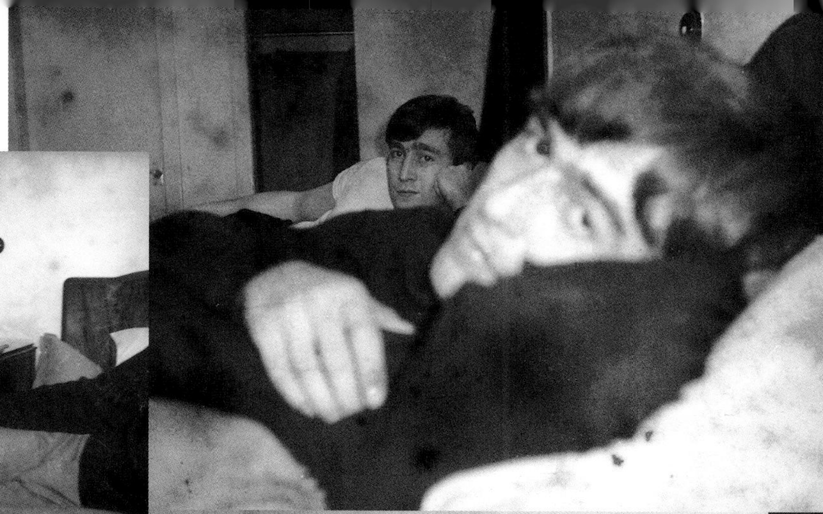

GEORGE: After the Hamburg period we were driving up and down, doing gigs at the BBC in London a lot. We got a better van and made more money and then a better van still.

RINGO: There are lots of driving stories. This is how a band gets close: in the van, going up and down the M1, freezing your balls off, fighting for the seats. A lot of madness went on in the van, but it got us together. We had a Bedford and Neil would drive. There'd be the passenger seat for one of us, and the other three – whichever three; the rest of us – would sit behind on the bench seat, which was pretty miserable.

We would go everywhere in the van and the amps and everything would fit in it with us. I remember sliding all over Scotland. It was bloody freezing in the winter.

JOHN: But we always got screams in Scotland. I suppose they haven't got much else to do up there. Touring was a relief – just to get out and break new ground. We were beginning to feel stale and cramped.[67]

RINGO: We never stopped anywhere. If we were in Elgin on a Thursday and needed to be in Portsmouth on Friday, we would just drive. We didn't know how to stop this van! If we had a day off and we were going to Liverpool from London, we would just drive.

There was only a small piece of motorway in those days, so we'd be on the A5 for hours. Some nights it was so foggy that we'd be doing one mile an hour, but we'd still keep going. We were like homing pigeons; we just had to keep getting home.

One night I remember, when it was very, very cold, the three of us on the bench seat were lying on top of each other with a bottle of whisky. When the one on top got so cold that hypothermia was setting in, it would be his turn to get on the bottom. We'd warm each other up that way; keep swigging the whisky, keep going home.

PAUL: Quite an image. People think of stardom as glamorous, and there's us freezing – lying literally on top of each other, as a Beatle sandwich.

GEORGE: There were a lot of good times in the van; all the rough-and-tumble stuff that happens. And there were some hysterical things that happened. I had a good crash once. We were coming over the Pennines, the roads were icy and and I was driving pretty quickly as we came through what turned out to be Goole in Yorkshire. Everything was fine until suddenly I went into a right-hand turn. It was a bit sharper than it looked and we went up onto the grass bank, which then sloped down to the left. The whole van tipped as we went down the embankment, at the bottom of which was a wire-mesh fence with concrete posts around a Burton's factory.

We bounced along – bump, bump, bump – knocking down all these concrete poles and finally came to a stop with Neil sitting in the front seat next to me, howling, 'Ow, ow, my arm!' The accident had ripped the filler cap off and the petrol was pouring out. We got out and had to shove T-shirts and things into the hole to try to stop the flow of petrol.

We'd started to push the van back up on the road when, out of nowhere, came, ''Allo, 'allo, 'allo, what's all this then?' It was a cop, and he booked us for crashing. A couple of months later I went to court; Brian came with me for moral support. (He did stand by his lads.) I think they banned me for three months.

RINGO: Another great van story was when George and Paul were both planning to drive the van; George got into the driving seat and Paul had the keys, and there was no way one was going to help the other. We couldn't go anywhere. We sat there for two hours. When you're touring, things can be pretty tense sometimes and the littlest thing can suddenly turn into a mountain; that was one of the great ones.

GEORGE: AS A BAND, WE WERE TIGHT. THAT WAS ONE THING TO BE SAID ABOUT US; WE WERE REALLY TIGHT, AS FRIENDS. WE COULD ARGUE A LOT AMONG OURSELVES, BUT WE WERE VERY, VERY CLOSE TO EACH OTHER, AND IN THE COMPANY OF OTHER PEOPLE OR OTHER SITUATIONS WE'D ALWAYS STICK TOGETHER.

If we were arguing, it was always about things like space: 'Who's going to sit on the spare seat?' – because everyone else had to sit on the wheel arches or the floor all the way to Scotland or somewhere. We used to get ratty with each other, pushing, protesting, 'It's *my* turn in the front.'

PAUL: There were a lot of laughs in the back of the car, just naming albums and chatting about birds and other groups' music and things. I can't remember many deep conversations. There was a lot of giggling though.

I do remember one incident: going up the motorway when the windscreen got knocked out by a pebble. Our great road manager Mal Evans was driving and he just put his hat backwards on his hand, punched the windscreen out completely, and drove on. This was winter in Britain and there was freezing fog and Mal was having to look out for the kerb all the way up to Liverpool – 200 miles.

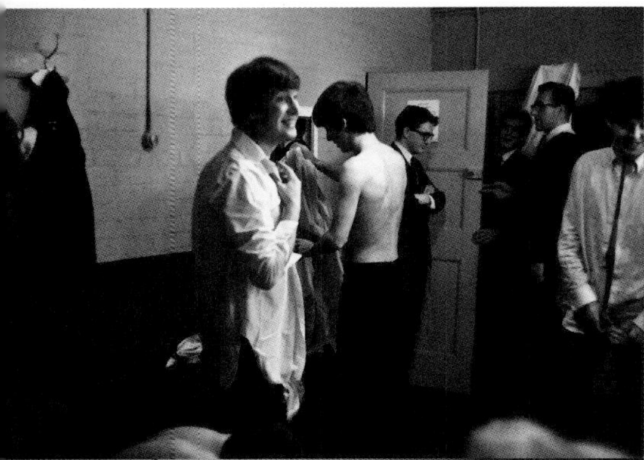

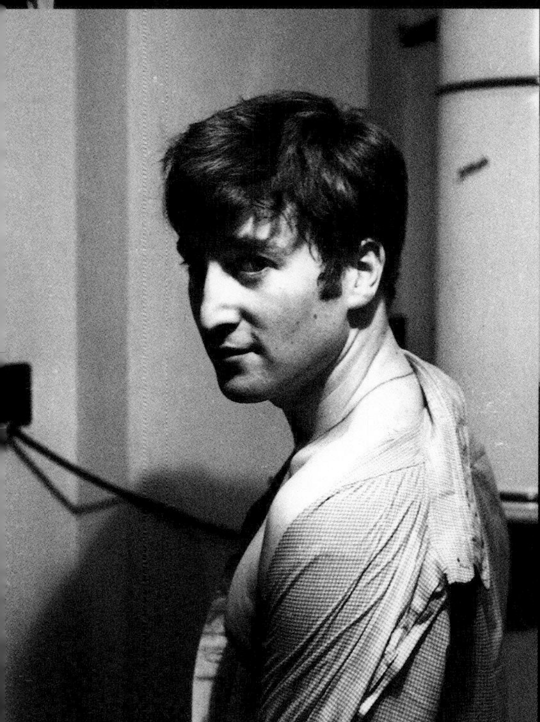
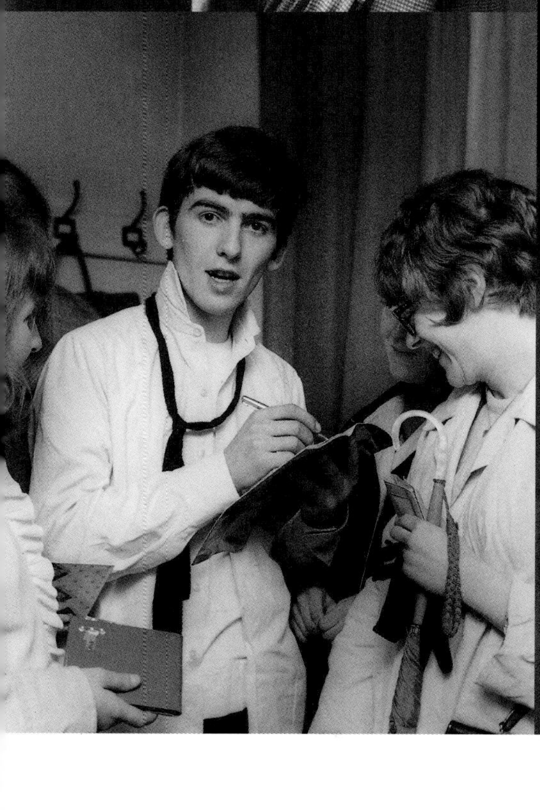

RINGO: Neil and Mal were all we ever had. Throughout our fame, we just had two guys looking after us. Mal joined us full-time in 1963. He was our bodyguard, but he was great at it because he would never hurt anyone. He was just big enough to say, 'Excuse me, let the boys through.' He was pretty strong. He could lift the bass amp on his own, which was a miracle. He should have been in the circus.

MAL EVANS: *I walked down this little street called Mathew Street that I'd never noticed before and came to this place, the Cavern Club. I'd never been inside a club, but I heard this music coming out – real rock it sounded, a bit like Elvis. So I paid my shilling and went in...*

GEORGE: Mal used to come into the Cavern. He worked as a telephone engineer around the corner and would come into the club in his lunch hour. He'd sit there among all the other people and request Elvis songs. After a while we caught on that here was this guy who always wanted Elvis songs, so we'd say, 'Well, now we'd like to do a request for Mal.' After a while he got a job there as a bouncer in the evenings.

One time Neil was sick and we needed someone to drive us to London, so we asked Mal. He was a nice bloke, and by this time we'd been chatting with him a lot. He had to take a couple of days off work to do it. Then as we were expanding with all the gigs we realised we had to get someone else to drive the van and leave Neil to look after us and our suits and all of that. It was a unanimous thought. So Mal left his job and came to work for us.

NEIL ASPINALL: *My weight went down to about eight stone on one tour, and I told Brian I needed somebody to help. That's when we got Mal Evans. We all knew Mal the bouncer, he was the 'gentle giant' – a good friend.*

*Mal started driving the van and looking after all the equipment and the stage-clothes, while I tended to look after The Beatles and the press and other people in our lives. And I had to teach Mal how to set up Ringo's drums! (Ringo has said that at first I wouldn't set up his drums. But I did.)*

PAUL:
MAL EVANS GOT SHOT BY THE LA POLICE DEPARTMENT IN 1976. IT WAS SO CRAZY, SO CRAZY. MAL WAS A BIG LOVEABLE BEAR OF A ROADIE; HE WOULD GO OVER THE TOP OCCASIONALLY, BUT WE ALL KNEW HIM AND NEVER HAD ANY PROBLEMS. THE LAPD WEREN'T SO FORTUNATE. THEY WERE JUST TOLD THAT HE WAS UPSTAIRS WITH A SHOTGUN AND SO THEY RAN UP, KICKED THE DOOR IN AND SHOT HIM. HIS GIRLFRIEND HAD TOLD THEM, 'HE'S A BIT MOODY AND HE'S GOT SOME DOWNERS.' HAD I BEEN THERE I WOULD HAVE BEEN ABLE TO SAY, 'MAL, DON'T BE SILLY.' IN FACT, ANY OF HIS FRIENDS COULD HAVE TALKED HIM OUT OF IT WITHOUT ANY SWEAT, BECAUSE HE WAS NOT A NUTTER. BUT HIS GIRLFRIEND – SHE WAS AN LA GIRL – DIDN'T KNOW HIM THAT WELL. SHE SHOULD NOT HAVE RUNG THE COPS, BUT THAT'S THE WAY IT GOES... A THUMP ON THE DOOR, 'WHERE IS HE? WHERE'S THE ASSAILANT?' BANG, BANG, BANG. THEY DON'T ASK QUESTIONS, THEY SHOOT FIRST.

MAL EVANS: *I'd never seen a drum-kit close up before. I didn't understand any of it. Neil helped me the first couple of days, but the first time I was on my own was terrible. It was a huge stage and my mind went blank. I didn't know where to put anything. I asked a drummer from another group to help me. I didn't realise each drummer likes his cymbals at a special height. He did them his own way, but they were useless to Ringo.*

*The worst of all was at the Finsbury Empire in London, when I lost John's guitar. It was one he'd had for years as well. It just disappeared. 'Where's my Jumbo?' he said. I didn't know – it's still a mystery.*

*It was great meeting all the people I'd seen on TV. I was really star-struck. I quickly realised of course that people were being nice, trying to get to know me, just to use me to get to The Beatles. I soon got to spot them a mile off.*

GEORGE: He loved his job, he was brilliant, and I often regret that he got killed. Right to this day I keep thinking, 'Mal, where are you?' If only he was out there now. He was such good fun, but he was also very helpful: he could do everything. He had a bag that he developed over the years, because it would always be: 'Mal, have you got an Elastoplast? Mal, have you got a screwdriver? Mal, have you got a bottle of this? Have you got that?' And he always had everything. If he didn't have it, he'd get it very quickly. He was one of those people who loved what he was doing and didn't have any problem about service. Everybody serves somebody in one way or another, but some people don't like the idea. Mal had no problem with it. He was very humble, but not without dignity; it was not belittling for him to do what we wanted, so he was perfect for us because that was what we needed.

PAUL: It was a saying of Mal's that: 'To serve is to rule.'

GEORGE: I remember once Mal put a guitar and some suitcases on a rack on the back of the Austin Princess held on with some bungee ropes. We were on the A1 in Yorkshire. The boot was open and I heard a noise. I remember looking out of the window and seeing the guitar, still in its case, bouncing down the road and me shouting to the driver to stop (we had about three or four different chauffeurs over all the years), but it was too late because there was a truck behind us that ran straight over it. I think it was a Gibson acoustic.

It was hard, organising all the equipment; although there wasn't much – just a drum-kit and three amplifiers. But there was still quite a lot to get in and out. Packing up, Neil would have to get the equipment, carry some out, open the van, put it in the van and then lock the van so it wouldn't get stolen; and then go back in, get the next bit and come back out, open the van, put it in, lock it again. That's why we needed an extra hand after a while; Neil had had to do everything.

Our early van became the centre of attention every time it pulled up. It was brush-painted in red and grey, and from head to foot was covered in graffiti – girls' names, and things like 'I love you John'. It looked interesting, but the moment anybody saw it they would feel free to write all over it. It also presented the problem that if anything was going to get nicked, it was obvious where it was kept. Neil always had to worry about that.

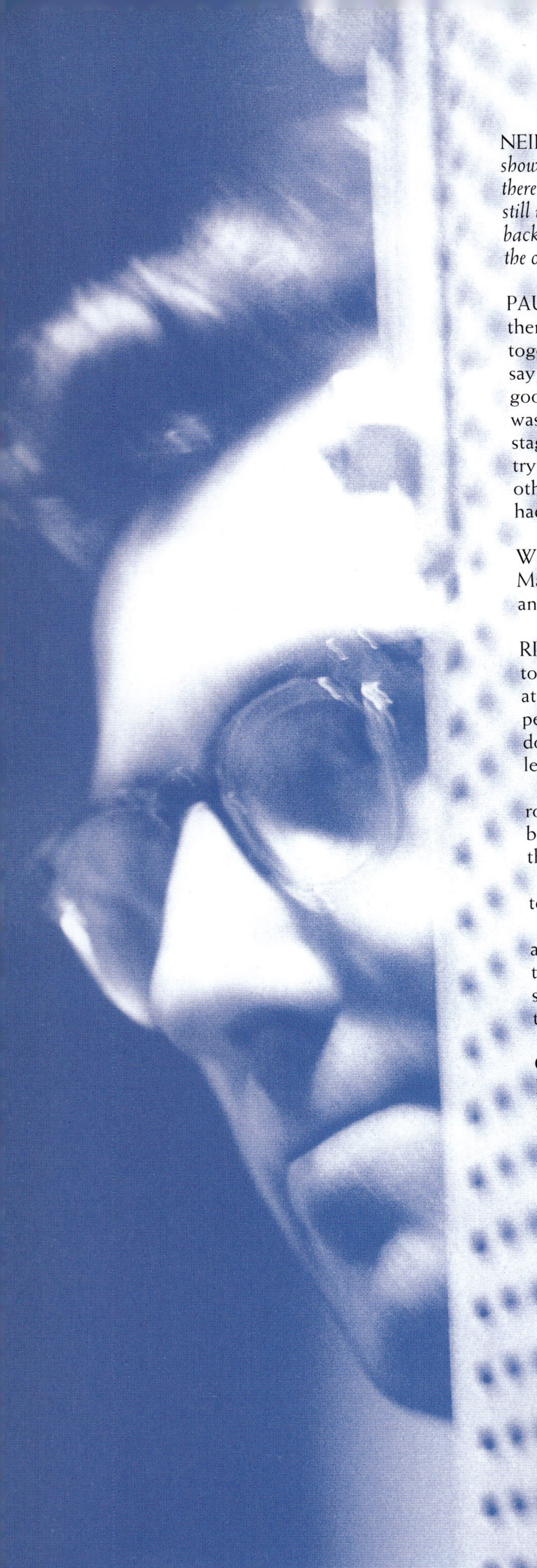

NEIL ASPINALL: *They did some funny gigs. I remember the worst show was when they played Crewe. There were only five people there. There were more of us than there were of the audience, but they still went on stage twice, and the five people stayed. When we went back there a month later, there were 700 people. (Probably including the original five.)*

PAUL: Birmingham was a hard gig. Whenever we played there, they would double book us: two places very close together, *they* thought – Wolverhampton and Birmingham, say, or Wolverhampton and Coventry. It would be quite good for us inasmuch as we'd get a double-pay night, but it was very hard. If the latter of the venues had a revolving stage, we'd have to set up while the other band was playing, trying to tune up by holding the guitar close to our ears, over the din of the other band. And when they swung the stage round we'd be praying we hadn't got all our leads caught up.

On the longer journeys we would stop at service stations such as the Watford Gap to get a nice greasy meal. Occasionally we might see Gerry Marsden and the guys or other Liverpool bands there, and we'd have a laugh and exchange jokes.

RINGO: Elgin was one of the strangest gigs we played. We'd got all the way to the outskirts of Scotland to find an L-shaped room – and we were playing at the wrong end! I have this vision of the audience all wearing wellies; farmers and country people. The bar was on one side and we were in the other, and you could tell which side was doing the business. In those days they were still laughing at us because we'd be out there in the leather and stomping. Then we got in my car and slid all the way to the next gig.

On that tour we were staying in one of those theatrical boarding-houses. The rumour went round that before we came they'd had a hunchback staying, and we all got a bit worried that we'd be having his bed. George and John went to stay in another place but Paul and I took a chance that we wouldn't catch the hunchback.

We stayed in guesthouses a lot. (We only started to stay in hotels from mid-1963.) We used to come down to London and stay at one in Russell Square.

We'd have two rooms; sharing two and two, and it could be any two. At the beginning it always used to be Paul with me, because I was the new boy and the other two didn't really want to deal with my sleeping habits, whatever they may have been. Maybe I snored, maybe my feet stank; maybe theirs did, but they knew each other. They'd been through a lot of life, I still had to get into it with them.

GEORGE: Doubling up rooms on the tours, after Pete Best left, I used to pair with John because I felt I'd been instrumental in talking them into getting Ringo into the band. I thought that rather than me hang out with Ringo, it would be best if he shared with one of them because that would integrate him better.

RINGO: Often at small hotels, when we got back from a gig there'd be nothing to eat. We would have to beg for a sandwich that had been made at four in the afternoon. They'd say, 'We've had Alma Cogan here, you know, and *she* didn't put up a fuss. Dinner's over by eight.' So we'd say, 'Hey, man, we've been playing, we just want something to eat. Couldn't you open the bar or something?' – 'Oh, no, sir, I don't think we could open the bar. We couldn't do that – you're not in London now.' The night staff were terrible – poor people.

The next morning Neil would wake us up and get us to the gig on time, do the lights and the sound. Executive material.

RINGO: First you play every free gig in the world. Then you start playing clubs and fighting for some money. Then you play dance halls, and suddenly you are in a theatre with a seated audience (that didn't last long). I loved the theatres; I still do. I love playing venues like Radio City Music Hall. I love the contact. (We lost the contact, playing stadiums. I don't really ever want to play stadiums again. It was thrilling in 1964, because we were the first to do it. Now, I don't like going to see bands if they're playing in a stadium. It's like television – you might as well wait until the video comes out.)

THE BE TLES engagements w/c 26.3.63
Tuesday March 26th
HOTEL & RESTAURANT ENTRANCE
Thursday March 28th
ABC THEATRE, EXETER
Friday March 29th
GAUMONT THEATRE, LEWISHAM Royal Court Hotel, Sloane Square, LONDON
Please remember that several reporters and photographers will be here.
Also Tony Barrow.
Saturday March 30th
GUILD HALL, PORTSMOUTH. Keppels Hotel, The Hard, Portsmouth.
Sunday March 31st
DE MONT FORT HALL, LEICESTER. Royal Court Hotel, London
Monday April 1st
Recordings for programme "SIDE BY SIDE" at the Paris Studios, Lower Regent Street, London. You will be recording two programmes from 2.30 p.m. finishing at approximately 10.30. Royal Court Hotel, London, presumably.
Azena Ballroom, SHEFFIELD.
Recording EASY BEAT BBC LONDON.
Recordings for SIDE BY SIDE, BBC, LONDON.
Stowe College
Press reception EMI.
Pavilion BUXTON.
Savoy SWANSEA.
Thank Your Lucky Stars (Recording)
Riverside Dancing Club, TENBURY WELLS WORCS.
Scene at 6.30. Granada, MANCHESTER.
Majestic LUTON.
BBC Albert Hall Concert, LONDON.
Kings Hall, STOKE.
Mersey View Pleasure Grounds FRODSHAM.
NME Poll Winners Concert WEMBLEY and
Pigalle Restaurant, LONDON.
Floral Hall, SOUTHPORT.
Majestic FINSBURY PARK.
Fairfield Ballroom, CROYDON.
Music Hall, SHREWSBURY.
Memorial Hall, NORTHWICH.
GRAND HOTEL
LEOPOLD STREET, SHEFFIELD 1
THE FREDERICK HOTELS LIMITED
(And Subsidiary Companies)
Telephone:
SHEFFIELD 21001
HOTEL RUSSELL, LONDON
GRAND HOTEL, SHEFFIELD
GRAND HOTEL, MANCHESTER
HOTEL MAJESTIC, HARROGATE
VICTORIA STATION HOTEL, NOTTINGHAM
CROWN HOTEL, SCARBOROUGH
VICTORIA HOTEL, BRADFORD
NORTH STAFFORD HOTEL, STOKE-ON-TRENT
HOTEL METROPOLE, LEEDS
KINDLY DELIVER YOUR KEY TO THE OFFICE BEFORE LEAVING THE H
DATE
REF. NO.
CODE
McCartney
Accounts are due on the day they are presented
APTS
M = Meeting/Stockrooms
B = Breakfast
FISH & CHIPS

GROSVENOR HOUSE
PARK LANE
LONDON W.1.

Telephone: Grosvenor 636
Telegrams: *Inland*: Grovh
*Overseas*: Grovh

SAW HER STANDING TH
straight in . . . . .
FROM ME TO YOU
Good Evenin etc . . .
THIS BOY,
HOLD YOUR HAND
TIL' THERE WAS YOU
Coloured gospel singer. Ve
SHE LOVES YOU
TWIST AND SHOUT.

NEIL ASPINALL: *They started touring with the Arthur Howes Agency. He put on tours playing all the Gaumont Theatres, Odeons and other cinemas around the country. The first person that they toured with was Helen Shapiro.*

*I was now suddenly supposed to be handling complicated lighting systems. It wasn't computerised as it is today. Then there were the footlights, batons at the side and overhead lights. On the first night, Johnny Clapson, the Shapiro tour manager, asked who The Beatles' road manager was. There was no answer. In the end he said, 'Well, is* anybody *with The Beatles?' I said, 'Yeah, I am,' and he said, 'Well, you're their road manager.' So then Clapson asked, 'Where's your lighting plot?' – 'What lighting plot?' – 'Look, we're on in half an hour,' he said. 'I'll do the lights for the first house. You watch what I do and after that you're on your own.'*

*That's how and when I became The Beatles' official road manager. I never thought about the title before. I'd just done everything that they didn't do. I did whatever was needed, and that's how it's always been.*

*I had to do a different lighting plot every night, because every time we got to a new theatre (depending, say, on what pantomime they'd had on at Christmas) they had differently coloured or operated lights. If we played a cinema, the projection guys – who normally showed the movie – would use the projectors as the spotlights. They would always have the spotlight on John when Paul was singing, and on Paul when John was singing. They would never get it right; but they would be up there and I would be down in the house trying to scream through a little microphone with thousands of kids screaming too. It was always chaotic. I used to try and sort them out at the beginning of the show: take them something to drink; bribe them into getting it right.*

GEORGE: The sound situation was bad. In some places all they had was one microphone. The Empire Theatre in those days had only one, coming up from the floor in the front centre of the stage. (I remember seeing The Everly Brothers there, both singing into this one mike. They'd sing 'Wake up, little Susie, wake up…' and then both reach forward with their guitars and hold them up to the big old mike and strum away. We used to have to do that.) Later, when they upgraded the sound system, venues started having two microphones and then the mikes came on moveable stands. We used to specify two mikes after a while, so that we could do our routine. It's funny, though; we never had the drums or the amplifiers miked up.

JOHN: There was always trouble with mikes on every tour. No theatre ever got it how we liked it. Even rehearsing in the afternoon first and telling them how we wanted it, it still wouldn't be right. They'd either be in the wrong position or not loud enough. They would just set it up as they would for amateur talent night. Perhaps we had a chip about them not taking our music seriously. Brian would sit up in the control room and we'd shout at him. He'd signal back that that was all they could do. It drove us mad.[67]

RINGO: The single 'Please Please Me' went to Number One in February 1963, when we were touring with Helen Shapiro. We used to open for her, then hang out until the next show; it was always a bore – then, suddenly, we had a Number One!

GEORGE: That tour was when we first did the Moss Empire circuit, the biggest gigs that there were in England at the time, other than the Palladium. We were quite happy with that – Helen Shapiro was established, she'd been around and had a bunch of hits. But when 'Please Please Me' got to Number One, all the people coming to the show were just waiting for The Beatles. It was embarrassing, because she was a very nice person.

JOHN: We'd had a Top Thirty entry with 'Love Me Do' and we really thought we were on top of the world. Then came 'Please Please Me' – and wham! We tried to make it as simple as possible. Some of the stuff we've written in the past has been a bit way-out, but we aimed this one straight at the hit parade.[63]

It was my attempt at writing a Roy Orbison song. I remember the day I wrote it. I remember the pink eiderdown over the bed, sitting in one of the bedrooms in my house on Menlove Avenue, my auntie's place. I heard Roy Orbison doing 'Only The Lonely' on the radio. I was also always intrigued by the words to a Bing Crosby song that went, 'Please lend a little ear to my pleas.' The double use of the word 'please'. So it was a combination of Roy Orbison and Bing Crosby.[80]

But what made it more exciting was that we almost abandoned it as the B side of 'Love Me Do'. We changed our minds only because we were so tired the night we did 'Love Me Do'. We'd been going over it a few times and when we came to the question of the flipside, we intended using 'Please Please Me'. Our recording manager, George Martin, thought our arrangement was fussy, so we tried to make it simpler. We were getting very tired, though, and we just couldn't seem to get it right. We are conscientious about our work and we don't like to rush things.[63]

GEORGE MARTIN: *In the first year, I had the final decision on songs (I didn't later on, but I did then), but they persuaded me to let them have their own songs on both sides of their first single. I was still thinking that we should release their recording of 'How Do You Do It'. They said, 'Couldn't we do one of our own, "Please Please Me"?' When I heard it originally, it was a Roy Orbison type of song, a very slow rocker, with a high vocal part; rather dreary, to be honest.*

PAUL: We sang it and George Martin said, 'Can we change the tempo?' We said, 'What's that?' He said, 'Make it a bit faster. Let me try it.' And he did. We thought, 'Oh, that's all right, yes.' Actually, we were a bit embarrassed that he had found a better tempo than we had.

JOHN: Eventually, George Martin suggested we do another song. 'Leave "Please Please Me" until some other time,' he said, 'and see if you can tidy it up a bit.'

In the following weeks we went over it again and again. We changed the tempo a little, we altered the words slightly and we went over the idea of featuring the harmonica, just as we'd done on 'Love Me Do'. By the time the session came around we were so happy with the result, we couldn't get it recorded fast enough.[63]

VOX

POST OFFICE TELEGRAM

____s. ____d. RECEIVED

Prefix. Time handed in. Office of Origin and Service Instructions. Words.

OFFICE STAMP LIVERPOOL 19 FE 63

C 179 3.40 REGENT TS 20/20

From BEATLES CAVERN CLUB MATHEW STREET

JOHN: THE FIRST ALBUM WAS RECORDED IN ONE LONG TWELVE-HOUR SESSION.[76]

GEORGE: THE SECOND ONE TOOK EVEN LONGER!

GEORGE MARTIN: *They came back with a speeded-up version, and I said, 'OK, let's give it a whirl,' and at the end of that session I was able to say to them, 'You've got your first Number One. Great.'*

NEIL ASPINALL: *That's where they wanted to be – Number One; but with it came the beginning of Beatlemania. They'd had a lot of madness in Liverpool, but they knew all the kids there. They didn't try to jump on you or overturn the van or rip the wing mirrors off. Suddenly this absolute craziness was going on, which was very exciting, but difficult to deal with. Now I had to organise getting in and out of theatres, instead of just being able to walk in normally.*

*Now they had BBC shows and an office, and a fan club in London – Cliff Richard had his own fan club, so that's an indication of how things were going. The first move was to get hand-out photographs made, all posed in the collarless jackets. They signed them in front of the fans; I gave them away.*

*When they performed, it was just a permanent scream. It was mainly girls, but it was a strange thing about The Beatles that there were a lot of guys there as well. They appealed to everybody.*

JOHN: A YEAR AGO, BEFORE ALL THIS HAPPENED, WE COULD ENTER AND LEAVE ANY THEATRE, STAY IN AN HOTEL, HAVE A NIGHT OUT, AND GO SHOPPING WITHOUT BEING MOBBED. THINGS WE REALLY ENJOY DOING HAVE NOW BECOME PIPE DREAMS. PERHAPS ONE DAY IT WILL ALL DIE DOWN, THEN WE CAN GO BACK TO LIVING NORMAL, PEACEFUL LIVES.[63]

PAUL: We were quite glad for a short period that people were screaming; because with some of those early gigs, we wished that someone would cover the noise we were making. The equipment was often dreadful and we weren't always too good. I can't remember where it was but one night we were very out of tune and it was fairly disastrous, but we just soldiered on.

JOHN: The worst part is getting out of the theatre. When you think you can get away safely and you've managed to get into the coach, you find that some nut has let the tyres down.[63]

GEORGE: Some of these places, the big theatres, by the time we'd had a record or two out – on the tour with Chris Montez, say – there would be girls standing outside, the early birds. We would pull up at the gig and run through them to the stage door. And if you could quickly suss out the ones who looked half decent, you could push them in through the door with you, slam it behind, and then they'd come up to the room…

RINGO: After Number One, where else is there to go? Number One was It. After that, of course, every bloody thing we did was Number One and it got strange because in a weird way we were waiting for the one that wasn't Number One. And when that happened we felt, 'Thank God that's over.' It was a lot of pressure: we had a dozen in a row that went to Number One, so the one that didn't was a real relief.

NEIL ASPINALL: *From the early recording sessions they always worked in No. 2 Studio, at Abbey Road. The control room was on a higher level. There were stairs coming down into the studio; it was a quite big, barn-like room. I know The Beatles were very nervous at first, but then I guess anybody would be at their first recording session. It was really a learning process – not just for them but for George Martin too, and they worked pretty well.*

JOHN: We were in a recording studio for the first time in our lives, and it was done in twelve hours because they wouldn't spend any more money.

That record tried to capture us live, and was the nearest thing to what we might have sounded like to the audiences in Hamburg and Liverpool. Still, you don't get that live atmosphere of the crowd stomping on the beat with you; but it's the nearest you can get to knowing what we sounded like before we became the 'clever' Beatles.[76]

One of the things is we worked without echo. When they came out, we couldn't afford one. By the time we could afford it we didn't like it, so we never used it on stage. It was a good thing, not getting echo, because we would probably have sounded like all the other groups.[63]

GEORGE MARTIN: *I had been up to the Cavern and I'd seen what they could do; I knew their repertoire, knew what they were able to perform and I said, 'Let's record every song you've got; come down to the studios and we'll just whistle through them in a day.' We started about eleven in the morning, finished about eleven at night, and recorded a complete album during that time.*

*To begin with, The Beatles didn't really have much say in recording operations. It was only after the first year that they started getting really interested in studio techniques. But they always wanted to get the thing right, so it wasn't a one-take operation. They would listen to it, and then do two or three takes until they got it. It was only later on that they were able to afford the indulgence of more time and lots of re-takes.*

RINGO: For me it is all a bit of a blur. The sessions and those times until we did the album – and that, too – are a bit of a blur.

We didn't rehearse for our first album. In my head, it was done 'live'. We did the songs through first, so they could get some sort of sound on each one; then we had to just run, run them down.

GEORGE: We were permanently on the edge. We ran through all the songs before we recorded anything. We'd play a bit and George Martin would say, 'Well, what else have you got?'

'Do You Want To Know A Secret' was 'my song' on the album. I didn't like my vocal on it. I didn't know how to sing; nobody told me how to sing: 'Listen, do da do, Do you want to know a secret? do da do, Do you promise not to tell…'

= TO A GREAT GROUP FROM A HAPPY GUV
CONGRATULATIONS ON A WONDERFUL ACHIEVEMENT =
BRIAN +

JOHN: I can't say I wrote 'Do You Want To Know A Secret' *for* George. I was in the first apartment I'd ever had that wasn't shared by fourteen other students – gals and guys at art school. I'd just married Cyn, and Brian Epstein gave us his secret little apartment that he kept in Liverpool for his sexual liaisons; separate from his home life.

So I had this thing in my head and I wrote it and gave it to George to sing.[80]

GEORGE: We might have run through 'Keep Your Hands Off My Baby' (Little Eva's follow-up to 'The Loco-Motion') by Goffin and King at that session. Sometimes we learnt songs and did them once or twice and then gave them up: like Paul at the Aintree Institute singing 'That's When Your Heartaches Begin', the Elvis record where he talks in the middle. Have you ever heard such a dumb line? – 'Love is a thing that we never can share.'

'Anna' by Arthur Alexander was on the album, too. I remember having several records by him, and John sang three or four of his songs. ('Soldier Of Love' was one; it appears on the BBC recordings.) Arthur Alexander used a peculiar drum pattern, which we tried to copy; but we couldn't quite do it, so in the end we'd invented something quite bizarre but equally original. A lot of the time we tried to copy things but wouldn't be able to, and so we'd end up with our own versions. (I'm sure that's how reggae came about. I think people were playing calypso music and listening to rock'n'roll in the Sixties and thought, 'We'll try that,' but they couldn't do it and it came out as reggae. Now we all try to play reggae and can't.)

RINGO: We started around about noon and finished at midnight, in my book, with John being really hoarse by 'Twist And Shout'. We knew the songs, because that was the act we did all over the country. That was why we could easily go into the studio and record them. The mike situation wasn't complicated either: one in front of each amp, two overheads for the drums, one for the singer and one for the bass-drum. You still never hear the bass-drum and, now I think about it, I'm not sure if it's not just a confused memory of mine that there ever was one.

GEORGE MARTIN: *I knew that 'Twist And Shout' was a real larynx-tearer and I said, 'We're not going to record that until the very end of the day, because if we record it early on, you're not going to have any voice left.' So that was the last thing we did that night. We did two takes, and after that John didn't have any voice left at all. It was good enough for the record, and it needed that linen-ripping sound.*

JOHN: The last song nearly killed me. My voice wasn't the same for a long time after; every time I swallowed, it was like sandpaper. I was always bitterly ashamed of it, because I could sing it better than that; but now it doesn't bother me. You can hear that I'm just a frantic guy doing his best.[76] We sang for twelve hours, almost non-stop. We had colds, and we were concerned how it would affect the record. At the end of the day, all we wanted to do was drink pints of milk.

Waiting to hear that LP played back was one of our most worrying experiences. We're perfectionists: if it had come out any old way, we'd have wanted to do it all over again. As it happens, we were very happy with the result.[63]

GEORGE: The LP cover was photographed with us looking over the balcony at the EMI offices in Manchester Square. It was by Angus McBean – and I've still got the suit I wore then. (I wore it in 1990 to a party. It was a Fifties party but I cheated and wore a Sixties suit. It looked as if it fitted, but I had to have the trousers open at the top.)

We went back in 1969 and did the same picture for the 'Red' and the 'Blue' albums, although we had planned it to be the *Let It Be* cover at one point.

Right up to and even through the psychedelic period, EMI was like the Civil Service. They did train all their engineers properly. They would start on tape copies, and then would become tape operators, and then assist with demo sessions, and only after they had been through all the different departments, they might be allowed to engineer a demo session, before finally becoming an engineer. Or, if suddenly there was no engineer available, a trainee might get his big break. They trained them well, but to still have to go into work in a suit and tie in 1967 was a bit silly.

PAUL: I remember being pretty nervous on most occasions in the recording studio, but very excited; a nervous excitement. It was fantastic to be in Abbey Road. I remember meeting Sir Donald Wolfit on the front steps: we were coming in, he was going out, and it struck me as something from out of the 'Just William' books – the great man! He had a coat with a big astrakhan collar – very theatrical – and great big bushy eyebrows. He looked down at us from beneath these eyebrows, rather patronisingly but benevolently, and said in a deep voice, 'Hello, how are you?'

We weren't even allowed into the control room, then. It was Us and Them. They had white shirts and ties in the control room, they were grown-ups. In the corridors and back rooms there were guys in full-length lab coats, maintenance men and engineers, and then there was us, the tradesmen. We came in through the tradesman's entrance and were helped by the lower people in the organisation to set up our stuff. That's how it was and stayed like until we became *very* famous (and even then those conditions still existed except that we were doing late-night recordings from the time of *Sgt Pepper*).

We gradually became the workmen who took over the factory. In the end, we had the run of the whole building. It would be us, the recording people on our session and a doorman. There would be nobody else there. It was amazing, just wandering around, having a smoke in the echo chamber. I think we knew the place better than the chairman of the company, because we *lived* there. I even got a house just round the corner, I loved it so much. I didn't want ever to leave.

ROY ORBISON FROM THE UNITED STATES

THE BEATLES THE HIT PARADE STARS

GEORGE: In March we toured with Tommy Roe and Chris Montez, who were supposed to share equal top billing: one of them closing the first house and one the second house for the show. Chris Montez had a big hit, 'Let's Dance', and Tommy Roe had 'Sheila'.

The Beatles were getting more and more popular – unfortunately for Tommy and Chris. Barking in London was the opening night of the tour and there was a big huddled meeting after the show because Arthur Howes, the promoter, said The Beatles had better close the first half. I think Chris Montez was closing the end of the performance and Tommy Roe the end of the first half. We said, 'No, no, Tommy and Chris close,' because they still sounded like big names to us. I remember Tommy Roe getting all uptight, saying, 'I'm contracted, and I'm going to leave if I don't close the show!'

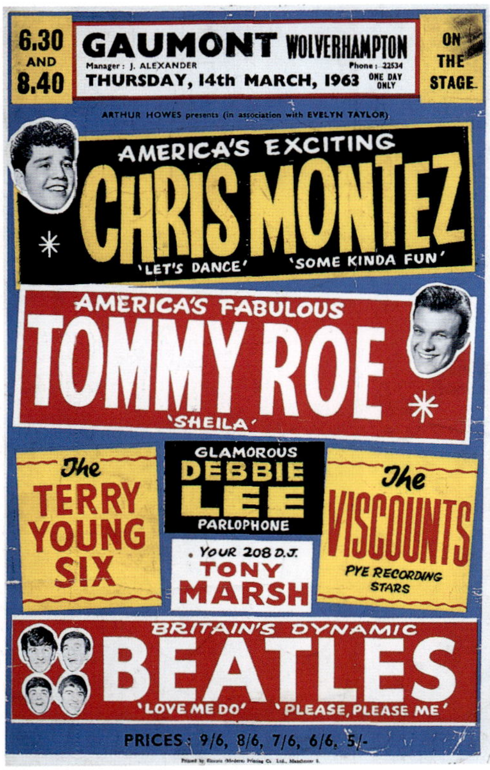


I felt sorry for Chris Montez; he was just a little Mexican bloke. He did a slow song on a chair, a Spanish tune, and the Teds were all shouting, 'Boo, fuck off.' He said, 'Oh, you don't like it, OK,' and he stopped and put down his guitar and tried something else. It was sad really, but Beatlemania was coming on; 'Please Please Me' had been a hit and 'From Me To You' was on the way.

NEIL ASPINALL: *The next big-name tour was with Roy Orbison, in May…*

PAUL: At the back of the bus Roy Orbison would be writing something like 'Pretty Woman', so our competitiveness would come out, which was good. He would play us his song, and we'd say, 'Oh, it's great, Roy. Have you just written that?' But we'd be thinking, 'We have to have something as good.' The next move was obvious – write one ourselves. And we did. It was 'From Me To You'.

JOHN: We were selling records but we were still second on the bill, and one of our first big tours was second on the bill to Roy Orbison. It was pretty hard to keep up with that man. He really put on a show; well, they all did, but Orbison had that fantastic voice.[75]

GEORGE: Even right up to when he died he was a killer, because of his songs, and he had the most incredible voice. He'd had so many hit songs and people could sit and listen to him all night. He didn't have to do anything, he didn't have to wiggle his legs, in fact he never even twitched; he was like marble. The only things that moved were his lips – even when he hit those high notes he never strained. He was quite a miracle, unique.

We soon took over as top of the bill. We had to come on after Roy. They had a trick in those theatres where they would close some of the curtains on the stage so we could set up behind them while the other bloke was still out there doing his tunes. I can't remember where his backing group was, but Roy would be out there every night and at the end he'd be singing, 'She's walking back to me, do do do do da do do-do…' And the audience would go wild. We'd be waiting there and he'd do another big encore and we'd be thinking, 'How are we going to follow this?' It was really serious stuff.

JOHN: Until now we'd never topped a bill. You can't measure success, but if you could, then the minute I knew we'd been successful was when Roy Orbison asked us if he could record two of our songs.[63]

RINGO: It was terrible, following Roy. He'd slay them and they'd scream for more. As it got near our turn, we would hide behind the curtains whispering to each other, 'Guess who's next, folks. It's your favourite rave!' But once we got on stage it was always OK.

JOHN: I'VE WRITTEN THINGS WITHOUT PAUL FOR YEARS. WE'VE ALWAYS WRITTEN TOGETHER AND SEPARATELY. ANOTHER WRITER, I DON'T NEED – GEORGE MAYBE; I'D WRITE WITH HIM.

RINGO: The real thrill, after we'd made 'Love Me Do' (even though I wasn't on it), 'Please Please Me' and 'From Me To You' – the first three singles – was that we always knew when they were going to be on the radio. Brian would say, 'Boys, it's on at twenty past seven.' We'd be in the car and stop wherever we were to listen. The other great deal was that every time a record of ours moved up the charts, we would have a celebratory dinner. You'll notice if you look at The Beatles from when we started recording, in the first eighteen months our weight went right up because we were eating all this food. That's when I discovered smoked salmon. I never ate salmon that hadn't come out of a tin until I was twenty-two; I still like it out of a tin.

GEORGE: We had four hits in 1963. Records were going gold before they had even been released – all kinds of things were happening.

The third single 'From Me To You' was really important, because that put the stamp on it. We'd had the first one, 'Love Me Do', which did well. Then they let us back in the studio and we did 'Please Please Me', then we had the album, and then 'From Me To You', the success of which assured us some fame.

JOHN: The night Paul and I wrote 'From Me To You', we were on the Helen Shapiro tour, on the coach, travelling from York to Shrewsbury. We weren't taking ourselves seriously – just fooling about on the guitar – when we began to get a good melody line, and we really started to work at it. Before that journey was over, we'd completed the lyric, everything. I think the first line was mine and we took it from there. What puzzled us was why we'd thought of a name like 'From Me To You'. It had me thinking when I picked up the *NME* to see how we were doing in the charts. Then I realised – we'd got the inspiration from reading a copy on the coach. Paul and I had been talking about one of the letters in the 'From You To Us' column.

We'd already written 'Thank You Girl' as the follow-up to 'Please Please Me'. This new number was to be the B side. We were so pleased with it, we knew we just had to make it the A side, 'Thank You Girl' the B.[63] It was far bluesier when we wrote it; today you could arrange it pretty funky.[80]

PAUL: We'd had a fair bit of practice writing over the years, though our legendary 'first one hundred' was probably in reality less than half that amount of songs. 'Please Please Me' was more John than me; I didn't have such a hand in it. 'PS I Love You' was more me. 'From Me To You' was both of us, very much together. (I remember being very pleased with the middle eight because there was a strange chord in it, and it went into a minor: 'I've got arms that long…' We thought that was a very big step.) 'She Loves You' was custom-built for the record we had to make. 'Love Me Do' was a bit of a 'two-song'.

Crediting the songs jointly to Lennon and McCartney was a decision we made very early on, because we aspired to be Rodgers and Hammerstein. The only thing we knew about songwriting was that it was done by people like them, and Lerner and Loewe. We'd heard these names and associated songwriting with them, so the two-name combination sounded interesting.

I wanted it to be 'McCartney/Lennon', but John had the stronger personality and I think he fixed things with Brian before I got there. That was John's way. I'm not saying there is anything wrong with that; I wasn't quite as skilful. He was one and a half years older than me, and at that age it meant a little more worldliness.

I remember going to a meeting and being told: 'We think you should credit the songs to "Lennon/McCartney".' I said, 'No, it can't be Lennon first, how about "McCartney/Lennon"?' They all said, '"Lennon/McCartney" sounds better; it has a better ring.' I said, 'No, "McCartney/Lennon" sounds good, too.' But I had to say, 'Oh, all right, sod it!' – although we agreed that if we ever wanted it could be changed around to make me equal. In fact, the *Please Please Me* album went out with the tracks all credited 'McCartney/Lennon'. Lennon/McCartney became a blanket term, but nowadays I occasionally fancy switching it on songs like 'Yesterday' to show who did what. So everything became Lennon/McCartney. But by now, we'd achieved our aim, we'd become like Rodgers and Hammerstein. We were now a songwriting duo.

JOHN: Paul and I saw eye to eye musically a lot in the old days. Geminis and Libras are supposed to get on well together, according to the astrologers' theories. And I suppose we worked well together because we both liked the same music.[71]

We sometimes wrote together and sometimes didn't.[70] In the early days, we'd write things separately because Paul was more advanced than I was. He was always a couple of chords ahead and his songs usually had more chords in them. His dad played the piano. He was always playing pop and jazz standards and Paul picked things up from him.[71] Some of Paul's he wrote separately. 'The One After 909' on the whatsit LP [*Let It Be*] is one that I wrote separately from Paul, when seventeen or eighteen in Liverpool.

We wrote together because we enjoyed it a lot sometimes.[70] It was the joy of being able to write, to know you could do it. There was also the bit about what they would like. The audience was always in my head: 'They'll dance to this,' and such. So most of the songs were oriented just to the dances.[74] And also they'd say, 'Well, are you going to make an album?' and we'd knock off a few songs, like a job.[70] Though I always felt that the best songs were the ones that came to you.

If you ask me to write a song for a movie or something, I can sit down and sort of make a song. I wouldn't be thrilled with it, I find it difficult to do, but I can do it. I call it craftsmanship. I've had enough years at it to put something together, but I never enjoyed that. I like it to be inspirational, from the spirit.[80]

PAUL: SOMETIMES I'VE GOT A GUITAR IN MY HANDS; SOMETIMES I'M SITTING AT A PIANO. IT DEPENDS, WHATEVER INSTRUMENT I'M ON I WRITE WITH. EVERY TIME IT'S DIFFERENT. 'ALL MY LOVING' I WROTE LIKE A BIT OF POETRY, AND PUT A SONG TO IT LATER.[65]

JOHN: Usually, one of us writes most of the song and the other helps finish it off, adding a bit of tune or a bit of lyric.[71] If I've written a song with a verse and I've had it for a couple of weeks and I don't seem to be getting any more verses, I say to Paul, and then we either both write, or he'll say, 'We'll have this, or that.'

It's a bit haphazard. There's no rules for writing. We write them anywhere, but we usually just sit down, Paul and I, with a guitar and a piano, or two guitars, or a piano and a guitar and Geoff (that's George).[65] It's all the combinations you can think of; every combination of two people writing a song. And we obviously influence each other, like groups and people do.[68]

GEORGE MARTIN: *As producer I didn't have tremendous input in their lyrics. I would tell them if I didn't think a lyric sounded good or suggest they ought to write another eight bars or so, but they tended to give me the finished songs. My work was mainly a question of contributing arrangement ideas.*

PAUL: John and I wrote 'She Loves You' together. There was a Bobby Rydell song out at the time and, as often happens, you think of one song when you write another.

We were in a van up in Newcastle. I'd planned an 'answering song' where a couple of us would sing 'She loves you...' and the other one answers, 'Yeah, yeah.' We decided that that was a crummy idea as it was, but at least we then had the idea for a song called 'She Loves You'. So we sat in the hotel bedroom for a few hours and wrote it.

We took it to George Martin and sang 'She loves you, yeah, yeah, yeah, yeah, yeeeeeaah...' with that tight little 6th-cluster we had at the end. (The 6th chord idea was George's – George Harrison's.) George Martin said, 'It's very corny, that end; it's like the old days, "De de dum dum wowww" – I would never end on a 6th.' But we said, 'It's such a great sound it doesn't matter; we've got to have it. It's the greatest harmony sound ever.'

He would often give us parameters, like, 'You mustn't double a 3rd,' or, 'It's corny to end with a 6th, and a 7th is even cornier.' We'd say, 'We like it, man; it's bluesy.' It was good that we could override a lot of his so-called professional decisions with our innocence. If anyone now asks, 'What is the sign of a great songwriter?' I say, 'If the songs sound good.' So we never listened to any rules.

My father said when he heard the song, 'Son, there's enough Americanisms around. Couldn't you sing "Yes, yes, yes" just for once?' I said, 'You don't understand, Dad, it wouldn't work.'

JOHN: Ever heard anyone from Liverpool singing 'Yes'? It's 'YEAH!'

That was the main catchphrase. We'd written the song and we needed more, so we had 'yeah, yeah, yeah', and it caught on.[67]

It was Paul's idea: instead of singing 'I love you' again, we'd have a third party. That kind of little detail is still in his work. He will write a story about someone. I'm more inclined to write about myself.[80]

PAUL: Brian Matthew, the radio presenter, reviewed 'She Loves You' in *Melody Maker*, and called it 'banal rubbish'. None of us had heard the word 'banal' and we thought, '"Banal"? What's that? Soppy? Too rebellious? What does "banal" mean?' But when the record zoomed to Number One in the *Melody Maker* chart the next week, he was on the front page disclaiming his comments: 'No, no – at first I thought maybe it was a little banal... but it grows on you.'

I'm sure we paid attention to the critics, so that's a golden memory for me. Criticism didn't really stop us and it shouldn't ever stop anyone, because critics are only the people who can't get a record deal themselves.

Later, William Mann in the *Times* wrote of the descending 'Aeolian cadence' in our song 'Not A Second Time' and the 'pandiatonic clusters' that came flying out of us at the end of 'This Boy'. We hadn't been conscious of any of that. We just did our songs in hotel rooms, whenever we had a spare moment; John and I, sitting on twin beds with guitars. He on one bed, me on another.

JOHN: Don't ask me what I think of our songs. I'm just not a good judge. I suppose the trouble is that we're so close to them. But I can't help having a quiet giggle when straight-faced critics start feeding all sorts of hidden meanings into the stuff we write. William Mann wrote the intellectual article about The Beatles. He uses a whole lot of musical terminology and he's a twit.[65] I still don't know what it means at the end, but he made us acceptable to the intellectuals. It worked and we were flattered. I wrote 'Not A Second Time' and, really, it was just chords like any other chords. To me, I was writing a Smokey Robinson or something at the time.[72]

Intellectuals have the problem of having to understand it. They can't feel anything. The only way to get an intellectual is to talk to him and then play him the record. You couldn't put a record on and just let him hear it.[73]

GEORGE: 'This Boy' was one of our three-part harmony numbers. There were a lot of harmony songs around. Harmony in Western music is natural. Paul claimed that his father taught us three-part harmony, but that's not the case from my memory. When you think back to early rock'n'roll there was always stuff like Frankie Lymon and the Teenagers, The Everly Brothers, The Platters. Everybody had harmonies. It was natural to sing a harmony sometimes – with the Everlys, it was a permanent thing.

JOHN: That was the thing about The Beatles: they never stuck to one style. They never did just blues, or just rock. We loved all music. We did 'In My Life', 'Anna' on the early things and lots of ballady things. My image was more rocky but if you look down those Beatle tracks, I'm right there with all the sentimental things, the same as Paul. I love that music just as much.[80]

PAUL: I could often be a foil to John's hardness. But it could be the other way round, too. People tend to have got it one way; but John could be very soft, and I could do the hard stuff. (One of the things I didn't like about the film *Backbeat* is that they gave 'Long Tall Sally' to the John character. I was not amused. I always sang that: me and Little Richard.)

It's funny; the myth developed that I was the melodic, soft one and John was the hard, acerbic one. There was some surface truth to that; but, in actual fact, back then one of his favourite tunes was 'Girl Of My Dreams'. That was through his mum. Another was 'Little White Lies', which was certainly not cool either, but was a good, well-crafted song. 'This Boy' was one of those.

RINGO: I used to wish that I could write songs, like the others – and I've tried, but I just can't. I can get the words all right, but whenever I think of a tune the others always say it sounds like such-a-thing, and when they point it out, I see what they mean.

PAUL: George used to write his own songs, or (as in the case of 'Do You Want To Know A Secret') we'd write one for him. All the guys had their fans – Ringo had a big following because he's a nice guy, a great drummer, so he needed a song on each album. Likewise with George; a lot of the girls were mad on him, so we always wanted to give him at least one track. Then George started to catch on: 'Why should you write my songs?' And he started writing his own.

From when George first started, he would deliver one song per album. It was an option to include George in the songwriting team. John and I had really talked about it. I remember walking up past Woolton Church with John one morning and going over the question: 'Without wanting to be too mean to George, should three of us write or would it be better to keep it simple?' We decided we'd just keep to two of us.

He wrote 'Don't Bother Me'. That was the first one and he improved from that and became very good, writing a classic like 'Something'.

GEORGE: 'Don't Bother Me' I wrote in a hotel in Bournemouth, where we were playing a summer season in 1963, as an exercise to see if I could write a song. I was sick in bed. I don't think it's a particularly good song; it mightn't be a song at all. But at least it showed me that all I

DIRECTORS E. C. SILVER (CHAIRMAN)
R. L. JAMES (MANAGING DIRECTOR)
B. S. EPSTEIN
J. T. ISHERWOOD

**NORTHERN** SONGS LIMITED

needed to do was keep on writing and maybe eventually I would write something good. I still feel now: I wish I could write something good. It's relativity. It did, however, provide me with an occupation.

I knew a little bit about writing from the others, from the privileged point of sitting in the car when a song was written or coming into being. I remember once sitting with Paul in the cinema on the corner of Rose Lane, not far from where he lived, near Penny Lane. They showed an ad for Link Furniture: 'Are you thinking of Linking?' Paul said, 'Oh, that would make a good song,' and he wrote one that went, 'Thinking of linking my life with you.'

John was always helpful. He said things like, 'When you're writing, try to finish the song immediately, because once you leave it it's going to be harder to complete,' which is true. Sometimes, anyway. He gave me a few good pointers and I did actually do some writing with him later on. I was at his house one day – this is the mid-Sixties – and he was struggling with some tunes. He had loads of bits, maybe three songs, that were unfinished, and I made suggestions and helped him to work them together so that they became one finished song, 'She Said, She Said'. The middle part of that record is a different song: 'She said, "I know what it's like to be dead," and I said, "Oh, no, no, you're wrong…"' Then it goes into the other one, 'When I was a boy…' That was a real weld. So I did things like that. I would also play him, on occasion, songs I hadn't completed. I played him a tune one day, and he said, 'Oh, well, that's not bad.' He didn't do anything at the time, but I noticed in the next song he wrote that he'd nicked the chords from it!

Writing on my own became the only way I could do it, because I started like that. Consequently, over the years, I never really wrote with anyone else and I became a bit isolated. I suppose I was a bit paranoid because I didn't have any experience of what it was like, writing with other people. It's a tricky thing. What's acceptable to one person may not be acceptable to another. You have to trust each other.

GEORGE: I'VE GOT A TAPE-RECORDER IN THE CAR, SO I CAN SING ON TO THAT AND WORK ON IT WHEN I GET HOME.[66]

JOHN: NORTHERN SONGS IS A LONG-TERM THING AND IT RESTS ON PAUL AND I WRITING SONGS UNTIL WE'RE SIXTY. UNLESS SOMETHING HAPPENS, THERE'S NOTHING TO STOP PAUL AND I WRITING HITS WHEN WE'RE OLD. IT'S SO PROFITABLE AND, ANYWAY, WE'RE GOOD FRIENDS – THERE'S NO REASON ON EARTH WHY WE SHOULD GIVE IT UP.[65]

NEIL ASPINALL: *Brian knew Dick James, who was famous for singing 'Robin Hood' on the TV series and had started his own music-publishing company. John and Paul were beginning to write their own songs and Brian played him some tapes of theirs.*

*Dick James got the rights to the single 'Please Please Me', and all the subsequent songs, too. We were all pretty naive back then and I think that The Beatles have all since regretted the deals they got into regarding song ownership.*

PAUL: We were desperate to get a deal. It's like any young novelist who just wants to be published. They would just die for Doubleday; they wouldn't care what the deal was, so long as they could say to their friends, 'Oh, my new book's coming out on Doubleday.' – 'What, the real Doubleday?' – 'Yeah!' So that's all we wanted; to be published: 'Our record's coming out on EMI.' – 'What, *the* EMI?'

But Brian did do some lousy deals and he put us into long-term slave contracts which I am still dealing with. For 'Yesterday', which I wrote totally on my own, without John's or anyone's help, I am on 15%. To this day I am only on 15% because of the deals Brian made; and that is really unjust, particularly as it has been such a smash. It is possibly the smash of this century.

But you can't be bitter. George Martin didn't get much at all off the Beatles deal and I've asked him, 'In retrospect, aren't you bitter about it, George?' He says, 'No, I had a great time. At one point during the boom I had thirteen solid weeks at Number One with you, Cilla, Billy J. Kramer, Gerry and the Pacemakers – all Brian's acts – but I didn't get a bonus or anything.' He got a straight contract fee. I said, 'You are a good man not to be bitter,' which is true; he has kept his karma together that way. So I feel the same, but I think if Brian did have a failing then it was this: he wasn't astute enough.

JOHN: I think Dick James might have carved Brian up a bit. I mean, what happened after Brian died? Dick James Music Company – a fucking multi-million music-industry company. Northern Songs, not owned by us; and NEMS, not owned by us. That was all Brian and his advisors' setting up.[72]

And Dick James has actually said that he made us! I'd like to hear Dick James's music, please. Just play me some.[70]

GEORGE: Brian didn't get very good deals on anything. For years EMI were giving us one old penny between us for every single and two shillings for every album. And there was the fiasco where Brian's father gave away the rights to The Beatles' merchandising. His father didn't have any authority to give away the rights, yet he gave them to some guy who gave them to somebody else, who gave them to somebody else.

If we'd known in 1962/3 what we know now, or even what we knew back in 1967, it would have made a real difference. We would have got better royalties if only we had known what was happening; and the royalty rate we got caused so much trouble and so many lawsuits later. We could have had a proper royalty rate.

I wasn't writing songs then, but John and Paul were. When I first started writing songs, it was presented to me like this: 'Do you want your song published?' and as John's and Paul's songs were being published by Dick James, I said, 'Yeah, OK, I'll have my songs published.' Nobody actually says, 'And when you sign this bit of paper to have your song published I am going to steal the copyright of your song from you.' So I signed this contract, thinking, 'Great, somebody's going to publish my song,' and then years later I'm saying, 'What do you mean, I don't own it?' I mean, that was terrible theft. Things like that went on all the time.

JOHN: We never talked in terms of finance. We were just a song-writing team; we started at sixteen and we decided that we'd call them 'Lennon/McCartney', and we said here's a song we wrote; because even with ones where we'd have it 90% finished, there's always something added in the studio. A song is – even now when I write a song – not complete. I can never give my song to a publisher before I've recorded it, however complete the lyrics and the tune and the arrangement are on paper, because it changes in the studio. So we just always did it like that, but nobody ever thought about the money. There was enough money for everybody in the world. Who's going to talk about money?[74]

PAUL: WE'VE GOT PEOPLE WE TRUST – OUR MANAGER. OUR RECORDING MANAGER, OUR PUBLISHER, OUR ACCOUNTANT – THEY'RE ALL TRUSTWORTHY PEOPLE, I THINK. SO WE LEAVE IT TO THEM AND I DON'T HAVE TO WORRY.[65]

RINGO: In April 1963 Paul, George and I decided to holiday together in Tenerife. Klaus Voormann's parents had a house there. They didn't have electricity, so we really felt we were Bohemians.

That was the first time I had been anywhere where there was black sand. I'd never seen the like of that before. It was a real good holiday. Paul has some great photos of us hanging out in Spanish hats, looking dramatic. That's what I love about the Spanish – they are so dramatic.

PAUL: We went out there and stayed there for a bit, but we got worried because nobody knew us in the Canaries and we were a bit put off: 'You know us? The Beatles?' And they were saying, 'No, no… don't know you.'

I got terrible sunburn: that British tan that hurts so much later. That gave me quite an uncomfortable time. And I got caught in a riptide. I was in the sea and thought, 'Now I'll swim back in,' but I realised I wasn't getting anywhere. In fact, I was getting further away.

GEORGE: I REMEMBER BLACK BEACHES. WE STAYED IN THE SUN TOO LONG AND GOT INCREDIBLY SUNBURNT; TYPICAL BRITISH. RINGO AND I BOTH HAD SUNSTROKE THE FIRST OR SECOND DAY AND I REMEMBER SHIVERING ALL NIGHT.

I drove around a lot. I was into sports cars and Klaus very kindly let me drive his Austin Healey Sprite. We've got some photographs of Paul and me in it – we took it up to the volcano. It was like the surface of the moon up there, and there were telescopes and a big observatory.

PAUL: Brian Epstein was going on holiday to Spain at the same time and he invited John along. John was a smart cookie. Brian was gay, and John saw his opportunity to impress upon Mr Epstein who was the boss of this group. I think that's why he went on holiday with Brian. And good luck to him, too – he was that kind of guy; he wanted Brian to know whom he should listen to. That was the relationship. John was very much the leader in that way, although it was never actually said.

JOHN: Cyn was having a baby and the holiday was planned, but I wasn't going to break the holiday for a baby: I just thought what a bastard I was and went. I watched Brian picking up boys, and I liked playing it a bit faggy – it's enjoyable.[70]

It was my first experience with a homosexual that I was conscious *was* a homosexual. We used to sit in a café in Torremolinos looking at all the boys and I'd say, 'Do you like that one? Do you like this one?' I was rather enjoying the experience, thinking like a writer all the time: 'I am experiencing this.' It was almost a love-affair, but not quite. It was not consummated. But it was a pretty intense relationship.[80]

But those rumours back in Liverpool! The first national press we got, the back page of the *Daily Mirror*, was me beating up Bob Wooler at Paul's twenty-first. That was the first 'Lennon hits out' story. I was so bad the next day. We had a BBC appointment; they all went down in the train, and I wouldn't come. Brian was pleading with me to go, and I was saying, 'I'm not!' – I was so afraid of nearly killing Wooler.

Bob had insinuated that me and Brian had had an affair in Spain. And I must have been frightened of the fag in me to get so angry. I was out of my mind with drink. (You know, when you get down to the point where you want to drink out of all the empty glasses; that drunk.) And Bob was saying, 'Come on, John, tell me about you and Brian – we all know.' You know when you're twenty-one, you want to be a man – if somebody said it now I wouldn't give a shit, but I was beating the shit out of him, hitting him with a big stick, and for the first time I thought, 'I can kill this guy.' I just saw it, like on a screen: if I hit him once more, that's going to be it. I really got shocked. That's when I gave up violence, because all my life I'd been like that.[72]

He sued me afterwards; I paid him £200 to settle it. That's probably the last real fight I've ever had.[67] From then on – apart from occasionally hitting my dear wife, in the early days when I was a bit crazy (I can't say I'm non-violent, because I will go crazy sometimes) – I stopped that.[72]

PAUL: So there was the homosexual thing – I'm not sure John did anything but we certainly gave him a lot of grief when he got back.

JOHN: Brian was in love with me. It's irrelevant. I mean, it's interesting and it will make a nice *Hollywood Babylon* someday about Brian Epstein's sex life, but it's irrelevant, absolutely irrelevant.[80]

GC-14112

PAUL: In September, Ringo and I went on holiday again, to Greece, with Jane Asher and Maureen.

RINGO: We went to Rhodes, Corfu and Athens. In Rhodes we wanted to see the Colossus so I asked the woman at the hotel bar, 'Excuse me, where's the Colossus?' She said, 'It's gone now, son' – that's how much we hadn't left home – 'but if you go down to the port…' which we did and we saw these two little plinths with two deers on, supposedly where the Colossus was. And I remember going around the Parthenon three times – I think to keep Jane happy – and it was really tiring.

*NEIL ASPINALL: The interesting music in the early Sixties for us was American R&B. They were very American-influenced when they went to the clubs, to find out what was happening in London, since it wasn't yet our scene. We were the new boys in town. Around then we met a guy called Andrew Oldham, whom Brian brought in as a press representative. Andrew took us out to Richmond to see a blues band: The Rolling Stones. (He went on to become their manager, of course.)*

JOHN: We made it and then the Stones came out doing things a little bit more radical than we'd done. They had their hair longer, they would be insulting on stage, which we'd given up.

We first went to see the Stones at the Crawdaddy Club in Richmond and then at another place in London. They were run by a different guy then, Giorgio Gomelsky. When we started hanging around London, the Stones were up and coming in the clubs, and we knew Giorgio through Epstein. We went down and saw them and became good friends.[74]

GEORGE: We'd been at Teddington taping *Thank Your Lucky Stars*, miming to 'From Me To You', and we went to Richmond afterwards and met them.

They were still on the club scene, stomping about, doing R&B tunes. The music they were playing was more like we'd been doing before we'd got out of our leather suits to try and get onto record labels and television. We'd calmed down by then.

RINGO: I remember standing in some sweaty room and watching them on the stage, Keith and Brian – wow! I knew then that the Stones were great. They just had *presence*. (And, of course, we could tell – we'd had five weeks in the business; we knew all about it!)

We talked to them. I don't know what about and I don't know if we ended up backstage.

PAUL: Mick tells the tale of seeing us there with long suede coats that we'd picked up in Hamburg, coats that no one could get in England. He thought, 'Right – I want to be in the music business; I want one of those coats.'

JOHN: I remember Brian Jones came up and said, 'Are you playing a harmonica or a harp on "Love Me Do"?' because he knew I'd got this bottom note. I said, 'A harmonica with a button,' which wasn't really funky-blues enough; but you couldn't get 'Hey! Baby' licks on a blues harp and we were also doing 'Hey! Baby' by Bruce Channel.[74]

*NEIL ASPINALL: The Stones that night were OK – like any band down the Cavern. They could do their stuff and that was all you needed to do. A lot of people couldn't.*

*I remember Ian Stewart was playing with them on piano and later I couldn't understand why he wasn't in any of the publicity photographs. He still seemed to be around, on the piano, but in another way he wasn't in the band at all. I suppose that's the way it worked best for them.*

PAUL: John and I were walking down Charing Cross Road one day. We used to hang out there because it was where all the guitar shops were; that was our Mecca. If we had nothing to do for an afternoon, we'd go down there window-shopping. I remember seeing Mick and Keith in a taxi and shouting, 'Hey, Mick – give us a lift!' We jumped in; they were on their way to the recording studio and Mick said, 'Here, you got any songs we could have? We've got a contract with Decca.' We thought, 'Hmmm.' We did have one we'd written for Ringo, 'I Wanna Be Your Man'.

Ringo always used to do a song in the show. Back then he had 'Boys'. It was a little embarrassing because it went, 'I'm talking about boys – yeah, yeah – boys.' It was a Shirelles hit and they were girls singing it, but we never thought we should call it 'Girls', just because Ringo was a boy. We just sang it the way they'd sung it and never considered any implications. So we tried to write something else for Ringo, something *like* 'Boys', and we came up with 'I Wanna Be Your Man' – a Bo Diddley kind of thing. I said to Mick, 'Well, Ringo's got this track on our album, but it won't be a single and it might suit you guys.' I knew that the Stones did 'Not Fade Away' and Bo Diddley numbers, and that Mick was into the maracas, from when we'd seen them down at the Crawdaddy. So we went to the studio with them.

JOHN: The story on 'I Wanna Be Your Man' was that they needed a record. They'd put out 'Come On' by Chuck Berry and needed a quick follow-up. We met Andrew Oldham, who used to work for Epstein then had gone to the Stones and probably got them off Giorgio Gomelsky. He came to us and said, 'Have you got a song for them?' And we said, 'Sure,' because we didn't really want it ourselves.

We went in and I remember teaching it to them.[74] We played it roughly and they said, 'Yeah, OK, that's our style.' So Paul and I just went off in the corner of the room and finished the song while they were all still there, talking. We came back and that's how Mick and Keith got inspired to write: 'Jesus, look at that. They just went in the corner and wrote it and came back!' Right in front of their eyes we did it.[80]

We used to write in the early days, when we had more time or seemed to, for other people. We thought we had some to spare. We wrote one for Cliff and *we* did it.[66]

PAUL: The idea of our being rivals with The Rolling Stones was newspaper talk. It was natural that we would *seem* to be rivals, but in fact George got them their recording contract. He was at a party with Dick Rowe, the man famous for having turned The Beatles down for Decca.

GEORGE: There was a big showcase, at the Liverpool Philharmonic Hall. The Beatles had become famous, and Gerry and a few others had had success and everybody thought, 'Bloody hell!' and was looking up to Liverpool. Nobody had *ever* played the Philharmonic – they wouldn't let you *in*, let alone do a rock concert. But suddenly every group in Liverpool was there – even ones that weren't groups before. (Groups were forming right, left and centre to try to cash in on Liverpool's supposedly swinging scene.)

Anyway, I remember meeting some executives from London, one of whom must have been Dick Rowe. He said, 'You'll tell us who the good groups are, will you?' And I said, 'I don't know about that, but you want to get The Rolling Stones.'

JOHN: WE DON'T THINK THERE IS SUCH A THING AS THE MERSEY SOUND. THAT'S JUST SOMETHING JOURNALISTS COOKED UP, A NAME. IT JUST SO HAPPENED WE CAME FROM LIVERPOOL AND THEY LOOKED FOR THE NEAREST RIVER AND NAMED IT. THE ONLY THING IS THAT WE WRITE OUR OWN SONGS.[64]

JOHN: We hung around with the Stones in two separate periods. The first was initially, when they were still playing in the clubs, and the later period was when we were both riding high and there was a discotheque scene in London. We were like kings of the jungle then, and we were very close to the Stones. I don't know how close the others were; I spent a lot of time with Brian and Mick and I admired them.[74]

RINGO: When we came down to London it was a little like Liverpool, because most of the bands had come from the North and we'd all jammed together. We'd all hang out at each other's places. We'd hang out with The Animals and the Stones and some jazz guys that we'd meet in clubs. There were good clubs: the Bag O'Nails and places like that.

(One odd thing: when we first started going to clubs in London we found people would be kissing you on the cheek. That was very weird for me, coming from up North. We shake hands up there; that's the manly thing to do. I soon got into it, but I remember being shocked at first. Brian Morris, who used to run the Ad Lib, went to give me a kiss on the cheek and I was mortified: 'Oh, my goodness!' But that was just the London way.)

JOHN: WE WERE THE FIRST WORKING-CLASS SINGERS THAT STAYED WORKING CLASS AND PRONOUNCED IT AND DIDN'T TRY AND CHANGE OUR ACCENTS, WHICH IN ENGLAND WERE LOOKED DOWN UPON. THE ONLY CHANGE WAS OUR IMAGE.[75]

JOHN: There have been offers of a spot on the Palladium show, but we don't feel that we are ready. We have seen others go and be torn to pieces.[63]

GEORGE: In October, the big one was *Sunday Night at the London Palladium*. That show had the biggest stars from America who were in England, and the biggest stars in England. We felt comfortable on the show. I think we had enough cockiness going, and we'd had enough success. We were always a little nervous before we went up each step of the ladder, but there was always that confidence. That was the good thing about being four together: we were able to share the experience.

RINGO: Going on the Palladium was amazing for me because, years and years before, the Eddie Clayton group and I would rehearse in the living room in our house and my mother's best friend, Annie Maguire, would always say, 'See you on the Palladium, son. See your name in lights.' So I always wanted to play there, to get on that roundabout stage.

There was nothing bigger in the world than making it to the Palladium. I'd say, 'Yeah, sure, Annie, that's where we're going to go.' And we played *Sunday Night at the London Palladium*, and we were on the roundabout and it was *dynamite*. Anyone who knew you would say, 'Fucking hell, hey, look at this!' – we would of ourselves.

Before the show I was so nervous with craziness and tension that I spewed up into a bucket; just like those old showbiz stories – I spewed up and went on stage. Even today, when the intro is playing I have to run on stage. Once I'm on, I'm OK. I often think I'd like to be like Frank Sinatra and saunter on and go, 'Hi.' But perhaps while he's sauntering his mind is running.

GEORGE:

TO GET ON THE PALLADIUM AND ALL THOSE PLACES WE WORE THE SUITS AND WE PLAYED THEIR GAME, BUT A LOT OF THE TIME WE WERE THINKING, 'HA, WE'LL SHOW THESE PEOPLE.'

RINGO: We came through showbusiness. Bands don't have to do that now – they can come through rock'n'roll. We had to go through the Shirley Bassey school, that was our battle. We could never have done the Palladium unless we'd have put the suits on. The real change of our clothes and our attitude was through our musical progression.

In your twenties you're just rolling, you feel that anything is possible; there's no obstacles. If they are in your way, you're determined just to knock them down.

GEORGE: At the time, there was a clique of people who were the stars and they were all basically conformists; the ones who played the game, the usual onslaught of the uninspired. If you look at the list of people who appeared on these things, it reads like the Grade or the Delfont organisation (the big London agencies); it was all their gang.

Early on, we were told by many a London band that it's all khaziland ten miles north of Watford. So the first thing we did on 'making it' was to give two fingers to all those bands who started out with a much better chance than us because they *were* from London.

It's typical even now that record companies don't know anything about trends or talent. All they know is the fear of signing up somebody who's a flop or not signing up somebody who's a hit. We were told all the time: 'You'll never do anything, you Northern bastards.' It was that kind of attitude. So although we didn't openly say, 'Fuck you!' it was basically our thing: 'We'll show these fuckers.' And we walked right through London, the Palladium, and kept on going through Ed Sullivan and on to Hong Kong and the world.

It was the same at school: my teachers expected nothing of me and didn't have it in them to be able to give me anything. My headmaster wrote on my school-leaving testimonial, 'I can't tell you what his work has been like because he hasn't done any. Has taken part in no school activity whatsoever.' Thanks a lot, pal, that'll really get me a job, won't it! So when Paul pulled out of a Ford showroom a couple of years later having bought a brand new Ford Classic and his old headmaster was standing there, Paul looked at him like, 'Ha ha, yes, it *is* me and I *do* have my own Ford Classic.' It was 'fuck you'. We made it in spite of him, in spite of the teachers, of Dick Rowe, of EMI (they didn't sign us up, either). We were hanging in there by the skin of our teeth, with no money or anything, and just got a bit of luck with George Martin. And we might have believed the crap, too – if it wasn't for the inner determination that we always had, that I always felt; a kind of assurance within that something was going to happen.

But that's the thing, as anybody knows who's had the experience of being down and being downtrodden (which we have, as working-class Liverpool lads), then making it big and seeing everybody brown-nosing you: everybody loves a winner, but when you lose, you lose alone.

JOHN: The class thing is just as snobby as it ever was. People like us can break through a little – but only a little. Once, we went into a restaurant and nearly got thrown out for looking like we looked, until they saw who it was: 'What do you want?' the head waiter said. 'We've come to bloody eat, that's what we want,' we said. Then the owner spotted us and said, 'Ah, a table, sir, over here, sir.' It took me back to when I was nineteen and I couldn't get anywhere without being stared at or remarked about. It's only since I've been a Beatle that people have said, 'Oh, wonderful, come in, come in,' and I've forgotten a bit about what they're really thinking. They see the shining star, but when there's no glow about you, they see only the clothes and the haircut again.

We weren't as open and as truthful when we didn't have the power to be. We had to take it easy. We had to shorten our hair to leave Liverpool. We had to wear suits to get on TV. We had to compromise. We had to get hooked to get in, and then get a bit of power and say, '*This* is what we're like.' We had to falsify a bit, even if we didn't realise it at the time.[66]

Ref. 4410 H.P.W. 55042

**Inter-Departmental MEMORANDUM** **Date** May 28th. 1963

**To** Miss E. Harwood. C/S9/JLS.

**Re:** THE BEATLES.

Thank you for your reminder regarding the Beatles' Contract.

We should like to exercise the Option at the same time increasing their royalty to 2d.

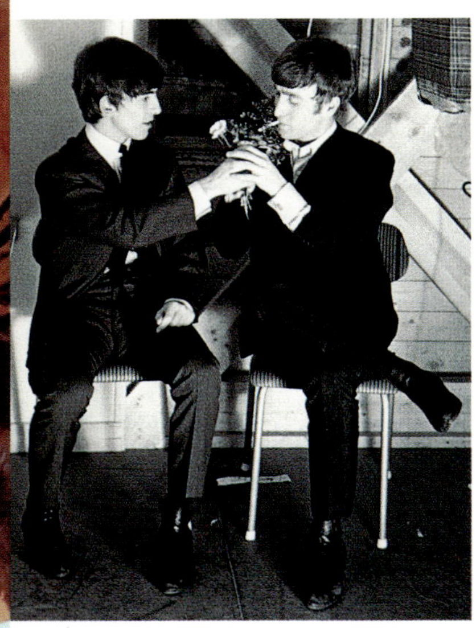

RINGO: We went to Sweden that October for a week, to do some shows. The hotel was a lot of fun. There was a memorable day when Paul dressed up in disguise; he had a camera and ran round the restaurants going, 'How do you do, Sweden?' He'd say some crazy mouthful and take photos of everybody and no one would recognise him, which we thought was pretty hip. He was handing out strange business cards that other people had given him – it was one of the grooves of life.

NEIL ASPINALL: *The popularity was escalating madly day by day. I can remember waiting outside stage doors when Eddie Cochran and Gene Vincent played in Liverpool and there'd be a lot of girls there, screaming and going wild – but never on the scale of Beatlemania. There were 10,000 people in London Airport when we came back from Sweden. It was just bigger. It began in 1963 but it hadn't yet reached its peak.*

RINGO: We'd started to fly really just that year. The first time we took a plane together as a group, with Brian Epstein, from Liverpool to London, the seat George Harrison was sitting in was a window seat, and the window opened... He was screaming; very strange.

We were flying from London to Glasgow once and there were only three seats left on the plane and in my naivety I said, 'I'll stand.' – 'I'm afraid you can't do that Mr Starr...'

# Royal Performance

## in the presence of Her Majesty The Queen Mother on the Evening of Monday November 4th 1963 at The Prince of Wales Theatre, London.

JOHN: FOR OUR LAST NUMBER I'D LIKE TO ASK YOUR HELP. THE PEOPLE IN THE CHEAPER SEATS CLAP YOUR HANDS, AND THE REST OF YOU IF YOU'D JUST RATTLE YOUR JEWELLERY. WE'D LIKE TO SING A SONG CALLED 'TWIST AND SHOUT'.[63]

NEIL ASPINALL: *To them, the show was just another way of plugging the records. Other people on the show reacted to The Beatles very well; they could spot a success when they saw one. Everybody wanted to be The Beatles' friend. That's showbusiness. I've always found it very transient. You meet people when you're doing a gig and you might not meet them again for another six months or a year.*

JOHN: We have met some new people since we've become famous, but we've never been able to stand them for more than two days. Some hang on a bit longer, perhaps a few weeks, but that's all. Most people don't get across to us.[67] We can't go around with anybody for a long time unless they are a friend, because we're so closely knit.[64] We talk in code to each other. We always did when we had strangers around us…

PAUL: If there was someone disastrous in the dressing room (because, occasionally, someone would get in who was a right pain and we didn't have time for all of that) we would have little signs. We'd say 'Mal…' and yawn, and that would be the sign to get rid of them. It was a very 'in' scene.

RINGO: A lot of established stars loved us; they really did. Shirley Bassey was a big star in those days and she was always at the gigs. Alma Cogan was always throwing parties and inviting us. I don't remember too many artists of the day putting us down – except for Noël Coward, who put his foot in it with his 'no talent' remark. We got him back later, when Brian came to us and said, 'Noël Coward is downstairs and he wants to say "hi".' – 'Fuck off!' We wouldn't see him. I mean, 'Sod off, Noël.'

PAUL: The fame really started from when we played the Palladium. Then we were asked to do the Royal Command Performance and we met the Queen Mother, and she was clapping.

NEIL ASPINALL: *They took off like a rocket. I remember the Royal Command Performance; they were very, very nervous because they weren't used to that kind of audience. This wasn't the Cavern; this was a big charity show and everybody had paid a lot of money to attend. It was a completely different set of people sitting in judgement.*

GEORGE: John did the line about 'rattle your jewellery' because the audience were all supposedly rich. I think he'd spent a bit of time thinking of what he could say. I don't think it was spontaneous. John also overdid the bowing as a joke, because we never used to like the idea of bowing; such a 'showbiz' thing.

JOHN: We had a few jokes in that one because people weren't screaming so they could hear what we were saying.[64]

We managed to refuse all sorts of things that people don't know about. We did the Royal Variety Show, and we were asked discreetly to do it every year after that, but we always said, 'Stuff it.' So every year there was a story in the newspapers: 'WHY NO BEATLES FOR THE QUEEN?' which was pretty funny, because they didn't know we'd refused. That show's a bad gig, anyway. Everybody's very nervous and uptight and nobody performs well. The time we did do it, I cracked a joke on stage. I was fantastically nervous, but I wanted to say something to rebel a bit, and that was the best I could do.[70]

PAUL: The Queen Mother said, 'Where are you playing tomorrow night?' I said, 'Slough.' And she said, 'Oh, that's just near us.'

RINGO: Marlene Dietrich was also on. I met her and I remember staring at her legs – which were great – as she slouched against a chair. I'm a leg-man: 'Look at those pins!'

NEIL ASPINALL: *On 14th December there was a performance at the Wimbledon Palais for the Southern Area Fan Club Convention. All 3,000 fans present got to shake hands with The Beatles – when they weren't bombarding them with jelly babies.*

JOHN: Somebody once asked what the kids had sent us and we said, 'Things like jelly babies.' 'But,' I said, 'George ate them.' And the next day I started getting jelly babies with a note saying, 'Don't give George any.' And George got some saying, 'Here's some for you, George; you don't need John's.' And then it went mad; they started throwing them all over the stage. Finally we got it round that we don't like them any more.[64]

RINGO: I remember we were in a cage at that gig, because it got so crazy. It was like being in a zoo, on stage! It felt dangerous. The kids were out of hand. It was the first time I felt that if they got near us we would be ripped apart.

NEIL ASPINALL: *Halfway through, George said, 'I'm not doing this,' and he packed up, went to the stage door and began looking for a cab.*

*I ran after him and said, 'What are you doing? You can't walk out, we've got to finish.' And then John turned up with his guitar. I said, 'What are you doing?' and he said, 'Well, if he's leaving, I'm leaving.'*

*But they did finish the gig and they shook hands with all the fans – about 10,000 of them, actually, because they kept going back to the end of the queue and coming round again.*

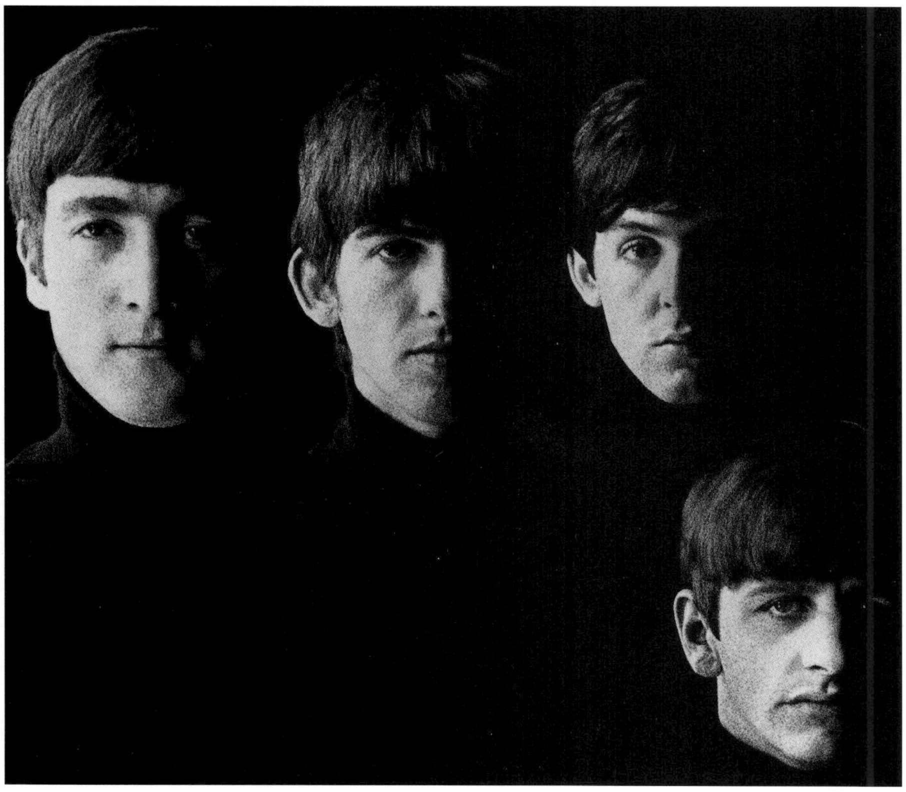

GEORGE MARTIN: *The first album was really a recital of their repertoire. We weren't thinking in terms of an album being an entity in itself back then. We would record singles, and the ones that weren't issued as singles would be put onto an album – which is how the second album,* With The Beatles, *was put together. It was just a collection of their songs, and one or two other people's songs as well.*

RINGO: The cover songs recorded for *With The Beatles* were chosen by whoever liked them. It was interesting that when I joined The Beatles we didn't really know each other (the other three knew each other, of course), but if you looked at each of our record collections, the four of us had virtually the same records. We all had The Miracles, we all had Barret Strong and people like that. I suppose that helped us gel as musicians, and as a group.

PAUL: We were all very interested in American music, much more so than in British. Ringo arrived in the band knowing more blues music. Coming from the Dingle, by the river, he'd known plenty of blokes in the Merchant Navy (that was a way for kids to get out of Liverpool, to places like New Orleans and New York) who would pick up a lot of blues records. It was Ringo who introduced us to old country-and-western; Jimmie Rodgers and those kind of people. Ringo had quite a good collection of that. But, as far as Elvis and other such music was concerned, our tastes were pretty much in common, each of us having slightly different leanings as well, which made life interesting.

GEORGE: The second album was slightly better than the first, inasmuch as we spent more time on it, and there were more original songs. We did 'Money' for that album, and other cover versions: 'Please Mr Postman', 'You Really Got A Hold On Me' and 'Devil In Her Heart' (an obscure American song by The Donays).

Because there were a lot of record companies in America, lots of records seemed only to be distributed on a local basis. It was very regional; some were lucky enough to get distributed nationwide and others weren't. However, many of the small companies were affiliated with major labels that had distribution in the UK, so some obscure American records ended up being sold in the UK but unknown in America. There are some incredible R&B records from America that I find most Americans have never heard of.

Brian had had a policy at NEMS of buying at least one copy of every record that was released. If it sold, he'd order another one, or five or whatever. Consequently he had records that weren't hits in Britain, weren't even hits in America. Before going to a gig we'd meet in the record store, after it had shut, and we'd search the racks like ferrets to see what new ones were there. That's where we found artists like Arthur Alexander and Ritchie Barrett ('Some Other Guy' was a great song), and records like James Ray's 'If You Gotta Make A Fool Of Somebody'. These were songs which we used to perform in the clubs in the early days, and which many British bands later started recording. 'Devil In Her Heart' and Barrett Strong's 'Money' were records that we'd picked up and played in the shop and thought were interesting.

I sang 'Roll Over Beethoven' for *With The Beatles* – it was a song I liked. I had the Chuck Berry record and I used to sing it in the clubs. I also wrote my first song, 'Don't Bother Me', for the album.

GEORGE MARTIN: *In those days, the boys tended to rehearse for the recording as we did it. I would meet up with them, go through the material, and say, 'OK, what's the next one we're doing?' And we'd go in and rehearse a song and record it. It was like a workshop.*

JOHN: We always record them exactly as we can play them. Even if we do put things on top, the basic thing we sing on a record we do live. We play and sing at the same time on the record, so if we can't do it there, we don't do it.[64]

The first set of tricks on the records was double-tracking on the second album. We discovered that, or it was told to us, 'You can do this,' and that really set the ball rolling. We double-tracked ourselves off the album.

The first [album] we did just as a 'group'; we went in and played and they put it on tape and we went. They remixed it, they did everything to it.[70]

GEORGE: The album cover for *With The Beatles* became one of the most copied designs of the decade. Robert Freeman took the cover picture. We showed him the pictures Astrid and Jürgen had taken in Hamburg and said, 'Can't you do it like this?' We did the photo session in a room with a piece of black background.

That cover was the beginning of us being actively involved in The Beatles' artwork. The *Please Please Me* album cover is crap; but at that time it hadn't mattered. We hadn't even thought it was lousy, probably because we were so pleased to be on a record. *With The Beatles* was the first one where we thought, 'Hey, let's get artistic.'

NEIL ASPINALL: *John lived upstairs from Robert Freeman when he moved down to London. Robert had just got out of art school, and John got him doing the album cover. They all told him the sort of effect that they wanted and he achieved it very well. From then on, they were involved with all aspects of album artwork.*

17th December, 1963.
C/I/SB

MR. R. DAWES

THE BEATLES

I hear so many different stories about how the Beatles came to E.M.I. that I thought I ought to set down on paper the true facts.

a) A Beatles Polydor recording was submitted by Brian Epstein to Mr. R.N. White.

b) Mr. R.N. White submitted this disc to Mr. Ridley and to Mr. Newell. Both turned it down on the basis that it sounded like a bad recording of The Shadows - and apparently it did!

c) Epstein then took the Polydor disc to Decca. Their "pop" A. & R. Manager, Dick Rowe, was in America, so his deputy decided to give theBeatles a test, and in fact did so.

d) Dick Rowe returned from America and the test recording was played to him. His reactinn was that electric guitars were now 'old hat' and he was not interested in the Beatles.

e) A depressed Brian Epstein then sent to our private recording department in the Oxford Street Store a tape of some of the Beatles own compositions which he wanted transferred to disc.

f) The engineer at Oxford Street was quite impressed with some of the compositions and referred them to Syd Colman.

g) Colman then phoned George Martin, said he thought he ought to hear the tape, and Martin agreed.

h) Brian Epstein then took the tape to George who agreed to give the Beatles a recording test - Martin took the test himself - was impressed with what he heard, signed them to a contract and the rest is public knowledge.

L.G. WOOD
E.M.I. RECORDS LTD.

RINGO: In 1963 the attitude of my whole family changed. They treated me like a different person.

One absolutely clear vision I had was round at my auntie's, where I'd been a thousand times before. We were having a cup of tea one night and somebody knocked the coffee table and my tea spilt into my saucer. Everyone's reaction was, 'He can't have that. We have to tidy up.' That would never have happened before. I thought then, 'Things are changing.' It was absolutely an arrow in the brain.

SUDDENLY I WAS 'ONE OF THOSE', EVEN WITHIN MY FAMILY, AND IT WAS VERY DIFFICULT TO GET USED TO. I'D GROWN UP AND LIVED WITH THESE PEOPLE AND NOW I FOUND MYSELF IN WEIRDLAND.

GEORGE: My family changed, but in a nice way. They were so knocked out with the whole idea of what was happening. Anybody would be. Everybody likes success, but when it came on *that* scale it was ridiculous. They loved it.

My mother was a nice person, but she was naive; as we all were in Liverpool in those days. She used to write to anybody who'd written to us, answering the fan mail. She'd answer letters from people saying, 'Dear Mr Harrison, can you give us one of Paul McCartney's toenails?' Still, to this day, people come up to me brandishing letters that my mother once wrote to them. Even back when I was a kid, she had pen-pals, people who lived in Northumberland or New Zealand or somewhere, people she'd never met: just writing and sending photographs to each other.

RINGO: Home and family were the two things I didn't want to change, because it had all changed 'out there' and we were no longer really sure who our friends were, unless we'd had them before the fame. The guys and the girls I used to hang about with I could trust. But once we'd become big and famous, we soon learnt that people were with us only because of the vague notoriety of being 'a Beatle'. And when this happened in the family, it was quite a blow. I didn't know what to do about it; I couldn't stand up and say, 'Treat me like you used to,' because that would be acting 'big time'.

The other thing that happens when you become famous is that people start to think you know something. They all want to know what you think about this and that, and I would blah on – as a 22/23-year-old – as if suddenly I *knew*. I could talk about anything, I knew exactly how the country should be run, and why and how this should happen; suddenly I was a blaher: 'Yeah, Mr Blah here, what do you want to know?' It was so crazy. I remember endless discussions that went on for days and days – nights and days, actually, discussing the world, discussing music. Suddenly people give you all this credit! But we weren't any different; we'd just had a couple of Number Ones and millions loved us.

I had no schooling before I joined The Beatles and no schooling after The Beatles. Life is a great education.

PAUL: We're constantly being asked all sorts of very profound questions. But we're not very profound people. People say, 'What do you think of the H-bomb, of religion, of fan worship?' But we didn't really start thinking about these things until people asked us. And even then we didn't get much time to consider them. What do I think of the H-bomb? Well, here's an answer with the full weight of five O levels and one A level behind it: I don't agree with it.[64]

GEORGE: 'Let's get our kicks today, for tomorrow we die, man' – that's rot! Some people are like that; thick people blowing up the world. I'm interested in what will happen.[66]

NEIL ASPINALL: *We all gradually moved to London. Until the move they would keep going home and still play the leftover dates at the Cavern and whatever, but it very quickly became far more practical to live in London than in Liverpool. All the families were very proud of what everybody had done but I think they may have felt they'd lost them a bit once they moved away. I think Mal Evans and I were the last ones to get a flat, because we couldn't afford it. Eventually they had to get us a flat, because staying in hotels, as we did, was even more expensive.*

JOHN: When I left Liverpool with the group, a lot of Liverpool people dropped us and said, 'Now you've let us down.' It was the same in England. When we left England to go to America we lost a lot of fans. They begin to feel as though they own you, and the people in Liverpool did, and did until we decided to leave. A lot of people dropped us but, of course, we got a whole pile more; a different audience.[71]

RINGO: By the end of 1963, it was impossible to go home. And if you are in our business, you go to London. The recordings are there, the places to be seen are there, where it's happening is there; it's just a natural move.

George and I started out sharing an apartment in Green Street, Park Lane. £45 a week it cost – a fortune! John was living with Cynthia. (That's when they finally told me they were married – they'd kept it a secret in case I told somebody. They didn't really trust me, you know. Just joking!)

We were fed by Harry and Carol Finegold, who lived below us. We didn't know how to look after ourselves: we'd been living with our parents; they had done the cooking, and the tea was always ready. Now, suddenly, we had our own place in London. We'd go to the Saddle Room, a club where Prince Philip was a member. They used to keep a horse and coach outside so you'd often see two drunken little Beatles in the back of this coach being taken home up Park Lane. Clip clop. For two shit-kickers from Liverpool, this was far-out: 'Let's take the carriage!'

We met a lot of people as well. Phil Spector was one I was thrilled to meet. The DJ Tony Hall also lived on Green Street and when he had Phil and the Ronettes staying with him, George and I went over to meet them.

GEORGE: We had been living in hotels in London for so long that we decided we needed a flat. John got his first, because he was married; Ringo and I used to stay in the Hotel President in Russell Square, then we moved into the flat. It was such a buzz because we'd been brought up in little two-up two-down houses in Liverpool, and now to have a posh flat in Mayfair, and with a bathroom each, it was great.

John and Paul went through their intellectual phase between 1963 and 1966. Looking back at John, he was always interested in poetry and films, but when we moved to London he and Paul got into a bit of one-upmanship over who knew the most about everything. Paul started going to the Establishment Club and hanging out with Jane Asher. There was a time when they'd go to see plays and it was all, 'Did you see such and such? Have you read this?'

PAUL: Really, that was why we'd left Liverpool; London was the big capital city with everything going for it. If you went to a play, it could be at the National Theatre, watching some mind-blowing actors. Seeing Colin Blakely in *Juno and the Paycock* was a big eye-opener. I was going out with an actress – Jane Asher – at the time, so I did quite a lot of theatre-going.

I began to make little films on my own, too. We'd film home movies, and because I didn't like sound cameras (we didn't really have many then), I'd take the visuals and put any soundtrack on them, to experiment. I remember one I did of a gendarme directing traffic. I then ran that film through the camera again and just filmed the traffic, so where he'd try to stop the cars they would all run through him. Over the top I stuck on a crazy jazz sax player, who sounded out of tune, playing the Marseillaise – which is probably where the idea came from for the start of 'All You Need Is Love'. It was quite funny.

I have always been someone who gets into a steady relationship. I met Jane Asher when she was sent by the *Radio Times* to cover a concert we were in at the Royal Albert Hall – we had a photo taken with her for the magazine and we all fancied her. We'd thought she was blonde, because we had only ever seen her on black-and-white telly doing *Juke Box Jury*, but she turned out to be a redhead. So it was: 'Wow, you're a redhead!' I tried pulling her, succeeded, and we were boyfriend and girlfriend for quite a long time.

I always feel very wary including Jane in The Beatles' history. She's never gone into print about our relationship, whilst everyone on earth has sold their story. So I'd feel weird being the one to kiss and tell.

We had a good relationship. Even with touring there were enough occasions to keep a reasonable relationship going. To tell the truth, the women at that time got sidelined. Now it would be seen as very chauvinist of us. Then it was like: 'We are four miners who go down the pit. You don't need women down the pit, do you? We won't have women down the pit.' A lot of what we, The Beatles, did was very much in an enclosed scene. Other people found it difficult – even John's wife, Cynthia, found it very difficult – to penetrate the screen that we had around us. As a kind of safety barrier we had a lot of 'in' jokes, little signs, references to music; we had a common bond in that and it was very difficult for any 'outsider' to penetrate. That possibly wasn't good for relationships back then.

I was still living on my own in London when all the others started getting married and moving to the suburbs, on golf-club estates, which wasn't my idea of fun at all: one, because I wasn't married and there didn't seem any point. (I could see it for them: they were going to raise kids out there.) And two, because I was able to stay in London I was much more involved in going to the theatre and art galleries and whatever was going on in the big metropolis.

JOHN: I'm glad things got as big as they did, because when we got nearly big, people started saying to us: 'You're the biggest thing since...' I got fed up that we were the biggest thing 'since'. I wanted The Beatles to just be the biggest thing. It's like gold. The more you get, the more you want.[70]

RINGO: We knew we were a great band but no one could predict then where it was going. We were playing good music and making good money. With Rory, at Butlins, I was on sixteen quid a week, and as an apprentice engineer I would take home £2 10s a week with the prospect of £12 or £15 a week after finishing the apprenticeship. But, now, here I was with money. Money was great. It meant having a bathroom in my own house, having cars. I suppose the biggest expense was the apartment George and I used to share. There were many suits and shirts and shoes and shopping sprees. I counted thirty-seven shirts one time and I couldn't believe it.

The first year we were still getting fifty quid a week from Brian. It was £25 when I joined, and even that had been a fortune.

JOHN: We don't feel as though we've got money. You just feel as though you've got the material things. The money we don't feel as though we've got, because we've never seen it. I never see more than £100 at once. They usually give us about thirty or forty quid a week each. I usually give it to my wife because I never use money, because I'm always being taken around. I only handle money when I'm off on holiday.[66]

GEORGE: We were still not that wealthy, except that we were better off relative to how poor we'd been before. But it was by no means real wealth, from the cash we were being given. I recently found a piece of paper that shows how much we were actually earning in one period in 1963. From the starting figure of £72,000, we made about £4,000 each; Brian Epstein took £2,025 a week and Neil and Mal got £25 each. *So Brian got £2,000 more each week than Mal and Neil!*

But our lives were changing. The way that we measured success or wealth now was that we had motorcars and lived in Mayfair and had four suits when we travelled. That was not bad, really.

JOHN: You can be bigheaded, and say, 'Yeah, we're going to last ten years,' but as soon as you've said that, you think, 'You know, we're lucky if we last three months.'[63]

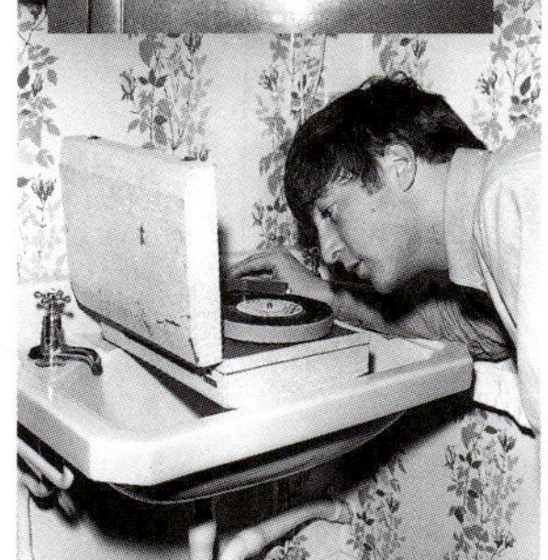

GEORGE MARTIN: *It was very difficult in 1963 to think The Beatles were going to last for ever and that I would be talking about them thirty years on. But it was very gratifying that they had made Number One. It took a whole year before they really conquered the world. It was 1964 before they had a Number One in America – the whole of 1963 was taken up with consolidating our work in England. They had four singles out during that time: 'Please Please Me', 'From Me To You', 'She Loves You', and 'I Want To Hold Your Hand'. As we recorded them, I would send each one to my friends at Capitol Records in America and say, 'This group is fantastic. You've got to issue them; you've got to sell them in the States.' And each time, the head of Capitol would turn it down: 'Sorry, we know our market better than you do, and we don't think they're any good.' Eventually, of course, they had to accede to public demand.*

NEIL ASPINALL: *Well, they had conquered Britain. The Beatles were everywhere – George even had his own column in the* Daily Express, *assisted by friend-to-be Derek Taylor.*

DEREK TAYLOR: *My first experience Beatle came earlier that year, and was extraordinary. I was still only thirty, but sufficiently unaware of the 'young' world in mid-Spring 1963 to have not heard of this rising phenomenon. I was working as a journalist for the* Daily Express *in Manchester and as such went to cover a one-night stand at the Odeon, starring The Beatles and Roy Orbison. I watched the show and when, two hours later, it was all over bar the screaming, I went to the telephone and dictated my review without a note, just as it came, and they printed it. I believed that in The Beatles the world had found the truest folk heroes of the century or, indeed, of any other time. From that day, 30th May 1963, I have never wavered in my certainty that they painted a new rainbow right across the world, with crocks of gold at each end and then some...*

*I was pleased when George's* Daily Express *column fell to me, but I started on the wrong foot. I did a real ghosting job. George's father was a bus driver, so I invented a conversation between his father and him in typical popular-newspaper style. It went like this: 'So my dad said to me, "Don't worry about me, son, you stick to your guitar and I'll carry on driving the big green jobs."'*

*I went down to London to deliver George's first column and I was asked by Brian, 'Oh, would you read it out for the boys? I'd like them to hear it.' So I had to take this column out of my pocket and, as if George had written it, I started reading it: '... you stick to your guitar and I'll carry on driving the big green jobs.' And George said, 'What are big green jobs?' I said, 'Um, buses – Liverpool buses.' George said, 'I didn't know they were called "big green jobs".' John said, 'I didn't know they were, either.' I said, 'Well, I don't know that they are.' I had just made it up. Which, of course, is what happens on newspapers and that's why all these things sound so phoney.*

*Anyway, the long and short of it was, after I'd passed the test by admitting that I'd made up 'big green jobs', George said, 'I'll help you write the column – we can do it together.'*

# 1964

nineteen sixty-four

JOHN:

# MERSEY BEAUCOUP!

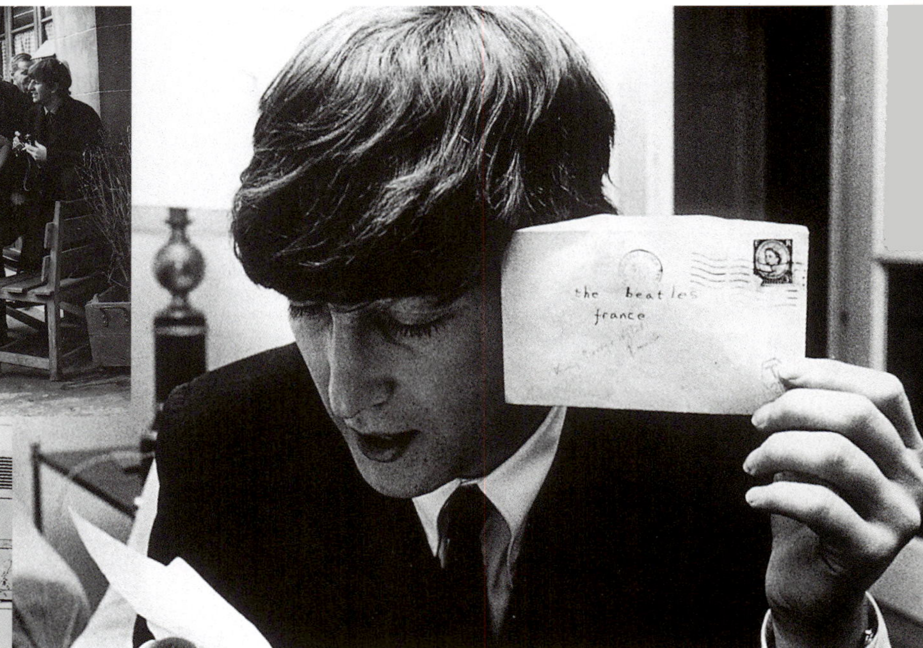


JOHN: If they want things like 'Sally' and 'Beethoven', we can do that standing on our ears. We might change the programme for the Olympia tomorrow, and put in some of the early rock numbers we used to do in Hamburg and at the Cavern – like 'Sweet Little Sixteen' and things. Easy.

We have a lot to live up to, especially being top of the bill at the Olympia. If we opened the show and didn't do so well, then we wouldn't have too much to live down, particularly as there are other acts following us. But topping the bill – well, let's hope it all works out.[64]

GEORGE: In January 1964 we played several concerts in Paris. The French audience was dreadful.

WE HAD VISIONS OF ALL THESE FRENCH GIRLS, *'OOH LÀ LÀ,'* AND ALL THAT, BUT THE AUDIENCE, AT LEAST ON THE OPENING NIGHT, WAS ALL TUXEDOED ELDERLY PEOPLE. AND A BUNCH OF SLIGHTLY GAY-LOOKING BOYS WERE HANGING ROUND THE STAGE DOOR SHOUTING, 'RINGO, RINGO!' AND CHASING OUR CAR. WE DIDN'T SEE ANY OF THE BRIGITTE BARDOTS THAT WE WERE EXPECTING.

RINGO: These boys chased us all over Paris. Before, we'd been more used to girls. The audience was a roar instead of a scream; it was a bit like when we played Stowe boys' school.

GEORGE: The sound went off in the hall and all the equipment blew up because it had been fused by the radio people (who were broadcasting us live without telling us).

It was all very disappointing, although it was made up for by our having, for the first time in our lives, the most enormous hotel suites, all with grand marble bathrooms. I think we were given two adjoining suites, with rooms that went on for ever.

Bill Corbett, our chauffeur then and a very nice fellow, wanted to be with us in Paris, so he told us he could speak French. He said, 'Oh, yeah, I speak it fluently, Paul.' So we sent him over on the boat with the car, and we flew over and he met us there.

RINGO: He said, 'You boys, you don't want to go over there with those frogs, they'll con you into all sorts of things. Let me go over there and I'll drive you round and interpret.' And we, of course, being so naive, said 'OK'.

When we got to Paris he stopped a policeman, and the first words out of his mouth were, 'Oi! May I park *ici?*'

GEORGE: One of us asked him for some honey, because his throat was getting sore and he needed a soothing drink, and Bill went up to a waiter and said, *'Avez-vous*... er, buzz-buzz?'

RINGO: We'd been done again. But Bill could get us anything – I remember once sending him for a selection of green socks. When George bought his house in Esher, with a swimming pool, he'd said to Bill, 'I'd like an eighty-foot diving stage.' And Bill had said, 'Sure, I'll have it round here in the morning, Mr Harrison. It will be right here.' So anything we wanted, he was good at getting for us.

GEORGE MARTIN: *When they were appearing at the Olympia Theatre I went over to Paris and arranged to record them in the EMI studio there. They were to record German versions of 'She Loves You' and 'I Want To Hold Your Hand'.*

*The German record company's head of A&R had told me that The Beatles would never sell records in Germany unless they actually sang in German. I was disinclined to believe this, but that's what he said and I told The Beatles. They laughed: 'That's absolute rubbish.' So I said, 'Well, if we want to sell records in Germany, that's what we've got to do.' So they agreed to record in German. I mean, really it was rubbish, but the company sent over one Otto Demmlar to help coach them in German. He prepared the translation of the lyrics, and 'She Loves You' became 'Sie Liebt Dich' – not terribly subtle!*

*On the appointed day I was waiting with Otto at the studios and they didn't turn up. It was the first time in my experience with them that they had let me down, so I rang the George V Hotel where they were staying, and Neil Aspinall answered. He said, 'I'm sorry, they're not coming, they asked me to tell you.' I said, 'You mean to tell me they're telling you to tell me? They're not telling me themselves?' – 'That's right.' – 'I'm coming right over,' I said.*

*So I went to see them and I had Otto with me. I was really angry and stormed in to find they were all having tea in the centre of the room. (They were, after all, very charming people.) It was rather like the Mad Hatter's Tea Party with Alice in Wonderland in the form of Jane Asher, with long hair, in the middle pouring tea.*

*As soon as I entered they exploded in all directions; they ran behind couches and chairs and one put a lampshade over his head. Then from behind the sofa and chairs came a chorus of: 'Sorry George, sorry George, sorry George...' I had to laugh. I said, 'You are bastards, aren't you? Are you going to apologise to Otto?' And they said, 'Sorry Otto, sorry Otto...'*

*They finally agreed to come down to the studio and work. They did record two songs in German. They were the only things they have ever done in a foreign language. And they didn't need to anyway. They were quite right. The records would have sold in English, and did.*

NEIL ASPINALL: *Whilst we were at the George V Hotel, a lot of exciting things were happening. As well as George Martin being there for the German recordings, Derek Taylor was around interviewing George for the* Daily Express *column he was doing for him. John was working on his second book,* A Spaniard in the Works. *At the same time they'd just got Dylan's first album and David Wynne was there, too; he did the sculptures of The Beatles' heads.*

*The Beatles played for three weeks at the Olympia, which apart from the Cavern and their stints in Hamburg, was the longest time they appeared at any single venue.*

GEORGE: One of the most memorable things of the trip for me was that we had a copy of Bob Dylan's *Freewheelin'* album, which we played constantly.

PROGRAMME
ET POURTANT (de Charles AZNAVOUR)
par DANIEL JANIN et son Orchestre
Nous irons de plus en plus haut
LARRY GRISWOLD
Année menée par le Twist et la Science, le Biologiste
ROGER COMTE
Nous resterons dynamique et... plutot coquin
PIERRE VASSILIU
Encore beaucoup d'équilibre à faire
LES HOGANAS
Inimitables dans leurs imitations de classe
GILL MILLER
et ARNOLD ARCHER
Paris verra pour la première fois, le Champion International du "SURF"
TRINI LOPEZ
A L'ENTR'ACTE : BARS • FUMOIRS
Achetez et faites dédicacer à notre stand dans le hall dès l'entr'acte et jusqu'à la fin du spectacle, les derniers disques de nos vedettes
Jolie, fraiche, avec du rythme elle vous insufle la joie de vivre
SYLVIE VARTAN
Une adresse extraordinaire le caractérise
VINICIO
Nous vivrons dans la fièvre, ils révolutionnent l'Angleterre et la France
LES BEATLES

JOHN: I think that was the first time I ever heard Dylan at all. I think Paul got the record from a French DJ. We were doing a radio thing there and the guy had the record in the studio. Paul said, 'Oh, I keep hearing about this guy,' or he'd heard it, I'm not sure – and we took it back to the hotel.[70] And for the rest of our three weeks in Paris we didn't stop playing it. We all went potty on Dylan.

The first time you hear Dylan you think you're the first to discover him. But quite a lot of people had discovered him before us.[64]

DEREK TAYLOR: *I got to Paris in 1964 to do George's column. He said, 'To make this column interesting, let's go out. We'll go to a nightclub and we'll go up the Eiffel Tower. We'll do French things.' They were new to travelling then. It was all new.*

*By Paris I was getting to be trusted, and one night John said to me, 'Are you pretending to be from Liverpool or something?' We were the last up and we'd had a few drinks and that's how the conversation took this difficult turn. I said, 'I don't know about pretending, but anyway, I am from Liverpool.' He said, 'Yeah, born in Manchester.' I said, 'Well, that's a narrow way of looking at it. At the moment I live in Manchester. A lot of people are not born where they happen to live later. I was born in Liverpool, lived in West Kirby; my wife's from Birkenhead.'*

*All this was local stuff, and it was surprisingly quick to get under that harsh exterior of John's to find a nice chap with whom (once you had proven you weren't from Manchester and therefore useless) you could have quite a pleasant conversation on a variety of subjects. None of which I remember, because we did get very drunk together. I enjoyed that night a lot, just him and me.*

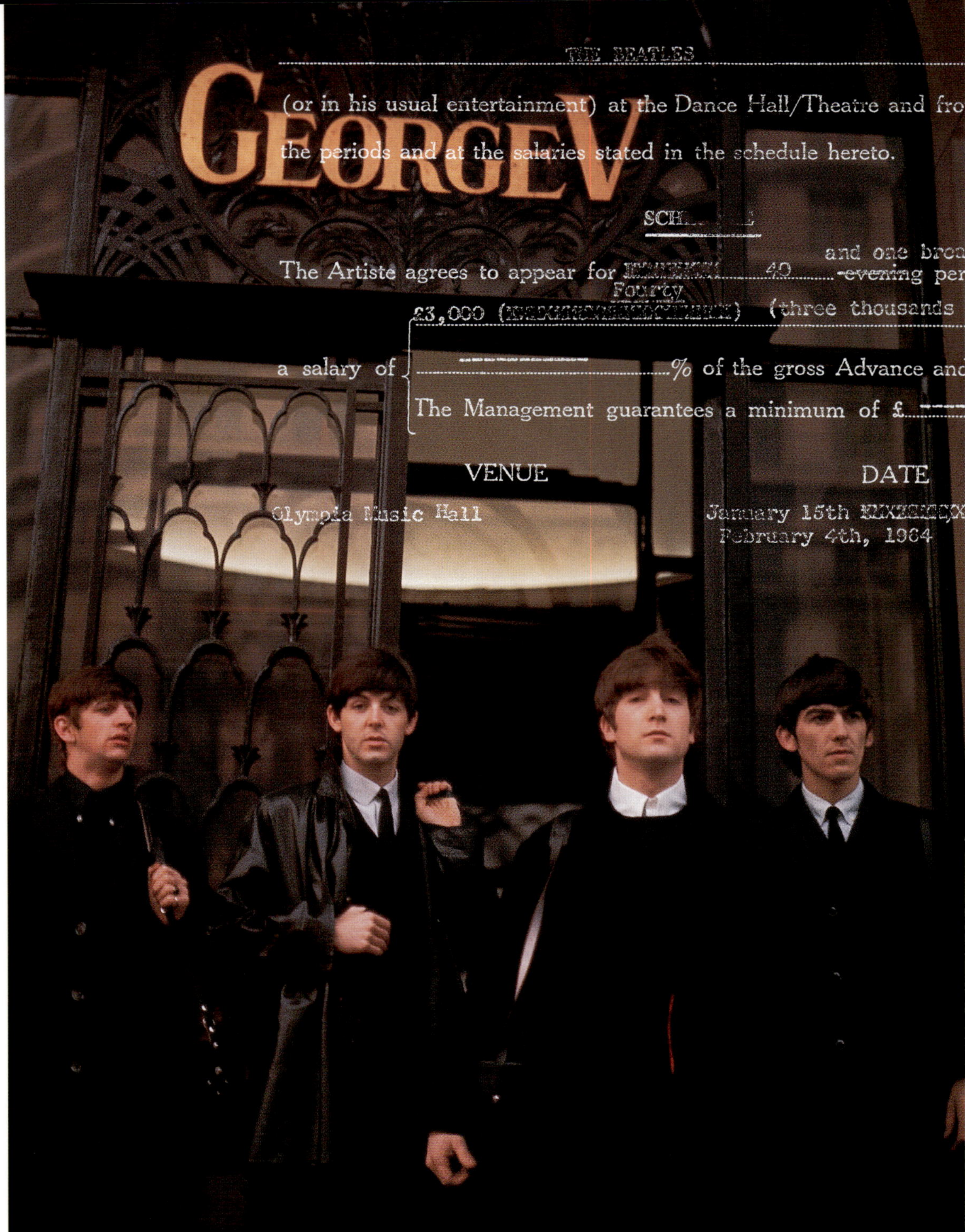


GEORGE: Besides the German versions of two songs, I remember recording 'Can't Buy Me Love'. We took the tapes from that back to England to do some work on them. I once read something that tries to analyse 'Can't Buy Me Love', talking about the double-track guitar – mine – and saying that it's not very good because you can hear the original one. What happened was that we recorded first in Paris and re-recorded in England. Obviously they'd tried to overdub it, but in those days they only had two tracks, so you can hear the version we put on in London, and in the background you can hear a quieter one.

GEORGE MARTIN: *I thought that we really needed a tag for the song's ending, and a tag for the beginning; a kind of intro. So I took the first few lines of the chorus and changed the ending, and said, 'Let's just have these lines, and by altering the end of the second phrase we can get back into the verse pretty quickly.' And they said, 'That's not a bad idea, we'll do it that way.'*

PAUL: PERSONALLY, I THINK YOU CAN PUT ANY INTERPRETATION YOU WANT ON ANYTHING, BUT WHEN SOMEONE SUGGESTS THAT 'CAN'T BUY ME LOVE' IS ABOUT A PROSTITUTE, I DRAW THE LINE. THAT'S GOING TOO FAR.

One night we arrived back at the hotel from the Olympia when a telegram came through to Brian from Capitol Records of America. He came running in to the room saying, 'Hey, look. You are Number One in America!' 'I Want To Hold Your Hand' had gone to Number One.

Well, I can't describe our response. We all tried to climb onto Big Mal's back to go round the hotel suite: 'Wey-hey!' And that was it, we didn't come down for a week.

RINGO: We couldn't believe it. We all just started acting like people from Texas, hollering and shouting, 'Ya-hoo!' I think that was the night we finished up sitting on a bench by the Seine; just the four of us and Neil. In those days we'd promise Neil £20,000 if he'd go for a swim. He'd go for a swim and we'd say, 'No, sorry.'

GEORGE: We knew we had a better chance of having a hit because we were finally with Capitol Records and they *had* to promote it. The smaller labels that had put out our earlier records didn't really promote them very much.

There had been cover stories on European Beatlemania in *Life* and *Newsweek* and other magazines, so it wasn't too difficult a job for Capitol to follow through. And the song itself was very catchy, anyway.

JOHN: I like 'I Want To Hold Your Hand', it's a beautiful melody.[70] I remember when we got the chord that made that song. We were in Jane Asher's house, downstairs in the cellar, playing on the piano at the same time, and we had, 'Oh, you-u-u… got that something…'

AND PAUL HITS THIS CHORD AND I TURN TO HIM AND SAY, 'THAT'S IT! DO THAT AGAIN!' IN THOSE DAYS, WE REALLY USED TO ABSOLUTELY WRITE LIKE THAT – BOTH PLAYING INTO EACH OTHER'S NOSES.[80]

GEORGE: It was such a buzz to find that it had gone to Number One. We went out to dinner that evening with Brian and George Martin. George took us to a place which was a vault, with huge barrels of wine around. It was a restaurant and its theme was… well, the bread rolls were shaped like penises, the soup was served out of chamber pots and the chocolate ice cream was like a big turd. And the waiter came round and tied garters on all the girls' legs. I've seen some pictures of us. There is a photograph around of Brian with the pot on his head.

It was a great feeling because we were booked to go to America directly after the Paris trip, so it was handy to have a Number One. We'd already been hired by Ed Sullivan, so if it had been a Number Two or Number Ten we'd have gone anyway; but it was nice to have a Number One.

We did have three records out in America before this one. The others were on two different labels. It was only after all the publicity and the Beatlemania in Europe that Capitol Records decided, 'Oh, we will have them.' They put out 'I Want To Hold Your Hand' as our first single, but in fact it was our fourth.

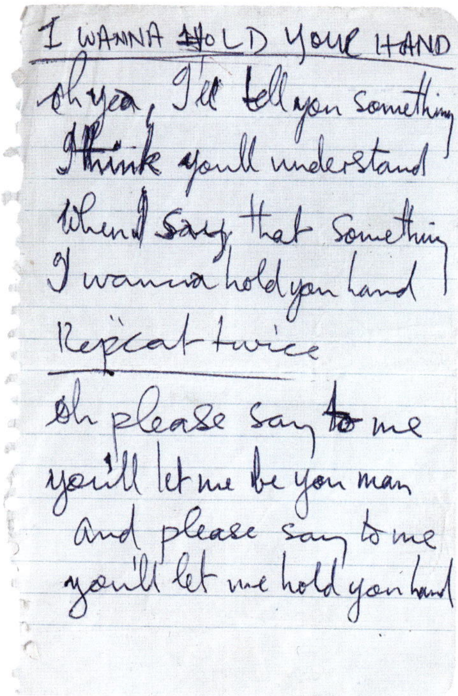
I WANNA HOLD YOUR HAND
oh yea, I'll tell you something
I think you'll understand
when I say that something
I wanna hold your hand
Repeat twice
Oh please say to me
you'll let me be your man
and please say to me
you'll let me hold your hand

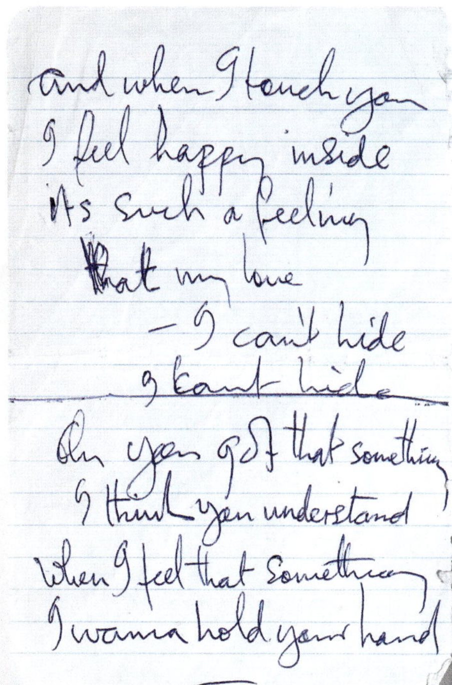
and when I touch you
I feel happy inside
its such a feeling
that my love
– I can't hide
I can't hide
Oh you got that something
I think you understand
when I feel that something
I wanna hold your hand

PAUL: 'From Me To You' was released – a flop in America. 'She Loves You' – a big hit in England, big Number One in England – a flop in the USA. 'Please Please Me' released over there – flop. Nothing until 'I Want To Hold Your Hand'.

JOHN: The thing is, in America, it just seemed ridiculous – I mean, the idea of having a hit record over there. It was just something you could never do. That's what I thought, anyhow. But then I realised that kids everywhere all go for the same stuff; and seeing we'd done it in England, there's no reason why we couldn't do it in America, too. But the American disc jockeys didn't know about British records; they didn't play them, nobody promoted them, so you didn't have hits.

It wasn't until *Time* and *Newsweek* came over and wrote articles and created an interest in us that disc jockeys started playing our records. And Capitol said, 'Well, can we have their records?' They had been offered our records years ago, and they didn't want them – but when they heard we were big over here they said, 'Can we have them now?' We said, 'As long as you promote them.' So Capitol promoted, and with them and all these articles on us, the records just took off.

DEREK TAYLOR: *I was now accepted by John. George and I had got along very well right from the start. He never did that 'you're from Manchester' stuff. He was anxious to please, and still is. If he is committed to something, he does it with enormous thoroughness. He has rather a 'straight-ahead' way. So my 'in' through George was very comfortable. I didn't know Ringo at all then, and Paul stood back a bit – he was very nice though. We seemed to have a lot in common: Merseyside grammar school boys, different ages, but we sort of fitted.*

*It was obvious to me in Paris that they were going to be red hot. They'd reached Number One in the Cashbox chart with 'I Want To Hold Your Hand', and the mania was spreading ahead of them. I did George's final before-America column, a 'tomorrow the world' kind of thing: 'Tonight we conquered Versailles, and by implication, all of France fell… How New York will view our visit, we can only guess!'*

*But the Daily Express didn't send me to America. They said, 'We've got David English there, he's the American correspondent.' I thought, 'He doesn't know them, he doesn't understand them, I'm the only one who understands them, I know these people.' However, I was asked to help Brian*

*Epstein with his book and we went down to Torquay for four days and wrote a pot-boiler – A Cellarful of Noise. And he said on the third day, 'I've had a lovely, lovely idea Derek, I want you to join us.'*

*I thought this was incredible. I'd given up the idea of joining them for the time being, thinking, 'If it happens, it happens.' So after about fifteen years on newspapers I dropped out and joined The Beatles as Brian's personal assistant, and eventually became The Beatles' press officer.*

BRIAN EPSTEIN: *We knew that America would make us or break us as world stars. In fact, she made us.*[64]

RINGO: Things used to fall right for us as a band. We couldn't stop it. The gods were on our side. We were fabulous musicians, we had great writers; it wasn't like a piece of shit was being helped, and things just fell into place. We were doing countries: we'd conquered Sweden, we'd conquered France, we conquered Spain and Italy; but we were worried about America.

George was the only one of us who'd been before and he'd been into record shops there and asked, 'Have you got The Beatles' records?' We had three out, on Vee-Jay and Swan, but nobody had them, or had even heard of us. He came back and said, 'They don't know us, it's going to be hard.' We were used to being famous by then, so we *were* worried about that.

But the deal went down with Capitol. Then Ed Sullivan was getting off a plane at Heathrow at the same time that we were getting off one from Sweden, saw all the fans at the airport and booked us on the spot. He didn't know us and we didn't know him.

All these forces started working so that when we landed in the US the record was Number One. We were booked five months ahead and you can't plan that kind of thing. We got off the plane and it was just like being at home, millions of kids again.

JOHN: We didn't think we stood a chance. We didn't imagine it at all. Cliff went to America and died. He was fourteenth on the bill with Frankie Avalon.[67] When we came over the first time, we were only coming over to buy LPs. I know our manager had plans for Ed Sullivan shows but we thought at least we could hear the sounds when we came over. It was just out of the dark. That's the truth; it was so out of the dark, we were knocked out.[64]

GEORGE: I'd been to America before, being the experienced Beatle that I was. I went to New York and St Louis in 1963, to look around, and to the countryside in Illinois, where my sister was living at the time. I went to record stores. I bought Booker T and the MGs' first album, *Green Onions*, and I bought some Bobby Bland, all kind of things.

Before we left for America for that first Beatle visit, Brian Epstein had said to Capitol, 'You can have The Beatles on condition that you spend thirty dollars advertising them.' And they did. It was actually something like $50,000, which sounded enormous. That was part of the deal.

PAUL: I think the money was mainly spent in LA getting people like Janet Leigh to wear Beatle wigs and be photographed in them, which started it all. Once a film star did that, it could get syndicated all across America: 'Look at this funny picture; Janet Leigh in this wacko wig – the "moptop" wig.' And so the whole 'moptop' thing started there. And it did get us noticed.

There were millions of kids at the airport, which nobody had expected. We heard about it in mid-air. There were journalists on the plane, and the pilot had rang ahead and said, 'Tell the boys there's a big crowd waiting for them.' We thought, 'Wow! God, we have really made it.'

I remember, for instance, the great moment of getting into the limo and putting on the radio, and hearing a running commentary on *us*: 'They have just left the airport and are coming towards New York City...' It was like a dream. The greatest fantasy ever.

RINGO: IT WAS SO EXCITING. ON THE PLANE, FLYING IN TO THE AIRPORT, I FELT AS THOUGH THERE WAS A BIG OCTOPUS WITH TENTACLES THAT WERE GRABBING THE PLANE AND DRAGGING US DOWN INTO NEW YORK. AMERICA WAS THE BEST.

It was a dream, coming from Liverpool.

I loved it. The radio was hip and bopping, the TV was on, we were going to clubs. And they loved Ringo over there. That's why it was so great for me, because when we got to America it wasn't JOHN, PAUL, GEORGE and Ringo; half the time it was RINGO, PAUL, GEORGE and JOHN, or whatever. Suddenly it was *equal*.

NEIL ASPINALL: *It has since been reported that their American record company had promised that every person who turned up at the airport would be given a dollar bill and a T-shirt. What really happened was that the receptionists at Capitol Records would answer the phone, 'Capitol Records – The Beatles are coming.' There was a lot of mention on the radio, too: 'The Beatles are coming!' It was the people handling the Beatles merchandise at the time who were offering the free T-shirt. I had no idea about that at the time, and it was nothing to do with the record company.*

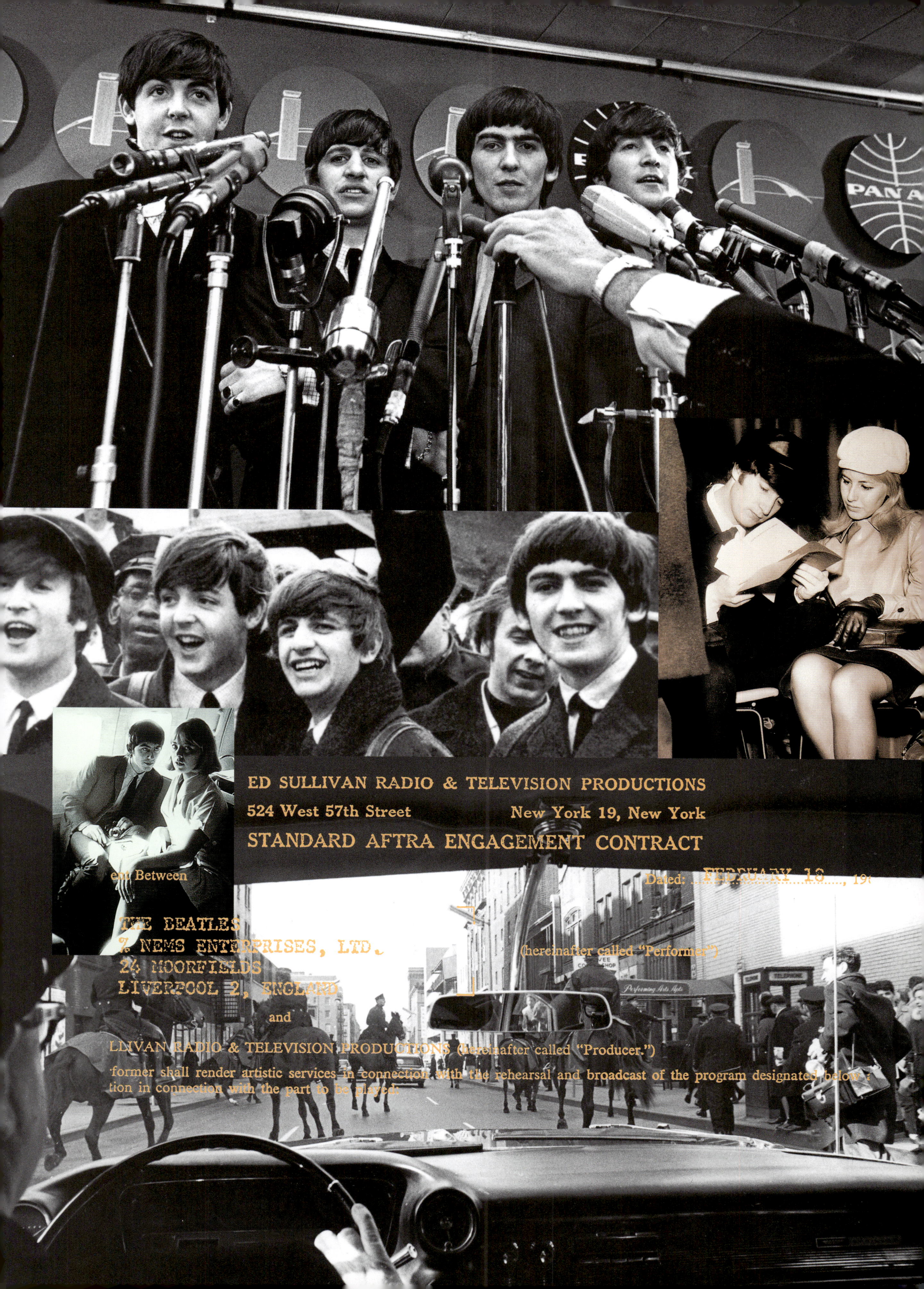
PAN A
ED SULLIVAN RADIO & TELEVISION PRODUCTIONS
524 West 57th Street New York 19, New York
STANDARD AFTRA ENGAGEMENT CONTRACT
ent Between
Dated: FEBRUARY 18
THE BEATLES
% NEMS ENTERPRISES, LTD.
24 MOORFIELDS
LIVERPOOL 2, ENGLAND
(hereinafter called "Performer")
and
LLIVAN RADIO & TELEVISION PRODUCTIONS (hereinafter called "Producer.")
former shall render artistic services in connection with the rehearsal and broadcast of the program designated below
tion in connection with the part to be played:

They've got so many programmes and we got on all the news. It was ridiculous. At first we had no idea, then when we got the first couple of hits we thought, 'Well, this is it, we'll probably flop now.' But we just seem to go on and on and on. Never in a million years did we think anything like this.

They expect you to be a big-time star, but I think most people prefer us being the way we are. They come in biased. Then we'll just be natural with them and they seem pleased. That's all we do: if we're tired, we look tired, if we're happy, we're happy; we don't kid on. If we're feeling a bit 'off' that day, we say to them, 'I'm feeling a bit "off", I'm sorry, I won't be quick-witted.'[64]

NEIL ASPINALL: *George had tonsillitis and didn't go to rehearsals for* The Ed Sullivan Show. *I stood in for him so that they could mark where everyone would stand, and I had a guitar strapped round me. It wasn't plugged in (nobody was playing anything) and it was amazing to read in a major American magazine a few days later that I 'played a mean guitar'.*

*The Beatles recorded a set in the afternoon, which was to be broadcast after they left, and then played a live* Ed Sullivan Show *that night.*

GEORGE: I had a bad throat and that's why I'm missing from the publicity shots in Central Park. There are pictures of just the three of them with the New York skyline behind. (The same with the rehearsal for Ed Sullivan: there are pictures of them rehearsing without me.) I could never figure out how, with swarms of people everywhere, with the mania going on, they actually did get out into the park for a photo session.

RINGO: The main thing I was aware of when we did the first *Ed Sullivan Show* was that we rehearsed all afternoon. TV had such bad sound equipment (it has still today, usually, but then it was *really* bad) that we would tape our rehearsals and then go up and mess with the dials in the control booth. We got it all set with the engineer there, and then we went off for a break.

The story has it that while we were out, the cleaner came in to clean the room and the console, thought, 'What are all these chalk marks?' and wiped them all off. So our plans just went out the window. We had a real hasty time trying to get the sound right.

GEORGE: We were aware that Ed Sullivan was the big one because we got a telegram from Elvis and the Colonel. And I've heard that while the show was on there were no reported crimes, or very few. When The Beatles were on Ed Sullivan, even the criminals had a rest for ten minutes.

PAUL: Seventy-three million people were reported to have watched the first show. It is still supposed to be one of the largest viewing audiences ever in the States.

It was very important. We came out of nowhere with funny hair, looking like marionettes or something. That was very influential. I think that was really one of the big things that broke us – the hairdo more than the music, originally. A lot of people's fathers had wanted to turn us off. They told their kids, 'Don't be fooled, they're wearing wigs.'

JOHN: If we do, they must be the only ones with real dandruff!

PAUL: A lot of fathers did turn it off, but a lot of mothers and children made them keep it on. All these kids are now grown-up, and telling us they remember it. It's like, 'Where were you when Kennedy was shot?' I get people like Dan Aykroyd saying, 'Oh man, I remember that Sunday night; we didn't know what had hit us – just sitting there watching Ed Sullivan's show.' Up until then there were jugglers and comedians like Jerry Lewis, and then, suddenly, The Beatles!

JOHN: They're wild; they're all wild. They just all seem out of their minds. I've never seen anything like it in my life. We just walk through it like watching a film. You feel as though it's something that's happening to somebody else, especially when you spot George and you think, 'Oh, that's George with all those people climbing all over him.'

PAUL: A New York DJ, Murray the K, was the man most onto the Beatle case; he had seen it coming and grabbed hold of it. Actually he was just a cheeky journalist who asked a few cheeky questions at the front of the press conference, instead of standing back and being aloof. His way was: 'Hey, OK, you guys? What do you think of… ?'

We were very impressed and we used to ring his radio show when he was on the air. We would give him all the exclusives because we loved him. And he had package shows on the road so he could talk about people like Smokey Robinson, who he'd met. Smokey Robinson was like God in our eyes.

GEORGE: I've often wondered how Murray could barge into the room and hang out with us for the entire trip. It's funny, really, I never quite understood how he did that.

RINGO: Murray the K was as mad as a hatter, a fabulous guy, a great DJ, and he knew his music. We practically killed him off, because he would come on the tour with us and hang about all the time we were up and about. Then *we* would pass out and go to sleep; and *he* would then have to start doing his shows. He was living on twenty minutes of sleep a night. We could see this man just *go*, disappearing in front of our eyes.

In New York there was him, and the DJ Cousin Brucie. Murray became the so-called 'fifth Beatle', because he was really big on playing our record: he helped to make it a hit.

NEIL ASPINALL: *We were all pretty naive when we arrived in America. We didn't know about advertising and all of that. People were pulling all sorts of strokes. There would be a press conference with big billboards behind, advertising something or other, and we'd not notice.*

*In England at that time there was only one radio station, the BBC. In the States you had radio stations coming out of your ears and they were hit on by all the DJs. Murray the K was from WINS in New York City, but there were loads of them. They would follow the guys into the lift with their microphones and, as they'd be talking to them, the conversation would be broadcast out of their hand-held radios.*

*The Beatles would ask, 'What radio station are you from?' and the DJ would tell them, which would promote the station. Then the other stations would get uptight, but as The Beatles did it for everybody anyway (because they didn't know any different), nobody could really complain. And they'd listen to the radio all the time, and call to request records.*

JOHN: We were so overawed by American radio, Epstein had to stop us: we phoned every radio [station] in town, saying, 'Will you play the Ronettes doing this?' We wanted to hear the music. We didn't ask for our own records, we asked for other people's.[74] In the old days we listened to Elvis, of course, Chuck Berry, Carl Perkins, Little Richard and Eddie Cochran, to name but a few; but now we liked Marvin Gaye, The Miracles, Shirelles, all those people.

We do nothing else all day. We have a transistor each, all on at various volumes, and whichever record we like, we just turn that one up. It's great. They've started in Britain now – 'pirate ships', they call them – off the British coast. They're similar, in a more modified, British way. But you get good records all day, which you never got before. I love it.

It does seem a lot of advertising when you just come out here. I suppose you get used to it. People come to Britain (people that haven't got commercial TV) and see the advertising on TV there and think it's awful; you just get used to it.[64]

RINGO: I loved New York at that time. We went into Central Park in a horse-drawn carriage. We had this huge suite of rooms in the Plaza Hotel, with a TV on in each room, and we had radios with earpieces. This was all so fascinating to me. It was too far out; the media was just so fast.

I remember that on one of the TV channels they were showing *Hercules Unchained*, an Italian 'Hercules' movie. When we got up in the morning and put the TV on there would be Hercules doing his stuff in ancient times. We'd go out and do something and come back in the afternoon and I'd switch on and he would *still* be doing his stuff. And then we'd go out at night, and come back, and I'd switch on this one channel, and it would be the same movie! I thought I was cracking up. In fact, this one channel had a Movie of the Week, and they would just keep showing it again and again. At the end of the credits they'd just start it at the top.

This was too far out, coming from England, where we'd only had a TV in our house for a couple of years. Now here was a channel doing something crazy like this.

GEORGE: The thing that bothered me about American TV was that in the morning you'd get up and there'd be a football match on that obviously didn't take place in the morning; it's not the appropriate time of day.

There are some things that I refuse to watch at certain times of day. I could never stand seeing *I Love Lucy*, and all those obviously night-time programmes, being on in the mornings. Or worse still, a movie at seven or eight in the morning. For me, movies don't come on until the evening.

NEIL ASPINALL: *After Ed Sullivan, we got on the train to Washington. They had their own carriage full of press and agents and others. It was very cold.*

RINGO: Being cheeky chappies saved our arses on many occasions, especially then, on the train to Washington, because the guys from the press had come to bury us. These reporters, being New Yorkers, would yell at us, but we just yelled back. When we got to know some of them they said, 'We came here to kill you, but you just started shouting back at us – we couldn't believe it.' Up until then pop groups had been milk and honey with the press: 'No, I don't smoke,' that kind of thing. And here *we* were, smoking and drinking and shouting at *them*. That's what endeared us to them.

JOHN: We'd learnt the whole game: we knew how to handle the press when we arrived. The British press are the toughest in the world – we could handle anything. We were all right. I know on the plane over I was thinking, 'Oh, we won't make it,' but that's that side of me: we knew we would wipe them out if we could just get a grip.[70]

I don't mind people putting us down; because if everybody really liked us, it would be a bore. You've got to have people putting you down. It doesn't give any edge to it if everybody just falls flat on their face saying, 'You're great.' We enjoy some of the criticisms as well, they're quite funny; some of the clever criticisms, not the ones that don't know anything, but some of the clever ones are quite fun.

The main thing that's kept us going when it's been real hard work is the humour amongst ourselves, we can laugh at anything – ourselves included. That's the way we do everything – everything's tongue in cheek. We're the same about ourselves; we never take it seriously.[64]

RINGO: We attended a miserable event in the British Embassy in Washington. In the early Sixties there was still a huge disparity between people from the North of England and 'people from Embassies'. They were all, 'Oh, *very* nice,' a bit like Brian Epstein, and we were, 'All right, lads, not so bad.' But we went, God knows why. Maybe because we'd suddenly become ambassadors and they wanted to see us, and I think Brian liked the idea that it was sort of big time.

We were standing around, saying, 'Hi, that's very nice,' and having a drink, when someone came up behind me and snipped off a piece of my hair, which got me very angry. Why was he carrying a pair of scissors? I just swung round and said, 'What the hell do you think you are doing?' He replied, 'Oh, it's OK, old chap... bullshit, bullshit.' That was a stupid incident: wanting to cut a Beatle's hair.

JOHN: People were touching us when we walked past, that kind of thing, and wherever we went we were supposed to be not normal. We were supposed to put up with all sorts of shit from Lord Mayors and their wives, and be touched and pawed like in *A Hard Day's Night*, only a million times more. At the American Embassy or the British Embassy in Washington, some bloody animal cut Ringo's hair. I walked out, swearing at all of them, I just left in the middle of it.[70]

PAUL: There were a lot of Hooray Henrys there, and we had never really met that kind before. We hadn't played arts balls or the Cambridge May Ball or anything like that; but we had heard about these guys who got a little stroppy after a few drinks: 'I say, play us a Rachmaninov Piano Concerto.' Oh, *yeah*, we love him...

There were a few of them at the Embassy. I remember girls wanting to cut bits off our hair, which was not entirely on – so there were a few little elbows in gobs.

JOHN: ONCE, IN NEW ZEALAND, IT WAS A BIT ROUGH, TOO, AND I THOUGHT A BIG CLUMP OF MY HAIR HAD DEFINITELY GONE; AND I DON'T MEAN JUST A BIT. I WAS HALFWAY ON THE GROUND AND I THOUGHT, 'HELLO, IT MUST BE LIKE A RAID WHEN YOU GET CRUSHED.' THEY'D PUT ABOUT THREE POLICEMEN ON PATROL FOR ABOUT THREE OR FOUR THOUSAND KIDS AND REFUSED TO PUT ANY MORE ON: 'WE'VE HAD ALL SORTS HERE. WE'VE SEEN THEM ALL.' AND THEY DID SEE THEM ALL – AS WE CRASHED TO THE GROUND![64]

NEIL ASPINALL: *The Washington show was difficult because they were in a boxing ring with the audience all round and they had to play to all four sides.*

*They had to go to a different side of the stage for every song, so we had to keep moving the mikes. Ringo was sitting on a round turntable in the middle of the stage, which we also had to turn round – and the bloody thing got stuck! All this chaos was going on, but it was actually a good show for all that. After that gig, it was back to New York.*

*I found out twenty years later that the show had been filmed for subsequent telecasting throughout America. Kids all over the States had paid to go to theatres and watch it. So when they went back and toured America in August, a lot of the people in the audiences had already seen them live in concert, via the telecast. The Beach Boys were on as well, and another act; put together and relayed to cinemas.*

PAUL: We played Carnegie Hall, because Brian liked the idea of playing a classical hall, and then we went to Miami and filmed the second *Ed Sullivan Show*.

Miami was like paradise. We had never been anywhere where there were palm trees. We were real tourists; we had our Pentax cameras and took a lot of pictures. I've still got a lot of photos of motorcycle cops with their guns. We'd never seen a policeman with a gun, and those Miami cops did look pretty groovy. We had a great time there. We played at one of the hotels. They always had cabarets down in the basements of the big hotels. And we'd look down on the beach where the fans would write 'I love John' in the sand, so big we could read it from our room.

JOHN: But if we waved, somebody always said, 'Stop that waving, you're inciting them!'

RINGO: Now, this was just the most brilliant place I'd ever been to. People were lending us yachts, anything we wanted. There were two great things in Florida. One: I was taken to my first drive-in in a Lincoln Continental by two very nice young ladies. Two: a family lent us their boat and let me drive. It was a sixty-foot speedboat, which I proceeded to bring into port head-on, not really knowing much about driving speedboats.

WELCOMES
THE BEATLES

Ludwig
THE
BEATLES

THE BEATLES
VOX

GEORGE: There were offshore powerboat races being held and we got a ride on one contender. It had two V12 engines and really went quickly when you floored it. Only the back of the boat, where the propellors were, stayed in the water at high speed. The boat just stood up on end whilst we hung on. I enjoyed that.

NEIL ASPINALL: *Ringo realised too late that you don't have brakes on boats and we just crashed into the jetty.*

RINGO: They have those pretty rails on the front, and I bent the bugger all over the place. But they didn't seem to mind, you know; they were just happy!

JOHN: We borrowed a couple of millionaires' houses there.[64]

PAUL: We'd told Brian we wanted a pool, and a guy from a record company had one. Looking back, it was quite a modest little pool for Miami. Not a huge affair. We would go round there in the afternoon and not get bothered. It was great – four Liverpool lads, you know: 'Get your cozzies on.' *Life* magazine was taking photos of us swimming.

I think, though, that we were hanging out with Mafiosi at that time. There was a critic giving us a hard time in the press; George Martin and Brian Epstein were discussing it when a big heavy guy came up and said, 'Mr Epstein, you want we should fix this guy?' – 'Er, no, that's OK.' That was the kind of crowd we were in: 'Yeah, I'm in the Mafia.' But *we* didn't know that: we just saw a nice man with a pool and a yacht. I must admit we were more interested in the yacht than in him.

At this stage, we started to meet people whom we'd only seen in newspapers and on film, and now we were rubbing shoulders with them.

GEORGE: Obviously we were having an effect, because all these people were clamouring to meet us – like Muhammad Ali, for instance. We were taken to meet him on that first trip. It was a big publicity thing. It was all part of being a Beatle, really; just getting lugged around and thrust into rooms full of press men taking pictures and asking questions. Muhammad Ali was quite cute, he had a fight coming up in a couple of days with Sonny Liston. There is a famous picture of him holding two of us under each arm.

RINGO: I sparred with Cassius Clay, as he was called then – I taught him everything he knew. That was a thrill, of course, and I was putting my money on Liston, so I *really* knew what was happening!

PAUL: We met a few people through Phil Spector. We met The Ronettes, which was very exciting, and various others, such as Jackie De Shannon, a great songwriter, and Diana Ross and the rest of The Supremes. They were people we admired and as we went on we met them all – all the people who were coming up as we were coming up. It was a matey sort of thing.

JOHN: We don't remember any of them, hardly.[65]

GEORGE: We met a few people who were famous that we didn't know. I mean, in America there were people – and there still are – who are really famous there, but whom you've never heard of in Britain. If you don't watch television or listen to the radio maybe, you'll never know who they are. A lot of people we met I certainly didn't know. And then there were the ones we met whom we did know, like The Supremes.

RINGO: Probably everyone has heard of Don Rickles now, but we hadn't in those days, and he was playing in the Deauville Hotel where we stayed. He was a vicious type of comedian. He would say, 'Hello, lady, where are you from?' and she'd say, 'Oh, I'm from Israel.' He'd go to another table, 'Where are you from?' They'd say, 'Germany,' and it'd be: 'Nazi, get out! What the hell is this?'

PAUL: Of course, he turned on us. We were all on one table with our policeman buddy, our chaperone (we had this one bodyguard who came everywhere with us; he was a good mate and we often went back to his house), and he started on him: 'Hey, cop, get a job! What's this? Looking after The Beatles? Great job you got, man; looking after The Beatles!' He went on, 'It's great. They just lie up there on the ninth floor, in between satin sheets and every time they hear the girls screaming they go "Oooohh".' *Very funny*, we thought. We were not amused, as I recall. Very cutting. I like him now but at first he was a bit of a shock.

GEORGE: We were all a bit taken aback. Also, we were trying to keep a low profile and suddenly he kept putting the spotlight on us, and embarrassing us. I think John felt a bit embarrassed, too, at the time. However, if we'd had him on our own terms we could have made mincemeat out of him.

He'd say, 'Nice people, these police. They're doing a great job.' And then he'd turn around and snap, 'I hope your badge melts.'

The manager of either Sonny Liston or Muhammad Ali was also watching the show and the fight was coming up, and Don Rickles would say, 'Well, if you ask me, Jack, I think the black guy will win.' And then suddenly he'd come back to our table and we'd be nervous, sitting there and he'd say, *'Look at that great personality!'*

RINGO: He asked me, 'Where are you from?' I said, 'Liverpool,' to silence, and he said, 'Oh, hear the applause!'

GEORGE: He did a great bit at the end. He said, 'Well, I see we've got some Arabs in the back of the room and there's always talk about fighting amongst Arabs and Jewish people. I'd just like to say that really we appreciate each other, and there's no hard feelings, and just to show it, gentlemen, would you please stand up and take a bow.' They all obeyed, honoured at such a gesture, and Rickles dived on the floor going, 'Drrrrrrrrrr… ' making the noise of a machine gun.

He turned out not to be that cool, though. He blew it all at the very end because he started apologising for everything he'd been saying, instead of just going off and leaving the buzz in the room.

RINGO: I had another disastrous evening in Miami. We went out to see The Coasters, who were heroes with 'Yakety Yak'. People were *dancing* to them in the club, and I just couldn't understand it. These were rock'n'roll gods to me, and people were dancing! I was just so disgusted. But The Coasters were great, and it was a thrill to see American artists. We'd never seen them before like this, *in America*.

GEORGE: When we were in New York, The Coasters were on there, and then when we were in Florida, they were there, too. Everywhere we went, even when we were in California, The Coasters were advertised.

There was a tendency in those days to have lots of different bands touring with the same name. Nobody knew who was who – they'd just go out and sing songs. I think there were hundreds of Shangri-Las and bands like that.

PAUL: All the excitement on that trip didn't confuse us, because the great thing about our career was that it had stepping stones. If we were going to get confused, it would have been when we became successful in the Cavern. We weren't confused there; it was a nice little local success. And when we were doing gigs like Peterborough Empire, *that* could have got confusing; but we took that also in our stride. Then we were on television shows and some important radio networks, and coped with all that, too; so America was really just a logical progression, only bigger and better than anything.

Americans all spoke with accents that we liked a lot and identified with. We felt we had a lot in common, phonetically. We say 'bath' and 'grass' with a short 'a' (we don't say 'bah-th'), and so do they. I think people from Liverpool do have an affinity with Americans, with the GIs and the war and that. There are a lot of guys in Liverpool walking around with cowboy hats. It is almost as if Liverpool and New York are twin towns.

RINGO: With my family, it didn't matter that we were now big in America. We were big in Liverpool and that was OK by them. It was just a carry-on from that. They didn't really care; I mean, once you'd played the Palladium you were set up in my family – that was *it* for them.

GEORGE: I didn't think beyond the moment during that US trip. I wasn't really aware of any change-over in our fame. I don't think I looked to the future much. I thought, 'We'll enjoy what's happening and go out there and do our thing.'

At first it was fun. We enjoyed it in the early days, but then it just became tiresome. When we went out on the first trip to America, it was the novelty of 'conquering' America. We went back later that year and toured, and then the next year we did another tour and by that time it was just too much. We couldn't move.

RINGO:

## GEORGE MARTIN HAS GONE DEAF IN ONE EAR. NOW HE CAN ONLY WORK IN MONO!

GEORGE MARTIN: *The Beatles didn't get totally immersed in record production until later on, when they stopped touring. Until then, they didn't have time. They would dash into the studio and put down their tracks and then leave all the work to us.*

*The very first records we made were mono, though I did have stereo facilities. To make mixing easier I would keep the voices separate from the backing, so I used a stereo machine as a twin-track. Not with the idea of stereo – merely to give myself a little bit more flexibility in remixing into a mono. So the first year's recordings were made on just two tracks and were live; like doing broadcasts. With the great advance of four-track we were able to overdub and put on secondary voices and guitar solos afterwards. By the time we did* A Hard Day's Night *we would certainly put the basic track down and do the vocals afterwards. Invariably, I was putting all the rhythm instruments onto either one or two tracks (generally one track) so you would have bass lumped with guitar. It wasn't until later still that we began putting bass on afterwards as well, giving Paul the opportunity of using his voice more.*

VOX

EXIT

JOHN: WHEN PEOPLE START COMPARING US TO THE MARX BROTHERS, THAT'S A LOAD OF RUBBISH! THE ONLY SIMILARITY IS THAT THERE WERE FOUR OF THEM AND THERE ARE FOUR OF US.[65]

FIRST
OVERALLS
JOHN RUTTER LTD.

PAUL: For a while we had been thinking about making a film. We'd progressed to success in America. Now it was a film. We'd loved *The Girl Can't Help It* and we knew that you *could* make a rock'n'roll film. We'd seen those little American productions and, although they were low budget and not very good, they did have music and we always went to see them.

So we wanted to be in one, but we wanted it to be a good one. Most were knocked together with a loose story about a DJ who has to go around with a band. They were always terrible stories.

JOHN: We didn't even want to make a movie that was going to be bad, and we insisted on having a real writer to write it.[67]

PAUL: We were offered one early on called *The Yellow Teddy Bears*. We were excited but it turned out that the fella involved was going to write all the songs, and we couldn't have that. But we were still interested in a film, so Brian started talking to people and came up with Dick Lester's name. Brian told us he had made *The Running, Jumping & Standing Still Film*, a short with Spike Milligan – a classic little comedy. We'd loved it, so we all said, 'He's in. That's our man.'

Dick came round to see us and we found that he was also a musician: he could play a bit of jazz piano, which made him even more interesting. He was American but had been working in England; he'd worked with The Goons, that was enough for us.

JOHN: WE WERE THE SONS OF *THE GOON SHOW*. WE WERE OF AN AGE. WE WERE THE EXTENSION OF THAT REBELLION, IN A WAY.[72]

PAUL: For the script, Dick Lester got hold of Alun Owen, a likeable Liverpool-Welsh playwright who had written *No Tram to Lime Street*, a very good television play with Billie Whitelaw.

JOHN: Lime Street is a famous street in Liverpool where the whores used to be. We auditioned people to write for us, and they came up with this guy and he was famous for writing Liverpool dialogue. We knew his work and we said 'all right'. Then he had to come round with us to see what we were like – he was like a professional Liverpool man – and wrote the characters.[70]

RINGO: Brian also got the producer, Walter Shenson; or Walter Shenson got him – everyone wanted to make the movie. And we started hanging out with Alun Owen. He came on part of our British tour and wrote down the chaos that went on around us and how we lived, and gave us a caricature of ourselves.

So *A Hard Day's Night* was like a day in the life; or, really, two days and two nights of our life. We'd go to the recording studio, then go to the TV studio; all the things that happened to us were put in, and he threw in parts for other people.

JOHN: That was a comic-strip version of what was actually going on. The pressure was far heavier than that.[71] I dug *A Hard Day's Night*, although Alun Owen only came with us for two days before he wrote the script. We were a bit infuriated by the glibness of it.

It was a good projection of one façade of us – on tour, in London and in Dublin. It was of us in that situation together, having to perform before people. We *were* like that. Alun Owen saw the press conference so he recreated it in the movie – pretty well; but we thought it was pretty phoney then, even.[70]

PAUL: Alun picked up lots of little things about us. Things like: 'He *is* late but he is very clean, isn't he?' Little jokes, the sarcasm, the humour, John's wit, Ringo's laconic manner; each of our different ways. The film manages to capture our characters quite well, because Alun was careful to try only to put words into our mouths that he might have heard us speak. When he'd finished a scene he would ask us, 'Are you happy with this?' and we'd say, 'Yeah, that's good, but could I say it this way?' I think he wrote a very good script.

GEORGE: There was one piece of dialogue where I say, 'Oh, I'm not wearing that – that's grotty!' Alun Owen made that up; I didn't. People have used that word for years now. It was a new expression: grotty – grotesque.

JOHN: We thought the word was really weird, and George curled up with embarrassment every time he had to say it.

GEORGE: I suppose he thought that being from Liverpool, he knew our kind of humour. If there was something we *really* didn't like, I don't suppose we would have done it – though by the time we got to *Help!* (in 1965) we were cocky enough to change the dialogue as we liked. Alun wrote a scene about us being harassed by the press – which was a real part of our daily duty. They would ask things like, 'How did you find America?' and we'd say, 'Turn left at Greenland.'

I think that was an important part of The Beatles – people associate humour with us. When all the new bands first came out, Gerry and the Pacemakers and others, nobody could tell who was who; one hit was the same as another, everybody got the same amount of coverage. So even if you had a hit you needed something else to carry you. The Beatles actually were very funny, and even when our humour was transposed to New York or somewhere else, it was still great. We were just being hard-faced, really, but people loved it.

EVERYONE IN LIVERPOOL THINKS THEY'RE A COMEDIAN. JUST DRIVE THROUGH THE MERSEY TUNNEL AND THE GUY ON THE TOLL BOOTH WILL BE A COMEDIAN. WE'VE HAD THAT BORN AND BRED INTO US.

And in our case the humour was made even stronger by the fact that there were four of us bouncing off one another. If one dried up, somebody else was already there with another fab quip.

RINGO: It was a lot of fun. It was incredible for me, the idea that we were making a movie. I loved the movies as a kid. I used to go to a hell of a lot, in the Beresford and Gaumont cinemas in Liverpool. I have great memories from Saturday-morning pictures. I'd be into whatever was showing: if it was a pirate movie, I would be a pirate, and if it was a Western I would be a cowboy; or I'd come out as D'Artagnan and fence all the way home. It was a great fantasy land for me, the movies, and suddenly we were in one. It was all so romantic, with the lights and coming to work in the limo.

I think because I loved films I was less embarrassed than the others to be in one; John really got into the movie, too. I felt a lot of the time that George didn't want to be there. It was something he was doing because we were doing it.

GEORGE: I don't know what he's talking about, I loved it! The only thing I didn't like was having to get up at five in the morning.

It was a very early start. We'd have to arrive and get dressed and have our hair and faces done. While all this was going on they would set up with stand-ins. They wouldn't call us until they were ready to rehearse us for a scene.

There was always so much happening that I never knew how many cameras there were. We didn't take too much notice of every detail – we were in the middle, surrounded by everything.

RINGO: Getting up early in the morning wasn't our best talent and there's an example of that in one scene: the one for which I got really good credit, walking by the river with a camera – the 'lonely guy' piece.

I had come directly to work from a nightclub (very unprofessional) and was a little hungover, to say the least. Dick Lester had all his people there, and the kid that I was supposed to be doing the scene with, but I had no brain. I'd gone.

We tried it several ways. They tried it with the kid doing his lines and someone off camera shouting mine. Then they had me doing the lines of the kid and the kid going 'blah blah blah'. Or me saying, 'And another thing, little guy…' I was so out of it, they said, 'Well, let's do *anything*.' I said, 'Let me just walk around and you film me,' and that's what we did. And why I look so cold and dejected is because I felt like shit. There's no acting going on; I felt that bad.

GEORGE: There were some things that we made up as we went along (although I must say they don't look very spontaneous) – for example, the press conference scene. We made up a lot of answers and Dick Lester said, 'Keep that one, use that one.' He was very good like that.

JOHN: The bit in the bathtub was spontaneous. The idea wasn't; they just ran it and I had to do whatever I thought of in the background. Quite a lot of it *is* spontaneous. There were a lot of ad lib remarks, but in a film you don't get ad lib because you've always got to take it eight times. You ad lib something quite good and everybody laughs, the technicians laugh, and the next minute you're told to 'take it again', so your 'ad lib' gets drier and drier until it doesn't sound funny any more. We stuck quite a lot to the script, but some of the gags were us, or the director – he threw quite a bit in, too.[64]

RINGO: Most of it was scripted. What we did lose was the ends of scenes, because they'd put the four of us in a room and we'd all go off in different directions. We'd make things up because of our being comfortable with each other. And the problem with Wilfrid Brambell, a fabulous actor, was that once the scene had finished he just stopped. It looked stupid with the rest of us going, 'Blah de blah, yeah, and another thing…' while, as a professional, he was having nothing to do with it.

PAUL: We got on a train at Marylebone Station one day and the train took off – and suddenly we were in a film! And in the film there were little schoolgirls in gym-slips who were actually models, and we were quite fascinated with them – George even married one: Pattie Boyd.

It was a great day out. We filmed the scene where all the fans run into the train station then the train pulls off, leaving the fans, so then we could get on with the rest of the filming. The train took us somewhere and back, and we had all the scenes made.

JOHN: The train bit embarrasses us now. I'm sure it's less noticeable to people watching in the cinema, but *we* know that we're dead conscious in every move we make, we watch each other. Paul's embarrassed when I'm watching him speak and he knows I am. You can see the nervous bits normally in pictures: things like the end – you make that on one day, and on the next day you do the beginning. But we did it almost in sequence. The first [scene] we did was the train, which we were all dead nervous in. Practically the whole of the train bit we were going to pieces.

It's as good as anybody who makes a film who can't act. The director knew we couldn't act, and we knew. So he had to try almost to catch us off guard; only you can't do that in a film, you've got to repeat things over and over. But he did his best. The minutes that are natural stand out like a sore thumb.[64]

We were always trying to get it more realistic, make the camerawork more realistic. They wouldn't have it – but they made the movie so that's how it happened. It was OK. We knew it was better than other rock movies.[70] The best bits are when you don't have to speak and you just run about. All of us liked the bit in the field where we jump about like lunatics because that's pure film, as the director tells us; we could have been anybody.

We enjoyed doing it, but we'd been the kind of people who didn't like musicals when all of a sudden a song started. We tried to get away from that – from saying, all of a sudden, 'How about a song?' – but we could only to an extent. It felt embarrassing to get into a number. There's a bit in the film where I say the American-musical cliché: 'Say, kids, why not do the show right here?' It was a joke originally that we threw in. Norman Rossington said it used to happen in all the old pop films. They'd be in the middle of a desert and somebody would say, 'I've got a great idea, kids, how about doing the show right here?' I stuck that bit in but it doesn't work; it looks as though I meant it. We thought the gag-line would break it down and everybody would get the joke and a number would follow.[64]

NEIL ASPINALL: *Norman Rossington played me – little Norm. I liked Norm. He was a nice guy. He didn't talk to me about the part; he just went by the script, which was a bit embarrassing because it was nothing like the reality.*

*For The Beatles, the film was six weeks' hard work. They seemed to do everything in quick time. It wasn't just the movie – it was writing the music, recording the album and everything else that went into it as well.*

*John and Paul wrote songs all the time, but that doesn't mean that they would have fourteen or sixteen songs all ready to record. They had some and wrote the rest as they went along. It was a question of being in the studio on Wednesday writing one song, and by Friday having written a couple more. They were writing all the time, on planes, sitting for days in hotel rooms, by a pool, wherever. There were always guitars around.*

JOHN: Paul and I enjoyed writing the music for the film. There were times when we honestly thought we'd never get the time to write all the material. But we managed to get a couple finished while we were in Paris. And three more completed in America, while we were soaking up the sun on Miami Beach. There are four I really go for: 'Can't Buy Me Love', 'If I Fell', 'I Should Have Known Better' – a song with harmonica we feature during the opening train sequence – and 'Tell Me Why', a shuffle number that comes at the end of the film.[64]

PAUL: That wasn't usually the way we worked, because we didn't write songs to order. Usually, John and I would sit down and if we thought of something we'd write a song about it. But Walter Shenson asked John and me if we'd write a song specially for the opening and closing credits. We thought about it and it seemed a bit ridiculous writing a song called 'A Hard Day's Night' – it sounded funny at the time, but after a bit we got the idea of saying it had been a hard day's night and we'd been working all the days, and get back to a girl and everything's fine… And we turned it into one of those songs.

JOHN: I was going home in the car and Dick Lester suggested the title from something Ringo had said. I had used it in *In His Own Write*, but it was an off-the-cuff remark by Ringo, one of those malapropisms – a Ringoism – said not to be funny, just said. So Dick Lester said, 'We are going to use that title,' and the next morning I brought in the song.[80]

GEORGE: Ringo would always say grammatically incorrect phrases and we'd all laugh. I remember when we were driving back to Liverpool from Luton up the M1 motorway in Ringo's Zephyr, and the car's bonnet hadn't been latched properly. The wind got under it and blew it up in front of the windscreen. We were all shouting, 'Aaaargh!' and Ringo calmly said, 'Don't worry, I'll soon have you back in your safely-beds.'

RINGO: I seem to be better now. I used to, while I was saying one thing, have another thing come into my brain and move down fast. Once when we were working all day and then into the night, I came out thinking it was still day and said, 'It's been a hard day,' and looked round and noticing it was dark, '...'s night!'

'Tomorrow Never Knows' was something I said, God knows where it came from. 'Slight bread' was another: 'Slight bread, thank you.' John used to like them most. He always used to write them down.

GEORGE MARTIN: *It was the first film for which I wrote the score, and I had the benefit of having a director who was a musician. We recorded the songs for the film just as we would ordinary recordings, and Dick used a lot of songs we'd already recorded. 'Can't Buy Me Love', for example, which was used twice in the picture.*

*I had scored an instrumental version of 'This Boy' as part of the background music, and I used it for the sequence where Ringo is wandering by the river. We called it 'Ringo's Theme', and it got into the charts in America as an orchestral record – that pleased me somewhat. It was recorded and mixed using a four-track.*

PAUL: The film had an American producer. It worked for American audiences and was an international success as well, but they altered one or two words for the American release. We had plenty of arguments about that. They'd tell us that an American audience wouldn't understand some English phrase. We said, 'Are you kidding? We watch all your cowboy pictures and you go "Yep..." and we know exactly what you're saying. The kids will figure it out,' and of course they did. They went to see it over and over again. We'd get letters saying, 'I've seen *A Hard Day's Night* seventy-five times and I love it!'

JOHN: The first time we saw it was the worst, because there were producers and directors of the film there, and cameramen and all the other people concerned. When you first see yourself on the big screen you watch yourself, thinking, 'Oh, look at that ear, oh, look at my nose, look at my hair sticking out...' and each one of us did that. By the end of the film we didn't know what had happened and we hated it.[64]

PAUL: I don't know what the exact deal was for the movie, but I recall we didn't get a royalty. We were given a fee. Looking back, it would have been better to have taken a small percentage. Our accountants got 3% and we were on a fee. But we didn't really care: 'We are artists, we don't look back...' We just figured, 'Get us some money, Brian. Get us the best deal you can.'

(I only ever once complained to Brian. We'd heard that The Rolling Stones got a slightly better deal at Decca than we did from EMI – sixpence a record or something. I complained to Brian. I remember it hurting him, too. It was a learning experience for me: don't do that

again. It got to him a bit too much. And he was probably right as well: he had done so much for us and there was me bitching about a penny or two.)

RINGO: They'd started to plan the movie months before we actually did it, so we'd got a lot bigger by the time it was made, and by the time it came out we were huge.

When *A Hard Day's Night* was released, or even before that, we felt, 'Yes, we're established. We've conquered all these countries, we're selling a lot of records and they love us.' But I didn't feel like it was going to last forever. I never thought, 'It's going to end tomorrow,' or, 'It's going to go on forever.' It was happening *now*. I wasn't making plans for the future, we were on a roll, and we were all in our early twenties and just going with it.

GEORGE: I HAD MY TWENTY-FIRST BIRTHDAY WHEN WE GOT BACK, JUST AS WE WERE STARTING TO MAKE *A HARD DAY'S NIGHT*. I GOT ABOUT 30,000 CARDS AND PRESENTS – I'M STILL OPENING THEM. I'M STILL WEARING THE WATCH THAT I WAS GIVEN BY MR EPSTEIN.

JOHN: Paul got me a Wimpy and Coke for *my* twenty-first.[64]

DEREK TAYLOR: *The* Daily Express *booked me to cover George's twenty-first birthday. I was supposed to stake it out and report on the guests, the food and so on.*

*At a press conference at the EMI studios, George chatted about the New Experience of Being Twenty-One. There was a great deal of whispering, about the party I supposed – but nothing more for the press. 'Sorry, Derek, know you're a friend of the family, but...' But writing George's column didn't entitle me to hang out at private parties.*

GEORGE: John's book, *In His Own Write*, was published in March. Some of it came from his schooldays, from the *Daily Howl*, a comic full of his jokes and avant-garde poetry, but a lot of the book was new. It turned up in *A Hard Day's Night*. That was the best plug you could have for a book – to put it in a hit movie.

JOHN: It's about nothing. If you like it, you like it; if you don't, you don't. That's all there is to it. There's nothing deep in it, it's just meant to be funny. I put things down on sheets of paper and stuff them in my pocket. When I have enough, I have a book.

There was never any real thought of writing a book. It was something that snowballed.[64] If I hadn't been a Beatle I wouldn't have thought of having the stuff published; I would have been crawling around broke and just writing it and throwing it away. I might have been a Beat Poet.[65] What success really does for you is to give you a feeling of confidence in yourself. It's an indescribable feeling; but once you've had it, you never want it to stop.[64]

It's just my style of humour. It started back in my schooldays. Three people I was very keen on were Lewis Carroll, [James] Thurber and the English illustrator, Ronald Searle. When I was about eleven I was turned on to these three. (I think I was fifteen when I started 'Thurberising' the drawings.)

I used to hide my real emotions in gobbledegook, like in *In His Own Write*. When I wrote teenage poems, I wrote in gobbledegook because I was always hiding my real emotions from Mimi.[71] And when I was about fourteen they gave us this book in English literature – Chaucer, or some guy like him – and we all thought it was a gas. Whenever the teacher got that book out we would all collapse. After that I started to write something on the same lines myself. Just private stuff for myself and my friends to laugh at.[64]

PAUL: I used to go round to Aunt Mimi's house and John would be at the typewriter, which was fairly unusual in Liverpool. None of my mates even knew what a typewriter was. Well, they knew what one *was*, but they didn't have one. *Nobody* had a typewriter.

JOHN: Then when the group started going on the road, I used to take out my typewriter after the show and just tap away as the fancy took me. Sometimes one of the others would say something, like Ringo thought of the film title, 'Hard Day's Night' – I used that in the book.[64]

I typed a lot of the book and I can only type very slowly, so the stories are short because I couldn't be bothered going on. And all my life, I never quite got the idea of spelling. English and writing, fine, but actually spelling the words... I'd spell it as you say it – like Latin, really. Or just try and do it the simplest way, to get it over with, because all I'm trying to do is tell a story and what the words are spelt like is irrelevant. And if it makes you laugh because the word is spelt like that – great. The thing is the story and the sound of the word.[68]

Then came the illustrations. That's the most amount of drawings I've done since I left college.[64] I used to draw with almost anything; usually black pen, or an ordinary fountain pen with black ink. So when it came to doing the book I said, 'Well, I can draw as well, you know,' since they'd mainly taken just the writing; and the drawings were very scrappy because I'm heavy-handed. I draw like I write. I just start to draw and if it looks like something vaguely to do with the story, I do it.[65]

An awful lot of the material was written while we were on tour, most of it when we were in Margate. I suppose it was all manifestations of hidden cruelties. They are very *Alice in Wonderland* and *Winnie the Pooh*. I was very hung-up; it was my version of what was happening then. Sheets of writing and drawings got lost. Some I gave away. A friend, an American who shall remain nameless called Michael Braun, took all the remaining material to the publishers and the man there said, 'This is brilliant. I'd like to do this.' And that was before he even knew who I was.

There's a wonderful feeling about doing something successfully other than singing. I don't suppose the royalties will ever amount to much, but it doesn't matter.[64] I like writing books. I got a big kick out of the first one. There was a literary lunch to which I was invited and at which I couldn't think of anything to say – I was scared stiff, that's why I didn't. I got as big a kick out of seeing that book up there in the writing world's Top Ten as I do when The Beatles get a Number One record. And the reason is that it's part of a different world.[65] Up to now we've done everything together and this is all my own work.[64]

BRIAN EPSTEIN: *John was guest of honour at a Foyle's lunch to mark the success of his splendid book. And made no speech. In answer to the toast, John stood, held the microphone and said, 'Thank you all very much; you've got a lucky face.' John was behaving like a Beatle. He was not prepared to do something which was not only unnatural to him, but also something he might have done badly. He was not going to fail.*

There was no reason for Michael to be sad tha
morning, (the little wretch); everyone liked him, (th
scab). He'd had a hard days night that day, for Michae
was a Cocky Watchtower. His wife Bernie, who was wel

JOHN: I had a holiday after we first made it big, in Tahiti.[68] The sun's there if you want to go and get it – I don't give a damn about the sun. You go out to these places and waste your time lying on the beach; I did it with George for three weeks. We were as brown as berries and we got home and it had gone the next day, so what's the point? I didn't feel any healthier – I was dead beat.[65]

GEORGE: IN 1964 WE SEEMED TO FIT A WEEK INTO EVERY DAY. In May, John and Cynthia and Pattie and I went on holiday. By now we were so famous that we couldn't get on an aeroplane without everyone knowing where we were going.

BRIAN EPSTEIN: *The Beatles' holiday was to be gloriously private. We hired a company and told them we wanted a fool-proof secret route plotting for four young men and three girlfriends and a wife. The men, we explained, would travel in pairs, the girls one pair, two singles. We wanted two destinations, at which two sets of couples would link up.*

*None of the arrangements were to be made by phone, and code names were created for the eight. Mr McCartney was Mr Manning; Mr Starr was Mr Stone. Their companions were to be Miss Ashcroft and Miss Cockcroft. Mr Lennon was Mr Leslie; and his wife, Mrs Leslie. Mr Harrison was Mr Hargreaves, and his girlfriend became Miss Bond. Manning and Stone, Ashcroft and Cockcroft were to holiday in the Virgin Islands; the Leslies, Hargreaves and Bond would go to Tahiti.*

GEORGE: We took a private plane to Amsterdam and caught a flight going to Honolulu via Vancouver. After a long flight we got off the plane in Vancouver for twenty minutes while they refuelled, and by the time we reached Honolulu the whole American disc-jockey network had got us covered.

We had to stay in Honolulu for a couple of days awaiting the connection to Tahiti, so to get away from Waikiki we drove up to the north of the island to a beach where no one knew us. Then we flew to Tahiti, and at Papeete was waiting the sailing boat that we'd booked. We went to a couple of shops there, where John and I bought cool-looking, dark green oilskin macs.

We slept on the boat that night and started sailing first thing the next morning – but as soon as we were out of the harbour we got into a really rough channel of water. We had to keep the engine going, and the boat had just been painted so it stunk of diesel and paint. We couldn't go below because of the fumes, so we lay holding on to the deck. Soon Cynthia and I were feeling sick and puked everywhere. The day seemed long, but eventually, as the sun was setting, we anchored at the next island. We were so ill that we just got into our bunks and went to sleep.

The next morning I woke and looked out of the porthole. It was fantastic. At that time we'd hardly been anywhere out of England, and never to anywhere that was tropical. It was incredible; a smooth lagoon with the island in the background, with mountains and coconut palms. Five or six Tahitians were paddling an outrigger canoe, gliding across the calm sea. It blissed me out.

JOHN: We had to go through Honolulu to get to Tahiti and the outer islands. In Tahiti we were OK; we escaped there. Once we were on the boat, no one got near us – except for one fella from Sydney who we didn't speak to. He swam with us, saying, 'Can I come on your boat?' We said 'no' and he had to swim miles back![64]

GEORGE: We had a great time swimming, snorkelling and sailing from island to island. John spent some of the time writing *A Spaniard in the Works*, and I remember coming up with a lot of little phrases while he sat at the table making it up and speaking it out. If anybody said anything it would go in the book.

JOHN: I'd get to some word, I'd get a sentence and it didn't work somehow, so I'd say to George, 'What's another word for "fly"?' and he'd suggest something.

I was writing 'The Singularge Experience of Miss Anne Duffield', the Sherlock Holmes piece; it was the longest one I'd ever done. I was seeing how far I could go. I would have gone on and on and made a whole book out of it, but I couldn't.

I read one or two Conan Doyle books when I was younger, but on the boat that we'd hired there was a set of them.[65] There was nothing else on the boat but books (half of them were in French and half of them in English). Tahiti and all those islands – great, but I still got into reading. I read every book that was in English whether I liked it or not; through boredom, really. There just happened to be a big volume of Sherlock Holmes, a sort of madman's Sherlock Holmes where you get all the stories in one; and I realised that every story was the same.[68] They're all pretty similar; and that's what I was doing, writing all of them into one.[65] So I wrote one Shamrock Womlbs after three weeks of Sherlock Holmes in Tahiti.[68]

GEORGE: Cynthia and Pattie had long black wigs which they wore as disguises. John and I put their wigs on, and our oilskin macs, and made a little 8mm film about natives on an island with a missionary (John) who comes out of the ocean to convert them.

The holiday was fantastic, but after four weeks we'd had enough. By now we'd drifted further and further from Tahiti and didn't relish the thought of a long boat ride home, so we hopped on a flying boat and went back and spent a day around Tahiti. We then caught a Pan Am 707 coming from New Zealand which took us to Los Angeles. The four of us were the only passengers on the plane and I remember lying on the floor, sleeping, as we had so much space to ourselves. In Los Angeles we went on a bus trip that took us around Sunset Strip, Beverly Hills and all the stars' homes: 'On your left is Jayne Mansfield's house,' and all that.

We were only back in London for about a week before we left for Denmark, Holland, Hong Kong, Australia and New Zealand on tour. Soon we were back about a stone's throw away from where we'd just been in Tahiti.

RINGO: Paul and I went to the Virgin Islands. It was great. The funny part was that we'd been given John's and George's passports, and they'd been given ours. It was still: 'Oh, it's just one of them, give them any passport; they're all the same.' Somehow we got to Lisbon and were checking into the hotel; Paul was wearing a disguise and the guy at reception said, 'Who's that?' looking at the passport suspiciously, 'That's not you.'

We had a 30-foot motor boat that we'd rented. It came with a captain and his wife, and a deck-hand. It was nothing palatial, but we cruised around having a great time. I was with Maureen, and Paul was with Jane Asher. Jane couldn't go in the sun and Paul got sunburnt one day and was screaming all night. Our bedrooms were either side of the passageway with only curtains dividing them, so you could hear everything.

We'd been already with Paul and Jane to Greece; we buddied up for a while. And Maureen and I went with John and Cynthia to Trinidad and Tobago in 1966. I never really went on holiday with George.

RINGO: We had the top five records in the US charts by April 1964, which was amazing.

PAUL: In June 1964, the world tour began. We went to Scandinavia, Holland, Hong Kong, Australia and New Zealand. Ringo missed part of the tour because he was in hospital with tonsillitis. We couldn't cancel, so the idea was to get a stand-in. We got Jimmy Nicol, a session drummer from London. He played well – obviously not the same as Ringo, but he covered well.

It wasn't an easy thing for Jimmy to stand in for Ringo, and have all that fame thrust upon him. And the minute his tenure was over, he wasn't famous any more: 'I was the guy who stood in for Ringo!' But he did great and Ringo joined us out in Australia when he had recovered.

RINGO: My illness was a real big event. It was miserable. I remember it really well: my throat was *so* sore, and I was trying to live on jelly and ice-cream. I was a smoker in those days, too. That was pretty rough, being hooked on the weed.

It was very strange, them going off without me. They'd taken Jimmy Nicol and I thought they didn't love me any more – all that stuff went through my head.

GEORGE: Of course, with all respect to Jimmy, we shouldn't have done it. The point was, it was the Fabs. Can you imagine The Rolling Stones going on tour: 'Oh, sorry. Mick can't come.' – 'All right, we'll just get somebody else to replace him for two weeks.' It was silly, and I couldn't understand it. I really despised the way we couldn't make a decision for ourselves then. It was just: 'Off you go.' – 'But Ringo *must* come with us.' – 'No, sorry, you'll get a new drummer.' As we grew older, I suppose, we would have turned round and said we wouldn't go; but in those days it was the blind leading the blind.

GEORGE MARTIN: *They nearly didn't do the Australia tour. George is a very loyal person, and he said, 'If Ringo's not part of the group, it's not The Beatles. I don't see why we should do it, and I'm not going to.' It took all of Brian's and my persuasion to tell George that if he didn't do it he was letting everybody down.*

*Jimmy Nicol was a very good drummer, who came along and learnt Ringo's parts well. Obviously, he had to rehearse with the guys. They came and worked through all the songs at Abbey Road so he got to know them. He did the job excellently, and faded into obscurity immediately afterwards.*

ASSOCIATED ARTISTES INTERNATIONAL
431 - 432, PRESIDENT HOTEL
KOWLOON, HONG KONG.

JOHN: It was some kind of scene on the road. *Satyricon!* There's photographs of me grovelling about, crawling about Amsterdam on my knees, coming out of whorehouses, and people saying, 'Good morning, John.' The police escorted me to these places, because they never wanted a big scandal. When we hit town, we hit it – we were not pissing about.[70]

We had them [the women]. They were great. They didn't call them groupies, then; I've forgotten what we called them, something like 'slags'.[75]

PAUL: The tour was generally not that different from the others. Hong Kong was different – it was all Army personnel, which was very funny. We had expected Asian people in Hong Kong, but the Army must have got the tickets first, or must have known about us (maybe the Hong Kong people hadn't heard about The Beatles). Each of us had a couple of suits made overnight, and we also had capes made there, which turned out to be disasters, because the dye in them ran so badly.

NEIL ASPINALL: *We'd seen some students in Amsterdam wearing these capes. I found out where they got them from and bought some. They hired a 24-hour tailor to make up more, and they were the model for the ones that The Beatles later used in* Help!.

JOHN: The first one we saw was in Amsterdam – when we were going through the canals, some lad had one on – but we couldn't get any. We could only get ones which weren't the right colour – green ones. So we had four copies made in Hong Kong.[64]

GEORGE: We were boating along the canals, waving and being fab and we saw a bloke standing in the crowd with a groovy-looking cloak on. We sent Mal to find out where he got it from. Mal jumped off or swam off the boat and about three hours later turned up at our hotel with the cloak, which he'd bought from the guy. When we flew from there to Hong Kong we all had copies made, but they were in cheap material which melted in the rain storm at Sydney Airport.

The best flight I remember was that one to Hong Kong. It took several hours and I remember them saying, 'Return to your seats, we are approaching Hong Kong.' I thought, 'We can't be there already.' We'd been sitting on the floor, drinking and taking Preludins for about thirty hours and it seemed like a ten-minute flight.

On all those flights we were still on uppers; that's what helped us get through, because we'd drink a whisky and Coke with anyone, even if he was the Devil – and charm the pants off him!

JOHN: In Hong Kong, the paper said, 'The Beatles fought a losing battle against the screams.' Compared with other audiences, they were quite quiet.[64]

PAUL: As for the show, Hong Kong was a slightly flat performance in a smallish place. They behaved themselves, and it looked like a khaki audience. We played, but I don't think we enjoyed the show too much – although at least we could be heard.

JOHN: When they told us how well our records were going in Australia, we could hardly believe it. Naturally, we're looking forward to the visit. We had a marvellous time water-skiing in Florida, and everyone says the Aussie beaches are great.

I like to keep my work and my private life separate, which is why I keep Cynthia out of the picture. I took her to America, because a trip like that comes once in a lifetime, and she deserved it. I'd dearly have loved to take her to Australia, but the schedule looks too gruelling. My auntie came with us because she's got relatives in New Zealand I have never met.[64]

PAUL: John's Aunt Mimi came to Australia with us, so he behaved himself for a change. She was a good woman, a very strong woman: she had a mind of her own.

GEORGE: WE WERE WATCHING ON TV, AND THEY WERE SAYING, 'I WONDER WHY THEY'RE NOT COMING OUT TO WAVE.' THERE'S NO WAY WE COULD TELL THEM THAT WE DIDN'T HAVE ANY DRY TROUSERS! [64]

The women in John's family were quite strong people. Mimi was very forthright and didn't mince her words. She always had a little twinkle in her eye over John, because she knew he was a bit roguish, and she let him do things – 'Boys will be boys.' She loved him as if he were her own son. But she would tell him off. And he'd say sheepishly, 'Sorry, Mimi.' There was no change in Mimi wherever she was. She was her own character and she was not going to be intimidated by anything. She died in 1991.

DEREK TAYLOR: *Australia was the first big tour for me. It was all very exciting, but I think only a madman would have volunteered to join such a thing. I had no insight into what it would actually mean.*

*The boys in the band were happy enough to have me along. They were fine, which was a relief. They had a press officer, Tony Barrow, who was very suitable, but he'd got very busy because of all the other contemporary stars around the place. Brian had Billy J. Kramer, Gerry and the Pacemakers, Cilla Black and others – and they were all getting Number Ones by then. Busy times.*

JOHN: We've never had more than one PR fella with us, ever. Brian's only got one for each of his artists, and they don't work together. Derek we've known for about a year, but he's one of those people that clicks as soon as you meet him.[64]

NEIL ASPINALL: *When we arrived in Sydney it was pissing down with rain. We got off the plane and they put The Beatles on the back of a flat-back truck so the crowd could see them. They were carrying umbrellas and wearing the capes made in Hong Kong. The driver was doing one mile an hour, and John kept leaning over and saying, 'Faster, faster!' but he wouldn't go any faster. I was saying, 'Go faster – it's pouring down,' and he said, 'These kids have been waiting here for twenty-four hours to see these guys.'*

*Nothing was going to make this big Australian trucker go any faster. By the time they got to the hotel everybody was blue because the dye in the capes had run and soaked right through; they all looked like old Celtic warriors covered in blue dye.*

JOHN: We were having hysterics, laughing. It was so funny, coming to Australia and getting on a big van, all soaking wet; we thought it was going to be sunny. We only got wet for about fifteen minutes, but the kids got wet for hours. How could we be disappointed when they came out to see us and stood in all the rotten wind and rain to wave to us? They were great, really great. I've never seen rain as hard as that, except in Tahiti. (It rained there for a couple of days and I thought it was the end of the world.)[64]

Australia was a high moment, like the first time in America: us appearing on every channel and ten records in the charts. This was another one. It's funny, but there were more people came to see us there than anywhere. I think the whole of Australia was there.[73]

We must have seen a million million people before they let us go. There was good security and everybody was happy and shouting, but we still saw everybody, everywhere we went – and nobody got hurt.[64]

GEORGE: I used to hate waving from balconies. 'Wave,' they'd say. 'You've got to go and wave.' Derek used to wave for me out of hotel windows.

Paul was good at waving and signing autographs. We'd be waiting in the car: 'Come on, Paul, let's go. Where is he? Oh, bugger, there he is.' – 'Oh, yes, what's your name? Betty. To Betty, love Paul.' – 'Come on and get in the fucking car. Let's get out of here!'

PAUL: Three hundred thousand people welcomed us to Adelaide. It was like a heroes' welcome. George waved too. That was the kind of place where we would go to the town hall and they would all be there in the centre of the city. If it had happened suddenly, overnight, it might have gone to our heads; but we had come up bit by bit, so it didn't (not too much). We were just very pleased that everyone had turned out.

We were still close enough to our Liverpool roots to know how it would feel, and what it would mean, if we had showed up in the middle of town to see a group; so we could feel it in their spirit. I think we quite enjoyed it all. It can get a bit wearing, but it certainly wasn't then.

We came in from the airport – it was the same in Liverpool for the première of *A Hard Day's Night*, with the whole city centre full of people – and the crowds were lining the route and we were giving them the thumbs up. And then we went to the Adelaide town hall with the Lord Mayor there, and gave the thumbs up again. In Liverpool it was OK, because everyone understands the thumbs up – but in Australia it's a dirty sign.

RINGO: I hated to leave the other three. I followed them out to Australia and there were people at the airport, but I was on my own and just automatically I looked round for the others. I couldn't stand it. I met up with them in Melbourne. The flight was horrendous. It still is – they may have shaved a couple of hours off the flight, but it's still a hell of a long way. I remember the plane felt like a disaster area to me.

It was fabulous in Australia, and of course, it was great to be back in the band – that was a really nice moment. And they'd bought me presents in Hong Kong.

PAUL:

SYDNEY WASN'T VERY GOOD WEATHER, WAS HE? I THINK IT MUST HAVE BEEN THE MONGOOSE SEASON.[64]

GEORGE: THERE ARE REEFERS ALONG THE WEST COAST, AREN'T THERE?[64]

JOHN: I THOUGHT IT WAS A KIWI BECAUSE IT STARTED POLISHING MY SHOES.[64]

JOHN: Melbourne was as wild as Adelaide, and I think that makes it equal. They were both about the wildest we'd ever seen. We never ask for civic receptions; we don't expect them. If people do it, we're flattered; but if they don't, that's that. There were crowds outside the hotel there. A lot of them got in – we'd find them in bathrooms.

We were all shoving our dirty rags into a case when I heard a knock on the window. I thought it must have been one of the others mucking around so I didn't take any notice, but the knocking kept on so I went over to the balcony – and there was this lad who looked just like a typical Liverpool lad. I knew before he opened his mouth where he was from, because nobody else would be climbing up eight floors. This lad – Peter – walked in and said, 'Hullo dere,' and I said, 'Hullo dere,' and he told me how he'd climbed up the drainpipe, from balcony to balcony. I gave him a drink because he deserved one and then I took him around to see the others, who were quite amazed. They thought I was joking when I told them.[64]

NEIL ASPINALL: *There were people in the crowds, lining the streets, shouting out, 'I'm from Blackpool. If you go up there, say "hello" to our Bill.' But The Beatles were getting used to a lot of people. They'd been to Holland before Australia, with huge crowds on the banks of the canals, and the States as well.*

GEORGE: We took photographs of them all – from the balcony, and on the back of the car in the motorcade. We were stunned, but happy that there was a nice feeling, and that we were popular there. Everybody was saying, 'There are more people here than came to see the Queen.' Well, she didn't have any hit records.

When we were flying in to New Zealand, it looked like England – like Devon, with cows and sheep. But in those days we were looking for some action, and there was absolutely nothing happening.

We were in the hotel room, sitting around eating fish and chips with peas, and watching television. And suddenly, at about nine o'clock at night, the channels all closed down. So we threw our dinners at the TV.

The most notable thing that happened in New Zealand (although it wasn't very good) was that the drummer from Sounds Incorporated had a girl in his room who tried to slash her wrists whilst he was out at the pub. I remember Derek panicking as the story was immediately on the wire service all over the world: 'SUICIDE ATTEMPT IN BEATLE HOTEL'.

JOHN: It was one of the quickest and most pleasant receptions we've ever been to. We went out onto a balcony and waved to the crowd, and some Maoris danced for us, and away we went.

The Lord Mayor was very nice and said, 'I wouldn't have blamed you if you hadn't come, with all the fuss they've been making round here about how much it's costing.'[64]

RINGO: I remember us standing on the roof of a building in one of the cities in Australia, and all the fans were down there, chanting. We were having fun with them and one guy, who was on crutches, threw his crutches away and went into: 'I can walk, I can walk!' What he felt I

don't know, but it was as if he was healed – and then he fell right on his face. He just fell over. Maybe that's why it stuck in my head.

Crippled people were constantly being brought backstage to be touched by 'a Beatle', and it was very strange. It happened in Britain as well, not only overseas. There were some really bad cases, God help them. There were some poor little children who would be brought in in baskets. And also some really sad Thalidomide kids with little broken bodies and no arms, no legs and little feet.

The problem was, people would bring in these terrible cases and leave them in our dressing room. They'd go off for tea or whatever, and they would leave them behind. If it got very heavy we would shout, 'Mal, cripples!' and that became a saying – even when there were no handicapped people present. If there were any people around we didn't like, we'd shout, 'Mal, cripples!' and they'd be escorted out.

PAUL: John used to do the spastic impersonations on stage a lot. He had a habit of putting a clear plastic bag on his foot with a couple of rubber bands. Brian wouldn't like it – he had gone through RADA so he was straight showbiz and he wanted us to behave accordingly, not be too far out. But John would do his cripples impression just crossing a zebra crossing, which would make people stop.

We used to think certain words were very funny that out of teenage nervousness made us laugh: 'cripple', 'harelip', 'cleft palate', 'club-foot' – when a guitar came out, a Club 40, we used to call it a Club-Foot. A sign on the way down to London used to make us howl: 'Cripples crossing'. We used to think it was a place rather than an event.

I remember John and I, shortly after we'd listened to Gene Vincent's album, walking out in the street near Penny Lane and seeing a woman with elephantiasis, and it was so sort of terrifying we had to laugh. A lot of what we did was based in that. And that was the kind of thing that separated us from other people. It meant we had our own world. A world of black humour and of nervousness at other people's afflictions. The way we got through our lives was laughing at them.

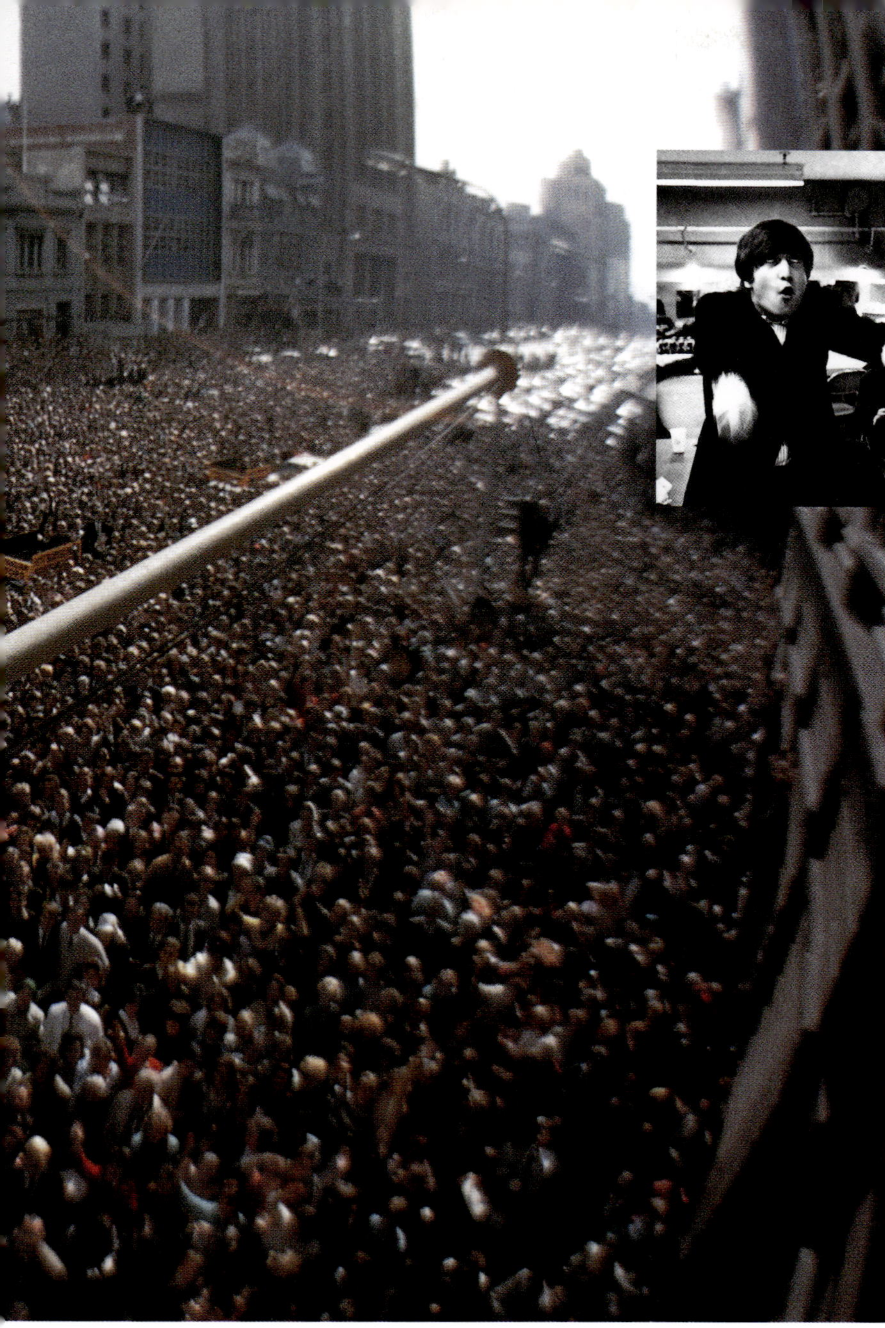

to touch you. And it's always the mother or nurse pushing them on you. They would push these people at you like you were Christ, as if there were some aura about you that would rub off on them.

It got to be like that, and we were very callous about it. It was just dreadful. When we would open up, every night, instead of seeing kids there, we would see a row full of cripples along the front. When we'd be running through, people would be lying around. It seemed that we were just surrounded by cripples and blind people all the time, and when we would go through corridors they would all be touching us. It was horrifying.[70]

In the States, they were bringing hundreds of them backstage, and it was fantastic. I can't stand looking at them. I have to turn away. I have to laugh, or I'd just collapse from hate. They'd line them up, and I got the impression The Beatles were being treated as bloody faith healers. It was sickening.[65] It was sort of the 'in' joke that we were supposed to cure them. It was the kind of thing that we would say. I mean, we felt sorry for them – anybody would – but it was awful. There's a kind of embarrassment when you're surrounded by blind, deaf and crippled people – and there is only so much we could say with the pressure on to perform.[70]

PAUL: I THINK THAT, PARTICULARLY IN THE OLD DAYS, THE SPIRIT OF THE BEATLES SEEMED TO SUGGEST SOMETHING VERY HOPEFUL AND YOUTHFUL. So, often, someone would ask us to say 'hello' to handicapped kids; to give them some kind of hope, maybe. But it was difficult for us, because part of our humour was a sick kind of humour. We were almost having to bless the people in wheelchairs; so there was this dual inclination going on for us.

JOHN: We're not cruel. We've seen enough tragedy in Merseyside. But when a mother shrieks, 'Just touch my son and maybe he will walk again,' we want to run, cry, empty our pockets. We're going to remain normal if it kills us.[65]

GEORGE: John was allergic to cripples. You could see he had a thing about them; I think it was a fear of something. You can see in all our home movies, whenever you switch a camera on John, he goes into his interpretation of a spastic. It's not very nice to be afflicted, so John had this thing that he'd always joke about it. I think the reality was too much for him.

We were only trying to play rock'n'roll and they'd be wheeling them in, not just in wheelchairs but sometimes in oxygen tents. What did they think that we would be able to do? I don't know. I think it was that those people whose job it was to push them around wanted to see the show, and this was a way to get in. It was a case of, 'How many have we got tonight, Brian?' We'd come out of the band room to go to the stage and we'd be fighting our way through all these poor unfortunate people.

John didn't like it. After a while, we used to call even normal people 'cripples', because most people are crippled in a way; in their brains, or in their legs. It's somewhere. Like John wrote: 'One thing you can't hide, is when you're crippled inside.' When you look at some of the old footage of John, and read *In His Own Write*, and with a few other clues in his lyrics, you can piece it together that he definitely had a phobia about it. Most people do. It's a question of, 'There but for the grace of God go I.'

JOHN: I don't think I'd know a spastic from a Polaroid lens. I'm not hung up about them. When I use the term 'spastic' in general conversation, I don't mean to say it literally. I feel terrible sympathy for these people – it seems the end of the world when you see deformed spastics, and we've had quite a lot of them in our travels.[65]

Wherever we went on tour, there were always a few seats laid aside for cripples and people in wheelchairs. Because we were famous, we were supposed to have people, epileptics and whatever, in our dressing room all the time. We were supposed to be good for them.

You want to be alone and you don't know what to say, and they're usually saying, 'I've got your record,' or they can't speak and just want

MEMORANDUM

TO : BEATLES

DATE: 1st JULY, 1964.

FROM : J. A. TAYLOR

SUBJECT: LIVERPOOL PREMIERE

REPLY (if applicable)

Herewith details of Film Premiere in Liverpool.

JULY 10th FRIDAY

Depart London Airport:
STW.161 at 16.00. Party must be at Airport
not later than 15.30

Arrive Liverpool : 17.00
Press Conference : 17.10
Leave Airport : 18.00
Arrive Town Hall : 18.30
Civic Reception : 19.00
Leave for Cinema : 20.15
Film Commences : 21.00
Film Ends : 22.55

Aircraft departs for London when party is aboard.

NEIL ASPINALL: *After Australia and New Zealand it was back to England for the world première of* A Hard Day's Night *in Piccadilly. Big crowds of people again. After London was the Northern première in Liverpool.*

PAUL: I remember Piccadilly being completely filled. We thought we would just show up in our limo, but it couldn't get through for all the people. It wasn't frightening – we never seemed to get worried by crowds. It always appeared to be a friendly crowd; there never seemed to be a violent face.

We weren't *really* apprehensive about going back to Liverpool, for the other première. We'd heard one or two little rumours that people felt we'd betrayed them by leaving, and shouldn't have gone to live in London. But there were always those detractors.

JOHN: We couldn't say it, but we didn't really like going back to Liverpool. Being local heroes made us nervous. When we did shows there, they were always full of people we knew. We felt embarrassed in our suits and being very clean. We were worried that friends might think we'd sold out – which we had, in a way.[67]

GEORGE: I remember us flying up there. When we first started flying to London, we went on Starways Airline. We'd take off from Liverpool and go up over the Mersey, over Port Sunlight. I remember the first time I went on that flight: as the plane was hammering down the runway, the back window opened, right where I was sitting. I freaked out, thinking I was going to get sucked out. I shouted and a stewardess came down, got hold of the window and slammed it shut again. I think by the time we went up for the première they'd started using the Dakota turbo-prop planes.

PAUL: We landed at the airport and found there were crowds everywhere, like a royal do. It was incredible, because people were lining the streets that we'd known as children, that we'd taken the bus down, or walked down. We'd been to the cinema with girls down these streets. And here we were now with thousands of people – for us. There was a lot of, 'Hello, how are you? All right?' It was strange because they were our own people, but it was *brilliant*.

We ended up at Liverpool Town Hall on the balcony, with throngs of people – 200,000, in fact – all out there between the Town Hall and the Cavern. Very familiar territory for us.

JOHN: It was marvellous. I don't know how many it was – just enough to make it fantastic. And it was better when we were in the car, because we were right near them.

We had all been keyed up for days, wondering what sort of reception we would get. We never expected so many people would turn out. We thought there would be only a few people standing on the odd street corner. We heard that we were finished in Liverpool, you see. And after a bit we began to believe it and we thought, 'We don't want to go home if they're going to do that; we'll just sneak home to our houses.' And they kept on, saying, 'I've been down the Cavern, and they don't like you any more.' Of course, they were talking to people who hadn't even known us before anyway. We went back and it was one of the best ever.

What really delighted us more than anything is that everybody, from the top nobs down to the humblest Scouser, has been so nice and friendly and sung praise after praise, which I'm sure we really don't deserve.[64]

GEORGE: It was funny, because the roads I'd driven down all my life were lined with people waving. We stood on the balcony of the Town Hall for the civic reception and John did the salute.

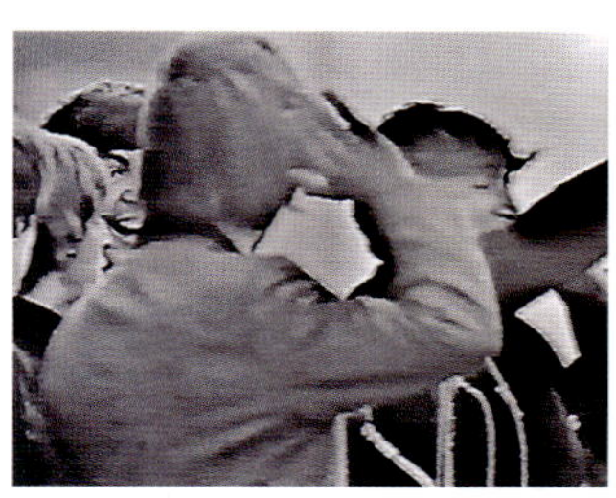

NEIL ASPINALL: *John got away with his Hitler bit on the balcony. Nobody seemed to pick up on it. John was always like that, a bit irreverent. Anybody in nerve-racking situations tends to do things to relieve the tension.*

PAUL: Liverpool was the place we loved, and the reception was great. There was apparently a little bit of sour grapes on the day, but it served only to give the newspaper a story.

# JOHN: THANKS FOR THE PURPLE HEARTS, HAROLD.

GEORGE: We had no reason to be guarded or defensive with the press because we were just having fun and it wasn't any big deal. So, consequently, when The Beatles did a press conference that was part of our charm. We were straightforward, down-to-earth and pretty honest.

JOHN: We were funny at press conferences, because it was all a joke. They'd ask joke questions so you'd give joke answers, but we weren't really funny at all. It was just fifth-form humour, the sort you laugh at at school. The press were putrid. If there were any good questions about our music we took them seriously. We *were* nervous, though I don't think people thought so.

Our image was only a teeny part of us. It was created by the press and us. It had to be wrong, because you can't put over how you really are. Newspapers always get things wrong. Even when bits were true, it was always old. New images would catch on as we were leaving them.[67]

We're past being bugged by questions, unless they're very personal – and then you just over-react: human reactions. There used to be one: 'What will you do when the bubble bursts?' We'd have hysterics, because someone *always* asked it. I'm still looking for the bubble.[68]

On our first [American] tour there was an unspoken thing that Mr Epstein was preventing us talking about the Vietnam War. Before we came back for the second, George and I said to him, 'We don't go unless we answer what we feel about the war.' We were being asked about it all the time and it was silly – we had to pretend to be like in the old days when artists weren't meant to say anything about anything. We couldn't carry it through, we couldn't help ourselves; things would come out even though there was an unspoken policy not to say anything.[72] We spoke our minds after that: 'We don't like it, we don't agree with it, we think it is wrong.'[68]

GEORGE: We were always saying we should speak out about Vietnam, and I think we did at times. I remember talking to the press all the way round the American tours – we used to have them on the plane with us. I would be rabbiting on about everything. But, generally, in the early days there was that concept that pop stars shouldn't rattle their audience: you can't be married; don't let them see your girlfriend – and don't mention the war! Maybe we were naive. Maybe there was a lot of stuff that people weren't ready for...

JOHN: All our songs are anti-war.[64]

GEORGE: I think about it every day, and it's wrong. Anything to do with war is wrong. They're all wrapped up in their Nelsons and their Churchills and their Montys – always talking about war heroes. Look at *All Our Yesterdays*. How we killed a few more Huns here or there. It makes me sick. They're the sort who are leaning on the walking sticks and telling us a few years in the army would do us good.[66]

GEORGE: Everywhere we went, the police were putting on their display. Everybody got into the mania. You could make a film, just showing how idiotic everybody else was whenever The Beatles came to town.

In America, the police would be directing the traffic. They'd drive ahead of the motorcade; they'd come to a crossroads, put both hands up and blow their whistles. Then another bike would pass and go to the next link, but they'd all try to be flash, going in and out and racing up the road. They loved the feeling of: 'It's the President coming!' But they were all crashing, falling off. It was happening everywhere – even in Sweden! Wherever we went it was that kind of thing.

JOHN: We always called it 'the eye of the hurricane' – it was calmer right in the middle.[74]

GEORGE: ON TOUR THAT YEAR, IT WAS CRAZY. NOT WITHIN THE BAND. IN THE BAND WE WERE NORMAL, AND THE REST OF THE WORLD WAS CRAZY.

NEIL ASPINALL: *The film* A Hard Day's Night *and the soundtrack album were both hits by the time they got back to America for the August tour. America was now very aware of The Beatles and things were crazy. There were lots of people trying to touch the band. Everywhere they went, the local dignitaries would want to meet them, and would bring their children with them.*

*Sometimes they didn't have time for it, and it was much less disciplined than it was in England, because everything was bigger. If they were playing a stadium, the dressing room would be the players' locker room. It wasn't like the back of the Hammersmith Odeon where they could isolate themselves; you could get 200 people in a locker room. So, there would be five or six of us, the people from GAC (the tour agency), the security staff, the local promoter, people bringing food in and out – and bands wanting to say 'hello': The Lovin' Spoonful, The Grateful Dead and other bands.*

PAUL: WE WERE GETTING A LITTLE CRAZY WITH IT ALL.

JOHN: It just really built up: the bigger that we got, the more unreality we had to face, the more we were expected to do – until when you didn't shake hands with a mayor's wife she starts abusing you and screaming, 'How dare they!'

There is one of Derek's stories where we were asleep after the session, in a hotel somewhere in America, and the mayor's wife comes and says, 'Get them up, I want to meet them!' Derek said, 'I'm not going to wake them up,' and she started to scream, 'You get them up or I'll tell the press!'

There was always that. They were always threatening what they would tell the press, to make bad publicity about us if we didn't see their bloody daughter with braces on her teeth. And it was always the police chief's daughter or the Lord Mayor's daughter; all the most obnoxious kids, because they had the most obnoxious parents. We had these people thrust on us and were forced to see them all the time. Those were the most humiliating experiences.[70]

RINGO: I found the tour madness exciting. I loved it. I loved the decoy cars and all the intricate ways of getting us to the gigs. It was just so much fun. Also, we were meeting a lot of great people, musicians and actors; and finding great bars. We could still go out. That was the amazing thing, we were not trapped. We went out all the time – well, I was out quite a lot.

JOHN: We just can't get out on our own – but we had seventeen years of being able to walk to the shops. Occasionally, one of us slips out on his own and we take a chance there, because people think we travel in fours all the time. When they see us on our own, they often don't recognise us.

People think fame and money bring freedom, but they don't. We're more conscious now of the limitations it places on us rather than the freedom. We still eat the same kind of food as we did before, and have the same friends. You don't change things like that overnight. We can't even spend the allowance we get, because there's nothing to spend it on. What can you spend on in a room?

When you're on tour, you exist in this kind of vacuum all the time. It's work, sleep, eat and work again. We work mad hours, really, but none of us would have it any other way. When I look back, I can't remember a time when I wasn't in the business – it seems years to me, now.[64]

RINGO: We would go to bars or clubs – or on police-car drives; drive with the cops. (The police were very good to us in those days, because they would take all the pills or stuff off the kids and give it to me. I loved the police!)

There was one time in San Francisco which was great. We went to a bar and Dale Robertson was there. I mean, *Dale Robertson!* It was, 'Hey, Dale, how you doing?' – 'I'm fine.' We were having a drink and then they said, 'OK, that's the end, everyone has to leave the bar.' California closes down at 2am; that's the end of the night. So they closed the bar and the barman and everyone went out and then we went back in and carried on. I loved all that.

I loved meeting Burt Lancaster, too. He was great. The first time in LA, we'd rented a huge house and I turned into a cowboy. I had a poncho and two toy guns and was invited over to Burt Lancaster's, and that was how I went. I was all, 'Hold it up there now, Burt, this town ain't big enough for both of us,' and he said, 'What have you got there? Kids' stuff.' Later he sent me two real guns, and a real holster: he didn't like me playing with kids' guns. I just wanted to be a cowboy.

He had an amazing house. It had a pool outside, but you could swim into the living room if you went under the glass. LA was a mind-blower. We used to walk up and down Sunset Strip; we'd get out of the limo and people would come up to us, but it was still quite cool. It wasn't like a crazy feeding frenzy; there would be a lot of 'hellos'. Of course, as it got into 1965/66 and substances came into play, the attitude was changing and it was cool to be cool, to just go shopping. Everyone would be pleased to see you walk down Sunset. And Sunset was great. We went to the Whisky A Go Go, and all the clubs.

JOHN: Something like Ringo's saying, 'Burt Lancaster's genuine,' sounds like a showbusiness or actors' or film stars' cliché, but it isn't. Because the people we meet and don't think are genuine we either don't meet or we don't mention on tape or we tell them that they're lousy.[64]

RINGO: We played the Hollywood Bowl. The shell around the stage was great. It was *the* Hollywood Bowl – these were impressive places to me. I fell in love with Hollywood then, and I am still in love with Hollywood – well, Beverly Hills, Hollywood, California. I prefer it to New York.

Hollywood has palm trees – there aren't many palm trees in Liverpool. The weather was hot and the lifestyle was really, really cool.

JOHN: Showbiz is a bit potty, and the whole of showbiz stuck in one area must be potty. We saw a couple of film stars: Edward G. Robinson, Jack Palance, Hugh O'Brian. We were expecting to see more. We were a bit choked.

The Hollywood Bowl was marvellous. It was the one we all enjoyed most, I think, even though it wasn't the largest crowd – because it seemed so important, and everybody was saying things. We got on, and it was a big stage, and it was great. We could be heard in a place like the Hollywood Bowl, even though the crowd was wild: good acoustics. There's a couple of places we've been heard quite well, better than we've been for years.[64] But we don't want them quiet. There's no point in doing a show if they're just going to sit there listening – they can listen to their record. I like a riot.[66]

GEORGE MARTIN: *I thought we should record the Hollywood Bowl concert, and I arranged for Capitol to provide their engineers. The technique we used was three-track, half-inch tape, and the separation wasn't too great. To begin with, we had the voices in the centre with a mixture of drums, bass and guitars on separate side-tracks. But pervading the whole lot was the enormous welter of screams from the audience. It was like putting a microphone at the tail of a 747 jet. It was one continual screaming sound, and it was very difficult to get a good recording.*

PAUL: People were saying, 'Doesn't it drive you mad, all these girls screaming?' We didn't mind it, because sometimes it covered a multitude of sins: we were out of tune. It didn't matter – we couldn't hear it, nor could they.

GEORGE MARTIN: *The Hollywood Bowl tapes weren't issued at that time. The Beatles didn't think it was right to do so; and it wasn't until 1977 that I dug them up, refurbished them and issued a record.*

*They were great as a live band, especially when you consider that one of their problems was that they couldn't hear themselves. In concerts today, everyone has a fold-back speaker at their feet, so that they can hear what's going on. They didn't have that in the days of The Beatles' live shows, so John, Paul and George would be standing at microphones in front of a screaming crowd of 60,000 and Ringo would be at the back on the drums.*

*Ringo once said to me how difficult following was: 'I couldn't do anything clever. I couldn't do great drum kicks or rolls or fills, I just had to hang onto the backbeat all the time to keep everybody together. I used to have to follow their three bums wiggling to see where we were in the song.'*

RINGO: There was nothing else I could do through the numbers bar play the off-beat and try to lip-read where they were up to in the songs, or read by their movements where the hell we were. If I tried to do anything on the toms it was lost in the din. But it never disappointed me because when we toured in the Sixties, it was to sell records, which the fans could then go off and listen to and we would get our royalty, a penny a record.

GEORGE: ALL THE TOURS MERGE INTO ONE IN MY MIND.

We had Jackie De Shannon on tour with us; I remember playing guitar with her. We went to Los Angeles, where we stayed in a big old shady house in Bel Air. Somebody conned us into going to the Whisky A Go Go. It seemed to take us twenty minutes to get from the door to the table and instantly the whole of Hollywood paparazzi descended. It was a total set-up by Jayne Mansfield to have pictures taken with us. John and I were sitting either side of her and she had her hands on our legs, by our groins – at least she did on *mine*. We'd been sitting there for hours, waiting to get a drink; we had glasses with ice in them, and the ice had all melted. A photographer came and tried to get a picture and I threw the glass of water at him. He took a photo of the water coming out of the glass and soaking (accidentally) the actress Mamie Van Doren, who just happened to be passing. We got out of there; it was hell. We left town the next day, and I remember sitting on the plane, reading the paper and there was the photo of me throwing the water.

RINGO: Which any normal fella would do, but because George did it and he was in The Beatles, it got all that publicity. You go to a club and there's some little photographers with big cameras, and none of them say, 'Can I take a picture?' They run up and put their flash about four inches from your eyes and flash a dirty big light which blinds you.

**1964**
Five week tour of USA and CANADA

.............San Francisco, Cow Palace
.............Las Vegas, Convention Hall
.............Seattle, Municipal Stadium
.............Vancouver, Empire Stadium
..........Los Angeles, Hollywood Bowl
..........................Rest Days
.............Denver, Red Rock Stadium
..............Cincinnati, The Gardens
.........New York, Forest Hills Stadium
..........Atlantic City, Convention Hall
..........................Rest Days
..........Philadelphia, Convention Hall
.......Indianapolis, State Fair Coliseum
................Milwaukee, Auditorium
.....Chicago, International Amphitheatre
..............Detroit, Olympic Stadium
...........Toronto, Maple Leaf Gardens
.....................Montreal, Forum
..........................Rest Days
...............Jacksonville, Gator Bowl
...............Boston, Boston Gardens
................Baltimore, Civic Centre
................Pittsburgh, Civic Arena
...........Cleveland, Public Auditorium
........New Orleans, City Park Stadium
............................Rest Day
.............Dallas, Memorial Coliseum
....New York City, Charity Performance

JOHN: Anywhere we go we're going to get people coming up with their flashes. You take it once, twice, maybe three times and then you say, 'OK, whatever-your-name-is, have you done yet? We're not going to do anything else, we're just sitting here, you've got all the pictures you need,' which is what happened in that club in Hollywood. We said 'go away' and he goes. But he comes back again. It's embarrassing for us, because they say, 'Oh, they're big headed, how dare they ask somebody to go away?' So the manager of the club comes up and says, 'Is he bothering you?' And we say, 'Yeah, will you just move him? Tell him to drop his camera; come over and join the table; anything, *but stop flashing!*'[64]

RINGO: I REMEMBER ONCE LOOKING INTO A MIRROR AND SAYING TO MYSELF: "ERE, IT'S NOT THAT BIG, IS IT?' YOU COULD SAY NOW I'VE COME TO TERMS WITH MY NOSE. IT'S THE TALKING POINT WHEN PEOPLE DISCUSS ME. I HAVE TO LAUGH – IT GOES UP ONE NOSTRIL AND OUT THE OTHER.[65]

GEORGE: Before LA we went and played in Las Vegas, where Liberace visited us. I think the first four rows of that concert were filled up by Pat Boone and his daughters. He seemed to have hundreds of daughters.

There was all kinds of trouble in the States. There was everyone trying to sue us. There were girls trying to get into our rooms so they could sue us for totally made-up things. There was always this very peculiar suing consciousness. I'd never heard about suing people until we went to America.

We went to Key West from French Canada, where we'd thought Ringo was going to get shot. A Montreal newspaper reported that somebody was going to kill Ringo. Because they didn't like his nose or something? Because he was probably the most British of The Beatles? I don't know. Anyway, we decided, 'Fuck this, let's get out of town,' and we flew a day early, instead of staying the night in Montreal.

RINGO: Some people decided to make an example of me, as an English Jew. (The one major fault is I'm not Jewish.) Threats we took in our stride. I mean, suddenly there would be a few more cops; but this was one of the few times I was really worried. We were playing the gig and, as always, I was on a high-riser. I had the cymbals up towards the audience to give me a bit of protection; usually I had them flat on. I also had a plain-clothes policeman sitting there with me. But I started to get hysterical, because I thought, 'If someone in the audience has a pop at me, what is this guy going to do? Is he going to catch the bullet?' I found this was getting funnier and funnier all the time, and the guy just sat there.

GEORGE: We got on the plane to Jacksonville, Florida. But we found that there was a hurricane hitting Jacksonville, so they diverted us to Key West, announcing, 'Fasten your seat belts. The runway isn't big enough for this plane. We're going to have to go in with full reverse thrust.' This was on an Electra, a plane that we later discovered has a very high accident record. But we landed at Key West all right and had our day off there.

They said the hurricane had passed when we flew into Jacksonville, but it was as windy as hell and it was dark with very heavy black clouds all over. It had cleared a bit, but there were still turbulent winds, and as we were approaching we could see the devastation: palm trees fallen over and mess laying everywhere.

We'd discovered that there was a group of people following us around America, filming us, and we'd told them not to. They were in Florida and by this time we were saying, 'Look, we told these people to bugger off and they're here again and right out front.' They had actually been given priority with their camera, right in front of the stage. The winds were howling and there was Mal, nailing the drum kit to the platform, about ten or twelve feet off the ground; and we were really pissed that the film crew was there, so we said that we weren't going on. The promoters were getting stroppy with *us*, instead of kicking the camera people out. In the end Derek Taylor went on stage and was like Adolf Hitler up there, shouting to the crowd: 'These camera people are not wanted, they must be removed.' He was yelling, 'Do you want The Beatles on this stage?' – 'Yeah!' – 'Well then, do you want to get rid of the cameras?' – 'Yeah!' It was like a big Nuremberg rally, and I suppose the police and promoters thought that we were causing the trouble; but, even in those days, we knew there were some things you couldn't control.

There were riots in every city. Students rioting, blacks rioting; in Canada the French were trying to split from the British. Every place we went, there seemed to be something going on.

All the time, constantly, I felt frightened by things. I remember when we were going for that trip to America and they were saying, 'Oh, yeah, we're going to start in San Francisco with a ticker-tape parade.' That was once when I actually said, 'I'm not going.' I mean, it was less than a year since they'd assassinated Kennedy, and you know how mad it is in America. And with ticker-tape, somebody has got to sweep it up later. I don't like littering the streets, so I just said: 'I'm not doing that, I don't want a ticker-tape parade; it's silly.'

GEORGE MARTIN: *There had been death threats. I remember going to one of their concerts at the Red Rock Stadium in Denver where Brian and I climbed up on a gantry overlooking the stage, and we looked down at the boys below during the performance; and the amphitheatre is such that you could have a sniper on the hill who could pick off any of the fellows at any time – no problem. I was very aware of this, and so was Brian, and so were the boys.*

JOHN: We get battered mostly by people trying to guard us – they get in the way half the time. They are always grabbing us and shoving us in the wrong thing. We have hysterics when they [the fans] get on stage. One got George, and I could hear all wrong notes coming out. He was trying to carry on playing – with a girl hanging round his neck! But I always feel safe on stage, even when they break through. I just feel as though I'm all right when I'm plugged in.[64]

PAUL: I was got once by a cigarette lighter. It clouted me right in the eye and closed my eye for the stay. In Chicago a purple and yellow stuffed animal, a red rubber ball and a skipping rope were plopped up on stage. I had to kick a carton of Winston cigarettes out of the way when I played.[64]

JOHN: You feel a clonk on the back of the head and you look and it's a shoe. Then once one comes they all start thinking, 'Shoes: that'll attract their attention. If they get a shoe on the head, they're bound to look over here.' I always scout round looking on stage and tell Mal. He usually picks them all up at the end before the scavengers leap on and all the attendants pinch anything that's worth having.[66]

DEREK TAYLOR: *From Dallas our next official stop was New York. Our secret interim destination was the Arkansas/Missouri border, where Reed Pigman (whose Lockheed Electra had been our travelling home for the last month) had a ranch.*

GEORGE: We flew from Dallas to an intermediate airport where Pigman met us in a little plane with the one wing, on top, and with one or maybe two engines. It was so like Buddy Holly, that one; that was probably the closest we came to that sort of musicians' death. I don't mean it nearly crashed because it didn't, but the guy had a little map on his knee, with a light, as we were flying along and he was saying, 'Oh, I don't know where we are,' and it's pitch black and there are mountains all aroud and he's rubbing the windscreen trying to get the mist off. Finally he found where we were and we landed in a field with tin cans on fire to guide us in.

AMERICAN FLYERS AIRLINE CORP.
MEACHAM FIELD • FORT WORTH, TEXAS
MA 4-7258

September 18, 1964

THE BEATLES
Attention: Paul Mc Cartney

Dear Paul;

I hope the enclosed recap of your U.S. tour will serve to remind you of the many experiences you have had while in America. It has been a real pleasure to have participated in your travel arrangements, by keeping four "Down To Earth" up in the air so much of the time.

I have enjoyed meeting and talking with you personally and sincerely hope that I may again take part in planning your ups and downs.

Sincerely,

J. E. Linnell

DEREK TAYLOR: *After a night awake, dawdling through poker and cigarettes and beer into the early hours, we took our pick of some wild and rugged horses. Watched with amusement by Mrs Pigman, we chose our nags according to whim; Beatles first, aides next, Brian last because – alone among us – he did know something about riding horses.*

GEORGE: With the concerts and the Beatlemania, after a while the novelty wore off and then it was very boring. It wasn't just the noise on stage, not hearing the music and playing the same old songs; it was too much everywhere we went. Even when we got away from the screaming fans, there were all the screaming policemen and the Lord Mayors and their wives and the hotel managers and their entourages.

THE ONLY PLACE WE EVER GOT ANY PEACE WAS WHEN WE GOT IN THE SUITE AND LOCKED OURSELVES IN THE BATHROOM. THE BATHROOM WAS ABOUT THE ONLY PLACE YOU COULD HAVE ANY PEACE.

DEREK TAYLOR: *I was very, very good at helping the press and very anxious to oblige and let people in on the story and share it out. But there were too many people, tens of thousands, clamouring to get at the band. One weekend in America, 20,000 people phoned the switchboard in the hotel in New York to get through, and many of them did. To me. Just too much. Too many. Too often.*

*The Beatles handled that extreme pressure well. I didn't know then how difficult it was for them because, again, I had no time to get an insight into what it was really like.*

*I did make great demands on them, which they met somewhat, balcony-waving, etc.: 'Come on, guys, try and give them one more wave. Let's get you out there.' There were those moments when someone, George in particular, would rebel, would do that: 'Get your arm and bloody wave for me, I'm not going up there,' that sort of thing; or, 'I'm not meeting Shirley Temple!' – 'Don't shout, she's listening, she'll hear you.' – 'I don't care. I don't know Shirley Temple; she doesn't mean anything to me!'*

JOHN: We make more money out of writing songs than we do out of appearing and running round waving and that.[64]

DEREK TAYLOR: *George later said, 'If we'd known of, or were ready to be impressed by, Hedda Hopper or George Raft or Edward G. Robinson, we wouldn't have had the guts to go out. It was because we really didn't know a lot of those people, hadn't heard of them, that we weren't scared of them.' I, of course, had heard of them and was scared of them, so while The Beatles were pirates, I was still a bit middle class.*

*In the heyday of Beatlemania, there was a view that if you got to know The Beatles, your life would become sublime. It was a mania of some size. In 1964, because it was the first huge year, they did meet all kinds of people whom they would eventually shut out of their lives.*

*I still saw things as a journalist and got The Beatles to people in numbers, which is why I was really so good at the job, because I wanted to give the boys and the girls of the press what they wanted.*

GEORGE MARTIN: *I've seen the stresses to which they were subjected, and it was absolute hell. Wherever they went, there were hordes of people trying to get hold of them, trying to get their autographs, trying to touch them.*

*They were besieged by reporters, who aren't very nice people; they tend to use their elbows and feet to kick people, and each other, out of the way. I remember being escorted by police cars, or almost being kicked out of an aircraft by reporters who wanted to get on. Another time, I was in a lift, stuck between floors because too many people had crowded in.*

*It was just some giant three-ring circus from which there was no let-up.*

*The only peace they got was when they were alone in their hotel room, watching television and hearing the screams outside. That was about it. A hell of a life, really.*

JOHN: Our life isn't like a tour, or like *A Hard Day's Night*, or any of those things. Only when we do that is all that created. When we're just living, it's calm. We never saw anything – just different rooms all over the place.[68]

If you're on tour, you don't get any time off. Even if we're touring America and it says 'a day off', you don't play that night, it's no good; because we're in the hotel room and to go out is a big operation involving the police and everything. And you're still 'on' because you're in contact with people who are looking at you and wanting autographs, or wanting a smile, or wanting something. So that's still a strain and still work.

You get used to it, like a prisoner must do. We play guitars, sing, have people round, play cards, draw; we do everything. Now and then, you get sick and tired – like anybody does; but no more sick and tired of it than I got sick and tired of school, or I got sick and tired of having no money.[65]

NEIL ASPINALL: *Brian was very much in control; in control of what I'm not sure – but he was in control. If he said they were playing Milwaukee, then they were playing Milwaukee. Brian was the manager and if he booked an engagement they'd do it and complain afterwards: 'Don't get us a gig like that again,' or, 'We don't want to do a double-shuffle' – two gigs on the same night – 'it's getting too crazy to do that.' But the words would always be said afterwards and not before. If something was booked for The Beatles, they turned up and did it.*

THE BEATLES 1964 TOUR
OF U.S.A. AND CANADA
STATEMENT OF ACCOUNT
Gross Receipts - Tour
- "Shindig"
$ 1,187,123.8
50,000.0
$ 1,237,123.8
Less: Commissions
Expenses paid
Less: Taxes witheld
Less: Commission

NEIL ASPINALL: *I remember the Kansas offer – for them to play an additional, unscheduled gig – kept coming up. It started out at $60,000 and they were saying 'no' because they had so few days off. Already that year they'd been to Paris, the States, appeared on the Ed Sullivan shows, come home and made the A Hard Day's Night record and movie. Then flown straight off on a world tour, and back to England for more concerts, TV and radio shows. And a visit to Sweden and straight after that an American tour.*

*They weren't getting any rest. A day off was precious; so if Brian wanted to fill one of their days off with an extra gig, they'd have to stop and think. To play thirty-five American cities was a big tour in those days. They'd play a gig on Monday, Tuesday, Wednesday, Thursday, Friday, in different cities all over the States – flying in, hotel, press conference, gig, back to the hotel, flying out.*

*Brian had booked a 35-gig tour and they knew what they were doing and were committed to that. But to shove one more show in the middle was another story. So, The Beatles kept saying 'no', and the money kept going up. They agreed to do it in the end. The offer started at $60,000 and finally went to $150,000.*

JOHN: Wherever we went, there was always a whole scene going. Derek's and Neil's rooms were always full of fuck knows what, and policemen and everything.[70] All those people that went into Derek's room originally came with the intention of getting to *our* room, and they expect free drinks, free food, free anything that's going. You get to know them and can tell them apart from the others. Some of them are good fun because they are such clever imposters and con men. You can admire them; but all of them are just bums, and that's why they're in Derek's room and not ours.[64] We had our four bedrooms separate to keep them out.

We had to do something, and what do you do when the pill doesn't wear off, when it's time to go?[70]

MAL EVANS: *During that American tour each of us lost one and a half stone in sweat.*

NEIL ASPINALL: *We did have a laugh, and it was good, and though it got tense and tiring it didn't become a bore. We had a good time overall, and if anybody really got tense they took it out on me.*

JOHN: We were bastards. You can't be anything else in such a pressurised situation, and we took it out on Neil, Derek and Mal. They took a lot of shit from us because we were in such a shitty position. It was hard work and somebody had to take it. Those things are left out, about what bastards we were. Fucking big bastards, that's what The Beatles were. You have to be a bastard to make it, and that's a fact. And The Beatles were the biggest bastards on earth.

We were the Caesars. Who's going to knock us when there's a million pounds to be made, all the hand-outs, the bribery, the police and the hype?[70]

DEREK TAYLOR: *By the end of the US tour in September, Brian and I had a falling out. We actually fell out a lot, because I still had an independent spirit. I knew about trade-union rights and holidays and speaking your mind and that sort of thing. I knew also about blundering into situations which were not tactful, making commitments for one or other of them which, really, only a manager should do: 'Sure, John can give away a South Australian opal on camera.' – 'Well, that's an engagement,' Brian said. 'How dare you commit John to giving away a South Australian opal on camera?' – 'I didn't realise.' – 'Well, you should have realised. You're usurping your power, and I didn't hire you for that, I hired you for this; you shouldn't be working with the boys, anyway, you should be with me all the time.' – 'Oh, this is crazy, I'm off!'*

*So, I left in New York. I resigned at the end of the tour, in September; but Brian made me work three months' notice, though, until just before Christmas. He tortured me by sending me to America on tour with Tommy Quickly and a song called 'The Wild Side Of Life'.*

*He made me work out my time, but he also asked me to stay, with, 'Derek... you and I, we do get along, when we get along.' – 'Well, we do, Brian, but...' And it was such a relief to leave; I couldn't imagine why I'd ever wanted to join them. As long as we could still be friends, that was fine; let's get out of here and go back to newspapers.*

*So I went on to the* Daily Mirror *as a reporter, almost as just an ordinary reporter: happy, too.*

PAUL: Our days off were sacred. If you look at our 1964 timetable you can see why. I didn't realise until recently that we used to have a whole year of work, and then get something like 23rd November off – and then have to judge a beauty competition that day. So, by the time we got to Kansas City, we probably needed a day off. I can't actually remember falling out with Brian about him wanting us to work on a day off; we'd talk to each other rather than fall out.

DEREK TAYLOR: *Occasionally The Beatles and I socialised with the public on tour. Just a bit. I wanted them to do it more. Ringo and Paul would, quite a lot – relatively so. George would do none of it. John would, if he was up all night. If you could keep him up he would do things first thing in the morning, which is when I couldn't get the others; so we used to stay up on pills and drink together a lot, and that's when we really got very friendly, in an extremely wholesome sort of way. It was the kind of friendship that men have when they are drinking together, whatever that means.*

*I think all of The Beatles enjoyed some of the touring. They liked meeting people like Fats Domino and others they met; they had quite a time.*

PAUL: Fats Domino we admired. We met him in New Orleans. He had a very big diamond watch in the shape of a star, which was very impressive.

GEORGE: He was sweet, just like a little boy. On the tours we liked to listen to Tamla Motown: Marvin Gaye and the others. Stevie Wonder was just coming around in those days, and Ray Charles we'd liked from the Fifties. We were also meeting people like Chuck Berry and Carl Perkins.

And Indianapolis was good. As we were leaving, on the way to the airport, they took us round the Indy circuit, the 500 oval, in a Cadillac. It was fantastic. I couldn't believe how long the straightway was; and to be on the banking and see all the grandstands was great.

DEREK TAYLOR: *They loved going to New York, when we stayed at the Del Monico Hotel, flying by helicopter into Forest Hills, the great tennis stadium. Those New York dates were exciting. They did enjoy that excitement, the city lights, the pace of events. Or so it seemed to me.*

GEORGE: The Righteous Brothers were on stage singing 'You've Lost That Loving Feeling', when we came hovering over in this sodding big Chinook. All the people were up in the stands, pointing up to the sky, screaming and shouting, paying not a blind bit of notice to The Righteous Brothers – which pissed them off a little. In fact, they got so pissed off that they decided to leave the tour. Righteous indignation.

JOHN:

GOOD NIGHT, AND THANKS FOR THE BREAD.[64]

Less: Paid out, 11th February
bank charges,
Cheque to Beatles Limited - £ 85,273.18. 5.

## RINGO: IN NEW YORK WE MET BOB DYLAN. THAT WAS THE FIRST TIME THAT I'D REALLY SMOKED MARIJUANA AND I LAUGHED AND I LAUGHED AND I LAUGHED. IT WAS FABULOUS.

RINGO: Bob was our hero. I heard of him through John, who'd played his records to me. He was just great; he was this young dude with great songs. Songs of the time, poetry, and a great attitude.

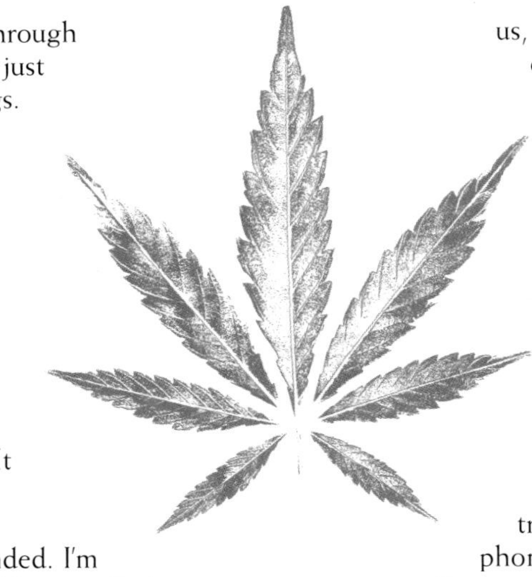

PAUL: Bob came round one evening, whilst we were in New York. He was our idol. I had seen early programmes on Granada TV, when we were in Liverpool, about the New York Beat Poets' scene, where he had been singing along with Allen Ginsberg. So we were into him as a poet, and we all had his first album with his floppy cap. I'm sure that's where the Lennon cap came from. John was a particularly big admirer. It shows in songs like 'Hide Your Love Away'.

JOHN: When I met Dylan I was quite dumbfounded. I'm pretty much a fan type myself, in a way; I stopped being a 'fan' when I started doing it myself. I never went collecting people's autographs or any of that jive. But if I dig somebody, I really dig them.[71]

'You've Got To Hide Your Love Away' is my Dylan period.[74] It's one of those that you sing a bit sadly to yourself, 'Here I stand, head in hand...' I'd started thinking about my own emotions. I don't know when exactly it started, like 'I'm A Loser' or 'Hide Your Love Away', those kind of things. Instead of projecting myself into a situation, I would try to express what I felt about myself, which I'd done in my books. I think it was Dylan who helped me realise that – not by any discussion or anything, but by hearing his work.

I had a sort of professional songwriter's attitude to writing pop songs; we would turn out a certain style of song for a single, and we would do a certain style of thing for this and the other thing. I'd have a separate songwriting John Lennon who wrote songs for the meat market, and I didn't consider them (the lyrics or anything) to have any depth at all; to express myself I would write *A Spaniard in the Works* or *In His Own Write*, the personal stories which were expressive of my personal emotions. Then I started being *me* about the songs, not writing them objectively, but subjectively.[70]

PAUL: Vocally and poetically Dylan was a huge influence. Lyrically he is still one of the best. Some of the long rambling poems he set to music are still some of my favourite pieces of work.

One thing that he did introduce us to was pot. I mean, we'd heard all the jokes: that the Ray Charles band had been at the Hammersmith Odeon and the cleaner said, 'He must be really tight, that Ray Charles – there are two of his musicians sharing a ciggy in the toilet!' We thought it was funny, but it wasn't us. Then Bob came round to our hotel, and he said to us, 'Here, try a bit of this.' It is very indiscreet to say this, because I don't know whether Bob is telling people he turned The Beatles on to marijuana. But it *was* funny.

JOHN: The drugs were around a long time. All the jazz musicians had been into heavy dope for years and years – it's just that they got in the media in the Sixties. People were smoking marijuana in Liverpool when we were still kids, though I wasn't too aware of it at that period. All these black guys were from Jamaica, or their parents were, and there was a lot of marijuana around. The beatnik thing had just happened. Some guy was showing us pot in Liverpool in 1960, with twigs on it. And we smoked it and we didn't know what it was. We were drunk.[75]

GEORGE: We first got marijuana from an older drummer with another group in Liverpool. We didn't actually try it until after we'd been to Hamburg. I remember we smoked it in the band room in a gig in Southport and we all learnt to do the Twist that night, which was popular at the time. We were all seeing if we could do it. Everybody was saying, 'This stuff isn't doing anything.' It was like that old joke where a party is going on and two hippies are up floating on the ceiling, and one is saying to the other, 'This stuff doesn't work, man.'

JOHN: Bob Dylan had heard one of our records where we said, 'I can't hide,' and he had understood, 'I get high.' He came running and said to us, 'Right, guys, I've got some really good grass.' How could you not dig a bloke like that? He thought that we were used to drugs.

We smoked and laughed all night. He kept answering our phone, saying, 'This is Beatlemania here.' It was ridiculous.[69]

GEORGE: We had a mutual friend, Al Aronowitz, whom we'd met first in 1963, who worked for the *Saturday Evening Post*. Al Aronowitz and Bob were part of a beatnik crowd. We had always liked Bohemians and beatniks. I still do – I still like anyone who is not the run of the mill. One of the things Al did was to take Beatles and Bob Dylan records to Russia and try to be subversive. He was a friend of Bob's and he phoned us up and said that Bob was around and we could all get together. He brought him over to the hotel. It was a real party atmosphere. We all got on very well and we just talked and had a big laugh.

PAUL: We had a crazy party the night we met. I went around thinking I'd found the meaning of life that night. I kept saying to Mal, 'Get a pencil and paper, I've got it.' Mal, who was a bit out of it too, couldn't find a pencil or paper anywhere. Eventually he found some and I wrote down The Message of the Universe and told him, 'Now keep that in your pocket.' Next morning Mal said, 'Hey, Paul, do you want to see that bit of paper?' I had written: 'There are seven levels.' Yeah, OK, maybe it didn't exactly sum it all up after all, but we had a great time.

Drugs have now become such a serious menace that it is very difficult to write about the subject; I don't want to influence anyone in this day and age – I've got kids of my own. (When we used to talk about it, it was a bit lightweight; you could talk about pot and wine as opposed to scotch and Coke.) But it *is* part of the truth.

JOHN: I don't remember much what we talked about. We were smoking dope, drinking wine and generally being rock'n'rollers and having a laugh, you know, and surrealism. It was party time.

I remember one little nugget. We were up one of these hotels in New York (he'd bring his demos every time he made a new record) and he'd be saying, 'Hey, John, listen to the lyrics, man.' – 'Forget the lyrics!' You know, we're all out of our minds, are we supposed to be listening to lyrics? No, we're just listening to the rhythm and how he does it.[74]

PAUL: I'm sure that the main influence on both Dylan and John was Dylan Thomas. That's why Bob's not Bob Zimmerman – his real name. We all used to like Dylan Thomas. I read him a lot. I think that John started writing because of him, and the fact that Bob Dylan wrote poetry added to *his* appeal. John was already doing it 'in his own right'. He was writing before he'd heard of Bob Dylan.

We were always interested in that kind of thing. We were slightly studenty. We used to make fun of the other bands who weren't. I received a poetry book once, in Hamburg: Yevtushenko. A girlfriend sent it to me. We were sitting in the communal dressing room, where everyone stuck their saxophones and equipment. We were waiting to go on, and a sax player from one of the other groups was knocking to come in. We said, 'Come in,' and we were all in various poses, 'Yeah, ah, ah,' as I was reading: 'The yellow flower graces thoughtlessly the green steps.' The guy was creeping past, 'Sorry, don't want to disturb you...'

The point was that we *had* a book of poetry; it was part of our equipment. It was part and parcel of what we all liked – art. John had been to art college. I had won a little art prize at school. (I was never very swotty but I occasionally did quite well in things. In 1953, there was a Coronation essay competition. All the kids in Britain were invited to write essays about the monarchy or something, to celebrate our Queen's glorious accession to the throne. And I won a prize: a book on modern art.)

I'm sure this kind of thing found its way into our music, and into our lyrics, and influenced whom we were interested in; people like Dylan. That's where it all led.

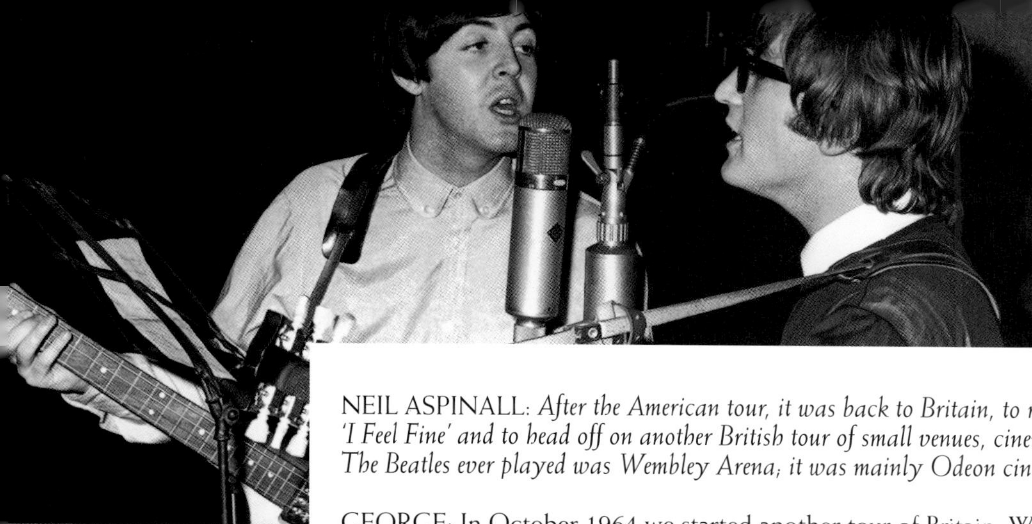

NEIL ASPINALL: *After the American tour, it was back to Britain, to record the album* Beatles For Sale, *the single 'I Feel Fine' and to head off on another British tour of small venues, cinemas and theatres. I think the largest UK gig The Beatles ever played was Wembley Arena; it was mainly Odeon cinemas and the like.*

GEORGE: In October 1964 we started another tour of Britain. We had a lot of shows booked from before, and so, having played huge stadiums in America, we were now coming back to Britain and playing the working men's club in Accrington for tuppence a month. After having some success, we still fulfilled the obligations that we had *before* we got really famous. That was one of the things everybody was proud of.

RINGO: It was the same in 1963. That was a great thing with Brian. If we'd been booked to play a small club anywhere, we still went and played it for the price agreed originally. We were honourable folk, and so was Brian. It was pretty strange, though, because we'd be playing in some daft dance hall in the middle of nowhere, and it would be packed. But we played all those gigs.

I felt we were progressing in leaps and bounds, musically. Some of the material on *Beatles For Sale* and the 1965 *Rubber Soul* album was just brilliant; what was happening elsewhere was nothing like it. It was getting to be really exciting in the studio. We did it all in there: rehearsing, recording and finishing songs. We never hired a rehearsal room to run down the songs, because a lot of them weren't finished. The ideas were there for the first verse, or a chorus, but it could be changed by the writers as we were doing it, or if anyone had a good idea.

The first form in which I'd hear a newly written tune would be on the guitar or piano. It's great to hear the progression through takes of various songs. They'd change dramatically. First of all, whoever wrote it would say, 'It goes like this.' They would play it on guitar or piano, singing it every time – they would be learning to sing the song while we were all learning to play it, over and over again.

Most of our early recordings were on three tracks because we kept one track for overdubs. That also kept us together as a band – we played and played and played. If one of them could sing it, the four of us could play it till the cows came home. There was none of this, 'We'll put the bass on later, or the guitars.' We put most of it on then and there, including the vocals. And songs were written anywhere.

PAUL: Recording *Beatles For Sale* didn't take long. Basically it was our stage show, with some new songs – 'Eight Days A Week', for example. I remember writing that with John, at his place in Weybridge, from something said by the chauffeur who drove me out there. John had moved out of London, to the suburbs. I usually drove myself there, but the chauffeur drove me out that day and I said, 'How've you been?' – 'Oh, working hard,' he said, 'working eight days a week.' I had never heard anyone use that expression, so when I arrived at John's house I said, 'Hey, this fella just said, "eight days a week".' John said, 'Right – "Oooh, I need your love, babe..."' and we wrote it. We were always quite quick to write. We would write on the spot. I would show up, looking for some sort of inspiration; I'd either get it there, with John, or I'd hear someone say something.

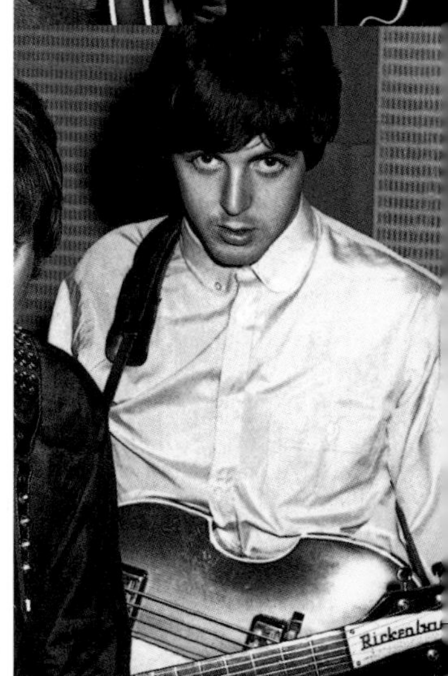

John and I were always looking for titles. Once you've got a good title, if someone says, 'What's your new song?' and you have a title that interests people, you are halfway there. Of course, the song has to be good. If you've called it 'I Am On My Way To A Party With You, Babe', they might say, 'OK...' But if you've called it 'Eight Days A Week', they say, 'Oh yes, that's good!' With 'A Hard Day's Night', you've almost captured them.

So we would start with a title. I would turn up at John's house. He'd get up when I arrived. I'd have a cup of tea and a bowl of cornflakes with him and we'd go up to a little room, get our guitars out and kick things around. It would come very quickly, and in two or three hours' time I'd leave.

We would normally play it to Cynthia, or to whoever was around. We couldn't put it down on a cassette because there weren't cassettes then. We'd have to remember it, which was always a good discipline, and if it was a rubbish song we'd forget it.

JOHN: EVERYBODY THINKS YOU MOVE POP STARS INTO WHAT THEY CALL 'THE STOCKBROKER AREA'. I DON'T KNOW WHY OTHER POP STARS MOVE INTO AREAS LIKE THAT; I MOVED IN BECAUSE IT WAS ABOUT THE THIRD HOUSE I'D LOOKED AT AND I HAD TO GET OUT OF A FLAT QUICK, AND I DIDN'T CARE WHERE. I WANTED TO LIVE IN LONDON, BUT I WOULDN'T RISK IT UNTIL IT'S QUIETENED DOWN.

[THE HOUSE] IS QUITE BIG. I ONLY REALISE HOW BIG IT IS WHEN I GO HOME TO LIVERPOOL OR VISIT RELATIONS AND REALISE THE SIZE OF MY HOUSE COMPARED WITH THEIRS. IT'S THREE FLOORS. I'VE GOT ONE ROOM WITH ABOUT FOURTEEN GUITARS IN IT, TWENTY PIANOS, ORGANS, TAPE RECORDERS, EVERYTHING. THE NEXT ROOM'S FULL OF RACING CARS. THE NEXT ROOM'S GOT A DESK IN WHERE I WRITE AND DRAW AND THE NEXT'S GOT ONE-ARMED BANDITS AND FOOTBALL GAMES AND ALL THOSE THINGS THAT YOU PUT TANNERS IN. THE REST OF THE HOUSE IS NORMAL; BUT IT'S NOT BIG ENOUGH. I NEED A GIANT PLACE.[65]

JOHN: 'Eight Days A Week' was Paul's effort at getting a single for the movie. That luckily turned to 'Help!', which I wrote – bam! bam! like that – and got the single. 'Eight Days A Week' was never a good song. We struggled to record it and struggled to make it into a song. It was his initial effort, but I think we both worked on it.[80]

'I'm A Loser' is me in my Dylan period, because the word 'clown' is in it. I objected to the word 'clown', because that was always artsy-fartsy, but Dylan had used it so I thought it was all right, and it rhymed with whatever I was doing.[74] Part of me suspects I'm a loser, and part of me thinks I'm God Almighty.

'No Reply' was my song. Dick James, the publisher, said, 'That's the first complete song you've written where it resolves itself.' You know, with a complete story. It was my version of 'Silhouettes': I had that image of walking down the street and seeing her silhouetted in the window and not answering the phone. Although I never called a girl on the phone in my life – phones weren't part of the English child's life.[80]

GEORGE: Our records were progressing. We'd started out like anyone spending their first time in a studio – nervous and naive and looking for success. By this time we'd had loads of hits and a few tours and were becoming more relaxed with ourselves, and more comfortable in the studio. And the music was getting better.

For this album we rehearsed only the new ones. Songs like 'Honey Don't' and 'Everybody's Trying To Be My Baby', we'd played live so often that we only had to get a sound on them and do them. But with songs like 'Baby's In Black', we had to learn and rehearse them. We were beginning to do a little overdubbing, too, probably a four-track. And George Martin would suggest some changes; not too many, but he was always an integral part of it.

PAUL: We got more and more free to get into ourselves. Our student selves rather than 'we must please the girls and make money', which is all that 'From Me To You', 'Thank You Girl', 'PS I Love You' is about. 'Baby's In Black' we did because we liked waltz-time – we'd used to do 'If You Gotta Make A Fool Of Somebody', a cool three-four blues thing. And other bands would notice that and say, 'Shit man, you're doing something in three-four.' So we'd got known for that. And I think also John and I wanted to do something bluesy, a bit darker, more grown-up, rather than just straight pop. It was more 'baby's in black' as in mourning. Our favourite colour was black, as well.

RINGO: We all knew 'Honey Don't'; it was one of those songs that every band in Liverpool played. I used to love country music and country rock; I'd had my own show with Rory Storm, when I would do five or six numbers. So singing and performing wasn't new to me; it was a case of finding a vehicle for me with The Beatles. That's why we did it on *Beatles For Sale*. It was comfortable. And I was finally getting one track on a record: my little featured spot.

JOHN: I wrote 'I Feel Fine' around that riff going on in the background. I tried to get that effect into practically every song on the LP, but the others wouldn't have it. I told them I'd write a song specially for the riff. So they said, 'Yes, you go away and do that,' knowing that we'd almost finished the album. Anyway, going into the studio one morning, I said to Ringo, 'I've written this song, but it's lousy.' But we tried it, complete with riff, and it sounded like an A side, so we decided to release it just like that.

George and I play the same bit on guitar together – that's the bit that'll set your feet a-tapping, as the reviews say. I suppose it has a bit of a country-and-western feel about it, but then so have a lot of our songs. The middle-eight is the most tuneful part, to me, because it's a typical Beatles bit.[64]

GEORGE: The guitar riff was actually influenced by a record called 'Watch Your Step' by Bobby Parker. But all riffs in that tempo have a similar sound. John played it, and all I did was play it as well, and it became the double-tracked sound.

JOHN: 'Watch Your Step' is one of my favourite records. The Beatles have used the lick in various forms. The Allman Brothers used the lick straight as it was.[74]

GEORGE: John got a bit of feedback unintentionally and liked the sound and thought that it would be good at the start of the song. From then on he started to hold the guitar to create the feedback for every take that we recorded.

JOHN: The record had the first feedback anywhere. I defy anybody to find a record – unless it's some old blues record in 1922 – that uses feedback that way. I mean, everybody played feedback *on stage*, and the Jimi Hendrix stuff was going on long before [him]. In fact, the punk stuff now is only what people were doing in the clubs. So I claim for The Beatles – before Hendrix, before The Who, before anybody – the first feedback on any record.

The B side, 'She's A Woman', was Paul's, with some contribution from me on lines, probably. We put in the words 'turns me on'. We were so excited to say 'turn me on' – you know, about marijuana, using it as an expression.

There was a little competition between Paul and me as to who got the A side, who got the hit singles. If you notice, in the early days the majority of singles – in the movies and everything – were mine. And then, only when I became self-conscious and inhibited, and maybe the astrology wasn't right, did Paul start dominating the group a little. But in the early period, obviously, I'm dominating. I did practically every single with my voice except for 'Love Me Do'. Either my song, or my voice or both. The only reason Paul sang on 'Hard Day's Night' was because I couldn't reach the notes – 'When I'm home, everything seems to be right. When I'm home...' – which is what we'd do sometimes: one of us couldn't reach a note but he wanted a different sound, so he'd get the other to do the harmony.

It wasn't resentment, but it *was* competitive. I mean, rivalry between two guys is always there: it was a creative rivalry, like there was a rivalry between The Beatles and the Stones. I used this 'sibling rivalry', from youth, to create a song. In that respect it was not a vicious, horrible vendetta, because it's not on that level.[80]

PAUL: The album cover was rather nice: Robert Freeman's photos. It was easy. We did a session lasting a couple of hours and had some reasonable pictures to use. We showed up in Hyde Park by the Albert Memorial. I was quite impressed by George's hair there. He managed to create his little turnip top. The photographer would always be able to say to us, 'Just show up,' because we all wore the same kind of gear all the time. Black stuff; white shirts and big black scarves.

RINGO: We'd all go to the same shop. I'd get the shirt in blue, and someone would get it in pink, and someone would get it in button-down. If you look at all the photos, we are all dressed in the same style because that's how it happened.

For example, with the famous round-necked jackets, we had our *Thank Your Lucky Stars* gig to do – the TV show – and we were somewhere around Shaftesbury Avenue. We saw the suits in a window and just went in and got them. We all got one, and suddenly that was a uniform. We were going to all these shops and buying little uniforms for ourselves. That's also why we looked like Beatles; beside the haircut, we were all looking the same.

JOHN: We're really pleased with the record and with the new LP. There was a lousy period when we didn't seem to have any material for the LP and didn't have a single. Now we're clear of things and they're due out, it's a bit of a relief.[64]

NEIL ASPINALL: *No band today would come off a long US tour at the end of September, go into the studio and start a new album, still writing songs, and then go on a UK tour; finish the album in five weeks, still touring, and have the album out in time for Christmas. But that's what The Beatles did at the end of 1964. A lot of it was down to naivety, thinking that this was the way things were done: if the record company needs another album, you go and make one. Nowadays, if a band had as much success as The Beatles had by the end of 1964, they'd start making a few demands.*

*John once said, 'We gave the whole of our youth to The Beatles.'*

*If you look at the work schedule in late 1963, and right through 1964, you'll see it really was incredible. On top of the tours and the records and the film, they did a Christmas show and all the TV shows:* Top of the Pops *and* Thank Your Lucky Stars *and* Around The Beatles *(thirty-seven of them). And all the BBC radio shows (twenty-two). It was non-stop.*

*Brian was beginning to plan quite far ahead. At Christmas 1964 he would be planning the tour of America for 1965, trying to get a script together for* Help!*; and he would have been planning whatever other tours they were doing. Somebody would suggest, 'Can we have a holiday as well, Brian?' while all this was going on.*

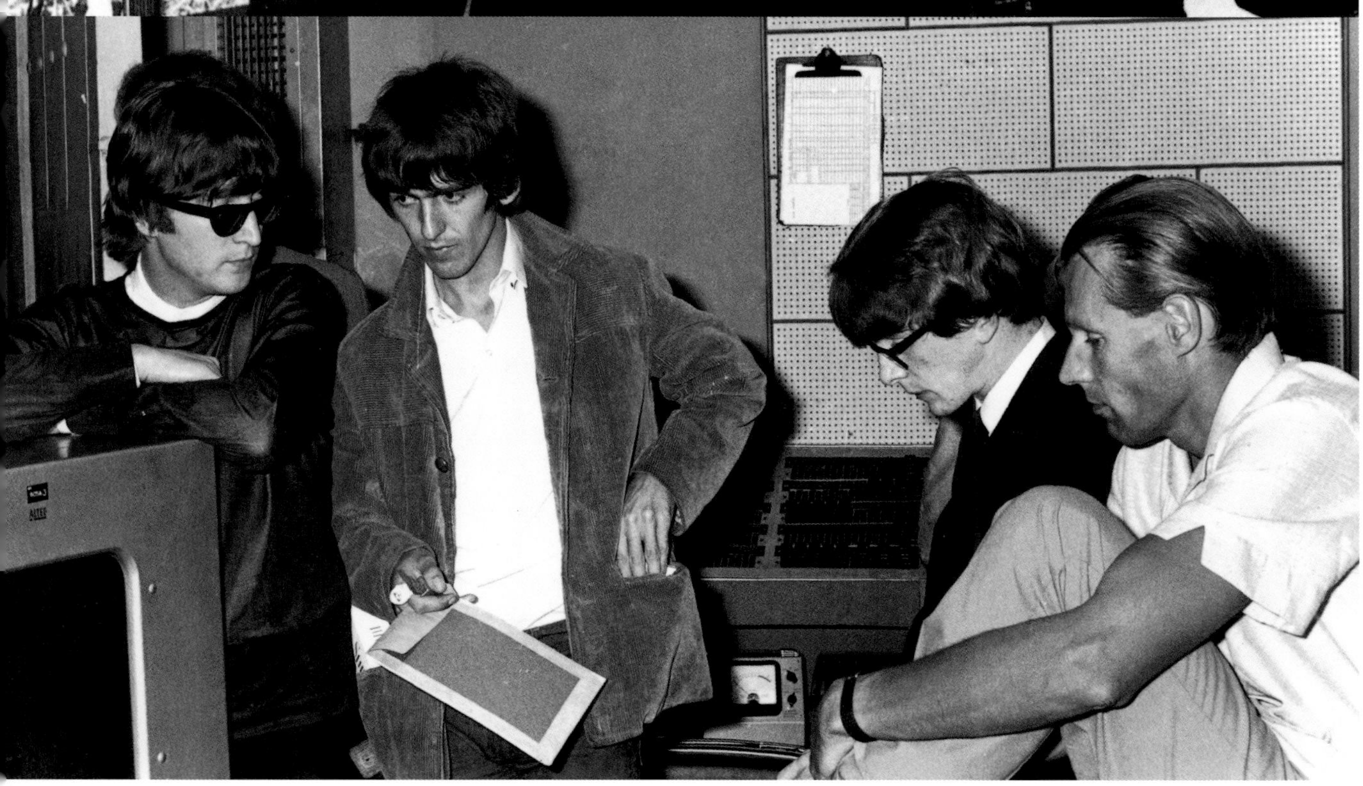

# 1965

nineteen sixty-five

## RINGO: I MARRIED MAUREEN IN FEBRUARY 1965.

We had met in the Cavern. She was in the audience and I had taken her home (and her friend). There was always that Liverpool thing: 'I'll take you home, love.' – 'Sure, can you take my friend too?' – 'Er, all right.' Then one day you'd ask, 'Can we go out alone?'

We started going steady; more or less. How could you go steady in my job? I kept leaving and going on tour. In the early days we didn't have much time off, but any time we *did* have off I spent with her. We'd have Mondays, because nobody booked gigs for a Monday, so I'd dash up to Liverpool and we'd go to a pub, to the movies or see a show, and then go to a restaurant. Just fill up that whole time.

When I came back from the States and went into hospital to have my tonsils out, Maureen stayed with my mother in my London flat. It was then I said, 'Do you want to get married?' and she said 'yes'. It was a gradual build-up; but we married and had three kids. I was with Maureen right through till 1975.

JOHN: I don't think the two of us being married has had any bad results on our popularity. Remember that when it was announced Ringo and I were both married there hadn't been anybody in such a position as us who had got married. Before us, it was silver-disc people (as opposed to gold-disc people) who'd married – people who relied mainly on the fact that they wiggled, all sexy, in their acts. We didn't rely on wiggling and we still don't. We were never dependent on fans being in love with us so much.[65]

Mr. Webb,
Bryce Hanmer & Co.
23, Albemarle Street,
London W.1.

Dear Mr. Webb,

I would be grateful if you would send an extra 48/- this week
to the cleaning lady for John Lennon.

Yours sincerely,

Peter Brown

THE BEATLES
HELP!

GEORGE: In February we started filming our second film, *Help!*. It was shot in the Bahamas, Austria and England. It was real fun doing the movie on location. We started off in the Bahamas and, as with most filming, we spent a lot of time hanging about; but *there* we could hang about on the beach.

We shot some incredible scenes that were never used. We've been trying to get hold of some of the out-takes. We rented sports cars which we used to drive around the island; I think they were Triumph Spitfires and MGBs. And as the police were all in the movie, we never had any trouble with speeding.

One day we found a disused quarry and started driving madly around it; skidding, doing doughnuts, going up the sides and spinning out. We made Dick Lester come and set up the camera so he could film us. He shot it with a fish-eye lens and it looked amazing: a big golden quarry with blue and red cars – like little toys – going round the bottom and up the sides. It was never used in the film, but we could sure use it now.

We've since found that they destroyed all that footage. People were so short-sighted in the old days; it was that 'they'll never last' concept.

RINGO: The problem was that we went to the Bahamas to film all the hot scenes, and it was freezing. We had to ride around and run around in shirts and trousers, and it was absolutely bloody cold.

NEIL ASPINALL: *And they couldn't get tanned, because afterwards they had to go to Europe to shoot scenes that would appear earlier in the movie. They always had to sit in the shade or wear hats.*

*We found in the Apple archives Brian's notes about the Bahamas trip, dictated at the time.*

BRIAN EPSTEIN: *I travelled out from London with Paul and Ringo. John and George had arrived at Heathrow airport a couple of minutes before us. As our car approached the back of Queens' Building, we saw a packed group of fans on its roof. When we turned the corner and walked onto the tarmac, there it was: an unbelievable crowd of wonderful fans; cheering, waving and holding banners. A thrilled Paul and Ringo joined up with an equally-amazed John and George, who were already acknowledging the crowd.*

*The group posed for the mass of photographers, continuing to wave to the fans as long as the airline would allow them. It was the most wonderfully loyal demonstration the group could receive of their fans' affection.*

*Our unit travelling to the Bahamas numbered seventy-eight, making for a full load. Amongst these were: Eleanor Bron; actors Victor Spinetti, John Bluthal and Patrick Cargill; producer and director duo Walter Shenson and Dick Lester; and fave photographer Robert Freeman. Also present were Beatles' road managers Neil Aspinall and Malcolm Evans, suitably equipped with the usual stack of photos, throat sweets, ciggies and other touring Beatle gear.*

*The cold air of New York gusted in as we touched down to refuel. Then, about eleven hours after leaving England – seven o'clock local time – our chartered Boeing touched down in Nassau. We disembarked to receive the warm welcome and weather. The Beatles and I were then whisked off by the authorities to a press conference without so much as the option to get a bit nearer to the waiting crowd – this is usually the true story when you read of artists 'ignoring their fans'.*

*The group started shooting the morning following their arrival. Among the first scenes shot were those of the group cycling on a public thoroughfare, chatting away. Personally, I was greatly impressed with what seemed to be improved naturalness of speech and movement. Ringo proved as good an actor as was apparent in the first film. Another day, the four enjoyed a swim fully clothed (well, shirt, jeans and shoes). John said he'd always wanted to try this and thought it might be even better to bathe in a suit, with tie and all.*

*Before leaving Nassau on Friday, I took a speedboat out to a tiny island where the boys were working. I arrived just in time to get a boxed lunch, used on these occasions, and to join up with the group for a break. No doubt about it, I thought, they're enjoying making this film very much; relaxed, inventive and effervescent as ever. I left the Bahamas with no doubts that my clients are being well looked after by the gentle and brilliant Mr Lester and the efficient and understanding Mr Shenson, not forgetting the people of Nassau, their sea and sun.*

RINGO: The storyline to *Help!* was written around me and the theme of the ring, and of course, Kaili. I had the central part. I think it helped that I'd been enthusiastic about the first film.

JOHN: He comes in possession of this ring, and whoever wears it has to be sacrificed by this big mob. We're trying to save him and get the ring off his finger, and there's other people trying to get it off for various reasons. It's very complicated, but that's basically what it is – to stop him being sacrificed.[65]

PAUL: While we'd really tried to get involved and learn the script for *A Hard Day's Night*, by the time *Help!* came along we were taking it as a bit of a joke. I'm not sure anyone ever knew the script, I think we used to learn it on the way to the set.

JOHN: The movie was out of our control. With *A Hard Day's Night*, we had a lot of input, and it was semi-realistic. But with *Help!*, Dick Lester didn't tell us what it was about. I realise, looking back, how advanced it was. It was a precursor for the *Batman* 'Pow! Wow!' on TV – that kind of stuff. But he never explained it to us. Partly, maybe, because we hadn't spent a lot of time together between *A Hard Day's Night* and *Help!*, and partly because we were smoking marijuana for breakfast during that period. Nobody could communicate with us; it was all glazed eyes and giggling all the time. In our own world.[80] It's like doing nothing most of the time, but still having to rise at 7am; so we became bored.[70]

RINGO: A hell of a lot of pot was being smoked while we were making the film. It was great. That helped make it a lot of fun.

GEORGE: Brandon De Wilde was an actor, a James Dean type. (He died in a car crash in 1972.) He liked The Beatles' music and he heard we were going to film in the Bahamas, so he came over from the States with a big bag of reefer. We smoked on the plane, all the way to the Bahamas. It was a charter flight, with all the film people – the actors and the crew – and we thought, 'No, nobody will notice.' We had Mal smoking cigars to drown out the smell.

GEORGE: Austria was next. It was the first and last time on skis for me. It was really dangerous. Nowadays when people make movies, everybody's got to be insured and you're not supposed to do this, that and the other in case you get injured and hold up the budget of the movie. And yet they took us to Austria, took us up a mountain, gave us our boots (that nobody even laced up), gave us our skis, said, 'Turn over, take one. Action!' – and gave us a push.

RINGO: It was the first time we'd been to Austria – first time I'd been on skis. I loved that.

In one of the scenes, Victor Spinetti and Roy Kinnear are playing curling; sliding along those big stones. One of the stones has a bomb in it and we find out that it's going to blow up, and have to run away. Well, Paul and I ran about seven miles, we ran and ran, just so we could stop and have a joint before we came back. We could have run all the way to Switzerland.

If you look at pictures of us you can see a lot of red-eyed shots; they were red from the dope we were smoking. And these were those clean-cut boys!

Dick Lester knew that very little would get done after lunch. In the afternoon we very seldom got past the first line of the script. We had such hysterics that no one could do anything. Dick Lester would say, 'No, boys, could we do it again?' It was just that we had a lot of fun – a lot of fun in those days.

JOHN: All the best stuff is on the cutting-room floor, with us breaking up and falling about all over the place, lying on the floor, incapable of saying a word.[70]

PAUL: We showed up a bit stoned, smiled a lot and hoped we'd get through it. We giggled a lot.

I remember one time at Cliveden (Lord Astor's place, where the Christine Keeler/Profumo scandal went on): we were filming the Buckingham Palace scene where we were all supposed to have our hands up. It was after lunch, which was fatal because someone might have brought out a glass of wine as well. We were all a bit merry and all had our backs to the camera and the giggles set in. All we had to do was turn around and look amazed, or something. But every time we'd turn round to the camera there were tears streaming down our faces. It's OK to get the giggles anywhere else but in films, because the technicians get pissed off with you. They think, 'They're not very professional.' Then you start thinking, 'This isn't very professional – but we're having a great laugh!'

GEORGE: We were filming that scene for days. There is a pipe with red smoke coming through and we have the window open and all the guards fall over. That scene just went on forever. We were in stitches – in hysterics laughing – and I think we pushed Dick Lester to the limit of his patience. And he was very, very easygoing; a pleasure to work with.

JOHN: We went wrong with the picture somehow. I enjoyed filming it; I'm sort of satisfied, but not smug about it. It'll do. There's good photography in it. There's some good actors – not us, because we don't act, we just do what we can. Leo McKern is exceptional; and Victor Spinetti and Roy Kinnear – the thin and the fat fella – they're good together. The first half of the film is much better than the end, and it's a bit of a let-down when it gets to the Bahamas.

I think there is a lot of scope for us in films which hasn't been exploited. It took us three or four records before we really got our sound. I suppose it will be the same with films. We do feel that if we prove ourselves we'll stay with it. If Elvis Presley could do it, we don't mind following him to the screen. The main point is to keep our films different. We'll always have a shock in store for the audience; this is where we stray from the Presley plan. But I wouldn't want to concentrate on films. It isn't our speed; we like to move. I still prefer playing for a live audience to anything else.

One final thing, you may as well discount Hollywood – we've all decided that if we win Oscars for this film, we're all going to send them back![65]

JOHN: The first time that we were aware of anything Indian was when we were making *Help!*. There was an odd thing about an Indian and that Eastern sect that had the ring and the sacrifice; and on the set in one place they had sitars and things – they were the Indian band playing in the background, and George was looking at them.

We recorded that bit in London, in a restaurant. And then we were in the Bahamas filming a section and a little yogi runs over to us. We didn't know what they were in those days, and this little Indian guy comes legging over and gives us a book each, signed to us, on yoga. We didn't look at it, we just stuck it along with all the other things people would give us.

Then, about two years later, George had started getting into hatha yoga. He'd got involved in Indian music from looking at the instruments on the set. All from that crazy movie. Years later he met this yogi who gave us each that book; I've forgotten what his name was because they all have that 'Baram Baram Badoolabam', and all that jazz. All of the Indian involvement came out of the film *Help!*.[72]

GEORGE: I suppose that was the start of it all for me. It was a chance meeting – the guy had a little place on Paradise Island, and somebody must have whispered in his inner ear to give us his book, *The Illustrated Book of Yoga*. We were on our bikes on the road, waiting to do a shoot, when up walked a swami in orange robes: Swami Vishnu Devananda, the foremost hatha yoga exponent. It was on my birthday.

Later, when I got involved with Indian philosophy and got the desire to go to Rishikesh, I picked up the book again and couldn't believe that that was where he was from – the Shivananda Ashram in Rishikesh. His main place was in Montreal, but he had a little aeroplane and flew himself in and around different countries, getting arrested and put in jail; gaining publicity for what he called his 'Boundary-Breaking Tour'. He opposed the whole idea of having borders between countries, and even issued us all with Planet Earth passports. Peter Max, the pop artist who became famous by copying the *Yellow Submarine*-type pictures, painted Vishnu Devananda's aeroplane.

I read his book after I became vegetarian. The thing that repelled me about eating meat was the idea of killing animals. But the main issue is that meat-eating is not healthy and it's not natural. In the book he says things like: monkeys don't get headaches; all human ailments and diseases come from an unnatural diet.

Also in his book, he illustrates things like how to cleanse the nasal passage, where he threads a string up his nose and pulls it out of his throat.

There's another one which involves swallowing a bandage that's been soaked in salt and water. You swallow it all the way down, and then you pull it back out. It's all to do with getting the body perfect. John had the idea of combining the two: the nasal-passage one, pulling on each end, with swallowing the bandage – and pulling it out of your arse! John was very funny, he was brilliant.

PAUL: The songwriting for the album was done mainly at John's place in Weybridge. With *A Hard Day's Night* John went home and came back with a lot of it, but with *Help!* we sat down and wrote it together. I remember us all sitting round trying to think, and John getting the idea for the title track. I helped with the structure of it and put in little counter melodies. When we'd finished, we went downstairs and played it to Cynthia and Maureen Cleave, and they thought it was good. We'd got it then; that was it.

From something he said later, I think 'Help!' reflected John's state of mind. He was feeling a bit constricted by the Beatle thing.

JOHN: Most people think it's just a fast rock'n'roll song. I didn't realise it at the time – I just wrote the song because I was commissioned to write it for the movie – but later I knew, really I was crying out for help. 'Help!' was about me, although it was a bit poetic.[71] I think everything comes out in the songs.

THE WHOLE BEATLE THING WAS JUST BEYOND COMPREHENSION. I WAS EATING AND DRINKING LIKE A PIG, AND I WAS FAT AS A PIG, DISSATISFIED WITH MYSELF, AND SUBCONSCIOUSLY I WAS CRYING FOR HELP. IT WAS MY FAT ELVIS PERIOD.

You see the movie: he – I – is very fat, very insecure, and he's completely lost himself. And I am singing about when I was so much younger and all the rest, looking back at how easy it was; but then things got more difficult.[80]

Happiness is just how you feel when you don't feel miserable. There's nothing guaranteed to make me happy. There's no one thing I can think of that would go 'click' and I'd be happy.[66] Now I may be very positive, but I also go through deep depressions where I would like to jump out of the window. It becomes easier to deal with as I get older; I don't know whether you learn control or, when you grow up, you calm down a little. Anyway, I was fat and depressed and I *was* crying out for help. It's real.[80]

GEORGE: John never said that when he wrote it; he said it retrospectively. That was how he was feeling. He was plump and he had his glasses. He just didn't feel right. He looked like Michael Caine with horn-rimmed glasses.

He was paranoid about being short-sighted and we'd have to take him into a club and lead him to his seat, so that he could go in without his glasses on and look cool. It was funny when Cynthia was out with him: they'd sit outside in the car, arguing as to whose turn it was to put the glasses on to go in and see where we were sitting. So he did go through that period when he was feeling, 'I was younger than today…'

JOHN: The lyric is as good now. It makes me feel secure to know I was that sensible; not sensible – *aware of myself*. That was with no acid, no nothing (well, pot).

I don't like the recording that much. The real feeling of the song was lost because it was a single; we did it too fast, to try and be commercial. I've thought of doing it again sometime and slowing it down. I remember I got very emotional at the time, singing the lyrics. Whatever I'm singing, I really mean it. I don't mess about. Even if I'm singing 'awop-bop-alooma-awop-bam-boom' I really mean it. And then there's always that very emotional music going on at the same time.[71]

I remember Maureen Cleave – a writer, the one who did the famous 'Jesus' story in the *Evening Standard* – said to me, 'Why don't you ever write songs with more than one syllable in the words?' I never considered it before, so after that I put a few three-syllable words in, but she didn't think much when I played the song for her, anyway. I was insecure then, and things like that happened more than once.[80]

PAUL: THE THING ABOUT JOHN WAS THAT HE WAS ALL UPFRONT. YOU NEVER SAW *JOHN*. ONLY THROUGH A FEW CHINKS IN HIS ARMOUR DID I EVER SEE HIM, BECAUSE THE ARMOUR WAS SO TOUGH. JOHN WAS ALWAYS, ON THE SURFACE, TOUGH, TOUGH, TOUGH.

Unfortunately, I think the world has to have a false impression of John. I think John was a really nice guy – covering up. He didn't dare let you see that nice side. So it was always rock'n'roll… till you actually caught him in the right moment.

JOHN: I really don't want to be labelled a cynic. They [the press] are getting my character out of some of the things I write or say. I hate tags. I'm slightly cynical, but I'm not a cynic. One can be wry one day and cynical the next and ironic the next. I'm a cynic about things that are taken for granted: society, politics, newspapers, government; but I'm not cynical about life, love, goodness, death.[66]

Paul can be very cynical and much more biting than me when he's driven to it. Of course, he's got more patience, but he can carve people up in no time at all, when he's pushed. He hits the nail right on the head and doesn't beat about the bush, does Paul.[69]

PAUL: One of my great memories of John is from when we were having some argument. I was disagreeing and we were calling each other names. We let it settle for a second and then he lowered his glasses and he said, 'It's only me…' and then he put his glasses back on again. To me, that was John. Those were the moments when I actually saw him without the façade, the armour, which I loved as well, like anyone else. It was a beautiful suit of armour. But it was wonderful when he let the visor down and you'd just see the John Lennon that he was frightened to reveal to the world.

GEORGE MARTIN: *I produced all the tracks for the film, but I wasn't asked to do the scoring – another guy was offered the job. Dick Lester and I didn't hit it off too well on* A Hard Day's Night, *and the fact that I got an Academy Award nomination for musical direction probably didn't help either.*

JOHN: I do think the songs in the film are better. One I do which I like is 'You've Got To Hide Your Love Away' – but it's not commercial. 'The Night Before' that Paul does' is good.[65]

I used to like guitars; I didn't want anything else on the album but guitars and jangling piano, or whatever, and it's all happening. 'Ticket To Ride' was slightly a new sound at the time. It was pretty fucking heavy for then, if you go and look in the charts for what other music people were making. You hear it now and it doesn't sound too bad; but it'd make *me* cringe. If you give me the A track and I remix it, I'll show you what it is really, but you can hear it there. It's a heavy record and the drums are heavy too. That's why I like it.[70]

RINGO: I recorded a song for the *Help!* album that was never released – 'If You've Got Trouble'. George Martin found it in the vaults of EMI studios.

GEORGE: We've just come across that, and it's the most weird song. I've no recollections of ever recording it. It's got stupid words and is the naffest song. No wonder it didn't make it onto anything.

RINGO: I sang 'Act Naturally' in *Help!* I found it on a Buck Owens record and I said, 'This is the one I am going to be doing,' and they said 'OK'. We were listening to all kinds of things. John sang 'Dizzy Miss Lizzy'. We were all listening to that, too. Paul, of course, had written his 'Yesterday'; the most recorded song in history. What a guy!

JOHN: *Help!* as a film was like 'Eight Days A Week' as a record for us. A lot of people liked the film, and a lot of people liked that record. But neither was what we really wanted – we knew they weren't really *us*. We weren't ashamed of the film, but close friends know that the picture and 'Eight Days' weren't our best. They were both a bit manufactured.

The 'Help!' single sold much better than the two before it: 'I Feel Fine' and 'Ticket To Ride.'[65] But there were still a lot of fans who didn't like *Help!*. They said, 'Ah, The Beatles are dropping us. This isn't as good as *A Hard Day's Night*.' So you can't win. Trying to please everybody is impossible – if you did that, you'd end up in the middle with nobody liking you. You've just got to make the decision about what you think is your best, and do it.

People think of us as machines. They pay 6s 8d for a record and we have to do what they say – like a jack-in-the-box. I don't like that side of it much. Some people have got it all wrong. We produce something, a record, and if they like it, they get it. The onus isn't on us to produce something great every time. The onus is on the public to decide whether they like it or not. It's annoying when people turn round and say, 'But we *made* you, you ungrateful swines.' I know they did, in a way, but there's a limit to what we're bound to live up to, as if it's a duty.

I don't want to sound as if we don't like being liked. We appreciate it. But we can't spend our lives being dictated to. We make a record, and if you like it you buy it. If you don't, you don't buy it. It's up to the public to decide.

JOHN: WE KNOW ALL ABOUT 'YESTERDAY'. I HAVE HAD *SO* MUCH ACCOLADE FOR 'YESTERDAY'. THAT'S PAUL'S SONG AND PAUL'S BABY. WELL DONE. BEAUTIFUL. AND I NEVER WISHED I'D WRITTEN IT.[80]

PAUL: I was living in a little flat at the top of a house and I had a piano by my bed. I woke up one morning with a tune in my head and I thought, 'Hey, I don't know this tune – *or do I?*' It was like a jazz melody. My dad used to know a lot of old jazz tunes, I thought maybe I'd just remembered it from the past. I went to the piano and found the chords to it (a G, F#minor7 and a B), made sure I remembered it and then hawked it round to all my friends, asking what it was: 'Do you know this? It's a good little tune, but I couldn't have written it because I dreamt it.' I took it round to Alma Cogan, a friend of ours (I think she may have thought I was writing it for her), and she said, 'I don't know it, but it is rather nice.'

It didn't have any words at first so I blocked it out with 'scrambled eggs': 'Scrambled eggs, oh, my baby, how I love your legs – diddle diddle – I believe in scrambled eggs.' Over the next couple of weeks I started to put in the words. I liked the tune and I thought I'd like to take some time over the words, get something that fitted like 'scrambled eggs'. And then, one day, I had the idea of 'Yesterday'.

JOHN: This song was around for months and months before we finally completed it. Every time we got together to write songs for a recording session, this would come up. We almost had it finished. Paul wrote nearly all of it, but we just couldn't find the right title. We called it 'Scrambled Egg' and it became a joke between us.

We had made up our minds that only a one-word title would suit, we just couldn't find the right one. Then one morning Paul woke up and the song and the title were both there; completed. I was sorry in a way, we'd had so many laughs about it. And it has been issued in America as an orchestral piece by George Martin – called 'Scrambled Egg'! Now we are getting letters from fans telling us they've heard a number called 'Scrambled Egg' that's a dead copy of 'Yesterday'.[65]

PAUL: I remember thinking that people liked sad tunes; they like to wallow a bit when they're alone, to put a record on and go, 'Ahh.' So I put the first verse together, then all the words fitted and that was it.

It was my most successful song. It's amazing that it just came to me in a dream. That's why I don't profess to know anything; I think music is all very mystical. You hear people saying, 'I'm a vehicle; it just passes through me.' Well, you're dead lucky if something like that passes through you.

I brought the song into the studio for the first time and played it on the guitar, but soon Ringo said, 'I can't really put any drums on – it wouldn't make sense.' And John and George said, 'There's no point in having another guitar.' So George Martin suggested, 'Why don't you just try it by yourself and see how it works?' I looked at all the others: 'Oops. You mean a *solo* record?' They said, 'Yeah, it doesn't matter, there's nothing we can add to it – do it.'

GEORGE MARTIN: *Paul went down to No. 2 Studio at EMI, sat on a high stool with his acoustic guitar and sang 'Yesterday'. That was the master to begin with. Then I said, 'Well, what we can do with it? The only thing I can think of is adding strings, but I know what you think about that.' And Paul said, 'I don't want Mantovani.' I said, 'What about a very small number of string players, a quartet?' He thought that was interesting, and I went and worked on it with him and made suggestions for the score. He had ideas too, and we booked a string quartet and overdubbed the strings – and that was the record.*

PAUL: Writing a song out with George Martin was nearly always the same process. For 'Yesterday' he had said, 'Look, why don't you come round to my house tomorrow? I've got a piano, and I've got the manuscript paper. We'll sit down for an hour or so, and you can let me know what you're looking for.' We'd sit down and it would be quite straightforward because I'd have a good idea of how I wanted to voice it. Or George would show me possibilities: very wide apart or very gungy and very close, and we'd choose. He would say, 'This is the way to do the harmony, technically.' And I'd often try to go against that. I'd think, 'Well, why *should* there be a proper way to do it?'

'Yesterday' was typical. I remember suggesting the 7th that appears on the cello. George said, 'You definitely wouldn't have that in there. That would be very *un*-string-quartet.' I said, 'Well? Whack it in, George, I've got to have it.'

That was the way the process worked. He'd show me how to write the song 'correctly' and I'd try to sabotage the correct method and move towards the way I like music; make it original. I still think that's a good way to work.

Once, when George Martin was figuring out what a particular note was in 'A Hard Day's Night' (not for one of *our* arrangements; this was later, when he was writing out our songs to record them himself, orchestrally), I remember his saying to John: 'It's been a hard day's night and I've been working... Is that a 7th, or another note, or is it somewhere in-between?' John would say, 'It's between those two.' And George would have to put down 'blue note' or something.

It was great fun. I'm still fascinated by that. I don't have any desire to learn. I feel it's like a voodoo, that it would spoil things if I actually learnt how things are done.

GEORGE MARTIN: *'Yesterday' was a breakthrough; it was recorded by just Paul and a group of other musicians. No other Beatle was on that recording and no other Beatle heard the song until we played it back. John listened to it, and there's a particular bit where the cello moves into a bluesy note which he thought was terrific, so it was applauded.*

*But it wasn't really a Beatles record and I discussed this with Brian Epstein: 'You know, this is Paul's song... Shall we call it Paul McCartney?' He said, 'No, whatever we do we are not splitting up The Beatles.' So even though none of the others appeared on the record, it was still The Beatles – that was the creed of the day.*

PAUL: I wouldn't have put it out as a solo 'Paul McCartney' record. We never entertained those ideas. It was sometimes tempting; people would flatter us: 'Oh, you know you should get out front,' or, 'You should put a solo record out.' But we always said 'no'. In fact, we didn't release 'Yesterday' as a single in England at all, because we were a little embarrassed about it – we were a rock'n'roll band.

I am proud of it. I get made fun of because of it a bit. I remember George saying, 'Blimey, he's always talking about "Yesterday", you'd think he was Beethoven or somebody.' But it is, I reckon, the most complete thing I've ever written.

JOHN: I sat in a restaurant in Spain and the violinist insisted on playing 'Yesterday' right in my ear. Then he asked me to sign the violin. I didn't know what to say so I said, 'OK,' and I signed it, and Yoko signed it. One day he's going to find out that Paul wrote it.[71] But I guess he couldn't have gone from table to table playing 'I Am The Walrus'.[80]

Thank you for your letter of December 1st.

The illustration missing from "Spaniard" (Pages 34/35) was given by John to George; who in trun gave it to the man who constructed his swimming pool. I spoke to Mr. Herrick today and he assures me he mailed it to Jonathan Cape, by registered post, some months ago.

Actually, Mr. Maschler said that he thinks it can be managed without the originals -- so, unless I hear from you to the contrary, I will let the matter rest.

Many thanks for returning the odd drawing. I will send it to John as soon as he returns to London.

With all best wishes.

Sincerely,

Wendy Hanson
Personal Assistant to Brian Epstein

JOHN: The second book was more disciplined because it was started from scratch. They said, 'You've got so many months to write a book in.'[65] I wrote *In His Own Write* – at least some of it – while I was still at school, and it came spontaneously. But once it became: 'We want another book from you, Mr Lennon,' I could only loosen up to it with a bottle of Johnnie Walker, and I thought, 'If it takes a bottle every night to get me to write...' That's why I didn't write any more.[80] I'm not very keen on being disciplined. (It seems odd, being a Beatle; we're disciplined but we don't feel as though we are. I don't mind being disciplined and not realising it.)

The longest thing I've written is in this book. It's one about Sherlock Holmes and it seemed like a novel to me, but it turned out to be about six pages. Most of *A Spaniard in the Works* is longer than the bits in the first book. But my mind won't stay on the same thing. I forget who I've brought in, I get lost and I get fed up and bored. That's why I usually kill the lot off. I killed them off in the first book, but with the second book I tried not to; I tried to progress.[65]

I'd done most of it and they needed a bit more, so the publisher sent along a funny little dictionary of Italian. He said, 'See if you get any ideas from this.' I looked in, and it was just a howl on its own. So I changed a few words (which is what I used to do at school with Keats or anything; I'd write it out almost the same and change a few words) but then they put in the reviews: 'He's pinched the whole book!'[67]

I hardly ever alter anything because I'm selfish about what I write, or big-headed about it. Once I've written it, I like it. And the publisher sometimes says, 'Should we leave this out, or change that?' and I fight like mad, because once I've done it I like to keep it. But I always write it straight off. I might add things when I go over it before it's published, but I seldom take anything out. So it *is* spontaneous.[65]

One of the reviews of *In His Own Write* tried to put me in this satire boom with Peter Cook and those people that came out of Cambridge, saying, 'Well, he's just satirising the normal things, like the Church and the State,' which is what I did. Those *are* the things that keep you satirising, because they're the *only* things.[70] I'm not a do-gooder about things: I won't go around marching, I'm not that type.[65]

PAUL: John was irreligious. He had a drawing that he'd done when he was younger of Jesus on the cross with a hard-on, which was brilliant. It was very hard-hitting teenage stuff, which at the time we all took just as black comedy. There was always an edge to John's stuff.

JOHN: I always set out to write a children's book; I always wanted to write *Alice in Wonderland*.[80] I was determined to be Lewis Carroll with a hint of Ronald Searle.[68] I think I still have that as a secret ambition.[80] Lewis Carroll I always admit to, because I love *Alice in Wonderland* and *Alice Through the Looking-Glass*.

I read a lot; things that you should read that everybody's reading. Dickens I don't like much; I've got to be in a certain mood. I'm too near school to read Dickens or Shakespeare. I hate Shakespeare; I don't care whether you should like him or not. I don't know if it's because of school or because it doesn't mean anything to me.

I was ignorant. I'd heard the name of Lear somewhere, but we didn't do him at school. The only classic or highbrow things I'd read or I knew of were at school.[65] I must have come across James Joyce at school, but we hadn't done him like I remember doing Shakespeare. The first thing they say is, 'Oh, he's read James Joyce,' but I hadn't. So I thought the thing to do would be to buy *Finnegans Wake* and read a chapter. And it was great, and I dug it and felt as though he was an old friend, but I couldn't make it right through the book.

I bought one book on Edward Lear, and a big book on Chaucer – so now I know what they [the reviewers] are talking about.[68] But I couldn't see any resemblance [in my own work] to any of them. A little bit of *Finnegans Wake*. But *Finnegans Wake* was so way-out and so different – a few word changes, and anyone who changes words has got to be compared; but his stuff is something else.

Ringo hasn't read anything I've written. Paul and George have. They were more interested in the first book, obviously. Paul was, because at the time a lot of people were beginning to say, 'Is that all they do?' Paul was dead keen, and that keen to write the intro, even – and he helped with a couple of stories, but was only mentioned on one because they forgot.

There's nothing to stop *them* doing something. I was doing this kind of thing before I was a Beatle, or before I had a guitar. When they met me I was already doing it. After a week of friendship with them or after a couple of weeks, I probably brought out things and said, 'Read this.' So this came before the other: the guitars came second. Now the guitars come first because this is still a hobby.

*A Spaniard in the Works* gave me another personal boost. OK, it didn't do as well as the first, but then what follow-up book ever does? In any case, I had a lot of the stories in the book bottled up in my system and it did me good to get rid of them – 'better out than in'. The book is more complicated; there are some stories and bits in it that even I don't understand, but once I've written something what's the point of letting it hang around in a drawer when I know I can get it published? The plain unvarnished fact is that I like writing, and I'd go on writing even if there wasn't any publisher daft enough to publish them.[65]

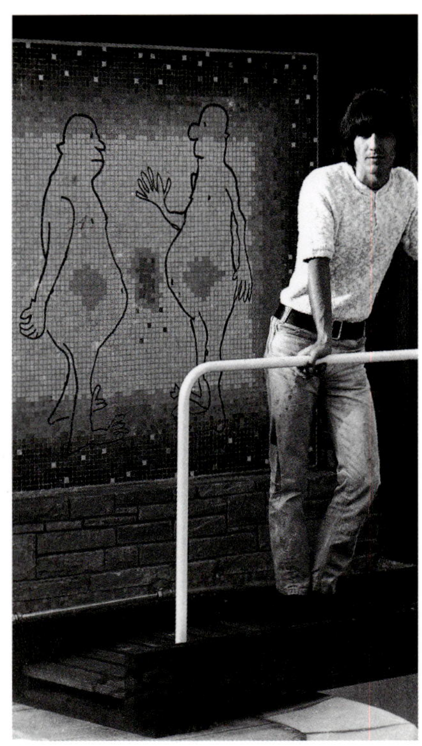

GEORGE: The first time we took LSD was an accident. It happened sometime in 1965, between albums and tours. We were innocent victims of the

**wicked dentist**

whom we'd met and had dinner with a few times. There'd been discos and similar events; everybody knew each other.

One night John, Cynthia, Pattie and I were having dinner at the dentist's house. Later that night we were going down to a London nightclub called the Pickwick Club. It was a little restaurant with a small stage where some friends of ours were playing: Klaus Voormann, Gibson Kemp (who became Rory Storm's drummer after we stole Ringo) and a guy called Paddy. They had a little trio.

After dinner I said to John: 'Let's go – they're going to be on soon,' and John said 'OK', but the dentist was saying,

*'Don't go; you should stay here.'* And then he said, *'Well, at least finish your coffee first.'*

So we finished our coffee and after a while I said again, 'Come on, it's getting late – we'd better go.' The dentist said something to John and John turned to me and said,

'WE'VE HAD LSD.'

I just thought, 'Well, what's that? So what? *Let's go*!'

This fella was still asking us to stay and it all became a bit seedy – it felt as if he was trying to get something happening in his house, that there was some reason he didn't want us to go. In fact, he had obtained some lysergic acid diethylamide 25. It was, at the time, an unrestricted medication – I seem to recall that I'd heard vaguely about it, but I didn't really know what it was, and we didn't know we were taking it. The bloke had put it in our coffees: mine, John's, Cynthia's and Pattie's. *He* didn't take it. He had never had it himself. I'm sure he thought it was an aphrodisiac. I remember his girlfriend had enormous breasts and I think he thought that there was going to be a big gang-bang and that he was going to get to shag everybody. I really think that was his motive.

So the dentist said, 'OK, leave your car here. I'll drive you and then you can come back later.' I said 'No, no. We'll drive.' And we all got in my car and he came as well, in his car. We got to the nightclub, parked and went in.

We'd just sat down and ordered our drinks when

SUDDENLY I FELT THE MOST INCREDIBLE FEELING COME OVER ME

It was something like a very concentrated version of the best feeling I'd ever had in my whole life.

It was FANTASTIC.

*I felt in love*, not with anything or anybody in particular, but with *everything*. Everything was perfect, in a perfect light, and I had an overwhelming desire to go round the club telling everybody how much I loved them – people I'd never seen before.

One thing led to another, then suddenly it felt as if a bomb had made a direct hit on the nightclub and the roof had been blown off: 'What's going on here?' I pulled my senses together and I realised that the club had actually closed – all the people had gone, they'd put the lights on, and the waiters were going round bashing the tables and putting the chairs on top of them. We thought, 'Oops, we'd better get out of here!'

We got out and went to go to another disco, the Ad Lib Club. It was just a short distance so we walked, but things weren't the same now as they had been. It's difficult to explain: it was very Alice in Wonderland – many strange things. I remember Pattie, half playfully but also half crazy, trying to smash a shop window and I felt, 'Come on now, don't be silly...' Then we got round the corner and saw just all lights and taxis. It looked as if there was a big film première going on, but it was probably just the usual doorway to the nightclub. *It seemed very bright, with all the people in thick make-up, like masks.*

VERY STRANGE.

We went up into the nightclub and it felt as though the elevator was on fire and we were going into hell (and it was and we were), but at the same time we were all in hysterics and crazy. Eventually we got out at the Ad Lib, on the top floor, and sat there, probably for hours and hours.

Then it was daylight and I drove everyone home – I was driving a Mini with John and Cynthia and Pattie in it. I seem to remember we were doing eighteen miles an hour and I was really concentrating – because some of the time I just felt normal and then, before I knew where I was, it was all crazy again. Anyway, we got home safe and sound, and somewhere down the line John and Cynthia got home. I went to bed and lay there for, like, three years.

That is what became known as *'The Dental Experience'*.

JOHN: A dentist in London laid acid on George, me and our wives.

HE JUST PUT IT IN OUR COFFEE OR SOMETHING.

[It was] all the thing with the middle-class London swingers who'd heard all about it and didn't know it was any different from pot and pills. He gave us it, and he was saying, 'I advise you not to leave.' We thought he was trying to keep us for an orgy in his house, and we didn't want to know. We went out to the Ad Lib and these discotheques, and there were incredible things going on.

We got out and the guy came with us, and he was nervous and we didn't know what was going on, and that we were going crackers. *It was insane, going around London on it.* We thought when we went to the club that it was on fire, and then we thought there was a premiere and it was just an ordinary light outside. We thought, 'Shit, what's going on here?' And we were cackling in the streets, and then people were shouting, 'Let's break a window.' We were just insane. We were out of our heads.

We finally got on the lift. We all thought there was a fire on the lift: it was just a little red light, we were all screaming, 'AAAAAAAARGH!', all hot and hysterical. And we all arrived on the floor (because this was a discotheque that was up a building), and the lift stops and the door opens, and we were all, 'AAAAAAAARGH!' and we just see that it's the club, and we walk in and sit down and the table's **elongating**. I think we went to eat before that and it was like the thing I read, describing the effects of opium in the old days, where the table... I suddenly realised it was only a table, with four of us around it, but it went long, just like I had read, and I thought, 'Fuck! It's happening.' Then we went to the Ad Lib and all of that, and some singer came up to me and said, 'Can I sit next to you?' I said, 'Only if you don't talk,' because I just couldn't think.

*It seemed to go on all night.* I can't remember the details; it just went on."

*And George somehow or other managed to drive us home in his Mini,*

but we were going about ten miles an hour and it seemed like a thousand. And Pattie was saying, 'Let's jump out and play football' – there were these big rugby poles and things. And I was getting all these hysterical jokes coming out, like [I did on] speed, because I was always on that, too. George was going, 'Don't make me laugh. Oh, God!'

IT WAS TERRIFYING,

*but it was fantastic.*

I did some drawings at the time (I've got them somewhere) of four faces saying, *'We all agree with you!'* – things like that. I gave them to Ringo, the originals. I did a lot of drawing that night. They all went to bed, and then George's house seemed to be just like a big submarine I was driving.[70]

RINGO: I was actually there in the club when John and George got there shouting,

'THE LIFT'S ON FIRE!'

Acid was the best thing we could take after that!

GEORGE: That first time I had acid, a light-bulb went on in my head and I began to have realisations which were not simply, 'I think I'll do this,' or, 'I think that must be because of that.' The question and answer disappeared into each other. An illumination goes on inside: in ten minutes I lived a thousand years. My brain and my consciousness and my awareness were pushed so far out that the only way I could begin to describe it is like an astronaut on the moon, or in his spaceship, looking back at the Earth. I was looking back to the Earth from my awareness.

Because acid wasn't illegal back then and nobody really knew much about it, there wasn't the big panic about 'heaven and hell' that people talk about – *we* didn't conjure up heaven and hell. But everything in the physical world is governed by duality: everything is heaven and hell. Life is heaven and it is hell; that's the nature of it. And so all that acid does is shoot you into space, where everything is so much greater. The hell is more hell, if that's what you want to experience, or the heaven is more heaven.

JOHN: WE MUST ALWAYS REMEMBER TO THANK THE CIA AND THE ARMY FOR LSD, BY THE WAY. EVERYTHING IS THE OPPOSITE OF WHAT IT IS, ISN'T IT? THEY BROUGHT OUT LSD TO CONTROL PEOPLE, AND WHAT THEY DID WAS GIVE US FREEDOM. SOMETIMES IT WORKS IN MYSTERIOUS WAYS, ITS WONDERS TO PERFORM. BUT IT SURE AS HELL PERFORMS THEM. IF YOU LOOK AT THE GOVERNMENT REPORT BOOK ON ACID, THE ONLY ONES WHO JUMPED OUT OF WINDOWS BECAUSE OF IT WERE THE ONES IN THE ARMY. I NEVER KNEW ANYBODY WHO JUMPED OUT OF A WINDOW OR KILLED THEMSELVES BECAUSE OF IT.[80]

GEORGE: I can't say how this experience has affected others. We are all individuals, and it's become more apparent to me over the years that while we may all experience a certain thing, we don't actually know if we have experienced it in the same way as each other. I made the mistake of assuming that my experience with LSD would be the same as anybody else's. Prior to that, I'd known that if you all drink whisky, you all get drunk, you all feel dizzy and you all start slipping around. So I presumed, mistakenly, that everybody who took LSD was a most illuminated being. And then I started finding that there were people who were just as stupid as they'd been before, or people who hadn't really got any enlightenment except a lot of colours and lights and an Alice in Wonderland type of experience.

The thing is, after you've had it a couple of times there doesn't seem to be any point to taking it again. Although the tablecloth might keep moving or the chairs get small, the basic thing that I first experienced was the thought: 'You shouldn't need this, because it's a state of awareness.' To change consciousness with a chemical obviously isn't a path to self-realisation. I think in some cases it can have a positive effect, but it is also dangerous. People later didn't have the ability to cope with it – the bogeyman within them would have the 'hell', and the 'hell' would come out. There were always reports of people jumping under cars and out of buildings. I can understand that, because you do suddenly experience the soul as free and unbound. You can have that feeling, that consciousness of what it must be like to leave your body, like experiencing death – but you have to remember that you're still *in* your body.

In 1966, I was in India on the day that they all worship Shiva. Amongst the little items being sold in the street I came across a small cactus covered with little hooks, the size of the top of a big poppy. I said to Ravi Shankar, who I was with, 'What's that?' and he said, 'Shiva would eat that, in mythology.' I thought, 'Ah, it's mescaline, peyote or something like that,' and I said, 'I'll try one of them.' But Ravi said, 'No, no, don't eat it – people who've eaten it have gone mad.' Well, *that* fits the bill for a psychedelic, because the down side of it can be that you go so far out in your mind that you think you've lost your grip and that you're never going to get back to the normal state of consciousness. And, in a way, you don't ever really return to how you were before.

The great thing about it for me was that, whereas with other drugs and alcohol you're under an influence and you feel intoxicated, with psychedelics you don't. It has an effect on your system but you're not feeling intoxicated; you're straight, with a twist – taken out of focus. Suddenly you can see through walls and you can see your body as if it isn't a solid. Like when you peel a slice of orange and you take the skin off the slice, you see tiny droplets that all just fit together, but are separate pieces. You can look at your body like that – I can almost see it now, just by recall – and you can see it's all moving; it's all pulsating with energy. It's amazing. Or, you know how it is when you can see a heat haze? It's like that – you can actually *see* heat. I tried sunbathing on acid once, at the house in LA, and after about ten seconds I could hear my skin frying, a sound like bacon sizzling in a pan. People will say, 'Well, he was under the influence of a drug,' but I believe it is actually the senses getting heightened to such a degree.

It must be like that for people who have attained a 'cosmic consciousness'. All the time, they can see through the trees and see the roots of the trees in the ground and see the sap flowing up through the ground and through the tree – as Superman can see through walls. Because the essence and the cause of everything in the physical world is that pure intelligence that is manifested externally as all these different parts. It's the ego identity that fools us into thinking, 'I am this body.' LSD gave me the experience of: 'I am not this body. I am pure energy soaring about everywhere, that happens to be in a body for a temporary period of time.'

This was something that I didn't know about back then. I just got born and did what I was doing, and I came along just as The Beatles were coming along and as acid and everything else was coming along; so you could call it karma. And, although it has a down side, I see my acid experience more as a blessing because it saved me many years of indifference. It was the awakening and the realisation that the important thing in life is to ask: 'Who am I?', 'Where am I going?' and 'Where have I come from?' All the rest is, as John said, 'just a little rock'n'roll band'. It wasn't that important. All the other bullshit – that was just bullshit. All the governments and all the people running round the planet doing whatever they're doing – all just a waste of time. They're all chasing their tails in some big illusion. If you can live by an inner rule and become centred on some kind of cosmic law, you don't need governments or policemen or anybody laying down rules. If I had half a chance, I'd put acid in the Government's tea.

RINGO: I think LSD changes everybody. It certainly makes you look at things differently. It makes you look at yourself and your feelings and emotions. And it brought me closer to nature, in a way – the force of nature and its beauty. You realise it's not just a tree; it's a living thing. My outlook certainly changed – and you dress differently, too!

JOHN: I must have had a thousand trips. I just used to eat it all the time. I stopped taking it because of bad trips. I just couldn't stand it. I dropped it for I don't know how long, and I started taking it again just before I met Yoko.

I got a message on acid that you should destroy your ego, and I did. I was reading that stupid book of Leary's [*The Psychedelic Experience*], all that shit. We were going through the whole game that everybody went through, and I destroyed myself. I destroyed my ego and I didn't believe I could do anything, and I let people do and say what they wanted, and I was nothing; I was shit. Then Derek tripped me out at his house after he got back from LA. He said, 'You're all right,' and he pointed out songs I had written and said, 'You wrote this, and you said this, and you *are* intelligent; don't be frightened.' And then next week I went down with Yoko and we tripped again, and she filled me completely to realise that I was me, and that it was all right. That was it, and I started fighting again and being a loudmouth again, and saying, 'Well, I can do this,' and, 'Fuck you, this is what I want. I want it and don't put me down.'[70]

[I haven't taken LSD] in years. A little mushroom or peyote is not beyond my scope; maybe twice a year or something. But acid is a chemical. People are taking it, though, even though you don't hear about it any more. People are still visiting the cosmos. It's just that nobody talks about it; you get sent to prison.

I've never met anybody who's had a flashback in my life and I took millions of trips in the Sixties, and I've never met anybody who had any problem. I've had bad trips, but I've had bad trips in real life. I've had a bad trip on a joint. I can get paranoid just sitting in a restaurant; I don't have to take anything.

Acid is only real life in CinemaScope. Whatever experience you had is what you would have had anyway. I'm not promoting, all you committees out there, and I don't use it because it's a chemical, but all the garbage about what it did to people is garbage.[80]

GEORGE: I don't think John had a thousand trips; that's a slight exaggeration. But there was a period when we took acid a lot – the year we stopped touring, the year of the Monterey Pop Festival, we stayed home all the time, or went to each others' houses.

In a way, like psychiatry, acid could undo a lot – it was *so* powerful you could just *see*. But I think we didn't really realise the extent to which John was screwed up. For instance, you wouldn't think he could get bitter, because he was so friendly and loving; but he could also be really nasty and scathing. As a kid, I didn't think, 'Oh well, it's because his dad left home and his mother died,' which in reality probably did leave an incredible scar. It wasn't until he made that album about Janov, primal screaming, that I realised he was even more screwed up than I thought.

After taking acid together, John and I had a very interesting relationship. That I was younger or I was smaller was no longer any kind of embarrassment with John. Paul still says, 'I suppose we looked down on George because he was younger.' That is an illusion people are under. It's nothing to do with how many years old you are, or how big your body is. It's down to what your greater consciousness is and if you can live in harmony with what's going on in creation. John and I spent a lot of time together from then on and I felt closer to him than all the others, right through until his death. As Yoko came into the picture, I lost a lot of personal contact with John; but on the odd occasion I did see him, just by the look in his eyes I felt we were connected.

Dear Mr. Epstein,

Under contract to this agency, to write his life story, is Mr. Alfred Lennon, father of John.

Mr. Lennon is deeply resentful of letters he has received from relatives, and others, accusing him of trying to sponge on the now famous son he neglected as a child.

He is anxious that his own viewpoint should be fully put in his story of John's early homelife, the time they spent together in Blackpool etc...

However, before going ahead, he has asked us to try and arrange a meeting with John so that he can give his own explanation of what happened when the family split up.

Mr Lennon asked us to emphasise that he is not interested in his son's wealth, but only in "putting himself straight" in the eyes of John - and the rest of the world. Something, he says, that he was not able to do in the brief, highly publicised meeting, they had some time ago.

Such a meeting, he feels, would clear the air of acrimony, and be of advantage to both.

I'm sure you would agree that no harm could come of this, and on our part we would make sure that the general press would not have access to Mr Lennon.

Perhaps you would let me know what you and John decide.

JOHN: I never knew my father. I saw him twice in my life till I was twenty-two, when he turned up after I'd had a few hit records. I saw him and spoke to him and decided I still didn't want to know him.[66]

He turned up after I was famous, which I wasn't very pleased about. He knew where I was all my life – I'd lived in the same house in the same place for most of my childhood, and he knew where. I thought it was a bit suspicious, but I gave him the benefit of the doubt after he'd put a lot of pressure on me in the press. I opened up the paper – the front page news is: 'JOHN'S DAD IS WASHING DISHES, WHY ISN'T JOHN LOOKING AFTER HIM?' I said, 'Because he never looked after me.' So I looked after him for the same period he'd looked after me; about four years.[72]

I started supporting him, then I went to therapy and re-remembered how furious I was in the depths of my soul about being left as a child. (I understand about people leaving their children because they can't cope or whatever happens, the reasons, when you're feeling your own misery.) So I came out of the therapy and told him to get the hell out, and he did get the hell out, and I wish I hadn't really because everyone has their problems – including wayward fathers. I'm a bit older now and I understand the pressure of having children or divorces and reasons why people can't cope with their responsibility.[76]

He died a few years later of cancer. But at sixty-five he married a 22-year-old secretary that had been working for me or The Beatles, and had a child, which I thought was hopeful for a man who had lived a life of a drunk and almost a Bowery bum.[80]

PAUL: We were at Twickenham Film Studios one afternoon when Brian showed up and took us to the dressing room rather secretively. We wondered what that was all about. He said, 'I've got some news for you – the Prime Minister and the Queen have awarded you an MBE,' and we said, 'What's that?' – 'It's a medal!'

RINGO: He said, 'What do you think, boys?' I had no problem with it – none of us had any problems with it in the beginning. We all thought it was really thrilling:

> WE'RE GOING TO MEET THE QUEEN AND SHE'S GOING TO GIVE US A BADGE. I THOUGHT, 'THIS IS COOL.'

PAUL: At first we were very impressed, but we asked, 'What will it mean?' Someone said, 'You become a Member of the British Empire,' and we *were* genuinely honoured. Then the cynicism started to creep in a little and we asked, 'What do you get for it?' They said, 'Well, £40 a year, and you get to go into St Paul's Whispering Gallery for nothing.' So we said, 'How much does that cost, anyway?' and were told, 'About a shilling.' There are two ways to look at it: either it's a great honour that's being bestowed on you – and I think to some degree we did believe that – or (if you want to be cynical) it's a very cheap way to reward people.

JOHN: When my envelope arrived marked OHMS, I thought I was being called up!

Before you get an MBE, the Palace writes to ask if you're going to accept it – because you're not supposed to reject it publicly, and they sound you out first. I chucked the letter in with all the fan mail, until Brian asked me if I had it. He and a few other people persuaded me that it was in our interests to take it.[65]

I was embarrassed. Brian said, 'If you don't take it, nobody will ever know you refused.' The same as nobody ever knows the people that have refused every Royal Variety Performance since the one we did. Every year they asked us and every year Brian went through hell telling Lew Grade we wouldn't do it. (Brian was on his knees, saying, 'Please do the Royal Variety Show,' after getting so much pressure from Lew and the rest of them. We said, 'We've done them all.' We only did one of everything, once was enough.)[67]

It was hypocritical of me to accept it, but I'm glad, really, that I did – because it meant that four years later I could use it to make a gesture.[70]

GEORGE: It's as if a bit of bargaining goes on behind the scenes before they issue it to the press. We were sworn to secrecy, but the press knew something was on; they were on to it before it was announced.

Probably it was Harold Wilson that put us up for it. He was Prime Minister and was from Liverpool, Huyton – 'two dogs fightin', one is black and the other's a white un'.

JOHN: We had to do a lot of selling-out then. Taking the MBE was a sell-out for me.[70] We thought being offered the MBE was as funny as everybody else thought it was. Why? What for? It was a part we didn't want. We all met and agreed it was daft. 'What do you think?' we all said. 'Let's not.' Then it all just seemed part of the game we'd agreed to play, like getting the Ivor Novello awards. We'd nothing to lose, except that bit of you which said you didn't believe in it.[67]

Although we don't believe in the Royal Family, you can't help being impressed when you're in the palace, when you know you're standing in front of the Queen. It was like in a dream. It was beautiful. People were playing music, I was looking at the ceiling – not bad, the ceiling. It was historical. It was like being in a museum.[70] There was this Guardsman telling us how to march, how many steps, and how to curtsey when you met the Queen. Left foot forward. Every time he was reading out the names and he got to Ringo Starr he kept cracking up. We knew in our hearts she was just some woman, yet we were going through with it. We'd agreed to it.[67]

To start with, we wanted to laugh. But when it happens to you, when you are being decorated, you don't laugh any more. We, however, were giggling like crazy because we had just smoked a joint in the loos of Buckingham Palace, we were so nervous. We had nothing to say. The Queen was planted on a big thing. She said something like 'ooh, ah, blah, blah' we didn't quite understand. She's much nicer than she is in the photos.[70]

I must have looked shattered. She said to me, 'Have you been working hard lately?' I couldn't think what we had been doing, so I said, 'No, we've been having a holiday.' We'd been recording, but I couldn't remember that.[65]

GEORGE: We never smoked marijuana at the investiture. What happened was we were waiting to go through, standing in an enormous line with hundreds of people, and we were so nervous that we went to the toilet. And in there we smoked a cigarette – we were all smokers in those days.

Years later, I'm sure John was thinking back and remembering, 'Oh yes, we went in the toilet and smoked,' and it turned into a reefer. Because what could be the worst thing you could do before you meet the Queen? Smoke a reefer! But we never did.

PAUL: Some equerry to the Queen, a Guards officer, took us to one side and showed us what we had to do: 'Approach Her Majesty like this and never turn your back on her, and don't talk to her unless she talks to you.' All of those things. For four Liverpool lads it was, 'Wow, hey man!' It was quite funny. But she was sweet. I think she seemed a bit mumsy to us because we were young boys and she was a bit older.

JOHN: I SHALL KEEP IT IN THE SMALLEST ROOM IN THE HOUSE – MY STUDY.[65]

RINGO: I went up and the Queen said to me, 'You started the group, did you?' and I said, 'No, I was the last to join.' And then she asked, 'Well, how long have you been together as a band?' and without the blink of an eye, Paul and I said, 'We've been together now for forty years and it don't seem a day too much.' She had this strange, quizzical look on her face, like either she wanted to laugh or she was thinking, 'Off with their heads!'

I'm not sure if we had a joint or not. It's such a strange place to be, anyway, the palace.

JOHN: I really think the Queen believes in it all. She must. I don't believe in John Lennon, Beatle, being any different from anyone else, because I know he's not. I'm just a fella. But I'm sure the Queen thinks she's different.[67] Imagine being brought up like that for 2,000 years! It must be pretty freaky. They must have a hard time trying to be human beings. I don't know if any of them ever make it, because I don't know much about them, but you feel sorry for people like that, because it's like us – only worse. If they believe they're royal, that's the joke.[68]

I always hated all the social things. All the horrible events and presentations we had to go to. All false. You could see right through them all, and all the people there. I despised them. Perhaps it was partly from class. No, it wasn't. It was because they really *were* all false.[67]

RINGO: Our families loved it. Some old soldiers sent their medals back, I don't know why! I think a lot of Australian soldiers sent theirs back. They just thought that it was too much that we should get the MBE: loud-mouthed rock'n'rollers.

JOHN: Lots of people who complained about us getting the MBE received theirs for heroism in the war. Ours were civil awards. They got them for killing people. We deserve ours for not killing people. If you get a medal for killing, you should certainly get a medal for singing and keeping Britain's economics in good nick! And we signed autographs for everybody waiting to get their MBEs and OBEs.[65]

PAUL: There was only one fella who said, 'I want your autograph for my daughter. I don't know what she sees in you.' Most other people were pleased about us getting the award. There were one or two old blokes from the RAF who felt it had slightly devalued their MBEs – these long-haired twits getting one. But most people seemed to feel that we were a great export and ambassadors for Britain. At least people were taking notice of Britain; cars like Minis and Jaguars, and British clothes were selling. Mary Quant and all the other fashions were selling, and in some ways we'd become super salesmen for Britain.

GEORGE: After all we did for Great Britain, selling all that corduroy and making it swing, they gave us that bloody old leather medal with wooden string through it. But my initial reaction was, 'Oh, how nice, how nice.' And John's was, 'How nice, how nice.'

I brought it home and put it in the drawer, and later I wore it on the *Sgt Pepper* album-cover picture session. So did Paul. It then remained pinned onto my 'Pepper' jacket for a year or so before I put it back in the box and back in the drawer.

RINGO: When they gave us the MBE, they gave us a certificate, and also a little note to say that you can't wear this one in public but you can buy a dress MBE, if you want to go out in your bow-tie. Which I thought was real strange. I never did wear it going out, but you would have thought that they would have thrown in the little one as well.

I wondered whether Brian minded not getting the MBE. But he was always happy for what we got, really. I suppose if he'd hung on, he'd have been going for a knighthood.

GEORGE: Brian didn't even go to the palace or get invited. I think you could invite somebody from your family. So he was probably very annoyed, secretly. But he didn't show any signs of it.

PAUL: Having grown up with this whole idea of the Queen as monarch, from when she flew back from Kenya to take over in 1952, we were always pretty keen on her.

'HER MAJESTY'S A PRETTY NICE GIRL, BUT SHE DOESN'T HAVE A LOT TO SAY' – WELL, THAT'S WHAT I'D SAY.

MEMO

OM

BILL OAKES

TO

DEREK TAYLOR

OUR REFERENCE | YOUR REFERENCE

September 25th 1969

DEREK TAYLOR: *Four years later, in November 1969, John sent his MBE back to attract attention to his causes.*

RINGO: I was never going to send mine back, I knew that. John did, he had his reasons, but not me. At the time, I was very proud. It meant a lot to me – not that it gave *me* anything, but it gave Harold Wilson the election. It was a groove meeting the Queen, and it was far out – now she meets *anybody*!

JOHN: I had been mulling it over for a few years. Even as I received it, I was mulling it over. I gave it to my auntie who proudly had it over the mantelpiece, which is understandable – she was very proud of it. She won't understand this move I've made probably, but I can't not do it because of my auntie's feelings. So I took it a few months back and didn't tell her what I was going to do with it – no doubt she knows now – and I'm sorry Mimi, but that's the way it goes.

Anyway, I sold out, so it was always worrying me, and then the last few years I'd been thinking, 'I must get rid of that, must get rid of that.' I was thinking how to do it, and I thought if I did it privately the press would know anyway, and it would come out; so instead of hiding it, just make an event of the whole situation. So I did it with the MBE. I was waiting for some event to tie it up with, but I realise that this *is* the event, this is the next peace event going on now.

Neither of us [Yoko and I] want to make the mistake that Gandhi and Martin Luther King did, which is get killed one way or the other. Because people only like dead saints, and I refuse to be a saint or a martyr. So I'm just protesting as a British citizen with his wife against British involvement in Biafra, and voicing the protest in the loudest way I can.[69]

**John Lennon has returned his MBE award in protest against Britain's involvement in the Nigerian and Vietnamese conflicts. In identical letters addressed to Her Majesty The Queen, the Prime Minister, and the Secretary of the Central Chancery, John Lennon writes"I am returning this MBE in protest against Britain's involvement in the Nigeria - Biafra thing, against our support of Amertca in Vietnam and against Cold Turkey slipping down the charts." The letter is signed "with love John Lennon", in his handwriting. Tayped underneath is "John Lennon of Bag". The letters are written on notepaper headed "Bag Productions, 3 Savile Row, London, W.1" Bag is the company set up by Lennon and his wife Yoko Ono to handle their films, records and other merchandise. John Lennon and the other three Beatles were awarded the MBE in the Queen's Birthday Honours list in the Summer of 1965.**

HOW TO SEND BACK AN M.B.E.

The medal, with a brief explanation, should be sent to - The Secretary of the Central Chancery
8 Buckingham Gate,
London, SW1.

Two optional letters should be sent to:
a) Harold Wilson
The main protest should be lodged here - presumably this letter would become public

b) H.M.The Queen
Solicitors advise no more than a respectful, regretful note..

JOHN: THE QUEEN'S INTELLIGENT. IT WON'T SPOIL HER CORNFLAKES.[69]

Derek Taylor.

BAG PRODUCTIONS 3, SAVILE ROW, LONDON W.1. 7348232

PEACE

TO

Her Majesty the Queen

25th November 1969

Your Majesty,

I am returning this MBE in protest against Britain's involvement in the Nigeria - Biafra thing, against our support of America in Vietnam and against Cold Turkey slipping down the charts.

with love
John Lennon.

John Lennon of Bag

GEORGE: At one time, all we wanted to do was make a record and that would have done us. People always think you go about dreaming that you're going to be a star – well, I think that's daft.[64]

JOHN: We wanted to be bigger than Elvis. At first we wanted to be Goffin and King, then we wanted to be Eddie Cochran, then Buddy Holly, but finally we arrived at wanting to be bigger than the biggest – Elvis Presley.

It was making it big in Liverpool, and then being the best group in the country, then being the best group in England. The goal was always just a few yards ahead rather than right up there. Our goal was to be as big as Elvis, but we didn't believe we were going to do it.[72]

RINGO: WE'D GET IN THE CAR. I'D LOOK OVER AT JOHN AND SAY, 'CHRIST. LOOK AT YOU. YOU'RE A BLOODY PHENOMENON!' AND JUST LAUGH – BECAUSE IT WAS ONLY HIM.[65]

JOHN: WHEN I FEEL MY HEAD START TO SWELL I LOOK AT RINGO – THEN I KNOW WE'RE NOT SUPERHUMAN![64]

PAUL: We knew something would happen sooner or later; we always had this little blind Bethlehem star ahead of us. Fame is what everyone wants, in some form or another; there must be millions of people all over the world annoyed that people haven't discovered them.

The thing is, we never believed in Beatlemania, never took the whole thing that seriously, I suppose. That way, we managed to stay sane.

JOHN: When I see old friends of mine, they keep laughing. The ones who knew me at school just keep looking at me and saying: 'Is it really you?'[64]

When people meet you in a restaurant, or anywhere, and you're trying to order something, you find they are so struck by, 'Is it really you?' that they don't really hear you order. So when I'm talking to them I'm saying, 'I'd like a steak, medium, and two elephants came and a policeman bit my head off, and a cup of tea please,' and they're saying, 'Yes, thank you.'[71]

RINGO: We very seldom get one waiter, because they all seem to queue up to give you a different portion of the meal so they can all have a look.

GEORGE: That is the main problem with fame – that people forget how to act normally. They are not in awe of you, but in awe of the thing that they think you've become. It's a concept that they have of stardom and notoriety. So they act crazy. All you have to do is go on the radio or television once, and when people see you down the street, they act differently. And The Beatles had been on the front page of the papers every day for a year or so. Everybody changes; they are so impressed by it.

It was difficult going to the same places we'd been before. People were starting to 'hey man' us a lot. We went back to Liverpool and we were in the same club where we used to be a year earlier. We just went in for a drink, and now suddenly there was a lot of: 'Hey man, hey man,' and we couldn't get a minute's peace.

JOHN: We were always pretty aware of what our effect was on people. (You learn about audience reaction in your early days of playing. You either get to be able to play an audience or the public, or you don't.) So we were always pretty aware in a way of what we were doing, although it was pretty hard to keep up when you're going at 2,000 miles an hour. Sometimes you get dizzy. But we usually hung together somehow. There'd always be somebody to lean on when there's four of you. There'd always be somebody that would be together enough to pull you through the difficult phases.[71]

RINGO: Elvis went downhill because he seemed to have no friends, just a load of sycophants. Whereas with us, individually we all went mad, but the other three always brought us back. That's what saved us. I remember being totally bananas thinking *I am the one* and the other three would look at me and say, ''Scuse me, what are you doing?' I remember each of us getting into that state.

PAUL: FAME, IN THE END, IS GETTING OFF YOUR PARKING FINE BECAUSE THE ATTENDANT WANTS YOUR AUTOGRAPH, AND FAME IS BEING INTERRUPTED WHEN YOU'RE EATING BY A 50-YEAR-OLD AMERICAN LADY WITH A PONY-TAIL. THE FOUR OF US ARE KNOWN TO ALMOST EVERYBODY IN THE WORLD, BUT WE DON'T *FEEL* THAT FAMOUS.[66]

# JOHN: WE TOUR THE PLACES OUR MANAGER WANTS TO SEE – HE TAKES HIS CAMERA.[65]

PAUL: I remember playing a big bullring in Barcelona, the Plaza de Toros, where the Lord Mayor had great seats and all the rich people had seats but the kids, our real audience, were outside. We used to get upset about that: 'Why are we playing to all these bloody officials? We should be playing to the people outside. Let them in...' But of course they wouldn't.

JOHN: I couldn't stand it if the audiences were too old. If that's what it looks like out front, I reckon I'll be off. It doesn't really seem natural to see older people out there looking at us like that. It's nice to see anybody, but I always think old people should be at home doing the knitting or something.[65]

RINGO: The thing I remember about Madrid, where we played another bullring, was that the police were so violent. It was the first time I'd really seen police beating kids up.

I went to a bullfight there, and it was the saddest thing I ever saw. It was really sorrowful to see the bull just getting weakened and weakened. And then, when they finally kill the bugger, they wrap a chain round its leg and bring in a couple of cart-horses and drag the corpse away. I always thought it was such a miserable end. That's the only bullfight I ever went to, and I've never been interested in seeing one again.

NEIL ASPINALL: *They toured France, Italy and Spain. All I remember about Italy is some rally drivers taking us to Milan. The next tour after the European tour was America, where they played their first gig at Shea Stadium.*

JOHN: If we're playing to audiences of 55,000 – which is the size of the crowd in the opening show in New York – there are bound to be some wild scenes. Even if the crowd was watching ping-pong, there'd be a scene because of the size of the crowd. It's still amazing to hear the row they make.

It's a drag going away from home, but if you have got to go anywhere, it might as well be America. It's one of the best places there is. I'd sooner be off there than go to Indonesia.[65]

GEORGE: Shea Stadium was an enormous place. In those days, people were still playing the Astoria Cinema at Finsbury Park. This was the first time that one of those stadiums was used for a rock concert. Vox made special big 100-watt amplifiers for that tour. We went up from the 30-watt amp to the 100-watt amp and it obviously wasn't enough; we just had the house PA.

RINGO: Now we were playing stadiums! There were all those people and just a tiny PA system – they couldn't get a bigger one. We always used to use the house PA. That was good enough for us, even at Shea Stadium. I never felt people came to *hear* our show – I felt they came to *see* us. From the count-in on the first number, the volume of screams drowned everything else out.

PAUL: Now it's quite commonplace for people to play Shea Stadium or Giants Stadium and all those big places, but this was the first time. It seemed like millions of people, but we were ready for it. They obviously felt we were popular enough to fill it.

Once you go on stage and you know you've filled a place that size, it's magic; just walls of people. Half the fun was being involved in this gigantic event ourselves. I don't think we were heard much by the audience. The normal baseball-stadium PA was intended for: 'Ladies and gentlemen, the next player is...' But that was handy in that if we were a bit out of tune or didn't play the right note, nobody noticed. It was just the spirit of the moment. We just did our thing, cheap and cheerful, ran to a waiting limo and sped off.

NEIL ASPINALL: *In the States the venues had their own lights and sound, and Mal was taking care of the equipment. Now it was just me and a briefcase. Circumstances had changed. In England, because we didn't go on the coach, we'd drive ourselves around, and in some places I still had to plot the lights. In America it was more security and press, and taking care of the general madness. I'd be talking to the chief of police, working out how The Beatles were going to get in and out, and taking care of whatever else came down the pike.*

GEORGE: We went by helicopter, but they wouldn't allow us to drop right into the arena so we had to land on the roof of the World's Fair. From there we went into the stadium in a Wells Fargo armoured truck. (I didn't think Wells Fargo were still going; I thought the Indians had got them all years ago.) When we got into the helicopter at Wall Street, instead of going right to the show the fella started zooming round the stadium, saying, 'Look at that, isn't it great?' And we were hanging on by the skin of our teeth, thinking, 'Let's get out of here!'

PAUL: We got changed into our semi-military gear: beige outfits with high collars. Then, rather nervously, we ran out onto the field. We just went through the paces and did our act. We sweated up a lot.

JOHN: We'd get dead nervous before we'd go on stage, and nine times out of ten we suddenly get tired about half an hour before we have to get changed. All of a sudden, everybody's tired. Changing into suits and putting the shirts on, you feel, 'Oh, no,' but as soon as we get on, it's all right.[64]

GEORGE: They weren't really military jackets, it was just that they were beige-coloured and we had sheriff's badges on them.

We were in and out of the place in no time. As always. I watched the film of us at Shea Stadium, and suddenly the King Curtis band came on, and I thought, 'Wow! That's a good band.' King Curtis was travelling in our aeroplane on the tour, but I never even saw him play. We never saw anyone play because we were always stuck inside the basement of one of the stadiums.

| | | |
|---|---|---|
| 15.8.65 | Shea Stadium New York | $4.50; $5.10; $5.65 |
| 17.8.65 | Maple Leaf Gardens Toronto | $4.50; $5.00; $5.50 |
| 18.8.65 | Atlanta Stadium Atlanta | $4.55; $5.50 |
| 19.8.65 | Sam Houston Coliseum Houston | $5.00 |
| 20.8.65 | Comisky Park Chicago | $2.50; $3.50; $4.50; $5.50 |
| 21.8.65 | Metropolitan Stadium Minneapolis | No ticket prices stated |
| 22.8.65 | Coliseum Portland | $4.00; $5.00; $6.00 |
| 28.8.65 | Balboa Stadium San Diego | No ticket prices stated |
| 29.8.65 | The Hollywood Bowl Los Angeles | No ticket prices stated |
| 31.8.65 | Cow Palace San Francisco | Between $4.50 – $6.50 |

PAUL: IT'S LIKE THIS: YOU MAKE A NOISE AND THEY MAKE A NOISE, AND IT'S THE NOISE TOGETHER THAT COUNTS. IT'S THE BIBLE, REALLY, WITH CECIL B. DE MILLE AND 60,000 EXTRAS.[65]

RINGO: If you look at the film footage you can see how we reacted to the place. It was very big and very strange. I feel that on that show John cracked up. He went mad; not mentally ill, but he just got crazy. He was playing the piano with his elbows and it was really strange.

JOHN: I was putting my foot on it and George couldn't play for laughing. I was doing it for a laugh. The kids didn't know what I was doing.

Because I did the organ on 'I'm Down', I decided to play it on stage for the first time. I didn't really know what to do, because I felt naked without a guitar, so I was doing all Jerry Lee – I was jumping about and I only played about two bars of it.

It was marvellous. It was the biggest crowd we ever played to, anywhere in the world. It was the biggest live show anybody's ever done, they told us. And it was fantastic, the most exciting we've done. They could almost hear us as well, even though they were making a lot of noise, because the amplification was tremendous.

Nothing really reached us because we were so far away, but we could see all the posters. It's still the same: up there with the mike, you don't try to work out what it all means, you forget who you are. Once you plug in and the noise starts, you're just a group playing anywhere again and you forget that you're Beatles or what your records are; you're just singing.[65]

PAUL: John was having a good time at Shea. He was into his comedy, which was great. That was one of the great things about John. If there was ever one of those tense shows, which this undoubtedly was (you can't play in front of that many people for the first time and not be tense), his comedy routines would always come out. He'd start the faces, and the shoulders would start going, and it was very encouraging: 'OK, that's good – at least we're not taking it seriously.' He kept us jolly.

NEIL ASPINALL: *John was very good at doing that; whether it was a comment, a remark or an action. The others were aware of it. When he was bowing, his hand would be flapping about; but other people tended not to notice.*

One interesting point is that Barbara, now my wife, was at that show with her sister Marjorie. Marjorie had a Beatle wig and Barbara was a Rolling Stones fan.

PAUL: Linda was also there – but as she was a real music fan she was quite pissed off with everyone screaming. I think she enjoyed the experience but she genuinely wanted to hear the show. That wasn't the deal, though. Not then.

JOHN: We played for four or five years being completely heard and it was good fun. And it's just as good fun to play being not heard and being more popular. They pay the money; if they want to scream – scream. We scream, literally; we're just screaming at them, only with guitars. Everybody's screaming – there's no harm in it.[64]

NEIL ASPINALL: *I remember my ears ringing for a while after, with the high-pitched sound of the screaming going on for an hour. It was a good experience, though. I didn't realise until later that it was the first really big open-air show that had happened. It was the most spectacular gig that The Beatles played on that tour.*

JOHN: It [the San Francisco show] was wild. Some little lad got my hat. Somebody like him doesn't really care about the show anyway, or the kids there – he just grabbed my hat from behind and dived full-length onto some kids at the front. He could have killed one of them. That kind of fool nobody needs.

I don't think it would have been as bad if the photographers hadn't been standing in the front so that the kids had to stand up to see. And the photographers got higher so as to photograph the kids standing up and that's when it started.

At the beginning I was nervous, because I get nervous thinking, 'Well, the show's going to be no good, anyway.' I could tell that. For us it was just a drag – we knew they wouldn't hear anything and the guitars were knocked out of tune by our own people running in and saving us, amplifiers were pulled out.[65]

RINGO: What I remember most about the concert was that we were so far away from the audience. They were all across the field, all wired in. When I tour now, I like the audience right in my face. I like to have some reaction, something going on together between me and them. It was just very distant at Shea. Sure, we were big-time, and it was the first time we'd played to thousands and thousands of people, and we were the first band to do it; but it was totally against what we had started out to achieve, which was to entertain, right *there*, up close. And screaming had just become the thing to do. We didn't say, 'OK, don't forget, at this concert – everybody scream!' Everybody just screamed.

The services of THE BEATLES
for presentation thereof by PURCHASER:
(a) at SHEA STADIUM,
(Place of Engagement)
(b) on SUNDAY, AUGUST 15th,
(Date(s) of Engagement)
Ludwig
THE BEATLES
FULL PRICE AGREED UPON:
gross box office
and Local Admission taxes, if
All payments shall be paid by
(a) $ 25,000.00

complete supporting
W YORK
(See Attached Rider)
y-Five Thousand Dollars ($35,000.00) guaranteed XXXXXXX
ver $167,000.00, after deduction of all Federal, State
(See attached Rider)
ck, money order, bank draft or cash as follows:
be paid by PURCHASER to and in the name of PRODUCER'S agent,

RINGO: America always had something for me. California ended up like it was our base. I've always loved it in California.

The first time in America had been absolutely marvellous. Our personal road crew then was Neil, Mal and Brian, with Derek to look after the press. Brian was the manager, but he didn't actually do anything. Neil would get us a cup of tea, and Mal would fix the instruments. There were four people with us. Now when I go out on tour there are forty-eight people with me.

But the shows were just the shows – you went on and you got off. You'd arrive just before, and do it. It was a great way to tour; I wish I could do that now. It's so much now; you carry so much luggage with you. The Beatles used to just run on, do their stuff and get off and then boogie. It was silly: the actual things we were there to do, the shows, were breaking up our day, because we were having a lot of fun outside.

NEIL ASPINALL: *When we got to California at the end of the tour, they rented a house in LA where we stayed for a week. We met Peter Fonda there. He had a trick in the swimming pool that we'd never seen anybody do before. He went in at the deep end, down to the bottom of the pool, and walked across the bottom to the other side. 'Wow! Could you do that again?' He could.*

GEORGE: We stayed in the house that Hendrix later stayed in. It was a horseshoe-shaped house on a hill off Mulholland. It had a little gatehouse, which Mal and Neil stayed in, decorated by Arabian-type things draped on the walls.

There was one very important day at that house. John and I had decided that Paul and Ringo had to have acid, because we couldn't relate to them any more. Not just on the one level – we couldn't relate to them on *any* level, because acid had changed us so much. It was such a mammoth experience that it was unexplainable: it was something that had to be *experienced*, because you could spend the rest of your life trying to explain what it made you feel and think. It was all too important to John and me. So the plan was that when we got to Hollywood, on our day off we were going to get them to take acid. We got some in New York; it was on sugar cubes wrapped in tinfoil and we'd been carrying these around all through the tour until we got to LA.

Paul wouldn't have LSD; he didn't want it. So Ringo and Neil took it, while Mal stayed straight in order to take care of everything. Dave Crosby and Jim McGuinn of The Byrds had also come up to the house, and I don't know how, but Peter Fonda was there. He kept saying, 'I know what it's like to be dead, because I shot myself.' He'd accidentally shot himself at some time and he was showing us his bullet wound. He was very uncool.

RINGO: I'd take anything. John and George didn't give LSD to me. A couple of guys came to visit us in LA, and it was them that said, 'Man, you've got to try this.' They had it in a bottle with an eye-dropper, and they dropped it on sugar cubes and gave it to us. That was my first trip. It was with John and George and Neil and Mal. Neil had to deal with Don Short while I was swimming in jelly in the pool. It was a fabulous day. The night wasn't so great, because it felt like it was never going to wear off. Twelve hours later and it was: 'Give us a break now, Lord.'

JOHN: The second time we had it was different. Then we took it deliberately – we just decided to take it again, in California. We were in one of those houses like Doris Day's house, and the three of us took it, Ringo, George and I – and maybe Neil. Paul felt very out of it, because we are all slightly cruel: 'We're all taking it and *you're* not.' It was a long time before Paul took it.

We couldn't eat our food, I couldn't manage it, just picking it up with our hands. There were all these people serving us in the house and we were knocking food on the floor and all of that. There was a reporter, Don Short, when we were in the garden. It was only our second [trip] – we still didn't know anything about doing it in a nice place, and to cool it and that – we just took it. Then suddenly we saw the reporter and thought, 'How do we act normal?' We imagined we were acting extraordinarily, which we weren't. We thought surely somebody could *see*. We were terrified, waiting for him to go, and he wondered why he couldn't come over. Neil, who had never had acid either, had taken it and he still had to play road manager. We said, 'Get rid of Don Short,' and he didn't know what to do; he just sort of sat with it.[70]

Peter Fonda came in when we were on acid and kept coming up and sitting next to me, and whispering, 'I know what it's like to be dead.' We didn't want to hear about that! We were on an acid trip, and the sun was shining, and the girls were dancing (some from *Playboy*, I believe) and the whole thing was really beautiful and Sixties. And this guy – who I didn't really know, he hadn't made *Easy Rider* or anything – kept coming over, wearing shades, saying, 'I know what it's like to be dead,' and we kept leaving him, because he was so boring. It was scary, when you're flying high: 'Don't tell me about it. I don't want to know what it's like to be dead!'

I used it for the song 'She Said, She Said'. But I changed it to 'she' instead of 'he'.[80] That's how I wrote, 'She said, she said, I know what it's like to be dead.' It was an acidy song.[70]

PAUL: Peter Fonda seemed to us to be a bit wasted; he was a little out of it. I don't know if we'd expected a bit more of Henry's son, but he was certainly of our generation, and he was all right. I don't think there were many people we hated – we just got on with them. If we didn't get on with them that much, we didn't see them again.

GEORGE: I had a concept of what had happened the first time I took LSD, but the concept is nowhere near as big as the reality, when it actually happens. So as it kicked in again, I thought, 'Jesus, I remember!' I was trying to play the guitar, and then I got in the swimming pool and it was a great feeling; the water felt good. I was swimming across the pool when I heard a noise (because it makes your senses so acute – you can almost see out of the back of your head). I felt this bad vibe and I turned around and it was Don Short from the *Daily Mirror*. He'd been hounding us all through the tour, pretending in his phoney-baloney way to be friendly but, really, trying to nail us.

Neil had to go and start talking to him. The thing about LSD is that it distorts your perception of things. We were in one spot, John and me and Jim McGuinn, and Don Short was probably only about twenty yards away, talking. But it was as though we were looking through the wrong end of a telescope. He seemed to be in the very far distance, and we were saying, 'Oh fuck, there's that guy over there.' Neil had to take him to play pool, trying to keep him away. And you have to remember that on acid just a minute can seem like a thousand years. A thousand years can go down in that minute. It was definitely not the kind of drug which you'd want to be playing pool with Don Short on.

Later on that day, we were all tripping out and they brought several starlets in and set up a movie for us to watch in the house. By the evening, there were all these strangers sitting around with their make-up on – and acid just cuts through all that bullshit. The movie was put on, and – of all things – it was a drive-in print of *Cat Ballou*. The drive-in print has the audience response already dubbed onto it, because you're all sitting in your cars and don't hear everybody laugh. Instead, they tell you when to laugh and when not to. It was bizarre, watching this on acid. I've always hated Lee Marvin, and listening on acid to that other little dwarf bloke with a bowler hat on, I thought it was the biggest load of baloney shite I'd ever seen in my life; it was too much to stand. But you just trip out. I noticed that I'd go 'out there'; I'd be gone somewhere, and then – bang! – I'd land back in my body. I'd look around and see that John had just done the same thing. You go in tandem, you're out there for a while and then – boing! whoa! – 'What happened? Oh, it's still *Cat Ballou*.' That is another thing: when two people take it at the same time; words become redundant. One can see what the other is thinking. You look at each other and know.

PAUL: We met Elvis Presley at the end of our stay in LA. We'd tried for years to, but we could never get to him. We used to think we were a bit of a threat to him and Colonel Tom Parker, which ultimately we were. So although we tried many times, Colonel Tom would just show up with a few souvenirs and that would have to do us for a while. We didn't feel brushed off; we felt we *deserved* to be brushed off. After all, he was Elvis, and who were we to dare to want to meet him? But we finally received an invitation to go round and see him when he was making a film in Hollywood.

JOHN: We were always in the wrong place at the wrong time to meet him, and we would have just gone round or something, but there was a whole lot of palaver about where we were going and how many people should go and everything, with the managers Colonel Tom and Brian working everything out.[65]

GEORGE: Meeting Elvis was one of the highlights of the tour. It was funny, because by the time we got near his house we'd forgotten where we were going. We were in a Cadillac limousine, going round and round along Mulholland, and we'd had a couple of 'cups of tea' in the back of the car. It didn't really matter where we were going: it's like the comedian Lord Buckley says, 'We go into a native village and take a couple of peyote buds; we might not find out *where* we is, but we'll sure find out *who* we is.'

Anyway, we were just having fun, we were all in hysterics. (We laughed a lot. That's one thing we forgot about for a few years – laughing. When we went through all the lawsuits, it looked as if everything was bleak; but when I think back to before that, I remember we used to laugh all the time.) We pulled up at some big gates and someone said, 'Oh yeah, we're going to see Elvis,' and we all fell out of the car laughing, trying to pretend we weren't silly: just like a Beatles cartoon.

JOHN: It was very exciting, we were all nervous as hell, and we met him in his big house in LA – probably as big as the one we were staying in, but it still felt like, 'Big house, big Elvis.' He had lots of guys around him, all these guys that used to live near him (like we did from Liverpool; we always had thousands of Liverpool people around us, so I guess he was the same). And he had pool tables! Maybe a lot of American houses are like that, but it seemed amazing to us; it was like a nightclub.[76]

NEIL ASPINALL: *The Colonel was there and all of Elvis's buddies, the so-called 'Memphis Mafia', and Priscilla. The first thing they did was show us their pool table that swivelled and became a craps table.*

*We went into this other room with a television set that seemed to be twenty foot by twenty foot. Then Brian walked in and the Colonel said, 'A chair for Mr Epstein,' and about fifteen people came with chairs.*

*Everybody was sitting around talking. Elvis was drinking water and I think a couple of The Beatles played guitar with him. I was up the other end of the room with Mal, talking to a couple of the other guys.*

RINGO: I was pretty excited about it all, and we were lucky because it was the four of us and we had each other to be with. The house was very big and dark. We walked in and Elvis was sitting down on a settee in front of the TV. He was playing a bass guitar, which even to this day I find *very* strange. He had all his guys around him and we said, 'Hi Elvis.' He was pretty shy and we were a little shy; but between the five of us, we kept it rolling. I felt I was more thrilled to meet him than he was to meet me.

PAUL: He showed us in, and he was great. I mean, it was Elvis. He just looked like Elvis – we were all major fans, so it was hero worship of a high degree. He said, 'Hello lads – do you want a drink?' We sat down and we were watching telly and he had the first remote switcher any of us had ever seen. You just aimed it at the telly and – wow! That's Elvis! He was playing 'Mohair Sam' all evening – he had it on a jukebox.

JOHN: He had his TV going all the time, which is what I do; we always have TV on. We never watch it – it's just there with no sound on, and we listen to records. In front of the TV he had a massive big bass amplifier, with a bass plugged into it, and he was up playing bass all the time with the picture up on the TV. So we just got in there and played with him. We all plugged in whatever was around and we played and sang and he had a jukebox, like I do, but I think he had all his hits on it – but if I'd made as many as him, maybe I'd have all mine on.[76]

PAUL: That was the great thing for me, that he was into the bass. So there I was: 'Well, let me show you a thing or two, El...' Suddenly he was a mate. It was a great conversation piece for me: I could actually talk about the bass, and we sat around and just enjoyed ourselves. He *was* great – talkative and friendly, and a little bit shy. But that was his image: we expected that; we hoped for that.

MAL EVANS: *It was a thrill, but it was the biggest disappointment of my life in one way. I really am a big Elvis fan – at six foot three I'm one of the biggest. So I prepare my outfit to go and meet Elvis – send the suit to the cleaners, nice white shirt and tie – really ponce myself up. But when the suit came back from the cleaners, they'd sewn the pockets up. Now, I always carry plectrums – picks, they call them in the States. It's just a habit. I'm not even working for them now and I've still got a pick in my pocket at the moment.*

*So when we get there, Elvis asks, 'Has anybody got a pick?' and Paul turns round and says, 'Yeah, Mal's got a pick. He's always got a pick. He carries them on holiday with him!' I went to go in my pocket for one – and there they were, all sewn up.*

*I ended up in the kitchen breaking plastic spoons, making picks for Elvis!*

*That was a disappointment: I'd have loved to have given Elvis a pick, have him play it, then got it back and had it framed.*

*Charlie Rich was there. I loved Charlie Rich, and so did Elvis. They had a record-player with the arm up the middle, and Muddy Waters just seemed to be playing all night. And the colour TV in one corner with the sound off, and there was Elvis playing bass, Paul and John on guitars – and I was just sat there with my mouth open all night.*

JOHN: At first we couldn't make him out. I asked him if he was preparing new ideas for his next film and he drawled, 'Ah sure am. Ah play a country boy with a guitar who meets a few gals along the way, and ah sing a few songs.' We all looked at one another. Finally Presley and Colonel Parker laughed and explained that the only time they departed from that formula – for *Wild in the Country* – they lost money.[65]

PAUL: We played a bit of pool with a few of his motorcycle mates, and at about ten o'clock Priscilla was brought in. To demonstrate the respect that country-and-western people have for their wives? Sometimes it's a bit on the surface – as maybe their situation was shown to be later. It was like, 'Here's Priscilla.'

She came in and I got this picture of her as a sort of Barbie doll – with a purple gingham dress, and a gingham bow in her very beehive hair, with lots of make-up. We all said 'hello' and then it was, 'Right lads, hands off – she's going.' She didn't stay long.

I can't blame him, although I don't think any of us would have made a pass at her. That was definitely not on – Elvis's wife, you know! That was unthinkable – she didn't need to be put away quite so quickly, we thought.

GEORGE: I don't remember even seeing Priscilla. I spent most of the party trying to suss out from his gang if anybody had any reefers. But they were 'uppers and whisky' people. They weren't really into reefer-smoking in the South.

RINGO: I don't remember seeing Priscilla there at all. I think it wouldn't have mattered to me if she was there, because it was him I came to see. I don't really remember the boys he had with him either.

NEIL ASPINALL: *I thought Priscilla had a long dress on, and a tiara. I remember that when Brian told the Colonel that he managed bands other than The Beatles, the Colonel was quite shocked. He said he didn't understand how Brian could handle more than The Beatles, because it took him all his time to handle Elvis.*

JOHN: It was nice meeting Elvis. He was just Elvis, you know? He played a few songs, and we were all playing guitars. It was great. We never talked about anything – we just played music. He wasn't bigger than us, but he was 'the thing'. He just wasn't articulate, that's all.[72]

He seemed normal to us, and we were asking about his making movies and not doing any personal appearances or TV. I think he enjoys making movies so much. We couldn't stand not doing personal appearances; we'd get bored – we get bored quickly. He says he misses it a bit. He's just normal. He was great, just as I expected him.[65]

PAUL: It was one of the great meetings of my life. I think he liked us. I think at that time he may have felt a little bit threatened, but he didn't say anything. We certainly didn't feel any antagonism.

I only met him that once, and then I think the success of our career started to push him out a little; which we were very sad about, because we wanted to co-exist with him. He was our greatest idol, but the styles were changing in favour of us. He was a pretty powerful image to British people. You'd look at photos of him doing American concerts and the audience would not even be jumping up and down. We used to be amazed, seeing them sitting in the front row – not even dancing.

RINGO: The saddest part is that, years and years later, we found out that he tried to have us banished from America, because he was very big with the FBI. That's very sad to me, that he felt so threatened that he thought, like a lot of people, that we were bad for American Youth. This is Mr Hips, *the man*, and he felt *we* were a danger. I think that the danger was mainly to him and his career.

I saw him again. I remember one time I got really angry with him because he just wasn't making any music. He'd stopped everything and was just playing football with his guys. So I said, 'Why don't you go into a studio and give us some music here? What are you doing?' I can't remember what he said – he probably just walked away and started playing football again.

PAUL: I've seen those famous Nixon transcripts where Elvis actually starts to try to shop us – The Beatles! He's in the transcript saying – to Richard Nixon, of all people – 'Well, sir, these Beatles: they're very un-American and they take drugs.'

I felt a bit betrayed by that, I must say. The great joke was that *we* were taking drugs, and look what happened to him. He was caught on the toilet full of them! It was sad; but I still love him, particularly in his early period. He was very influential on me.

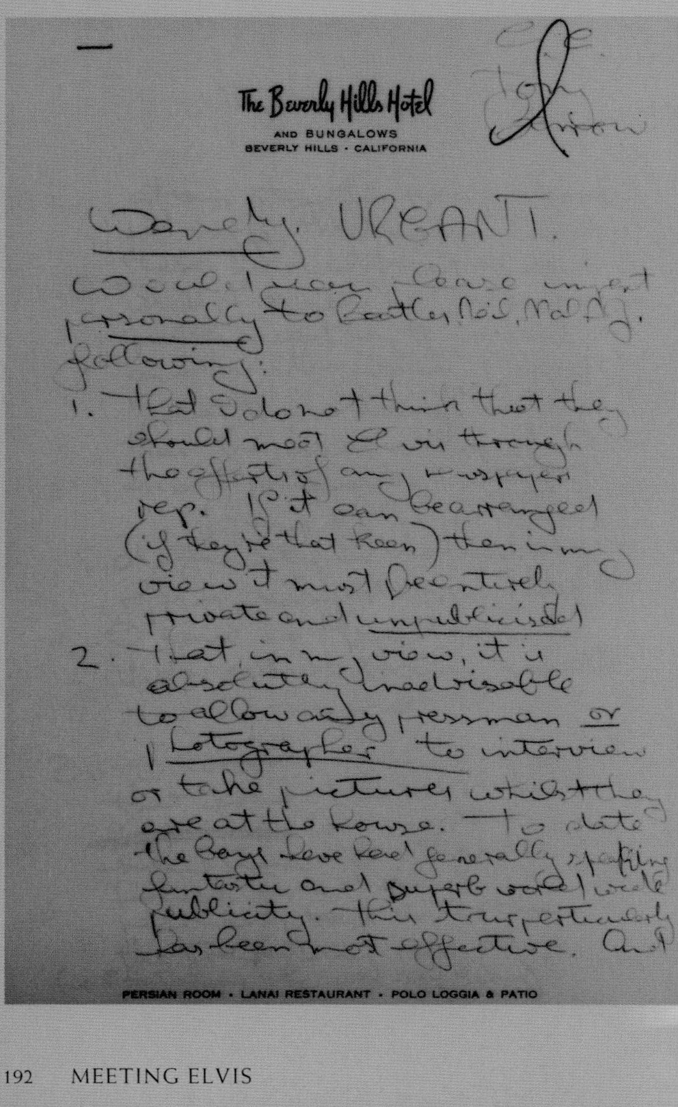
The Beverly Hills Hotel
AND BUNGALOWS
BEVERLY HILLS · CALIFORNIA

Wendy. URGENT.
Would you please impart personally to Beatles, Neil, Mal & A.J. following:
1. That I do not think that they should meet Elvis through the efforts of any newspaper rep. If it can be arranged (if they're that keen) then in my view it must be entirely private and unpublicised.
2. That, in my view, it is absolutely inadvisable to allow any pressman or photographer to interview or take pictures whilst they are at the house. To date the boys have had generally speaking fantastic and superb world wide publicity. This tour particularly has been most effective. And

PERSIAN ROOM · LANAI RESTAURANT · POLO LOGGIA & PATIO

JOHN: When I first heard 'Heartbreak Hotel' I could hardly make out what was being said. It was just the experience of hearing it and having my hair stand on end. We'd never heard American voices singing like that. They'd always sung like Sinatra or enunciated very well. Suddenly there's this hillbilly hiccuping on tape echo and all this bluesy background going on. And we didn't know what the hell Presley was singing about, or Little Richard or Chuck Berry. It took a long time to work out what was going on. To us, it just sounded like a noise that was great.[71]

Up until Elvis joined the army I thought it was beautiful music, and Elvis was for me and my generation what The Beatles were to the Sixties.[77] But after he went into the army, I think they cut 'les bollocks' off. They not only shaved his hair off, but I think they shaved between his legs, too. He played *some* good stuff after the army, but it was never quite the same. It was like something happened to him psychologically.[75]

Elvis really died the day he joined the army. That's when they killed him, and the rest was a living death.[77]

PAUL: These were great times, so even if you didn't enjoy all of the events that much you could still go home to Liverpool and say, 'Well, you know who I met?' I mean, to meet Elvis, or anybody like that, or to say you've been to Sunset Strip – it was very impressive.

JOHN: It sort of dawned on me that love was the answer, when I was younger, on the *Rubber Soul* album. My first expression of it was a song called 'The Word'. The word is 'love'. 'In the good and the bad books that I have read,' whatever, wherever, the word is 'love'. It seems like the underlying theme to the universe. Everything that was worthwhile got down to this love, love, love thing. And it is the struggle to love, be loved and express that (just *something* about love) that's fantastic.

I think that whatever else love is – and it's many, many things – it is constant. It's been the same forever. I don't think it will ever change. Even though I'm not always a loving person, I want to be that; I want to be as loving as possible.

PAUL: 'THE WORD' COULD BE A SALVATION ARMY SONG. THE WORD IS 'LOVE' BUT IT COULD BE 'JESUS'. (IT *ISN'T*, MIND YOU, BUT IT COULD BE.)[65]

JOHN: We were getting better, technically and musically. We finally took over the studio. In the early days, we had to take what we were given; we had to make it in two hours, and one or three takes was enough and we didn't know how you could get more bass – we were learning the techniques.[70] Then we got contemporary. I think *Rubber Soul* was about when it started happening.

Everything I, any of us, do is influenced, but it began to take its own form. *Rubber Soul* was a matter of having all experienced the recording studio; having grown musically as well, but [getting] the knowledge of the place, of the studio.[73] We were more precise about making the album, that's all, and we took over the cover and everything.

It was Paul's title. It was like 'Yer Blues', I suppose, meaning English soul, 'Rubber soul'. Just a pun.[70]

PAUL: I think the title *Rubber Soul* came from a comment an old blues guy had said of Jagger. I've heard some out-takes of us doing 'I'm Down' and at the front of it I'm chatting on about Mick. I'm saying how I'd just read about an old bloke in the States who said, 'Mick Jagger, man. Well you know they're good – but it's plastic soul.' So 'plastic soul' was the germ of the *Rubber Soul* idea.

In October 1965, we started to record the album. Things were changing. The direction was moving away from the poppy stuff like 'Thank You Girl', 'From Me To You' and 'She Loves You'. The early material was directly relating to our fans, saying, 'Please buy this record,' but now we'd come to a point where we thought, 'We've done that. Now we can branch out into songs that are more surreal, a little more entertaining.' And other people were starting to arrive on the scene who were influential. Dylan was influencing us quite heavily at that point.

GEORGE MARTIN: *By the time of* Rubber Soul *they were ready for new musical directions. In the early days they were very influenced by American rhythm-and-blues. I think that the so-called 'Beatles sound' had something to do with Liverpool being a port. Maybe they heard the records before we did. They certainly knew much more about Motown and black music than anybody else did, and that was a tremendous influence on them.*

*And then, as time went on, other influences became apparent: classical influences and modern music. That was from 1965 and beyond.*

RINGO: There was a lot of experimentation on *Rubber Soul*, influenced, I think, by the substances. George Martin knew about it and used to get annoyed; well, not really annoyed, he would just go, 'Oh God,' because things would take a little longer.

He was very good. In the early days he'd had an assistant who'd go through rehearsals with us and George would just come in for the take, to press the tape button. That changed and he was there all the time; and then, as we went on, we would just be playing, and playing great, and we'd say, 'Did you get that, George?' I believe we taught George Martin how to keep the tape rolling. He lost that old attitude that you only press the button when you are going to do the take. We began to have the tape rolling all the time and we got a lot of good takes that way.

PAUL: George Martin was very understanding, even though we were going to change style and get more psychedelic or surreal. It never seemed to throw him, even though sometimes it was not quite his taste in music.

We did occasionally get pissed off with him. As time went by, things crept in. In an out-take I heard recently – recording 'Dizzy Miss Lizzy' – John is saying, 'What's wrong with that?' and George Martin says, 'Erm... it wasn't exciting enough, John,' and John mumbles, 'Bloody hell,' – that kind of thing was creeping in a bit – 'it wasn't exciting enough, eh? Well, you come here and sing it, then!' I think that's just pressure of work. When you've been working hard for a long time, you really start to need a break.

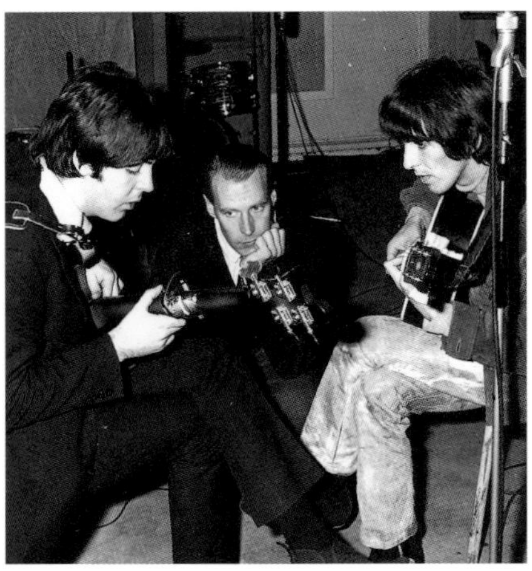

RINGO: Like everyone else, we get a bit edgy, but it never goes too far. None of us have ever gone to hit each other or anything like that.[65]

JOHN: We have plenty of arguments, but we're all so attuned to each other, and we know each other so well through the years, that an argument never reaches a climax. It's like mind-reading. If an argument's building up between Ringo and I, say, it comes to a point where we know what's going to come next and everybody packs in. So we have arguments, like other people, but there's no conflict. All the people that have conflict in showbusiness either get married about nineteen times, or they leave the group and go solo.[65]

RINGO: When we did take too many substances, the music was shit, absolute shit. At the time we'd think it was great, but when we came to record the next day we'd all look at each other and say, 'We'll have to do that again.' It didn't work for The Beatles to be too deranged when making music. There's very little material where we were out to lunch. It was good to take it the day before – then you'd have that creative memory – but you couldn't function while under the influence.

GEORGE: It used to make us feel ill as well. John would pick us up in his big Rolls Royce with blacked-out windows when we were living out in the stockbroker belt. (Ringo, John and I had all moved out of town to Surrey.) He'd pick up Ringo and then me and we'd head into town. Because a Rolls Royce doesn't have the proper springs, it just rolls around; and the black windows would be shut, so we'd be getting double doses of reefers. By the time we got to Hammersmith, we were loaded and feeling ill. We would pull up at the Abbey Road studios and fall out of the car.

Reefers are hard to avoid in The Beatles' story. All the time, Mal and Neil would sit in Studio No. 2 behind the sound baffles while we were working, rolling them up and smoking. You can hear on one of the tapes from the sessions: a song starts and John goes, 'Hang on, 'ang on...' And Paul starts filling in for him. Then John comes back: 'Ahhhh. OK, OK.' And by the time the engineers have rewound the tape you're thinking, 'I'll just go and have another hit...'

But *Rubber Soul* was my favourite album, even at that time. I think that it was the best one we made; we certainly knew we were making a good album. We did spend a bit more time on it and tried new things. But the most important thing about it was that we were suddenly hearing sounds that we weren't able to hear before. Also, we were being more influenced by other people's music and everything was blossoming at that time; including us, because we were still growing.

RINGO: Grass was really influential in a lot of our changes, especially with the writers. And because they were writing different material, we were playing differently. We were expanding in all areas of our lives, opening up to a lot of different attitudes. I feel that we made it on love songs (all the initial songs were love songs). Now we get to *Rubber Soul* and begin stretching the writing and the playing a lot more. This was the departure record. A lot of other influences were coming down and going on the record.

'Nowhere Man' was good. 'Girl' was great – weird breathy sounds on it. 'The Word', another great track – George Martin on harmonium, Mal 'Organ' Evans on Hammond. We were really getting into a lot of different sounds and I think the lyrics were changing, too, with songs like 'Drive My Car', 'Norwegian Wood', 'You Won't See Me', 'Nowhere Man' and, of course, 'Michelle'.

JOHN: *Rubber Soul* was the pot album, and *Revolver* was the acid. It was like pills influenced us in Hamburg, drink influenced us in so and so; I mean, we weren't all stoned making *Rubber Soul*, because in those days we couldn't work on pot. We never recorded under acid.

It's like saying, 'Did Dylan Thomas write *Under Milk Wood* on beer?' What does that have to do with it? The beer is to prevent the rest of the world from crowding in on you. The drugs are to prevent the rest of the world from crowding in on you. They don't make you write any better. I never wrote any better stuff because I was on acid or not on acid.[72]

GEORGE: Songwriting for me, at the time of *Rubber Soul*, was a bit frightening because John and Paul had been writing since they were three years old. It was hard to come in suddenly and write songs. They'd had a lot of practice. They'd written most of their bad songs before we'd even got into the recording studio. I had to come from nowhere and start writing, and have something with at least enough quality to put on the record alongside all the wondrous hits. It was very hard.

PAUL: John and I were writing quite well by 1965. For a while we didn't really have enough home-made material, but we did start to around the time of *Rubber Soul*.

Most of the time we wrote together. We'd go and lock ourselves away and say, 'OK, what have we got?' John might have half an idea, something like for 'In My Life': 'There are places I remember...' (I think he had that first as a lyric – like a poem, 'Places I Remember') and we'd work out the extra melody needed, and the main theme, and by the end of three or four hours we nearly always had it cracked! I can't remember coming away from one of those sessions not having finished a song.

One of the stickiest was 'Drive My Car', because we couldn't get past one phrase that we had: 'You can buy me golden rings.' We struggled for hours; I think we struggled too long. Then we had a break and suddenly it came: 'Wait a minute: "Drive my car!"' Then we got into the fun of that scenario: 'Oh, you can drive my car.' What is it? What's he doing? Is he offering a job as a chauffeur, or what? And then it became much more ambiguous, which we liked, instead of golden rings, which was a bit poofy. 'Golden rings' became 'beep beep, yeah'. We both came up with that. Suddenly we were in LA: cars, chauffeurs, open-top Cadillacs, and it was a whole other thing.

GEORGE: I played the bassline on 'Drive My Car'. It was like the line from 'Respect' by Otis Redding.

PAUL: SONGWRITING IS A THING WE CAN'T STOP – IT'S A HABIT, ALMOST.[65]

JOHN: 'Girl' is real. There is no such thing as *the* girl; she was a dream, but the words are all right. It wasn't just a song, and it was about *that* girl – that turned out to be Yoko, in the end – the one that a lot of us were looking for.

It's about, 'Was she taught when she was young that pain would lead to pleasure, did she understand it?' Sort of philosophy quotes I was thinking about when I wrote it. I was trying to say something or other about Christianity, which I was opposed to at the time because I was brought up in the Church.

I was pretty heavy on the Church in both books, but it was never picked up, although it was obviously there. I was talking about Christianity, in that you have to be tortured to attain heaven. That was the Catholic Christian concept: be tortured and then it'll be all right; which seems to be true, but not in their concept of it. I didn't believe in that: that you *have* to be tortured to attain anything; it just so happens that you are.[70]

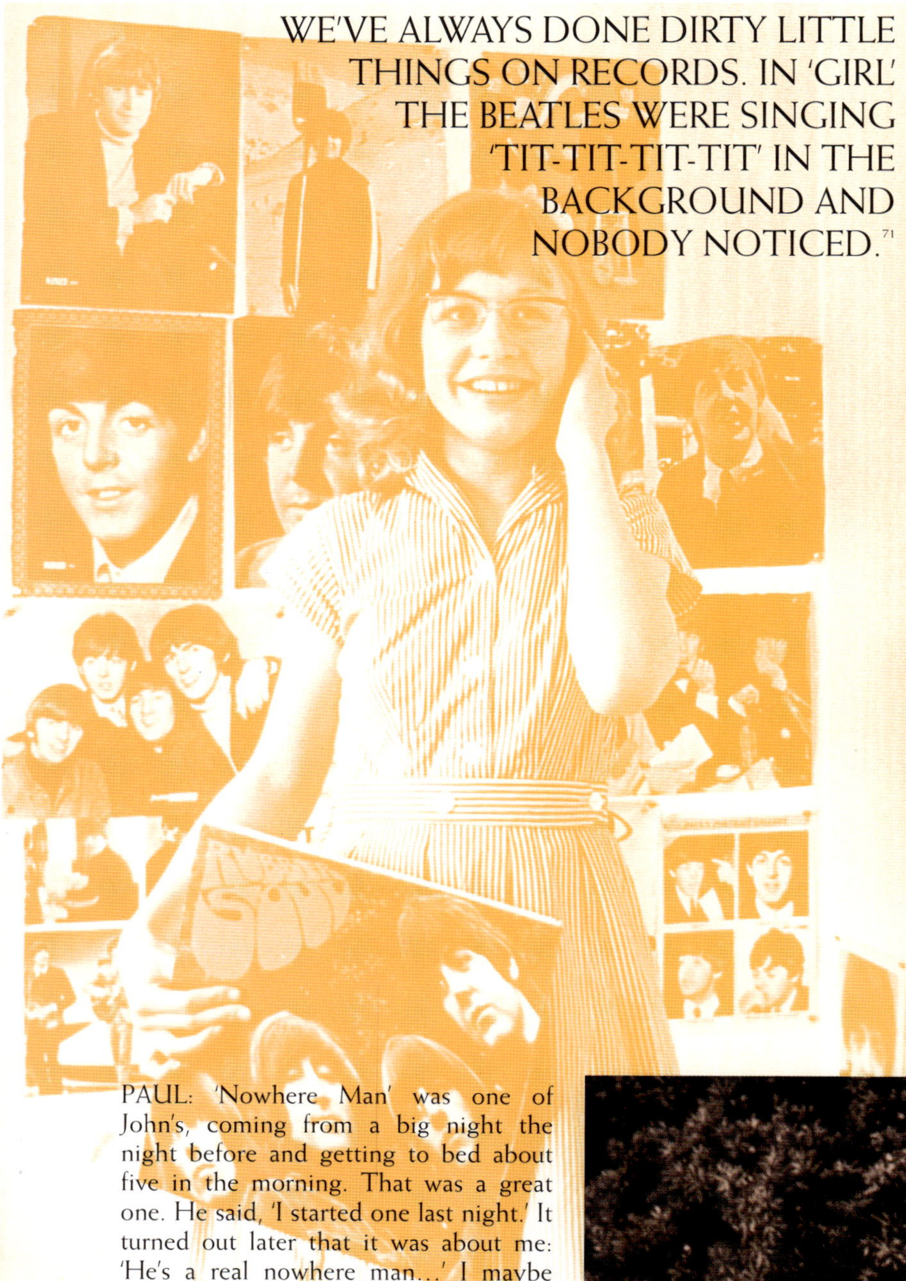

WE'VE ALWAYS DONE DIRTY LITTLE THINGS ON RECORDS. IN 'GIRL' THE BEATLES WERE SINGING 'TIT-TIT-TIT-TIT' IN THE BACKGROUND AND NOBODY NOTICED.[71]

PAUL: 'Nowhere Man' was one of John's, coming from a big night the night before and getting to bed about five in the morning. That was a great one. He said, 'I started one last night.' It turned out later that it was about me: 'He's a real nowhere man...' I maybe helped him with a word here or there, but he'd already got most of it.

Nobody ever had any notes written down; we just used to sing a tune and it would come out good. Part of the secret collaboration was that we liked each other. We liked singing at each other. He'd sing something and I'd say, 'Yeah,' and trade off on that. He'd say, 'Nowhere land,' and I'd say, 'For nobody.' It was a two-way thing.

JOHN: I'd spent five hours that morning trying to write a song that was meaningful and good.[80] I was just sitting, trying to think, and I thought of myself sitting there, doing nothing and going nowhere. Once I'd thought of that, it was easy, it all came out. No – I remember now; I'd actually stopped trying to think of something. Nothing would come. I was cheesed off and went for a lie down, having given up. Then I thought of myself as Nowhere Man – sitting in this Nowhere Land.[67]

'Nowhere Man' came, words and music, the whole damn thing. The same with 'In My Life'. I'd struggled for days and hours, trying to write clever lyrics. Then I gave up, and 'In My Life' came to me – letting it go is the whole game.[80]

GEORGE: In Studio No. 2 there is a steep staircase that goes up to the control room. Underneath is a cupboard where they used to keep all kinds of different equipment. Most of it has gone now, but there is still a wind machine where you wind the handle. There were strange tambourines and Moroccan drums and all kinds of little things. The studio itself was full of instruments: pedal harmoniums, tack (jangly) pianos, a celeste and a Hammond organ. That's why we used all those different sounds on our records – because they were *there*. So when we'd get to an overdub we'd look around the cupboard and see if there was something that would fit, like the funny drum sound on 'Don't Bother Me'.

Paul used a fuzz box on the bass on 'Think For Yourself'. When Phil Spector was making 'Zip-A-Dee-Doo-Dah', the engineer who'd set up the track overloaded the microphone on the guitar player and it became very distorted. Phil Spector said, 'Leave it like that, it's great.' Some years later everyone started to try to copy that sound and so they invented the fuzz box. We had one and tried the bass through it and it sounded really good.

GEORGE MARTIN: *The Beatles were always looking for new sounds, always looking to a new horizon and it was a continual but happy strain to try and provide new things for them. They were always waiting to try new instruments even when they didn't know much about them.*

GEORGE: 'Norwegian Wood' was the first use of sitar on one of our records, though during the filming of *Help!* there were some Indian musicians in a restaurant scene and I first messed around with one then.

Towards the end of the year I'd kept hearing the name of Ravi Shankar. I heard it several times, and about the third time it was a friend of mine who said, 'Have you heard this person Ravi Shankar? You may like the music.' So I went out and bought a record and that was it: I thought it was incredible.

When I first consciously heard Indian music, it was as if I already knew it. When I was a child we had a crystal radio with long and short wave bands and so it's possible I might have already heard some Indian classical music. There was something about it that was very familiar, but at the same time, intellectually, I didn't know what was happening at all.

So I went and bought a sitar from a little shop at the top of Oxford Street called Indiacraft – it stocked little carvings, and incense. It was a real crummy-quality one, actually, but I bought it and mucked about with it a bit. Anyway, we were at the point where we'd recorded the 'Norwegian Wood' backing track (twelve-string and six-string acoustic, bass and drums) and it needed something. We would usually start looking through the cupboard to see if we could come up with something, a new sound, and I picked the sitar up – it was just lying around; I hadn't really figured out what to do with it. It was quite spontaneous: I found the notes that played the lick. It fitted and it worked.

JOHN: 'Norwegian Wood' was about an affair I was having. I was very careful and paranoid because I didn't want my wife, Cyn, to know that there really was something going on outside the household. I'd always had some kind of affairs going, so I was trying to be sophisticated in writing about an affair, but in such a smokescreen way that you couldn't tell. I can't remember any specific woman it had to do with.[80] I was writing from my experiences; girls' flats, things like that.[70]

George had just got the sitar and I said, 'Could you play this piece?' We went through many different versions of the song. It was never right and I was getting very angry about it; it wasn't coming out like I said. They said, 'Just do it how you want,' and I did the guitar very loudly into the mike and sang it at the same time. And then George had the sitar and I asked him could he play the piece that I'd written. He was not sure whether he could play it yet because he hadn't done much on the sitar, but he was willing to have a go, as is his wont, and he learnt the bit and dubbed it on after.

RINGO: It was such a mind-blower that we had this strange instrument on a record. We were all open to anything when George introduced the sitar: you could walk in with an elephant, as long as it was going to make a musical note. Anything was viable. Our whole attitude was changing. We'd grown up a little, I think.

JOHN: I wrote the middle eight of 'Michelle', one of Paul's songs. He and I were staying somewhere and he walked in and hummed the first few bars, with the words, and he says, 'Where do I go from here?' I had been listening to Nina Simone – I think it was 'I Put A Spell On You'. There was a line in it that went: 'I love *you*, I love *you*, I love *you*.' That's what made me think of the middle eight: 'I *love* you, I *love* you, I *l-o-ove* you.'

My contribution to Paul's songs was always to add a little bluesy edge to them. Otherwise 'Michelle' is a straight ballad. He provided a lightness, an optimism, while I would always go for the sadness, the discords, the bluesy notes. There was a period when I thought I didn't write melodies; that Paul wrote those and I just wrote straight, shouting rock'n'roll. But of course, when I think of some of my own songs – 'In My Life', or some of the early stuff, 'This Boy' – I was writing melody with the best of them.[80]

PAUL: We'd just put out 'Michelle' and I remember one night at the Ad Lib club David Bailey hearing it and saying, 'You've *got* to be joking – it *is* tongue in cheek, isn't it?' My reaction was: 'Piss off! That's a real tune,' and was quite surprised that he'd think that. Looking at the Sixties now, I can see why he did, because everything was very 'Needles And Pins', 'Please Please Me', and suddenly – 'Michelle'. It came a bit out of left field, but those are often my favourites. I mean, one of Cliff Richard's best ones was 'Living Doll'. When he came out with that it was quite a shock, with its acoustics; but it was a well-formed little song.

JOHN: We did a lot of learning together. George Martin had a very great musical knowledge and background, and he could translate for us and suggest a lot of things. He'd come up with amazing technical things, slowing down the piano and things like that. We'd be saying, 'We want it to go un, un and ee, ee,' and he'd say, 'Well, look, chaps, I thought of this, this afternoon, and last night I was talking to… whoever, and I came up with this.' And we'd say, 'Great, great, come on, put it on here.' He'd also come up with things like, 'Have you heard an oboe?' and we'd say, 'Which one's that?' and he'd say, 'This one.'[75]

In 'In My Life' there's an Elizabethan piano solo – we'd do things like that. We'd say, 'Play it like Bach,' or, 'Could you put twelve bars in there?' He helped us to develop a language a little, to talk to musicians. Because I'm very shy and for many, many reasons I didn't much go for musicians, I didn't like to have to go and see twenty guys and try and tell them what to do. They're all so lousy, anyway.[70]

GEORGE MARTIN: *'In My Life' is one of my favourite songs because it is so much John. A super track and such a simple song. There's a bit where John couldn't decide what to do in the middle and, while they were having their tea-break, I put down a baroque piano solo which John didn't hear until he came back. What I wanted was too intricate for me to do live, so I did it with a half-speed piano, then sped it up, and he liked it.*

JOHN: 'In My Life' was, I think, my first real, major piece of work. Up until then it had all been glib and throw-away. I had one mind that wrote books and another mind that churned out things about 'I love you' and 'you love me', because that's how Paul and I did it. I'd always tried to make some sense of the words, but I never really cared.

It was the first song that I wrote that was really, consciously, about my life. It was sparked by a remark a journalist and writer in England made after *In His Own Write* came out. He said to me, 'Why don't you put some of the way you write in the book in the songs? Or why don't you put something about your childhood into the songs?'[80]

I wrote the lyrics first and then sang it. That was usually the case with things like 'In My Life' and 'Across The Universe' and some of the ones that stand out a bit. I wrote it in Kenwood, upstairs, where I had about ten tape recorders, all linked up. I'd mastered them over the period of a year or two – I could never make a rock'n'roll record, but I could make some far-out stuff.[70]

It started out as a bus journey from my house on 251 Menlove Avenue to town. I had a complete set of lyrics, naming every sight. It became 'In My Life', a remembrance of friends and lovers of the past. Paul helped with the middle eight, musically.[80]

PAUL: Funnily enough, this is one of the only songs John and I disagree on. I remember writing the melody on a mellotron that was parked on his half-landing.

JOHN: Most of my good songs are in the first person.[71] 'In My Life', 'I'm A Loser', 'Help!', 'Strawberry Fields' – they're all personal records. I always wrote about me when I could. I didn't really enjoy writing third-person songs about people who lived in concrete flats and things like that. I like first-person music. But because of my hang-ups, and many other things, I would only now and then write specifically about me.

From the same period, same time, I never liked 'Run For Your Life', because it was a song I just knocked off. It was inspired from – this is a very vague connection – 'Baby Let's Play House'. There was a line on it: 'I'd rather see you dead, little girl, than to be with another man,' so I wrote it around that. I didn't think it was all that important, but it was always a favourite of George's.[70]

GEORGE: I wouldn't say that my songs are autobiographical. 'Taxman' is, perhaps. Some of them were later on, after The Beatles. The early ones were just any words I could think of.

GEORGE MARTIN: *They had a great time in the studio and, in the main, they were enormously happy times. They would fool around a lot and have a laugh, particularly when overdubbing voices. John was funny; they all were. My memory is of a very joyful time.*

PAUL: Later, when we made *Sgt Pepper*, I remember taking it round to Dylan at the Mayfair Hotel in London; I went round as if I were going on a pilgrimage. Keith Richards was in the outer room and we had to hang around and then went in to meet Dylan. It was a little bit like an audience with the Pope. I remember playing him some of *Sgt Pepper* and he said, 'Oh, I get it – you don't want to be cute any more.' That was the feeling about *Rubber Soul*, too. We'd had our cute period and now it was time to expand.

The album cover is another example of our branching out: the stretched photo. That was actually one of those little exciting random things that happen. The photographer Robert Freeman had taken some pictures round at John's house in Weybridge. We had our new gear on – the polo necks – and we were doing straight mug shots; the four of us all posing. Back in London Robert was showing us the slides; he had a piece of cardboard that was the album-cover size and he was projecting the photographs exactly onto it so we could see how it would look as an album cover. We had just chosen the photograph when the card that the picture was projected onto fell backwards a little, elongating the photograph. It was stretched and we went, 'That's it, *Rubber So-o-oul*, hey hey! Can you do it like that?' And he said, 'Well, yeah. I can print it that way.' And that was it.

GEORGE: I liked the way we got our faces to be longer on the album cover. We lost the 'little innocents' tag, the naivety, and *Rubber Soul* was the first one where we were fully-fledged potheads.

GRANADA TELEVISION LIMITED

Address reply to

PO Box 494, 36 GOLDEN SQUARE LONDON W1

Granada London. Telephone: Regent 8080 (STD code 01)

27th October 1965.

PAUL: We did a television programme in November: *The Music of Lennon and McCartney*. It was planned as a kind of tribute, a showcase of stars singing songs that John and I had written. The idea had come from the director, Johnny Hamp; a mate. (We knew a lot of people at his company, Granada; the first TV show we did was with them. The Granada studios were only half an hour away from us in Liverpool, so we would just go up the road.)

We weren't really that keen, but Johnny was very persuasive and a nice bloke, so we were happy to do it for him. He'd told us he had Cilla Black doing one of the songs – Cilla was an old mate – and that Henry Mancini was to be another on the show. It was a great honour that someone as good as Henry would be doing our songs; so, altogether, we couldn't really turn it down.

It was great to meet Hank Mancini, because like most people we'd loved 'Moon River'. The line 'My huckleberry friend' had done us in: after *Breakfast at Tiffany's* he was a hero.

Fritz Spiegl was on the show. He did a baroque version of one of our tunes. People were doing a lot of that at the time: dressing in white wigs and pretending they were a baroque string quartet. Baroque and Roll! We'd actually met Fritz quite a few years earlier, at a party; which is something of a story.

John was at art school then, and the only people at that time who had parties were the art-school people. (*Our* school didn't have parties – you just went home after school.) I remember this party was at John's tutor's house. It was very sophisticated for me and George, so we were trying to hang in there and pretend we knew what was going on. The Liverpool Philharmonic Orchestra had finished a concert and some of the musicians had come to the party in full evening dress from the concert. They were all a bit grand for us. There we were, looking as suave as we could and a guy walked over and it was Fritz Spiegl. He came over and was putting a record on the record-player: Liszt's 'Hungarian Rhapsodies', and I remember George looking over to him and saying, 'Hey, Geraldo – got any Elvis?' Fritz was not amused…

Also in the TV show was Peter Sellers. I didn't know him too well. (Ringo got to know him; Ringo hung out with the showbiz people a bit more. He has been to dinner with Marlon Brando, Richard Burton, Elizabeth Taylor – he could hold his own with all of them.) But I met Peter later: a very nice bloke, pretty hung up, and, like a lot of comedians, he wanted to be a musician. He was a drummer, as I recall, but on this show he did a very funny impression of Larry Olivier doing 'A Hard Day's Night'.

Then there was Ella Fitzgerald. She was at the opposite end of the spectrum from us. That was another honour – Ella Fitzgerald singing 'Can't Buy Me Love'. I'd been a fan of hers for years; she had such a great voice.

Before the show, Johnny Hamp had asked us if we had any real favourites of the Lennon/McCartney cover versions out at the time. Esther Phillips was my big favourite. She'd changed our 'And I Love Her' to 'And I Love Him' and did a great version of it. The sort of people we were listening to then were on Stax and Motown; black American, mainly. George used to have a great collection of Stax records on his jukebox. I liked Marvin Gaye, Smokey Robinson, people like that. The Miracles were a big influence on us, where Little Richard had been earlier. Now, for us, Motown artists were taking the place of Richard. We loved the black artists so much; and it was the greatest accolade to have somebody with one of those *real* voices, as we saw it, sing our own songs (we'd certainly been doing theirs). So I turned Johnny on to Esther Phillips, and he got her over for the show.

A lot of people covered our songs. If you've written something, it's good to be covered. It doesn't matter if Pinky and Perky do it, it shows someone liked it enough in the first place. So I'm amused rather than annoyed – I've never been annoyed with any cover version. Obviously some of them are more successful than others – like Ray Charles or Esther Phillips. Roy Redmond did a really brilliant version of 'Good Day Sunshine'. And *Count Basie Plays The Beatles*, too. Those are the ones we really got serious about and loved, and the others we just put up with and enjoyed.

JOHN: Sinatra's not for me; it just doesn't do it, you know? Some of his things I have liked, some of the arrangements of the bands. But Peggy Lee I could listen to all day, as much as I can to rock'n'roll. Ella Fitzgerald is great. I couldn't understand what people liked about her for years and then I heard something of hers and I said, 'That's great,' and they said, 'That's Ella Fitzgerald.' I didn't believe them; I thought it was some R&B singer.[64]

NEIL ASPINALL: *It was good that they could still get involved in shows like this, and those funny little sketches at Christmas. For a rock'n'roll band, it was amazing. That came from art-school days and the rag night. They could still join in that sort of fun in 1965.*

PAUL: In December we did the last tour of Britain we would ever do. We'd worked nearly every day for a long time doing live sets, so after a few years of that we were now much more intrigued with recording.

It's as if we were painters who had never *really* been allowed to paint – we'd just had to go selling our paintings up and down the country. Then, suddenly, we had somebody telling us, 'You can have a studio and you can paint and you can take your time.' So, obviously, being in a recording studio became much more attractive to us than going on the road again.

JOHN: I always was a record man. I always liked the studio best, once I got the hang of it and the control. I like it because it's complete control.[75]

NEIL ASPINALL: *As time went by, they began to find that, technically, they couldn't produce on stage what they could do in the studio. I think the guys were getting pissed off with just churning out performances and tracks, however good, as though they were on some sort of conveyor belt. They didn't want that any more.*

JOHN: 'Day Tripper' was [written] under complete pressure, based on an old folk song I wrote about a month previous. It was very hard going, that, and it sounds it.[69] It wasn't a serious message song. It was a drug song. In a way, it *was* a day tripper – I just liked the word.[70]

'We Can Work It Out': Paul wrote that chorus, I wrote the middle bit. You've got Paul writing 'we can work it out', real optimistic; and me, impatient: 'Life is very short and there's no time for fussing...'[80]

RINGO: By the end of 1965 the touring started to hit everybody. I remember we had a meeting during which we all talked about how the musicianship was going downhill, never mind the boredom of doing it; going away and hitting all those hotels.

Bands go on the road nowadays and do a press conference one day and shows for the next four days. But, for The Beatles, it was *always* the press and those sorts of people: there was so much pressure. From the minute we opened our eyes people were trying to get at us.

The pressure was on. I don't remember having any time off, except when we rented the house in LA and spent a week or so there; but even then we'd had to put the barriers up – that is, Neil and Mal and whoever else they had around them. It was, 'OK, lock the door; let's just have a break here.'

JOHN: I enjoy playing, really, but in America it was spoiled for me because of the crap there – meeting people we don't want to meet. I suppose I'm a bit intolerant. But is it any wonder I got fed up when they kept sending in autograph books and we signed them only to find they belonged to officials – promoters, police and the rest of that lot. The real fans, they'd waited for hours, days. They were treated like half-wits because they wanted our autographs – but the cops made sure they got theirs. I bet every policeman's daughter in Britain has got our autographs. Half of them aren't our fans. It's bloody unfair on the kids who really want them.[64]

It would hurt me; I would go insane, swearing, whatever. I'd always do *something*. I couldn't take it; it was awful, all that business was awful. One has to completely humiliate oneself to be what The Beatles were, and that's what I resent. I mean, I did it, I didn't know, I didn't foresee; it just happens bit by bit, gradually, until this complete craziness is surrounding you and you're doing exactly what you don't want to do with people you can't stand; the people you hated when you were ten.[70]

NEIL ASPINALL: *Anybody near to the band at that time could sense their dissatisfaction with touring life, which is why they'd made a little holiday of their visit to LA this time.*

GEORGE: In LA there'd been a lot of people and a lot of things to dodge – stars' sons wanting to hang out with us, journalists wanting to know what we were on, parties to attend, the whole showbiz thing. But we had friends there, too; people like David Crosby and Jim McGuinn, whom we liked to spend time with. So there were pros and cons to that lifestyle; but mainly cons.

PAUL: Looking for birds: I think that's what I was doing judging all those beauty contests. Think... I *know* that's what I was doing!

1963–65 was ridiculous. It was: make a movie, tour Europe, tour England twice, make four singles, three EPs and a couple of albums, tour America, tour the Far East... it was unbelievable. We were going all the time. And as Paul points out, on his one day off he would be judging a beauty competition or something.

We'd been everywhere, Australia and Tokyo and America and Europe, and yet the biggest tour we ever did at the top was only six weeks long, including travel time. It was always hit and run. We nipped about very quickly and then we were back home. Only then were we able to have personal lives, and we liked that, and wanted more of that.

The studio was where it was all going on. And we were still very close. We'd all ride to London together – this was the period when I got a Ferrari – and we'd go to the studio, be at the studio together, go out to dinner, go to the clubs and drive home, all together. We'd work all day and then go home and change and then all meet each other back at the club at about 10.30. From around 1964 I had given up whisky and Coke and started drinking red wine, and out had come the 'jazz Woodbines'. But still we were going to the clubs.

RINGO: A lot was changing – our attitudes, our lives – at this time, and the *Rubber Soul* sessions were the start of the build-up to the end, in a way. We *were* doing great stuff and it was really a joy in the studio and the results were great; but the time was getting longer and longer, taking up a lot of space, and as it built up, over five or six years, I was getting fed up with the studios, too.

I'd just got married in 1965 and was driving up to Abbey Road every day. I think that's where I started the resentment for the studio. We would go in there and it would be a beautiful day, and we'd come out and days had gone by.

# 1966

nineteen sixty-six

JOHN: The Sixties saw a revolution among youth – not just concentrating in small pockets or classes, but a revolution in a whole way of thinking. The youth got it first and the next generation second. The Beatles were part of the revolution, which is really an evolution, and is continuing.[69]

We were all on this ship in the Sixties. Our generation – a ship going to discover the New World. And The Beatles were in the crow's-nest of that ship. We were part of it and contributed what we contributed; I can't designate what we did and didn't do. It depends on how each individual was impressed by The Beatles, or how shock waves went to different people. We were going through the changes, and all we were saying was, 'It's raining up here!' or, 'There's land!' or, 'There's sun!' or, 'We can see a seagull!' We were just reporting what was happening to us.[75]

GEORGE: The Sixties was a good period, and in Europe at least it had a lot to do with the fact that we were the generation that hadn't been in the war. We'd been born during the Second World War, and as we grew up we became sick of hearing about it. To this day the newspapers and television love the war and wars in general – they can't get enough of them. They keep putting programmes on about them. There's about fifty-four wars happening right now, and even if there's a lull in one of the fifty-four wars they'll show us the re-runs of the Second World War or Pearl Harbor.

We were the generation who didn't suffer from the war and we didn't want to have to keep being told about Hitler. We were more bright-eyed and hopeful for the future, breaking out of the leftover Victorian mould of attitudes and poverty and hardship. We were the first generation to experience that, so in that respect it was good. And then we had Little Richard and Elvis and Fats Domino and all that music – because up until then it had all been pretty silly music from the Fifties. I was a bit disappointed the way the Seventies seemed to hit a brick wall and turn into headbanging and spitting on each other.

And then we bumped right into Vietnam around that time when we were starting to have had enough experience as The Beatles to have grown up a bit and realised that there's more to life than being noddy-head Beatles.

PAUL: There was a big period of freedom, which I always liken to God opening up the waves for Moses and then closing them again. AIDS has closed down the sexual freedom we had then, just as VD had shut it off for an earlier generation. I remember my dad saying he was quite envious of me because there was no longer any need to fear VD. It had been a major threat when he was a kid. We didn't have to worry about it – you just went down the clinic and got a jab. And all the girls were on the Pill, which removed another traditional worry, so we had an amazing sexual freedom.

JOHN: People are just uptight because the kids are having fun. They didn't have the same freedom because they didn't take it; they just followed the lives laid down by their parents. And they're jealous of the people that didn't do that. It's a simple sexual jealousy.

I don't know what age it was, the Twenties or the Thirties, [when] most of the pop music was about the sort of illusory romantic love that was basically nonexistent. The songs were always about love and a boy/girl relationship, but they just happened to miss out the most important thing, which was sex. I think now the kids sing and want to hear about reality, whether that's love or sex, or whatever it is.

I think the music reflects the state that the society is in. It doesn't *suggest* the state. I think the poets and musicians and artists are of the age – not only do they lead the age on, but they also reflect that age. And I think that's what the pop music is doing: it's reflecting.

Like The Beatles. We came out of Liverpool and we reflected our background and we reflected our thoughts in what we sang, and that's all people are doing.[71]

PAUL: I suppose the fashion thing was a kind of eruption. We were erupting anyway, as The Beatles; and it's very difficult to separate The Beatles' eruption from the fashion or the cultural or the mind eruption. It was all happening at once, as a whirlpool. If we got invited to places, generally it was because we were The Beatles; it wouldn't be because of the clothes, which were secondary.

Pot and LSD were the two other major influences. Instead of getting totally out of it and falling over, as we would have done on Scotch, we'd end up talking very seriously and having a good time till three in the morning. Now it's reverted and in many ways it's as though that period didn't happen. It's come full circle: the waters have closed over again and we've got militaristic things in the air instead of people putting flowers down the barrels of guns. When will they ever learn?

RINGO: I feel The Beatles were doing what they wanted to do, and a lot of it was that youthfulness of trying to change ideas. I think it allowed people to do things they wouldn't have done if we hadn't been out there. Because so many people have always said, 'Oh, it's OK for *you* to dress like that or to do that,' but it's OK for anyone, really.

The Sixties were it for me, but the Forties were best for my dad. For him, no one topped Glenn Miller, including The Beatles. If I play records I don't really play a lot after 1970. I go for blues, some jazz, people who were around in the Sixties. It's Bob from then, Eric from then – some Elton, not a lot. I don't play a lot of Beaky, Beaky, Nosey, Ducky, Dicky and Tich, all that stuff. I'd got it all nailed by 1970.

NEIL ASPINALL: *Easing up on their breakneck schedule in early 1966, when they took a couple of months off, meant we all had more time. For them it meant time to hang around with friends, get into other things, have personal lives, even time to go on holiday.*

JOHN: We were all at the prime, and we used to go around London in our cars and meet each other and talk about music with The Animals and Eric [Burdon] and all those. It was a really good time. That was the best period, fame-wise. We didn't get mobbed so much. It was like a men's smoking club, a very good scene.[70]

PAUL: FOR A TIME IT WAS GREAT: WE WERE INTRODUCED TO A WHOLE SET OF PEOPLE WE COULDN'T HAVE EXPECTED TO MEET IN OTHER TIMES OR CIRCUMSTANCES. IT WAS A GOOD SET, TOO; A VERY COSMOPOLITAN GROUP – GAY WOULD MIX WITH HETERO WITHOUT EVEN THINKING ABOUT IT, CERTAINLY AMERICAN WOULD MIX WITH BRITISH. ALL NATIONALITIES WOULD MIX.

JOHN: The main club we all went to was the Ad Lib. The Bag O'Nails was another. There were a couple more but they were never as big. We used to go there and dance and talk music, get drunk, stoned and high. One of the records we always played in the Ad Lib, with all of us sitting there, and dancing, looking superstoned, was 'Daddy Rolling Stone' by Derek Martin, which The Who later did a version of, like the English usually do all these great records: not too good – that's including us. That's all we ever played: American records. There was no such thing as English records in those days.[74]

PAUL: We're very friendly with all the other groups. When we go to the Ad Lib and The Rolling Stones are there, or The Animals or The Moody Blues, it's good to have a chance to sit down and talk about music and our latest record or their new record.[65]

JOHN: The thing about clubs like the Ad Lib is that we go there and we meet other people – we meet The Rolling Stones and The Animals and any visiting American artists – and we're not bothered there. I think I've signed one autograph at the Ad Lib and we've been going there a year. No one bothers us, and you can get drunk or you can fall on your face if you like and nobody's going to bother. You know that you're OK and you relax there, even though it's rowdy and heavy.[65]

PAUL: After recording sessions, at two or three in the morning, we'd be careering through the villages on the way to Weybridge, shouting 'wey-hey' and driving much too fast. George would perhaps be in his Ferrari – he was quite a fast driver – and John and I would be following in his big Rolls Royce or the Princess. John had a mike in the Rolls with a loudspeaker outside and he'd be shouting to George in front: 'It is foolish to resist, it is foolish to resist! Pull over!' It was insane. All the lights would go on in the houses as we went past – it must have freaked everybody out.

When John went to make *How I Won The War* in Spain, he took the same car, which he virtually lived in. It had blacked-out windows and you could never see who was in it, so it was perfect. John didn't come out of it – he just used to talk to the people outside through the microphone: 'Get away from the car! Get away!'

Once we were going through Regent's Park on our way to North London to do a session. We were in John's Rolls and we'd just come from his house in Weybridge. Suddenly we pulled up behind Brian Jones, who was sitting quietly in the back of his Austin Princess. John was a very funny guy, and he shouted through the microphone: 'Brian Jones, do not move! You have been under surveillance – you are under arrest!' Brian leapt up about eight feet and went as white as a sheet, going, 'Oh my God! Oh my God!' Then he saw it was us – 'You bunch of bastards!' It nearly killed him that day, John was so official-sounding.

JOHN: When I first got the original black Rolls, I couldn't drive; I hadn't passed my test. I'd never bothered because I wasn't very interested in driving, but when the others passed I thought I'd better do it or I'd get left. So I got the first Rolls and it used to be embarrassing, sitting in a Rolls. People think they've got black windows to hide. It's partly that, but it's also for when you're coming home late. If it's daylight when you're coming in, it's still dark inside the car – you just shut all the windows and you're still in the club.[65]

GEORGE: I had a couple of Ferraris and later John suddenly decided that he wanted a Ferrari, too. We used to race together but I always regarded myself as slightly better because, first of all, John was as blind as a bat and, secondly, he was never really very good at driving. But he wanted to drive his Ferrari and I would always be fearing some huge crash. We'd come down Piccadilly at about ninety miles an hour and go under the underpass on Hyde Park Corner like bats out of hell and he'd be right behind me, trying to keep up, with his contact lenses in, or whatever. And all the way home, back down the A3; I remember that a few times. Sometimes I'd slow down, because I was afraid that he was going to have an enormous 'sausage'.

Once John was driving his Ferrari with Terry Doran in the passenger seat. Terry was a car dealer from Liverpool (a 'man from the motor trade'), and an old friend of Brian Epstein; he was with us all the time around that period. He and John were coming down the M1, doing about ninety, when a bird flew across their path and splattered itself on the windscreen. John instinctively ducked and threw up his hands – 'Whoa!' – and Terry was forced to grab hold of the steering wheel and steer the car out of a crash.

Brian Epstein had a big posh car. Early on it was great because Paul and I had learnt how to drive and we always wanted to drive his car. That's one of the reasons we signed up with him – because he had a good car. Brian was the worst driver. He knocked down the little 'Keep Left' bollard going into Liverpool Airport. He also had a problem with traffic lights. When they were green he'd stop, and when they went to red he'd go. He had a Maserati, which in the early Sixties was a pretty potent car, and as he went down Piccadilly in it one day the light went to red and he went across the junction. A cop was standing at the side and he shouted, 'Hey!' but Brian drove off down to the next green light and stopped. The cop came running almost up to him, but as the light changed to red he pulled away again. The cop ran all the way down Piccadilly, trying to get him, but Brian didn't even know the cop was after him. He was totally on his own agenda.

PAUL: We'd be hanging out with the Stones, working on their sessions; it was a very friendly scene. There must have been a bit of competition because that's only natural, but it was always friendly. We used to say, 'Have you got one coming out?' and if they had we'd say, 'Well, hold it for a couple of weeks, because we've got one.' It made sense, really, to avoid each other's releases. John and I sang on the Stones' song 'We Love You' – Mick had been stuck for an idea and he asked us to come along. So we went down to Olympic Studios and made it up.

We and the Stones were part of the same crowd. We used to go to a flat in Earl's Court, the late-night hangout. Actually there were a few of these – there was Robert Fraser's place, my place, Mick and Keith's place or maybe Brian's. I remember Mick bringing in 'Ruby Tuesday' as a demo; they'd just done it and it was great. We'd get everything hot off the press. They said, 'What do you think of this one?' and we said, 'Yeah, great, "Ruby Tuesday" – lovely.'

When we asked Brian Jones to one of our sessions, to our surprise he brought along a sax. He turned up in a big Afghan coat at Abbey Road. He played sax on a crazy record, 'You Know My Name (Look Up The Number)'. It's a funny sax solo – it isn't amazingly well played but it happened to be exactly what we wanted: a ropey, shaky sax. Brian was very good like that.

GEORGE: I always used to see Brian in the clubs and hang out with him. In the mid-Sixties he used to come out to my house – particularly when he'd got 'the fear', when he'd mixed too many weird things together. I'd hear his voice shouting to me from out in the garden: 'George, George…' I'd let him in – he was a good mate. He would always come round to my house in the sitar period. We talked about 'Paint It Black' and he picked up my sitar and tried to play it – and the next thing was he did that track.

We had a lot in common, when I think about it. We shared the same date of birth, or nearly, so he must have been a Pisces as well. We also shared the same positions in the most prominent bands in the universe: him with Mick and Keith, and me with Paul and John. I think he related to me a lot, and I liked him. Some people didn't have time for him, but I thought he was one of the most interesting ones.

JOHN: He was different over the years as he disintegrated. He ended up the kind of guy that you dread he'd come on the phone because you knew it was trouble. He was in a lot of pain. But in the early days he was all right because he was young and confident. He was one of those guys that disintegrates in front of you. He was all right. Not brilliant or anything, just a nice guy.[70]

PAUL: Brian was a nervous guy, very shy, quite serious and maybe into drugs a little more than he should have been, because he used to shake a bit. He was lovely, though. We knew he was on heroin. I knew about heroin but I couldn't have been very clear about it because I remember asking Robert Fraser about it. I think it was he who said to me, 'Heroin's no problem as long as you can afford it. There are millions of addicts, man,' and for a second I almost thought that might just be true. But thank goodness something said to me, 'No, that doesn't sound right,' so I didn't get into it. I was lucky.

I was round at John Dunbar's house when one of their friends came round and got out the rubber, tied his arm up, got out the needle and did the whole thing. I was so scared, but I just had to look. I couldn't tell him not to do it because it was his life, but it was frightening to witness. I was told that the guy died the next week, so I could see what they were getting into.

GEORGE: I GOT MARRIED TO PATTIE ON 21ST JANUARY 1966. PAUL WAS THE BEST MAN. WE GOT MARRIED IN EPSOM, AND THEN WENT TO BARBADOS FOR OUR HONEYMOON.

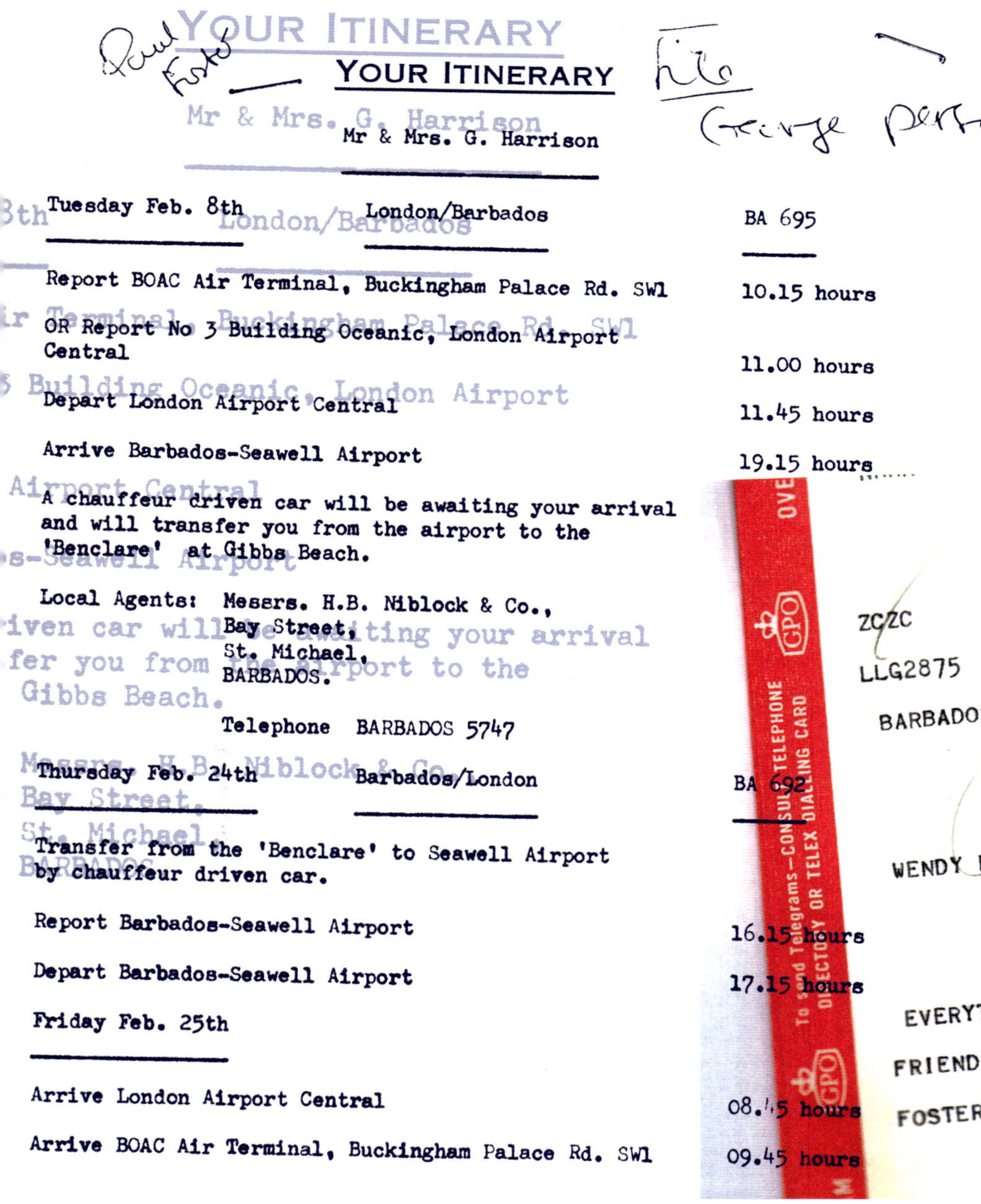

YOUR ITINERARY

George personal

Mr & Mrs. G. Harrison

| | | | |
|---|---|---|---|
| Tuesday Feb. 8th | London/Barbados | | BA 695 |
| Report BOAC Air Terminal, Buckingham Palace Rd. SW1 | | | 10.15 hours |
| OR Report No 3 Building Oceanic, London Airport Central | | | 11.00 hours |
| Depart London Airport Central | | | 11.45 hours |
| Arrive Barbados-Seawell Airport | | | 19.15 hours |

A chauffeur driven car will be awaiting your arrival and will transfer you from the airport to the 'Benclare' at Gibbs Beach.

Local Agents: Messrs. H.B. Niblock & Co., Bay Street, St. Michael, BARBADOS.
Telephone BARBADOS 5747

| | | | |
|---|---|---|---|
| Thursday Feb. 24th | Barbados/London | | BA 692 |
| Transfer from the 'Benclare' to Seawell Airport by chauffeur driven car. | | | |
| Report Barbados-Seawell Airport | | | 16.15 hours |
| Depart Barbados-Seawell Airport | | | 17.15 hours |
| Friday Feb. 25th | | | |
| Arrive London Airport Central | | | 08.45 hours |
| Arrive BOAC Air Terminal, Buckingham Palace Rd. SW1 | | | 09.45 hours |

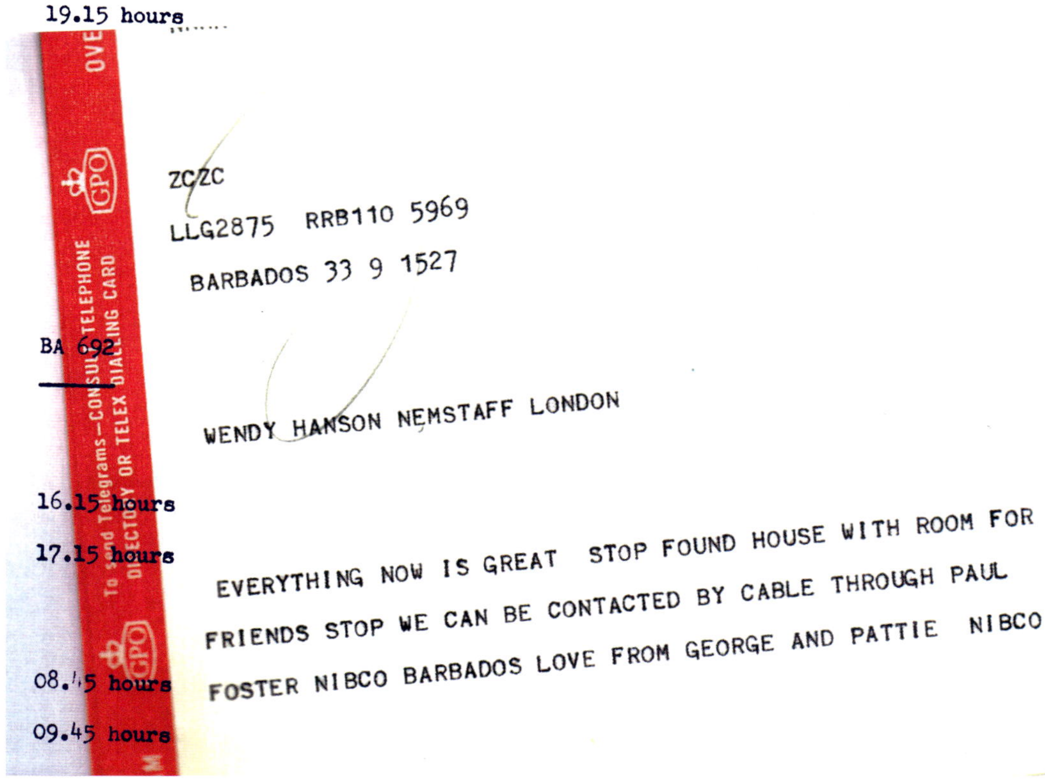



ZCZC
LLG2875 RRB110 5969
BARBADOS 33 9 1527

WENDY HANSON NEMSTAFF LONDON

EVERYTHING NOW IS GREAT STOP FOUND HOUSE WITH ROOM FOR FRIENDS STOP WE CAN BE CONTACTED BY CABLE THROUGH PAUL FOSTER NIBCO BARBADOS LOVE FROM GEORGE AND PATTIE NIBCO

JOHN: MY ORIGINAL IDEA FOR THE COVER WAS BETTER – DECAPITATE PAUL– BUT HE WOULDN'T GO ALONG WITH IT.

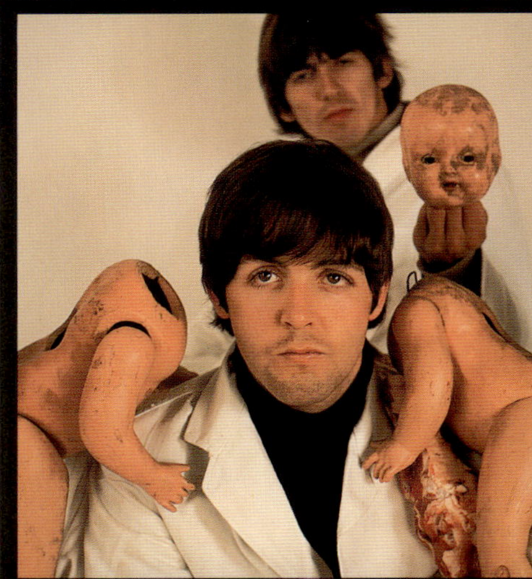

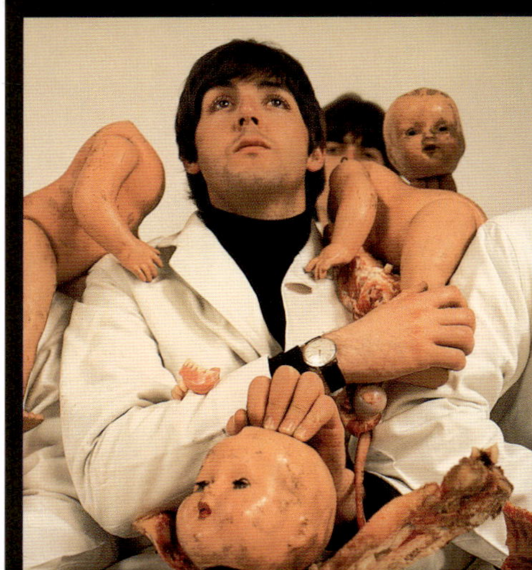

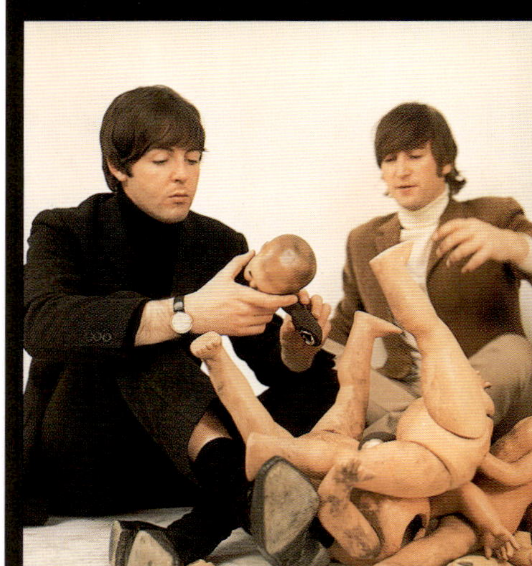

GEORGE: The 1966 American album, *Yesterday and Today*, was the one with the controversial sleeve. I think Brian Epstein had met a photographer in Australia called Robert Whitaker, who came to London where Brian introduced him to us. He was avant-garde and took a lot of photographs. He set up a photo session which I never liked personally at the time.

I thought it was gross, and I also thought it was stupid. Sometimes we all did stupid things, thinking it was cool or hip when it was naïve and dumb; and that was one of them. But again, it was a case of being put in a situation where one is obliged, as part of a unit, to co-operate.

So we put on those butchers' uniforms for that picture. In the photograph we're going, 'Ugh!' That's what I'm doing, isn't it? I'm disgusted, and especially so by the baby dolls with their heads off. What the bloody hell is that all about?

Quite rightly somebody took a look at it and said, 'Do you think you *really* need this as an album cover?' So the record company said: 'You don't want to do a cover like that. We want to have a nice one with you all sitting in a little box.'

NEIL ASPINALL: *The 'butcher' sleeve was Bob Whitaker's idea. He was trying to get across some sort of earthy idea. It was on the American album – Capitol Records issued different versions from the English ones then – and the retailers were horrified. I'm not sure how many copies they pressed, but the reaction to it was: 'What is this?'*

*Capitol pasted a new cover over the original sleeves they had already pressed, and then the next pressings had only the new image. But people who bought one of the first batch steamed off the new cover to reveal the 'butcher' picture. There are not that many of them out there.*

PAUL: In those days you'd turn up at a session and the photographer would normally have an idea. In the very early days Dezo Hoffmann asked us to put glasses on. I said, 'I don't wear glasses, Dezo.' He said, 'Yeah, but I'll be able to sell these to eyeglass magazines all over the world.' We were getting all these little clues of how it was done. So we were used to photographers giving us bizarre ideas; sometimes we'd ask why we should do it, and they'd say, 'It'll be OK,' and we'd agree.

We'd done a few sessions with Bob before this, and he knew our personalities: he knew we liked black humour and sick jokes. It was very prevalent at that time. And he said, 'I've had an idea – stick these white lab coats on.' It didn't seem too offensive to us. It was just dolls and a lot of meat. I don't know really what he was trying to say, but it seemed a little more original than the things the rest of the people were getting us to do – eyeglasses!

He had a little history of doing that kind of shoot. I remember we came in once and he had some polystyrene that he wanted us to break, and he took action photos of us doing it. I suppose when the photos came out, it looked as if we were wrecking everything, but it was only because we were asked to do it as an idea for a photo session; and that's what the 'butcher' cover was. So we liked it – we thought it was stunning and shocking, but we didn't see all the connotations.

It was Capitol Records that didn't want it, but you have to remember the climate then. I remember Sir Edward Lewis, head of Decca, not wanting the Stones' album cover because it had graffiti on a toilet seat on it. Mick came round to talk to us about it, and I actually rang up Sir Edward and said that I thought they should put it out, but he wasn't having any of it. We weren't against a little shock now and then; it was part of our make-up.

RINGO: I don't know how it came about. I don't know how we ended up sitting in butchers' coats with meat all over us. If you look at our eyes, you realise none of us really knew what we were doing. It was just one of those things that happened as life went on.

The sleeve was great for us because we were quite a nice bunch of boys and we thought, 'Let's do something like this!' What was crazy about that sleeve was that, because it was banned, they glued paper over it and everyone started steaming it off. They made it into a really heavy collector's item – which, I'm afraid to say, I don't have a copy of, because in those days we never thought, 'We'd better save this.'

JOHN: We took the pictures in London at one of those photo sessions. By then we were really beginning to hate it – a photo session was a big ordeal, and you had to try and look normal and you didn't feel it. The photographer was a bit of a surrealist and he brought along all these babies and pieces of meat and doctors' coats, so we really got into it, and that's how we felt – 'Yeah!'

I don't like being locked in to one game all the time, and there we were supposed to be sort of angels. I wanted to show that we were aware of life, and I really was pushing for that album cover. I would say I was a lot of the force behind it going out and trying to keep it out.

I especially pushed for it to be an album cover, just to break the image. And it got out in America: they printed it and about 60,000 got out, and then there was some kind of fuss, as usual, and they were all sent back in or withdrawn, and they stuck that awful-looking picture of us looking just as deadbeat but supposed to be a happy-go-lucky foursome. We tried to do something different. We would design a cover or have control of more of our own covers in England, but America always had more albums so they always needed another picture, another cover. We used to say, 'Why can't we put fourteen [tracks] out in America?' Because we would sequence the albums – how we thought they should sound – and we put a lot of work into the sequencing too. They wouldn't let us put fourteen out; they said there was some rule or something. And so we almost didn't care what happened to the albums in America until we started coming over more, and noticing [for instance that] on the eight tracks they'd have out-takes and mumbling on the beginning – which is interesting now, but it used to drive us crackers. We'd make an album and they'd keep two from every album.[74]

Capitol RECORDS

EXECUTIVE AND GENERAL OFFICES
CAPITOL RECORDS DISTRIBUTING CORP.
HOLLYWOOD AND VINE • HOLLYWOOD, CALIFORNIA 90028

June 14, 1966

Dear Reviewer:

In the past few days, you may have received an advance promotional copy of The Beatles' new album, "The Beatles Yesterday And Today." In accordance with the following statement from Alan W. Livingston, President, Capitol Records, Inc., the original album cover is being discarded and a new jacket is being prepared:

"The original cover, created in England, was intended as 'pop art' satire. However, a sampling of public opinion in the United States indicates that the cover design is subject to misinterpretation. For this reason, and to avoid any possible controversy or undeserved harm to The Beatles' image or reputation, Capitol has chosen to withdraw the LP and substitute a more generally acceptable design."

All consumer copies of The Beatles' album will be packaged in the new cover, which will be available within the next week to 10 days. As soon as they are, we will forward you a copy. In the meantime, we would appreciate your disregarding the promotional album and, if at all possible, returning it, C.O.D., to Capitol Records, 1750 N. Vine Street, Hollywood, Calif. 90028.

Thank you in advance for your cooperation.

Sincerely,

Ron Tepper
Ron Tepper
Manager
Press & Information Services

RT:s

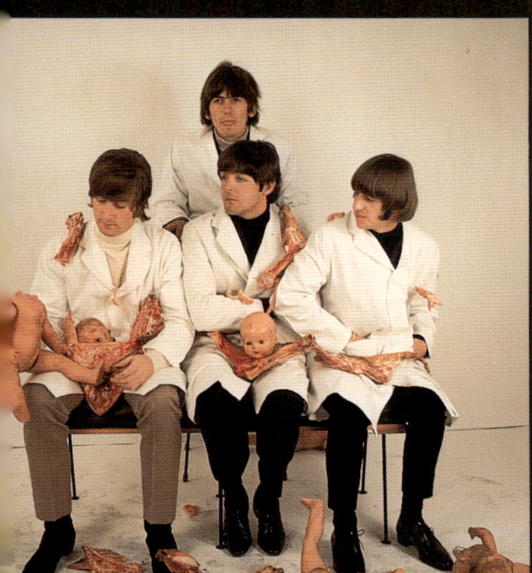

I'll send you a copy of the new L.P. as soon as its out ('spose you heard the whole Pop world awaits in vigil,) and Matt and Frankie will be well pleased. Called 'Revolver' for some unknown reason, has fourteen new songs specially written by the boys themselves some up tempo rock a' shuffle protest folk and more ballads in the 'Do You want a' no a neggro' vein. Altogether I'd say its quite good but not as good as their last one – "Boss Sounds Man". Still give it a spin and see what you say!

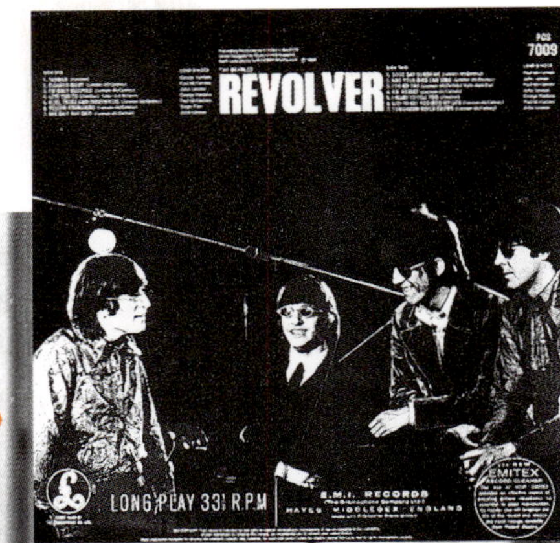

JOHN: One thing's for sure – the next LP is going to be very different. We wanted to have it so that there was no space between the tracks – just continuous. But they wouldn't wear it.

Paul and I are very keen on this electronic music. You make it clinking a couple of glasses together, or with bleeps from the radio, then you loop the tape to repeat the noises at intervals. Some people build up whole symphonies from it. It would have been better than the background music we had for the last film. All those silly bands. Never again![66]

GEORGE MARTIN: *Their ideas were beginning to become much more potent in the studio. They started telling me what they wanted, and pressing me for more ideas and for more ways of translating those ideas into reality.*

*With* Revolver *you can hear that the boys were listening to lots of American records and saying, 'Can we get this effect?' and so on. So they would want us to do radical things, but this time they'd shove in high EQ on mixing, and for the brass they'd want to have a really 'toppy' sound and cut out all the bass. The engineers would sometimes wonder whether there should be that much EQ.*

*We would go through the complete range of EQ on a disc, and if that wasn't enough we'd put it through another range of EQ again, multiplied, and we'd get the most weird sound, which The Beatles liked and which obviously worked.*

GEORGE: EQ is equalisation – when you want to add a bit of top, or roll off a bit of bottom. It's bass, treble and middle, but equalisation is the posh way of saying it.

I have a very high EQ – something like 3,000 hertz. If I think too hard my brain hertz.

PAUL: Originally, George Martin was the Supreme Producer In The Sky and we wouldn't even dare ask to go into the control room. But, as things loosened up, we got invited in and George gave us a bit of the control of the tools; he let us have a go.

GEORGE: George Martin had a strong role in our lives in the studio, but as we got more confidence he and the others in EMI became more relaxed with us. I suppose as time went on they believed more in our ability because it was obvious that we'd had success. They eased off on the schoolteacher approach.

Also, George Martin had become more our friend as well; we socialised with him. We gained more control each time that we got a Number One, and then when we'd go back in the studio we'd claw our way up until we took over the store.

JOHN: We got knowledge of the studio. [At first, I'd] go in there and think, 'It's just like a tape recorder. I'm going to sing and play to you, and you're the one that knows about the tape-recorder – just put it on and I'll sing.' But as soon as you tell me, 'Well, if we do that we can get a little reverb on it,' or if I stand over there it'll sound different than if I stand here, you start learning all that.[73]

I used to play the first four albums one after the other to see the progression musically, and it was interesting. I got up to about *Revolver* and it got too many. It would be too much listening time, but you could hear the progression as we learnt about recording and the techniques got refined.[72]

GEORGE: It was in April 1966 that we started recording *Revolver.* 'Taxman' was on *Revolver*. I had discovered I was paying a huge amount of money to the taxman. You are so happy that you've finally started earning money – and then you find out about tax.

In those days we paid nineteen shillings and sixpence out of every pound (there were twenty shillings in the pound), and with supertax and surtax and tax-tax it was ridiculous – a heavy penalty to pay for making money. That was the big turn-off for Britain. Anybody who ever made any money moved to America or somewhere else.

We got twenty-five quid a week in the early Sixties when we were first with Brian Epstein, when we played the clubs. But twenty-five quid a week each was quite good. My dad earned ten pounds a week, so I was earning two and a half times more than my father. Then we started earning much more, but Brian would keep it and pay us wages. He once tried to get us to sign a deal saying he would guarantee us fifty pounds a week forever and he would keep the rest. We thought, 'No, we'll risk it, Brian. We'll risk earning a bit more than fifty pounds a week.'

PAUL: 'Taxman' was very George. In business meetings, the solicitors and accountants would be explaining to us how things worked. We were very naive, as you can see by any of our business deals, and George would say, 'Well, I don't want to pay tax,' and they'd say, 'You've got to, like everyone else – and the more you make, the more they take.' And George would reply, 'Well, that's not very fair.'

They said, 'Look, when you're dead you're going to pay taxes.' – 'What?' – 'Death duties.' So he came up with that great line: 'Declare the pennies on your eyes,' which was George's righteous indignation at the whole idea of having got here, made all this money and half of it was about to be removed by force.

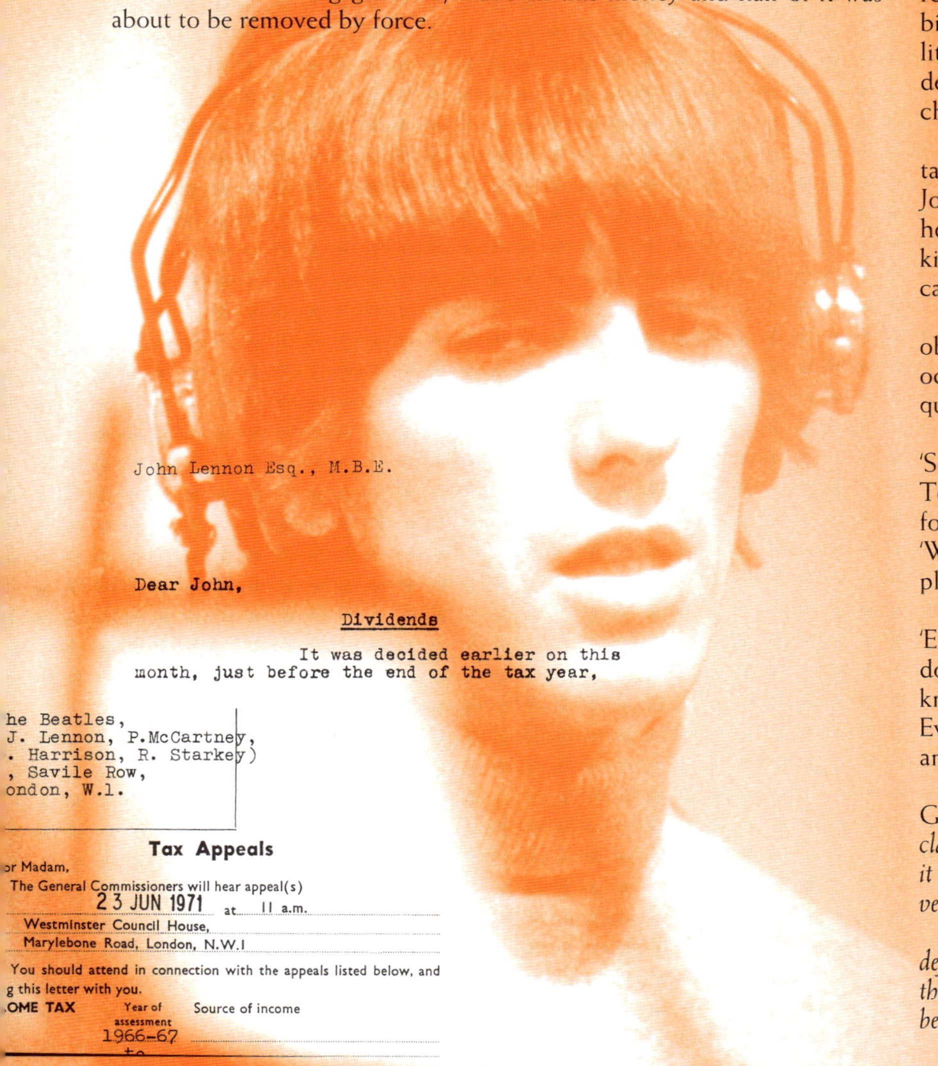


RINGO: WE WERE PISSED OFF WITH THE TAX SITUATION. WE WENT INTO ONE MAD SCHEME WHERE WE PAID A GUY TO GO AND LIVE IN THE BAHAMAS AND HOLD OUR MONEY FOR US SO IT WOULD BE TAX-FREE. AND IN THE END WE HAD TO BRING ALL THE MONEY BACK, PAY THE TAXES ON IT AND PAY THIS GUY. SO WE MIGHT AS WELL HAVE JUST LEFT IT WHERE IT WAS. IT WAS A SCHEME THAT SOMEONE HAD PUT FORWARD WITH BRIAN AND WE WENT FOR IT.

Bryce Hanmer have now confirmed our fears and they have greed with the Inspector of Taxes that there is an excess dividend of 68,204 under Section 83 of the Finance Act 1965. This excess dividend s deemed to have been payable on April 6, 1966 and Schedule F tax f £28,134. 3. 0. in respect of this dividend is due to the Collector of axes.

The Beatles are in the 90% tax bracket. Accordingly, in der for them to personally give the £15,000 gift, they ald have to earn £150,000. It is possible to obtain a cash

JOHN: 'Taxman' was an anti-Establishment tax song, where we said, 'If you walk the street, they'll tax your feet.' George wrote it and I helped him with it. At the time, we weren't aware of the whole tax scene. I'm still not really aware of what goes on with taxes. We believe that if you earn it, you may as well keep it, unless there's a communal or Communist or real Christian society. But while we're living in this, I protest against paying the Government what I have to pay them.[68]

PAUL: I can remember more about writing *Revolver* than about recording it. I was in Switzerland on my first skiing holiday. I'd done a bit of skiing in *Help!* and quite liked it, so I went back and ended up in a little bathroom in a Swiss chalet writing 'For No One'. I remember the descending bass-line trick that it's based on, and I remember the character in the song – the girl putting on her make-up.

Occasionally we'd have an idea for some new kind of instrumentation, particularly for solos. On 'You've Got To Hide Your Love Away' John had wanted a flute. On 'For No One' I was interested in the French horn, because it was an instrument I'd always loved from when I was a kid. It's a beautiful sound, so I went to George Martin and said, 'How can we go about this?' And he said, 'Well, let me get the very finest.'

That was one of the great things about George. He knew how to obtain the best musicians and would suggest getting them. On this occasion he suggested Alan Civil, who, like all these great blokes, looks quite ordinary at the session – but plays like an angel.

George asked me, 'Now, what do you want him to play?' I said, 'Something like this,' and sang the solo to him, and he wrote it down. Towards the end of the session, when we were getting the piece down for Alan to play, George explained to me the range of the instrument: 'Well, it goes from here to this top E,' and I said, 'What if we ask him to play an F?' George saw the joke and joined in the conspiracy.

We came to the session and Alan looked up from his bit of paper: 'Eh, George? I think there's a mistake here – you've got a high F written down.' Then George and I said, 'Yeah,' and smiled back at him, and he knew what we were up to and played it. These great players will do it. Even though it's officially off the end of their instrument, they *can* do it, and they're quite into it occasionally. It's a nice little solo.

GEORGE MARTIN: *On 'For No One', the track was laid down on my own clavichord. I brought it in from my home, because I thought it had a nice sound, it was a very strange instrument to record, and Paul played it. But we wanted a very special sound, and French horn was what he chose.*

*Paul didn't realise how brilliantly Alan Civil was doing. We got the definitive performance, and Paul said, 'Well, OK, I think you can do it better than that, can't you, Alan?' Alan nearly exploded. Of course, he didn't do it better than that, and the way we'd already heard it was the way you hear it now.*

PAUL: I DON'T KNOW WHETHER POETS THINK THEY HAVE TO EXPERIENCE THINGS TO WRITE ABOUT THEM, BUT I CAN TELL YOU OUR SONGS ARE NEARLY ALL IMAGINATION – 90% IMAGINATION. I DON'T THINK BEETHOVEN WAS IN A REALLY WICKED MOOD ALL THE TIME.[66]

PAUL: I was never able to write out music, although I took lots of lessons when I was a kid. First of all I learnt from the old lady who gave me the homework. Then I tried it again when I was sixteen, with a young neighbour. But when he took me back to the five-finger exercises, I became bored because I was already writing little melodies like 'When I'm Sixty-Four'. So I'd got into the fun of it, and having to be pulled back to the discipline of it came too late.

Later, when I'd written 'Eleanor Rigby', I tried learning with a proper bloke from the Guildhall School of Music whom I was put on to by Jane Asher's mum (Margaret Elliot, an oboe teacher). But I didn't get on with him either. I went off him when I showed him 'Eleanor Rigby' because I thought he'd be interested, and he wasn't. I thought he'd be intrigued by the little time jumps.

I wrote 'Eleanor Rigby' when I was living in London and had a piano in the basement. I used to disappear there and have a fiddle around, and while I was fiddling on a chord some words came out: 'Dazzie-de-da-zu picks up the rice in the church where a wedding has been...' This idea of someone picking up rice after a wedding took it in that poignant direction, into a 'lonely people' direction.

I had a bit of trouble with the name, and I'm always keen to get a name that sounds right. Looking at my old school photographs I remembered the names, and they all work: James Stringfellow, Grace Pendleton. Whereas when you read novels, it's all 'James Turnbury' and it's not real. So I was very keen to get a real-sounding name for that tune and the whole idea.

We were working with Eleanor Bron on *Help!* and I liked the name Eleanor; it was the first time I'd ever been involved with that name. I saw 'Rigby' on a shop in Bristol when I was walking round the city one evening. I thought, 'Oh, great name, Rigby.' It's real, and yet a little bit exotic. So it became 'Eleanor Rigby'.

I thought, I swear, that I made up the name Eleanor Rigby like that. I remember quite distinctly having the name Eleanor, looking around for a believable surname and then wandering around the docklands in Bristol and seeing the shop there. But it seems that up in Woolton Cemetery, where I used to hang out a lot with John, there's a gravestone to an Eleanor Rigby. Apparently, a few yards to the right there's someone called McKenzie.

It was either complete coincidence or in my subconscious. I suppose it was more likely in my subconscious, because I will have been amongst those graves knocking around with John and wandering through there. It was the sort of place we used to sunbathe, and we probably had a crafty fag in the graveyard. So subconscious it may be – but this is just bigger than me. I don't know the answer to that one. Coincidence is just a word that says two things coincided. We rely on it as an explanation, but it actually just names it – it goes no further than that. But as to why they happen together, there are probably far deeper reasons than our little brains can grasp.

JOHN: 'Eleanor Rigby' was Paul's baby, and I helped with the education of the child.[80]

PAUL: I remember lying in bed one night, in that moment before you're falling asleep – that little twilight moment when a silly idea comes into your head – and thinking of 'Yellow Submarine': 'We all live in a yellow submarine...'

I quite like children's things; I like children's minds and imagination. So it didn't seem uncool to me to have a pretty surreal idea that was also a children's idea. I thought also, with Ringo being so good with children – a knockabout uncle type – it might not be a bad idea for him to have a children's song, rather than a very serious song. He wasn't that keen on singing.

JOHN: Donovan helped with the lyrics. I helped with the lyrics, too. We virtually made the track come alive in the studio, but based on Paul's inspiration. Paul's idea, Paul's title – so I count it as a Paul song.[80]

GEORGE: 'Yellow Submarine' was written by Paul and John, but even in the early days they were writing large portions on their own. Then one would help the other one finish it off; but that became more apparent later on.

RINGO: I don't actually know where they got the idea for it; I just felt it was a really interesting track for me to do. I'd been doing a lot of covers. At that time I did either covers or something they wrote specifically for me.

It usually happened that we'd be well into an album – and we all knew that I'd be doing a number somewhere, usually about three-quarters of the way through – and either I'd say, 'Have you got a song?' or they'd say, 'We've got this for you,' or, 'We haven't got anything – is there anything you want to do?' So through the years we did the Carl Perkins numbers and the Buck Owens numbers, and then it ended up that mainly John and Paul would write songs for me.

At that time it was hard to bring your own songs in when you had Lennon and McCartney. It used to be a bit of a joke, really – I would bring in the songs I'd written and they'd all be rolling on the floor laughing because I'd rewritten an old standard again. I was great at rewriting Jerry Lee Lewis songs. It was me getting my craft together.

At first George went through the same problems presenting his songs that I went through. But that didn't last long, and then he started coming up with great songs. 'Taxman' was great – it's not a bad opening act for *Revolver*, is it?

GEORGE: I didn't have too many songs. I'd always had a couple of ones I was working on or thinking about, and in the later years I did have a huge backlog. But in the mid-Sixties I didn't have too many.

JOHN: 'She Said She Said' was mine. It's an interesting track. The guitars are great on it. That was written after an acid trip in LA during a break in The Beatles' tour where we were having fun with The Byrds and lots of girls.

'Doctor Robert' was another of mine. Mainly about drugs and pills. It was about myself: I was the one that carried all the pills on tour and always have done. Well, in the early days. Later on the roadies did it, and we just kept them in our pockets loose, in case of trouble.[80]

PAUL: 'Doctor Robert' is like a joke. There's some fellow in New York, and in the States we'd hear people say, 'You can get everything you want off him – any pills you want.' It was a big racket, but a joke too about this fellow who cured everyone of everything with all these pills and tranquillisers, injections for this and that. He just kept New York high. That's what 'Doctor Robert' is all about, just a pill doctor who sees you all right. It was a joke between ourselves, but they go in in-jokes and come out out-jokes, because everyone listens and puts their own thing on it, which is great. I mean, when I was young I never knew what 'gilly gilly otsen feffer catsa nell a bogen' was all about, but I still enjoyed singing it.[67]

JOHN: 'Good Day Sunshine' is Paul's. Maybe I threw a line in or something – I don't know. 'For No One' is Paul's. One of my favourites of his – a nice piece of work. 'And Your Bird Can Sing' was another of my throwaways.

'Got To Get You Into My Life' was Paul's again. I think that was one of his best songs, too, because the lyrics are good – and I didn't write them. When I say that he could write lyrics if he took the effort, here's an example. It actually describes his experience taking acid. I think that's what he's talking about. I couldn't swear to it, but I think it was a result of that.[80]

PAUL: It was a song about pot, actually.

JOHN: 'Here, There and Everywhere' was Paul's song completely, I believe – and one of my favourite songs of The Beatles.[80]

PAUL: One of my special memories is when we were in Obertauern, Austria, filming for *Help!*. John and I shared a room and we were taking off our heavy ski boots after a day's filming, ready to have a shower and get ready for the nice bit, the evening meal and the drinks. We were playing a cassette of our new recordings and my song 'Here, There And Everywhere' was on. And I remember John saying, 'You know, I probably like that better than any of my songs on the tape.' Coming from John, that was high praise indeed.

GEORGE: 'I Want To Tell You' is about the avalanche of thoughts that are so hard to write down or say or transmit.

I wrote 'Love You To' on the sitar, because the sitar sounded so nice and my interest was getting deeper all the time. I wanted to write a tune that was specifically for the sitar. Also it had a tabla part, and that was the first time we used a tabla player.

PAUL: The Indian sounds are definitely mainly George. We started off just hearing Indian music and listening to things, and we liked the drone idea because we'd done a bit of that kind of thing in songs before. But George got very interested in it, and went to a couple of Ravi Shankar concerts, and then he met Ravi and said, 'I was knocked out by him!' – just as a person. He's an incredible fellow. He's one of the greatest. He didn't know that George was serious about it, and so when he found out George was serious *he* was knocked out, too. So the two of them were having a great time! And that's how we brought Indian sounds on. It's nice to start bridging the two kinds of music, because we've just started off in a very simple way, and then this album's got a bit better. It's a little bit more like Indian music. And it helps people to understand it, too – because it's very hard to understand. But once you get into it, it's the greatest.[66]

JOHN: It's amazing, this – so cool. Don't the Indians appear cool to you? This music is thousands of years old; it makes me laugh, the British going over there and telling them what to do. Quite amazing.[66]

GEORGE: To me it is the only really great music now, and it makes Western three-or-four-beat type stuff seem somehow dead. You can get so much more out of it if you are prepared really to concentrate and listen. I hope more people will try to dig it.[66]

PAUL: The final track on *Revolver*, 'Tomorrow Never Knows', was definitely John's. Round about this time people were starting to experiment with drugs, including LSD. John had got hold of Timothy Leary's adaptation of *The Tibetan Book of the Dead*, which is a pretty interesting book. For the first time we got the idea that, as with ancient Egyptian practice, when you die you lie in state for a few days, and then some of your handmaidens come and prepare you for a huge voyage. Rather than the British version, in which you just pop your clogs. With LSD, this theme was all the more interesting.

JOHN: Leary was the one going round saying, take it, take it, take it. And we followed his instructions in his 'how to take a trip' book. I did it just like he said in the book, and then I wrote 'Tomorrow Never Knows', which was almost the first acid song: 'Lay down all thought, surrender to the void,' and all that shit which Leary had pinched from *The Book of the Dead*.

I read George Martin was saying that John was into *The Book of the Dead*. I'd never seen it in my life. I just saw Leary's psychedelic handout – it was very nice in them days.

We'd had acid on *Revolver*. Everybody is under this illusion – even George Martin was saying, '*Pepper* was their acid album.' But we'd had acid, including Paul, by the time *Revolver* was finished.[72]

The expression 'tomorrow never knows' was another of Ringo's. I gave it a throwaway title because I was a bit self-conscious about the lyrics. So I took one of Ringo's malapropisms, which was like 'a hard day's night', to take the edge off the heavy philosophical lyrics.[80]

GEORGE: I've been wondering lately why it was supposed to be from *The Tibetan Book of the Dead*. It was, I think, based more upon the book by Timothy Leary called *The Psychedelic Experience*. The lyrics are the essence of Transcendentalism.

You can hear (and I am sure most Beatles fans have) 'Tomorrow Never Knows' a lot and not know really what it is about. Basically it is saying what meditation is all about. The goal of meditation is to go beyond (that is, transcend) waking, sleeping and dreaming. So the song starts out by saying, 'Turn off your mind, relax and float downstream, it is not dying.'

Then it says, 'Lay down all thoughts, surrender to the void – it is shining. That you may see the meaning of within – it is being.' From birth to death all we ever do is think: we have one thought, we have another thought, another thought, another thought. Even when you are asleep you are having dreams, so there is never a time from birth to death when the mind isn't always active with thoughts. But you can turn off your mind, and go to the part which Maharishi described as: 'Where was your last thought before you thought it?'

The whole point is that *we* are the song. The self is coming from a state of pure awareness, from the state of being. All the rest that comes about in the outward manifestation of the physical world (including all the fluctuations which end up as thoughts and actions) is just clutter. The true nature of each soul is pure consciousness. So the song is really about transcending and about the quality of the transcendent.

I am not too sure if John actually fully understood what he was saying. He knew he was onto something when he saw those words and turned them into a song. But to have experienced what the lyrics in that song are actually about? I don't know if he fully understood it.

Indian music doesn't modulate; it just stays. You pick what key you're in, and it stays in that key. I think 'Tomorrow Never Knows' was the first one that stayed there; the whole song was on one chord. But there is a chord that is superimposed on top that does change: if it was in C, it changes down to B flat. That was like an overdub, but the basic sound all hangs on the one drone.

PAUL: John showed up with a song after we'd had a couple of days off. I remember being in Brian Epstein's house in Chapel Street in Belgravia. We met up and John had a song that was all on the chord of C, which in our minds was a perfectly good idea.

I was wondering how George Martin was going to take it, because it was a radical departure; we'd always had at least three chords, and maybe a change for the middle eight. Suddenly this was John just strumming on C rather earnestly – 'Lay down your mind...' And the words were all very deep and meaningful – certainly not 'Thank You Girl'; a bit of a change from all that.

George Martin took it very well. He said, 'Rather interesting, John. Jolly interesting!' So we got in and recorded it as a fairly straightforward rock'n'roll band thing.

We needed a solo, and I was into tape loops at the time. I had two Brennell machines and I could create tape loops with them. So I brought in a little plastic bag with about twenty tape loops, and we got machines from all the other studios, and with pencils and the aid of glasses got all the loops to run. We might have had twelve recording machines where we normally only needed one to make a record. We were running with these loops all fed through the recording desk.

JOHN: He [Paul] made them at home on his tape, in whatever the key was, and we had six fellows with pencils holding them on, on six machines. Very desirable, the whole effect, I thought.[66]

GEORGE: Everybody went home and made up a spool, a loop: 'OK, class, now I want you all to go home and come back in the morning with your own loop.' We were touching on the Stockhausen kind of 'avant garde a clue' music.

So we made up our little loops and brought them to the studio. They were put through the board, on to a different fader, and mixed. You always get a slightly different mix – a spontaneous thing – and those 'seagulls' are just weird noises.

I don't exactly recall what was on my loop; I think it was a grandfather clock, but at a different speed. You could do it with anything: pick a little piece and then edit it, connect it up to itself and play it at a different speed.

RINGO: I had my own little set-up to record them. As George says, we were 'drinking a lot of tea' in those days, and on all my tapes you can hear, 'Oh, I hope I've switched it on.' I'd get so deranged from strong tea. I'd sit there for hours making those noises.

GEORGE MARTIN: *'Tomorrow Never Knows' was a great innovation. John wanted a very spooky kind of track, a very ethereal sound. When we constructed the original version of the tape, we started off with just the tamboura drone and Ringo's very characteristic drumming.*

RINGO: I was proud of my drumming on 'Tomorrow Never Knows', but I was quite proud of my drumming all the way through really.

GEORGE MARTIN: *Paul at that time was probably more avant garde than the other boys. We always think of John as being the avant-garde one, with Yoko and so on; but at that time Paul was heavily into Stockhausen and John Cage and all the avant-garde artists, while John was living a comfortable suburban life in Weybridge.*

PAUL: I don't want to sound like Jonathan Miller going on, but I'm trying to cram everything in, all the things that I've missed. People are saying things and painting things and writing things and composing things that are great, and I must *know* what people are doing. I vaguely mind people knowing anything I don't know.[66]

JOHN: Weybridge won't do at all. I'm just stopping at it, like a bus stop. Bankers and stockbrokers live there; they can add figures, and Weybridge is what they live in and they think it's the end, they really do. I think of it every day – me in my Hansel and Gretel house. I'll take my time; I'll get my real house when I know what I want.

You see there's something else I'm going to do, something I must do – only I don't know what it is. That's why I go round painting and taping and drawing and writing and that, because it may be one of them. All I know is, this isn't it for me.[66]

GEORGE MARTIN: *It was Paul, actually, who experimented with his tape machine at home, taking the erase-head off and putting on loops, saturating the tape with weird sounds. He explained to the other boys how he had done this, and Ringo and George would do the same and bring me different loops of sounds, and I would listen to them at various speeds, backwards and forwards, and select some.*

*That was a weird track, because once we'd made it we could never reproduce it. All over the EMI studios were tape machines with loops on them, and people holding the loops at the right distance with a bit of pencil. The machines were going all the time, the loops being fed to different faders on our control panel, on which we could bring up the sound at any time, as on an organ. So the mix we did then was a random thing that could never be done again. Nobody else was doing records like that at that time – not as far as I knew.*

*John never liked his voice. I don't know why, because he had the greatest of voices. I guess it's the same problem you have when you wake up in the morning and look in the mirror and think, 'What an awful face!' It's a self-destructive thing. He was always wanting to distort his vocal, asking me to do things to it: double-track it, or artificially double-track it, or whatever: 'Don't give me that thing again, George, give me another one.' He was always wanting something different.*

*For 'Tomorrow Never Knows' he said to me he wanted his voice to sound like the Dalai Lama chanting from a hilltop, and I said, 'It's a bit expensive, going to Tibet. Can we make do with it here?' I knew perfectly well that ordinary echo or reverb wouldn't work, because it would just put a very distant voice on. We needed to have something a bit weird and metallic. When I thought of the Dalai Lama, I thought of alpenhorns and those people with funny things on their heads; I'd never been to Tibet, but I imagined what the voice would sound like, coming out of one of those horns. I spoke to Geoff Emerick, the engineer, and he had a good idea. He said, 'Let's try putting his voice through a Leslie speaker and back again and re-recording it.' A Leslie speaker is a rotating speaker, a Hammond console, and the speed at which it rotates can be varied according to a knob on the control. By putting his voice through that and then recording it again, you got a kind of intermittent vibrato effect, which is what we hear on 'Tomorrow Never Knows'. I don't think anyone had done that before. It was quite a revolutionary track for* Revolver.

*Geoff Emerick used to do things for The Beatles and be scared that the people above would find out. Engineers then weren't supposed to play about with microphones and things like that. But he used to do really weird things that were slightly illegitimate, with our support and approval.*

JOHN: Often the backing I think of early on never comes off. With 'Tomorrow Never Knows' I'd imagined in my head that in the background you would hear thousands of monks chanting. That was impractical, of course, and we did something different. I should have tried to get near my original idea, the monks singing. I realise now that was what it wanted.[67]

We were always asking George Martin, 'Please give us double tracking without having to track it – save time.' And then one of the engineers who was working with us [Ken Townsend] came in the next day with this machine. We'd got ADT – and that was beautiful.[73]

GEORGE MARTIN: *Artificial Double Tracking is taking an image of the sound and delaying it slightly, or advancing it slightly, so that it forms double. If you think in photographic terms, it's like having two negatives: when you get one negative exactly on top of the other there's just one picture. So if you have one sound image on top of the other exactly, then it becomes only one image. But move it slightly, by a few milliseconds, and around eight or nine milliseconds it gives you a boxy telephone-like quality. Below that, depending on the frequency you are signalling, it will give you a phasing effect, rather like the broadcasts that used to come from Australia – a kind of 'in-and-out' effect. If you take the image even further away, to about twenty-seven milliseconds, you get what we call Artificial Double Tracking – two definite voices.*

JOHN: Phasing is great! 'Double-flanging', we call it.[67]

JOHN: I DON'T MIND WRITING OR READING OR WATCHING OR SPEAKING, BUT SEX IS THE ONLY PHYSICAL THING I CAN BE BOTHERED WITH ANY MORE.[66]

PAUL: People were starting to lose their pure-pop mentality and mingle with artists. We knew a few actors, a few painters; we'd go to galleries because we were living in London now. A kind of cross-fertilisation was starting to happen.

While the others had got married and moved out to suburbia, I had stayed in London and got into the arts scene through friends like Robert Fraser and Barry Miles and papers like the *International Times*. We opened the Indica gallery with John Dunbar, Peter Asher and people like that. I heard about people like John Cage, and that he'd just performed a piece of music called *4'33"* (which is completely silent) during which if someone in the audience coughed he would say, 'See?' Or someone would boo and he'd say, 'See?' It's not silence – it's music.

I was intrigued by all of that. So those things started to be part of my life. I was listening to Stockhausen; one piece was all little plink-plonks and interesting ideas. Perhaps our audience wouldn't mind a bit of change, we thought, and anyway, tough if they do! We only ever followed our own noses – most of the time, anyway. 'Tomorrow Never Knows' was one example of developing an idea.

I always contend that I had quite a big period of this before John really got into it, because he was married to Cynthia at that time. It was only later when he went out with Yoko that he got back into London and visited all the galleries.

GEORGE: For the *Revolver* sleeve we moved away from Robert Freeman, who prepared the original artwork (not used on the album, but pictured here), to Klaus Voormann. Klaus was a good artist and a really good friend of ours. I can't remember how we arrived at Klaus, but he did a good job and it became quite a classic album cover.

*Revolver* was accepted well. I don't see too much difference between *Rubber Soul* and *Revolver*. To me, they could be Volume One and Volume Two.

PAUL: Klaus had been a great friend since Hamburg days – he'd been one of the 'exi's', the existentialists whom we'd got to know then. We knew he drew and he'd been involved in graphic design; I must admit we didn't really know what he did, but he'd been to college. We knew he must be all right and so we said, 'Why don't you come up with something for the album cover?'

He did, and we were all very pleased with it. We liked the way there were little things coming out of people's ears, and how he'd collaged things on a small scale while the drawings were on a big scale. He also knew us well enough to capture us rather beautifully in the drawings. We were flattered.

RINGO: *Revolver* has that quality of *Rubber Soul* because it's the follow-on. We were really starting to find ourselves in the studio. We were finding what we could do, just being the four of us and playing our instruments. The overdubbing got better, even though it was always pretty tricky because of the lack of tracks. The songs got more interesting, so with that the effects got more interesting.

I think the drugs were kicking in a little more heavily on this album. I don't think we were on anything major yet; just the old usual – the grass and the acid. I feel to this day that though we *did* take certain substances, we never did it to a great extent at the session. We were really hard workers. That's another thing about The Beatles – we worked like dogs to get it right.

NEIL ASPINALL: *Quite a bit of marijuana was being smoked. I guess it made recording a bit slower, but it didn't affect the quality of the work.*

*At this time I was in the studio with them when they were making records, and the pattern changed over the years. At the time of* Revolver *it was getting so that sessions would start at about two or three in the afternoon and go on until they finished, whatever the time was.*

*At the beginning of the session, if there was a new song, whoever had written it would play the chords to George Martin on either guitar or piano, or they'd all be around a piano, playing it, learning the chords. If they were halfway through a song, they'd go straight in and do harmonies, or double-tracking, or a guitar solo or whatever. Sometimes, because it was all on four-track, they would have to mix down on to one track to give a bit of space to do the rest of it.*

*The critics thought* Revolver *was a step forward in some ways, breaking new ground. I think they all listened to critics. They'd pretend not to take notice – but they did.*

JOHN: Like anything, people go in trends, and the trend now is to think that it [*Revolver*] was the change. And the trend before was to think *Rubber Soul* was the change, and then the other trend was *Sgt Pepper*. But the whole thing was a gradual change. We were conscious that there was some formula or something – it was moving ahead. That was for sure, that we were on the road – not physically; I mean 'on the road' in the studio – and the weather was clear.[74]

PAUL: In this period 'Paperback Writer' and 'Rain' were also recorded. John and I wrote together. I remember showing up at his house with the idea for 'Paperback Writer'. Because I had a long drive to get there, I would often start thinking away and writing on my way out, and I developed the whole idea in the car. I came in, had my bowl of cornflakes, and said, 'How's about if we write a letter: "Dear Sir or Madam," next line, next paragraph, etc?' I wrote it all out and John said, 'Yeah, that's good.' It just flowed.

JOHN: 'Paperback Writer' is son of 'Day Tripper' – meaning a rock'n'roll song with a guitar lick on a fuzzy, loud guitar – but it is Paul's song.[80]

GEORGE MARTIN: *'Paperback Writer' had a heavier sound than some earlier work – and very good vocal work, too. I think that was just the way it worked out, that the rhythm was the most important part of their make-up by this time.*

RINGO: The drumming on 'Rain' stands out for me because I feel as though that was someone else playing – I was possessed!

PAUL: I don't think 'Rain' was just John's. We sat down and wrote it together. It was John's vocal and John's feel on the song, but what gave it its character was collaboration. I think it's all too easily said: 'It's a John song. It's a Paul song. Paul does ballads – John does rockers. John's the hard one – Paul's the soft one.' That's a fallacy.

There were certain songs that were very much mine and others that were definite collaborations with John, where we'd actually sit down and spend three hours. Then there were ones that were very much John's. I think it roughly splits somewhere down the middle.

On 'Rain', I remember we couldn't get a backing track and we decided to play it fast and slow it down, which is why it's so 'goo goo goo' and ploddy. We had to play it fast and accurately, but I don't think that was John's idea. I don't remember whose it was, but it was very collaborative.

I suppose the way things did go was that each of us would say, 'Mine's "Strawberry Fields", yours is "Penny Lane".' That did start to happen, but before then, on things like 'Rain', it was that we *all* wanted to do it. It wasn't only John who wanted to make that kind of record. It was probably just that we'd all get an excuse to do it on his track.

JOHN: People ask me what music I listen to. I listen to traffic and birds singing and people breathing. And fire engines. I always used to listen to the water pipes at night when the lights were off, and they played tunes.

Half the musical ideas I've had have been accidental. The first time I discovered backwards guitar was when we made 'Rain'. This was a song I wrote about people moaning about the weather all the time. I took the tracks home to see what gimmicks I could add, because the song wasn't quite right.[69]

I got home from the studio stoned out of my mind on marijuana, and, as I usually do, I listened to what I'd recorded that day. Somehow I got it on backwards and I sat there, transfixed, with the earphones on, with a big hash joint. I ran in the next day and said, 'I know what to do with it, I know… Listen to this!' So I made them all play it backwards.[80]

I wanted to do the whole song backwards. We ended up with a bit of the voice at the end backwards and half the guitar backwards.[69]

That one was the gift of God – of Jah, actually, the god of marijuana. Jah gave me that one. The first backwards tape on any record anywhere. Before Hendrix, before The Who, before *any* fucker. Maybe there was that record about 'They're coming to take me away, ha ha'; maybe *that* came out before 'Rain', but it's not the same thing. 'I'm Only Sleeping' has got backwards guitars, too.[80]

GEORGE: Usually if we were working on a song we'd take a little rough mix of it home. In those days you never used cassettes; it was always on

reel-to-reel. John, Paul and I each had little reel-to-reel tape machines at home. They were quite good machines, with three speeds. We were halfway through 'Rain' when we left the studio at night, so John said, 'Can I have a rough mix of that?'

In those days they made a three- or four-inch spool, the copy tape. That means they would play the rough mix onto a little spool, and when they finished they would cut the tape off and hand it to you in a box so the tail was sticking out – it's called 'tails out'. John didn't know that at the time (I don't think I knew it, either), so when he got home he threaded it on his machine as if it were 'heads out', and played it. He heard the song backwards, and heard enough to think, 'Wow, amazing!'

ss Brenda Young,
4 Harrow Road,
embley
ddsx.

May 10, 1966.

ar Miss Young,

ank you so much for returning the harmonica that you found in the dressing
om after the New Musical Express Concert. Actually it did not belong to
an Lennon, but to Mal Evans (the Beatles Road Manager).

I was very happy to have it back and John asked me to thank you for your
ry sweet letter.

It obviously gave him a buzz because he came in raving about it the next morning, and so we experimented. We turned the tape over and put it on backwards, and then played some guitar notes to it. I think he and I both plugged in guitars, just playing little bits, guessing, hoping it fitted in. George Martin turned the master upside down and played it back. We were excited to hear what it sounded like, and it was magic – the backwards guitarist! The way the note sounded, because of the attack and the decay, was brilliant. We got very excited and started doing that on overdub. And then there was a bit of backwards singing as well, which came out sounding like Indian singing.

As time went by, the technology we were now using on records didn't allow us to play a lot of songs live on tour. In those days there was no technology on stage as there is now. There were two guitars, bass and drums, and that was it. If we did stuff in the studio with the aid of recording tricks, then we couldn't reproduce them on tour.

You could do it now. You could do 'Tomorrow Never Knows' – have all the loops up there on the keyboards and emulators. You can have as many piano players and drummers and orchestras and whatever as you want; but back then, that was it.

We were just a little dance-hall band and we never really thought of augmenting ourselves. We thought, 'Well, we can't. We'll do it to the best of our ability until the point where we can't really do it, and then we'll miss it out.' So around this time we were starting to miss out a lot of record tracks on live shows.

'Paperback Writer', for instance, was all double-tracked, and it sounded pretty crummy on stage. So what we did with it (in the American tour at least) was get to the point where it was particularly bad, and then we'd do our 'Elvis legs' and wave to the crowd, and they'd all scream and it would cover that. As Paul has said, the screaming did cover a lot of worrying moments.

RINGO: The idea of making promotional films for 'Paperback Writer' and 'Rain' was that we didn't have to go out. We felt it was a great idea to send the film out there. I don't think we even thought of calling them 'videos'. They were just going to be on TV.

It was really exciting with 'Rain' – with Klaus Voormann, who did that whole set-up. It was a lot of fun. The 'Penny Lane' one on the horses wasn't quite that exciting for me; it was a bit real!

GEORGE: The mania made it pretty difficult to get around, and out of convenience we decided we were not going to go into the TV studios to promote our records so much because it was too much of a hassle. We thought we'd go and make our own little films and put them on TV.

So we started getting a film crew and shooting. There are a number of those films. I think the first proper ones we did were 'Paperback Writer' and 'Rain' in Chiswick House. They were the forerunner of videos.

The idea was that we'd use them in America as well as the UK, because we thought, 'We can't go everywhere. We're stopping touring and we'll send these films out to promote the record.' It was too much trouble to go and fight our way through all the screaming hordes of people to mime the latest single on *Ready, Steady, Go!*. Also, in America, they never saw the footage anyway.

Once we actually went on an Ed Sullivan show with just a clip. I think Ed Sullivan came on and said, 'The Beatles were here, as you know, and they were wonderful boys, but they can't be here now so they've sent us this clip.' It was great, because really we conned the Sullivan show into promoting our new single by sending in the film clip. These days obviously everybody does that – it's part of the promotion for a single – so I suppose in a way we invented MTV.

GEORGE: We went back to Hamburg in June 1966, for the first time since 1962. We played concerts in Munich and Essen first, and then got on a train to Hamburg. It was the train that was used when the royal party toured Germany, and it was very nice; we each had our own little compartment with marble bathtubs, really luxuriously decorated.

Hamburg had a good and bad feeling for me. The good side was that we were coming back to play after all our fame and fortune, and when we'd been there before we'd been playing dirty nightclubs to work our way up. The bad bit was that a lot of ghosts materialised out of the woodwork – people you didn't necessarily want to see again, who had been your best friend one drunken Preludin night back in 1960. It's 1966, you've been through a million changes, and suddenly one of those ghosts jumps out on you.

PAUL: We had an old booking that had to be honoured. It was strange to see all our old friends in Hamburg. It was as if we'd mutated into something different *and yet* we were still just the boys. But *we* knew and *they* knew that we'd got famous in the meantime, and that we shouldn't really be playing that sort of gig.

It was good, though. I remember it being a very crazy evening, very steamy. There was a lot of crying from our German gangster friends, nostalgia for the old days. I'm not sure how good a gig it was from a musical point of view, but it was quite nice to go back one last time.

RINGO: To this day Hamburg doesn't seem to have changed. In 1992 I played there and it feels just the same. Every year or two I've always gone back, and the Reeperbahn still has that feel about it; it's still thrilling for me. It was the most exciting place a twenty-year-old could go – the red-light district of Germany – to play the nightclubs, with all the booze and the pills, the hookers and the atmosphere. It was pretty incredible, and great to be back in 1966.

NEIL ASPINALL: *I wasn't there in 1962, so it was the first time for me. There were all the Germans who'd been in the Reeperbahn and in the clubs, people like Bettina who had worked behind the bar or in the cloakroom. People like that were there, old friends of theirs whom I didn't know.*

GEORGE: John enjoyed going back. It was still hit-and-run, though; *everything* was hit-and-run in those days. The day after the Hamburg concert we had a flight to Tokyo, so we were driven straight out of the concert, out of Hamburg to a *schloss* – a big castle of a hotel – where we stayed the night, and then we were flown to Heathrow and put on the plane to Japan. Unfortunately there was a hurricane hitting Tokyo and our plane got diverted to Alaska.

RINGO: Anchorage, Alaska, was like a cowboy town to us; it was really like a backwater. My only great memory of Alaska is that at the airport they have a huge, magnificent white polar bear in a glass case.

GEORGE: I remember looking out of the window on the flight in, and Alaska was incredible: mountains, lush green pine forests, wonderful lakes and rivers. As we were coming lower and lower, the lakes and the trees were thinning out a bit, but when we landed suddenly there was a huge, bulldozed mess that Man had made in the middle of the lush beauty.

I thought, 'Oh, here we are again.' Mankind keeps giving us real tacky things until eventually the planet's covered in them. The nasty little hotels that they throw up – boxes made out of concrete. It was so obvious there in Alaska. Normally they are absorbed into the city, but in the middle of a million acres of pristine forest they stick out a bit.

For me caring about the planet probably began in a previous life. When I was a kid, I used to walk around on my own and I was very much in touch with nature and the sky and the trees and the plants and the insects.

We were there for about twelve hours. I've never been back, but I'd like to some day. We went on to Tokyo. When we came off the plane, we were put in little 1940s-type cars along with policemen dressed in metal helmets, like Second World War American soldiers' helmets. We were driven in convoy into town and taken to the Tokyo Hilton where we were put in our upstairs suite – and that was it. We were only allowed out of the room when it was time for the concert.

To get our own back on the people who weren't letting us out, we used to get them to bring tradesmen up to our suite. They would bring big boxes and trunks full of golden kimonos, jade, incense-holders and little carved objects, which we would buy: 'We'll show them!' We wanted to go shopping.

The promoter was very generous. He gave movie cameras to Mal and Neil, and he gave us Nikons (and in those days a Nikon was a pretty good toy to have).

Everywhere we were going, there was a demonstration about one thing or another. In America the race riots were going on when Beatlemania had come to town. In Japan there were student riots, plus people were demonstrating because the Budokan (where we were playing) was supposed to be a special spiritual hall reserved for martial arts. So in the Budokan only violence and spirituality were approved of, not pop music.

PAUL: We were locked up in the hotel for a long time, with various merchants coming around and showing us ivory and various gifts. People go to Tokyo to go shopping, but we couldn't get out of the hotel. I once tried and a policeman came running after me. I did actually manage it, but he organised half the Tokyo police force to come with us. I had wanted to go and see the Emperor's palace, but the policeman wasn't too keen on the idea.

NEIL ASPINALL: *John and I sneaked out of the hotel – and Paul and Mal, too. I think the security got Paul and Mal, but John and I made it down to the local market, and it was great. It was such a relief to get out. We were looking around and buying things, but then the police got us and said, 'Naughty boys – come back with us.'*

PAUL: In the hotel room we did a communal painting; we all started a corner of the piece of paper and drew in towards the middle where the paintings met. This was just to pass the time away. I've seen it recently: it's a psychedelic whirl of coloured doodles.

The way the Japanese had organised going to the gig was very efficient. They all had walkie-talkies, at a time when you didn't often see those. They came for us at exactly the time on the schedule.

RINGO: The fun in Tokyo was the timing. The Japanese have a dedication to time. They would like us to leave the room at 7:14, get to the elevator by 7:15 and a half, and the elevator took one minute eight seconds to get us down to the car, and so on. We were expected to be prompt. But when they knocked on the door, we would never come out. We'd totally wreck their timings, and we'd see all these guys going absolutely barmy because we hadn't walked down the corridor at 7:14 and a third!

We knew we were doing that to them. It was the way we had fun on the road, by having our own little side trips going on. We could only leave the hotel room when we played a gig.

PAUL: They had the seating exactly arranged in all the cars. Amazing efficiency, that we'd never seen the like of in Britain. When we went to the gig they had the fans organised with police patrols on each corner, so there weren't any fans haphazardly waving along the streets. They had been gathered up and herded into a place where they were allowed to wave, so we'd go along the street and there'd be a little 'eeeeek!' and then we'd go a few more hundred yards and there'd be another 'eeeeek!'

At the Budokan we were shown the old Samurai warriors' costumes, which we marvelled at dutifully in a touristy kind of way: 'Very good! Very old!'

We were more amazed to see the women leaping up out of the seats for the promoter, because we'd never seen that in the West. The subservience of the women was amazing. They'd say, 'Oh God, I'm sorry – was I in your seat?' I remember us getting back to Britain and saying to our wives and girlfriends, 'I wouldn't want you to do that, but maybe it's a direction worth considering?' Promptly rejected.

We got into our yellow shirts and natty bottle green suits. The thing about suits was that they always made us feel part of a team. When we arrived we were in our civvies, but once we put those on we were The Beatles! – the four-headed monster. It was good for me that we all wore the same, in that I really felt part of a unit.

Peeping from behind the stage to watch the place fill up, we saw police walk in from either side and fill the whole of the front row, upstairs and downstairs. After them, the crowd was allowed to come in. They were very well behaved compared to what we'd seen of Western crowds, but they seemed to enjoy it.

There was a funny local group on stage before us. This was in the days when the Japanese didn't really know how to do rock'n'roll, although they've now got the hang of it pretty well. They sang a song that went, 'Hello Beatles! Welcome Beatles!' – something pretty naff in rock'n'roll terms, but it was very nice of them to do it. Our show went down quite well.

NEIL ASPINALL: *The show was a bit weird! There were the jujitsu people who used the Budokan, so they felt it was their temple. This was the first time they'd had a rock band in there, and they didn't like it. There were threats from them, and so there were a lot of police around. The Japanese were very disciplined. There were 3,000 police for 10,000 fans. The police were all over the place, keeping them under control.*

GEORGE MARTIN: *It was upsetting. I remember when George was in Germany he got a letter saying, 'You won't live beyond the next month.' And when they went to Japan they had such heavy guards that they couldn't move anywhere. The Japanese took those death threats very seriously.*

RINGO: The audience was very subdued. If you look at the footage from the shows you'll see a cop on every row. They'd all get excited in their seats as we were playing, but they couldn't express it.

NEIL ASPINALL: *For the first time in a long while the audience could hear. There was no loud screaming, which came as a surprise: the band suddenly realised they were out of tune and they had to get their act together. The second show was pretty good – they had got it together by then – but the first one, in the afternoon, was a bit of a shock.*

GEORGE: The audience were reserved, but they were up on their feet – or they tried to be, but there were police all around the stadium with cameras with telephoto lenses, and anybody who stood up and looked like they were going to run toward the stage was photographed. The people were very restricted as to what they could do and how they could respond to us. It was a warm reception – but a bit clinical, as Japan is.

Getting back to the hotel was the same procedure in reverse: do the show, back to our room and that was it. It was worked out like a military manoeuvre.

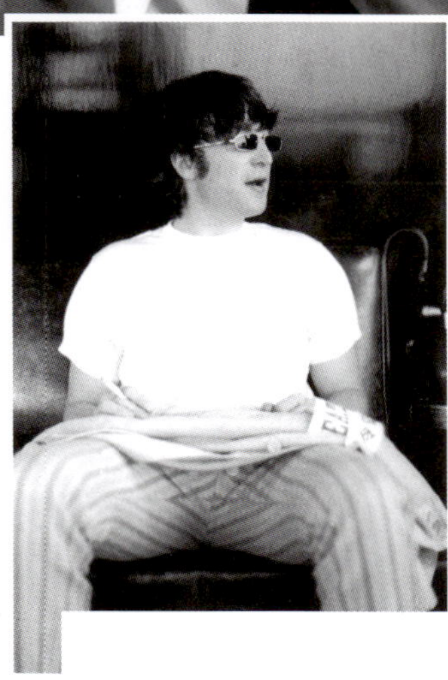

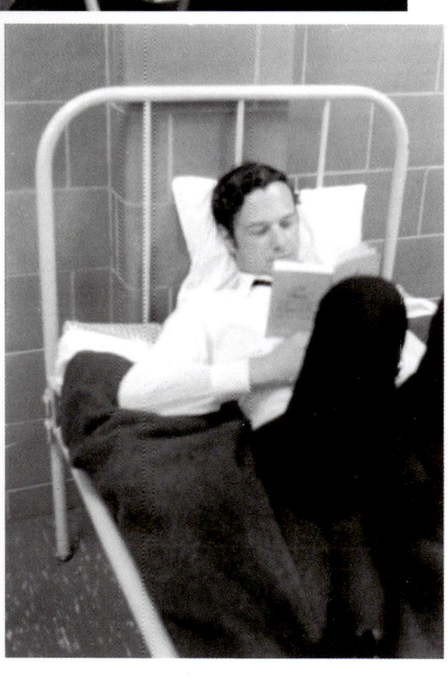

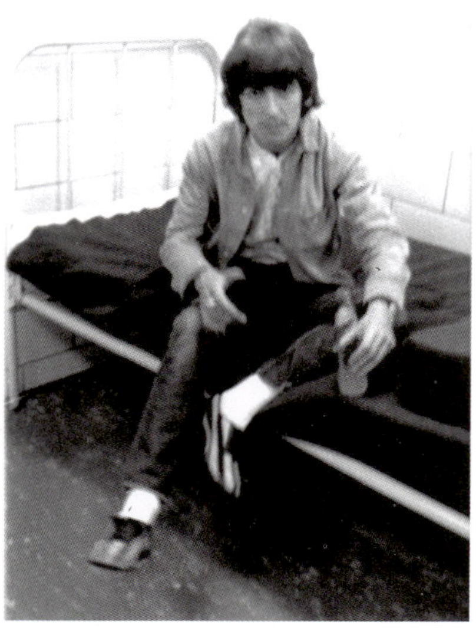

RINGO: I hated the Philippines. We arrived there with thousands upon thousands of kids, with hundreds upon hundreds of policemen – and it was a little dodgy. Everyone had guns and it was really like that hot/Catholic/gun/Spanish Inquisition attitude.

GEORGE: As soon as we got there it was bad news. There were tough gorillas – little men – who had short-sleeved shirts and acted very menacingly.

The normal proceedings in those days were that, because the mania was everywhere, we didn't pull up at an airport and get off the plane like normal people. The plane would land and it would go to the far end of the airfield where we would get off, usually with Neil and our 'diplomatic bags' (we carried our shaving gear – and whatever – in little bags), get in a car, bypass passport control and go to the gig. Mal Evans with Brian Epstein and the rest would go and do our passports and all that scene.

But when we got to Manila, a fellow was screaming at us, 'Leave those bags there! Get in this car!' We were being bullied for the first time. It wasn't respectful. Everywhere else – America, Sweden, Germany, wherever – even though there was a mania, there was always a lot of respect because we were famous showbiz personalities; but in Manila it was a very negative vibe from the moment we got off the plane, so we were a bit frightened.

We got in the car, and the guy drove off with us four, leaving Neil behind. Our bags were on the runway and I was thinking, 'This is it – we're going to get busted.'

NEIL ASPINALL: *The army was there, and also some thugs in short-sleeved shirts over their trousers, and they all had guns; you could see the bulges. These guys got the four Beatles and stuck them in a limo and drove off, and wouldn't let them take their briefcases with them. They left them on the runway – and those little briefcases had the marijuana in them. So while the confusion was going on, I put them in the boot of the limo that I was going in, and said, 'Take me to wherever you've taken The Beatles.'*

GEORGE: They took us away and drove us down to Manila harbour, put us on a boat, took us out to a motor yacht that was anchored out in the harbour and they put us in this room.

It was really humid, it was Mosquito City, and we were all sweating and frightened. For the first time ever in our Beatle existence, we were cut off from Neil, Mal and Brian Epstein. There was not one of them around, and not only that, but we had a whole row of cops with guns lining the deck around this cabin that we were in on the boat. We were really gloomy, very brought down by the whole thing. We wished we hadn't come here. We should have missed it out.

RINGO:

# THE PHILIPPINES VISIT WAS REALLY FRIGHTENING. IT'S PROBABLY THE MOST FRIGHTENING THING THAT'S HAPPENED TO ME.

GEORGE:

# AS SOON AS WE GOT THERE IT WAS BAD NEWS.

**BEATLES TOUR INFORMATION**

blank

where else?

tough

**1966 Summer Tour Germany and Japan**

| | |
|---|---|
| JUNE 24 | Munich, Circus Krone |
| JUNE 25 | Essen, Grugahalle |
| JUNE 26 | Hamburg, Ernst Merck Halle |
| JUNE 27 | Journey to Tokyo |
| JUNE 30 | Tokyo, Budo Kan Hall |
| JULY 1 | Tokyo, Budo Kan Hall |
| JULY 2 | Tokyo, Budo Kan Hall |
| JULY 3 | Journey to Manila |
| JULY 4 | [illegible] Araneta Coliseum |
| JULY 5 | Depart for London |

torture

nearly fucking killed by the government

**1966 American Tour**

| | |
|---|---|
| AUGUST 12 | Chicago, International Amphitheatre |
| AUGUST 13 | Detroit, Olympic Stadium |
| AUGUST 14 | Cleveland, Municipal Stadium |
| AUGUST 15 | Washington, Washington Stadium |
| AUGUST 16 | Philadelphia, Philadelphia Stadium |
| AUGUST 17 | Toronto, Maple Leaf Gardens |
| AUGUST 18 | Boston, Suffolk Downs Racetrack |
| AUGUST 19 | Memphis, Memphis Coliseum |
| AUGUST 20 | Cincinnati, Crosley Field |
| AUGUST 21 | St. Louis, Busch Stadium |
| AUGUST 23 | New York, Shea Stadium |
| AUGUST 24 | New York, Shea Stadium |
| AUGUST 25 | Seattle, Seattle Coliseum |
| AUGUST 28 | Los Angeles, Dodger Stadium |
| AUGUST 29 | San Francisco, Candlestick Park |
| AUGUST 30 | Depart for London |

and its just another Beatle day in His Book



after manila george said in London} Press "they should drop an H. World} Bomb on Manila" we all silently agreed...

We found out later that it was Imelda Marcos (with her shoes and her bras) waiting for us. Somebody had invited us and we (gracefully, we thought) had declined the offer. But there was the TV announcer – their equivalent of Richard Dimbleby – saying, 'And the First Lady is waiting with the Blue Ladies…' (it was like America – they had Pink Ladies and Blue Ladies and First Ladies – and they were *all* waiting there) '… and pretty soon the famous pop group will be arriving.' And we're going, 'Shoot – nobody's told them!' and the promoters are saying, 'Well, you've got to go now. It's only a limo to get there.' And we said, 'We can't.' We stuck to our guns and sat the rest of the day out in the hotel. We turned the telly off and got on with our day off.

RINGO: Personally I didn't know anything about Madame Marcos having invited us to dinner. But we'd said 'no' and Brian Epstein had told her 'no'. John and I were sharing a room, and we woke up in the morning and phoned down for eggs and bacon (or whatever we were eating in those days) and all the newspapers, because we always liked to read about ourselves.

WE WERE JUST HANGING OUT IN OUR BEDS, CHATTING AND DOING WHATEVER WE WERE DOING, AND TIME WENT BY SO WE CALLED DOWN AGAIN: 'EXCUSE ME, CAN WE HAVE THE BREAKFAST?' STILL NOTHING HAPPENED, SO WE PUT THE TV ON, AND THERE WAS A HORRIFIC TV SHOW OF MADAME MARCOS SCREAMING, 'THEY'VE LET ME DOWN!' THERE WERE ALL THESE SHOTS WITH THE CAMERAMAN FOCUSING ON EMPTY PLATES AND UP INTO THE LITTLE KIDS' FACES, ALL CRYING BECAUSE THE BEATLES HADN'T TURNED UP. WE VERY NICELY HAD SAID 'NO' TO THE INVITATION.

NEIL ASPINALL: *They drove me to the end of a pier, and I got out of the car and said, 'Where are they?' They pointed: 'There they are,' and there was a big boat miles away, in the middle of the harbour. There were what seemed to be rival militia gangs One gang had taken them and put them on this boat to meet some people who weren't the people putting on the show. It was all very strange. I never really understood why they got put on a boat.*

GEORGE: We've no idea why they took us to the boat; I still don't know to this day. An hour or two later, Brian Epstein arrived, really flustered, with the Philippine promoter, and he was yelling and shouting. Everyone was shouting and then they took us off the boat, put us in a car and drove us to a hotel suite.

The next morning we were woken up by bangs on the door of the hotel, and there was a lot of panic going on outside. Somebody came into the room and said, 'Come on! You're supposed to be at the palace.' We said, 'What are you talking about? We're not going to any palace.' – 'You're supposed to be at the palace! Turn on the television.'

We did, and there it was, live from the palace. There was a huge line of people either side of the long marble corridor, with kids in their best clothing, and the TV commentator saying, 'And they're still not here yet. The Beatles are supposed to be here.'

We sat there in amazement. We couldn't believe it, and we just had to watch ourselves not arriving at the presidential palace.

PAUL: I went out on my own in the morning, down to the kind of 'Wall Street' area. I remember taking a lot of photographs because right up against it was the shanty-town area. There were cardboard dwellings right up against this 'Wall Street', which I'd never seen so well juxtaposed. I got the camera out: 'Wow, this is good stuff!' And I bought a couple of paintings from the shanty town as presents to go back home, and went back to the hotel to have lunch.

Everyone was up and about then, and we were in our hotel room when they started saying, 'You've got to go to the President's Palace now! Remember that engagement?' We said, 'No, no, no.' The promoters, with those white shirts with lace that everyone in Manila seemed to wear, looked a little heavy to us. A couple of them carried guns, so it was a bit difficult.

We were used to each different country doing it their own way. They were starting to bang on the door: 'They will come! They must come!' But we were saying, 'Look, just lock the bloody door.' We were used to it: 'It's our day off.'

NEIL ASPINALL: *I think they'd been invited and Brian had telexed them or sent a telegram saying 'no' – The Beatles didn't do that sort of stuff for anybody. They wouldn't get involved in politics and they wouldn't go to the palace. But it was ignored as if he hadn't said it.*

*I remember waking up in the morning and having breakfast, and the television was on with the news that The Beatles were about to turn up at Imelda Marcos's party for a lot of children. It was saying, 'OK, they'll be here in five minutes.' They were looking at each other and asking, 'What are they talking about?' They didn't turn up.*

*After it was all over, and they hadn't turned up, and people were going barmy, we asked Brian what had happened, and he said, 'I cancelled it. You weren't supposed to go there.'*

*It turned nasty in the Philippines. I didn't eat for three days. They would bring up food that was terrible. Even if it was cornflakes for breakfast, you'd pour the milk out and it would come out in lumps. They had given you sour milk. I remember once ordering dinner and it came up on one of those big trays with the rolled lid on it, and I rolled back the lid, and – 'Ohhhhh!' – just by the smell of it I knew we couldn't eat it.*

*Paul and I sneaked out there as well; we must have been very brave or very naive. We got in a car and drove for miles – it was like Manhattan for five minutes and then a dreadful shanty town for a long way out – to some sand dunes. We bought a couple of pictures, sat in the sand dunes and had a smoke, and then drove back to the hotel with everybody freaking out (especially the security): 'Where have you been? How did you get out?'*

*Although people kept saying it was a failure in the Philippines, The Beatles did two gigs to a total of about 100,000 people (after the Marcos thing), and all the fans had a really good time. They really enjoyed it. There were still thugs about, organising things (nothing to do with the army), but they seemed to be organising the fans rather than us. The cars were going the wrong way and the dressing room was in a mess.*

GEORGE: Again, we had a big problem with the concert. Brian Epstein had made a contract for a stadium of so many thousand people, but when we got there it was like the Monterey Pop Festival. There were about 200,000 people on the site, and we were thinking, 'Well, the promoter is probably making a bit on the side out of this.' We went back to the hotel really tired and jet-lagged and pretty cheesed off. I don't recall much of what happened after that, until the newspapers arrived and we saw the TV news.

PAUL: The next morning someone brought in a newspaper, and on the front it just said in massive letters: 'BEATLES SNUB PRESIDENT'. Oh dear! 'Well, we didn't mean to,' we thought. We'll just say we're sorry.

We were scheduled to leave Manila that morning, and as we were leaving the hotel everyone was a bit nasty at reception, so we had to scuffle out as if we hadn't paid our bill.

RINGO: Things started to get really weird. 'Come on! Get out of bed! Get packed – we're getting out of here.' And as we got downstairs and started to get to the car – we really had no help – there was only one motorbike compared to the huge motorcade that had brought us in.

GEORGE: It was 'BEATLES SNUB FIRST FAMILY' – that's how they decided to present it. Nobody ever said, 'Well, they were never asked.' It was quite likely it was the promoter or the agent who had done a deal; brown-nosing Mrs Marcos, probably. She was later quoted as saying, 'Oh, I never liked them anyway – their music is horrible!'

THE WHOLE PLACE TURNED ON US. WE HAD PEOPLE YELLING AND SCREAMING WHEN WE TRIED TO GET TO THE AIRPORT. NOBODY WOULD GIVE US A RIDE. WE COULDN'T GET ANY CARS; THERE WAS NOTHING AVAILABLE.

Finally somebody managed to get a car or two and they put our baggage in one and we got in the other. We were driven to the airport. Two things were happening simultaneously: there were all the government officials or police, who were trying to punch us and yelling and waving fists at us, and then underneath that were the young kids who were still around doing the mania.

NEIL ASPINALL: *They were really putting obstacles in our way. When we were on the way to the airport, a soldier kept sending us round and round the roundabout until in the end I told the driver to pull over.*

PAUL: We got down to the airport and found they'd turned the escalators off. So we had to walk up the escalators. 'What's wrong?' – 'We don't know – we're not sure.' 'Would someone take the luggage, then? There don't appear to be any luggage people around.' It was a case of, 'Carry your own luggage.' All right – let's get out of here, then, if that's what it's going to be.

Behind a huge plate-glass window, the sort they have in airports, and on the taxi rank outside there were all the Filipino taxi guys banging on the window – and we're all going 'gibber, gibber'.

NEIL ASPINALL: *Nobody would help us with all this equipment and so we started using the escalators and then they stopped. So we had to lug all the stuff up the stairs, and once we got it all up the stairs the escalators started to work again. The Beatles were going to Delhi and the equipment was going back to England. So at the check-in desk we kept saying, 'OK, that's going to Delhi,' and they kept putting it on the pile that was going to England. In the end Mal jumped over the counter and sorted it all out for us because nobody was going to do it.*

GEORGE: We were all carrying amplifiers and suitcases – nobody was helping us to do anything – but the mania was going on with people trying to grab us, and other people trying to hit us, and we finally got checked in.

It seemed like forever at the check-in desk. We eventually got into the departure lounge, which was a huge room, but then the thugs appeared again – the same people with the short-sleeved shirts who had been shouting at us as soon as we had got off the plane when we arrived in Manila. As well as Mal and Neil, we had Alf Bicknell with us, helping out, and I saw him get punched by one of the thugs.

There were a number of them coming up to us, pushing, and screaming, 'Get over there!' They forced us back, and then another one would come around the other way, doing it again: 'Get over there!' I was trying to keep my eye on all the people, keep moving ahead of them to stay out of their way. It was all really negative. I saw a couple of Buddhist monks, and went and hid behind them.

RINGO: There was chanting, with people hating us all the way – and now at the airport they started spitting at us, spitting *on* us, and there's the famous story of John and me hiding behind these nuns, because we thought, 'It's a Catholic country – they won't beat up the nuns.'

JOHN: All along the route to the airport there were people waving at us, but I could see a few old men booing us. When they started on us at the airport, I was petrified. I thought I was going to get hit, so I headed for three nuns and two monks, thinking that might stop them. As far as I know I was just pushed around, but I could have been kicked and not known it.

'You treat like ordinary passenger! Ordinary passenger!' they were saying. We were saying: 'Ordinary passenger? He doesn't get kicked, does he?' I saw five in sort of outfits who were doing it, all the kicking and booing and shouting. I was petrified, and pushed a lot. I was very delicate, and moved every time they touched me.[66]

That was Brian's cock-up. Because he'd had the invitation given to him, and declined it, and never told us. And the next day they wouldn't accept that we'd declined it, and were hustling and pushing us around at the airport, and wouldn't help us with our bags. It was terrifying.[72]

PAUL: We were quite frightened. Most of the aggression (luckily for us) was directed towards our people. I think Alf got thrown down the stairs violently by one of them. But mostly it wasn't overt – though they *were* annoyed.

We felt a bit guilty, but we didn't feel it was our cock-up. Now, knowing more about the regime, what I think is that they had ignored our telling them we weren't coming: 'Let them just try and not come – we'll make it difficult for them.'

There was a group of nuns in the corner of the airport, and when all the fisticuffs broke out, and with the taxi drivers behind the plate-glass window, we went over to the nuns. (It was rather a nice little shot – nuns and Beatles in the corner. We had a lot in common in many ways: black outfits, and little groups obviously in the same mould.) We stood behind them: 'You'll have to get through them to get to us. You'll have to get through *them*, mate.'

They didn't actually protect us; they just stood there looking a bit bemused. Whenever they moved, we moved the other side of them.

NEIL ASPINALL: *All the thugs in their Hawaiian shirts were pushing and shoving and punching. It was dreadful. I'm sure nobody got badly hurt, but that was because we didn't fight back, so we got pushed and shoved. We knew not to fight back.*

*If we had fought back it could have been very bad. It was very, very scary, and nothing like this had ever happened before – and nothing like it has ever happened since.*

GEORGE: Finally they announced the flight and we boarded the plane – and that was the greatest feeling, just to be on that plane. It was a sense of relief. Then the plane sat there.

Eventually, there was an announcement on the speaker saying, 'Will Mr Epstein and Mr Evans and Mr Barrow...' (Tony, who was our press agent at that time) '... get off the plane.' They all had to get off, and they looked terrified.

Mal went past me down the aisle of the plane breaking out in tears, and he turned to me and said, 'Tell Lil I love her.' (Lil was his wife.) He thought that was it: the plane was going to go and he would be stuck in Manila. The whole feeling was, 'Fucking hell, what's going to happen?'

PAUL: When we got on the plane, we were all kissing the seats. It was feeling as if we'd found sanctuary. We had definitely been in a foreign country where all the rules had changed and they carried guns. So we weren't too gung-ho about it at all.

Then the announcement came over. Tony Barrow had to go back into the lion's den, and they made him pay an amazing airport-leaving Manila tax that I think they just dreamed up. Strangely enough, I think it came to the same amount as the receipts for the trip. I think that was the story.

GEORGE: We sat there for what seemed like a couple of hours. It was probably only thirty minutes or an hour, but it was humid and hot.

Finally they reboarded, the front door was closed and the plane was allowed to leave. They took the money that we had earned at the concert and that was it; we got out of there and it was such a relief. I felt such resentment against those people.

PAUL: I remember when we got back home a journalist asked George, 'Did you enjoy it?' And he said, 'If I had an atomic bomb I'd go over there and drop it on them.'

It was an unfortunate little trip, but the nice thing about it was that in the end (when we found out what Marcos and Imelda had been doing to the people, and the rip-off that the whole thing allegedly was) we were glad to have done what we did. Great! We must have been the only people who'd ever dared to snub Marcos. But we didn't really know what we were doing politically until many years later.

RINGO: We had fantasies that we were going to be put in jail, because it was a dictatorship there in those days, not a democracy. You lose your rights in a dictatorship, no matter who you are. So we weren't going to get off the plane. Our people were allowed back on, and that was my first and last time in Manila.

NEIL ASPINALL: *I'm sure it made the band think hard about touring. It might have been one of the last nails in the touring coffin.*

GEORGE MARTIN: *When they got out of the country they said, 'Never again. This is it.' They said to Brian then that they would not tour again. Brian said, 'Sorry, lads, we have got something fixed up for Shea Stadium. If we cancel it you are going to lose a million dollars...' Oops – and they did do Shea Stadium.*

JOHN: NO PLANE'S GOING TO GO THROUGH THE PHILIPPINES WITH ME ON IT. I WOULDN'T EVEN FLY OVER IT. WE'LL JUST NEVER GO TO ANY NUT-HOUSES AGAIN.[66]

Apple

21st October, 1971.

J. Lennon, Esq.,
c/o ABKCO Industries Inc.,
1700 Broadway,
NEW YORK, N.Y. 10019.

Dear John,

You probably remember the chaos which surrounded your visit to Manila in the Philippines in 1966 but I am wondering whether you can remember one specific incident that was supposed to have occurred.

Apparently your plane was grounded by the authorities until certain tax had been paid on the income of the tour. I understand that in fact a representative of the Manila promoter boarded the plane and Brian actually handed to him in cash $17,000 for the payment of the tax. It is this incident that I am wondering whether you remember because since then efforts have been made on your behalf to recover the money and they have now reached the stage where the lawyers in the Philippines are trying to produce evidence of actual payment.

Can you recall Brian handing over any cash on the plane ?

For the sake of convenience, could you please write either yes or no on this letter and return it to me and we can discuss it in more detail when you return.

Yours sincerely,

Peter

I think Brian gave them money.
anyway they NEVER paid us at all
for 'insulting the 1st family.'
They stopped the plane for other reasons
than tax! They wanted to FRIGHTEN US!

Apple Corps Ltd., 3 Savile Row, London, W.1. 01-734 8232. Cables Apcore London, W.1. Telex 27121
Directors: J. O. Lennon G. Harrison

We popped of at India for sitars hookers etc.. and you can imagine that scene - it was great and we all spent a bomb! Brian caught malaria or some other mystical eastern disease, and Neil came second with Oriental Crabs.

GEORGE: Before the tour was planned, I had an arrangement made that on the return journey from the Philippines to London I would stop off in India, because I wanted to go and check it out and buy a good sitar. I had asked Neil if he would come with me, because I didn't want to be in India on my own. He agreed, and we had booked for the two of us to get off in Delhi.

Somewhere between leaving London and going through Germany and Japan to the Philippines, one by one the others had all said, 'I think I'll come, too.' But we got to Delhi and, after the experience in the Philippines, the others didn't want to know. They didn't want another foreign country – they wanted to go home.

I was feeling a little bit like that myself; I could have gone home. But I was in Delhi, and as I had made the decision to get off there I thought, 'Well, it will be OK. At least in India they don't know The Beatles. We'll slip in to this nice ancient country, and have a bit of peace and quiet.'

The others were saying, 'See you around, then – we're going straight home.' Then the stewardess came down the plane and said, 'Sorry, you've got to get off. We've sold your seats on to London,' and she made them all leave the plane.

So we got off. It was night-time, and we were standing there waiting for our baggage, and then the biggest disappointment I had was a realisation of the extent of the fame of The Beatles – because there were so many dark faces in the night behind a wire mesh fence, all shouting, 'Beatles! Beatles!' and following us.

We got in the car and drove off, and they were all on little scooters, with the Sikhs in turbans all going, 'Oh, Beatles, Beatles!' I thought, 'Oh, no! Foxes have holes and birds have nests, but Beatles have nowhere to lay their heads.'

Delhi was a really funny feeling. I'm sure a lot of people have had this experience when they go there. In the parts of New Delhi that were built by the British, it isn't the little streets you might expect: we were on big wide roads, dual carriageways with roundabouts.

The amazing thing was that there were so many people out there. All the roundabouts had hundreds and hundreds of people sitting in the dark, a lot of them squatting in groups, including old guys with pipes. There were crowds of people everywhere. I was thinking, 'God! What's happened?' It was as if the Superbowl was on, or there'd been a big disaster, with all the people milling around. Then you get to realise that's how it is – there are a lot of people there.

The next day I bought a sitar. I had a guy bring them over – again, we couldn't really get out easily. I bought a sitar off a man called Rikhi Ram, whose shop is still there in Delhi to this day.

We got in cars and had a ride out of Delhi to see what it looked like. That was quite an eye-opener. We were in enormous old late-1950s Cadillacs, and we went to a little village and got out of the cars. We all had Nikon cameras, and that was when it first sunk into me about the poverty. There were little kids coming up to us with flies all over them and asking for money: 'Baksheesh! Baksheesh!' Our cameras were worth more money than the whole village would earn in a lifetime. It was a very strange feeling seeing this: Cadillacs and poverty.

RINGO: That was our first time in India, and it was quite interesting; but we had a bad day when the guys from British Airways took us out to see a camel drawing water – they go round in circles to work the pump where the water comes out. You could always tell the people who worked for BA in Delhi, because they all wore ties even though it was about 300 degrees in the shade. One guy thought it would be a bit of fun to jump on the poor animal that was walking round – probably that was all it would ever do in its life, drag this harness and draw the water. It was crazy, so we all got a bit angry with him.

But then we went shopping, and going around looking at the shops is probably the biggest memory of that time in Delhi. We were offered huge pieces of ivory carvings, and we thought it was all too expensive – huge chess pieces, which would now be antiques and worth fortunes. But I'm glad we didn't buy it; even in those days we were thinking *not* to buy ivory.

**Dear Paul,**

**Welcome home. Hope you had a marvelous time.**

**Sorry to bother you so quickly, but could you please see Maureen Cleeve on Monday? She would like to invite you to lubbh. She has done all the boys, and Monday is her latest deadline.**

**Could you leave a message so that, when I phone monday morning, I have your answer.**

JOHN: CHRISTIANITY WILL GO. IT WILL VANISH AND SHRINK. I NEEDN'T ARGUE ABOUT THAT; I'M RIGHT AND I WILL BE PROVED RIGHT. WE'RE MORE POPULAR THAN JESUS NOW; I DON'T KNOW WHICH WILL GO FIRST – ROCK'N'ROLL OR CHRISTIANITY. JESUS WAS ALL RIGHT, BUT HIS DISCIPLES WERE THICK AND ORDINARY. IT'S THEM TWISTING IT THAT RUINS IT FOR ME.[66]

GEORGE: Why can't we bring all this out in the open? Why is there all this stuff about blasphemy? If Christianity's as good as they say it is, it should stand up to a bit of discussion. [MARCH 1966]

PAUL: John used to know Maureen Cleave of the London *Evening Standard* quite well. We'd gravitate to any journalists who were a little better than the average, because we could talk to them. We felt we weren't stupid rock'n'roll stars. We were interested in other things, and were seen as spokesmen for youth. So Maureen Cleave's article with John touched on religion, and he started to say something that we'd all felt quite keenly: that the Anglican Church had been going downhill for years. They themselves had been complaining about lack of congregations.

Maureen was interesting and easy to talk to. We all did an in-depth interview with her. In his, John happened to be talking about religion because, although we were not religious, it was something we were interested in.

We used to get a number of Catholic priests showing up at our gigs, and we'd do a lot of debating backstage, about things like the church's wealth relative to world poverty. We'd say, 'You should have gospel singing – that'll pull them in. You should be more lively, instead of singing hackneyed old hymns. Everyone's heard them and they're not getting off on them any more.'

So we felt quite strongly that the church should get its act together. We were actually very pro-church; it wasn't any sort of demonic, anti-religion point of view that John was trying to express. If you read the whole article, what he was trying to say was something that we all believed in: 'I don't know what's wrong with the church. At the moment The Beatles are bigger than Jesus Christ. They're not building Jesus enough; they ought to do more.' But he made the unfortunate mistake of talking very freely because Maureen was someone we knew very well, to whom we would just talk straight from the shoulder. Was it a mistake? I don't know. In the short term, yes. Maybe not in the long term.

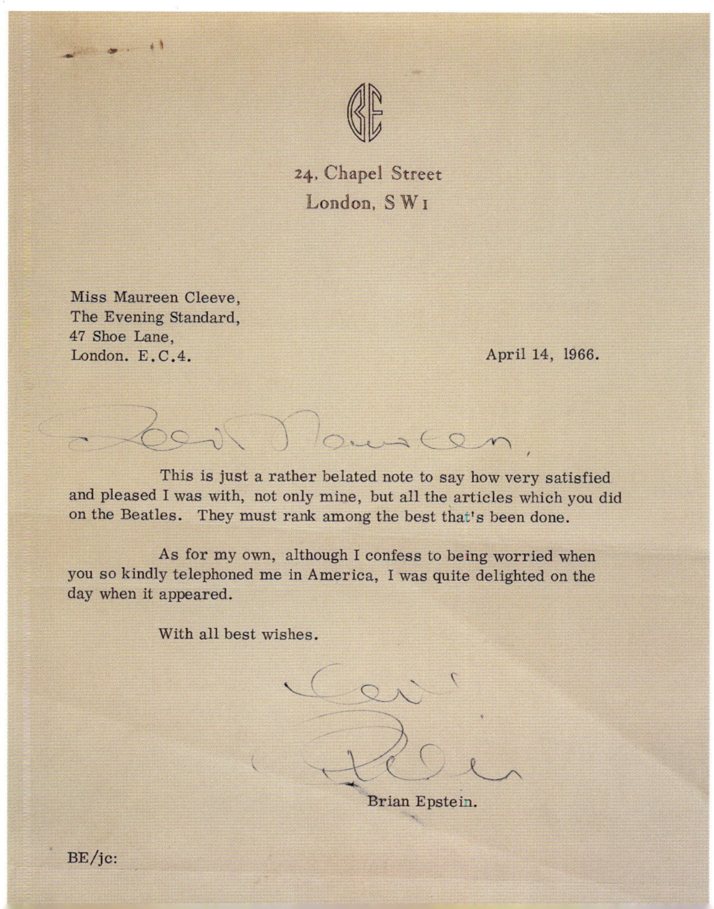

BE

24, Chapel Street
London, S W 1

Miss Maureen Cleeve,
The Evening Standard,
47 Shoe Lane,
London. E.C.4.

April 14, 1966.

Dear Maureen,

This is just a rather belated note to say how very satisfied and pleased I was with, not only mine, but all the articles which you did on the Beatles. They must rank among the best that's been done.

As for my own, although I confess to being worried when you so kindly telephoned me in America, I was quite delighted on the day when it appeared.

With all best wishes.

Brian Epstein.

BE/jc:

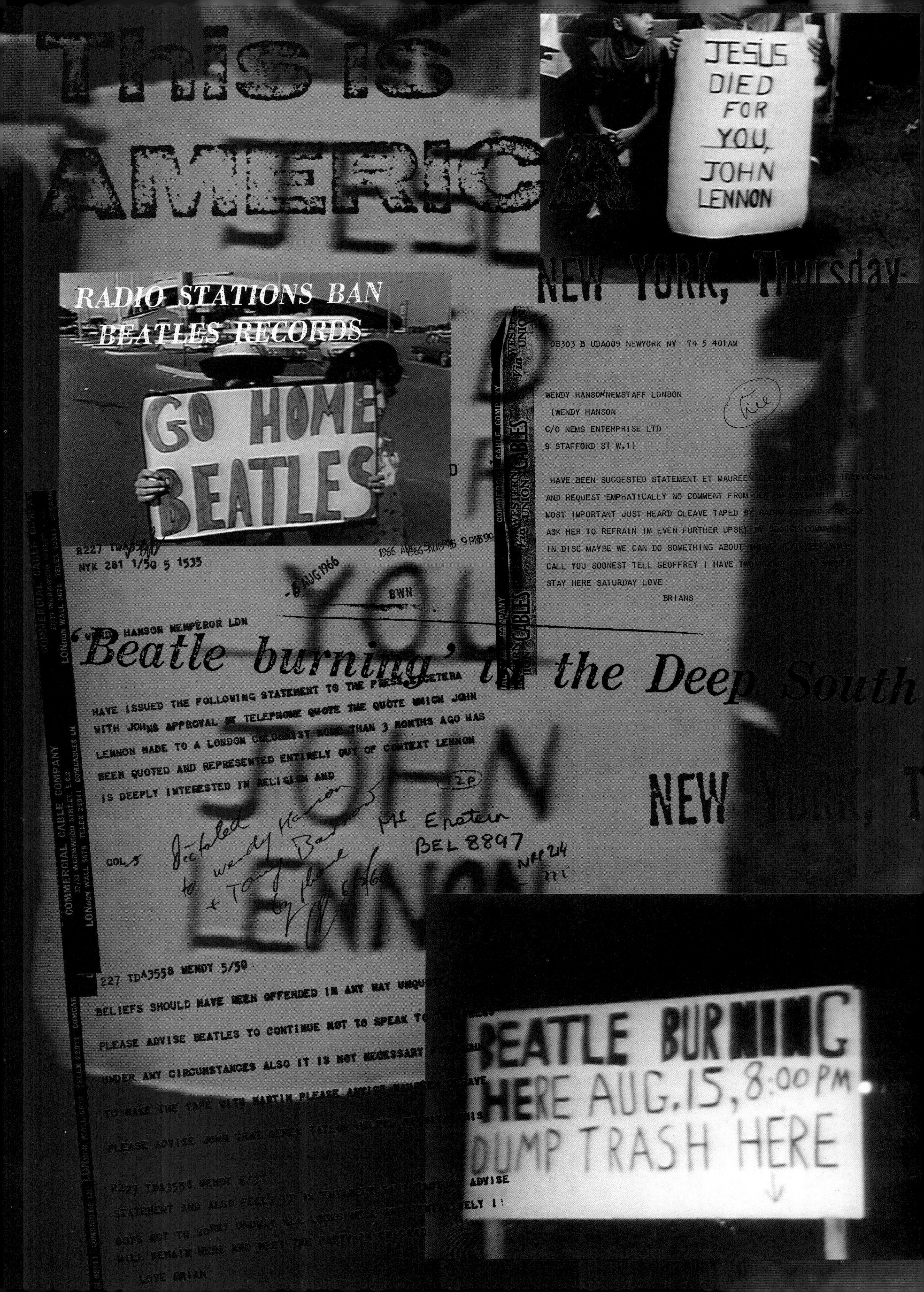


0B303 B UDA009 NEWYORK NY 74 5 401AM

WENDY HANSON NEMSTAFF LONDON
(WENDY HANSON
C/O NEMS ENTERPRISE LTD
9 STAFFORD ST W.1)

HAVE BEEN SUGGESTED STATEMENT ET MAUREEN CLEAVE CONSIDER INADVISABLE AND REQUEST EMPHATICALLY NO COMMENT FROM HER OR BOYS THIS IS MOST IMPORTANT JUST HEARD CLEAVE TAPED BY RADIO STATPONS PLEASE ASK HER TO REFRAIN IM EVEN FURTHER UPSET BY GEORGE COMMENTS IN DISC MAYBE WE CAN DO SOMETHING ABOUT THOSE NEXT WEEK WILL CALL YOU SOONEST TELL GEOFFREY I HAVE TWO ROOMS SO HE SHOULD STAY HERE SATURDAY LOVE

BRIANS

R227 TDA
NYK 281 1/50 5 1535

-6 AUG 1966

BWN

HANSON NEMPEROR LDN

HAVE ISSUED THE FOLLOWING STATEMENT TO THE PRESS ETCETERA WITH JOHNS APPROVAL BY TELEPHONE QUOTE THE QUOTE WHICH JOHN LENNON MADE TO A LONDON COLUMNIST MORE THAN 3 MONTHS AGO HAS BEEN QUOTED AND REPRESENTED ENTIRELY OUT OF CONTEXT LENNON IS DEEPLY INTERESTED IN RELIGION AND

COL

Dictated to Wendy Hanson & Tony Barrow by phone Mr Epstein BEL 8897

227 TDA3558 WENDY 5/50

BELIEFS SHOULD HAVE BEEN OFFENDED IN ANY WAY UNQUOTE

PLEASE ADVISE BEATLES TO CONTINUE NOT TO SPEAK TO

UNDER ANY CIRCUMSTANCES ALSO IT IS NOT NECESSARY

TO MAKE THE TAPE WITH MARTIN PLEASE ADVISE

PLEASE ADVISE JOHN THAT

R227 TDA3558 WENDY

STATEMENT AND ALSO FEELS IT IS

BOYS NOT TO WORRY UNDULY ALL

WILL REMAIN HERE AND

LOVE BRIAN

JOHN: When the bad news comes they shoot the messenger and they don't listen to the message. Whether it be Christianity, Mohammedanism, Buddhism, Confucianism, Marxism, Maoism, everything. It's always about the person and never about what they said.[80]

DEREK TAYLOR: *The Maureen Cleave article was first printed in the London* Evening Standard *back in March, but it appeared in America just before the American tour in August that year. John's comment about The Beatles being bigger than Christ was turned into a big headline in a teen magazine called* Datebook. *Brian was in North Wales recuperating from Manila, among other things – because it had made him ill – and he got the message that the Americans were going bananas about John's comment, which was only one line in a two-page spread.*

GEORGE MARTIN: *It got picked up in America, and reported on various radio stations and magnified, and a storm of protest hit The Beatles hard: 'Who do they think they are, comparing themselves to the Lord?' Records were burned in public bonfires and banned by radio stations, and it reached such a pitch that Brian had to prevail upon John to make a statement and an apology.*

GEORGE: The 'bigger than Jesus' quote wasn't really said the way it came out in America, where they took that one thing and blew it out of context. But the repercussions were big, particularly in the Bible Belt. In the South they were having a field day. There's footage of the disc jockey who started all the uproar saying, 'Come and bring your Beatle trash and deposit it here! We will have different sites all around the States to deposit this trash and we'll be burning it.' And the Ku Klux Klan were out there saying, 'We're going to get them.'

NEIL ASPINALL: *As the Americans had taken exception to the comment, Brian suggested to John that he record a taped statement explaining what he had meant and regretting all the fuss. Studio time was booked with George Martin, but then there was a change of plan.*

*Brian went over to the States prior to the tour and made apologies, and in a press conference told promoters that if they wanted to cancel a show they could do so. Nobody did.*

BRIAN EPSTEIN'S PRESS STATEMENT: *The quote which John Lennon made more than three months ago to a London columnist has been quoted and misrepresented entirely out of context. Lennon is deeply interested in religion, and was at the time having serious talks with Maureen Cleave, who is both a friend of The Beatles and a representative for the London* Evening Standard.

*What he said, and meant, was that he was astonished that in the last fifty years the Church in England, and therefore Christ, had suffered a decline in interest. He did not mean to boast about The Beatles' fame. He meant to point out that The Beatles' effect appeared to be, to him, a more immediate one upon certain of the younger generation.*

RINGO: It was a real mess in America because they took it the wrong way. We read it and it passed us by. It wasn't blasphemous – it was a point of view. If we took it on a worldwide view the church would still be winning. There weren't more people coming to see us than going to church.

It was a valid point. We were punks and said a few things, but not to cause what it caused. It only did so in America because someone took that one line and shot it to the moon.

JOHN: In England nobody took any notice: they know this guy's blabbing off – who is he? But over here some lunatic gets his Klan mask on and starts running round burning crosses.[74]

GEORGE: Although there was a big palaver, we got to America and held a press conference where John apologised. Under the pressure of the cameras and the press, despite the stress of having to deal with what he'd caused, he gave his apology or explanation. He got through it and we decided, 'We'll go and do the gig.'

RINGO: WE ALL HAD TO PAY FOR IT AND IT WAS A PRETTY SCARY TIME. JOHN HAD TO APOLOGISE, NOT BECAUSE OF WHAT HE'D SAID, BUT TO SAVE OUR LIVES BECAUSE THERE WERE A LOT OF VERY HEAVY THREATS – NOT ONLY TO HIM, BUT TO THE WHOLE BAND. SOMETIMES YOU'VE GOT TO TAKE YOUR CAP IN YOUR HAND AND SAY, 'EXCUSE ME.'

"You had a serious and long talk about religion (in which you are very interested) and the quote came out of the fact that you were astonished and surprised that Christianity in the last 50 years in this country has gone off in its appeal. When you said the Beatles are more popular than Jesus you were not trying to upset anyone, but merely suggesting that your appeal is more immediate.* He felt you shouldn't mention the Disciples being "thick" as that would cause more offence. Also that you could conlude with "Profound and sincere apologies to Americans and to all people throughout the world who may have misinterpreted this quote, which was taken out of contest."

George Martin has said he will do the tape with you and has booked Number 3 Studio at Abbey Road for 2.30PM tomorrow (as your BBC thing at Paul's is for 4PM).

Brian wanted to discuss this with you. If he doesn't call you and you want to reach him, (remembering NY is 5 hours BEHIND us) he's at the Waldorf TOWERS which is EL 5-3000. Our office there is 212-563-6767. I'll be home (HYDe Pk 6440) til around 7.45 tonight....anyway will see you at Abbey Road tomorrow.

JOHN: I didn't want to talk because I thought they'd kill me, because they take things so seriously here. I mean, they shoot you and then they realise that it wasn't that important. So I didn't want to go, but Brian and Paul and the other Beatles persuaded me to come. I was scared stiff. I saw a couple of press conferences on film where I'm saying, 'Well, what I really meant was I wasn't condoning that we were bigger than Jesus. I was just saying the fact that kids follow us and not Jesus.' Going through all this hypocrisy – and terrified. I was really scared.[74]

Even I doubted how much sense the whole article meant because I'd forgotten. It was that unimportant – it had been and gone. I had to reread the whole article to make sure I hadn't said anything I didn't mean.

I said we were more popular than Jesus, which is a fact. I believe Jesus was right, Buddha was right and all of those people are right. They're all saying the same thing – and I believe it. I believe what Jesus actually said – the basic things he laid down about love and goodness – and not what people say he said. If Jesus being more popular means more control, I don't want that. I'd sooner they all follow us, even if it's just to dance and sing for the rest of their lives. If they took more interest in what Jesus – or any of them – said, if they did that, we'd all be there with them.[66]

RINGO: John did not want to apologise, because he didn't say what they said. But what was happening around us was getting too violent, and so Brian asked him and kept asking him to say something, and in the end John realised that he'd have to go out and do it.

JOHN: I don't need to go to church. I respect churches because of the sacredness that's been put on them over the years by people who do believe. But I think a lot of bad things have happened in the name of the church and in the name of Christ. Therefore I shy away from church, and as Donovan once said, 'I go to my own church in my own temple once a day.' And I think people who need a church should go. And the others who know the church is in your own head should visit that temple because that's where the source is. We're all God. Christ said, 'The Kingdom of Heaven is within you.' And the Indians say that and the Zen people say that. We're all God. I'm not *a* god or *the* God, but we're all God and we're all potentially divine – and potentially evil. We all have everything within us and the Kingdom of Heaven is nigh and within us, and if you look hard enough you'll see it.[69]

PAUL: We all discussed it. We knew it wasn't really a big issue for us, but because it had become so big we couldn't deny it.

I've never seen John so nervous. He realised the full import of what had happened. So he had to say, 'I didn't mean it like *that*. I meant I'm actually quite supportive...' – which people were able to accept as an answer, except in the Bible Belt.

JOHN: If I'd have said, 'Television is more popular than Jesus,' I might have got away with it. I am sorry I opened my mouth. I just happened to be talking to a friend and I used the word 'Beatles' as a remote thing – 'Beatles', like other people see us. I said they are having more influence on kids and things than anything else, including Jesus. I said it in that way, which was the wrong way. I'm not anti-God, anti-Christ, or anti-religion. I was not knocking it. I was not saying we are greater or better. I think it's a bit silly. If they don't like us, why don't they just not buy the records?

It was part of an in-depth series she was doing, and so I wasn't really thinking in terms of PR or translating what I was saying. It was going on for a couple of hours, and I said it just to cover the subject. It's so complicated, and it got out of hand.

When I first heard about the repercussions I thought, 'It can't be true – it's just one of those things.' And then when I realised it was serious, I was worried stiff because I knew how it would go on, and the things that would get said about it, and all those miserable pictures of me looking like a cynic, and it would go on and on and on and get out of hand, and I couldn't control it. I can't answer for it when it gets that big, because it's nothing to do with me then.

I'm sorry I said it for the mess it's made, but I never meant it as an anti-religious thing. My views are from what I've read or observed of Christianity, and what it was, and what it has been, and what it could be. I'm not knocking it or saying it's bad. I'm just saying it seems to be shrinking and losing context. Nothing seems to be replacing it. It's no good going on and saying, 'Yes, it's all fine, we're all Christians and we're all doing this,' and we're *not* doing it!

I don't profess to be a practising Christian. I think Christ was what he was, and if anyone says anything great about him, I believe, but I'm not a practising Christian like I was brought up to be.

I got away with it in England inasmuch as nobody took offence and saw through me, but in America it went the other way. We forget we're Beatles sometimes.

GEORGE:

IF EVERYBODY WHO HAD A GUN JUST SHOT THEMSELVES THERE WOULDN'T BE A PROBLEM.

PAUL: THREATS WERE HARD FOR US TO COMPREHEND. WE WEREN'T INTO PREJUDICE. WE WERE ALWAYS VERY KEEN ON MIXED-RACE AUDIENCES. I REMEMBER A WOMAN COMING TO OUR SCHOOL ONCE, GIVING A LECTURE ON SOUTH AFRICA, SAYING, 'IT'S MARVELLOUS – YOU CAN GET A BOY TO DO THE TEA, AND WE HAVE BOYS CLEANING UP, AND BOYS IN THE CRICKET NETS...' WE SAID, 'DON'T YOU FEEL A LITTLE EMBARRASSED? IT'S LIKE SLAVES, ISN'T IT?' – 'NO, NO, NO. THEY LOVE IT, THE LITTLE BOYS.'

GEORGE: I THINK WE WERE OFFERED GIGS IN SOUTH AFRICA BUT WE WOULDN'T GO, AND BECAUSE OF THAT THEY BANNED OUR RECORDS THERE.

JOHN: MUSICIANS DON'T USUALLY HAVE THIS THING ABOUT WHAT STREET YOU LIVE ON. THEY GET THAT SCENE SORTED OUT AS SOON AS THEY MEET OTHER MUSICIANS. IT'S THE MUSIC THAT COUNTS. BUT THERE'S NO COMMON DENOMINATOR FOR SOCIETY LIKE IN MUSIC.[68]

PAUL: WITH THAT BEING OUR ATTITUDE, SHARED BY ALL THE GROUP, WE NEVER WANTED TO PLAY SOUTH AFRICA OR ANY PLACES WHERE BLACKS WOULD BE SEPARATED. PEOPLE SAID TO US LATER THAT EVEN IF YOU LET EVERYBODY IN, ALL THE BLACK PEOPLE TENDED TO STICK TOGETHER AND ALL THE WHITE PEOPLE. YOU DON'T INTEGRATE JUST BECAUSE SOMEONE SAYS IT'S NICE – YOU SIT WITH YOUR MATES. THAT WAS ALL RIGHT, BUT WE DIDN'T WANT ANY SEGREGATION. WE WERE VERY KEEN ON PEOPLE'S RIGHTS.

IT WASN'T OUT OF ANY GOODY-GOODY THING; WE JUST THOUGHT, 'WHY SHOULD YOU SEPARATE BLACK PEOPLE FROM WHITE? THAT'S STUPID, ISN'T IT?'

You can't help it, and if you say something like, 'Britain's becoming a police state,' you say it exactly the same as two friends in a pub across the bar.

I don't like supposing that somebody like Jesus was alive now and pretending and imagining what he'd do. But if he was Jesus and he held that he was the real Jesus that had the same views as before – well, 'Eleanor Rigby' wouldn't mean that much to him. [CHICAGO PRESS CONFERENCE, 11TH AUGUST 1966]

PAUL: We don't care about those who don't like us because of the statement. We'd rather perform for people who do like us. We found out that the guy who started it did it purely as an unashamed publicity stunt.[66]

JOHN: It doesn't matter about people not liking our records or not liking the way we look or what we say. They're entitled to not like us – and we're entitled not to have anything to do with them if we don't want to, or not to regard them. We've all got our rights... Harold.[64]

RINGO: It shows us where people are at, because they love you and love you, but then when something like that happens millions of kids start burning their Beatles records. There were bonfires of them – which was OK for us because later they rebought them! But we knew it was getting pretty rough.

The repercussions were that we played a lot of places where people were getting really angry. The Ku Klux Klan were out in force, which was pretty frightening. There was always that edge in America – we knew that they did have guns.

I don't think we contemplated cancelling the tour. We never cancelled anything. Brian would say, 'Here you go,' and we would say, 'Oh, we're off again.' I think we just moaned: 'This is enough.' But it was a routine: 'It's autumn, you make a record and get it out for Christmas.' There were all these strange rules, and we'd keep on going. But it was starting to get too much. It was building up to us saying, 'This is it.'

GEORGE: With the stress and all the things we had to go through anyway, it was something we could have done without. There was a consideration that we might not bother with the tour because we felt we were going to get threatened.

We thought we could actually pull out of one concert in the South, in Memphis – and in Memphis there was film of a guy from the Ku Klux Klan with his shades on, saying, 'We have ways of dealing with this...' But apparently the members of the Klan who were outside the stadium got chased away by the fans. So although we were feeling quite frightened (I remember sitting in a little minibus on the way to the gig, feeling a bit scared) we did the show. Nothing happened. We got out there and that was it.

PAUL: By the time we got to the Bible Belt, down South, there were people banging on our windows. I particularly remember a young boy, maybe eleven or twelve years old, banging on the window of our coach. If he could have got to us, I think he would have killed us; he was fired up with the Spirit of the Lord. And we were saying, 'No, we *love* you. It's OK.'

It made us wonder about touring. It was a case of how much of a good thing can you have? How long can you sustain things? Every tour had gone great, marvellous, but we were becoming a bit fed up anyway because we'd been at it so long – and it gets gruelling: one Holiday Inn after another. Now other things were starting to happen: Manila and threats – and people thinking we're anti-Christ!

JOHN: We dare not go out on the streets. We just stay in the hotel room until the car or coach calls to take us to the show. We miss an awful lot, but I suppose we will see it one day.

We seem to have gone back every August, as far as I can see. Like our annual trip. The longest tour we ever do is three weeks, and it's usually America where we do the longest tours. Three weeks – if you're busy, it's all over before you know what's happened, and you're back home.[66]

NEIL ASPINALL: *The American tour was a repetition of what they'd done the year before, and therefore it was boring, really. It was the same good old exciting America, but it's like anything else – if you've done it once or twice, the third time is a bit old hat.*

*When they played Shea Stadium again, for me it blended in with the first one, though it was said there were slightly fewer people there than the year before. For some reason I missed the police van that was taking us. I had gone back for something, and before I could get in the van, they slammed the doors and off it went. I was left at the hotel, so I got a cab, but that broke down in Harlem. Another cab took me to the stadium, but there were thousands of people, and I thought: 'Oh God, they're really going to let me in! I'm going to just knock on the door and say, "I'm with The Beatles?"' Then I saw the four of them hanging out of a window, and they saw me wandering round the car park. It was like magic; they were shouting, 'There he is! Let him in!'*

*In the Washington gig there had been a Ku Klux Klan demonstration, but it turned out to be six guys in white sheets and conical hats walking round with a placard. It really didn't amount to much. But the assassination threats in Memphis were more scary.*

JOHN: One night on a show in the South somewhere [Memphis] somebody let off a firecracker while we were on stage. There had been threats to shoot us, the Klan were burning Beatle records outside and a lot of the crew-cut kids were joining in with them. Somebody let off a firecracker and every one of us – I think it's on film – look at each other, because each thought it was the other that had been shot. It was that bad.[74]

GEORGE: Cincinnati was an open-air venue, and they had a bandstand in the centre of the ballpark, with a canvas top on it. It was really bad weather, pouring with rain, and when Mal got there to set up the equipment he said, 'Where's the electricity power feed?' And the fella said, 'What do you mean, electricity? I thought they played guitars.' He didn't even know we played electric guitars.

It was so wet that we couldn't play. They'd brought in the electricity, but the stage was soaking and we would have been electrocuted, so we cancelled – the only gig we ever missed. But we did it the next morning. We had to get up early and get on and play the concert at midday, then take all the gear apart and go to the airport, fly to St Louis, set up and play the gig originally planned for that day. In those days all we had were three amps, three guitars, and a set of drums. Imagine trying to do it now!

MAL EVANS: *Open-air concerts in the States were terrible. When it looked like rain in the open air, I used to be scared stiff. Rain on the wires and everybody would have been blown up; yet if they'd stopped the show, the kids would have stampeded.*

PAUL: When we played one place it rained quite heavily, and they put bits of corrugated iron over the stage, so it felt like the worst little gig we'd ever played at even before we'd started as a band. We were having to worry about the rain getting in the amps and this took us right back to the Cavern days – it was worse than those early days. And I don't even think the house was full.

After the gig I remember us getting in a big, empty steel-lined wagon, like a removal van. There was no furniture in there – nothing. We were sliding around trying to hold on to something, and at that moment everyone said, 'Oh, this bloody touring lark – I've had it up to here, man.'

I finally agreed. I'd been trying to say, 'Ah, touring's good and it keeps us sharp. We need touring, and musicians need to play. Keep music live.' I had held on to that attitude when there were doubts, but finally I agreed with them.

George and John were the ones most against touring; they got particularly fed up. So we agreed to say nothing, but never to tour again. We thought we'd get into recording, and say nothing until some journalist asked, 'Are you going out on tour?' – 'Not yet.' We wouldn't make The Big Announcement that we'd finished touring forever, but it would gradually dawn on people: 'They don't appear to be going on tour, do they? How long was that? Ten years? Maybe they've given it up.'

That was the main point: we'd always tried to keep some fun in it for ourselves. In anything you do you have to do that, and we'd been pretty good at it. But now even America was beginning to pall because of the conditions of touring and because we'd done it so many times.

RINGO: In 1966 the road was getting pretty boring and it was also coming to the end for me. Nobody was listening at the shows. That was OK at the beginning, but it got that we were playing really bad, and the reason I joined The Beatles was because they were the best band in Liverpool. I always wanted to play with good players. That was what it was all about. First and foremost, we were musicians: singers, writers, performers. Where we ended up on a huge crazy pedestal was not really in my plan. My plan was to keep playing great music. But it was obvious to us that the touring had to end soon, because it wasn't working any more.

On the last tour of America the most exciting thing was meeting people who came to the shows, not the shows themselves. We'd played the stadiums, we'd played to the big crowds, and still we were only doing our thirty-minute show!

JOHN: The Beatles were famous for doing fifteen-minute shows; we could speed it up to fifteen minutes over in America. Fifty thousand people, and we'd be off. That was our record. We got our kicks from seeing how fast we could do the whole show. And if we were really counting them in too fast, or were too speedy to deal with it, we'd run off and realise we'd only been on fifteen minutes.

There were times when your voice was so bad (through losing your voice) you virtually wouldn't be singing at all, and nobody would notice because there'd be so much noise going on. You could never hear what we were doing. It would just become a sort of happening – like Shea Stadium was a happening. You couldn't hear any music at all. That got boring; that's why we stopped it.[71]

## PAUL: BY CANDLESTICK PARK IT WAS LIKE, 'DON'T TELL ANYONE, BUT THIS IS PROBABLY OUR LAST GIG.'

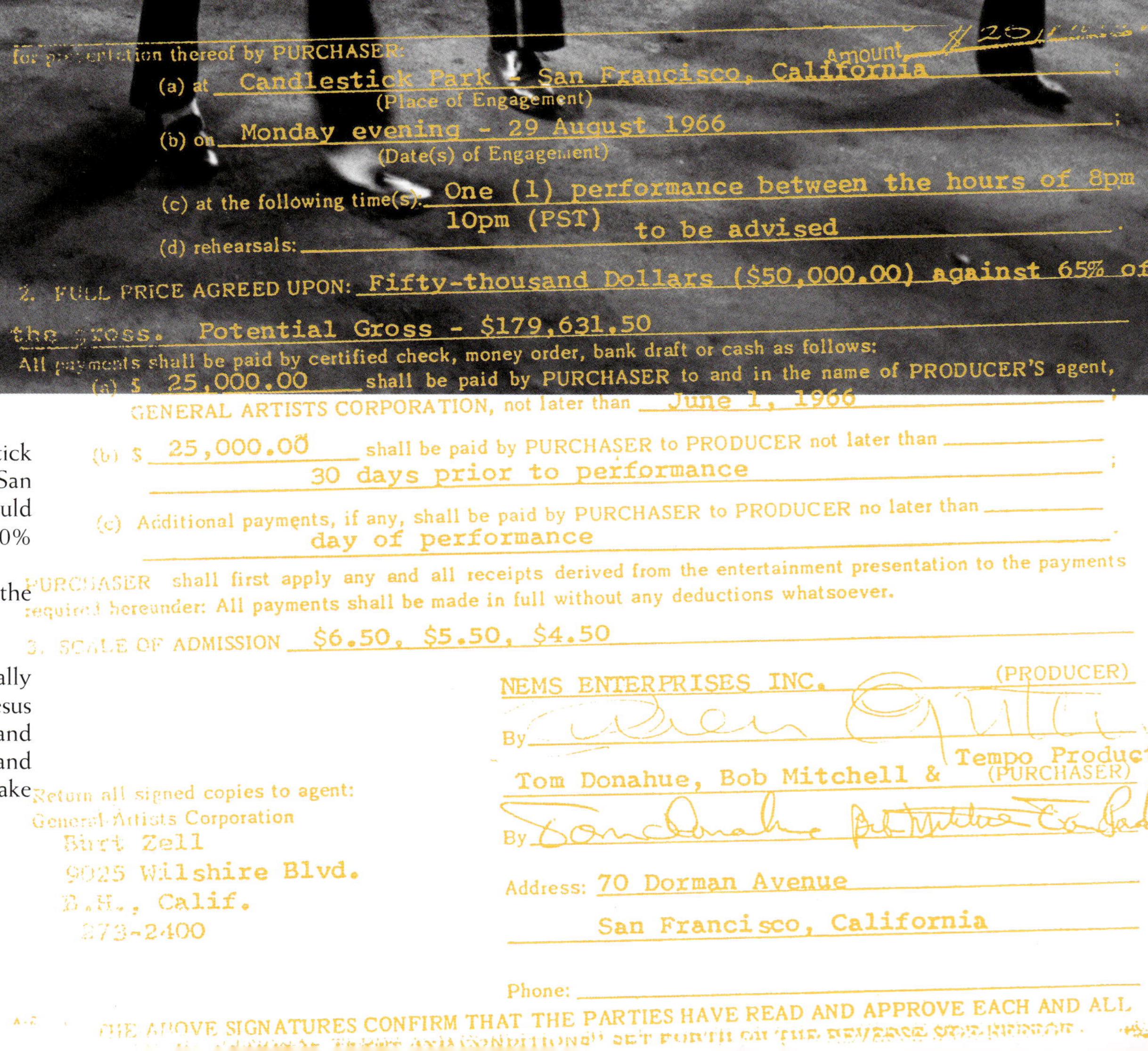

for presentation thereof by PURCHASER: Amount

(a) at Candlestick Park - San Francisco, California;
(Place of Engagement)

(b) on Monday evening - 29 August 1966;
(Date(s) of Engagement)

(c) at the following time(s) One (1) performance between the hours of 8pm
10pm (PST)

(d) rehearsals: to be advised.

2. FULL PRICE AGREED UPON: Fifty-thousand Dollars ($50,000.00) against 65% of the gross. Potential Gross - $179,631.50

All payments shall be paid by certified check, money order, bank draft or cash as follows:

(a) $ 25,000.00 shall be paid by PURCHASER to and in the name of PRODUCER'S agent, GENERAL ARTISTS CORPORATION, not later than June 1, 1966;

(b) $ 25,000.00 shall be paid by PURCHASER to PRODUCER not later than 30 days prior to performance;

(c) Additional payments, if any, shall be paid by PURCHASER to PRODUCER no later than day of performance.

PURCHASER shall first apply any and all receipts derived from the entertainment presentation to the payments required hereunder: All payments shall be made in full without any deductions whatsoever.

3. SCALE OF ADMISSION $6.50, $5.50, $4.50

NEMS ENTERPRISES INC. (PRODUCER)

By

Tom Donahue, Bob Mitchell & Tempo Product (PURCHASER)

By

Return all signed copies to agent:
General Artists Corporation
Burt Zell
9025 Wilshire Blvd.
B.H., Calif.
273-2400

Address: 70 Dorman Avenue
San Francisco, California

Phone:

THE ABOVE SIGNATURES CONFIRM THAT THE PARTIES HAVE READ AND APPROVE EACH AND ALL

RINGO: There was big talk at Candlestick Park that this had got to end. At that San Francisco gig it seemed that this could possibly be the last time, but I never felt 100% certain till we got back to London.

John wanted to give up more than the others. He said that he'd had enough.

JOHN: I didn't want to tour again, especially after having been accused of crucifying Jesus when all I'd made was a flippant remark, and having to stand with the Klan outside and firecrackers going on inside. I couldn't take any more.[80]

RINGO: I don't think anyone *didn't* want to stop touring, but Paul would have gone on longer than George and I. I was feeling such a bad musician and I was fed up playing the way I was playing. That was my criteria for ending it. I just wasn't working on the road any more because I couldn't play.

I don't think any of the decisions were made quickly. We'd all expressed them and moaned about them, laughed about them and cried about them. Then it had got to a head where it was 'yes' or 'no' time – and we seemed to do that with the touring, with the recording and with the breaking-up. None of those things ended with someone turning round and saying it without talking about it first. We didn't make a formal announcement that we were going to stop touring, because it was just something we decided and then we let it go away.

GEORGE: When we got to Candlestick Park we placed our cameras on the amplifiers and put them on the timer. We stopped between tunes, Ringo got down off the drums, and we stood facing the amplifiers with our back to the audience and took photographs. We knew. 'This is it – we're not going to do this again. This is the last concert.' It was a unanimous decision.

It was too much, with all those riots and hurricanes. Beatlemania took its toll, and we were no longer on the buzz of fame and success. 'The Dental Experience' had made us see life in a different light, and touring was no longer fun.

We'd done about 1,400 live shows and I certainly felt that was it. I never really projected into the future; I was thinking, 'This is going to be such a relief – not to have to go through that madness any more.'

It was nice to be popular, but when you saw the size of it, it was ridiculous, and it felt dangerous because everybody was out of hand and out of line. Even the cops were out of line. They were all caught up in the mania. It was as if they were all in a big movie and we were the ones trapped in the middle of it. It was a very strange feeling. For a year or so I'd been saying, 'Let's not do this any more.' And then it played itself out, so that by 1966 everybody was feeling, 'We've got to stop this.' I don't know exactly where in 1966, but obviously after the Philippines we thought, 'Hey, we've got to pack this in.'

We were all still pretty friendly; we were just tired. It had been four years of legging around in a screaming mania. We'd had a couple of small vacations, but we'd only had one big holiday during that whole four years. We needed a rest. I don't think anybody was regretting it, thinking, 'This is the end of an era.' I think we welcomed it.

JOHN: I reckon we could send out four waxwork dummies of ourselves and that would satisfy the crowds. Beatles concerts are nothing to do with music any more. They're just bloody tribal rites.[66]

## GEORGE: WHILE EVERYBODY ELSE WAS GOING MAD, WE WERE ACTUALLY THE SANEST PEOPLE IN THE WHOLE THING.

NEIL ASPINALL: *It was in India that I heard for the first time that they might not tour in 1967. We were all in a hotel suite with Brian, talking about going to America. It was George who asked Brian, 'Is this touring becoming an annual event?' because he wasn't prepared to do it again. Probably they'd all spoken about it among themselves and decided that it wasn't a good idea. And they decided then and there that they weren't going to do America the next year.*

*So when we got to Candlestick Park we knew that was the last gig. For me that wasn't The Last Gig Ever; it was just that they weren't going to tour for a while. I never knew what my role was, so I figured their not touring wouldn't affect me.*

*I'm not sure whether or not Brian was at the last show. Maybe he was trying to find his briefcase. It was reported that money and other personal items had been stolen from his room. Brian was robbed on occasions.*

*With no more live shows planned, the idea was that they could make more records. All The Beatles' albums, with the possible exception of* Revolver, *had been fitted in between coming off the road and getting back on. They would have to make an album in two or three weeks, including the cover and everything. Then they were back on the road with no real time to concentrate on it.*

GEORGE MARTIN: *Curiously enough the second Shea Stadium concert had about 11,000 seats unsold. So it was a pretty unsettling time. And it was against this background that they said, 'Right, we definitely won't do any more. We are going to have a break and then we are going into the studio to make a record.'*

PAUL: I don't remember having a negative feeling about the band. I did about touring. But you always forget the bad bits. It's like a holiday when it rains all the time; you just remember the fine days.

George has said, 'We weren't musicians any more. We were just moptops and rag dolls,' and I think that was true. We were getting fed up with that aspect, but I think I could have handled it. I expect that when you become famous.

But the quality of the music wasn't good, and it wasn't getting any better with the touring. We all agreed that maybe going into recording would be the new thing to turn us all on.

JOHN: We are not goody-goody boys. We are not possessed of limitless patience. One has to have the quality of an angel to cheerfully submit to the demands of some fans. We're not trying to pass off as kids, and we're human as the next fellow. Whether we look our age or not, very often we feel a lot older than we really are.

We can't go on holding hands forever. We have been Beatles as best we ever will be – those four jolly lads. But we're not those people any more. We are old men. We can't go on hopping on *Top of the Pops* forever. We still enjoy it, but sometimes we feel silly. We can't develop the singing because none of us can sing the tune. We've got to find something else to do. Paul says it's like leaving school and finding a job. It's just like school, actually, because you have the group to lean on, and then suddenly you find you're on your own.

I shouldn't worry if I was rejected by the public. It's rejection on the part of *me* that would get me. Suppose I suddenly found out I was a useless bum. What I have done is fine – I know I wasn't a useless bum, but now I have to do something else. We sort of half hope for The Downfall – a nice downfall. Then we would just be a pleasant old memory.[66]

RINGO: For Brian Epstein, our not touring sure left a void, because part of his gig was to get us out there, and that was a huge management thing for him. That's when he was 'Big Bri' – on the road. Once we hit all those towns, it was 'Mr Epstein: The Beatles' Manager'.

I think Brian (like the rest of us) was getting tired of doing the same old thing. What fun could it have been for him to rebook us at Candlestick Park or Shea Stadium?

After deciding not to tour I don't think we cared a damn. We'd been having more fun in the studio, as you can hear from *Revolver* and *Rubber Soul*. As it was building up, it was getting more experimental. We were starting to spend more time there, and the songs were getting better and more interesting. Instead of being pulled out of the studio to go on the road, we could now spend time there and relax.

JOHN: We've had enough of performing forever. I can't imagine any reason which would make us do any sort of tour again. We're all really tired. It does nothing for us any more – which is really unfair to the fans, we know, but we've got to think of ourselves.[67]

I'm just sorry for the people that can't see us live. Sometimes you haven't missed anything because you wouldn't have heard us, but sometimes I think you might have enjoyed it. I'm sorry for them.[64]

When we were away from it for a while, it was like the school holidays. You hadn't done any work for a bit and you'd just remember the laughs. You'd quite look forward to it again. Until you got back and were fed up. It's like the army. One big sameness which you have to go through. One big mass. I can't remember any tours.[67]

## THE MUSIC WASN'T BEING HEARD. IT WAS JUST A SORT OF A FREAK SHOW: THE BEATLES *WERE* THE SHOW, AND THE MUSIC HAD NOTHING TO DO WITH IT.[69]

MICHAEL CRAWFORD · JOHN LENNON
HOW I WON THE WAR X
If you think Richard Lester's 'HOW I WON THE WAR' is just another war film - forget it.
Co-starring ROY KINNEAR · LEE MONTAGUE
JACK MacGOWRAN · MICHAEL HORDERN · JACK HEDLEY
Also starring KARL MICHAEL VOGLER · SCREENPLAY BY CHARLES WOOD
BASED ON THE NOVEL BY PATRICK RYAN · PRODUCED AND DIRECTED BY RICHARD LESTER · ASSOCIATE PRODUCER DENIS O'DELL
EASTMAN COLOUR
A Petersham Films Ltd. Production
United Artists
NOW SHOWING
LONDON PAVILION
PICCADILLY CIRCUS PHONE 437-2982
Progs. at 10.35, 12.25, 2.55, 5.30, 8.10. Late Show Sat. 11 p.m.
Sunday: Progs. at 2.55, 5.30, 8.10. Last Screening daily 8.50.

Dear Mr. Brown...

"HOW I WON THE WAR"

JOHN LENNON is

This is to confirm that ~~xxxxxxx~~ called for post-synching

WEDNESDAY 28th Dec. at 9 a.m. for all day

at Twickenham Studios on THURSDAY, 29th Dec. at 9 a.m. for day.

Yours sincerely,
For PETERSHAM FILMS LTD.,

Mr. Lennon is at present abroad making a film in Spain and I do not expect him back in England for quite some time. However, if you would send me some idea of the information you require I may be able to help through other members of his family.

With appreciation of your interest and with all best wishes.

Yours sincerely,

Wendy Hanson
Personal Assistant to Brian Epstein

NEIL ASPINALL: *I went with John to make* How I Won the War *in the autumn of 1966. While John was filming I was dressed up as a dead soldier, coloured orange in the convention of the film.*

*We went back to Hamburg again, because we did some filming on location near there. That was really nice because it was just John and me in Hamburg, without fans or shows or Beatles, and we went round to all their old places and shops. We did it for a day or so, then we got the train to Paris.*

*We also filmed in Spain. During the time there, John wrote 'Strawberry Fields Forever' on a beach and played it to me.*

JOHN: We were in Almeria, and it took me six weeks to write the song. I was writing it all the time I was making the film. (And as anybody knows about film work, there's a lot of hanging around.) I have an original tape of it somewhere – of how it sounded before it became the psychedelic-sounding song it became on record.[80]

As an artist, I always, in the most real moments, try to express myself, and to show *myself* and not somebody else. If I knew myself less I could express it less, that's all.

In 'Strawberry Fields' I'm saying, 'No, always think it's me,' and all that bit, and, 'Help!' I was trying to describe myself, how I felt, but I wasn't sure how I felt. So I'd be saying, 'Sometimes, no always, think it's real but ...' but I'm expressing it haltingly because I'm not sure what I'm feeling. But now I was sure: 'Yeah, that was what I'm feeling – it hurts, that's what it's about.' So then I could express myself.[70]

The second line goes, 'No one I think is in my tree.' Well, what I was trying to say in that line is, 'Nobody seems to be as hip as me, therefore I must be crazy or a genius.' It's the same problem as I had when I was five.[80]

'Strawberry Fields' was psychoanalysis set to music, really. I think most analysis is just symptomatic, where you just talk about yourself. I don't need to do that because I've done a lot of it with reporters. I never had time for psychiatrists and those people, because they're all cracked.

Instead of penting up emotion or pain, feel it – rather than putting it away for a rainy day. I think everyone's blocked. I haven't met anybody that isn't a complete blockage of pain, from childhood, from birth on. Why shouldn't we cry? They tell us to stop crying about twelve: 'Be a man.' What the hell's that? Men hurt.[70]

NEIL ASPINALL: *There had been a big storm during one night. Everything had been washed out to sea, and all the roads were really muddy. Then they had all become rutted when it dried. We were coming back from location in John's black Rolls Royce and we had Dylan on the car stereo, but switched it over to the tannoy so the song played outside. We were going down the road with Dylan blaring out all over the place. (We found out later that everyone called it the 'Carriage of Death' – for them the car was like a hearse.) As we went over a narrow bridge, a motorbike came round the corner, and the rider saw a big black object looming with music coming out of it. There was a gap between a mountain and the little wall over the bridge, and the motorbike went straight through it – the guy just took off!*

*While John had been in Spain, the others had all been doing their own things. Paul was working on the soundtrack of* The Family Way. *George was in India.*

*Ringo came to Spain when John and I were there. So did another guy, with a box of chocolates full of marijuana. He opened it and said, 'Brian and I really packed this well for you.' The contents then erupted and went all over the floor into a thick pile carpet: 'Oh, thank you!'*

RINGO: Towards the end of 1966, with John being in Spain filming *How I Won the War*, I went and hung out with him because he was lonely. We really supported each other a lot.

Maureen and I decided to go out and stay with Michael Crawford, who was with John in the film, and every five or six days we would move house. All of us were living in the same house and there was always something wrong with it – that was the most boring part about it, and it was damn hot.

In 1965 Maureen and I had bought a house in Weybridge. John lived out there and George lived in Esher, which was five miles away, so we all ended up in the same area, which was dynamite for me. We had had Zak by then, and when we were living in London we couldn't put him outside; and also we were a family now, so it was time to move on.

We had a building firm decorating and remodelling it, and we thought, 'We'll buy the building firm – that way they'll really work!' And so I went into partnership and we called the company Brickey Building, and did all the work on my house, thinking it would be less expensive. The foreman used to cook us dinner every night because he was the only one who could cook; Maureen couldn't in those days.

That's how we got the building – but buying the house and doing it up was probably the daftest thing I ever did. I bought it for £37,000, which was quite a fortune in those days, but it had cost me £90,000 by the time we'd finished it, and we sold it for £47,000. And the other part about the building firm was that we did some work for George Harrison – who still hasn't paid the bloody bill! (Joke.)

I really enjoyed having time off in 1966, getting used to the idea: 'OK, that's it for touring – let's have fun with my wife and child.' I now had time to do other things.

JOHN: I was always waiting for a reason to get out of The Beatles from the day I made *How I Won the War* in 1966. I just didn't have the guts to do it, you see. Because I didn't know where to go. I remember why I made the movie. I did it because The Beatles had stopped touring and I didn't know what to do. Instead of going home and being with the family, I immediately went to Spain with Dick Lester because I couldn't deal with not being continually onstage. That was the first time I thought, 'My God, what do you do if this isn't going on? What is there? There's no life without it.' And that's when the seed was planted that I had to somehow get out of this, without being thrown out by the others. But I could never step out of the palace because it was too frightening.

I was really too scared to walk away. I was thinking, 'Well, this is the end, really. There's no more touring. That means there's going to be a blank space in the future.' At some time or other that's when I really started considering life without The Beatles – what would it be? And I spent that six weeks thinking about that: 'What am I going to do? Am I going to be doing Vegas? But *cabaret*?' I mean, where do you go? So that's when I started thinking about it. But I could not think what it would be, or how I could do it. I didn't even consider forming my own group or anything, because it didn't enter my mind. Just what would I do when it stopped?[80]

OW I WON THE WAR

A Film by

RICHARD LESTER

Screenplay by

CHARLES WOOD

From the Novel by

PATRICK RYAN

RHINE (LEAGUER) (COLOUR) GERMANY 1945 NIGHT A

Infantrymen in battle order move up silently in the dark. Officers stand behind a small group of searchlights and whisper their unit designations over and over again. LIEUTENANT GOODBODY says his piece as if he loves the rolling sound of it which he does.

GOODBODY

Third Troop the Fourth Musketeers
Third Troop the Fourth Musketeers
Third Troop the Fourth Musketeers

OTHER OFFICERS

First Troop
First Troop
First Troop

Headquarter Fighting
Headquarter Fighting
Headquarter Fighting

Fourth Troop
Fourth Troop
Fourth Troop

GOODBODY

Third Troop the Fourth Musketeers
Third Troop the Fourth Musketeers
Third Troop the Fourth Musketeers

B THE RHINE (LEAGUER) (COLOUR) NIGHT B

A normal voice cuts through the tension.

STOREMAN

Any oil ?

Far away behind the front line near the river and searchlights down the lines of tanks in leaguer some insensitive fool of a tech storeman loads clanging jerry cans on a P.O.L. three tonner and tosses in the cans while tank crews refuel. The TECH STOREMAN bangs with his feet on the deck of the three tonner ... Arc welding is going on as the troops advance.

STOREMAN

... the next.

PAUL: John's now trying acting again, and George has got his passion for the sitar and all the Indian stuff. He's lucky. Like somebody's luck who's got religion. I'm just looking for something I enjoy doing. There's no hurry. I have the time and the money.[66]

GEORGE: I went to India in September 1966. When I had first come across a record of Ravi Shankar's I had a feeling that, somewhere, I was going to meet him. It happened that I met him in London in June, at the house of Ayana Deva Angadi, founder of the Asian Music Circle. An Indian man had called me up and said that Ravi was going to be there. The press had been trying to put me and him together since I used the sitar on 'Norwegian Wood'. They started thinking: 'A photo opportunity – a Beatle with an Indian.' So they kept trying to put us together, and I said 'no', because I knew I'd meet him under the proper circumstances, which I did. He also came round to my house, and I had a couple of lessons from him on how to sit and hold the sitar.

So in September, after touring and while John was making *How I Won the War*, I went to India for about six weeks. First I flew to Bombay and hung out there. Again, because of the mania, people soon found out I was there.

I stayed in a Victorian hotel, the Taj Mahal, and was starting to learn the sitar.

Ravi would give me lessons, and he'd also have one of his students sit with me. My hips were killing me from sitting on the floor, and so Ravi brought a yoga teacher to start showing me the physical yoga exercises.

It was a fantastic time. I would go out and look at temples and go shopping. We travelled all over and eventually went up to Kashmir and stayed on a houseboat in the middle of the Himalayas. It was incredible. I'd wake up in the morning and a little Kashmiri fellow, Mr Butt, would bring us tea and biscuits and I could hear Ravi in the next room, practising.

(After I'd had LSD a lingering thought stayed with me, and the thought was 'the yogis of the Himalayas'. I don't know why it stuck. I had never thought about them before, but suddenly this thought was in the back of my consciousness: it was as if somebody was whispering to me, 'Yogis of the Himalayas.' That was part of the reason I went to India. Ravi and the sitar were excuses; although they were a very important part of it, it was a search for a spiritual connection.)

Ravi had a really sweet brother called Raju, who gave me a lot of books by wise men, and one of the books, which was by Swami Vivekananda, said: 'If there's a God you must see him and if there's a soul we must perceive it – otherwise it's better not to believe. It's better to be an outspoken atheist than a hypocrite.'

All my early life they'd tried to bring me up as a Catholic, but I wasn't really into that. The whole 'Christian' attitude (and I say 'Christian' in inverted commas, because there are a lot of people who represent themselves as Christians who aren't – who don't really, to my mind, have the franchise on Christ, and are not necessarily representative of what He was trying to say) seemed to be telling you to believe what *they're* telling you and not to have the direct experience.

For me, going to India and reading somebody saying, 'No, you can't believe anything until you have direct perception of it' – which was obvious, really – made me think, 'Wow! Fantastic! At last I've found somebody who makes some sense.' So I wanted to go deeper and deeper into that. That's how it affected me – I read books by various holy men and swamis and mystics, and went around and looked for them and tried to meet some.

PAUL: If you are blessed with the ability to write music, you can turn your hand to various forms. I've always admired people for whom it's a craft – the great songwriting partners of the past, such as Rodgers and Hammerstein, or Cole Porter. I've admired the fact that they can write a musical and they can do a film score.

So film scores were an interesting diversion for me, and with George Martin being able to write and orchestrate – and being pretty good at it – I got an offer through the Boulting Brothers for him and me to do some film music for *The Family Way*.

I had a look at the film and thought it was great. I still do. It's very powerful and emotional – soppy, but good for its time. I wanted brass-band music; because with The Beatles we got into a lot of different kinds of music, but maybe brass band was a little too Northern and 'Hovis'. I still loved it. My dad had played trumpet and his dad had been in a brass band, so I had those leanings. For the film I got something together that was sort of 'brassy bandy', to echo the Northernness of the story, and I had a great time.

We got an Ivor Novello Award for the score – for the best film song that year, a piece called 'Love In The Open Air', which Johnny Mercer was *nearly* going to put lyrics to, but I didn't know who he was. Later I realised, 'Oh, *that* Johnny Mercer! You mean the greatest lyricist on the planet!' I should have done that. Never mind – it fell through – but it was good fun doing the music.

You can see them in India. It's unbelievable: you can go down the street and there's somebody driving a bus or a taxi, or riding a bicycle, and there's a chicken and a cow, and someone in a business suit with a briefcase – and an old sannyasi with a saffron robe. All mixed together. It's an incredible place, with layers and layers and layers of sounds and colours and noises, and it all bombards your senses. It was amazing then. I felt as if I was back in time.

It was the first feeling I'd ever had of being liberated from being a Beatle or a number. It comes back to *The Prisoner* with Patrick McGoohan: 'I am not a number.' In our society we tend, in a subtle way, to number ourselves and each other, and the government does so, too. 'What's your Social Security number?' is one of the first things they ask you in America. To suddenly find yourself in a place where it feels like 5000 BC is wonderful.

I went to the city of Benares, where there was a religious festival going on, called the Ramlila. It was out on a site of 300 to 500 acres, and there were thousands of holy men there for a month-long festival. During this festival the Maharajah feeds everybody and there are camps of different people, including the sadhus – renunciates. In England, in Europe or the West, these holy men would be called vagrants and be arrested, but in a place like India they roam around. They don't have a job, they don't have a Social Security number, they don't even have a name other than collectively – they're called sannyasis, and some of them look like Christ. They're really spiritual; and there are also a lot of loonies who look like Allen Ginsberg. That's where he got his whole trip from – with the frizzy hair, and smoking little pipes called chillums, and smoking hashish. The British tried for years to stop Indians smoking hashish, but they'd been smoking it for too long for it to be stopped.

I saw all kinds of groups of people, a lot of them chanting, and it was a mixture of unbelievable things, with the Maharajah coming through the crowd on the back of an elephant, with the dust rising. It gave me a great buzz.

JOHN: Yoko had been invited to London by some group of artists called Destruction in Art Symposium. They had some big thing going on in London. She had an exhibition put on by Indica Gallery, by John Dunbar – Marianne Faithfull's ex-husband. I used to go down there occasionally to see things like Takis, who'd made flashing lights and sold them for a fortune. It would be garbage. But they sent me this pamphlet, or he called me – I don't know which – about this Japanese girl from New York, who was going to be in a bag, doing this event or happening. I thought, 'Hmm,' you know, 'sex.' So I went down.[80]

I was in a highly unshaved and tatty state. I was up three nights. I was always up in those days, tripping. I was stoned.[69]

I walked in and there was nobody there. It turns out that it was the night before the opening night. The place wasn't really opened, but John Dunbar was all nervous, like: 'The millionaire's come to buy something!' He's flittering around like crazy. Now I'm looking at this stuff. There's a couple of nails on a plastic box. Then I look over and see an apple on a stand with a note saying 'apple'. I thought, 'This is a joke, this is pretty funny.' I was beginning to see the humour of it. I said, 'How much is the apple?' – '£200.' – 'Really? Oh, I see. So how much are the bent nails?'[80]

I wasn't quite sure what it was about. I knew there was some sort of con game going on somewhere. She calls herself a concept artist, but with the 'cept' off it's a con artist. I saw that side of it, and that was interesting.[72]

So I was wandering around having a good time and I went downstairs and there's just a couple of scruffy people sitting around in jeans. I was feeling a bit defensive, thinking, 'They must be the hip ones.' It turns out they were just assistants putting all this stuff together for her, but I was like, 'I'm the famous, rich pop star and these must be the ones that know what those nails and apples are about.' I took it humorously, which turned out to be fine, but I was reacting like a lot of people react to her humour, which is they get angry at her and say she's got no sense of humour. Actually, she's hysterically funny.

Then Dunbar brings her over because The Millionaire is here, right? And I'm waiting for the bag. Where's the people in the bag? All the time I was thinking about whether I'd have the nerve to get in the bag with whoever. You don't know who's gonna be in the bag!

So he introduced me, and of course there was supposed to be this event happening, so I asked, 'Well, what's the event?' She gives me a little card. It just says 'breathe' on it. And I said, 'You mean [*panting*]?' She says, 'That's it. You've got it.' And I'm thinking, 'I've got it!' But I'm all geared up to *do* something. I did the breathing, but I wanted more than putting my consciousness on my breathing, which is an intellectual way of looking at it. I saw the nails and I got the humour – maybe I didn't get the depth of it, but I got a warm feeling from it. I thought, 'Fuck, I can make that. I can put an apple on a stand. I want more.'

Then I saw this ladder on a painting leading up to the ceiling where there was a spyglass hanging down. It's what made me stay. I went up the ladder and I got the spyglass and there was tiny little writing there. You really have to stand on the top of the ladder – you feel like a fool, you could fall any minute – and you look through and it just says 'yes'.

Well, all the so-called avant-garde art at the time and everything that was supposedly interesting was all negative, this smash-the-piano-with-a-hammer, break-the-sculpture, boring, negative crap. It was all anti, anti, anti. Anti-art, anti-establishment. And just that 'yes' made me stay in a gallery full of apples and nails instead of walking out saying, 'I'm not gonna buy any of this crap.'

Then I went up to this thing that said, 'Hammer a nail in.' I said, 'Can I hammer a nail in?' and she said 'no', because the gallery was actually opening the next day. So the owner, Dunbar, says, 'Let him hammer a nail in.' It was, 'He's a millionaire. He might buy it.' She's more interested in it looking nice and pretty and white for the opening. That's why she never made any money on the stuff – she's always too busy protecting it. There was this little conference and she finally said, 'OK, you can hammer a nail in for five shillings.' So smart-arse here says, 'Well, I'll give you an imaginary five shillings and hammer an imaginary nail in.' And that's when we really *met*. That's when we locked eyes and she got it and I got it and that was it.

It took a long time. We were both very shy. The next time we met was a Claes Oldenburg opening with a lot of soft objects like cheeseburgers made out of rubber and garbage like that. And we met again and made eye contact. But it was eighteen months or two years before we really got it together.

The rest, as they say in all the interviews we do, is history.[80]

RINGO: THESE LITTLE SLUGS WERE GONNA TURN INTO BUTTERFLIES.

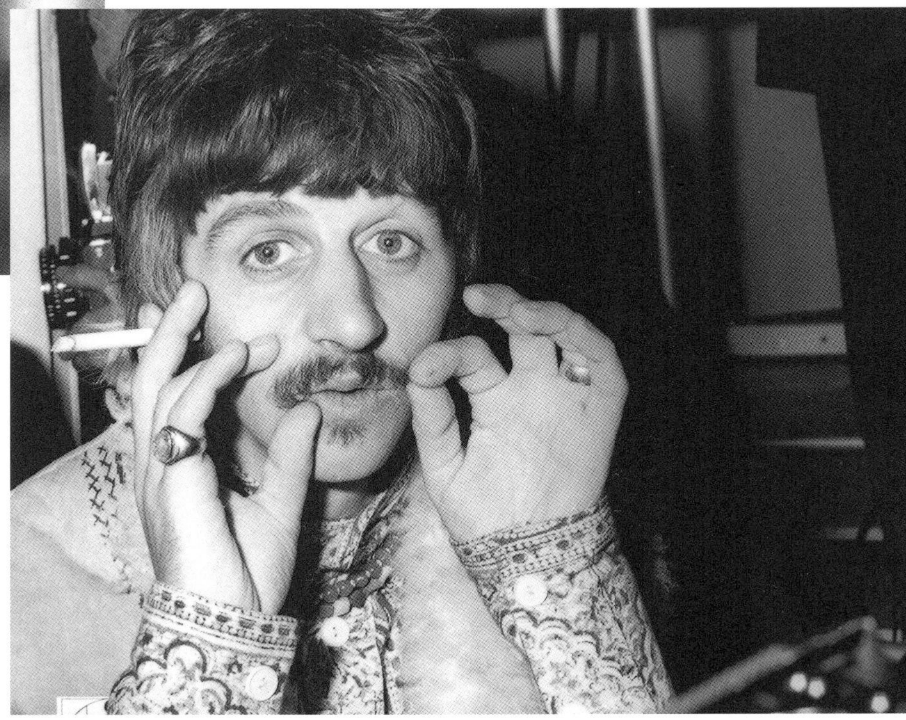

PAUL: I had an accident when I came off a moped in Wirral, near Liverpool. I had a very good friend who lived in London called Tara Browne, a Guinness heir – a nice Irish guy, very sensitive bloke. I'd see him from time to time, and enjoyed being around him. He came up to visit me in Liverpool once when I was there seeing my dad and brother. I had a couple of mopeds on hire, so we hit upon the bright idea of going to my cousin Bett's house.

We were riding along on the mopeds. I was showing Tara the scenery. He was behind me, and it was an incredible full moon; it really was huge. I said something about the moon and he said 'yeah', and I suddenly had a freeze-frame image of myself at that angle to the ground when it's too late to pull back up again: I was still looking at the moon and then I looked at the ground, and it seemed to take a few minutes to think, 'Ah, too bad – I'm going to smack that pavement with my face!' Bang!

There I was, chipped tooth and all. It came through my lip and split it. But I got up and we went along to my cousin's house. When I said, 'Don't worry, Bett, but I've had a bit of an accident,' she thought I was joking. She creased up laughing at first, but then she went 'Holy...!' I'd really given my face a good old smack; it looked like I'd been in the ring with Tyson for a few rounds. So she rang a friend of hers who was a doctor.

He came round on the spot, took a needle out and, after great difficulty threading it, put it in the first half of the wound. He was shaking a bit, but got it all the way through, and then he said, 'Oh, the thread's just come out – I'll have to do it again!' No anaesthetic. I was standing there while he rethreaded it and pulled it through again.

In fact that was why I started to grow a moustache. It was pretty embarrassing, because around that time you knew your pictures would get winged off to teeny-boppery magazines like *16*, and it was pretty difficult to have a new picture taken with a big fat lip. So I started to grow a moustache – a sort of Sancho Panza thing – mainly to cover where my lip had been sewn.

It caught on with the guys in the group: if one of us did something like growing his hair long and we liked the idea, we'd all tend to do it. And then it became seen as a kind of revolutionary idea, that young men of our age definitely ought to grow a moustache! And it all fell in with the Sgt Pepper thing, because he had a droopy moustache.

I was originally trying to grow a long Chinese one, but it was very difficult. You have to do a lot of work waxing it, and it takes about sixty years – I never did get one of them.

John had a moustache cup. It had a little hole underneath the lip so you could drink tea from it without getting your moustache in it – rather fetching!

RINGO: Growing moustaches was just part of being a hippy: you grow your hair, you grow a moustache, and in my case you grow a beard. That was the Sixties coming to the fore.

I always hated shaving anyway, but the moustache was not special for me. The moustache was growing and the beard was growing – hair was growing. It was just part of the set. We were gradually turning into Sgt Peppers. It was as if we were going through a metamorphosis.

NEIL ASPINALL: *Their appearance was still changing – moustaches and so on – but it was nobody's decision. It was just everybody influencing everybody else. Somebody would come in with something new and the others would go, 'That's nice. Where did you get that?' It was like that.*

*Occasionally Paul used to disguise himself when we were on the road. He and I would go out into the audience, up the stairs and into the gallery or the circle with all the fans, watching the other acts that were on the show. Paul would have his hair back and a moustache, glasses, and an overcoat on, and nobody would expect him to be there so nobody took any notice.*

*When he was in the Wirral, Paul had a moped accident and he grew a moustache to hide his split lip and, because he had a moustache, the next thing everybody's got one. That's how it happened for me, anyway. That's my story. I had a moustache, too.*

GEORGE: Moustaches were part of the synchronicity and the collective consciousness. What happened to me was that Ravi Shankar wrote to me before I went out to Bombay, and in the letter said, 'Try to disguise yourself – couldn't you grow a moustache?' I thought, 'OK, I'll grow a moustache. Not that it's going to disguise me, but I've never had a moustache before, so I'll grow it.'

If you see the photographs of the *Sgt Pepper* sessions, we've all got funny things happening and hair breaking out on the face. And then everybody had a moustache; I think even Engelbert Humperdinck got one.

NEIL ASPINALL: *The band at this time started to appeal to a more turned-on audience, because they themselves were turned on. Brian loved it all. He had great faith in The Beatles and what they were doing, and loved them as a band, as musicians and as artists. Brian was a fan.*

*They influenced people right from the very early days, when everybody suddenly seemed to have collarless jackets and Cuban-heeled boots and Beatle haircuts. That influence always seemed to be there.*

JOHN: That bit about 'we changed everybody's hairstyles' – something influenced us, whatever was in the air. Pinpointing who did what first doesn't work. We were part of whatever the Sixties was. It was happening itself. *We* were the ones chosen to represent what was going on 'on the street'. It could have been somebody else but it wasn't: it was us and the Stones and people like that.[74]

RINGO: The Beatles were *the* influence on other bands in 1966/67. It is interesting that when we got to LA and relaxed more and started hanging out with people like David Crosby, Jim Keltner, Jim McGuinn, we realised how much people were trying to be like us. Not those *particular* people, but they were telling us about other bands. We heard that producers were telling everyone to sound like The Beatles.

GEORGE: I came back to England towards the end of October and John got back from Spain. It was all predetermined when we'd meet again. Then we went in the studio and recorded 'Strawberry Fields'. I think at that point there was a more profound ambience to the band.

JOHN: Lots of people ask me what will be the new sound. I personally haven't a clue as to how the scene will progress – what, if anything, will replace it. In any case, I don't like predictions; they are always vague, and invariably wrong. If I knew, I could make a fortune.[66]

## PAUL: WE COULDN'T DO ANY BETTER THAN WE'VE DONE ALREADY, COULD WE?[66]

GEORGE MARTIN: *In November The Beatles returned to the studio for the first time after they had decided to stop touring. They were generally fed up with their lives. They'd had a lot of aggro in that past year, coupled with Brian Epstein worrying that they were going down the pan. He thought that it was the end of The Beatles, and there were all sorts of signs of that in 1966. There was the Philippines disaster, and the falling attendance in some of their shows, and they were fed up with being prisoners of their fame.*

*We started off with 'Strawberry Fields', and then we recorded 'When I'm Sixty-Four' and 'Penny Lane'. They were all intended for the next album. We didn't know it was* Sgt Pepper *then – they were just going to be tracks on The New Album – but it was going to be a record created in the studio, and there were going to be songs that couldn't be performed live.*

NEIL ASPINALL: *As with* Revolver, *or any of the other albums, they just went into a studio and started recording, and the album title and the artwork for the cover came later.*

RINGO: Every time we went back into the studios there was a period of wondering whose song we would start with. Nobody wanted to submit the first song, because by then it was 'Lennon or McCartney' more than 'Lennon *and* McCartney'. So they'd say, 'What have you got?' – 'Well, what have *you* got?!'

It was up to about 80% separately written songs. I could tell which were John's songs. I always preferred to play on them; they always had a bit more rock'n'roll to them.

PAUL: I don't think we were very worried about our musical ability. The world was a problem, but we weren't. That was the best thing about The Beatles: I don't think any of us worried *musically*. I think we were itching to get going.

Now we were off the road and in the studio with new songs. 'Strawberry Fields' is the song that John had, about the old Salvation Army home for kids he used to live next door to in Liverpool. We related it to youth, golden summers and fields of strawberry. I knew what he was talking about.

The nice thing is that a lot of our songs were starting to get a little bit more surreal. I remember John having a book at home called *Bizarre*, about all sorts of weird things. We were opening up artistically and taking the blinkers off.

We used a mellotron on 'Strawberry Fields'. I didn't think it would get past the Musicians' Union, so we didn't advertise it; we just had it on the sessions. It had what would now be called 'samples' of flute, which are actually tapes that play and then rewind. We had eleven seconds on each tape, which could be played on each key.

GEORGE MARTIN: *When John sang 'Strawberry Fields' for the first time, just with an acoustic guitar accompaniment, it was magic. It was absolutely lovely. I love John's voice anyway, and it was a great privilege listening to it.*

PAUL: We did a few versions of it. John wasn't totally happy with the first couple of takes that we did, so we remade the whole track, and in the end John and George Martin stitched two different versions together. We could hardly hear the join, but it's one of those edits where the pace changes slightly: it goes a bit more manic for the second half of the song.

'Penny Lane' was a little more surreal, too, although in a cleaner way. I remember saying to George Martin, 'I want a very clean recording.' I was into clean sounds – maybe a Beach Boy influence at that point.

The 'fireman with his hourglass' and all that imagery was us trying to get into a bit of art. The lyrics were all based on real things. There was a barber called something like Bioletti (I think he's actually still there in Penny Lane) who, like all barbers, had pictures of the haircuts you could choose. But instead of saying, 'The barber with pictures of haircuts in his windows,' it was changed round to: 'Every head he's had the pleasure to have known.' A barber showing photographs – like an exhibition.

It was twisting it to a slightly more artsy angle, more like a play. Like the nurse who's selling poppies from a tray (which some Americans thought was 'selling *puppies* from a tray') for Remembrance Day. Then 'she feels as if she's in a play' – which 'she is anyway'. These were all the trippy little ideas that we were trying to get in.

They're both songs about Liverpool as well. It was always a good thing for us, because we were a group that had been together for a long time, that we could do that: 'Strawberry Fields' *and* 'Penny Lane' – wow! A lot of our formative years were spent walking around those places. Penny Lane was the depot I had to change buses at to get from my house to John's and to a lot of my friends. It was a big bus terminal which we all knew very well. I sang in the choir at St Barnabas Church opposite.

Those two songs were the lead singles. They were the first things we tried in the batch of new recordings.

## PAUL: IT'S PART FACT, PART NOSTALGIA FOR A GREAT PLACE – BLUE SUBURBAN SKIES, AS WE REMEMBER IT, AND IT'S STILL THERE. AND WE PUT IN A JOKE OR TWO: 'FOUR OF FISH AND FINGER PIE'. THE WOMEN WOULD NEVER DARE SAY THAT, EXCEPT TO THEMSELVES. MOST PEOPLE WOULDN'T HEAR IT, BUT 'FINGER PIE' IS JUST A NICE LITTLE JOKE FOR THE LIVERPOOL LADS WHO LIKE A BIT OF SMUT.[67]

# 1967

nineteen sixty-seven

NEIL ASPINALL: *The double A side 'Strawberry Fields Forever' and 'Penny Lane' was The Beatles' first release of 1967.*

GEORGE: It was pretty bad, wasn't it, that Engelbert Humperdinck stopped 'Strawberry Fields Forever' from getting to Number One? But I don't think it was a worry. At first, we wanted to have good chart positions, but then I think we started taking it for granted. It might have been a bit of a shock being Number Two – but then again, there were always so many different charts that you could be Number Two in one chart and Number One in another.

JOHN: The charts? I read them all. There's room for everything. I don't mind Humperbert Engeldinck. They're the cats. It's their scene.[67]

PAUL: It's fine if you're kept from being Number One by a record like 'Release Me', because you're not trying to do the same kind of thing. That's a completely different scene altogether.[67]

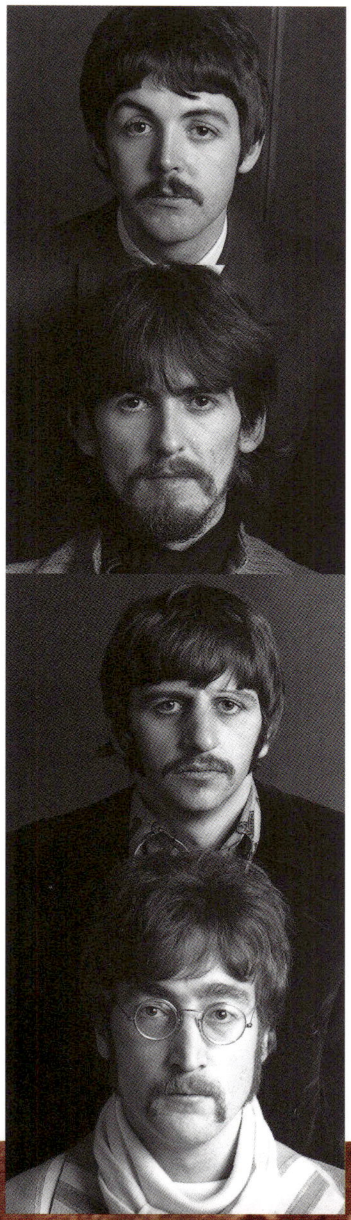

JOHN: When [singles] first come out, we follow how much the initial sales were. Not for the money reason, just to see how it's doing compared to the last one; just because we made it. We need that satisfaction, not the glory of Number One.[68]

GEORGE MARTIN: *The only reason that 'Strawberry Fields Forever' and 'Penny Lane' didn't go onto the new album was a feeling that if we issued a single, it shouldn't go onto an album. That was a crazy idea, and I'm afraid I was partly responsible. It's nonsense these days, but in those days it was an aspect that we'd try to give the public value for money.*

*The idea of a double A side came from me and Brian, really. Brian was desperate to recover popularity, and so we wanted to make sure that we had a marvellous seller. He came to me and said, 'I must have a really great single. What have you got?' I said, 'Well, I've got three tracks – and two of them are the best tracks they've ever made. We could put the two together and make a smashing single.' We did, and it was a smashing single – but it was also a dreadful mistake. We would have sold far more and got higher up in the charts if we had issued one of those with, say, 'When I'm Sixty-Four' on the back.*

NEIL ASPINALL: *The charts didn't worry the band; but if you're going to be in the entertainment business, you do want to be successful. They realised that splitting the sales with the double A side had made it Number Two. But it had to happen at some time, and for it to happen then wasn't a bad idea.*

RINGO: I don't think it was important to categorise the songs into A and B sides any more. We just felt: 'This is the record.' The other attitude was an old trap that people were put into when they made records.

JOHN: The people who have bought our records in the past must realise that we couldn't go on making the same type forever. We must change, and I believe those people know this.

I've had a lot of time to think, and only now am I beginning to realise many of the things I should have known years ago. I'm getting to understand my own feelings. Don't forget that under this frilly shirt is a hundred-year-old man who's seen and done so much, but at the same time knowing so little.[67]

PAUL: We were now in another phase of our career, and we were happy. We'd been through all the touring, and that was marvellous; but now we were more into being *artists*. We didn't have to be performing every night, so instead we could be writing or chatting with our mates or visiting an art exhibition. (For instance, John and Yoko would never have met if we hadn't had all that time spare for him to look around exhibitions and 'bang a nail in'.) Having the time off gave us a lot of freedom to come in with crazy ideas.

I spent a lot of time listening to avant-garde artists and going to places like Wigmore Hall, where I saw the composer Luciano Berio (I remember meeting him afterwards, and he was a very unassuming bloke). George was into Indian music. We were all opening our minds to different areas, and then we'd come together and share it all with each other. It was exciting, because there was a lot of cross-fertilisation.

JOHN: 'Sgt Pepper' is Paul, after a trip to America. The whole West Coast long-named group thing was coming in, when people were no longer The Beatles or The Crickets – they were suddenly Fred and His Incredible Shrinking Grateful Airplanes. I think he got influenced by that. He was trying to put some distance between The Beatles and the public – and so there was this identity of Sgt Pepper. Intellectually, that's the same thing he did by writing 'she loves you' instead of 'I love you'.[80]

PAUL: It was at the start of the hippy times, and there was a jingly-jangly hippy aura all around in America. I started thinking about what would be a really mad name to call a band. At the time there were lots of groups with names like 'Laughing Joe and His Medicine Band' or 'Col Tucker's Medicinal Brew and Compound'; all that old Western going-round-on-wagons stuff, with long rambling names. And so, in the same way that in 'I Am The Walrus' John would throw together 'choking smokers' and 'elementary penguin', I threw those words together: 'Sgt Pepper's Lonely Hearts Club Band'.

I took an idea back to the guys in London: 'As we're trying to get away from ourselves – to get away from touring and into a more surreal thing – how about if we become an alter-ego band, something like, say, "Sgt Pepper's Lonely Hearts"? I've got a little bit of a song cooking with that title.'

JOHN: How can we tour when we're making stuff like we're doing on the new album? We can only do what we're doing. We've toured – that was then. If we do another tour, we'll probably hire London for one big happening, and we'd have us and the Stones and The Who, and everybody else on it. Unless that happens, forget it. I don't want to be a moptop. For those who want moptops, The Monkees are right up there, man.[67]

PAUL: AT THE MOMENT WE HAVEN'T AN ACT TO SUIT THE ORDINARY TYPE OF TOUR THAT GOES ON. IF WE CAN THINK OF A WAY OF GETTING FOUR FLYING SAUCERS LANDING ON THE TOP OF THE ALBERT HALL, IT WOULD BE POSSIBLE. BUT AT THE MOMENT THERE ISN'T MUCH HAPPENING IN THAT DIRECTION.[67]

JOHN: We didn't make any images for ourselves. You did the image-making – the papers, TV, and all that. I've never cared a toss about images. There's this big scoop about the new-look Lennon being photographed at the airport or somewhere. Who cares? I don't. If some photographer wants to take pictures of me and say that I've changed, let him. I'm there. I'm only answered to myself. Nobody else.[67]

NEIL ASPINALL: *I used to share a flat in Sloane Street with Mal. One day in February Paul called, saying that he was writing a song and asking if he and Mal could come over. The song was the start of 'Sgt Pepper'.*

*At my place he carried on writing and the song developed. At the end of every Beatles show, Paul used to say, 'It's time to go. We're going to go to bed, and this is our last number.' Then they'd play the last number and leave. Just then Mal went to the bathroom, and I said to Paul, 'Why don't you have Sgt Pepper as the compère of the album? He comes on at the beginning of the show and introduces the band, and at the end he closes it. A bit later, Paul told John about it in the studio, and John came up to me and said, 'Nobody likes a smart-arse, Neil.'*

GEORGE MARTIN: *The idea came about gradually. Basically it was Paul's idea: he came in and said he had the song 'Sgt Pepper's Lonely Hearts Club Band' and that he was identifying it with the band, with The Beatles themselves. We recorded the song first, and then the thought came to make it into an idea for the album. It was at a time when they wanted to concentrate on the studio, and that probably fomented the idea of the alter-ego group: 'Let Sgt Pepper do the touring.'*

PAUL: We would be Sgt Pepper's band, and for the whole of the album we'd pretend to be someone else. So, when John walked up to the microphone to sing, it wouldn't be the new John Lennon vocal, it would be whoever he was in this *new* group, his fantasy character. It liberated you – you could do anything when you got to the mike or on your guitar, because it wasn't *you*.

RINGO: The album was always going to have 'Sgt Pepper' at the beginning; and if you listen to the first two tracks, you can hear it was going to be a show album. It was Sgt Pepper and his Lonely Hearts Club Band with all these other acts, and it was going to run like a rock opera. It had started out with a feeling that it was going to be something totally different, but we only got as far as Sgt Pepper and Billy Shears (singing 'With A Little Help From My Friends'), and then we thought: 'Sod it! It's just two tracks.' It still kept the title and the feel that it's all connected, although in the end we didn't actually connect all the songs up.

JOHN: *Sgt Pepper* is called the first concept album, but it doesn't go anywhere. All my contributions to the album have absolutely nothing to do with this idea of Sgt Pepper and his band; but it works, because we *said* it worked, and that's how the album appeared. But it was not put together as it sounds, except for Sgt Pepper introducing Billy Shears, and the so-called reprise. Every other song could have been on any other album.[80]

I can't really get into writing *Tommy*. I read that Pete Townshend said that he had just a bunch of songs and they sort of melted into *Tommy* in the studio. It's like *Sgt Pepper* – a bunch of songs, and you stick two bits of *Pepper* in it and it's a concept.[75]

GEORGE: I felt we were just in the studio to make the next record, and Paul was going on about this idea of some fictitious band. That side of it didn't really interest me, other than the title song and the album cover.

RINGO: *Sgt Pepper* was our grandest endeavour. It gave everybody – including me – a lot of leeway to come up with ideas and to try different material. John and Paul would write songs at home, usually – or wherever they were – and bring them in and say, 'I've got this.' The actual writing process was getting to be separate by now, but they'd come in with bits and help each other, and we'd all help. The great thing about the band was that whoever had the best idea (it didn't matter who), that would be the one we'd use. No one was standing on their ego, saying, 'Well, it's mine,' and getting possessive. Always, the best was used. That's why the standard of the songs always remained high. Anything could happen, and that was an exciting process. I got to hang out and listen to it unfolding, although I wasn't there every day.

GEORGE MARTIN: *I'd been involved in a lot of avant-garde type recordings, and I did a lot of experimenting in the early days – long before Beatles – with electronic tracks and* musique concrète. *I introduced The Beatles to some new sounds and ideas; but when* Sgt Pepper *came along, they wanted every trick brought out of the bag. Whatever I could find, they accepted.*

RINGO: As we got up to *Sgt Pepper*, George Martin had really become an integral part of it all. We were putting in strings, brass, pianos, etc., and George was the only one who could write it all down. He was also brilliant. One of them would mention: 'Oh, I'd like the violin to go "de de diddle",' or whatever, and George would catch it and put it down. He became part of the band.

John, Paul and George – the writers – were putting whatever they wanted on the tracks, and we were spending a long time in the studio. We were still recording the basic tracks as we always did, but it would take weeks to do the overdubs for the strings or whatever, and then the percussion would be overdubbed later and later. *Sgt Pepper* was great for me, because it's a fine album – but I did learn to play chess while we were recording it (Neil taught me).

GEORGE: It was becoming difficult for me, because I wasn't really that *into* it. Up to that time, we had recorded more like a band; we would learn the songs and then play them (although we were starting to do overdubs, and had done a lot on *Revolver*). *Sgt Pepper* was the one album where things were done slightly differently. A lot of the time it ended up with just Paul playing the piano and Ringo keeping the tempo, and we weren't allowed to play as a band so much. It became an assembly process – just little parts and then overdubbing – and for me it became a bit tiring and a bit boring. I had a few moments in there that I enjoyed, but generally I didn't really like making the album much.

I'd just got back from India, and my heart was still out there. After what had happened in 1966, everything else seemed like hard work. It was a job, like doing something I didn't really want to do, and I was losing interest in being 'fab' at that point.

Before then everything I'd known had been in the West, and so the trips to India had really opened me up. I was into the whole thing; the music, the culture, the smells. There were good and bad smells, lots of colours, many different things – and that's what I'd become used to. I'd been let out of the confines of the group, and it was difficult for me to come back into the sessions. In a way, it felt like going backwards. Everybody else thought that *Sgt Pepper* was a revolutionary record – but for me it was not as enjoyable as *Rubber Soul* or *Revolver*, purely because I had gone through so many trips of my own and I was growing out of that kind of thing.

Throughout that period I was quite close to John (although people always saw the Lennon-McCartney aspect). We were the ones that had had 'The Dental Experience' together.

NEIL ASPINALL: *Spending six months on* Sgt Pepper *did allow them to experiment more, and take more time over the record. Sometimes being stuck together in the same place for too long can have an adverse effect; it can tend to be a bit disruptive rather than pulling things together. But that didn't happen; everything was OK – although it did get a bit boring for me, really.*

JOHN: I never took it [LSD] in the studio. Once I did, actually. I thought I was taking some uppers and I was not in the state of handling it. I took it and I suddenly got so scared on the mike. I said, 'What is it? I feel ill.' I thought I felt ill and I thought I was going cracked. I said I must go and get some air. They all took me upstairs on the roof, and George Martin was looking at me funny, and then it dawned on me that I must have taken some acid.

I said, 'Well, I can't go on. You'll have to do it and I'll just stay and watch.' I got very nervous just watching them all, and I kept saying, 'Is this all right?' They had all been very kind and they said, 'Yes, it's all right.' I said, 'Are you sure it's all right?' They carried on making the record.[70]

We didn't really shove the LP full of pot and drugs but, I mean, there *was* an effect. We were more consciously trying to keep it out. You wouldn't say, 'I had some acid, baby, so groovy,' but there *was* a feeling that something had happened between *Revolver* and *Sgt Pepper*. (Whether it would have happened anyway is pure speculation.)[68]

GEORGE MARTIN: *I was aware of them smoking pot, but I wasn't aware that they did anything serious. In fact, I was so innocent that I actually took John up to the roof when he was having an LSD trip, not knowing what it was. If I'd known it was LSD, the roof would have been the last place I would have taken him.*

*He was in the studio and I was in the control room, and he said he wasn't feeling too good. So I said, 'Come up here,' and asked George and Paul to go on overdubbing the voice. 'I'll take John out for a breath of fresh air,' I said, but of course I couldn't take him out the front because there were 500 screaming kids who'd have torn him apart. So the only place I could take him to get fresh air was the roof. It was a wonderful starry night, and John went to the edge, which was a parapet about eighteen inches high, and looked up at the stars and said, 'Aren't they fantastic?' Of course, to him I suppose they would have been especially fantastic. At the time they just looked like stars to me.*

*I suppose I was a big brother to them. I was fourteen years older than they were. I guess I was straight, and they knew I disapproved very strongly of drugs (although I'm afraid I used to smoke cigarettes, and that's pretty well as bad). They never smoked pot in front of me; they used to nip down to the canteen below and have a little drag and come out giggling a bit. I knew what they were doing, but it didn't make any difference.*

RINGO: The song 'With A Little Help From My Friends' was written specifically for me, but they had one line that I wouldn't sing. It was: 'What would you do if I sang out of tune? Would you stand up and throw tomatoes at me?' I said, 'There's not a chance in hell am I going to sing this line,' because we still had lots of really deep memories of the kids throwing jelly beans and toys on stage; and I thought that if we ever did get out there again, I was *not* going to be bombarded with tomatoes.

JOHN: Paul had the line about 'little help from my friends'. He had some kind of structure for it – and we wrote it pretty well fifty/fifty based on his original idea.[70]

RINGO: 'Lucy In The Sky With Diamonds' and all the madness that went on around it was absolutely bonkers. I was actually with John when Julian came in with this little kid's painting, a crazy little painting, and John (as the dad) said, 'Oh, what's that?' and Julian said, 'It's Lucy in the sky with diamonds.' And then John got busy.

PAUL: I showed up at John's house and he had a drawing Julian had done at school with the title 'Lucy in the Sky with Diamonds' above it. Then we went up to his music room and wrote the song, swapping psychedelic suggestions as we went. I remember coming up with 'cellophane flowers' and 'newspaper taxis' and John answered with things like 'kaleidoscope eyes' and 'looking glass ties'. We never noticed the LSD initial until it was pointed out later – by which point people didn't believe us.

JOHN: I saw Mel Tormé introducing a Lennon-McCartney show, saying how 'Lucy In The Sky With Diamonds' was about LSD. It never was, and nobody believes me. I swear to God, or swear to Mao, or to anybody you like, I had no idea it spelt LSD. *This* is the *truth*: my son came home with a drawing and showed me this strange-looking woman flying around. I said, 'What is it?' and he said, 'It's Lucy in the sky with diamonds,' and I thought, 'That's beautiful.' I immediately wrote a song about it. And the song had gone out, the whole album had been published, and somebody noticed that the letters spelt out LSD. I had no idea, and of course after that I was checking all the songs to see what the letters spelt out. They didn't spell out anything, none of the others. It wasn't about that at all.[71]

The images were from *Alice in Wonderland*. It was Alice in the boat. She is buying an egg and it turns into Humpty-Dumpty. The woman serving in the shop turns into a sheep, and the next minute they're rowing in a rowing boat somewhere – and I was visualising that. There was also the image of the female who would someday come save me – 'a girl with kaleidoscope eyes' who would come out of the sky. It's *not* an acid song.[80]

GEORGE: I liked 'Lucy In The Sky With Diamonds' a lot. John always had a way of having an edge to his songs. I particularly liked the sounds on it where I managed to superimpose some Indian instruments onto the Western music. There were specific things that I had written, like 'Within You Without You', to try to feature the Indian instruments; but under normal circumstances that wouldn't work on a Western song like 'Lucy', which has chord changes and modulations (whereas tambouras and sitars stay in the same key forever). I liked the way the drone of the tamboura could be fitted in there.

There was another thing: during vocals in Indian music they have an instrument called a sarangi, which sounds like the human voice, and the vocalist and sarangi player are more or less in unison in a performance. For 'Lucy' I thought of trying that idea, but because I'm not a sarangi player I played it on the guitar. In the middle eight of the song you can hear the guitar playing along with John's voice. I was trying to copy Indian classical music.

PAUL: There were all sorts of ideas: 'Let's use bass harmonicas on this,' or, 'Let's use comb and paper on this. Hey, we used to do that when we were kids, that's a laugh.'

GEORGE: John got the idea for 'Mr Kite' when we were filming in Sevenoaks in Kent. We had a lunch break, and we went in an antique shop on the way to the restaurant. We were looking around when John came out of the shop with a little poster which had more or less the whole lyric of the song 'Being For The Benefit Of Mr Kite!' on it.

JOHN: It was from this old poster for an old-fashioned circus from the 1800s that I'd bought at an antique shop. We'd been filming a TV piece to go with 'Strawberry Fields Forever'. There was a break and I went into this shop and bought an old poster advertising a variety show which starred Mr Kite.

It said the Hendersons would also be there, late of Pablo Fanques Fair. There would be hoops and horses and someone going through a hogshead of real fire. Then there was Henry the Horse. The band would start at ten to six. All at Bishopsgate. I hardly made up a word, just connecting the lists together. Word for word, really.

I wasn't very proud of that. There was no real work. I was just going through the motions because we needed a new song for *Sgt Pepper* at that moment.[67] I had to write it quick because otherwise I wouldn't have been on the album.[70] [Later] there were all kinds of stories about Henry the Horse being heroin. I had never seen heroin in that period.[80]

JOHN: GEORGE HAS DONE A GREAT INDIAN ONE. WE CAME ALONG ONE NIGHT AND HE HAD ABOUT 400 INDIAN FELLAS PLAYING THERE, AND IT WAS A GREAT SWINGING EVENING, AS THEY SAY.[67]

GEORGE: 'Within You Without You' came about after I had spent a bit of time in India and fallen under the spell of the country and its music. I had brought back a lot of instruments. It was written at Klaus Voormann's house in Hampstead after dinner one night. The song came to me when I was playing a pedal harmonium.

I'd also spent a lot of time with Ravi Shankar, trying to figure out how to sit and hold the sitar, and how to play it. 'Within You Without You' was a song that I wrote based upon a piece of music of Ravi's that he'd recorded for All-India Radio. It was a very long piece – maybe thirty or forty minutes – and was written in different parts, with a progression in each. I wrote a mini version of it, using sounds similar to those I'd discovered in his piece. I recorded in three segments and spliced them together later.

JOHN: ['Within You Without You' is] one of George's best songs. One of my favourites of his, too. He's clear on that song. His mind and his music are clear. There is his innate talent; he brought that sound together.

RINGO: 'WITHIN YOU WITHOUT YOU' IS BRILLIANT

I LOVE IT.

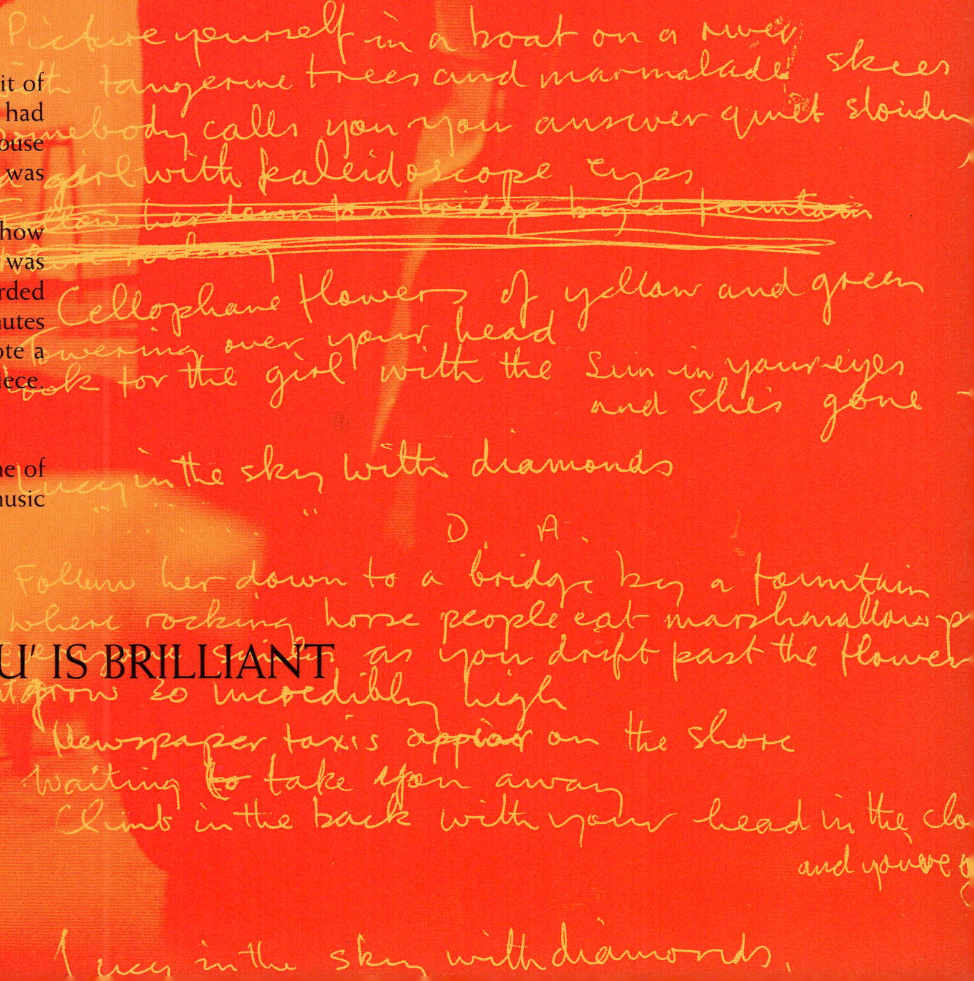

Ludwig

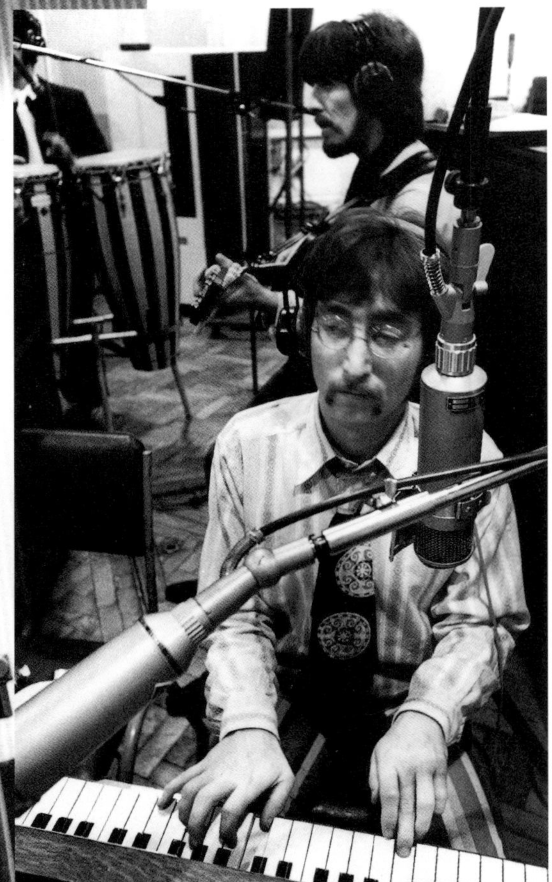

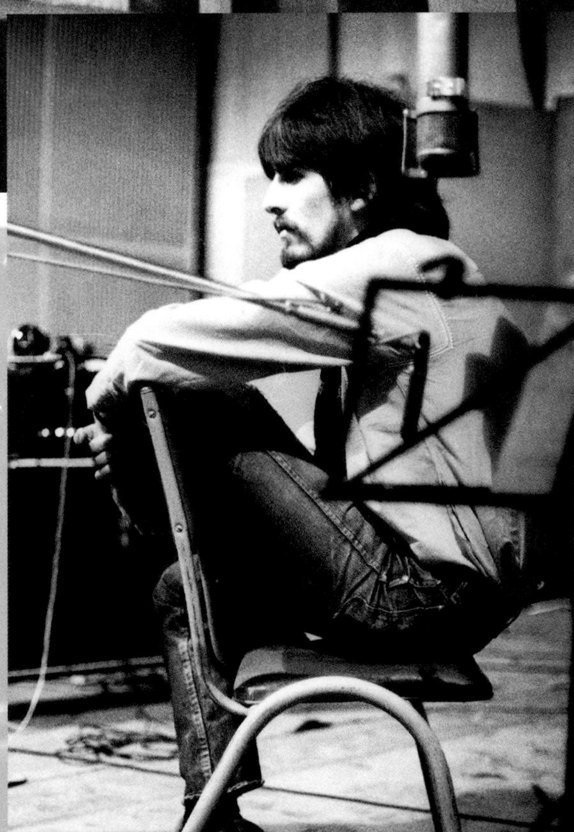

JOHN: 'When I'm Sixty-Four' was something Paul wrote in the Cavern days. We just stuck a few more words on it like 'grandchildren on your knee' and 'Vera, Chuck and Dave'. It was just one of those ones that he'd had, that we've all got, really; half a song. And this was just one that was quite a hit with us. We used to do them when the amps broke down, just sing it on the piano.[67]

PAUL: There was a story in the paper about 'Lovely Rita', the meter maid. She'd just retired as a traffic warden. The phrase 'meter maid' was so American that it appealed, and to me a 'maid' was always a little sexy thing: 'Meter maid. Hey, come and check my meter, baby.' I saw a bit of that, and then I saw that she looked like a 'military man'. The song got played around with and pulled apart, and I remember wandering around Heswall (where my dad lived and my brother now lives), trying to write the words to it. I pulled them all together and we recorded it.

JOHN: He makes them up like a novelist. You hear lots of McCartney-influenced songs on the radio – these stories about boring people doing boring things: being postmen and secretaries and writing home. I'm not interested in writing third-party songs. I like to write about me, because I *know* me.[80]

I was writing 'A Day In The Life' with the *Daily Mail* propped in front of me on the piano. I had it open at their News in Brief, or Far and Near, whatever they call it.[67] I noticed two stories. One was about the Guinness heir who killed himself in a car. That was the main headline story. He died in London in a car crash.[80]

PAUL: John got 'he blew his mind out in a car' from a newspaper story. We transposed it a bit – 'blew his mind out' was a bit dramatic. In fact, he crashed his car. But that's what we were saying about history: Malcolm Muggeridge said that all history is a lie, because every fact that gets reported gets distorted. Even in the Battle of Hastings, King Harold didn't die with an arrow in his eye; that's just what the Bayeux tapestry says – they put it in because it looked better. And now if you research Harold, you find he was off somewhere else – playing Shea Stadium, probably.

JOHN: On the next page was a story about 4,000 potholes in the streets of Blackburn, Lancashire.[80] There was still one word missing in that verse when we came to record. I knew the line had to go: 'Now they know how many holes it takes to – something – the Albert Hall.' It was a nonsense verse, really, but for some reason I couldn't think of the verb. What did the holes do to the Albert Hall? It was Terry [Doran] who said 'fill' the Albert Hall. And that was it. Perhaps I was looking for that word all the time, but couldn't put my tongue on it. Other people don't necessarily *give* you a word or a line, they just throw in the word you're looking for anyway.[67]

Paul and I were definitely working together, especially on 'A Day In The Life'. The way we wrote a lot of the time: you'd write the good bit, the part that was easy, like 'I read the news today' or whatever it was. Then when you got stuck or whenever it got hard, instead of carrying on, you just drop it. Then we would meet each other, and I would sing half and he would be inspired to write the next bit, and vice versa. He was a bit shy about it, because I think he thought it was already a good song. Sometimes we wouldn't let each other interfere with a song either, because you tend to be a bit lax with someone else's stuff; you experiment a bit.[70] Paul's contribution was the beautiful little lick in the song: 'I'd love to turn you on,' that he'd had floating around in his head and couldn't use. I thought it was a damn good piece of work.[80]

PAUL: John and I sat down, and he had the opening verse and the tune. He got the idea of how it would continue from the *Daily Mail*, where there was the mad article about the holes in Blackburn. Then the next article would be that Dame So-and-so had played the Albert Hall. So they all got mixed together in a little poetic jumble that sounded nice.

Then I threw in a little bit I played on the piano: 'Woke up, fell out of bed, dragged a comb across my head...' which was a little party piece of mine, although I didn't have any more written. Then we thought, 'Oh, we'll have an alarm clock to start it,' which we did on the session. We got Mal Evans to count out: 'Three, four – twenty-five,' and then the alarm went off and we knew that was the cue to go into the next bit of the song. We just divided it all up.

There was also the big orchestral build-up. I just sat down and thought, 'Oh, this is a great opportunity. This is the song, man!' It was a crazy song, anyway, with 'I'd love to turn you on' and lots of psychedelic references. We could go anywhere with this song; it was definitely going to go big places. I started to try to sell an idea to John: 'We take fifteen bars, just an arbitrary amount, and then we'll try something new. We'll tell the orchestra to start on whatever the lowest note on their instrument is, and to arrive at the highest note on their instrument. But to do it in their own time.' We actually put that in the score: 'From here you're on your own.'

I had to go round to all the session musicians and talk to them: 'You've got fifteen bars. If you want to go together, you can.' The trumpet players, always famous for their fondness of lubricating substances, didn't care, so they'd be there at the note ahead of everyone. The strings all watched each other like little sheep: 'Are you going up?' – 'Yes.' – 'So am I.' And they'd go up a little more, all very delicate and cosy, all going up together. But listen to those trumpets – they're just freaking out. The result was a crazy big swing storm, which we put together with all the other little ideas. It was very exciting to be doing that instead of twelve-bar blues. The whole album was made like that.

At that stage, we had just discovered stereo (which was just coming in), so we panned everything everywhere. I remember we asked why there were always little breaks between songs on a record. The engineers told us they were traditionally three seconds long, and they were there so the DJs could get their records lined up. We thought, 'You could put something in there, little funny sounds.' And then we heard the engineers talking about frequencies, and we asked about them. They said, 'Well, you've got low and high frequencies. Only your dog can hear the highest ones.' We said, 'You're kidding.' Then they told us that people had experimented with low frequencies as weapons – you can blow a city away if the right frequency is strong enough.

So we thought, 'Well, we've got to have a bit that only the dogs can hear. Why just make records for humans?' It got a bit insane and everyone added a bit more. We put those bits on the end of the record just for a laugh, really: 'Let's have a bit for Martha, Fluffy and Rover.'

JOHN: Was that the one ['A Day In The Life'] that everyone thought was something obscene, and never was? If you play it backwards and all that. We listened to it backwards and it seemed to say something obscene but we had no idea; it was just one of those things.[69]

I'd like to meet the man who banned this song of ours. I'd like to turn him on to what's happening. Why don't they charge the Electricity Board with spreading drugs because to get electricity you have to 'switch on'? Hidden meanings. Everything depends on the way you read a thing. If they want to read drugs into our stuff, they will. But it's *them* that's reading it, *them!*[67]

RINGO: People think things are hidden on the album. Well, I didn't think anything was hidden. We did put a lot of animal noises on, but a lot of the talking that was on there was only there because the state of the art was pretty primitive at that time. If we talked on one track, you could never get rid of it, and it would be moved onto the next track as you jumped across.

We did some talking that was absolutely up-front. We all went out and talked on a mike and turned it backwards. It was not as if it was that secretive; all those people who play records backwards and get something rude should play it the right way and it probably says something really nice.

GEORGE MARTIN: *In terms of asking me for particular interpretations, John was the least articulate. He would deal in moods, he would deal in colours, almost, and he would never be specific about what instruments or what line I had. I would do that myself. Paul, however, would actually sit down at the piano with me, and we'd work things out. John was more likely to say (as in the case of 'Being For The Benefit Of Mr Kite!'): 'It's a fairground sequence. I want to be in that circus atmosphere; I want to smell the sawdust when I hear that song.' So it was up to me to provide that.*

NEIL ASPINALL: *Brian was in America with his business partner, Nat Weiss. Being a bit nervous – as you sometimes are before flying – he left a note with Nat about the cover for the new album.*

GEORGE: Brian had a premonition that his plane was going to crash, so he sent a letter saying: 'Brown paper bags for *Sgt Pepper*.'

PAUL: This album was a big production, and we wanted the album sleeve to be really interesting. Everyone agreed. When we were kids, we'd take a half-hour bus ride to Lewis's department store to buy an album, and then we'd come back on the bus, take it out of the brown paper bag and *read* it cover to cover. They were the full-size albums then (not like CDs): you read them and you studied them. We liked the idea of reaching out to the record-buyer, because of our memories of spending our own hard-earned cash and really loving anyone who gave us value for money. So, for the cover, we wouldn't just have our Beatle jackets on, or we wouldn't just be suave guys in turtlenecks (looking like we did on *Rubber Soul*). It would now be much more pantomime, much more 'Mr Bojangles'.

For our outfits, we went to Berman's, the theatrical costumiers, and ordered up the wildest things, based on old military tunics. That's where they sent you if you were making a film: 'Go down to Berman's and get your soldier suits.' They had books there that showed you what was available. Did we want Edwardian or Crimean? We just chose oddball things from everywhere and put them together. We all chose our own colours and our own materials: 'You can't have that, he's having it...'

at the time, and I took the whole album-cover idea to him. He represented the artist Peter Blake, and he was very good friends with the photographer Michael Cooper. Robert said, 'Let Michael take some pictures. We'll get Peter to do a background, and then we'll collage it all together.'

I went down to Peter's house and gave him a little drawing of mine as a starting point. The cover was going to be a picture of a presentation somewhere up north: The Beatles being given the keys to the city by the mayor, beside a floral clock like the one they have in the municipal park. And then, inside the cover, we were going to be sitting there, with pictures of our favourite icons around us.

That was the original plan, but then Peter collaged it into one big idea. It all came together and we had the photo session in the evening. We had all the plants delivered by a florist; people think they're pot plants – marijuana plants – but they're not, it was all straight.

NEIL ASPINALL: *The sleeve was the result of conversations with Peter Blake. They had a list of the people they wanted standing in the background, so Mal and I went to all the different libraries and got prints of them, which Peter Blake blew up and tinted. He used them to make the collage, along with the plants and everything else you see on the cover.*

PAUL: The Fool were part of our crowd. They were a group of artists who later painted the Baker Street shop and used to make clothes for us. They had wanted to do a big psychedelic painting for the gatefold, and The Beatles loved the idea. But Robert Fraser hated it. He said, 'It's not

We went for bright psychedelic colours, a bit like the fluorescent socks you used to get in the Fifties (they came in very pink, very turquoise or very yellow). At the back of our minds, I think the plan was to have garish uniforms which would actually go against the idea of uniform. At the time everyone was into that 'I Was Lord Kitchener's Valet' thing; kids in bands wearing soldiers' outfits and putting flowers in the barrels of rifles.

JOHN: *Pepper* was just an evolvement of the Beatle boots and all that. It was just another psychedelic image. Beatle haircuts and boots were just as big as flowered pants in their time. I never felt that when *Pepper* came out, Haight-Ashbury was a direct result. It always seemed to me that they were all happening at once. Kids were already wearing army jackets on the King's Road; all we did was make them famous.[72]

PAUL: To help us get into the character of Sgt Pepper's band, we started to think about who our heroes might be: 'Well, then, who would this band like on the cover? Who would my character admire?' We wrote a list. They could be as diverse as we wanted; Marlon Brando, James Dean, Albert Einstein – or whoever. So we started choosing... Dixie Dean (an old Everton football hero I'd heard my dad talk about, I didn't really know him), Groucho Marx and so on. It got to be anyone we liked.

NEIL ASPINALL: *I remember being in the studio, and everybody was asking: 'Who do you want in the band?' All these crazy suggestions were coming out. John was talking about Albert Stubbins – and nobody quite knew who he was. He was a Liverpool centre forward.*

RINGO: *Sgt Pepper* was a special album, so when the time came for the sleeve we wanted to dress up, and we wanted to *be* these people, all the 'Peppers'. It was Flower Power coming into its fullest. It was love and peace; it was a fabulous period, for me and the world.

PAUL: We got artistic people involved. I was very good friends with Robert Fraser, the London art-dealer; a guy with one of the greatest visual eyes that I've ever met. It was a great thrill, being a friend of his

good art.' And I said, 'Well, I don't care about you, mate. You may not like it, but it's our bloody cover.' We stuck out, so The Fool did the painting. Robert kept saying, 'No, it's just not a good painting.' He did have a great eye for it, and I agree with him now, but it would have been OK for the time. Instead, Robert told us we had to have one of the big four-head photographs from the Michael Cooper session for the gatefold, and he was right. There was a lot of crossover with our friends, with everyone throwing in their twopenny worth.

When we started dreaming up ideas for the cover, the main problem was that people thought it would be too expensive. They'd never paid so much to have a cover put together. Normally it was about seventy quid: a good photographer like Angus McBean would come in and take your snap, and that would be his fee; seventy pounds.

NEIL ASPINALL: *When the cover was finished, Sir Joseph Lockwood had a meeting with Paul. I was there when he brought the album cover in. It had the flowers, the drum, the four Beatles – and a big blue sky. They'd wiped out all the people behind, because he was frightened that they might all sue or not want to be on the cover.*

PAUL: I said, 'Don't worry, Joe – it's going to be great, man.' He said, 'We'll have dozens of lawsuits on our hands – it will be absolutely terrible. The legal department is going mad with it.' I told him, 'Don't worry, just write them all a letter. I bet you they won't mind. So write to them, and *then* come back to me.'

NEIL ASPINALL: *Paul refused and said that no way would they lose all the people. In the end Brian's office wrote to everybody, saying: 'Sign here if you agree.' Everybody did, except Leo Gorcey of the Bowery Boys who wanted $500. He was on the back row, so they just put a bit of blue sky where he had been. Brian thought the sleeve was wonderful. It gave him a bit of a headache having to ask everybody's permission, but he thought the idea was great.*

GEORGE: There were those who refused to be on there, saying, 'I'm not a lonely heart,' or, 'I don't want to be on there.' Letters had to go out to get permission from everybody, and some people did turn us down.

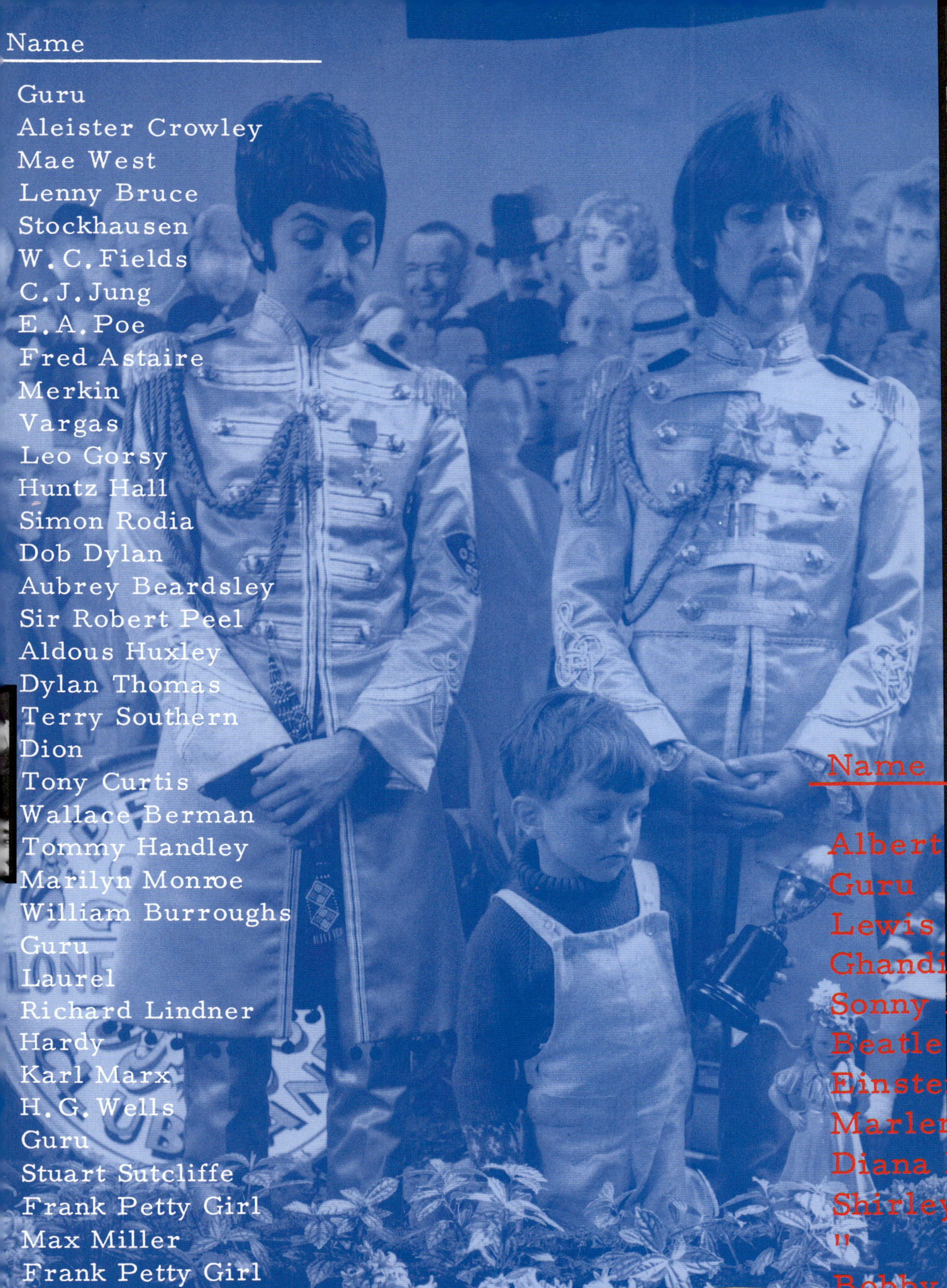

Name

Guru
Aleister Crowley
Mae West
Lenny Bruce
Stockhausen
W. C. Fields
C. J. Jung
E. A. Poe
Fred Astaire
Merkin
Vargas
Leo Gorsy
Huntz Hall
Simon Rodia
Dob Dylan
Aubrey Beardsley
Sir Robert Peel
Aldous Huxley
Dylan Thomas
Terry Southern
Dion
Tony Curtis
Wallace Berman
Tommy Handley
Marilyn Monroe
William Burroughs
Guru
Laurel
Richard Lindner
Hardy
Karl Marx
H. G. Wells
Guru
Stuart Sutcliffe
Frank Petty Girl
Max Miller
Frank Petty Girl
Marlon Brando
Tom Mix
Oscar Wilde
Tyrone Power
Larry Bell
Dr. D. Livingstone
Johnny Weissmuller
Stephen Crane
Issy Bonn
out
George Bernard Shav
out

Name

Albert Stubbins
Guru
Lewis Carroll
Ghandi
Sonny Liston
Beatles
Einstein
Marlene Deitrich
Diana Dors
Shirley Temple
" "
Bobby Breen
merican Legionn
Lawrence

I have been asked by Mr. Brian Epstein about the risks involved in this photograph.
Most of the people shouldevolve very little risk since they are dead and the photograph is probably not copyright or the copyright … ared.
The risk attaches in the case of copyrights of dead people … by proprietors
France has particularly restrictive legislation
have to be specially considered, but the damages in France are in relation to
the sort of damages paid in the United States - a cool million to a football
for a libel in the Saturday Evening Post - relatively small and should not be
specially worrying.
Robert Brownjohn
designed this letterheading
for Michael Cooper of
4 Chelsea Manor Studios
Flood Street London SW3
FLAxman 9762
INVOICE
TO
Hire and use of Michael Cooper Studios for 8 days including personnel (3 fulltime assistants) plus overtime and expenses to staff for additional work during Easter weekend
£ 625. 0. 0
54 copy negatives @ 10/6 each
28. 7. 0
54 20"x16" prints @ 17/6 each
47. 5. 0
Photography fee
SGT. PEPPER'S LONELY HEARTS BAND set and centre spread,
250. 0. 0
Art direction fee
(layout and co-ordination of sleeve and inserts, cutouts, song sheets. production of mechanical rough and artwork by Al Vandenberg for Michael Cooper Studios, including co-ordination and supervision of all aspects of design and artwork from Peter Blake and Simon & Marekka; supervision and co-ordination of printing, retouching and blockmaking)
350. 0. 0
Special fee to Peter Blake
200. 0. 0
£ 1,500.12. 0
£1,500
business and might resent their inclusion in a group of seeming "extras" to advertise a Beatle record. Also one can never be sure what complete nonentity out of the group may not cook up some allegation that the photograph has ruined him totally as his girl friend will no longer have anything to do with him, and he has been compelled to repay his overdraft.
It is too light-hearted to believe that no one will sue on account of this record or anyone will see what a splendid notion it is. There will be a
MONO
MONO/STEREO 4T
Sheet 1 of
Class :
ARTISTE(S) AND/OR CAST
THE
TITLES and MATRIX Nos.
SGT PEPPERS LONELY HEA
CLUB BA

2. MODEL RELEASES

As far as I can gather (tho have not been able to get a definite yes or not out of them) EMI only require these from living people. In France, for example, an estate can sue but in England it is not possible to libel a dead person. However, two difficulties could arise from Mrs. Dylan Thomas (who seems publicity mad) and Stuart Sutcliffe's mother.

Otherwise, here are the necessary explanations:

1. (27, 33 & 51) Have discussed the Gurus with George and we both felt, subject to another decision, the likelihood they would see the photos, let alone sue, was so remote that we have done nothing about them.

5. Stockhausen is somewhere between Davis California, Texas or Germany, am still trying to track him down.

Marlene Deitrich, c/o Marti Stephens, 1280 N. Wetherly Drive, Los Angeles, 69
wants to see picture before final 'yes'

Issy Bonn, 46A Maddock Street, London, W.1.

Bob Dylan, c/o Grossman in New York
Al Grossman, 75 East 55th Street, N.Y.

Fred Astaire, 1155 San Ysidro Drive, Beverly Hills, California

Mrs. Black, (Shirely Temple), 115 Lakeview Drive, Woodside, California
wants to see the cover (and HEAR record, said this impossible) also to receive autographed cover for her children

Johnny Weissmuller, 1700 East Oakland Park Boulevard, Fort Lauderdale, Fla.

PAUL: At that time, EMI was very much a colonial record company. It still is – they sell records in India and China – so they were/are very aware of Indian sensibilities. I remember Sir Joe (a good old mate, actually) coming round to my house in St John's Wood, and saying, 'I say, Paul, we really can't do it, old chap. You can't have Gandhi.' I said, 'Why not? We're revering him.' – 'Oh, no, no. It might be taken the wrong way. He's rather sacred in India, you know.' So Gandhi had to go.

NEIL ASPINALL: *Gandhi was sitting under the palm tree, so they just put another palm frond there in his place.*

GEORGE: I still have no idea who chose some of those people. I think Peter Blake put a lot of the more confusing people in there. It was just a broad spectrum of people. The ones I wanted were people I admired. I didn't put anybody on there because I *didn't* like them (unlike some people...)

PAUL: John wanted a couple of far-out ones like Hitler and Jesus, which was John just wanting to be bold and brassy. He was into risk-taking, and I knew what he was doing. I didn't agree with it, but he was just trying to be far out, really.

Robert Fraser and Michael Cooper were mates with The Rolling Stones, as were we, and they said, 'It would be great to have a reference to the Stones on there.' So we slung that in the corner.

JOHN: If you look closely at the album cover, you'll see two people who are flying, and two who aren't. (That's just a little 'in' joke. Two of them didn't share it with two others.)[75]

RINGO: Have a look at the cover and come to your own conclusion! There's a lot of red-eyed photos around.

PAUL: We wanted the whole of *Pepper* to be so that you could look at the front cover for years, and study all those people and read all the words on the back. And there were little hand-outs, little badges. We originally wanted to have an envelope stuck inside the sleeve with gifts in, but it became too hard to produce. It was hard enough, anyway, and the record company were having to bite the bullet: it was costing a little bit more than their usual two pence cardboard cover.

JOHN: *Sgt Pepper's Lonely Hearts Club Band* is one of the most important steps in our career. It had to be just right. We tried, and I think succeeded in achieving what we set out to do. If we hadn't, then it wouldn't be out now.[67]

GEORGE MARTIN: *Looking back on Pepper, you can see it was quite an icon. It was the record of that time, and it probably did change the face of recording; but we didn't do it consciously. I think there was a gradual development by the boys, as they tried to make life a bit more interesting on record. They felt: 'We don't have to go up onstage and do this; we can do it just for ourselves, and just for the studio.' So it became a different kind of art form – like making a film rather than a live performance. That affected their thinking and their writing, and it affected the way I put it together, too.*

*I think Pepper did represent what the young people were on about, and it seemed to coincide with the revolution in young people's thinking. It was the epitome of the Swinging Sixties. It linked up with Mary Quant and miniskirts and all those things – the freedom of sex, the freedom of soft drugs like marijuana and so on.*

JOHN: It took nine months. It wasn't nine months in the studio, but we'd work then stop a bit, work it out, rest, work... I just like to get in and get out. I get a bit bored. Generally, our other albums took three intensive weeks of work. Afterwards, we would slow down for one week, and then we could judge the whole thing. It was the most expensive [album] and, of course, the record company was screaming. They screamed at the price of the record cover, etc., etc. And now it's probably pinned all over the walls.[74]

PAUL: After the record was finished, I thought it was great. I thought it was a huge advance, and I was very pleased because a month or two earlier the press and the music papers had been saying, 'What are The Beatles up to? Drying up, I suppose.' So it was nice, making an album like *Pepper* and thinking, 'Yeah, drying up, I suppose. That's right.' It was lovely to have them on that when it came out. I loved it. I had a party to celebrate – that whole weekend was a bit of a party, as far as I recall. I remember getting telegrams saying: 'Long live *Sgt Pepper*.' People would come round and say, 'Great album, man.'

It certainly got noticed. It was released on the Friday, and on the Sunday Jimi Hendrix opened with 'Sgt Pepper' when we saw him at the Saville Theatre. That was the single biggest tribute for me. I was a big fan of Jimi's, and he'd only had since the Friday to learn it.

John was very pleased with the album. It fitted with what we were doing, and he certainly had some great tracks on it. 'A Day In The Life' is a classic.

GEORGE: I liked *Sgt Pepper* when it was finished. I knew it was different for the public, and I was very happy with the concept of the cover. 'A Day In The Life' had the big orchestra and the big piano chord, and 'Lucy In The Sky With Diamonds' I liked musically. But the rest of it was just ordinary songs.

JOHN: All the differences in *Pepper* were in retrospect. It wasn't sitting there thinking, 'Oh, we've had LSD,' so tinkle, tinkle...[67]

In those days, reviews weren't very important – because we had it made whatever happened. Nowadays, I'm as sensitive as shit, and every review counts. But those days, we were too big to touch. I don't remember the reviews at all. We were so blasé, we never even read the news clippings. I didn't bother with them or read anything about us. It was a bore.[70]

RINGO: *Sgt Pepper* seemed to capture the mood of that year, and it also allowed a lot of other people to kick off from there and to really go for it. When that album came out the public loved it. It was a monster. *Everybody* loved it, and they all admitted it was a really fine piece of work. Which it was.

While we were making the album, they thought we were actually in there self-indulging, just in the studio as the Fabs. Like in the movies, where people get famous and then end up in the studio writing huge operas that never work out. We, however, were actually in there recording this fine body of work, and making, I believe, one of the most popular albums ever.

PAUL: Other people were starting to get interested in what we were doing. I always felt that the Stones took our lead and followed. We would do a certain thing, like *Pepper*, then a year later they would do *Satanic Majesties*. There were others, Donovan for example, who were making some pretty funky little records at the time, but I don't think anyone was getting into the art and craziness of instrumentation as much as we were.

The biggest influence, as I've said a lot of times, was the Beach Boys' *Pet Sounds* album, and it was basically the harmonies that I nicked from there. Again it wasn't really avant-garde, it was just straight music, surf music – but stretched a bit, lyrically and melodically.

JOHN: When you get down to it, it was nothing more than an album called *Sgt Pepper* with the tracks stuck together. It was a beautiful idea then, but it doesn't mean a thing now.

I actively dislike bits of them which didn't come out right. There are bits of 'Lucy In The Sky' I don't like. Some of the sound in 'Mr Kite' isn't right. I like 'A Day In The Life', but it's still not half as nice as I thought it was when we were doing it. I suppose we could have worked harder on it, but I couldn't be arsed doing any more. 'Sgt Pepper' is a nice song, 'Getting Better' is a nice song, and George's 'Within You Without You' is beautiful. But what else is on it musically besides the whole concept of having tracks running into each other?[67]

PAUL: The mood of the album was in the spirit of the age, because we ourselves were fitting into the mood of the time. The idea wasn't to *do* anything to cater for that mood – we happened to be *in* that mood anyway. And it wasn't just the general mood of the time that influenced us; I was searching for references that were more on the fringe of things. The actual mood of the time was more likely to be The Move, or Status Quo or whatever – whereas outside all of that there was this avant-garde mode, which I think was coming into *Pepper*.

There was definitely a movement of people. All I am saying is: we weren't really trying to cater for that movement – *we were just being part of it*, as we always had been. I maintain The Beatles weren't the leaders of the generation, but the spokesmen. We were only doing what the kids in the art schools were all doing. It was a wild time, and it feels to me like a time warp – there we were in a magical wizard-land with velvet patchwork clothes and burning joss sticks, and here we are now soberly dressed.

GEORGE: The summer of 1967 was the Summer of Love for us. There were music festivals, and everywhere we went people were smiling and sitting on lawns drinking tea. A lot of it was bullshit; it was just what the press was saying. But there was definitely a vibe: we could feel what was going on with our friends – and people who had similar goals in America – even though we were miles away. You could just pick up the vibes, man.

RINGO: Of course the scene was a very small world – England, America, Holland and France – but we're talking about major cities. I had a guy working for me in Weybridge, the artist Paul Dudley, and when he was around me he had his beads on and his Afghan – but when he went back up North he put his brown suit on. A lot of Flower Power didn't translate in, say, Oldham or Bradford, and not really in Liverpool. But I felt it was universal, anyway.

PAUL: The year 1967 seems rather golden. I've got memories of bombing around London to all the clubs and the shops – of going down the King's Road, Fulham Road and to Chelsea and Mason's Yard (where we had the Indica art gallery and book store). It always seemed to be sunny and we wore the far-out clothes and the far-out little sunglasses. The rest of it was just music. Maybe calling it the Summer of Love is a bit too easy; but it *was* a golden summer.

There were posters coming in from San Francisco; all those psychedelic posters were great. George went to San Francisco that year, and I made a similar trip. It was a straight 'hello, hi there' visit: I woke Grace Slick up one morning, and I met Jack Casady of Jefferson Airplane, among others. I simply went there to see what the place was all about, just before the tour buses moved into Haight-Ashbury.

DEREK TAYLOR: *I'd left The Beatles in December 1964, and gone to live in Hollywood for three years. Things had got very 'successful', which means I took on too much: The Byrds, Beach Boys, Van Dyke Parks, Mamas and Papas, Chad and Jeremy – the intelligent side of US pop – and so I'd dropped out because it was all too much.*

*Then, to keep active, I became one of the three founders of the first International Pop Festival at Monterey which was to take place in June 1967. Very soon we had a billboard up outside our nice little gimcrack offices, and the first name on it was Petula Clark. Since we had already secured the Monterey showground for three days – five concerts at 8,000 seats each – filling the rest of the bill was a matter of some urgency. And now we had to ask ourselves, 'Why are we doing a festival? Why should anyone make any money out of it?' The festival should be for people, for music, love and, yes, flowers. That was my slogan and we were to put it on bumper stickers, posters and make it all come true. The festival became a charitable affair with no one being paid for appearing.*

*The preparations were easier to deal with because of the LSD experience; now it really was Music, Love and Flowers, not only on the bumper stickers but also in the air and in the offices and even on the telephone. We succeeded in eliminating the word 'problem' (as in 'Problem: how do we feed 8,000 people?'), not by pretending that things couldn't go wrong – we would never have got the festival into shape if we had lost our sense of reality – but by refusing absolutely to become 'hung up'.*

*My own time was spent knee-deep in the hardest of work, and I stayed very straight through all of it. The worst people to deal with, at first, were the police and the city fathers and mothers. Having squared and bribed and charmed them out of the way, we then had to take on the Diggers, who believed in free food and drink and music for all, man, and the Hell's Angels (free beer and dope for us, man) and finally other acid-heads who, previously drugged out of harm's way, now decided that they would take over 'security' and let everyone into the festival. 'Hey, man, why not?'*

*The police and fire departments, extremely negative at first, found they had nothing at all to trouble them and it soon became so cool and easy and peaceable that they were handing each other flowers. I presented a glass-prism necklace to the chief of police at the final press conference. 'This is from us to you and it makes us one,' I said without cracking up, and he took it without embarrassment. Imagine such times… I wonder if you can. It did happen in Monterey, a long time ago.*

*Musically, the festival was stunning beyond description. Almost all of the artists were beyond praise, not only for their offer of free services, but for the power of their performance. Anyone who saw every show – and I didn't because I was too busy – saw a parade of popular music stars that will never be equalled. Cloud-cuckoo-land? No! An earthly paradise? You bet! Every generation should be so lucky.*

PAUL: John Phillips and some others came to see me in London, asking if The Beatles would perform at Monterey. I said we couldn't, but recommended Jimi Hendrix. They'd never heard of him: 'Is he any good?' Jimi played it, and he was great.

GEORGE: I wasn't there and didn't know anything about it. We just took acid in St George's Hill and wondered what it could have been like.

PAUL: AFTER I TOOK IT, IT OPENED MY EYES. WE ONLY USE ONE-TENTH OF OUR BRAIN. JUST THINK WHAT WE COULD ALL ACCOMPLISH IF WE COULD ONLY TAP THAT HIDDEN PART. IT WOULD MEAN A WHOLE NEW WORLD. IF THE POLITICIANS WOULD TAKE LSD, THERE WOULDN'T BE ANY MORE WAR OR POVERTY OR FAMINE.

JUL 29 1967

## British Minister Of State Horrified By Beatle's Views

LONDON (UPI)—A woman government minister said Friday she was horrified by Beatle Paul McCartney's views on drugs.

"I was in the hairdressers yesterday and this magazine was passed to me to while away the time while I was under the hair dryer," said Miss Alice Bacon, minister of state at the Home Office, during a parliamentary debate on drug-taking.

"There was a long article in it called 'The Love Generation,' and statements from various people who are pop singers and managers of pop groups. I just say I was horrified by some of the things I read in it," she said.

She added McCartney had said God was in everything and he had realized this from LSD. Beatle Manager Brian Epstein had said he was wholeheartedly on the side of hallucinatory drugs, according to Miss Bacon.

Miss Bacon said: "Our young people do take what some of these pop stars say quite seriously.

"What sort of society are we going to create if everyone wants to escape from reality into a dream world?"

PAUL: When acid came around, we heard that you were never the same after you took it – it alters your life, and you can never think in the same way again. I think John was rather excited by this prospect, but I was rather frightened by it. 'Just what I need,' I thought. 'I'm going to have some funny little thing, and then I'll never be able to get back home again. Oh Jeez!'

So I delayed, and I think I was seen to stall a little bit within the group. Talk about peer pressure! I mean, The Beatles had got to be one of the ultimate peer pressures going; they were my mates, my fellow musicians. I remember in 1965 we'd had a few days off in Los Angeles and had hired a house in Hollywood. John, George and Ringo took acid there, but I wouldn't do it that day. It took me quite a while to get round to it, until I eventually thought, 'We can't all be in The Beatles, with me being the only one who hasn't taken it.'

On 19th June 1967, I was interviewed by ITN about drug-taking. That would be the day after my birthday – how wonderful for me! I remember a couple of men from ITN showed up, and then the newscaster arrived: 'Is it true you've had drugs?' They were at my door – I couldn't tell them to go away – so I thought, 'Well, I'm either going to try to bluff this, or I'm going to tell him the truth.' I made a lightning decision: 'Sod it. I'll give them the truth.'

I spoke to the reporter beforehand, and said, 'You know what's going to happen here: I'm going to get the blame for telling everyone I take drugs. But *you're* the people who are going to distribute the news.' I said, 'I'll tell *you*. But if you've got any worries about the news having an effect on kids, then don't show it. I'll tell you the truth, but if you disseminate the whole thing to the public then it won't be my responsibility. I'm not sure I want to preach this but, seeing as you're asking – yeah, I've taken LSD.' I'd had it about four times at that stage, and I told him so. I felt it was reasonable, but it became a big news item.

JOHN: Who gave the drugs to The Beatles? I didn't invent those things. I bought it from someone who got it from somebody. We never *invented* the stuff.

The big story about The Beatles and LSD came from when the British TV interviewed Paul and said, 'Have you ever taken LSD?' Paul said 'yes', and then the press said, 'And do you feel any responsibility about announcing this?' Paul said, 'Yes. Don't put the film out.' And, of course, they showed the whole film. The same type of people five years later are saying, 'Paul McCartney and The Beatles are propagating drugs.' We didn't do it. How dare they say *we* propagated it, when they twisted everything we did?[75]

I don't think we did anything to kids – anything somebody does, they do to themselves.[72] I never felt any responsibility, being a so-called idol. It's wrong of people to expect it. What they are doing is putting their responsibilities on us, as Paul said to the newspapers when he admitted taking LSD. If they were worried about him being responsible, *they* should have been responsible enough and not printed it, if they were genuinely worried about people copying.[67] There's an illusion that just because somebody buys your record that they're going to do what you tell them. It doesn't work that way.[75]

PAUL: I don't know whether people attacked me for it. It was half and half. A lot of people knew it was going on that year. My friends would say, 'Wow! I hear you told the news,' or something. I'm sure the newspapers attacked me for it, but I made a big disclaimer beforehand because I didn't want to excite people into taking LSD. I think even on the interview I mention that.

We had all taken it by then, and it was just that they happened to ask me. If they'd asked any of our friends, they would have said the same thing. I lived the most locally, I think: I was the shortest trip from ITN.

JOHN: I don't think there's any truth coming over about what's happening at all. The only true thing in a newspaper is the name of the newspaper. I'm not saying they're intentionally evil; they just can't control it. They just won't allow the truth to come out, so there's something wrong with the system.

Television is a little better, but it is still under the influence of the system that doesn't allow the truth to come out. You've still got a system which restricts and inhibits people speaking their minds. We can speak our minds now, but there will be limits imposed and rules which are to safeguard something or other. But safeguarding it has a side effect. And the choice is where to draw the line. We couldn't describe making love to somebody, because the system doesn't allow that.[68]

GEORGE: It was all over the newspapers. The press had a field day. I thought Paul should have been quiet about it – I wish he hadn't said anything, because it made everything messy. People were bugging us about it for ages. Somebody must have heard a rumour and then gone to ask him about it.

It seemed strange to me, because we'd been trying to get him to take LSD for about eighteen months – and then one day he's on the television talking all about it.

JOHN: He always times his big announcements right on the letter, doesn't he?[72]

PAUL: The others always thought I had announced it on purpose. The truth was that I got caught on camera by a news team and had to decide quickly whether to tell the truth or not.

RINGO: We weren't actually telling anybody about LSD, bar the people who knew us, and Paul decided to come out and tell people. He always mentioned things like that. Public reaction was pretty mixed. The problem was that it gave the press an excuse to be on all our cases. I personally didn't think it was any of their business; but once Paul said it (and this applied to anything anyone ever said in The Beatles), the other three had to deal with it – which we did with all love, because we loved each other. But I could have done without it, myself.

The press started asking all those questions: 'Do you think it's right to take drugs, because the public do what you say?' In those days, we felt everyone should be doing it. I felt they should all be smoking grass and taking acid. I was twenty-seven years old, and that's what I was doing. It was the drug of love – love towards our fellow man or woman.

JOHN: We don't give instructions on how to live your life. The only thing we can do – because we're in the public eye – is to reflect what we do, and they can judge for themselves what happens to us. If they're using us as a guideline, we can only try and do what's right for us and therefore, we hope, right for them.[68]

PAUL: I ADMIT THERE ARE DANGERS IN TAKING IT, BUT I TOOK IT WITH A DELIBERATE PURPOSE IN MIND: TO FIND THE ANSWER TO WHAT LIFE IS ALL ABOUT.

you
love is all
love is all
you need
ove is all you need love is all you need love is all yo
love is
all you
need
love is
all you
need
ove is all you need love is all
all you
love is
you need love is all you need
need
love is a
you neec
ove is all you need love is all
love is all
you neec
love is all
ALL
TOUT
YOU
POUR
NEED
VOUS
LIEBE
LOVE
ЛЮБОВ
AMOR
AMORE
you need love is all you need
you need love is all you need love is all
you need love is all you need love is all you need love is all you need

RINGO: WE WERE BIG ENOUGH TO COMMAND AN AUDIENCE OF THAT SIZE, AND IT WAS FOR LOVE. IT WAS FOR LOVE AND BLOODY PEACE. IT WAS A FABULOUS TIME. I EVEN GET EXCITED NOW WHEN I REALISE THAT'S WHAT IT WAS FOR: PEACE AND LOVE, PEOPLE PUTTING FLOWERS IN GUNS.

RINGO: The *Our World* broadcast was great, going out to hundreds of millions of people around the world. It was the first worldwide satellite broadcast ever. It's a standard thing that people do now; but then, when we did it, it was a first. That was exciting; we were doing a lot of firsts. They were exciting times.

PAUL: I stayed up all the night before the show, drawing on the shirt that I wore. I had some chemicals called Trichem – you could draw on a shirt with them, and then you could launder the shirt and the pattern stayed on. I used them a lot; many's the shirt or door I've painted with them. It was good fun. That shirt got nicked after the show; still – easy come, easy go.

GEORGE: I don't know how many millions of people saw the broadcast, but it was supposed to be a phenomenal number. It was probably the very earliest that technology enabled that kind of satellite link: they broadcast from Japan and Mexico and Canada – all over the place.

I remember the recording, because we decided to get some people in who looked like the 'love generation'. If you look closely at the floor, I know that Mick Jagger is there. But there's also an Eric Clapton, I believe, in full psychedelic regalia and permed hair, sitting right there. It was good: the orchestra was there and it was played live. We rehearsed for a while, and then it was: 'You're on at twelve o'clock, lads.' The man upstairs pointed his finger and that was that. We did it – one take.

NEIL ASPINALL: *It was a professional shoot. I remember camera crews and a lot of colourful people. It was psychedelic and all the rest of it, but the BBC filmed it in black and white! If we'd have known that, we'd have filmed it ourselves.*

RINGO: We loved dressing up, and we had suits made for the show. Simon and Marijke from The Fool made mine. It was so bloody heavy, I had all this beading on and it weighed a ton.

You can see the happy faces. I had Keith Moon next to me. Everyone was joining in – it was a fabulous time, both musically and spiritually. And for that show, the writers of the song were masters at hitting the nail on the head.

PAUL: The Beatles sang 'All You Need Is Love'. It was John's song, mainly; one of those we had around at the time. It fits very well, so it might have been written especially for the show (and once we had it, it was certainly tailored to suit the programme). But I've got a feeling it was just one of John's songs that was coming anyway. We went down to Olympic Studios in Barnes and recorded it, and everyone said, 'Ah, this is the one we should use for the show.'

BRIAN EPSTEIN: *I've never had a moment's worry that they wouldn't come up with something marvellous. The commitment for the TV programme was arranged some months ago. The time got nearer and nearer, and they still hadn't written anything. Then, about three weeks before the programme, they sat down to write. The record was completed in ten days.*

*This is an inspired song, because they wrote it for a worldwide programme and they really wanted to give the world a message. It could hardly have been a better message. It is a wonderful, beautiful, spine-chilling record.*

PAUL: It goes back a little in style to our earlier days, I suppose, but it's really next time around on the spiral. I'd sum it up as taking a look back with a new feeling.[67]

JOHN: We just put a track down. Because I knew the chords I played it on whatever it was, harpsichord. George played a violin because we felt like doing it like that and Paul played a double bass. And they can't play them, so we got some nice little noises coming out. It sounded like an orchestra, but it's just them two playing the violin and that. So then we thought, 'Ah, well, we'll have some more orchestra around this little freaky orchestra that we've got.' But there was no perception of how it sounded at the end until they did it that day, until the rehearsal. It still sounded a bit strange then.[80]

GEORGE MARTIN: *John wrote 'All You Need Is Love' especially for the television show. Brian suddenly whirled in and said that we were to represent Britain in a round-the-world hook-up, and we'd got to write a song. It was a challenge. We had less than two weeks to get it together, and then we learnt there were going to be over 300 million people watching, which was for those days a phenomenal figure. John came up with the idea of the song, which was ideal, lovely.*

GEORGE: Because of the mood of the time, it seemed to be a great idea to perform *that* song while everybody else was showing knitting in Canada or Irish clog dances in Venezuela. We thought, 'Well, we'll sing "All You Need Is Love", because it's a subtle bit of PR for God.' I don't know if the song was written before that, because there were lots of songs in circulation at the time.

GEORGE MARTIN: *In arranging it, we shoved 'La Marseillaise' on the front, and a whole string of stuff on the end. I fell into deep water over that. I'm afraid that amongst all the little bits and pieces I used in the play-out (which the boys didn't know about) was a bit of 'In The Mood'. Everyone thought 'In The Mood' was in the public domain, and it is – but the introduction isn't. The introduction is an arrangement, and it was the introduction I took. That was a published work. EMI came to me and said: 'You put this in the arrangement, so now you've got to indemnify us against any action that might be taken.' I said, 'You must be joking. I got fifteen pounds for doing that arrangement, that's all.' They saw the joke. I think they paid a fee to Keith Prowse, or whoever the publisher was, and I wrote the arrangements out. 'Greensleeves' was also there (at half tempo) to weave in with a bit of Bach and the bit of 'In The Mood'.*

PAUL: We went around to EMI for the show. We'd done a lot of pre-recording, so we sang live to the backing track. We'd worked on it all with George Martin's help, and it was a good day. We went in there early in the morning to rehearse with the cameras, and there was a big orchestra – for all that stuff with 'Greensleeves' playing on the way out of the song. The band was asked to invite people, so we had people like Mick and Eric, and all our friends and wifelets.

GEORGE MARTIN: *I was on camera for the broadcast. It was a bit of a panic because it was done in the big No. 1 studio at EMI. The control room was then just at the bottom of the stairs. It wasn't very large, and there was Geoff Emerick, the tape operator and myself in there. We had prepared a basic track of the recording for the television show, but we were going to do a lot live. There was a live orchestra, the singing was live, the audience certainly was, and we knew it was going to be a live television show. There was also a camera in the control room.*

*With about thirty seconds to go, there was a phone call. It was the producer of the show, saying: 'I'm afraid I've lost all contact with the studio – you're going to have to relay the instructions to them, because we're going on air any moment now.' I thought, 'My God, if you're going to make a fool of yourself, you might as well do it properly in front of 350 million people.' At that point I just laughed.*

NEIL ASPINALL: *'All You Need Is Love' went straight to Number One. I think that it expressed the mood of the time, with Flower Power and all that whole movement. It really was 'all you need is love' time.*

RINGO: In July, we all went on holiday to Greece to buy an island. We went with Alexis Mardas – 'Magic Alex'.

GEORGE: Alex wasn't magic at all, but John thought he had something, and he became friendly with us. His dad was something to do with the military in Greece, and Alex knew all the military there, very strange.

JOHN: I'm not worried about the political situation in Greece, as long as it doesn't affect us. I don't care if the government is all fascist, or communist. I don't care. They're all as bad as here; worse, most of them. I've seen England and the USA, and I don't care for either of their governments. They're all the same. Look what they do here. They stopped Radio Caroline and tried to put the Stones away while they're spending billions on nuclear armaments and the place is full of US bases that no one knows about.[67]

NEIL ASPINALL: *There was talk of getting an island. I don't know what it was all about – it was a bit silly, really. The idea was that you'd have four houses with tunnels connecting them to a central dome.*

JOHN: We're all going to live there, perhaps forever, just coming home for visits. Or it might just be six months a year. It'll be fantastic, all on our own on this island. There's some little houses which we'll do up and knock together and live communally.[67]

DEREK TAYLOR: *We were all going to live together now, in a huge estate. The four Beatles and Brian would have their network at the centre of the compound: a dome of glass and iron tracery (not unlike the old Crystal Palace) above the mutual creative/play area, from which arbours and avenues would lead off like spokes from a wheel to the four vast and incredibly beautiful separate living units. In the outer grounds, the houses of the inner clique: Neil, Mal, Terry and Derek, complete with partners, families and friends. Norfolk, perhaps; there was a lot of empty land there. What an idea! No thought of wind or rain or flood, and as for cold… there would be no more cold when we were through with the world. We would set up a chain reaction so strong that nothing could stand in our way. And why the hell not? 'They've tried everything else,' said John realistically. 'Wars, nationalism, fascism, communism, capitalism, nastiness, religion – none of it works. So why not this?'*

GEORGE: We rented a boat and sailed it up and down the coast from Athens, looking at islands. Somebody had said we should invest some money, so we thought: 'Well, let's buy an island. We'll just go there and drop out.'

It was a great trip. John and I were on acid all the time, sitting on the front of the ship playing ukuleles. Greece was on the left; a big island on the right. The sun was shining and we sang 'Hare Krishna' for hours and hours. Eventually we landed on a little beach with a village, but as soon as we stepped off the boat it started pouring with rain. There were storms and lightning, and the only building on the island was a little fisherman's cottage – so we all piled in: ''Scuse us, squire. You don't mind if we come and shelter in your cottage, do you?'

The island was covered in big pebbles, but Alex said, 'It doesn't matter. We'll have the military come and lift them all off and carry them away.' But we got back on the boat and sailed away, and never thought about the island again.

It was about the only time The Beatles ever made any money on a business venture. To make the purchase, we'd changed the money into international dollars or some currency. Then, when they changed the money back, the exchange rate had gone up and so we made about twenty shillings or so.

NEIL ASPINALL: *I was only there for a day. I said, 'I'm going home,' and so did Ringo.*

RINGO: It came to nothing. We didn't buy an island, we came home. We were great at going on holiday with big ideas, but we never carried them out. We were also going to buy a village in England – one with rows of houses on four sides and a village green in the middle. We were going to have a side each.

THAT WAS WHAT HAPPENED WHEN WE GOT OUT. IT WAS SAFER MAKING RECORDS, BECAUSE ONCE THEY LET US OUT WE'D JUST GO BARMY.

## JOHN: IT COULDN'T MAKE IT WITH A NAME LIKE HAIGHT-ASHBURY.[68]

GEORGE: We went to America in August, a couple of months after the Monterey Pop Festival. My sister-in-law at the time, Jenny Boyd (who was Jennifer Juniper in the Donovan song), had been living in San Francisco, and she'd decided she was going to come back to live in England. We all went for a day out to see her: Derek and Neil, the not-so-magic Alex, and myself and Pattie.

NEIL ASPINALL: *Haight-Ashbury is the meeting of two streets in a part of San Francisco. We'd heard all the rumours about the hippies and the way people were behaving there, so we just decided to drop in. We were going to see Pattie's sister, and when we got to San Francisco we went to check it out. We didn't make the trip just to go to Haight-Ashbury – it was one of the stops on the way.*

GEORGE: We went up to San Francisco in a Lear jet. Derek took us to visit a disc jockey, and we went straight from the airport to the radio station in a limo. The DJ gave us some concoction and then we went off to Haight-Ashbury. I went there expecting it to be a brilliant place, with groovy gypsy people making works of art and paintings and carvings in little workshops. But it was full of horrible spotty drop-out kids on drugs, and it turned me right off the whole scene. I could only describe it as being like the Bowery: a lot of bums and drop-outs; many of them very young kids who'd dropped acid and come from all over America to this mecca of LSD.

We walked down the street, and I was being treated like the Messiah. The Beatles were pretty big, and for one of them to be there was a big event. I became really afraid, because the concoction that the DJ had given me was having an effect. I could see all the spotty youths, but I was seeing them from a twisted angle. It was like the manifestation of a scene from an Hieronymus Bosch painting, getting bigger and bigger, fish with heads, faces like vacuum cleaners coming out of shop doorways… They were handing me things – like a big Indian pipe with feathers on it, and books and incense – and trying to give me drugs. I remember saying to one guy: 'No thanks, I don't want it.' And then I heard his whining voice saying, 'Hey, man – you put me down.' It was terrible. We walked quicker and quicker through the park and in the end we jumped in the limo, said, 'Let's get out of here,' and drove back to the airport.

NEIL ASPINALL: *We were walking past bikers and hippies, and there were arguments going on. We got to the park and sat on the grass. Someone said, 'That's George Harrison,' and a crowd started to build. Somebody came to George and handed him a guitar and said, 'Will you play us a tune?' and he played a little bit. Suddenly there were too many people and we thought: 'Hey, we'd better get out of here.'*

*They started to close in, and we realised we had about a mile to go to get back to the limo. We started off at a slow walk, but soon we looked round and there were a thousand people behind us, saying, 'Give us an autograph,' and patting us on the back. We walked a bit faster, until in the end we were running for our lives.*

*We realised that maybe the drug vibe had lowered our guard, and we'd put ourselves in a situation that we'd always avoided. We'd always stayed in hotel rooms and had limos and police escorts, and the crowds had been kept back. Now we'd almost deliberately put ourselves in the middle of a situation where a crowd had developed, and there were just six of us (including two women). We made it OK. They were a happy bunch of souls, and there was no harm intended, but when there's a lot of people you can get hurt in the crush.*

DEREK TAYLOR: *Photographs tell the story of this great visit by one of the Fab Pied Pipers; it is one of the best-known moments in The Great Novel. The crowds that gathered, well-meaning though they were, pressed upon the English visitors and made life difficult and a little dangerous. George didn't enjoy Haight-Ashbury, yet it was right and inevitable that one of Them should have been there in those times.*

GEORGE: It certainly showed me what was really happening in the drug culture. It wasn't what I'd thought – spiritual awakenings and being artistic – it was like alcoholism, like any addiction. The kids at Haight-Ashbury had left school and dossed out there, and instead of drinking alcohol they were on all kinds of drugs.

That was the turning-point for me – that's when I went right off the whole drug cult and stopped taking the dreaded lysergic acid. I had some in a little bottle (it was liquid). I put it under a microscope, and it looked like bits of old rope. I thought that I couldn't put that into my brain any more.

People were making concoctions that were really wicked – ten times stronger than LSD. STP was one; it took its name from the fuel additive used in Indy-car racing. Mama Cass Elliot phoned us up and said, 'Watch out, there's this new one going round called STP.' I never took it. They concocted weird mixtures and the people in Haight-Ashbury got really fucked-up. It made me realise: 'This is not it.' And that's when I really went for the meditation.

NEIL ASPINALL: *We went back by Lear jet. At the time, I was flying in more sense than one, and suddenly I saw all these red lights coming on in the cockpit. We had taken off like a rocket, and then we started coming down just as fast, with all the warning lights flashing and the pilots saying: 'We're going to be all right, Harry.' It was quite frightening, but they got it together.*

GEORGE: I was sitting right behind the pilots; two big brown-brogue-shoed Frank Sinatras. As it took off, the plane went into a stall – we hadn't got very high before we went into a steep turn and the plane made a lurch and dropped. The whole dashboard lit up saying 'UNSAFE' right across it. I thought, 'Well, that's it.' Alex was chanting, 'Hare Krishna, Hare Krishna,' and I was saying, 'Om, Christ, Om…'

Somehow it recovered itself, and we flew down to Monterey and stopped there. We went to the beach and became calm again.

DEREK TAYLOR: *Lear jets were the passion of young pop stars then – the Porsches of the air. Personally, I found them as terrifying as any other very fast, easily-manoeuvrable vehicle, but I went anyway.*

*We went on to Monterey, and had difficulty getting coffee in a coffee-shop. When the waitress, pretending not to see us in this Lytham-St-Anne's-on-Pacific, was hailed by George ('We have got the money, you know,' he said finally, not quietly, waving a thousand dollars in bills) she recognised him and dropped every piece of crockery she was holding. Dozens of plates and saucers and cups shattered on the floor – she had collected them, too many of them, as she busied herself to avoid the cloud of denim in the corner. Things hadn't loosened up everywhere yet, it seemed.*

## GEORGE: PEOPLE WERE SO OUT OF THEIR MINDS, TRYING TO SHOVE STP ON ME, AND ACID – EVERY STEP I TOOK THERE WAS SOMEBODY TRYING TO GIVE ME SOMETHING – BUT I DIDN'T WANT TO KNOW ABOUT THAT.[67]

MAHARISHI MAHESH YOGI:

*Love is the sweet expression of life. It is the supreme content of life. Love is the force of life, powerful and sublime. The flower of life blooms in love and radiates love all around.*

GEORGE: I had seen David Wynne again, and had been talking to him about yogis. He said he had made a sketch of one who was quite remarkable, because he had a lifeline on his hands that didn't end. He showed me a photograph of this fella's hand and said, 'He's going to be in London next week doing a lecture.' So I thought: 'Well, that's good. I'd like to see him.'

On August 24th, all of us except Ringo attended the lecture given by Maharishi at the Hilton Hotel. I got the tickets. I was actually after a mantra. I had got to the point where I thought I would like to meditate; I'd read about it and I knew I needed a mantra – a password to get through into the other world. And, as we always seemed to do everything together, John and Paul came with me.

PAUL: It was George's idea to go. During *Sgt Pepper*, George was the most interested in Indian culture. We were all interested in it – but for George it was a *direction*. But it was nice to hear Ravi Shankar's music, it was interesting and very beautiful – and it was deep, technically deep.

I remember Peregrine Worsthorne being there, and I read his article the next day to see what he thought. He was a little bit sceptical. But *we* were looking for something; we'd been into drugs, and the next step was to try to find a meaning for it all.

We'd seen Maharishi up North when we were kids. He was on the telly every few years on Granada's *People and Places* programme, the local current-affairs show. We'd all say, 'Hey, did you see that crazy guy last night?' So we knew all about him: he was the giggly little guy going round the globe seven times to heal the world (and this was his third spin).

I thought he made a lot of sense; I think we all did. He said that with a simple system of meditation – twenty minutes in the morning, twenty minutes in the evening – you could improve your quality of life and find some sort of meaning in doing so.

JOHN: We thought, 'What a nice man,' and we were looking for that. I mean, everyone's looking for it, but we were all looking for it that day. We met him and saw a good thing and went along with it. Nice trip, thank you very much.

The youth of today are really looking for some answers – for proper answers the established church can't give them, their parents can't give them, material things can't give them.[68]

RINGO: At that time Maureen was in hospital having Jason, and I was visiting. I came home and put on the answerphone, and there was a message from John: 'Oh, man, we've seen this guy, and we're all going to Wales. You've got to come.' The next message was from George, saying, 'Wow, man – we've seen him. Maharishi's great! We're all going to Wales on Saturday, and you've got to come.'

JOHN: Cyn and I were thinking of going to Libya, until this came up. Libya or Bangor? Well, there was no choice, was there?[67]

GEORGE: Maharishi happened to be having a seminar in Bangor and had said, 'Come tomorrow and I'll show you how to meditate.' So, the next day we jumped on a train and went.

Mick Jagger was also there. He was always lurking around in the background, trying to find out what was happening. Mick never wanted to miss out on what the Fabs were doing.

NEIL ASPINALL: *We were all at Euston; they were getting on a train. I was going to go up in the car, because I wanted the freedom of having wheels. John's wife Cyn got left behind in the crush, and as the train left the station she was just standing there, so I drove her to Bangor that day. Some friends of mine were staying in a caravan in North Wales, and after I dropped Cyn off I went to see them. I didn't go to any of the lectures.*

PAUL: At first it was a big outing. We rang our mates: 'Hey, come and see him!' It was like a good book you'd read: 'You ought to read it. I'll send you a copy!'

I remember Cynthia not making the train, which was terrible and very symbolic. She was the only one of our party not to get there. There's a bit of film of her not making it. That was the end of her and John, really, weirdly enough. There was a big crowd at the train station, and there was another to meet us in Bangor. We all wandered through in our psychedelic gear. It was like a summer camp.

The seminar was in a school: you sit around and he tells you how to meditate, then you go up to your room and try it. And, of course, you can't do it for the first half hour. You're sitting there and you've got a mantra, but you keep thinking: 'Bloody hell, that train was a bit much, wasn't it? – oh, sorry – mantra – du du du du du du – bloody hell – I wonder what our next record's going to be? – oh, stop, stop, stop...' You spend all your first few days just trying to stop your mind dealing with your social calendar. But it was good, and I eventually got the hang of it.

JOHN: You just sit there and let your mind go; it doesn't matter what you're thinking about, just let it go. And then you introduce the mantra, the vibration, to take over from the thought. You don't will it or use your will power.[67]

GEORGE: The moment you find yourself thinking about things, then you replace that thought with the mantra again.

JOHN: There's none of this sitting in the lotus position or standing on your head. You just do it as long as you like: *'Tventy minutes a day is prescribed for ze verkers. Tventy minutes in ze morning and tventy minutes after verk.'* It makes you happy, intelligent and [gives you] more energy. I mean, look how it all started. I believe he just landed in Hawaii in his nightshirt – all on his own, nobody with him – in 1958.[68]

One of his analogies is it's like dipping a cloth into gold. You dip it in and you bring it out. If you leave it in, it gets soggy, like you're just sitting in a cave all your life. And if you bring it out, it fades. So the meditation is going in and going out and going in. So after however many years when you bring it out, it's the same.

You don't have to go to Wales and do it, or even cut yourself off from society and reality. And you don't have to get so hung up about it that you go round in a trance. I can't understand why people are so stubborn and why they're not open-minded. If the Maharishi was asking people to devote their lives to meditation, that would be different. But what possible harm can it do anyone to try for half-an-hour a day?[67]

RINGO: Maureen had had the baby and everything was really cool, so we all went to Wales to meet Maharishi. He didn't know who we were then, which was really fabulous. Only when we got off the train and he saw all the kids running, I think then he may have felt, 'Wow, things are looking up for me.' They ran right past him and were looking in our faces, and I think he realised that these boys could get his message across real fast. And so after we met him, he brought up the idea of us going on tour again and opening up a place in every city. But we didn't do that, because things began to change.

There were lots of people there – Donovan was there. Everybody was very open: 'What's happening? Let's do this, let's look at that.'

I was really impressed with the Maharishi. I was impressed because he was laughing all the time. That really struck home the first time I saw him: this man is really happy and he's having a great time in life. So we listened to his lectures, we started meditating and we were given our mantras. It was another point of view. For the first time, we were getting into Eastern philosophies – and that was another breakthrough.

JOHN: Bangor was incredible. Maharishi reckons the message will get through if we can put it across. People know us, know how we think, how we were brought up and what we've done. We'll be able to explain it to them, and they'll understand, and they know we're not trying to trick them. The thing is, that the more people who do it, perhaps one day one of them will be prime minister or something. He'd be better than Harold Wilson, anyway, wouldn't he? If there's any possibility of getting this across, it's worth it. At the very least, it can't do any harm.

What he says about life and the universe is the same message that Jesus, Buddha and Krishna and all the big boys were putting over. If you ask Maharishi for a few laws for living by, they'd be the same as Christianity. Christianity is the answer as well; it's the same thing. All the religions are all the same, it's just a matter of people opening their minds up. Buddha was a groove, Jesus was all right (but Maharishi doesn't do miracles for a kick-off). I don't know how divine or how superhuman he is. He was born quite ordinary, but he's working at it.

Even if you go into the meditation bit just curious or cynical, once you go into it, you *see*. The only thing you can do is judge on your own experience. I'm less sceptical than I ever was. Mick came up and got a sniff, and he was on the phone saying: 'Send Keith, send Brian – send them all down.' You get a sniff and you're hooked.[68]

MAHARISHI MAHESH YOGI: *They came backstage after one of my lectures, and they said to me: 'Even from an early age we have been seeking a highly spiritual existence. We tried drugs and that didn't work.' They are such practical and intelligent young boys that it took them only two days to find that Transcendental Meditation is the answer.*

JOHN: Another groovy thing: everybody gives one week's wages when they join. I think it's the fairest thing I've ever heard of. And that's all you ever pay, just the once.[68]

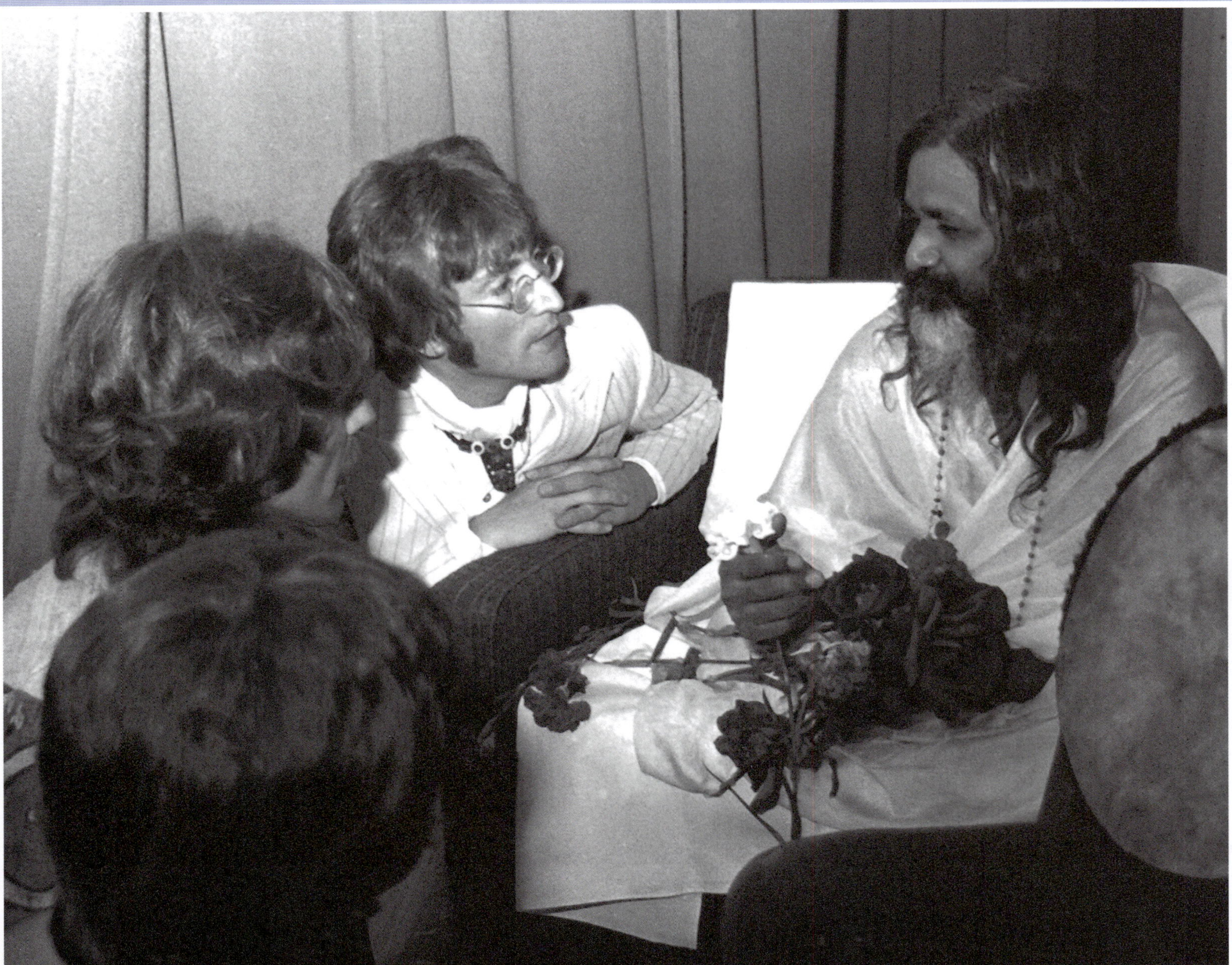

NEIL ASPINALL: Everybody *going to the Maharishi was like everybody ending up with moustaches on* Sgt Pepper. *A lot of it was follow-the-leader (whoever the leader was at the time). One got a moustache, and so everybody got a moustache. If somebody wore flared trousers, then within a couple of weeks everybody was wearing flared trousers. I think the Maharishi was in the same mode as that for some of us, but for George it was serious.*

GEORGE: I couldn't really speak for the others and their experiences, but, inasmuch as we'd collectively come through from Liverpool and gone through everything together, there *was* a collective consciousness within The Beatles. I assumed that whatever one of us felt, the others would not be far out of line with. So I handed over all the books about yogis to John, Paul and Ringo. And when we came to meet Maharishi, I got tickets for them all to go but I never really asked them what they thought or were experiencing.

In Bangor we had a press conference saying that we'd given up drugs. It wasn't really because of Maharishi. It came out of my desire to further the experience of meditation. I was doing yoga exercises anyway in order to learn how to play the sitar. I got a little bit down the line, and then Maharishi came along at the time I wanted to try meditation.

JOHN: If we'd met Maharishi before we had taken LSD, we wouldn't have needed to take it. We'd dropped drugs before this meditation thing. George mentioned he was dropping out of it, and I said, 'Well, it's not doing me any harm. I'll carry on.' But I suddenly thought: 'I've seen all that scene. There's no point, and [what] if it does do anything to your chemistry or brains?' Then someone wrote to me and said that whether you like it or not, whether you have no ill effects, something happens up there. So I decided that if I ever did meet someone who could tell me the answer, I'd have nothing left to do it with.

We don't regret having taken LSD. It was a stepping-stone. But now we should be able to experience things at first hand, instead of artificially with a wrong stepping-stone like drugs.[68]

PAUL: There was a press conference. It was suggested that as we were going with the Maharishi, it might be a good idea to accommodate the press; it also saved them waiting around outside our windows. I don't remember that we specifically said that we'd given up drugs – but at the time I think we probably had, anyway.

GEORGE: LSD isn't a real answer. It doesn't give you anything. It enables you to see a lot of possibilities that you may never have noticed before, but it isn't the answer. You don't just take LSD and that's it forever, you're OK. To get really high, you have to do it straight. I want to get high, and you can't get high on LSD. You can take it and take it as many times as you like, but you get to a point that you can't get any further unless you stop taking it.[67]

PAUL: You cannot keep on taking drugs forever. You get to the stage where you are taking fifteen aspirins a day, without having a headache. We were looking for something more natural. This is it.

It was an experience we went through. Now it's over and we don't need it any more. We think we're finding other ways of getting there.[67]

GEORGE: It helps you find fulfilment in life, helps you live life to the full. Young people are searching for a bit of peace inside themselves.[67]

JOHN: Don't believe that jazz about there's nothing you can do, and 'turn on and just drop out, man' – because you've got to turn on and drop in, or they're going to drop all over you.

GEORGE: We don't know how this will come out in the music. Don't expect to hear Transcendental Meditation all the time. We don't want this thing to come out like Cliff and Billy Graham.[67]

MAHARISHI MAHESH YOGI: *I can train them as practical philosophers of the present century, something very great and of use to the world. I see the possibility of a great future for them.*

GEORGE: I was only twenty-three when we made *Sgt Pepper*, and I'd already been through India and LSD and was on the road to transcendentalism. After having such an intense period of growing up and so much success in The Beatles and realising that this wasn't the answer to everything, the question came: 'What is it all about?' And then, purely because of the force-fed LSD experience, I had the realisation of God.

Nobody I know in the Christian religions seems to have a deep enough understanding of the science of God to be able to translate it into human terms. Church leaders are purveying a kind of nonsense because they don't really understand it themselves. So they blind you with ignorance, like a government does, as if the power of the Church has become reason enough for you not to question anything it says. It's like, 'You don't know anything about Christ and God because we're the ones who own the franchise.'

I had read enough from the Vivekenandas and Yoganandas to comprehend how to see God: by using the Yogic system of transcending through the relative states of consciousness (waking, sleeping, dreaming) to get to the most subtle level of pure consciousness. It is in that level that the individual experiences pure awareness, pure consciousness, the source of all being. We said it in 'Tomorrow Never Knows'.

The void is the transcendent, beyond waking, sleeping, dreaming. Everything in creation is the effect of that pure state of being, the transcendent or the God. God is the cause. And the effect is all three worlds: the causal, the astral and the physical.

I believe absolutely in the power of prayer, but it's like love: people say 'I love you', but it's a question of 'how deep is your love?' Maharishi used to say that if you have a bow and an arrow, and you can only pull back the bow a little, the arrow won't go far. But if you can draw the bow right back, you can get the maximum range from the arrow. With prayer, some people are so powerful at doing it that their prayers really work, whereas others might have the intention but not the ability. A strong bloke can lift a heavy weight dead easy. Another guy won't have the strength. Both have the same intention, but only one has manifested the ability to do it. For prayer to really work, you have to do it in the transcendent, as the more manifest the material world is (or the conscious level is), the less effect it has. So the power of prayer is subject to one's own spiritual development. That's why the transcendent level of consciousness is so important, and also why the mantra is so important in reaching that level. The mantra is like a prescription. If you have the right word on a prescription, you get the right medicine.

We go through life being pulled by our senses and our ego, seeking new experiences; because without experience we can't get knowledge, and without knowledge we can't gain liberation. But along the way we become entwined with ignorance and darkness because of our ego and our association with material energy. So, although we are made of God, we can't reflect God because of all the pollution that's gathered along the way; and it's such an epic battle to get all of that out of your system. A bee goes to a flower to collect pollen, and then tries to find one that's got more. It's the basic nature of the bee to seek more nectar, just as it's the soul's nature to always seek a better experience. When you've had all these experiences – met all the famous people, made some money, toured the world and got all the acclaim – you still think: 'Is that it?' Some people might be satisfied with that, but I wasn't and I'm still not.

Being in The Beatles did help speed up the process of God-realisation, but it also hindered it as there were more impressions and more entanglements to get out of. Every experience and thought has been recorded on your file within. Meditation is only a means to an end. You do it to release all the clutter out of your system, so that when it's gone you become that which you are anyway. That's the joke: we already *are* whatever it is we would like to be. All we have to do is *undo* it.

All we wanted to do was be in a rock band but, as Shakespeare said, all the world's a stage and the people are only players. We were just playing a part. Being The Beatles was like a suit that we wore for that period of time, but that isn't us really. None of us are. Our true nature is looking to re-establish that which is within. All knowing.

JOHN: ON ANY TRIPS – WHETHER THEY'RE CHEMICAL OR ANYTHING – THINGS THAT YOU DISCOVER ARE SELF-AWARENESS; ALL THE THINGS THAT YOU'VE ALREADY KNOWN. NOBODY'S TELLING YOU ANYTHING NEW. A SCIENTIST DOESN'T DISCOVER ANYTHING NEW, HE JUST TELLS YOU WHAT'S ALREADY THERE. NOBODY CAN TELL YOU NOTHING. EVEN SOMEBODY LIKE A DYLAN OR A SARTRE OR SOMEBODY LIKE THAT. THEY TELL YOU SOMETHING THAT IS LIKE A REVELATION – BUT IT ALWAYS IS SOMETHING THAT YOU KNOW INSIDE THAT THEY'VE JUST AFFIRMED FOR YOU.

JOHN: I can't find words to pay tribute to him. It is just that he was lovable, and it is those lovable things we think about now.[67]

PAUL: This is a terrible shock. I am terribly upset.[67]

RINGO: WE LOVED BRIAN. HE WAS A GENEROUS MAN. WE OWE SO MUCH TO HIM. WE HAVE COME A LONG WAY WITH BRIAN ALONG THE SAME ROAD.[67]

GEORGE: He dedicated so much of his life to The Beatles. We liked and loved him. He was one of us. There is no such thing as death. It is a comfort to us all to know that he is OK.[67]

RINGO: In Bangor we heard that Brian had died. That was a real downer because of the confusion and the disbelief: 'You're kidding me!' Your belief system gets suspended because you so badly don't want to hear it. You don't know what to do with it. If you look at our faces in the film shot at the time, it was all a bit like: 'What is it? What does it mean? Our friend has gone.' It was more 'our friend' than anything else. Brian was a friend of ours, and we were all left behind. After we arrived there with hope and flowers – now this. And then we all left – real slow.

GEORGE: There was a phone call. I don't know who took it; I think it might have been John. Blood drained from his face: 'Brian's dead.'

There was very little we knew, other than that he'd been found dead. It was very strange for it to happen at that precise moment, when we'd just got involved with meditation. That may not sound like a big deal, but it actually was. It is a very big change in your life when you start making the journey inward, and for Brian to kick the bucket that particular day was pretty far out. So we just packed up and went outside where the press were. There is footage of us saying we were 'shocked and stunned'. We got in the car and drove back to London.

PAUL: It was stunning because we were off on this 'finding the meaning of life' journey, and there he was dead. I remember us trying to deal with our grief; going for a policy talk with Maharishi to see whether he could throw any light on the matter. We said, 'Look, this is a real old friend of ours. He's been our manager for ever and ever – and he's died. Should we leave? Maybe we shouldn't stay here. What should we do, O Great One?'

And he said, 'Well, he's died. He's only passed on. It's all right, really.' That was in line with his thinking, so we had a talk with the press again and said that we were very sad – as we all were, because Brian was a great guy – but that there wasn't an awful lot you could do about it.

We were all gutted about him dying. I recall John being as shocked as all of us. Just gutted. It was sheer shock because he was one of the people we'd known longest; he was a huge confidant of ours and we knew him very well. When anyone dies like that there is the huge shock of them being wrenched out of the picture, when you think, 'I'm not going to see him any more.' I loved the guy.

JOHN: We loved him and he was one of us. Maharishi's meditation gives you confidence enough to withstand something like this, even after the short amount we've had.[67]

NEIL ASPINALL: *I remember meeting Gerry Marsden. He was on the beach at Bangor with a rubber dinghy, and it was pure coincidence that we met. I had heard on the car radio that Brian had died. I told Gerry, and it was a real shock for him. Then I went to where the guys were with the Maharishi. I said to John that Brian had died, and he said, 'I know – isn't it exciting?' and I thought, 'What?' But they were all in a state of shock.*

GEORGE MARTIN: *I was personally very fond of Brian, and I found out about it in quite a bizarre way, really. I have a country cottage (which is where I live permanently now) and after a heavy day in London I had gone down there and the local shopkeeper said, 'Sorry about the news.' I said, 'What news?' and he told me, 'Your friend has died.'*

*I hadn't known. It was just the time when my wife was having her first baby, Lucie. When she came out of hospital we went back to our flat in London, and there was a bouquet of flowers on the doorstep which hadn't been taken in. It had been sent by Brian and the flowers were dead. It was the day that we heard that Brian had died, so it was a pretty emotional time.*

RINGO: Maharishi told us not to hold on to Brian – to love him and let him go, because we are all powerful forces and we could stop him going on in the natural progression up to heaven. He said, 'You know you have to grieve for him and love him, and now you send him on his way.' And it really helped.

JOHN: We all feel very sad, but it's controlled grief and controlled emotion. As soon as I find myself feeling depressed, I think of something nice about him. But you can't hide the hurt – I went to the phone book and saw his name and it hit me a few minutes ago. The memory must be kept nice, but of course there's something inside that tells us that Brian's death is sad.

It hurts when someone close dies, and Brian was very close. We've all been through that feeling of wanting a good cry. But it wouldn't get us anywhere, would it?

We all feel it, but these talks on Transcendental Meditation have helped us to stand up to it so much better. You don't get upset when a young kid becomes a teenager, or a teenager becomes an adult, or when an adult gets old. Well, Brian is just passing into the next phase. His spirit is still around, and always will be. It's a physical memory we have of him, and as men we will build on that memory. It's a loss of genius, but other geniuses' bodies have died as well, and the world still gains from their spirits.

He was due to come up to Bangor and join us in these Transcendental Meditations with the Maharishi. It's a drag he didn't make it.[67]

RINGO: I've never thought Brian committed suicide. I've always thought Brian took his downers – that were probably prescribed by a doctor – then woke up and took some more. His night out is well documented. I feel that happened with Keith Moon, as well; just one too many downers: 'I can deal with it.' And to Jimi, Jim Morrison – all those people; I don't think any of them set out to die.

GEORGE: The last time I talked to Brian, he had gone through a change – which was inevitable. Whoever takes LSD, they change, and they don't go back to how they were before. The effect wears off over a period of time, but there's a certain change that's not going to go away. I felt with Brian that he was interested in India and in what I was thinking and feeling. Maybe he would have liked to meet Maharishi, but unfortunately it didn't work out like that.

I believe it was an accident. In those days everybody was topping themselves accidentally by taking uppers and/or amphetamine and alcohol – loads of whisky or brandy and uppers – and then they'd choke on sandwiches. That was the favourite thing, and that's the kind of thing that Brian did: he threw up and choked on the barf.

He was obviously very unhappy, and in a way the film *The Rutles* shows the situation just as much as the reality: 'Unable to raise some friends, he decided to take a teaching post in Australia.'

PAUL: I don't think there was anything sinister in his death. There were rumours of very sinister circumstances, but I personally think it was a drink-and-sleeping-pills overdose. I think what happened – and there's no evidence whatsoever except people I talk to – was that Brian was going down to his house in the country. It was a Friday night, and there were going to be friends there. Brian was gay and I think there were going to be young men at the house. Brian went down with one of his friends, but no one had showed up – so he thought: 'Ugh – it's Friday night! I've got time to get back to London if I rush. Then I can get back to the clubs.' It seems feasible to me, knowing Brian. Then he drove back up to London and went to the clubs, but they were all closing and there was not a lot of action.

So he had a few bevvies, then to console himself had a sleeping pill or two before going to bed (Brian always did that, he was quite into the pills). And then I think he woke up in the middle of the night and thought: 'My God, I can't sleep. I haven't had a pill.' Then he had a few more pills, and I think that could have killed him.

I went round a couple of days later and saw Brian's butler. He didn't seem to feel there was anything suspicious, nor that Brian was in any kind of black mood. My feeling was that it was an accident.

NEIL ASPINALL: *People had to break Brian's bedroom door down after he'd died. I don't believe he'd tried to kill himself. He was coming up the next day to Bangor.*

GEORGE MARTIN: *I had the same doctor as Brian did, and I knew the circumstances. I think that Brian used to take uppers and downers, and he used to drink a lot. He wasn't a terribly happy man.*

RINGO: Brian's role with us had changed because he wasn't booking us around the world any more. We were working in the studio; we'd make a record and the record would come out. What was there left for him to do? Book the studio – one phone call. That was the extent of it at that time.

In the beginning he was everywhere we were, and we were everywhere he was. George and I had an apartment in the same block as him in London; we would just walk in and out on each other. And then he got his place in the country and we'd go down for soirées; lovely technicoloured weekends. But then suddenly I was married with a kid; so I had a family *and* The Beatles *and* Brian, and by then he was taking third place in my book. It's just how it was, there were other priorities – and I think everyone else was feeling the same.

We were still as close to Brian as we had been in the early days. We would spend time in his house and he'd come out to us. We'd go out together. Of course, we weren't spending as much time with him because we weren't doing as much *out there* where he would come along.

GEORGE: Brian hadn't really done anything since we stopped touring. He was at a bit of a loss. We were in the studio after that, and he had never really hung out in the studio, although in the early days he might have come occasionally to hear tracks. And, with us being in the studio, there was very little for him to do with us. But we did meet him socially.

PAUL: Gradually, with The Beatles, we'd always wanted to get the tools of the art into our own hands. Even before we got into our own company, Apple, we were virtually managing ourselves. So Brian had become a bit redundant, and we said to him: 'Look, we don't want to put you out of a job, but we do like doing it ourselves.' So it got a bit difficult. And, without ever saying anything (he was still our manager), I think he felt a bit sidelined – and I'm sure it contributed to his unhappiness.

NEIL ASPINALL: *In a sense, he didn't have to work so hard; not on The Beatles' behalf, anyway. That was a good thing for him, as it was for everybody else; just getting a bit of a break, really.*

*Brian was very close to the band, but I always thought he did too much – not for The Beatles, but running careers for Cilla, Gerry and the Pacemakers, Billy J. Kramer and Tommy Quickly, and then going in with Robert Stigwood and Cream and The Bee Gees. I know Brian was trying to shift the emphasis in his business towards Robert Stigwood and Vic Lewis looking after all the other bands, leaving Brian with just The Beatles.*

GEORGE MARTIN: *It was thought he'd been losing control over them to a certain extent. They were getting so big, and so important, and his own affairs weren't being handled terribly well. At the same time, when he died, they knew that they'd lost their leader.*

*He was the guy who'd shepherded them from the beginning. Ironically, if he'd gone on living, I think it would have been even more tragic in a way; because he may have lost the boys anyway. But at that time it was a pretty awful disaster.*

RINGO: IT'S HARD TO SAY WHETHER WE WOULD HAVE LEFT BRIAN, BUT I DON'T THINK WE WOULD HAVE DONE. WE WERE SORT OF LEAVING EACH OTHER, ANYWAY, BECAUSE THERE WAS LESS FOR HIM TO DO. BUT I STILL THINK THAT IF BRIAN WAS AROUND TODAY, HE WOULD BE MANAGING US. AND IF WE'D BEEN WITH BRIAN, WE WOULDN'T HAVE HAD TO GO THROUGH ALLEN KLEIN TO BE OUR OWN MEN.

JOHN: We had complete faith in Brian when he was running us. I mean, if you're asking me in retrospect, and I say he made those mistakes, you'd say, 'Well, what a silly businessman.' But to us he was the expert.

I liked Brian. I had a very close relationship with him for years. In the group I was closest to him. He had great qualities and he was good fun. He was a theatrical man rather than a businessman, and he was a bit like that with us.

With a classy, well-spoken manager, The Beatles had that bit of a classy touch which was different. He literally cleaned us up. There were great fights between him and me, over years and years, about me not wanting to dress up. He and Paul had some kind of collusion to keep me straight.[72] They did have to cover up a lot for me, but I kept spoiling the image. I'm not putting Paul down, and I'm not putting Brian down: they did a good job in containing my personality from causing too much trouble.[80] It never got too bad like that, though. Brian was never overbearing, and if Brian and Paul and everybody said, 'Well, look, why don't we just trim our hair a bit and look like this,' you're going to say 'all right' in the end, or, 'Fuck it: I'll just loosen my collar.'

People always have images, like: George Martin did everything and The Beatles did nothing; or The Beatles did everything and George Martin was invisible; or Brian Epstein did everything. It was never like that. It was a combination. What I think about The Beatles is that if there had been even Paul and John and two other people, we'd never have been The Beatles. It had to be that combination of Paul, John, George and Ringo to make The Beatles. There's no such thing as, 'Well, John and Paul wrote all the songs, therefore they contributed more,' because if it hadn't been us, we would have got songs from somewhere else. And Brian contributed as much as us in the early days: we were the talent and he was the hustler. He sold us. He presented us. There was a lot of heavy grind for Brian in the early days, and he was good at handling the tours. (Though once we went to Italy and never got paid, and in Manila he nearly got us killed...) He did all that for us, so we would have never made it without him, and vice versa.[72]

*but whoever it was, I know what he meant and there was a time early this year when I almost gave it up.*

RINGO: Brian was great. You could trust Brian. He was a lot of fun, and he really knew his records; like the guy in the movie *Diner*. We used to have a game with Brian where we'd say to him: 'OK, "C'mon Everybody" – what was the B side?' and he'd tell us. So we'd say, 'What number did it reach?' and he'd know. It was thrilling.

He tried to educate us, taking us to different restaurants instead of the greasy spoon. He persuaded us to wear ties, he persuaded us to dress up a bit more, and it's true that he said: 'Don't drink on stage, and try not to smoke through the set.' He really was instrumental in bending our attitude this much, so that the public would bend theirs that much to accept us.

PAUL: We were all pretty close to Brian, but John might have been slightly closer. I think in the early days John had taken him aside and said, 'Look, if you want to deal with this group, then I'm the man you go through.' He could do that, John: he was wise to the possibility – whereas the rest of us would say, 'All right, man, sure.'

BRIAN EPSTEIN: *One did everything. One worked very hard. One shouted from the rooftops about the group when there was no enthusiasm for groups. People thought you were mad, but you went on shouting.*

DEREK TAYLOR: *There was a famous early story; one of those legends that may or may not have been true. I think it was at the EMI studios when Brian said, 'I think one of you is flat,' and John said, 'We'll do the songs, you keep on counting the percentages.' Brian told me that they'd said that, and it could have been said. But it would only happen once; he was quite nervous of them as well.*

*Nobody liked to be rounded upon by the four of them – in however jokey a way. It was not pleasant for those four buggers to be at you. It was 'whoosh' – and all the fangs were in you at once. It didn't last, but it was very painful. Crawl away quietly and lick your wounds.*

JOHN: Brian could never make us do what we *really, really* didn't want to do. He wasn't strong enough.

Brian came to us in Paris once and said he'd had enough, and he wanted to sell us to Delfont or Grade, I've forgotten which one. And we all told him – I told him personally – that we would stop. We all said it: 'Whatever you do, if you do that, we stop now. We don't play any more, and we disband. We're not going to let anybody else have us, especially them.'

They don't understand, the Richenbergs and the Grades. They couldn't handle people like us. They're used to the donkeys that they had after the war, Tommy Handley and all them people, and the poor old Crazy Gang who, like Derek used to say, look like they'd been injected with silicone to be brought on stage at eighty.

So whenever Brian tried to make us do something, we didn't care whether it was legal or not. It's the same now. If anything happened, I wouldn't give a shit whether it was legal or not. I'd fuck off, and let them catch me. Let them come and chase me to fucking Japan or Africa, and get me to fucking work if I don't want to. Piss on them. No contract would hold us.[72]

PAUL: It's a misconception that Brian and I put The Beatles in suits – we all showed up happily at the tailor's. And the haircut was me and John together in Paris.

BRIAN EPSTEIN: *I don't know whether it was William Shakespeare or Ringo Starr who said: 'When this business stops being fun, I'm giving it up,'*

The theory is that when John went off to Spain on holiday with Brian, that's what it was about – John trying to get his position clear as leader of the group. Also, I'm sure Brian was in love with John. We were all in love with John, but Brian was gay so that added an edge.

GEORGE MARTIN: *I was very, very good friends with Brian. I knew he was gay – but Brian, Judy (my wife) and I were a triangle of good friends. We used to go away together sometimes and it was great fun.*

*Wondering about his contribution to their success, I know I wouldn't have met them without him. Who's to say what would have happened if Brian hadn't been along? Who's to say whether Ringo would have ever been part of the group? There are so many ifs about that one cannot evaluate.*

JOHN: Would The Beatles be where they are today if it weren't for Epstein? Not the same as we know it, no. But the question doesn't apply, because we met him and what happened, happened. If he hadn't come along, we would all – the four of us and Brian – have been working towards the same thing, even though it might have been with different aims. We all knew what we wanted to get over, and he helped us and we helped him.[67]

PAUL: As for Brian's homosexuality, we were very innocent and I think Brian could see that, so he never hit on me at all: there was never any question of it. We would go to clubs and pubs that were open late, and looking back on it, they must have been gay clubs because there were friends of Brian's there that I knew later to be gay friends of his. But he wasn't overtly gay; he was rather macho, and his friends were just nice guys. I don't think any of us knew about the gay world.

It *was* always obvious Brian was gay and we could talk to him about gay things, but he would never come out with, 'Hello, Paul, you're looking nice today.' I was quite obviously un-gay, due to my hunting of the female hordes, and I think we all must have given the same impression. There has been a suggestion since that John had some homosexual thing with Brian, but I personally doubt it. All the intimate moments we shared were always about girls.

Somebody mentioned that show business is run by gays, and there is a lot of gay influence; many heads of companies and people in power are gay, and it must have helped us a lot having a gay contact. They felt happier with us because at least they could deal more easily with our manager. Looking back, I can see connections were formed with gay producers. Though, at the time, we didn't know.

Plugging into the gay network wasn't a bad thing, but it was Brian who would do the plugging in; we were just pawns in the game. It was very good for us, and anyone who says Brian wasn't a good manager is wrong: Brian was a great manager.

GEORGE: Brian was not on the same kind of journey that we were on. He was, *up to a point*, but he had his own set of karma that he had to work out, and it was as if we were the vehicle by which he could do what he wanted.

When you look at the Brian Epstein story – how he was kicked out of the Army, how he was a misfit at school, how he left RADA (he'd fancied himself as an actor), how he was given a job in the family business but wasn't really happy in it – you can see we were the ideal vehicle for him. It was a mutual thing that seemed to happen: we needed somebody to elevate us out of that cellar, and he needed somebody to get him out of the hole that he was in. It was a mutually beneficial meeting, but once we got to London and he became a theatre-goer and an impresario and a multi-millionaire, there wasn't really the same kind of relationship.

We didn't hang out together and try to discover what the folds in our trousers were doing (as in Aldous Huxley's *The Doors of Perception*). Brian was off into the gay world, and we didn't know too much about that. We knew that he was 'a friend of Dorothy's', but we didn't really go with him into that world. It was in the days when everything was in the closet. (And personally I'm glad it was. I mean, that's all you need, to have a gay manager poncing around the band room while everybody's in their undies!)

We never knew what he was up to, really; you'd just hear stories that he'd been robbed or he was beaten up by somebody. That happened to him when he took acid once, so I believe. I saw him a day or two afterwards. He'd been up in his room and he had all the newspapers and he'd ripped them all into little pieces, which says something. I'm sure an analyst would agree.

JOHN: Brian had hellish tempers and fits and 'lock-outs', and he'd vanish for days. He would just flip out. We weren't too aware of it. It was later on we started finding out about those things. He'd come to a crisis now and then, and the whole business would stop because he'd been on sleeping pills for days on end, and wouldn't be awake for days. Or beaten up by some docker on the Old Kent Road. Suddenly the whole business would stop because Brian would be missing.

I didn't watch him deteriorate. There was a period of about two years before he died when we didn't hardly see anything of him. After we stopped touring, he had nothing to do, really. The money just came in from records. Billy J. and all of them were sinking fast, and all his other protegés – his bullfighters and all those people – were vanishing. So, really, we grew apart.

Whenever somebody dies, you think, 'If only I'd spoken more to him, he might have been a bit happier.' I felt guilty because I was closer to him earlier, and then for two years I was having my own internal problems, and we didn't see him and I have no idea of the kind of life he was living.

It was always very embarrassing: 'Shall we have dinner together?' So we didn't see him. With the four of us and him, it was heavy. There would be an atmosphere, and we'd gradually break down, and turn him on to acid and all that jazz. Or try and straighten him out – which was what we were trying to do. But we didn't: he died instead.[72]

I introduced Brian to pills – which gives me a guilt association with his death – to make him talk; to find out what he was like. I remember him saying, 'Don't ever throw it back in my face,' which I didn't.[70]

GEORGE: It's shit. You can be a multi-millionaire and have everything you can think of in life, but it's shit – you're still going to die. You can go through life, go through millions of lives, and not even catch on to what the purpose is. You can try to see what the purpose is, and try to relate it back to Lime Street, Liverpool, just being a Scouse kid. That's what I thought: 'Well, this step from one to the other isn't really that difficult; it's just a change of attitude and a shift in perception.' I always felt really close to the people, to the public, and to where I grew up, and the people who had become Beatles fans around the world.

That is, I suppose, why I wrote some songs that were trying to say: 'Hey, you can all experience this, it's available for everyone.' But then you realise you can take the horse to the water, but you can't make him drink. You can be standing right in front of the truth and not necessarily see it,

and people only get it when they're ready to get it. Sometimes people took the songs the wrong way, as if I was trying to preach, but I wasn't.

PAUL: Brian would be really happy to hear how much we loved him.

JOHN: Brian has died only in body, and his spirit will always be working with us. His power and force were everything, and his power and his force will linger on. When we were on the right track he knew it, and when we were on the wrong track he told us so – and he was usually right. But anyway, he isn't really dead.[67]

JOHN: It is up to us, now, to sort out the way we, and Brian, wanted things to go. He might be dead physically, but that's a negative way of thinking. He helped to give us the strength to do what we did, and the same urge is still alive.

We have no idea of whether we'll get a new manager. We've always been in control of what we're doing, and we'll have to do what we have to, now. We know what we should do and what we shouldn't do. Brian was a natural guide, and we'll certainly miss him.[67]

GEORGE: After Brian died there was a huge void, because it was when he came along that we started to become professional and started advancing towards the record business and the London Palladium. We didn't know anything about our personal business and finances; he had taken care of everything, and it was chaos after that.

JOHN: We collapsed. I knew that we were in trouble then. I didn't really have any misconceptions about our ability to do anything other than play music, and I was scared. I thought, 'We've had it now.'[70]

RINGO: We wondered what we were going to do. We were suddenly like chickens without heads. What are we going to do? What are we going to do?

Then we heard that Clive Epstein felt he owned us, and so we went to see him to talk about his plans. But he said that he was more interested in his furniture store and his life in Liverpool. So, as time went on, we got free from Clive and started the whole Apple organisation. We didn't consider getting anybody else in to take Brian's place – not immediately, because the roles had changed now that we were recording instead of touring.

NEIL ASPINALL: *They decided they had to keep on trucking. They'd always discussed whatever they were doing with Brian, but now there was nobody. There was Brian's organisation, but they hadn't ever related to that; they'd only related to Brian. What were they going to do? They didn't have a single piece of paper to explain the nature of their contract.*

*There was a meeting of the six of us – the four guys, Mal and I. They were sitting in somebody else's office and they realised they didn't have anything. They didn't know where any of the money was, they didn't have a single contract for anything with Brian; not with a record company, not with a film company – Brian had them all. They were sitting there with nothing, in an office that didn't even belong to them.*

*It didn't make them vulnerable, but it did make them realise that they had to get it together. Suddenly the lunatics had got hold of the asylum.*

*There were several different sets of advice coming in at them about what they should do, but they decided they needed an office and an organisation of their own. And that's really why they expanded Apple.*

GEORGE MARTIN: *It was impossible for any one of the boys to become a manager of the group, because it was a democracy (and the other three wouldn't have stood for it, anyway). As for the rest of the people associated with them, neither Neil Aspinall nor Mal Evans was really 'up there' where Brian had been. Neil did eventually take over and he became manager of Apple, but at that time he wasn't of sufficient clout to be on first-name terms with someone like Joe Lockwood. So it was a very difficult time.*

*In the management vacuum there were all sorts of vultures flapping their wings over the body, but nothing really materialised. I'd never got involved with them on the managerial front; I didn't want to get involved. I thought that if I ever did, then I would lose the rapport I had with them in the studio (where we were mates). We were all on the same level and we could talk the same language. If ever I got into a managerial position of saying: 'You shouldn't do that, you should do this,' then I would lose the studio relationship.*

PAUL: I don't think I was too worried about the prospect of going ahead without Brian, because we'd been starting to have more of our own influence in the studio. We were almost managing ourselves, really. It was very sad to lose an old mate under those circumstances, but I don't think the major worry was: 'Oh, what are we going to do now? We haven't got a manager.' We'd been moving away from that, anyway.

GEORGE: That was when Neil stepped in and tried to figure out what was happening. Clive Epstein was forced into the situation where he had to take over NEMS – the management company – but he wasn't interested; he didn't really have the desire.

There was also another situation where Robert Stigwood had been involved. Brian was getting cheesed off with managing Billy J. Kramer and Cilla Black and all those people, so he'd got Stigwood in. After Brian's death, Robert thought he was going to take over the show and become our manager. He was actually poised on some deal with Deutsche Grammophon or Philips Records. They were going to give him money.

Brian kept trying to tell us something before he died – but he never got round to it. He had a big party down at his house and we were supposed to go there and have a meeting before the party. Unfortunately it was in the 'Summer of Love' and everybody was just wacko. We were in our psychedelic motor cars with our permed hair, and we were permanently stoned (Brian wasn't doing so badly himself, either) – so we never had the meeting.

Later, we found out that he'd given Stigwood the option to acquire 51% of NEMS, which in effect meant management of The Beatles. So we had a meeting with Robert Stigwood and we said: 'Look, NEMS is built basically on The Beatles, so bugger off. We'll have 51%, and you can have the 49%.' He backed off then, and formed his own company. He did very well, whereas NEMS just caved in. I think Neil, along with a couple of lawyers, was trying to find where everything was. There was also a big fiasco with Northern Songs, who published our music then.

PAUL: We told Brian that if he sold us to Stigwood, we would only ever record out-of-tune versions of 'God Save The Queen'.

JOHN: Brian did a few things that show he cooked us. We never got anything out of it, and Brian did. The fact that NEMS was a bigger company than The Beatles. We have no company. There's Northern Songs, NEMS and Dick James. What did *we* have? A couple of quid in the bank. That's where Brian fucked up. He's the one who would say: 'Sign for another ten years.' And who got the benefit? Not us. We're the ones who were tied by the balls.[72]

NEIL ASPINALL: *They could have just given up and said: 'Oh, Brian's dead. That's it. What do we do now? Oh, we don't do anything – right?' Or they could go out and do something to keep the organisation together. NEMS was still there, along with a lot of NEMS people (like Tony Barrow, who was later on the* Magical Mystery Tour *bus; organising things and looking after the press). They gave* Magical Mystery Tour *to NEMS to sell for them, and they were still their agents.*

*Robert Stigwood came to visit them when they were filming* Magical Mystery Tour. *We were in a hotel having dinner, sitting at the table, and Robert was intimating that he was now The Beatles' manager because he'd been Brian's partner (and therefore he had NEMS): 'So therefore,' he said, 'I'm your manager.' And they just said to him, 'No, you're not. You can have everything else, but you're nothing to do with us.'*

*In fact, Brian had set it up already that the company had split and become NEMS holding company and NEMS Enterprises. The Beatles had been put into the holding company, which was nothing to do with Stigwood. I think I'm simplifying that a bit, but that's what it was like. Anyway, he didn't have anything to do with The Beatles, but he tried. Good try, Robert.*

JOHN: I'm not going to have some stranger running the scene, that's all. I also like to be friends with whoever's going to run it. I like to work with friends.[72]

RINGO: Robert Stigwood was another person who, we suddenly realised, had a percentage. I don't know how it worked, but for a very reasonable price we got out of it. It was one of those magic moments. Stigwood felt he had a huge piece, we felt he didn't, and it got sorted out really quickly.

We heard that Allen Klein had expressed an interest. We didn't respond.

Nobody in the band itself said, 'Look, I'll run the thing for this period of time.' We never thought we would run it, we just thought we'd start things and then get other people in.

JOHN: Although Apple turned into The Beatles' baby, Apple was conceived by the Epsteins and NEMS before we took over; before we said, 'It's going to be like this.' They had it lined up so we would do the same as Northern Songs – sell ourselves to ourselves.

They were going to set it up, sell 80% to the public, and we were going to be minority shareholders with 5% each, and God knows who else running it.[72]

THE SOLICITORS' STATIONERY SOCIETY L^td

This DEED OF PARTNERSHIP is made the Nineteenth day of April One thousand nine hundred and sixty seve

BETWEEN THE BEATLES LIMITED whose Registered Office is situate at 23 Albemarle Street London W.1. (hereinafter called "the Company") of the one part and JOHN WINSTON LENNON of Kenwood House St.George's Hill Estate Weybridge Surrey JAMES PAUL McCARTNEY of 7 Cavendish Avenu London N.W.8. GEORGE HARRISON of Kinfauns Claremont Drive Esher Surre and RICHARD STARKEY of Sunny Heights South Road St.George's Hill Estat Weybridge Surrey (hereinafter collectively called "the Entertainers" and individually described by their proper names) of the other part

WHEREAS:

(1) The Entertainers are currently carrying on in partnership the business of exercising their skills and exploiting their talents as a group of entertainers in the entertainment industry under the name "The Beatles".

(2) The Entertainers have agreed to admit the Company to be a partner in the said partnership business upon the terms and in the manner hereinafter appearing.

NEIL ASPINALL: *I think the original plan for Apple came, as usual, from accountants. They'd told Brian that The Beatles should really diversify and invest in other things. So he'd set up a company in Baker Street called Apple Publishing; and that's all it was, just a little publishing company. Terry Doran was running it.*

JOHN: Our accountant came up and said, 'We've got this amount of money. Do you want to give it to the Government, or do something with it?' So we decided to play businessmen for a bit.[68]

Originally, we didn't want an Apple. Clive Epstein said, like they did every few years, 'If you don't do this, it will go in taxes.' So we really didn't want to go into fucking business, but the thing was: 'If we have to go in, let's go into something we like.'[72]

GEORGE: I've no idea who thought of Apple first. It was a bad idea, whoever thought of it! I think it came out of Brian dying, and then the thing about Stigwood and Clive Epstein coming along. We were thinking, 'Oh, well, we'd better just make our own thing.'

Because of the hippy period, everybody thought, 'Well, we can do this, and we can do that, and we can have a new way of doing things.' It was true, really, and it was a brave attempt in many ways. It was still very much a Britain with a post-war mentality, and in the mid-Sixties there was an awakening of interest and an awareness of people's abilities and their way of doing things. One example was Mary Quant.

Everybody was trying to break out of the old moulds and we thought that we'd be able to do that in a business sense. We thought we'd be able to develop and give other people a break and be able to make films ourselves. In fact, do everything ourselves!

You have to remember that in 1967 everybody was on such a buzz! I don't mean just The Beatles, but the whole planet (at least San Francisco, LA and London). There was a feeling about how everybody was going to change the world, and we had ideas along the lines of: 'Wouldn't it be nice if we could help other people, instead of them getting screwed around in business as we have been all the time?'

It was a problem with the hippy period – particularly with reefer – that you'd sit around and think of all these great ideas, but nobody actually did anything. Or if they did do something, then a lot of the time it was a failure. The idea of it was much better than the reality. It was easy to sit around thinking of groovy ideas, but to put them into reality was something else. We couldn't, because we weren't businessmen. All we knew was hanging around studios, making up tunes.

PAUL: The theory had been that we'd put all our affairs into one bundle in our own company. It would be all the things we'd ever wanted to do.

We were full of bright ideas: 'Yeah, we could do this. We could do that.' There was a lot of that around to give us all the enthusiasm; but there wasn't an awful lot of planning. So it soon started to get into budgetary problems with people spending too much, and there were hot and cold running secretaries. Occasionally it would get a bit weird, because you couldn't just fly on your enthusiasm alone, and I suppose Brian would have always handled all those things that we didn't plan for.

We actually started to try to run Apple ourselves, financially; and that was difficult, because we had to wear two hats. We all shared the responsibility, but I know John got a bit annoyed, saying, 'Paul's trying to be the leader of the group.' I don't think I was particularly trying to 'manage' us. What I think I was doing was getting us to *self-manage* from within the group.

It is possible that I was *there* more than anyone. When we did *Magical Mystery Tour*, for instance, I ended up directing it, even though we said that The Beatles had directed it. I was there most of the time, and all the late-night chats with the cameramen about what we were going to do tomorrow, and the editing etc., would tend to be with me rather than with the others.

JOHN: Now we're our managers, now we have to make all the decisions. We've always had full responsibility for what we did, but we still had a father figure, and if we didn't feel like it – well, Brian would do it. Now we've got to work out all our business, everything. It threw me quite a bit.[68]

PAUL:
ONE LOVELY SUNNY DAY WE WERE ALL OUT IN THE GARDEN WHEN ROBERT ARRIVED FOR A VISIT. HE'D BROUGHT A PICTURE BY MAGRITTE WHICH HE KNEW I'D LIKE, AND SO HE JUST PROPPED UP THE PICTURE ON THE TABLE AND LEFT. AND WHEN WE CAME IN WE SAW THE PICTURE: A BIG GREEN APPLE WITH 'AU REVOIR' WRITTEN ACROSS IT IN MAGRITTE'S HANDWRITING. IT WAS A DEAD COOL CONCEPTUAL THING OF ROBERT'S TO DO – HE KNEW I'D LOVE IT AND HE KNEW I'D PAY HIM LATER.
WE SHOWED MAGRITTE'S APPLE TO GENE MAHON, THE AD GUY, AND USED IT AS A BASIS FOR OURS.

PAUL: We had a lot of friends who used to make clothes for us, and, as lots of boutiques were opening at that time, it seemed natural for us to start a little clothes shop of our own. But a rude awakening comes in any venture like that. We started to meet with people from the rag trade and they said: 'Wow! We love this stuff, we're really interested. It will be massive next year.' We'd say, 'No! It's got to be ready next month. Our mates want it *now*, this summer!' They said that we should be thinking what was going to be fashionable *next* year, as they needed that long to gear up the factories. We told them: 'Oh, we couldn't tell you about next year, mate – it moves too fast for that, you know.' So we could never get into the trade proper, and we decided just to open a boutique ourselves.

JOHN: We ended up with a clothes shop. I don't know how. Initially, Clive Epstein came up to us and said, 'You've got so much money and we're thinking of investing it into retail shops for you.' You can just imagine The Beatles with a string of retail fucking shoe shops – that was the way they thought.

So we said, 'Imagine us owning fucking retail shops. At least if we're going to open a shop, let's open something that we'd want, that we'd like to buy.' We were thinking, 'Let's be the Woolworth of something,' or how great it was to go into Marks & Spencer and get a decent sweater when you were about eighteen. Cheap, but good quality. We wanted Apple to be that.

We said, 'Well, let's sell groovy clothes,' or something. Paul came up with a nice idea which was: 'Let's sell everything white.' You can never get anything white, like cups and all that. I've been looking for a decent set of white cups for five years.[72] It didn't end up with that. It ended up with Apple and all this junk and The Fool and all the stupid clothes and all that.[70]

DEREK TAYLOR: *I came over for the opening of the Apple boutique in December 1967. I took more acid and talked to George about Apple.*

*We went to the party at the opening of the boutique. We decided that we would all serve mankind as best we could. John said things like: 'We'll have a shop, and if anyone wants the counter – we'll sell them the counter. And if they want the chair, they can have it, you know, and that's the way it's going to be.'*

GEORGE: The Apple boutique started as an excellent idea. I'd still like to have a shop that sells worthwhile things. What we were trying to do was to sell all the stuff that we liked. Apart from the loony clothes and the hippy flower-power stuff, we were supposed to support all kinds of different music (which now they'd call 'world music'), and we'd sell books about various things we were into, as well as spiritual objects, incense and whatever.

PAUL: The shop in Baker Street was great, and we thought that to get people's attention we would put a beautiful big mural on the wall. The painting was gorgeous; it was done by The Fool.

GEORGE: TRYING TO INFLUENCE PEOPLE AND DOING THINGS LIKE PAINTING THE APPLE SHOP WAS ALL JUST PART OF THE TEDDY BOY IN US, THE TEDDY-BOY THEME OF 'WE'LL SHOW THEM'. WE THOUGHT, 'WE'LL PAINT THE BUILDING ONE NIGHT, AND THE NEXT MORNING PEOPLE WILL COME UP THE STREET AND THE WHOLE BLOODY BUILDING'S GOING TO BE PSYCHEDELIC.' THAT WAS WHAT IT WAS ALL ABOUT – I THINK WE WOULD HAVE BEEN PIRATES IN A DIFFERENT LIFE.

# MAGICAL MYSTERY TOUR

NEMS ENTERPRISES, LTD.
'MAGICAL MYSTERY TOUR'
REVISED UNIT LIST

| | | |
|---|---|---|
| ...UCER | NEMS ENTERPRISES | |
| ...CTORS | ...N LENNON | |
| | ...McCARTNEY | |
| ...IATE PROD. | DENIS O'DELL | |
| ...TION MANAGER. | GAVRIK LOSEY | |
| ...SSISTANT DIRECTOR. | ANDREW BIRKIN. | |
| ...SSISTANT DIRECTOR. | GERRY HARRISON. | |
| ...ING CAMERA-MAN | AUBREY DEWAR | |
| ...A OPERATOR (1) | TONY BUSBRIDGE. | |
| ...A OPERATOR (2) | MIKE SARASON | |
| ... PULLER (1) | DAVID LAWRENCE | |
| ... PULLER (2) | DAVID WALSH | |
| ...ER LOADER | BRYAN MITCHISON | |
| ...NUITY | PAT MOON | |
| ... MIXER | MICHAEL LAX | |
| ... CAMERA | ALAN HAYNES | |
| ...OPERATOR | TONY MILNE | |
| ... MAINTENANCE | MICHAEL COLUMN | |
| ...UP | | |
| ...RESSING | | |
| ...IRECTOR | KEITH LIDDIARD | c/o MA... |
| ...TION ADVISOR | ROGER GRAHAM | c/o MA... |
| | ROBYN STUBBS. | 948. |
| ...RTY BUYER | LEN SHORT | |
| ... (1) | CURLY HODGEN | c/o WALT... |
| ... (2) | JOHN HARRIS | " " |
| ...RUCTION MANAGER | DICK BROWN | c/o AIR... |
| ...TER (1) | LOU SAYERS | c/o " |
| ...TER (2) | BOB LANE | 7... |
| ...R (1) | DEL SMITH | 6... |
| ...R (2) | DANNY TUHEY | |
| ...AND | AL CHEATER | c/o WEST... |
| ... GRIP | GREG WELLEN | c/o WALT... |
| ...ICIAN | FRED MURDEN | ALDERSHO... |
| ...DRIVER | ALF MANDERS | 4... |
| ...RS | GEORGE COOK | c... |

WHO ARE THE EGGMEN ?

STRIPPER.
...........

The men have been separated from the women who are having tea on the coach. They are led through a door to a small club by the roadside where music is playing. Inside there is a stage on which a stripper strips alongside a singer. She does her act to the singer, who sings an unsuitable song. (or tries to tell jokes) The men clap loudly as she finishes her act with a flourish..and the curtain closes..When it opens again the women from the bus are there in her place. They look up to see what the applause is about.

The men stop clapping and walk out.

...........................

The new ... band
Denny L...'s band.
The crea...
Chris B...er's band

Bonzo Doo Dah ~~Dog~~ Band?

.................

Strip club....stripper... band...

...L SHEET NEMS ENTERPRISES LTD.
No.
...RY TOUR" PROD. No. NEM 1
CALL FOR DATE. 19 September 1967.
...IRFIELD, HANGAR NO:2: Mr.MAIDSTONE:KENT:
Tel. WEST MALLING 3658

| DRESSING ROOM No. | CHARACTER | TIME REQUIRED AT STUDIO | TIME REQUIRED ON SET |
|---|---|---|---|
| | PAUL | 9.00 | 9.05 |
| | GEORGE | 9.00 | 9.05 |
| | JOHN | 9.00 | 9.05 |
| | RINGO | 9.00 | 9.05 |
| | HOSTESS | 9.00 | 9.15 |
| | COURIER | 9.00 | 9.15 |
| | RINGO'S AUNT | 9.00 | 9.15 |
| | ACCORDIONIST | 9.00 | 9.15 |
| | PHANTOM COURIER | 9.00 | 9.15 |
| | PHOTOGRAPHER | 9.00 | 9.15 |
| | DRIVER | 9.00 | 9.15 |
| | RUBBER MAN | 9.00 | 9.15 |
| | STARLET | 9.00 | 9.15 |
| | PASSENGER. | 9.00 | 9.15 |
| | PASSENGER | 9.00 | 9.15 |
| | PASSENGER | 9.00 | 9.15 |
| | BOY PASSENGER | 9.00 | 9.15 |
| | PASSENGER | 9.00 | 9.15 |
| | PASSENGER | 9.00 | 9.15 |
| | PASSENGER | 9.00 | 9.15 |
| | PASSENGER | 9.00 | 9.15 |
| | PASSENGER | 9.00 | 9.15 |

COACH:
...ve Alsop Place
...on) at 7.30am.,
... to travel to the
... own transport do so
...nsibility.
...t Order with full
...sued by 5.30 pm.,
...ember.

DEAR SIRS,

THIS IS TO CONFIRM MY ORDER FOR FIVE VICARS' COSTUMES, ONE COLONELS' UNIFORM AND ONE SERGEANTS' UNIFORM FOR USE IN THE BEATLES PRODUCTION OF 'THE MYSTERY TOUR'.

PLEASE FORWARD ALL ACCOUNTS TO THIS OFFICE FOR PAYMENT.

YOURS FAITHFULLY,

...would like to underline that I am very keen on showing the film over the Christmas period on BBC-1. This would be at peak time and would, of course, have a family audience of more than 25 million. Because so many arrangements for our Christmas shows have already been made, we can only show the film at 45'.

PAUL: YOU KNOW, IT'S JUST GREAT TO BE BACK AT WORK AGAIN.[67]

JOHN: At the beginning of 1967, we realised that we wouldn't be doing any more concert tours, because we couldn't reproduce onstage the type of music that we'd started to record. So, if stage shows were to be out, we wanted something to replace them. Television was the obvious answer.[67]

GEORGE: For years we looked around for a screenplay that was suitable, but in the time that had elapsed since *A Hard Day's Night* and *Help!* – although it was probably only two years – it was as if we'd gone through five hundred years mentally. We didn't see any way of making a similar film of four jolly lads nipping around singing catchy little tunes. It had to be something that had more meaning.

I remember we had Patrick McGoohan around, and he'd written a couple of episodes of a series called *The Prisoner*, which we liked very much. We thought, 'Well, maybe he could write something for us.' Then there was David Helliwell, who wrote *Little Malcolm and His Struggle Against the Eunuchs* – we got him up and asked him to write us something. I know there was also a Joe Orton project, but I don't have any recollection of anybody meeting Joe Orton or ever seeing the screenplay (although it did come out later). I think that was probably a Brian Epstein kind of trip.

PAUL: I'm not sure whose idea *Magical Mystery Tour* was. It could have been mine, but I'm not sure whether I want to take the blame for it! We were all in on it – but a lot of the material at that time could have been my idea, because I was coming up with a lot of concepts, like *Sgt Pepper*. (I'm not saying that was *my* album – obviously we all worked on it – but I was coming up with a lot of ideas.)

Privately, I'd got a camera and I would go out in the park and make films. We'd show our little home movies to each other, and we'd put crazy soundtracks on them. I used to do a bit of editing at home – I had a little machine and I was getting very into it. So for the next Beatles project, I thought: 'Let's go and make a film – what a great thing to do.' It was all done on whims.

There wasn't a script for *Magical Mystery Tour*; you don't need scripts for that kind of film. It was just a mad idea. We said to everyone: 'Be on the coach on Monday morning.' I told them all, 'We're going to make it up as we go along, but don't worry – it'll be all right.' I did have to keep chatting to people, because the security of a script is obviously very helpful. But we knew we weren't doing a regular film – we were doing a crazy roly-poly Sixties film, with 'I am the eggman' and so on.

JOHN: WE HAVEN'T GOT A SCRIPT YET, BUT WE'VE GOT A BLOKE GOING ROUND THE LAVATORIES OF BRITAIN, CRIBBING ALL THE NOTES OFF THE WALLS.[67]

RINGO: *Magical Mystery Tour* was Paul's idea. It was a good way to work. Paul had a great piece of paper – just a blank piece of white paper with a circle on it. The plan was: 'We start *here* – and we've got to do something *here*...' We filled it in as we went along.

We rented a bus and off we went. There was *some* planning: John would always want a midget or two around, and we had to get an aircraft hangar to put the set in. We'd do the music, of course. They were the finest videos, and it was a lot of fun. To get the actors we looked through the actors' directory, *Spotlight*: 'Oh, we need someone like this, and someone like that.' We needed a large lady to play my auntie. So we found a large lady.

JOHN: It's about a group of common or garden people on a coach tour around everywhere, really, and things happen to them.[67]

GEORGE: It was basically a charabanc trip, which people used to go on from Liverpool to see the Blackpool lights – they'd get loads of crates of beer and all get pissed (in the English sense). It was very flimsy, and we had no idea what we were doing. At least, I didn't. I had no idea what was happening, and maybe I didn't pay enough attention because my problem, basically, was that I was in another world.

This is where Paul felt somebody had to try to do something; and so he decided he'd push what he felt. As for me, I didn't really belong; I was just an appendage. There were a number of people whose help we called upon. Denis O'Dell was one – I think he'd been an associate producer on *A Hard Day's Night*, and later he was brought in to have something to do with Apple. We were in need of having a grown-up person, a father figure, in the business side of the film. In one respect *Magical Mystery Tour* was probably quite good, because it got us doing something; it got us out and got us together.

JOHN: I was still under a false impression. I still felt every now and then that Brian would come in and say, 'It's time to record,' or, 'Time to do this.' And Paul started doing that: 'Now we're going to make a movie. Now we're going to make a record.' And he assumed that if he didn't call us, nobody would ever make a record. Paul would say, well, now *he* felt like it – and suddenly I'd have to whip out twenty songs. He'd come in with about twenty good songs and say, 'We're recording.' And I suddenly had to write a fucking stack of songs.[72]

NEIL ASPINALL: *Paul and John sat down in Paul's place in St John's Wood. They drew a circle, and then marked it off like the spokes on a wheel. It was a case of: 'We can have a song here, and a dream sequence there,' and so on. They mapped it out.*

JOHN: We knew most of the scenes we wanted to include; but we bent our ideas to fit the people concerned, once we got to know our cast. If somebody wanted to do something we hadn't planned, they went ahead. If it worked, we kept it in. There was a lovely little five-year-old girl, Nicola, on the bus. Because she was there, and because we realised she was right for it, we put in a bit where I just chat to her and give her a balloon.[67]

PAUL: I wandered off to France and did the 'Fool On The Hill' part one morning with a couple of mates. It wasn't quite 'union' – you were supposed to take millions of cameramen, but we didn't want to do that. We knew we were bucking the system and making a far-out, silly little film – and only occasionally did it get embarrassing.

Most of the time we were able to say to people: 'Look, this is very free-wheeling, so just go down to the beach...' We had Ivor Cutler, who played Buster Bloodvessel. His romantic interest was Jessie (the fat lady) and we got him on the sand, where he drew a big heart around her. We'd say, 'That's nice,' and it would be part of the sequence.

It did get a little hairy once or twice. I felt a bit sorry for people like Nat Jackley, whom we'd admired. He was an old music-hall comedian who used to do eccentric dancing and funny walks. He was great at all of that, and John and I really loved him. John wanted to do a sequence with him, but he got a bit annoyed because there wasn't enough script. Some of the older guys who were used to working with scripts – which, after all, is only sensible – were a little bit disappointed with the film.

RINGO: It was good. We would get off the bus: 'Let's stop here,' and go and do this and that. Go on the beach, draw a heart, dance. Then we'd put the music to it. It took two weeks to film and a *long* time to edit. We were a little unlucky with our first director. We had 'walking cameramen' – they'd walk and film the shots. When we looked at the first three or four days of rushes, we found he'd forgotten to turn the camera off – so we just had hours of pavement. Thank you, eh?

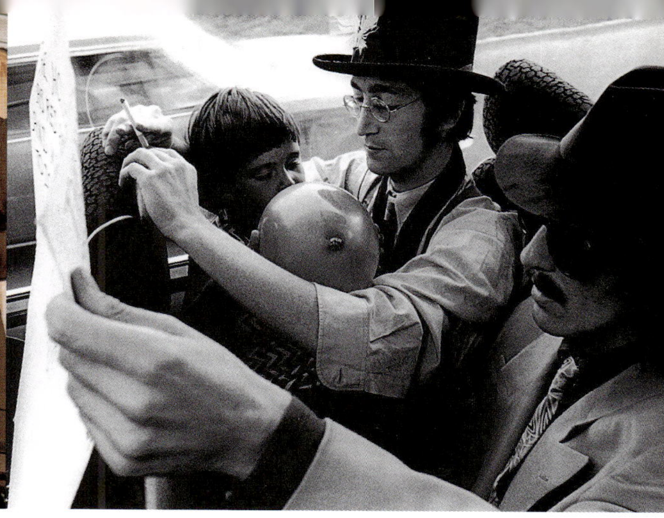

JOHN: We didn't get directors, we got cameramen who walked in. And what we say to them is, 'Are you a director?' And they say 'yes' and we say, 'Are you any good?' and he says 'yes'. And we say, 'Well, you're on.' And that's the big business scene.[72]

RINGO: I used three different drum kits. I had a kit made for a giant – and this is what happens when you don't really think it out: there was a giant bass drum and tom-toms and a giant snare. The snare was so big I couldn't get my leg to the bass drum and we could never use it as a kit. But it was fine for miming. Then I had the mini-kit; that was just my bit of fun. And there was a normal kit.

GEORGE: I remember the big hangar down in Kent when we were driving around the airfield in the Mini Cooper, and filming 'Your Mother Should Know', which was quite interesting. I enjoyed that scene.

NEIL ASPINALL: *All sorts of things happened. We were in the big coach with all the decoration on the side and we came to a little narrow bridge. The bus was too wide to go across the bridge so we got stuck, and we couldn't easily go forwards or backwards. The driver had to back off, but by then there was a trail of cars a hundred yards long in both directions and everybody was getting really cheesed off.*

*When John and Paul were editing the damned thing, they found out that nobody had filmed any linking shots. There wasn't one shot of the bus from the outside. So I said that I'd do it. I got Nick Knowland as cameraman, and Mal and I got the bus out again, put all the posters on the side, and drove off into the sunset.*

*We stopped by a little gypsy camp. I got a couple of children to wave at the bus going past, and because there was nobody on board I told the bus driver to drive fast. We did those shots with the bus driving up and over the camera, then of it going away. So, now we had a few links. That sort of thing was going on all the time, and I keep thinking, 'When did they do the music?'*

JOHN: *Magical Mystery Tour* is one of my favourite albums, because it was so weird. 'I Am The Walrus' is also one of my favourite tracks – because I did it, of course, but also because it's one of those that has enough little bitties going to keep you interested even a hundred years later.[74]

It's from 'The Walrus and the Carpenter'; *Alice in Wonderland*. To me, it was a beautiful poem. It never dawned on me that Lewis Carroll was commenting on the capitalist system. I never went into that bit about what he really meant, like people are doing with The Beatles' work. Later I went back and looked at it and realised that the Walrus was the bad guy in the story, and the Carpenter was the good guy. I thought, 'Oh, shit. I've picked the wrong guy.' But that wouldn't have been the same, would it? 'I am the Carpenter...'[80]

We saw the movie in LA, and the Walrus was a big capitalist that ate all the fucking oysters. I always had the image of the Walrus in the garden and I loved it, and so I didn't ever check what the Walrus was. He's a fucking bastard – that's what he turns out to be. But the way it's written, everybody presumes that means something. I mean, even I did. We all just presumed that because I said 'I am the Walrus' that it must mean 'I am God' or something. It's just poetry, but it became symbolic of me.[70]

'Walrus' is just saying a dream – the words don't mean a lot. People draw so many conclusions and it's ridiculous.[69] I've had tongue in cheek all along – all of them had tongue in cheek. Just because other people see depths of whatever in it... What does it really mean, 'I am the eggman'? It could have been the pudding basin, for all I care. It's not that serious.[80]

I'd seen some other people who liked Dylan and Jesus going on about Hare Krishna. It was Ginsberg in particular I was referring to. The words 'element'ry penguin' meant that it's naive to just go around chanting Hare Krishna or just putting your faith in one idol.

In those days I was writing obscurely, *à la* Dylan, never saying what you mean but giving the *impression* of something, where more or less can be read into it. It's a good game. I thought, '*They* get away with this artsy-fartsy crap.' There has been more said about Dylan's wonderful lyrics than was ever in the lyrics at all. Mine, too. But it was the intellectuals who read all this into Dylan or The Beatles. Dylan got away with murder. I thought, 'I can write this crap, too.'

You just stick a few images together, thread them together, and you call it poetry. But I was just using the mind that wrote *In His Own Write* to write that song.

There was even some live BBC radio. They were reciting Shakespeare or something and I just fed whatever lines were on the radio right into the song.[80] Do you know what they're saying at the end there? 'Everybody's got one, everybody's got one.' We did about half a dozen mixes and I just used whatever was coming through at that time. I never knew it was *King Lear* until, years later, somebody told me – because I could hardly make out what he was saying. It was interesting to mix the whole thing with a live radio coming through it. So that's the secret of that one.[74]

PAUL: It was shown on BBC1 on Boxing Day, which is traditionally music hall and Bruce Forsyth and Jimmy Tarbuck time. Now we had this very stoned show on, just when everyone's getting over Christmas. I think a few people were surprised. The critics certainly had a field day and said, 'Oh, disaster, disaster!'

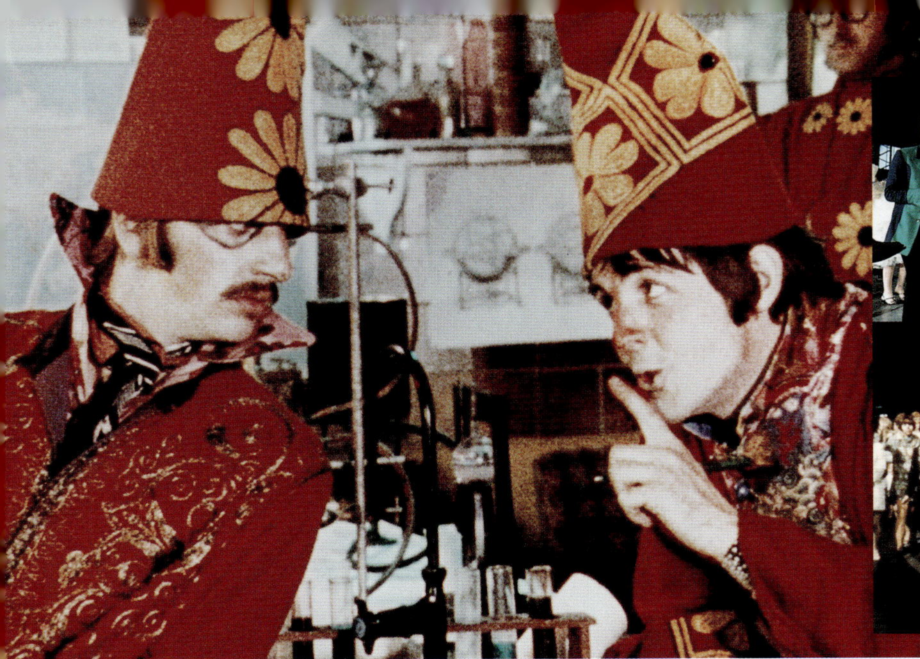

GEORGE MARTIN: Magical Mystery Tour *was not really a success – in fact, that's putting it mildly. When it came out originally on British television, it was a colour film shown in black and white; because they didn't have colour on BBC1 in those days. It looked awful and it was a disaster. Everyone said it was pretentious and overblown, but it was a kind of avant-garde video, if you like.*

*The Beatles were the first guys to make videos – they're accepted now as part of our business, and* Magical Mystery Tour *was a rather fanciful example.*

*It was a little bit pretentious – but it was also quite good fun. Maybe it was a little bit boring, and maybe some of the songs weren't great, but it was an attempt.*

RINGO: Being British, we thought we'd give it to the BBC (which in those days was the biggest channel), who showed it in black and white. We were stupid and they were stupid. It was hated. They all had their chance to say, 'They've gone too far. Who do they think they are? What does it mean?' It was like the rock-opera situation: 'They're not Beethoven.' They were still looking for things that made sense, and this was pretty abstract.

It was a crowd of people having a lot of fun with whatever came into mind. It was really slated but, of course, when people started seeing it in colour they realised that it was a lot of fun. In a weird way, I certainly feel it stood the test of time, but I can see that somebody watching it in black and white would lose so much of it – it would make no sense (especially the aerial ballet shot). We sent a guy out filming all over Iceland, and then it was shown in black and white – I mean, what is this? Painted silly clowns and magicians. What does it mean?

You have to remember that anything we did in the early days was a love song – 'Love Me Do', 'I Want To Hold Your Hand', 'Please Please Me', blah de blah, and now suddenly 'I Am The Walrus' and 'you let your knickers down'. 'Oh, my God, what *are* they doing? They've gone too far.' There were always a lot of people who said, 'They've gone too far this time.'

PAUL: WAS IT REALLY AS BAD AS THAT? IT WASN'T THE WORST PROGRAMME OVER CHRISTMAS. I MEAN, YOU COULDN'T CALL THE QUEEN'S SPEECH A GAS, EITHER, COULD YOU?[67]

JOHN: They thought we were stepping out of our roles. They'd like just to keep us in the cardboard suits that were designed for us. Whatever image they have for themselves, they're disappointed if we don't fulfil it. And we never do, so there's always a lot of disappointment.[68]

NEIL ASPINALL: *There was a whole flying sequence, a beautiful little tune where the clouds all change colour, but in black and white there are obviously no colour changes. So I could understand why an audience would say, 'What's this?' and be a bit disappointed.*

GEORGE: The press hated it. With all the success that we had, every time something came out (a new record or whatever), they'd all try to slam it; because once they've built you up that high, all they can do is knock you back down again. That's what happens; that's life.

They really didn't like the film, but that's understandable because from an artistic point of view it wasn't a brilliantly scripted affair that was executed well. It was like a little home movie; an elaborate home movie. We just had fun. We were supposed to; we were on the bus with the crates of beer and the accordionist.

I think the film had its moments. The bits that were good are still good, and the bits that weren't so good are still not so good. It hasn't matured with age, but there were always a couple of good songs, and there were a few funny scenes. To me, the scene that stands out is the one of John shovelling the spaghetti onto the fat woman's plate. That was the best bit of the movie for me. It was John's idea.

JOHN: Paul said, 'Well, here's the segment, you write a piece for that.' And I thought, 'Fucking Ada, I've never made a film. What does he mean, write a script?' So I ran off and wrote the dream sequence for the fat woman and all the things with spaghetti and all that.[70]

PAUL: People like Steven Spielberg have said since, 'When I was in film school, that was a film we really took notice of.' It was an art film rather than a proper film. I think we all thought it was OK. It wasn't the greatest thing we'd ever done, but I defend it anyway, on the lines that nowhere else do you see a performance of 'I Am The Walrus'. That's the only performance ever.

I think things like that are enough to make it an interesting film. And John's dream with the spaghetti, too. That was an actual dream where he came in and said, 'Hey, I had this wild dream last night. I'd like to do it. I'm a waiter…' So we just put all these ideas in and it was very haphazard. It's how you learn, by your mistakes.

Not that it was a mistake overall, but there were millions of *little* mistakes going along. We never had clapperboards, for instance, so when we came to edit – with music – it was very difficult. We put two weeks by to edit it – and it took eleven. So it went slightly over budget on the editing. I would be down in Soho with the editor all day – it was my job – and the guys would drop by, so I suppose I'm quite a bit to blame for that.

At the same time I'm quite proud of it. It was daring, even though back then it was certainly shown at the wrong time to the wrong audience.

JOHN: I don't think we have any responsibility to the fans. You give them the choice of liking what you're doing, or not liking it. If they don't like it, they let you know – fast. If you allow everything to be dictated by fans, you're just running your life for other people. All we do is try to give fans an even deal.[67]

RINGO: It was a good shoot. It was a lot of fun, and again we were making videos – making little movies – and it was to save us going on the road; going round the TV shows and saying 'hello' yet again to Cathy McGowan.

John's poetry in those songs was so great. In one line he could say what it takes most people a whole song or a novel to say with the same sharp bite. The songs were getting better, both melodically and musically.

JOHN: Every bloody record I put out was banned by the BBC for some reason or another. Even 'Walrus' was banned on the BBC at one time, because it said 'knickers'.[80] We chose the word because it is a lovely expressive word. It rolls off the tongue.

Somebody heard Joyce Grenfell talking yesterday about 'pull your knickers down'. So, listen, Sir Henry Fielding, or whoever it is running the BBC.[67]

| | | | | |
|---|---|---|---|---|
| 14.9.67 | | Location all day - Newquay | 40 | 0 |
| 14.9.67 | | Two wheel discs stolen by fans | 7 | 17 |
| 15.9.67 | | Newquay to London | 40 | 0 |

MR. J. LYNDON

From: ROSE HARDWAY

MR. CHICK LINTON
103 Granville Road,
London N22.

Home tel : 889:2197

Date: 10th Nov 1967

The above named gentleman called into the office yesterday afternoon and told me the following story :-

Paul McCartney had wanted 6 midget wrestlers for The Magical Mystery Tour. Great difficulty had been experienced in finding such artistes. Eventually Mrs. Lester managed to contact three - they needed a fourth to make up at least two pairs. One of those contacted by Mrs. Lester ~~a~~ ROY SMITH alias Jimmy Kay offered to get one of his friends to come along to film.

The friend he contacted was CHICK LINTON. He said "yes" he would do it, and was told that he would be paid. Chick Linton was on the film set working for two days - 22nd and 23rd September.

Up until 5 weeks or so ago, Roy Smith said that he had not yet received payment for the work - since then he has been missing somewhere in Europe and his own family does not know where he is.

Chick Linton's quandary is this :-

He has not been paid for his two day's work on the film.

He does not know exactly how much was being paid to the other wrestlers and so does not know how much is due to him.

He does not know whether Roy Smith has been paid for all four wrestlers or just for himself and Chick Linton.

He does not know whether Roy Smith has been paid at all.

However, if nothing has yet been paid out, he would like us to know that he exists and that pay is due to him.

And By the Bye, do we have any suggestions as to what he can do if Roy Smith does him Chick's pay and has disappeared with it.

I understand the Midgets worked more than one day.
Rate. £100 per day

2 days

I AM THE WALRUS
I am he as you are he as you are me and we are all together.
see how they run like pigs from a gun see how they fly,
I'm crying.
sitting on a cornflake - waiting for the van to come.
corporation teashirt, stupid bloody tuesday man you been a naughty boy
you let your face grow long.
I am the eggman they are the eggmen - - I am the walrus GOO GOO GOO JOOB.
city policeman sitting pretty little policeman in a row,
see how they fly like Lucy in the sky - see how they run
I'm crying - I'm crying I'm crying.
yellow matter custard driping from a dead dogs eye.
crabalocker fishwife pornographic priestess boy you been a naughty girl
you let your knickers down.
I am the eggman, they are the eggmen - - I am the walrus. GOO GOO GOO JOOB
Sitting in an english garden waiting for the sun.
If the sun dont come you get a tan from standing in the english rain,
I am the eggman, they are the eggmen I am the walrus GOOO GOO GOO JOOB ---
Expert texpert choking smokers dont you think the joker laughs at you?
see how they smile, like pigs in a sty, see how they snied.
semolina pilchard climbing up the Eifull Tower.
elementry penguin singing Hare Krishna man you should have seen them kicking
Edgar Allen POE.
I am the eggman they are the eggmen I am the walrus GOO GOO GOO JOOB
GOO GOO GOO JOOB GOO GOOGOOOOOOOOOOOOJOOOOOB

HOTEL NEGRESCO
37, Promenade des Anglais - NICE
Adresse Télégraphique : NEGRESCOTEL
Télex : 46040 NEGRESCO
Nom M. Mc CARTNEY
App' N° 304
HOTEL NEGRESCO
37, Promenade des Anglais - NICE
Adresse Télégraphique : NEGRESCOTEL
Télex : 46040 NEGRESCO
Nom M. EVANS
App' N° 806
Exhibited for Exchange Control Purposes Barclays Bank Limited.
Amount
Date
" NOS PRIX S'ENTENDENT " TOUS COMPRIS " TOUTES TAXES ET SERVICE 15 % ETANT INCLUS, TAXE DE SEJOUR F. O. 55 par PERSONNE ET PAR JOUR EN SUS.
OUR PRICES ARE ALL TAXES and SERVICE 15 % INCLUDED AT THE EXCEPTION OF THE CITY TAX F. 0.55 PER DAY AND PER PERSON.

PAUL: I directed the promo film we made for 'Hello, Goodbye'. Directing a film is something that everyone always wants to get into. It was something I'd always been interested in, until I actually tried it. Then I realised it was too much like hard work. Someone summed it up when they said: 'There's always someone arriving saying: "Do you want the *gold* pistols or the *silver* pistols?"' Then you think: 'Um, um…' There was so much of that going on – so many decisions to be made – that I ended up hating it.

I didn't really *direct* the film – all we needed was a couple of cameras, some good cameramen, a bit of sound and some dancing girls. I thought, 'We'll just hire a theatre and show up there one afternoon.' And that's what we did: we took our *Sgt Pepper* suits along and filmed at the Saville Theatre in the West End.

RINGO: At the end of the year I was off to Rome to film a movie: *Candy* – what a great movie. It was the mind-blowing thrill of my life. I was filming with Marlon Brando, Richard Burton, Walter Matthau and all those guys. Wow!

It was great. Marlon was such a lot of fun, he loved to play. We were all having lunch the day he was due to arrive; Elizabeth Taylor was there (because of Richard Burton), and she was dynamite. But with Marlon coming I was *really* excited – not just a little – because this was *Marlon Bloody Brando*, and I'm a big fan! He came, and he was so charming and so loving. What he did was to 'do Marlon' for me. He picked a spoon and really looked at it, doing his Brando. I just thought, 'It's Marlon Brando, it's Brando!' It was great. I love you, Marlon.

RINGO:
CANDY IS A YOUNG GIRL WHO GOES ROUND MAKING LOVE TO LOTS OF MEN, AND I'M THE FIRST.[67]

Richard and Elizabeth turned out to be really good friends. One fabulous thing he did was to read 'I Am The Walrus' off the album sleeve in that voice of his. It was just amazing. We'd go and stay with them on their boat, and that drove Richard crazy. Because I used to play games with his head. I would say, 'God, the English language, what a load of crap!' and he would explode. And I'd say, 'Shakespeare – give us a break.' It was just a little game I would play with him, and he'd always fall for it and get angry and send me off his boat: 'Get off my boat, you little whippersnapper.'

I loved acting, I really loved it. And I loved meeting all those great actors and sitting around and hanging out. They all gave me tips, that was my acting school: 'Oh, you know, maybe if you did it *this* way…'

**"Candy makes the mind boggle."**

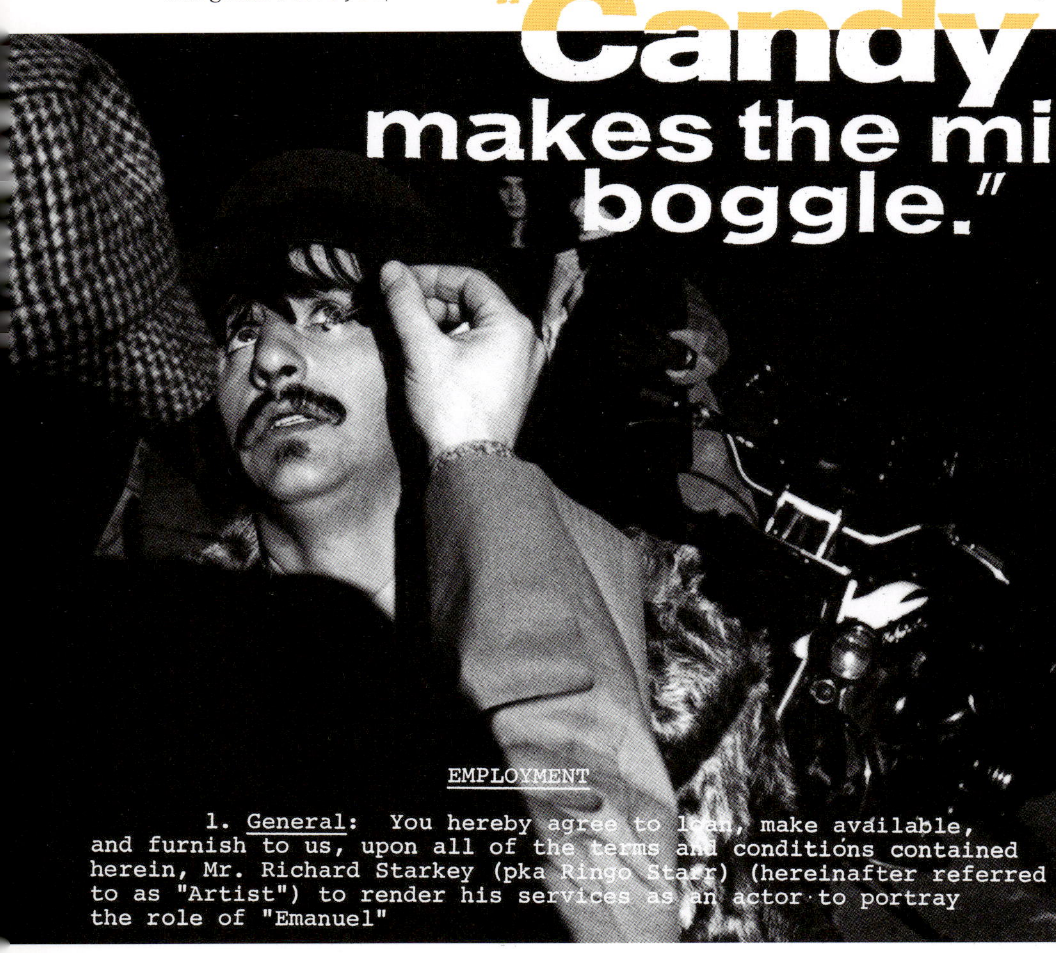

EMPLOYMENT

1. General: You hereby agree to loan, make available, and furnish to us, upon all of the terms and conditions contained herein, Mr. Richard Starkey (pka Ringo Starr) (hereinafter referred to as "Artist") to render his services as an actor to portray the role of "Emanuel" in the motion picture tentatively entitle "Candy", based on the novel of the same name by Terry Southern Mason Hoffenberg (hereinafter referred to as the "Photoplay").

RINGO: I'D READ THE BOOK OF THE FILM, AND I THOUGHT, 'YOU'RE JOKING. HOW CAN THEY MAKE THAT INTO A FILM?' RANDY ISN'T THE WORD FOR IT. NO WONDER IT'S BEEN BANNED![68]

# 1968

nineteen sixty-eight

GEORGE: In January 1968 I was in Bombay, working on the soundtrack for the film *Wonderwall* – a Sixties hippy movie directed by Joe Massot. He asked me if I would do the music, but I told him I didn't write music for films. Then he said that whatever I gave him, he would use. That sounded pretty simple, and I thought: 'I'll give them an Indian music anthology, and who knows, maybe a few hippies will get turned on to Indian music.'

I worked with Indian musicians at the EMI/HMV studios in Bombay. Mr Bhaskar Menon (later to become the head of EMI worldwide) brought a two-track stereo machine all the way from Calcutta on the train for me, because all they had in Bombay was a mono machine. It was the same kind of huge machine we used in Abbey Road; they're called STEEDs. I've got one in the kitchen now – the one that we recorded 'Paperback Writer' on. I came back and added a lot more in Abbey Road, and put the music on the film.

*Wonderwall* came out some time later, and probably died a death. Ringo came with me to the première in Cannes. (I know this because they've put out the CD and I've read Derek's liner notes. I didn't remember it until I saw the photos of us with a rather nice young lady called Jane Birkin who was in the movie.)

TO SHAMBHUDAS

~~BOMBAY MALABAR HILL~~ VILLA MANORAMA SWAMI VIVEKANANDA ROAD

BANDRA

BOMBAY 50.

TEXT:

ARRIVING 8th JANUARY 05.10 hrs. AIR INDIA 112 with TWO FRIENDS. LOOK FORWARD TO SEEING YOU AGAIN.

REGARDS GEORGE.

George – Personal.

INTERNAL MEMO

To: Neil Aspinall

From: Peter Brown

To Neil, c/o Shambhudas etc.

Subject: Indian Trip

Date: 5th January, 1968

You have all the details of the trip on the VIP Itinerary. The Managing Director of EMI in India is Mr. Bhaskar Menon. His office is in Calcutta, Tel. Calcutta 572431. The studios have been booked from the 9th - 12th inclusive and they have shipped the stereo equipment in for George's use. I have not yet been able to find out who the Studio Manager is in Bombay. I may know by this evening if you do not have the information I suggest you telephone Mr. Menon in Calcutta on Monday morning.

The name and address of the Indian friend of George's who has made all the arrangements for accommodation and has been informed of what time your flight arrives, is SHAMBHUDAS of VILLA MANORAMA SWAMI VIVEKANANDA ROAD BANDRA BOMBAY 50.

Can't think of anything else!

Everything arranged.

Regards,

Peter.

12th Jan. '68.

XX

TO:-

SHAMBHU DAS

VILLA MANORAMA

SWAMI VIVEKANANDA Road

BANDRA

BOMBAY 50

TEXT:- Will you be free from Tuesday 9th through till Friday 12th for recordings with musicians. 2 or 3 shanhai 3 sitar and one dha shanhai. Please confirm if this is possible so I can book E.M.I. Studio through London office. Grateful if you would arrange apartment for myself and one other for period 7th - 15th inclusive. Inform if you need any money as deposit. Please reply NEMSTAFF London. Regards George Harrison.

Sent: 29th December.

GEORGE: I BELIEVE I HAVE ALREADY EXTENDED MY LIFE BY TWENTY YEARS. I BELIEVE THERE ARE BODS UP HERE IN THE HIMALAYAS WHO HAVE LIVED FOR CENTURIES. THERE IS ONE SOMEWHERE AROUND WHO WAS BORN BEFORE CHRIST AND IS STILL LIVING NOW.[68]

JOHN: We're all going to India for a couple of months to study Transcendental Meditation properly. We want to learn properly so we can propagate it and sell the whole idea to everyone. This is how we plan to use our power now – they've always called us leaders of youth, and we believe that this is a good way to give a lead.

The whole world will know what we mean, and all the people who are worried about youth and drugs and that scene – all these people with the short back and sides – they can all come along and dig it too.

It's no gospel, Bible-thumping, singalong thing, and it needn't be religion if people don't want to connect it with religion. It's all in the mind. It strengthens understanding and makes people more relaxed. It's not just a fad or a gimmick, but the way to calm down tensions.[67]

PAUL: I think by 1968 we were all a bit exhausted, spiritually. We'd been The Beatles, which was marvellous. We'd tried for it not to go to our heads and we were doing quite well – we weren't getting too spaced out or big-headed – but I think generally there was a feeling of: 'Yeah, well, it's great to be famous, it's great to be rich – but what's it all for?'

So we were enquiring into all sorts of various things, and because George was into Indian music, the natural thing was to ask: 'Well, what is this meditation lark? Do they levitate? Can they really fly? Can the snake-charmer really climb up the rope?' It was really just pure enquiry, and after we met Maharishi and thought about it all, we went out to Rishikesh.

GEORGE: Each year, Maharishi had a course for Westerners who wanted to become Transcendental Meditation instructors. Although I wasn't going to become an instructor, I wanted to go and have a heavy dose of meditation.

John came, and Paul came after him, and then Richard followed with fifteen Sherpas carrying Heinz baked beans. There was also the world's press; I pretended to be asleep all the way to Delhi so I didn't have to talk to them.

It was a long drive from the airport to Rishikesh, and at that time they only had 1950s cars – Morris Cowleys or Morris Oxfords – so the journey took four or five hours.

Rishikesh is an incredible place, situated where the Ganges flows out of the Himalayas into the plains between the mountains and Delhi. There is quite a hefty flow of water coming out of the Himalayas, and we had to cross the river by a big swing suspension bridge.

Maharishi's place was perched up on a hill overlooking the town and the river. It was comprised of Maharishi's little bungalow and lots of little huts that he'd had built quickly for the Westerners coming out there, in a compound of about eight or ten acres. There was a kitchen with some outdoor seating and tables where we would all have our breakfast together. Nearby there was a large covered area with a platform where he'd give the lectures.

If you go to India you can't wear Western clothes. That's one of the best bits about India – having these cool clothes: big baggy shirts and pajama trousers. They also have tight trousers that look like drainpipes.

JOHN: The way George is going he will be flying on a magic carpet by the time he's forty. I am here to find out what kind of role I am now to play. I would like to know how far I can progress with it. George is a few inches ahead of us.[68]

RINGO: It was great; a lot of fun and a lot of meditation. It was pretty exciting. We were in a very spiritual place, meditating and attending seminars with Maharishi.

JOHN: We were really getting away from everything. It was a sort of recluse holiday camp right at the foot of the Himalayas. It was like being up a mountain, but it was in the foothills hanging over the Ganges, with baboons stealing your breakfast and everybody flowing round in robes and sitting in their rooms for hours meditating. It was quite a trip.

I was in a room for five days meditating. I wrote hundreds of songs. I couldn't sleep and I was hallucinating like crazy, having dreams where you could smell. I'd do a few hours and then you'd trip off; three- or four-hour stretches. It was just a way of getting there, and you could go on amazing trips.[74]

RINGO: We had breakfast outside and monkeys used to come and steal the bread. After breakfast, we'd usually have a morning of meditation in groups, on the roof. Then after lunch we'd do the same.

We did a lot of shopping. We all had Indian clothes made because they could do it right there: huge silly pants with very tight legs and a big body that you'd tie up tight, Nehru collars. We got right into it.

You'd have to fight off the scorpions and tarantulas to try to get in a bath, so there used to be amazing noise in the bathroom. To have a bath you'd start shouting – 'Oh yes, well, I think I'll be having a bath now' – and banging your feet. You'd keep shouting in the bath: 'Oh, what a time I'm having, yes it's wonderful!' Then you'd get out of the bath, get dry and get out of the room before all the insects came back in. At the time I was married to Maureen, who had a phobia of moths and flying things. It was pretty far out.

RINGO: We had a big party for George's birthday. It was crowded with people and we all got dressed up and had red and yellow paint on our foreheads.

GEORGE: I had my twenty-fifth birthday in Rishikesh (a lot of people had birthdays while we were there), and they had lots of flowers and garlands and things like that. Maharishi made me play my sitar.

PAUL: An average day there was very much like a summer camp. You would get up in the morning and go down to a communal breakfast. Food was vegetarian (which is good for me now), and I think we probably had cornflakes for breakfast.

After breakfast you would go back to your chalet, meditate for a little while, have a bit of lunch and then there might be a talk or a little musical event. Basically it was just eating, sleeping, and meditating – with the occasional little lecture from Maharishi thrown in.

There were probably about a hundred of us. There would be a lot of flowers on the stage and then Maharishi would come in. It was almost magical. He would say: 'This is only a system of meditation. I'm not asking you to believe in any great God or any great myth. It's merely a system to help you to be calmer in your own life.'

I still think it's good for that exact reason. I don't buy any of those other stories about flying and levitation, although it interests me now because you can actually take courses where you learn these 'siddhis', as they call them, and you fly – you bounce off the ground a bit. I well remember a little chat we had with Maharishi when we asked him if levitation was possible. He said, 'Well, *I* can't do it, but I know a fellow in the next village who can.' And we said, 'Can we get him here? We'd love to see it.' That would have been something to write home about, but we never did get to meet him.

There were question and answer sessions in the evenings. In one of these sessions a guy from America stood up and said: 'Maharishi, I've been having some trouble, but I've been listening to your advice. I was meditating the other day and a big snake was coming towards me. I'm from New York and I'm really scared of snakes, but I remembered what you told me and I looked at it – in my mind – I looked it straight in the eye and it turned into a bit of wiggly string.' I felt that was really symbolic: face your dangers and then you will see that they're not what you thought they were.

I learnt how to meditate. I don't meditate as much now, but I say to my kids that it's not a bad thing to learn, because if you're stuck somewhere or if you're a bit disturbed, it is a great thing to do.

Maharishi was very up with modern technology because he thought it would help him get round the world and get his message over quicker. Once he had to get into New Delhi, and a helicopter came to the camp and landed on the beach down by the river. We all traipsed down in our kaftans and then it was: 'One of you can go up for a quick ride with Maharishi. Who's it going to be?' And, of course, it was John. I asked him later, 'Why were you so keen to get up with Maharishi?' – 'To tell you the truth,' he said, 'I thought he might slip me the Answer.' That was very John!

JOHN: Regardless of what I was supposed to be doing, I did write some of my best songs while I was there. It was a nice scene. Nice and secure and everyone was always smiling. The experience was worth it if only for the songs that came out, but it could have been the desert or Ben Nevis.

The funny thing about the camp was that although it was very beautiful and I was meditating about eight hours a day, I was writing the most miserable songs on earth. In 'Yer Blues', when I wrote, 'I'm so lonely I want to die,' I'm not kidding. That's how I felt.[71] Up there trying to reach God and feeling suicidal.[80]

When you're born, you're in the pram and you smile when you feel like smiling. But the first game that you learn is to smile before you get touched. Most mothers actually torture the kid in the pram – make it smile when it doesn't want to: smile and you get fed. That isn't joy. You cannot be joyful unless you feel joyful, otherwise it's phoney. Mummy makes you smile or say 'Hare Krishna' before you feel good; then you've gone through a process, a falsification of your feelings. If you feel good you feel good, if you feel bad you feel bad. There's no way out. You can take drugs or get drunk, do whatever, but you're just suppressing the feelings. I haven't met anybody full of joy; neither the Maharishi nor any Swami or Hare Krishna singer. There is no constant. There's this *dream* of constant joy – it's bullshit as far as I'm concerned. There's no status, there's no absolute.

Pain is something like food in a way, or life; pain and joy. They go into your body and unless you feel it or express it, it remains there like constipation. You can't get away from the pain. There's no escape from it, it's there, in your body somewhere. It'll come out in your nerves or how many cigarettes you smoke or what you do, it'll make you go bald, or whatever. It expresses itself in *some* form. There's no getting rid of it.

I think we all go through heaven and hell every day; just accept that. To feel is to live. Life is made up of feeling all sorts of things. Every day's the same: there's some heaven and some hell. There's no complete joyful day. There's better days, worse days, and I think every day contains both. It's like the Yin and Yang or whatever you want to call it. It's both.[70]

PAUL: Mike Love was in Rishikesh. Donovan was there. I can remember people like that. Mia Farrow was there, and her sister, Prudence. John wrote the song 'Dear Prudence' for her because she had a panic attack and couldn't come out of her chalet.

RINGO: Prudence meditated and hibernated. We saw her twice in the two weeks I was there. Everyone would be banging on the door: 'Are you still alive?'

JOHN: No one was to know that sooner or later she was to go completely berserk under the care of Maharishi Mahesh Yogi. All the people around her were very worried about the girl because she was going insane. So we sang to her.[79]

They selected me and George to try and bring her out because she would trust us. She went completely mental. If she'd been in the West they would have put her away. We got her out of the house. She'd been locked in for three weeks and wouldn't come out, trying to reach God quicker than anybody else. That was the competition in Maharishi's camp: who was going to get cosmic first. (What I didn't know was I was already cosmic.)[80]

PAUL: I wrote a couple of little things while I was there. I had a song called 'I Will', but I didn't have any words for it. And I wrote a bit of 'Ob-La-Di, Ob-La-Da'. We went to a cinema show in a village where a guy put up a mobile screen and all the villagers came along and loved it. I remember walking down a little jungle path with my guitar to get to the village from the camp. I was playing: 'Desmond has a barrow in the market place…'

JOHN: 'The Continuing Story Of Bungalow Bill' was written about a guy who took a short break to go shoot a few poor tigers, and then came back to commune with God. There used to be a character called Jungle Jim, and I combined him with Buffalo Bill. It's a sort of teenage social-comment song and a bit of a joke.[80]

PAUL: RINGO CAME HOME EARLY; HE COULDN'T STAND THE FOOD AND HIS WIFE COULDN'T STAND THE FLIES. It was understandable; he was a very British lad. There were curries and spicy food – and he has a stomach that gets upset easily (probably due to the peritonitis when he was a kid). Maureen didn't like the flies – if there was one fly in the room, she would know exactly where it was at any given time. I remember her once being trapped in a room because there was a fly over the door. So obviously conditions in Rishikesh were not ideal for them.

RINGO: It's all a bit hard to remember now. I was only there for two weeks, then I left. I wasn't getting what I thought I would out of it.

The food was impossible for me because I'm allergic to so many different things. I took two suitcases with me, one of clothes and the other full of Heinz beans (there's a plug for you). Then one morning the guys who were dealing with the food said, 'Would you like some eggs?' And I said, 'Oh yeah, sure,' and the next morning they said it again. I thought, 'Oh yeah, great – things are looking up.'

Then I saw them burying the shells. That was the first of several incidents that made me think that it was not what I thought it would be. You weren't supposed to have eggs inside this religious and spiritual ashram. I thought: 'What do you mean, you're burying the shells? Can't God see that too?'

We came home because we missed the children. I wouldn't want anyone to think we didn't like it there. I said it was like Butlins holiday camp, we had learnt by then that you could say anything and they'd print it. It was a good experience – it just didn't last as long for me as it did for them.

PAUL: Being fairly practical, I had set a period for staying in Rishikesh. To start with I thought, 'Whoa, this could be it, man. I could never come back if this works.' Then I thought, 'Wait a minute, I'll go for a month. Even if it's incredible I'll still come back after a month.' If it had turned out to

be something we really had to go back for, I would have gone back. But at the end of my month I was quite happy to leave. Nobody got any blinding enlightenment. I thought: 'This will do me. If I want to get into it heavily, I can do it anywhere.' That's one of the nice things about meditation – you don't have to go to church to do it.

By saying I was only going to be there a month, I had to risk that the others would say that I wasn't into it. And George did; he was quite strict. I remember talking about the next album and he would say: 'We're not here to talk music – we're here to meditate.' Oh yeah, all right Georgie Boy. Calm down, man. Sense of humour needed here, you know. In fact, I loved it there.

GEORGE: Ringo only went for a couple of weeks – maybe just to put his toe in the water and see what it was like. Paul just came and went. I don't think he got much out of the trip because there's a bit of footage from *Let It Be* where he's grinning, and saying to John, 'Oh, and it was like being at school, you know: "Oh tell me, oh master".' Retrospectively, twenty years later, he may think back and the penny might have dropped as to what it was about, but I don't think it did at the time.

The idea of the course was that it lasted however many weeks in Rishikesh, and then at the end of that period they shifted the camp up to Kashmir. This was something they did every year. But I'd planned to go just for the Rishikesh trip and then go down to the South of India to do some filming with Ravi Shankar. He was making a movie called *Raga*.

I kept telling Maharishi, 'No, I'm not going to Kashmir – I went there last year.' And he was saying, 'No, no, you coming to Kashmir.' I told him I was going south, and that's when John and I left. It was only really John and I who were there from the beginning up until the end of the segment at Rishikesh, and I think John wanted to get back because – you can see it historically now – he had just started his relationship with Yoko before we went out to India.

JOHN: Yoko and me, we met around then. I was going to take her. I lost my nerve because I was going to take my ex-wife *and* Yoko, and I didn't know how to work it. So I didn't quite do it.[70]

PAUL: I was quite happy. I was wondering how the others were going to get out of it, though, and then they arrived back with a story that Maharishi had made a pass at an attractive blonde American girl with short hair (not Mia Farrow).

JOHN: There was a big hullabaloo about him trying to get off with Mia Farrow and a few other women, things like that. We'd stayed up all night discussing was it true or not true. And when George started thinking it might be true, I thought it must be true because if George is doubting him there must be something in it. So we went to see Maharishi. The whole gang of us the next day charged down to his hut; his very rich-looking bungalow in the mountains. As usual, when the dirty work came, I actually had to be leader. Whatever the scene was, when it came to the nitty-gritty, I had to do the speaking.

I said, 'We're leaving.' – 'Why?' – 'Well, if you're so cosmic, you'll know why.' Because all his right-hand men were always intimating that he did miracles. And I was saying, 'You know why.' He said, 'I don't know why, you must tell me.' And I just kept saying, 'You ought to know.' And he gave me a look like 'I'll kill you, you bastard'. He gave me *such* a look. And I knew then when he looked at me, because I'd called his bluff. I was a bit rough to him. I always expect too much – I'm always expecting my mother and I don't get her, that's what it is.[70]

GEORGE: Someone started the nasty rumour about Maharishi, a rumour that swept the media for years. There were many stories about how Maharishi was not on the level or whatever, but that was just jealousy about Maharishi. We'd need analysts to get into it. I don't know what goes through these people's minds, but this whole piece of bullshit was invented. It's probably even in the history books that Maharishi 'tried to attack Mia Farrow' – but it's bullshit, total bullshit. Just go and ask Mia Farrow.

There were a lot of flakes there; the whole place was full of flaky people. Some of them were us.

JOHN:
CUT TO MAHARISHI'S HEALTH FARM ON THE TIP OF THE HIMALAYAS. EYE-ING, EYE-ING, EYE-ING. HE PICKED THE RIGHT MANTRA FOR ME. OK, HE'S A LOT BALDER NOW THAN WHEN I KNEW HIM. HOW COME GOD PICKS ON THESE HOLI-MEN? ULCERS, ETC. 'HE'S TAKING ON SOMEONE ELSE'S KARMA.' I BET THAT'S WHAT ALL THE LITTLE SHEEP ARE BLEATING. HE'S GOT A NICE SMILE, THOUGH. THIS IS TURNING INTO *THE AUTOBIOGRAPHY OF A YOGURT*, BUT ISN'T EVERYTHING? I ASK MYSELF. HE MADE US LIVE IN SEPARATE HUTS FROM OUR WIVES… CAN'T SAY IT WAS TOO MUCH OF A STRAIN.[78]

The story stirred up a situation. John had wanted to leave anyway, so that forced him into the position of thinking: 'OK, now we've got a good reason to get out of here.' We went to Maharishi, and I said, 'Look, I told you I was going. I'm going to the South of India.' He couldn't really accept that we *were* leaving, and he said, 'What's wrong?' That's when John said something like: 'Well, *you're* supposed to be the mystic, you should know.'

We took some cars that had been driven up there. Loads of film crews kept coming because it was the world-famous 'Beatles in the Himalayas' sketch, and it was one of these film crews' cars we took to get back to Delhi.

We drove for hours. John had a song he had started to write which he was singing: 'Maharishi, what have you done?' and I said, 'You can't say that, it's ridiculous.' I came up with the title of 'Sexy Sadie' and John changed 'Maharishi' to 'Sexy Sadie'. John flew back to Yoko in England and I went to Madras and the South of India and spent another few weeks there.

The story was put around about our leaving and, of course, the newspapers jumped on that. As it says in *The Rutles*, 'The press got hold of the wrong end of the stick and started beating about the bush with it.' Now, historically, there's the story that something went on that shouldn't have done – but nothing did.

JOHN: I copped out and wouldn't write: 'Maharishi, what have you done, you've made a fool of everyone.'[70]

That was written just as we were leaving, waiting for our bags to be packed in the taxi that never seemed to come. We thought: 'They're deliberately keeping the taxi back so as we can't escape from this madman's camp.' And we had the mad Greek with us who was paranoid as hell. He kept saying, 'It's black magic, black magic. They're gonna keep you here forever.' I must have got away because I'm here.[74]

GEORGE MARTIN: *I don't go in for those kinds of things too much myself. Whether it's Maharishi, or dianetics, or whatever – I think it's a load of codswallop. But whatever you believe in is probably a good idea for you. And they did seem to believe in the Maharishi, and it seemed to work all right for them. Today, George still defends the Maharishi, even though the others were later disillusioned with his behaviour.*

PAUL: When people say, 'Wasn't he stashing it away in a Swiss bank?' I always say that I only ever saw him in one piece of cheesecloth. I never saw him in a decent suit in his life. You would have thought if he was doing it for the money you would catch him bombing off to a New Delhi nightclub in a Rolls. But he always appeared to be in his hut meditating, in a piece of cheesecloth, and I thought: 'You can't knock him for that.'

I remember us all sitting around and him asking us what would be a good make of car to buy. We said, 'Well, a Merc, Maharishi. Mercedes very good car.' – 'Practical? Long running? Good works?' – 'Yes.' – 'Well, we should get a Mercedes, then.' It was only one, it wasn't millions, and we were in on the discussions. He didn't say, 'What's the flashiest car that will pull all the birds?' He asked, 'What is practical?' He was very like that.

In my mind I was saying: 'What's the problem? He's not a god, he's not a priest. There are no rules in his religion that say he's not supposed to make a pass. He's only human, after all, and he's only given us a meditation system.'

John wrote 'Sexy Sadie' to get it off his chest. That was a veiled comment on it all, but personally I don't think Maharishi ever did make a pass. He didn't seem like the kind of guy who would. I've since wondered, 'How would a maharishi go about making a pass?' It's not so easy. I don't think any of that happened. Rishikesh was a good experience. I enjoyed it.

NEIL ASPINALL: *I visited them out in Rishikesh, but only to stop them making a movie, really. There was a suggestion they would make a movie with the Maharishi. I'm not quite sure what it was supposed to consist of, but they did have a three-picture deal with United Artists and they'd only made* Help! *and* A Hard Day's Night.

*I went in with Denis O'Dell. I stayed for a week, then I came home with Paul and Jane Asher, leaving John and George and their wives in Rishikesh. They came back later.*

PAUL: We thought there was more to him than there was, but he's human, and for a while we thought he wasn't.[68]

JOHN: We made a mistake there. We believe in meditation, but not the Maharishi and his scene. But that's a personal mistake we made in public. I think we had a false impression of Maharishi, like people do of us. What we do happens in public, so it's a different scene, slightly.

We thought he was something other than he was. But we were looking for it and we probably superimposed it on him. We were waiting for a guru, and along he came. But he was creating the same kind of situation for which he's giving recipes out to cure.

It was India, the meditation is good and it does what they say. It's like exercise or cleaning your teeth – it works. But we finished with that bit of it then. I think we're seeing him a bit more in perspective because we're as naive as the next person. I wouldn't say, 'Don't meditate.'

We're still a hundred per cent in favour of meditation, but we're not going to go potty and build a golden temple in the Himalayas. We will help where and when we can – we can't do everything overnight. But we're not going to empty the gold out of our pockets; there are other ways of helping.[68]

RINGO: WHEN I'M DRIVING I SOMETIMES CLOSE MY EYES AND MEDITATE – MY CHAUFFEUR DRIVES ME!

JOHN: I don't regret anything [about] meditation, I still believe in and occasionally use it. I don't regret any of that. I don't regret taking drugs, because they helped me. I don't advocate them for everybody because I don't think I should. But for me it was good, India was good for me, and I met Yoko just before I went to India and had a lot of time to think things out there. Three months just meditating and thinking, and I came home and fell in love with Yoko and that was the end of it. And it's beautiful.[69]

I DON'T KNOW WHAT LEVEL HE'S ON, BUT WE HAD A NICE HOLIDAY IN INDIA AND CAME BACK RESTED TO PLAY BUSINESSMAN.[68]

# JOHN: WE'D NEVER START OUR OWN LABEL, IT'S TOO MUCH TROUBLE.[65]

DEREK TAYLOR: *At the end of 1967 I got a call from all of The Beatles; a conference call from Hille House. That was where they had the big Apple launch meeting and they said, 'Come and join us, and you can run Apple Records.' It sounded like a wonderful treat. We had all changed. We'd been at a big housewarming party at Brian Epstein's house in Sussex in May, Sgt Pepper time. I had been given LSD by George, and John had given me a dose separately and earlier, so I had a big double dose and we did see wonderful things. We became hippies, really. And The Beatles had changed a lot from being rather charming but world-weary pop stars into being extremely nice, gentle, huggable souls. They really were very sweet in 1967, and we believed we were going to make everything very beautiful and that it was going to be, now, a wonderful world. So the idea of going back to England from California after having had three good years there was, I thought, like going to the Holy Land.*

*When all the stuff on the phone was over and done with – about what I was actually going to do, it was said: 'Well, you don't have to do anything, man. We don't believe in labels or structures or anything. Just come and be' – that sort of thing – 'and we'll pay your fare.' So I came over in April 1968. Work structures were still slightly important, but not very. 'The Lord will provide' was the idea.*

NEIL ASPINALL: *I didn't stay in Rishikesh because I was supposed to be running the Apple companies. We'd just taken some temporary offices in Wigmore Street, but we still didn't have a single piece of paper, not one contract. We didn't have anything about anything, and I was just trying to get all the information we needed – copies of the contracts and files – to find out what had happened in the past, so we could work out where we were going in the future.*

PAUL: In May, John and I went to New York to announce that Apple was starting: 'Send us your huddled talent.' We wanted a grand launch, but I had a strange feeling and I was very nervous. I had a real personal paranoia. I don't know if it was what I was smoking at the time, but it was very strange for me.

I remember sitting up there and being interviewed. John was wearing a bus driver's or a prefect's badge, and he was doing well. Linda was there taking photos, and afterwards I said, 'Couldn't you tell I was nervous?' but she said it was fine. For some reason I just felt very uneasy about the whole thing; maybe it was because we were out of our depth. We were talking to media like *Fortune* magazine, and they were interviewing us as a serious economic force – which we weren't. We hadn't done the business planning; we were just goofing off and having a lot of fun.

JOHN: We were just tripping off, having a joint and saying, 'Well, we could have films, and we could help young artists so they wouldn't have the trouble we had with all the tramping around being undiscovered.'[72]

George said, 'I'm sick of being told to stay out of the park,' so we're trying to make a park for people to come in and do what they want. That's what it's all about. You can't usually get through the door because of the colour of your shoes.[68]

PAUL: We're in the happy position of not really needing any more money, so for the first time the bosses aren't in it for the profit. We've already bought all our dreams, so now we want to share that possibility with others.[68]

JOHN: It's a business concerning records, films and electronics and, as a sideline, manufacturing or whatever. We want to set up a system whereby people who just want to make a film about anything don't have to go down on their knees in somebody's office (probably yours).

The aim of this company isn't really a stack of gold teeth in the bank. We've done that bit. It's more of a trick to see if we can actually get artistic freedom within a business structure, and to see if we can create nice things and sell them without charging three times our cost.[68]

NEIL ASPINALL: *I was in New York with them and it was a bit weird. We sailed round and round the Statue of Liberty on a Chinese junk, trying to figure out what we were going to do with Apple.*

*Then they appeared on* The Tonight Show, *but Johnny Carson was on holiday so it was hosted by Joe Garagiola. I think one of the things John said around that time was: 'We'll just spin it like a top and see where it goes,' and that's pretty much what actually happened at Apple.*

JOHN: It was terrible. There was a baseball player hosting the show, and they didn't tell us. He was asking, 'And which one's Ringo?' and all that shit. You'd expect to go on the Johnny Carson show... and then you'd get there, and there's this sort of football player, who doesn't know anything about you, and Tallulah Bankhead saying how beautiful we were. It was the most embarrassing thing I've ever been on.[72]

RINGO: We had a publishing company and a record company. The idea was that artists would come and see us and tell us their ideas and their schemes, and if any one of us felt it was OK, we'd give them the money and they could go and do it. We should have had a big sign saying: 'You don't have to beg.' I think we always felt that we'd had to beg a little in the early Sixties, and so we didn't want people begging from us.

GEORGE: I had very little to do with Apple. I was still in India when it started. I think it was basically John and Paul's madness – their egos running away with themselves or with each other. There were a lot of ideas, but when it came down to it, the only thing we could do successfully was write songs, make records and be Beatles.

By the time I came back they'd opened the offices in Wigmore Street. I went into the office and there were rooms full of lunatics: people throwing *I Ching* and all kinds of hangers-on trying to get a gig. And, because it was the hippy period, everybody was super-friendly. Basically it was chaos.

JOHN: I tried to see everyone. I saw everyone day in, day out; and there wasn't anybody with anything to offer to society or me. There was just 'I want, I want' and 'why not?' – terrible scenes going on in the office, with hippies and all different people getting very wild with me.[69]

NEIL ASPINALL: *In July, Apple moved to No. 3 Savile Row. It was a big building. The record division was on the ground floor and the studio was in the basement. On the first floor there was a room for me and each of The Beatles. The next floor up from me was the press office, and after that I can't remember.*

*It might have been exciting for everybody else, and for people that came in from the outside, but for me it was hard work setting it up and there was always a lot of chaos.*

*Before we went to New York for the official launch, we'd put an ad in the paper, saying: 'Send us your tapes and they will not be thrown straight into the wastepaper basket. We will answer.' We got inundated with tapes and poetry and scripts. We were overwhelmed by it all, in actual fact.*

This man has talent...
A is for Record
INTERNAL MEMO
One day he sang his songs to a tape recorder (borrowed from the man next door). In his neatest handwriting he wrote an explanatory note (giving his name and address) and, remembering to enclose a picture of himself, sent the tape, letter and photograph to apple music, 94 Baker Street, London, W.1.
If you were thinking of doing the same thing yourself – do it now!
This man now owns a Bentley!
Mr. Peter Brown,
C/O Messrs Beatle & Co.,
3, Savelie Row,
LONDON – W1.
PAR AVION
AEROGRAMME
TERRY DORAN
Assistant to George Harrison
3 Savile Row London W.1
01 734 8232
Hare Krishna
APPLE Films Ltd.
3 SAVILE ROW. LONDON. W.1.
INTERNAL MEMO
DATE 9/2/68
FROM STEPHEN
TO NEIL
RE: APPLE ELECTRONICS
ALEX THINKS THAT WE SHOULD BUY A MINI-VAN FOR APPLE TO BE USED AS A DELIVERY/MESSENGER VAN.
SO YOU THINK YOU'VE GOT TALENT?
So you think you're TALENTED?
a is for apple
apple

PAUL: We never really got much from the sent-in tapes, but at least people knew we were interested. So we got, for instance, James Taylor, who was brought in by Peter Asher.

Mary Hopkin was the main artist whom I produced at Apple, although I didn't really bring her in. She was on a big British television talent show, *Opportunity Knocks*. Twiggy, the model, was a friend of ours and she rang me up and said: 'There's a great girl who's just won *Opportunity Knocks* – you've got to watch her next week. She's fabulous, with a beautiful voice.' So I watched her, and I thought she really had got a lovely Welsh voice; it was very well pitched. And she looked nice with a folky guitar.

I had heard the song 'Those Were The Days' at a nightclub once, sung by an American couple who had a kind of Nina and Frederick act. The song had really stuck in my mind, and I'd always thought it could be a hit. It was a Russian folk tune that they'd done up, and they'd just played it as their finale and gone home. I said to someone in the office, 'Get hold of that song if you can.' They found the people and found the song. We recorded it with Mary and it was a very big hit.

I was also asked to write a theme tune for a London Weekend Television series that Stanley Holloway was going to be in, called *Thingumybob*. I've always loved brass bands, so I wrote and produced a song for the Black Dyke Mills Band. We went up North to Saltaire, near Bradford, where we recorded the B side (a version of 'Yellow Submarine') in a big echoey hall. For the A side, I wanted a really different sound so we went out and played it on the street. It was lovely, with very dead, trumpety-sounding cornets.

Later on, I also worked with Badfinger. I'd written the song 'Come And Get It', and I'd made a fairly decent demo. Because I lived locally, I could get in half an hour before a Beatles session at Abbey Road – knowing it would be empty and all the stuff would be set up – and I'd use Ringo's equipment to put a drum track down, put some piano down, quickly put some bass down, do the vocal, and double-track it. I said to Badfinger: 'OK, it's got to be exactly like this demo,' because it had a great feeling on it. They actually wanted to put their own variations on, but I said, 'No, this really is the right way.' They listened to me (I was producing, after all), and they were good. The song was a hit in 1970.

Pete Ham in the group was a very good writer. He wrote the Nilsson song 'Without You', which is a seriously good song. But the poor fellow topped himself. He was a lovely bloke, I can still see him now. It was a terrible loss.

John wanted to do more of the avant-garde work with Apple – things like Zapple, a funky label that he could do crazy stuff on. So that eventually became his area.

JOHN: In the old days at Apple we used to try and listen to everything, but then you find yourself spending your whole time listening to other people's stuff, and never doing any of your own.[71]

RINGO: The records Apple made were exciting. It started with Mary Hopkin, and then George brought Jackie Lomax and later Billy Preston. I put John Tavener on the label. His brother was working for me as a builder with a firm in Hampstead. He came to me and said, 'Would you like to hear my brother's tape?' I loved it. We were very open to all different kinds of music, so we thought we'd put it on Apple. That was my contribution.

Paul produced Badfinger. I later made the movie *The Magic Christian* with Peter Sellers, and Badfinger did the title track. How they got there I don't know; it wasn't through me.

PAUL: Anyone in The Beatles who wanted to show up and produce as much as he wanted was welcome to do so. Everyone was involved, but people didn't all do the same amount. I lived in London so I was there more. I probably did a little bit more production than Ringo, for instance. I'm not sure what Ringo actually did, but it was no sweat. He didn't *have* to do anything, it wasn't compulsory. But if you came up with an idea, you could carry it out.

Apple was quite a nice little record company, if that had been what we wanted to do. But, once the business hassles came in, we thought, 'Who needs a record company? I'd rather just have my freedom.'

DEREK TAYLOR: *They took on a lot with Apple. They took on business and pleasure and funding the arts, and did try to live up to some of their promises in person. There was a high quotient of sincerity in there, as well as a bit of madness.*

*But, after their promise to save mankind and to give people a start in show business, The Beatles tended to withdraw more or less from the front line. It was then a case of: 'Where are they? They've gone!' and there was only me. I had to make my place, my office, available to these supplicants, whatever, who came to the front office. And it just evolved that you'd come upstairs, I'd give you a drink – because I usually had a drink on the go – and a couple of jokes. 'There are the seats over there, make yourselves at home.'*

*I introduced people to other people, and inside six months we had quite a salon: a self-propagating, self-perpetuating salon of fun and games in the press office. The Beatles were making the 'White' album.*

*We'd get all the pests in our office. They'd call the reception, they'd ring Neil, but in the long run if people were actually in the building or there was something complex or somebody really barmy, I would get them (or the folk who worked with me would have to deal with them).*

*We had a very big staff in there – I had about four secretaries and an American assistant called Richard DiLello, and another press officer called Mavis Smith. It was a packed room – not a big room, but there were about eleven people in there. If anybody had been fired from another department, I'd bring them in; it was a kind of ark. Maybe forty people were in the whole building working there. Maybe fewer, but middle double-figures.*

*We could assimilate people. Frankie Hart (who was later the girlfriend of Bob Weir of The Grateful Dead) came in, and subsequently became a secretary in my office and then became George Harrison's assistant. And then there would be the press, and James Taylor, and Mary Hopkin would be in with her father and her sister and journalists covering her. Really, it was like an Altman film – where all over the place things are happening.*

PAUL: We were trying to get things under our own control. A lot of people do that now; they have their own companies and take lawyers to meetings and get good deals. It was the start of all of that but it was pretty haphazard and, because we hadn't ever really carefully budgeted in the background, most things fell through.

I once tried to sort it out. I remember checking out Derek's floor, and thinking: 'Derek's our publicist, but he doesn't really *need* four secretaries. He can lose one of them. We've got to make *some* sense out of this.' But, of course, it's never a popular guy who goes round trying to make that kind of sense. I was trying to save us money, so I felt justified and said: 'One secretary's got to go, Derek.' Derek told all the other guys and they came down to my office and said, 'If you sack her, we'll reinstate her.' So I said, 'OK, all right. We won't have any cutbacks, then.' I was put in my place there, you know.

I know now, from having my own company, that all that stuff isn't easy. It's the horrible bit. We were trying to make sense of it, and in the end we couldn't.

RINGO: I wasn't as involved as the others, but it was fun. A lot of what Apple did related to the four of us, but I wasn't hanging out there every day. At that time, I didn't really want to be in an office – I liked to be in the country. The problem was that we were giving out all that money and the cameras and equipment, and half of the people we never saw again – they just went off with it.

GEORGE: What it turned out to be was that we just gave away huge quantities of money. It was a lesson to anybody not to have a partnership, because when you're in a partnership with other people you can't do anything about it (or it's very difficult to), and at that point we were naive. Basically, I think John and Paul got carried away with the idea and blew millions, and Ringo and I just had to go along with it.

Some things made money, but very little compared to what was spent. That's been a problem all our lives: everything to do with The Beatles was always locked up in that partnership situation, and I don't recommend it. Other people have weird ideas and suddenly you find that you have to go along with it, or at least the part of it that rubs off on you. You get caught up in everybody else's trip and it's a pain in the arse. It works both ways, of course, and I suppose there's an upside and a downside to it. But it took me a while to get into Apple, and we were probably bankrupt by then.

Things were getting worse in 1968. We were heading for the big one. It was chaos. Brian Epstein used to manage us, and he had died. Even if he didn't *really* keep it together (because later we found out all the deals were bad and we were in a mess), at least he was the person we'd grown up with who was taking care of the shop. Suddenly Apple was a free-for-all, with every weirdo in the country heading into Savile Row and being given office space by John and Yoko. The Hare Krishnas, the Hell's Angels, the Diggers – everybody was in there. We had Paul and John going around Manhattan on a boat saying what they were going to do, and it was getting crazier and crazier with no management.

JOHN: It could never make sense to me to have money and yet think the way I thought. I had to give it away or lose it. I gave a lot of money away, which is one way of losing it; and the other way is disregarding it and not paying attention to it; not taking responsibility for what I really was, which is a guy with a lot of money.

DEREK TAYLOR: *It was frightfully busy. I mean, apart from the madness and the fact that we were smoking reefers and whatnot, it was a very, very active office because The Beatles were still red hot. They were all over the papers, and the press had started to turn against them very, very much by the middle of 1968: 'What's Happened To Our Boys?' Where have they gone? Why are they looking like this? They're freaking out – there's a broken marriage here, and there's all this Maharishi stuff and Indians. These aren't our boys any more. What's happened to them? What's happened to you, Derek? I mean, you're wearing dresses and things!*

*I wasn't wearing dresses, but I was wearing hippy things – not kaftans (I hated that word) but smocks, yes, with braid and jewels and bells on me. Bear in mind I was a man with five children by now, and people in the press world knew me from before. I met a fellow from the* Daily Mirror *at the* Yellow Submarine *party – the crime reporter Eddie Laxton. I'd got a particularly exotic suit on from Apple Boutique – a frock-coat, black-and-white shoes, a big ruffled shirt and scarves and, no doubt, badges. I didn't want Eddie to think I was being stand-offish because I was in this exotic company (of The Beatles) so I went over and said: 'Hello Eddie, you know me.' He said, 'No, I don't. I don't know this new guy at all.' I felt terrible, suddenly like Adam; you're naked, you haven't got any clothes on. 'Wow! He's right,' I thought, and I did feel weird – I'm not sure I've ever felt quite as free as I had until I met Eddie Laxton from the real world, so-called. But it was the spirit of the age. A lot of us who'd got free of grey suits (which I'm now happy to wear again) welcomed this freedom.*

NEIL ASPINALL: *I was running Apple, but I have no idea what my position was – probably the lotus position. Running Apple at that time was hard work, in the sense that there were so many different ideas coming in, and people had different criteria for how Apple should be run and what it should represent, and who should be on the label and what colour the room should be decorated... On that level it was pretty difficult. Talking about colours is maybe a bit superficial, but it's a symptom. There were big rooms at Savile Row, and somebody would say: 'Why don't you put a partition across the room so you can be here and the secretary can be in the other room.' So you would get a partition built, and then the next day somebody else (a different Beatle) would come in and say: 'What's this partition doing here?' and kick it down.*

*Someone would ask: 'Do we need a press office?' – 'Yes, we do.' – 'Well, maybe we don't...' – 'Should we sign this artist or shouldn't we?' Somebody would be signed because one person liked them, and then somebody else would be signed because somebody else liked them. It was anarchy, really. Some of my memories are happy; some are not. I can't say that I really enjoyed Savile Row that much.*

DEREK TAYLOR: *There's no doubt that by the end of 1968 (although I thought I was living for others; always martyring myself for the boys and all that), I was in my own egocentric way having an enormous amount of fun – ringmastering this circus for my own personal satisfaction, if you like. I was in a job that really suited me because it was chaotic. It was unmanageable, and yet it had a real press focus and the work was getting done. But, had I been one of the boys, coming in as they did now and again looking in on it, I'd have been shocked.*

*Sometimes (you had intercoms in those days in offices and anyone could flick through) people could hear what sounded like bedlam, because there was always a record-player playing, and a light show on the ceiling from a machine which we bought from the Hare Krishnas. But if anyone ever came in and said, 'God, this is a confusing place,' I would hit the roof. 'What do you mean, confusing? We know exactly what's going on in here!' And, in a way, we did.*

*Lots of people came in from the press and wrote long feature articles, and not all critical by any means. Careers were launched there – not only recording careers, but journalistic careers.*

## JOHN: AND THEN I BROUGHT IN MAGIC ALEX, AND IT JUST WENT FROM BAD TO WORSE.[72]

PAUL: 'Magic' Alex was a Greek bloke who was a friend of John's originally. I remember John coming to my house one day and saying: 'This is my new guru – Magic Alex.' And I said 'Oh, OK.'

It's a funny way to introduce anyone, it's very final. I thought, 'Oh yeah? What does he do, then?' He had a lot of knowledge about electronics. Other people disputed his ideas and said that they couldn't be done, but Alex said they could. We sat around expounding a lot of theories at the time – particularly late at night – and he had some great ones.

He thought of using wallpaper which would act as loudspeakers: you would paper your room with speakers. There is a lot of technology coming in now, but I don't think it existed then. It was just talked about in scientific journals that we didn't read, but Alex did. He was a nice bloke and we got on.

Alex became our man for Apple Electronics, because we thought if he could make loudspeakers out of wallpaper it would be great. But he never came up with it. He had a little laboratory and he did one or two fun things, but it didn't end up as he'd said it would. He's around still. He uses his proper name now.

RINGO: Magic Alex invented electrical paint. You paint your living room, plug it in, and the walls light up! We saw small pieces of metal as samples, but then we realised you'd have to put steel sheets on your living-room wall and paint them. Also, he had the 'talking telephone' (remember this is 1968) – a speaker-phone, which compensated so the volume always stayed at the same level as you walked round the room.

He had an idea to stop people taping our records off the radio – you'd have to have a decoder to get the signal. And then we thought we could sell the time and put commercials on instead. We brought EMI and Capitol in from America to look at it, but they weren't interested at all.

God knows what else he invented. He had this one idea that we all should have our heads drilled. It's called trepanning. Magic Alex said that if we had it done our inner third eye would be able to see, and we'd get cosmic instantly.

GEORGE: Magic Alex impressed John, and because John was impressed with him, Alex came into *our* lives. He was a charming fellow – for a while.

One invention he had was amazing, though. It was a small square of metal, like stainless steel, with two wires coming out of it to a flashlight battery. If you held the metal and connected the wires one way, it would very quickly become so hot you had to drop it. Then, if you reversed the wires, it got as cold as ice.

Another invention consisted of a thin piece of metal with something on it like a thick enamel paint, and it too had wires coming out of it. When it was connected, it lit up in a bright luminous greeny-yellow colour. Alex said, 'Imagine if that was the back end of the car and you'd just stepped on the brake.' So that's what I wanted him to do. The Ferrari was going to be rubbed down to the bare metal and Alex was

**APPLE CORPS LTD**
95 Wigmore Street
London W1

telephone 01-486 1931 INTERNAL MEMO

PAUL: APPLE WILL PRODUCE ELECTRONICS; NOT GIMMICKS BUT GREAT INVENTIONS. WE HAVE A FRIEND CALLED ALEXIS MARDAS WHO IS A GENIUS AT INVENTING THINGS.[68]

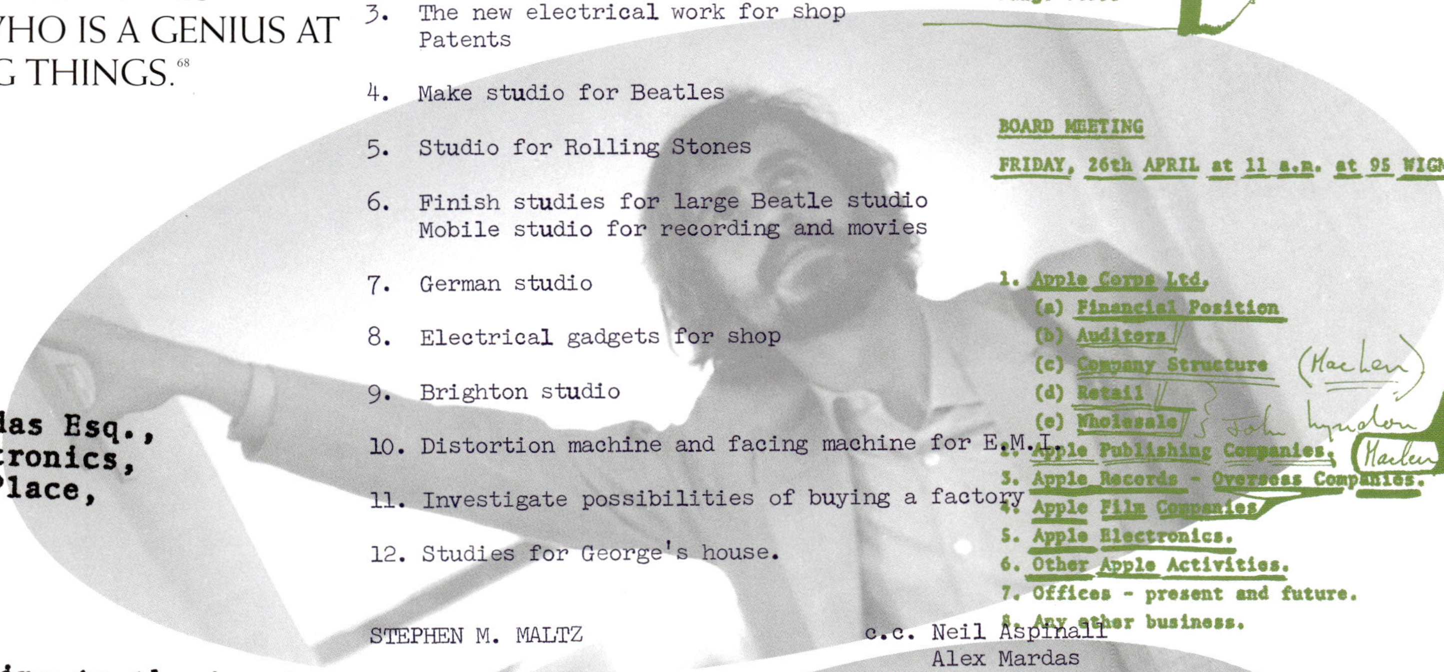

MEMORANDUM 19th January, 1968

Re: Future Plans of Apple Electronics Ltd.

1. Finish work at 34 Boston Place
2. Contract re Taj Mahal Hotel, India
3. The new electrical work for shop Patents
4. Make studio for Beatles
5. Studio for Rolling Stones
6. Finish studies for large Beatle studio Mobile studio for recording and movies
7. German studio
8. Electrical gadgets for shop
9. Brighton studio
10. Distortion machine and facing machine for E.M.I.
11. Investigate possibilities of buying a factory
12. Studies for George's house.

STEPHEN M. MALTZ c.c. Neil Aspinall
Alex Mardas

INTERN

DATE 23rd April, 1968
FROM Stephen Maltz
TO Neil Aspinall
Dennis O'Dell
Brian Lewis
John Lennon
Paul McCartney
George Harrison
Ringo Starr
RE:

BOARD MEETING

FRIDAY, 26th APRIL at 11 a.m. at 95 WIGMORE ST.

1. Apple Corps Ltd.
   (a) Financial Position
   (b) Auditors
   (c) Company Structure (Maclen)
   (d) Retail
   (e) Wholesale } John Lyndon
2. Apple Publishing Companies. (Maclen)
3. Apple Records – Overseas Companies.
4. Apple Film Companies
5. Apple Electronics.
6. Other Apple Activities.
7. Offices – present and future.
8. Any other business.

Alexis Mardas Esq.,
Apple Electronics,
34 Boston Place,
N.W.1

Dear Alexi

According to the invoices we have 200 light machines were ordered by you. I wonder if it would be possible for you to let me know what has happened to them.

going to apply the magic coating. We asked, 'Can you do other colours too?' – 'Sure, whatever you want.'

We decided he was going to connect a colour scheme for the whole body of the car. The back of the car would be red – but only when you stepped on the brake! The rest of the time the whole car would be connected to the revs on the gearbox – so the car would start off quite dull, and as you shifted through the gears it would become brighter. You could go down the A3 and pass somebody and it would look like a flying saucer. (And that's another thing: I was going to give him the V12 engine out of my Ferrari Berlinetta and John was going to give him his, and Alex reckoned that with those two engines he could make a flying saucer.)

But he didn't *do* anything (except he made a toilet with a radio in it, or something). When we finally got him to make a recording studio, we walked in and it was chaos. It was the biggest disaster of all time. He was walking round with a white coat on like some sort of chemist, but didn't have a clue what he was doing. It was a sixteen-track system, and he had sixteen little speakers all around the walls. You only need two speakers for stereo sound. It was awful. The whole thing was a disaster and had to be ripped out.

RINGO: Originally, the studio was going to be seventy-two track, which was pretty far out in 1968. We bought some huge computers from British Aerospace in Weybridge, and put them in my barn in St George's Hill. Birds lived in them, mice lived in them – but they never left that barn. It was a far-out idea, but once again Alex never came through. We'd just graduated to eight track – God knows what we thought we were going to do with seventy-two.

JOHN: I think some of his stuff has actually come true. They just haven't manufactured it. Maybe one of the whole midst is a saleable object. He was just another guy. That comes and goes around people like us. He's all right, but he's cracked. He means well.[70]

Directors:-
J.W. Lennon
J.P. McCartney
N.S. Aspinall
C J. Epstein

Registered Office:-
23 Albemarle Street
London, W.1

May 10th 1968

Dear Alex,

Recording Studio

As you are no doubt aware, we have been thinking of building a recording studio for some time and we think we might now have found some premises. I should like to know whether your company could built a studio for us and after having looked at our premises, if you could let us know how much it would cost.

Yours sincerely,

N S Aspinall

N.S. Aspinall

JOHN: THERE'S NO SUCH THING AS A GENIUS, BUT IF THERE ARE ANY, HE'S ONE. THE THINGS HE PRODUCES ARE FANTASTIC. I WISH I COULD TELL YOU ABOUT THEM, BUT WE'VE LEARNT IN THIS HAPPY BUSINESS-WORLD THAT SPIES IN BROWN RAINCOATS AND SUNGLASSES GO AROUND, AND SO YOU CAN'T SAY ANYTHING ABOUT A PRODUCT UNTIL IT'S OUT.[68]

GEORGE: *Yellow Submarine* came out in July. I remember meeting Heinz Edelmann and the main artists involved; they sketched some ideas and we talked about the characters in the cartoon. But we only had one or two meetings, maximum, with them and the producer, Al Brodax – basically there was very little involvement from us.

PAUL: Erich Segal, the author of *Love Story*, was one of the writers of the screenplay. It was good fun having a chat with him and seeing where he was going to go, but I was surprised when they took the psychedelic option. I thought that the producers were after something a little bit more commercial, which would have been OK by me. I wanted *Yellow Submarine* to be more of a classic cartoon. I thought they should have just had a man who sailed to sea and went to the land of submarines. He could have gone under the water, seen everything and met all the people – it sounds like a pretty good story.

I love the Disney films, so I thought this could be the greatest Disney movie ever – only with our music. That would be a lovely mix. They didn't want that, though, and luckily it wasn't my decision. Looking back on the film, I do like it now. It's really quite interesting. They felt they ought to pick up on where we had been up to, which was *Sgt Pepper* – but a *Bambi* would have been better for me at the time.

We told them we weren't going to get too heavily involved, and that we didn't want to do the voices – it was too much work. So instead, people like Lance Percival (a cabaret artist and voice-over man) did them. They could do a pretty good Ringo, but that's also where all that terrible fake Liverpool accent came from. It's like Americans trying to do Cockney: 'Wotcher, all right mate?' – the Dick Van Dyke syndrome.

GEORGE: Towards the end of the production we filmed the segment at the end of the film where I've got a hole in my pocket and all that stuff. Blue Meanies were seen leaving the theatre.

I liked the film. I think it's a classic. I'm not sure why we never did our own voices, but the actors probably did it better because they needed to be more cartoon-like. Our voices were pretty cartoon-like anyway, but the exaggeration that you've got with the actors' voices suits it. That film works for every generation – every baby, three or four years old, goes through *Yellow Submarine*.

RINGO: Eddie Yates from *Coronation Street* did the voices for John and me. They sound the same to me, I can't see any difference between them.

PAUL: At the end they wanted a bit where we came on and said: 'Hi, this is The Beatles here, we hope you've enjoyed the film.' We had to go and have it filmed in January 1968, which we weren't keen to do; but once we'd got ourselves involved we had to give them something.

I think if it had gone Disneyesque and they'd wanted a 'When You Wish Upon A Star' I would have been very keen to do it, but because they were going more in the *Pepper* direction, we said to use songs we'd already recorded, like 'All You Need Is Love'. They also wanted some new songs from us, so we recorded 'Only A Northern Song' in Abbey Road. I remember playing a silly trumpet. My dad used to play. I can't, but I can mess around a lot – and that song gave me the perfect framework. It was very tongue in cheek.

GEORGE: 'Only A Northern Song' was a joke relating to Liverpool, the Holy City in the North of England. In addition, the song was copyrighted Northern Songs Ltd., which I don't own, so: 'It doesn't really matter what chords I play… as it's only a Northern Song.'

RINGO: I loved *Yellow Submarine*. I thought it was really innovative, with great animation. The Sea of Holes, the Blue Meanie syndrome – it's still great and I'm glad we were involved with it.

The thing with the film that still blows me away is that in the first year it was out I had all these kids coming up to me, saying: 'Why did you press the button?' In the film I press a button and get shot out of the submarine – and kids from all over the whole bloody world kept shouting, 'Why did you press the button?' at me as if it was real. They actually thought it was me.

JOHN: Brodax got half of *Yellow Submarine* out of my mouth. The idea for the Hoover, the machine that sucks people up – all those were my ideas. They used to come to the studio and chat: 'Hi, John, old bean. Got any ideas for the film?' And I'd just spout out all this stuff, and they went off and did it.[72]

It was the third movie that we owed United Artists. Brian had set it up and we had nothing to do with it. But I liked the movie: the artwork. They wanted another song, so I knocked off 'Hey Bulldog'. It's a good-sounding record that means nothing.[80]

Nems Enterprises Ltd. and Subafilms hereby approve the use of the Lennon-McCartney song, YELLOW SUBMARINE as the title song and story theme of the film to be produced. Three other songs are to be written by THE BEATLES once the film treatment is complete, which songs are to relate to said story treatment. King agrees that it will provide a writer to meet with Paul McCartney to fully discuss said treatment, and thereupon write a screen treatment based upon these discussions.

November 1967

(1) Nems Enterprises Limited ('Nems')

(2) Mr. George Harrison
Mr. John Winston Lennon
Mr. James Paul McCartney
Mr. Richard Starkey
('The Beatles')

(3) Subafilms Ltd ('Suba')

(4) Hearst Corporation acting through its King Feature Syndicate Division of 235 East 45th Street, New York N.Y. 10017, U.S.A. ('King')

Dear Sirs:

YELLOW SUBMARINE

This agreement when signed by you and us shall constitute our agreement made in consideration of the respective obligations, facilitites and services which are herein set forth as follows:-

1. At your request and in consideration of 1/-d. now paid by each of you to us (receipt acknowledged) we agree to make available to Suba and King jointly without further charge on a non-exclusive basis tapes of the following recordings:

Hey Bulldog
ALL TOGETHER NOW
YOU ~~KNOW MY NAME, LOOK UP THE NUMBER~~
All Too Much
ITS ONLY A NORTHERN SONG
ALL YOU NEED IS LOVE
WHEN I'M 64
LOVELY RITA
NOWHERE MAN
ITS GETTING BETTER
MAGICAL MYSTERY TOUR
SGT. PEPPER'S REPRISE
YELLOW SUBMARINE
ELEANOR RIGBY
A LITTLE HELP FROM MY FRIENDS
PENNY LANE
STRAWBERRY FIELDS
LUCY IN THE SKY WITH DIAMONDS
YOU ~~ARE TOO MUCH~~
HELP
WAIT
YOUR MOTHER SHOULD KNOW
I AM THE WALRUS
FOOL ON THE HILL
FLYING
BLUE JAY WAY
DICK EMERY SINGING LUCY IN THE SKY WITH DIAMONDS

CROWD NOISES FROM THE SONG SGT. PEPPER'S LONELY HEARTS CLUB BAND

SOUND EFFECTS FROM YELLOW SUBMARINE

DOG BARKING & SOUNDS USED IN THE INTRODUCTIONS AND END OF THE SONG GOOD MORNING FROM THE SGT. PEPPER ALBUM

Notes
~~Clause~~ Page 4
1. "Beatles will be requested" to compose 3 songs?
2. E. Rudeff — was that him?
3. 50% Publishing to King?
4. p.5 3 other songs are to be written by Beatles and to "relate" ?!!

RINGO: WE WERE JUST HANGING OUT. JUST ANOTHER DAY IN THE PARK FOR THE BEATLE BOYS.

GEORGE: The painting on the side of the Baker Street shop looked amazing, but everything went wrong. A couple of nearby shopkeepers decided they didn't like the tone of the building, although others liked it because it brought a lot of attention and Baker Street suddenly became somewhere worth talking about. Before that, other than Sherlock Holmes, Baker Street was nothing – nobody went there except to catch a bus. Now, suddenly, it was really happening. But because of the complaints, the landlord or whoever owned the lease made us paint it out and get rid of it.

PAUL: The council got their knickers in a twist and said that we had to get rid of the mural. We said, 'Oh, you're kidding, it's beautiful – everyone loves it.' Some residents probably objected. Then we were going to paint the shop white and project the painting from the opposite side of the road. We were full of good ideas. Some of them we never got round to, but it was a great time for ideas.

GEORGE: If they'd protected it and the painted wall was there now, they would be saying, 'Wow, look at this. We've got to stop it chipping off.' But that's just typical of the narrow minds we were trying to fight against. That's what the whole Sixties Flower-Power thing was about: 'Go away, you bunch of boring people.' The whole government, the police, the public – everybody was so boring, and then suddenly people realised they could have fun.

Once we were told we had to get rid of the painting, the whole thing started to lose its appeal. The whole tone of the events around the Apple shop was going sour, and – as it was not working out – we decided to sell it. We ended up giving the contents away. We put an ad in the paper and we filmed people coming in and grabbing everything.

JOHN: It was a big event and all the kids came and just took everything that was in the shop. That was the best thing about the whole shop, when we gave it all away. But the night before, we all went in and took what we wanted. It wasn't much, T-shirts... It was great, it was like robbing. We took everything we wanted home.

And the next day we were watching, and there were thousands of kids all going in and getting their freebies. It was great. Of course, Derek and the others hated it but it so happened that I was running the office at that time, so we were in control. Paul had called me up one day and said, 'I'm going away. You take over.' It was as stupid as that.[72] We came up with the idea to give it all away and stop fucking about with a psychedelic clothes shop.[70]

PAUL: WE CAME INTO SHOPS BY THE TRADESMAN'S ENTRANCE, BUT WE'RE LEAVING BY THE FRONT DOOR. APPLE IS MAINLY CONCERNED WITH FUN, NOT FROCKS.[68]

RINGO: We went in the night before and took everything we wanted. We had loads of shirts and jackets – we cleaned a lot of the stuff out. It wasn't a sale, we just gave it all away, and that was the best idea. In the end, of course, people were coming with wheelbarrows. It was silly, but we *had* wanted to open a shop and dress everyone like us.

NEIL ASPINALL: *I think they got to the point where they didn't want it any more. It wasn't that it was losing money, it was just that the guys decided, for whatever reasons, that they didn't want to be in the retail business. They weren't retailers and it was taking up a lot of time.*

PAUL: The nice thing was that we weren't too fussed when it didn't work out. We suddenly realised we'd better cut our losses. It was great: giving the clothes to the people who showed up on the day. Michael J. Pollard, the actor, got a jacket (which Linda took a photograph of – it's in her book). The idea was that you could have one item each: 'You mustn't take *two* – stay in the spirit of the thing.'

Well, they cleaned out the shop. Personally, I think it was a good way to do it because it showed we weren't seriously trying to be in the rag trade: 'Look, it didn't work out so you can have the schmutter!'

DEREK TAYLOR: *The giving away of the clothing brought out that worst in people that I dread to see. Cabbies were grabbing kaftans and capes and silk ruffled shirts off rails: 'I want this' and 'I want that'. I thought it was one of the ugliest things I had ever heard of, this giving away of the clothes. It was awful and vulgar.*

*I didn't want them to close the shop at all, really, and I wrote an impassioned open letter: 'Dear boys, please don't...' I dreaded to see the thing falling apart.*

PAUL: WE FELT IT WAS TIME TO STEP BACK BECAUSE THAT WAS WHAT WE WANTED TO DO. YOU CAN STILL MAKE GOOD MUSIC WITHOUT GOING FORWARD. SOME PEOPLE WANT US TO GO ON UNTIL WE VANISH UP OUR OWN B SIDES.[68]

GEORGE: The Apple shop was now empty, and it was suggested that we advertise the new single in the window. So somebody went with whitewash and wrote 'Hey Jude' and 'Revolution' in big letters. The next day the shop window was smashed, apparently because somebody thought it was like '*Juden*' in the Nazi campaign before the war.

PAUL: I went into the Apple shop just before 'Hey Jude' was being released. The windows were whited-out, and I thought: 'Great opportunity. Baker Street, millions of buses going around...' So, before anyone knew what it meant, I scraped 'Hey Jude' out of the whitewash.

A guy who had a delicatessen in Marylebone rang me up, and he was furious: 'I'm going to send one of my sons round to beat you up.' I said, 'Hang on, hang on – what's this about?' and he said: 'You've written "Jude" in the shop window.' I had no idea it meant 'Jew', but if you look at footage of Nazi Germany, '*Juden Raus*' was written in whitewashed windows with a Star of David. I swear it never occurred to me.

I said: 'I'm really sorry,' and on and on... 'some of my best friends are Jewish, really. It's just a song we've got coming out. If you listen to the song you'll see it's nothing to do with any of that – it's a complete coincidence.' He was just about pacified in the end.

GEORGE: 'Hey Jude' was actually about Julian Lennon. It was written by Paul at the time John was splitting up with Cynthia. Julian was just a little boy – probably five years old – and Paul had gone out to John's house and been affected by seeing Julian, the innocent bystander in a divorce situation.

PAUL: When John and Cynthia got married it didn't really work. There was a beautiful kid, and they were quite happy for a while, but my estimation of it was that Cynthia wanted to tie John down to the pipe-and-slippers nice life. Of course, John was never ready for that.

John was a great jumper-off of cliffs. I often remember him saying, 'Look, you've come to a cliff. Why don't you jump off it?' I would say, 'You would probably get dead, John.' He was always coming up with hare-brained schemes, and so I developed a defence against them: 'I'll tell you what, you do it first and give us a shout. If it's OK, I'm jumping. If I hear nothing, I'm staying here.'

He came up to me once at a dinner and said, 'Have you ever thought about trepanning? It's an ancient Roman thing – you have a hole drilled in your skull.' And we talked about it a lot, as you did in the Sixties. I said, 'No, not really.' He said, 'I think we should all have it done.' I was still saying, 'I don't know about that. *You* have it done, and if it's fine we'll all have it done as well.' That was the only way to get rid of John's madcap schemes, otherwise he would have had us all with holes in our heads the next morning.

So, John and Cynthia were splitting up and I felt particularly sorry for Julian. I had known them for so long. We had hung out since John's art school days when I had a girlfriend called Dot and John had Cynthia, and we used to foursome it a lot and go to parties together. Since then, I'd seen them get married and seen them have Julian.

I thought, as a friend of the family, I would motor out to Weybridge and tell them that everything was all right: to try and cheer them up, basically, and see how they were. I had about an hour's drive. I would always turn the radio off and try and make up songs, just in case... I started singing: 'Hey Jools – don't make it bad, take a sad song, and make it better...' It was optimistic, a hopeful message for Julian: 'Come on, man, your parents got divorced. I know you're not happy, but you'll be OK.'

I eventually changed 'Jools' to 'Jude'. One of the characters in *Oklahoma* is called Jud, and I like the name. I played the song to John when I'd finished it – although I thought there might be a little more to do because there was one passage which went 'the movement you need is on your shoulder'. As I was playing it I looked at John and said, 'I'll fix that bit.' – 'What?' – 'I've used the word "shoulder" once already, and anyway, it's a stupid expression; it sounds like a parrot. I'll change it.' John said, 'You won't, you know. That's the best line in the song. I know what it means – it's great.' That was the good thing about John: whereas I'd definitely have knocked that line out, he would say it was great. Then I could see it through his eyes. So when I play that song, that's the line when I think of John; and I sometimes get a little emotional during that moment.

JOHN: 'Hey Jude' is one of his masterpieces. He said it was written about Julian, my child. He knew I was splitting with Cyn and leaving Julian. He was driving over to say 'hi' to Julian. He'd been like an uncle to him. Paul was always good with kids. And so he came up with 'Hey Jude'.

But I always heard it as a song to me. If you think about it, Yoko's just come into the picture. He's saying: 'Hey, Jude – hey, John.' I know I'm sounding like one of those fans who reads things into it, but you *can* hear it as a song to me. The words 'go out and get her' – subconsciously he was saying, 'Go ahead, leave me.' But on a conscious level, he didn't want me to go ahead. The angel inside him was saying, 'Bless you.' The devil in him didn't like it at all, because he didn't want to lose his partner.[80]

GEORGE MARTIN: *We recorded 'Hey Jude' in Trident Studios. It was a long song. In fact, after I timed it I actually said, 'You can't make a single that long.' I was shouted down by the boys – not for the first time in my life – and John asked: 'Why not?' I couldn't think of a good answer, really – except the pathetic one that disc jockeys wouldn't play it. He said, 'They will if it's us.' And, of course, he was absolutely right.*

PAUL: It *was* longer than any single had been, but we had a good bunch of engineers. We asked how long a 45 could be. They said that four minutes was about all you could squeeze into the grooves before it seriously started to lose volume and everyone had to turn the sound up. But they did some very clever stuff, squeezing the bit that didn't have to be loud, then allowing the rest more room. Somehow, they got seven minutes on there – which was quite an engineering feat.

I remember taking an acetate down to the Vesuvio, a three-in-the-morning-dossing-round-on-beanbags type club in Tottenham Court Road. As it was a suitable time in the evening, I got the DJ to put it on. I remember Mick Jagger coming up to me and saying: 'It's like two songs, man. It's got the song and then the whole "na na na" at the end. Yeah.'

I was always a bit in limbo with a new single; your heart's in your mouth when you first hear it played on the radio, for instance. I knew it was a lot to expect people to swallow the whole thing. Maybe they would want to fade it... but they didn't. I remember Stuart Henry on the Beeb saying: 'There you are my friends – either you like it or you don't.' Then he went on to the next record. I thought: 'Thank you! Couldn't you have thought of anything else, Stu?'

RINGO: 'Hey Jude' has become a classic. It felt good recording it. We put it down a couple of times – trying to get it right – and, like everything else, it just clicked. That's how it should be.

NEIL ASPINALL: *David Frost came down to Twickenham Film Studios where they were filming a performance of 'Hey Jude' and 'Revolution' and introduced it; like it was done for his show or something. It was filmed with an invited audience, and they all got up on stage and sang the chorus repeat for 'Hey Jude'.*

GEORGE: We made a film in front of an audience. They had brought people in for 'Hey Jude'. It wasn't done *just* for David Frost, but it was shown on his show and he was actually there when we filmed it.

GEORGE MARTIN: *The other side of 'Hey Jude' was 'Revolution'. We got into distortion on that, which we had a lot of complaints from the technical people about. But that was the idea: it was John's song and the idea was to push it right to the limit. Well, we went to the limit and beyond.*

GEORGE: The thing about 'Revolution' (and you could get into a debate about this), is that it's not so much the song but the attitude in which it was done. I think 'Revolution' is pretty good and it grooves along, but I don't particularly like the noise that it makes; and I say 'noise' because I didn't like the distorted sound of John's guitar.

I think that 'Revolution' – as with all the different styles of song – has its own merit. It's a good tune, but I don't think it is one of John's best songs. The only thing that may make it important is what it's actually saying, but at the same time there was a lot of other politically-aware music going around the world.

PAUL: I liked the sound on 'Revolution'.

MR DEREK TAYLOR APPLE RECORD COMPANY 3 SAVILE ROW
LONDONW1=

JOHN: When George and Paul and all of them were on holiday, I made 'Revolution' which is on the LP. I wanted to put it out as a single, but they said it wasn't good enough. We put out 'Hey Jude', which was worthy – but we could have had both.[70]

We recorded the song twice. The Beatles were getting real tense with each other. The first take, George and Paul were resentful and said it wasn't fast enough. Now, if you go into the details of what a hit record is and isn't, maybe. But The Beatles could have afforded to put out the slow, understandable version of 'Revolution' as a single, whether it was a gold record or a wooden record. But, because they were so upset over the Yoko thing and the fact that I was again becoming as creative and dominating as I was in the early days (after lying fallow for a couple of years), it upset the applecart. I was awake again and they weren't used to it.[80]

I wanted to put out what I felt about revolution. I thought it was about time we spoke about it, the same as I thought it was about time we stopped not answering about the Vietnamese war.

I had been thinking about it up in the hills in India. I still had this 'God will save us' feeling about it: 'It's going to be all right.' That's why I did it: I wanted to talk, I wanted to say my piece about revolutions. I wanted to tell you, or whoever listens, to communicate, to say, 'What do you say? This is what I say.'[70]

There were two versions of that song, but the underground left only picked up on the one that said 'count me out'. The original version which ends up on the LP said 'count me in' too; I put in both because I wasn't sure.

CONGRATULATIONS TO BEATLES ON NUMBER ONE WORLD
GROUP IN SPOTLIGHT POLL PLUS NUMBER ONE WORLD
RECORD HEY JUDE = JOHN COUGHLAN +

I didn't want to get killed. I didn't really know much about the Maoists, but I just knew that they seemed to be so few and yet they painted themselves green and stood in front of the police waiting to get picked off. I just thought it was unsubtle. I thought the original Communist revolutionaries coordinated themselves a bit better and didn't go around shouting about it.[71]

JOHN: You say, 'In order to change the world, we've got to understand what's wrong with the world and then destroy it. Ruthlessly.' You're obviously on a destruction kick. I'll tell you what's wrong with it – people. So, do you want to destroy them? Ruthlessly? Until you/we change your/our heads, there's no chance. Who fucked up Communism, Christianity, capitalism, Buddhism, etc.? Sick heads and nothing else. Do you think all the enemy wear capitalist badges so you can shoot them? [68]

RINGO: I never felt we'd gone too far, ever. Not musically and not in life, really. We didn't really do anything heavy in life. We didn't get radical. We were a little radical in our music, so it seems, with the backwards tapes and things like that, but we were not violent people.

JOHN: The statement in 'Revolution' was mine. The lyrics stand today. They're still my feeling about politics. I want to see the *plan*. That's what I used to say to Jerry Rubin and Abbie Hoffman. Count me out if it's for violence. Don't expect me on the barricades unless it's with flowers. As far as overthrowing something in the name of Marxism or Christianity, I want to know what you're going to do *after* you've knocked it down. I mean, can't we use *some* of it? What's the point of bombing Wall Street? If you want to change the system, change the system. It's no good shooting people.[80]

I know how I felt when I was at college at nineteen and twenty – I would have been for complete destruction. I always hoped for it anyway, just as a happening, just to go on the loot, to destroy it. I would have done then, but I don't know whether I would now – I still like stealing things; but I don't, because I can't be bothered. That's how I felt then, but if there was somebody like me I might listen.

If you want peace, you won't get it with violence. Please tell me one militant revolution that worked. Sure, a few of them took over, but what happened? Status quo. And if they smash it down, who do they think is going to build it up again? And then when they've built it up again, who do they think is going to run it? And how are they going to run it? They don't look further than their noses.[70] If someone showed me one that worked, then it might turn me a bit. I'd say, 'All right, that's the way to do it,' then turn the place upside down. But there isn't one.

The system-smashing scene has been going on forever. What's it done? The Irish did it, the Russians did it and the French did it – and where has it got them? It's got them nowhere. It's the same old game. Who's going to run this smashing-up? Who's going to take over? It'll be the biggest smashers. They'll be the ones to get in first and they'll be the ones to take over. I don't know what the answer is, but I think it's down to people.[72]

What I said in 'Revolution' – in all the versions – is 'change your head'. These people that are trying to change the world can't even get it all together. They're attacking and biting each others' faces, and all the time they're all pushing the same way. And if they keep going on like that, it's going to kill it before it's even moved.

It's silly to bitch about each other and be trivial. They've got to think in terms of at least the world or the universe, and stop thinking in terms of factories and one country.

The point is that the Establishment doesn't really exist, and if it does exist, it's old people. The only people that want to change it are young, and they're going to beat the Establishment. If they want to smash it all down, and have to be labourers as well to build it up again, then that's what they're going to get. If they'd just realise the Establishment can't last forever. The only reason it *has* lasted forever is that the only way people have ever tried to change it is by revolution. And the idea is just to move in on the scene, so they can take over the universities, do all the things that are practically feasible at the time. But not try and take over the state, or smash the state, or slow down the works. All they've got to do is get through and change it, because they will *be* it.[68]

If you think of the Establishment or whoever 'they' are, the Blue Meanies, you've got to remember that they're the sick ones. And if you've got a sick child in the family you don't kick it out the door – you've got to try and look after it or extend a hand to it. So somewhere along the line we've got to make a meeting point with whoever 'they' are, because even amongst them there are some human beings. In fact they're all human, but there's some that even look like it and respond like it. So it's up to us, if we're the aware generation, to extend a hand to the retarded child, and not just kick its teeth in because it happens to be a very big child.[72]

The only way to ensure a lasting peace of any kind is to change people's minds. There's no other way. The Government can do it with propaganda, Coca-Cola can do it with propaganda – why can't we? We are the hip generation.[69]

These left-wing people talk about giving the power to the people. That's nonsense – the people have the power. All we're trying to do is make people aware that they have the power themselves, and the violent way of revolution doesn't justify the ends.

All we're trying to say to people is to expose politicians and expose the people themselves who are hypocritical and sitting back and saying, 'Oh, we can't do anything about it, it's up to somebody else. Give us the answer, John.' People have to organise. Students have to organise voting. We have to be the Monday Club, only in a different way.[71]

They'll get peaceful revolution now if they put as much effort into that. The marching protests, where have they got us? The Grosvenor Square marches against Vietnam – the whole news was violence, the result of the marches.

CND were asking us: 'Well, what other ways can we promote peace? The marches seem to be going by the wind now and we have no result.' So I was saying: 'You've got a lot of sexy birds in the CND. The *Daily Mirror*, the biggest newspaper in Britain, has some bikini'd bird in every day. So when it says: "Pretty Polly for Peace" they'll stick it in so long as there's tits and arses on it. Promote peace *any* way – we've all got gimmicks in us.' Let them use sex for a change.[70]

EVENTUALLY IT WILL HAPPEN... IT HAS TO HAPPEN. IT MIGHT HAPPEN NOW, OR IT MIGHT HAPPEN IN FIFTY OR A HUNDRED YEARS.[70]

JOHN: SHE FORCED ME TO BECOME AVANT-GARDE AND TAKE MY CLOTHES OFF, WHEN ALL I WANTED WAS TO BECOME TOM JONES.[69]

PAUL: There was this girl called Yoko, Yoko Ono. She showed up at my house one day. It was John Cage's birthday, and she said she wanted to get hold of some manuscripts of various composers to give to him. She wanted one from me and John, so I said, 'Well, it's OK by me, but you'll have to go and see John.' And she did...

DEREK TAYLOR: *I went into Wigmore Street – and Yoko was in the office with John. I think they had been up all night. I didn't know of her and I hadn't seen her before, but she looked nice and John said: 'This is Yoko.' And: 'This is Derek, one of our friends.'*

*I went over and, for some reason or other, kissed her on top of the head, saying: 'Welcome to Apple,' and, 'How are you?' and so on. John said, 'I'll be with her now...' – one of those John things. Then he wandered off – he was always doing wanderings off – he put his hands on his hips, wandered off, and then came back: 'What do you think?' I said I was sure it would be fine.*

JOHN: I was too scared to break away from The Beatles, which I'd been looking to do since we stopped touring. I was vaguely looking for somewhere to go, but didn't have the nerve to really step out into the boat by myself, so I hung around. And when I met Yoko and fell in love: 'My God! This is different than anything before. This is more than a hit record. It's more than gold. It's more than everything...'[80]

Whatever I went through was worth it to meet Yoko. So, if I had to do all the things I did in my life – which is have a troubled childhood, a troubled teenage and an amazing whirlwind life with The Beatles, and then finally coming to land meeting Yoko – it was worth it.

I've never known love like this before, and it hit me so hard that I had to halt my marriage to Cyn. And don't think that was a reckless decision, because I felt very deeply about it and all the implications that would be involved. Some may say my decision was selfish. Well, I don't think it is. Are your children going to thank you when they are eighteen? Isn't it better to avoid rearing children in the atmosphere of a strained relationship?

My marriage to Cyn was not unhappy. But it was just a normal marital state where nothing happened and which we continued to sustain. You sustain it until you meet someone who suddenly sets you alight. With Yoko I really knew love for the first time. Our attraction was a mental one, but it happened physically too. Both are essential in the union.[68]

Being with Yoko makes me free. Being with Yoko makes me whole. I'm a half without her. Male is half without a female.[80] Before Yoko and I met, we were half a person. There's an old myth about people being half, and the other half being in the sky or in heaven or on the other side of the universe or a mirror image. But we are two halves, and together we're a whole.[69]

Yoko taught me about women. I was used to being served, like Elvis and a lot of the stars were. Always just being served by women, whether it was my Aunt Mimi, God bless you, or whoever – served by females, wives, girlfriends. You just flop in drunk and expect some girlfriend at college to make the breakfast the next morning. You know she'd been drunk as a dog too, with you at the party, but the female is supposed suddenly to get on the other side of the counter. It was quite an experience, and I appreciated what women have done for me all my life. I'd never even thought about it.

Yoko didn't buy that. She didn't give a shit about Beatles: 'What the fuck are The Beatles? I'm Yoko Ono! Treat me as *me*.' From the day I met her, she demanded equal time, equal space, equal rights. I didn't know what she was talking about. I said, 'What do you want, a contract? You can have whatever you want – but don't expect anything from me, or for me to change in any way.' 'Well,' she said, 'the answer to that is that I can't be here. Because there is no space where you are. Everything revolves around you, and I can't breathe in that atmosphere.' I'm thankful to her for the education.

I was used to a situation where the newspaper was there for me to read, and after I'd read it, somebody else could have it. It didn't occur to me that somebody else might want to look at it first. I think that's what kills people like Presley and others of that ilk. The king is always killed by his courtiers, not by his enemies. The king is over-fed, over-drugged, over-indulged; anything to keep the king tied to his throne. Most people in that position never wake up. They either die mentally or physically, or both. And what Yoko did for me was to liberate me from that situation.

And that's how The Beatles ended. Not because Yoko split The Beatles, but because she showed me what it was to be Elvis Beatle and to be surrounded by sycophants and slaves who were only interested in keeping the situation as it was. She said to me, 'You've got no clothes on.' Nobody had dared tell me that before.

With us, it's a teacher-pupil relationship. That's what people don't understand. She's the teacher and I'm the pupil. I'm the famous one, I'm supposed to know everything – but she taught me everything I fucking know.

When I met Yoko is when you meet your first woman and you leave the guys at the bar, and you don't go play football any more, and you don't go play snooker and billiards. Once I found *the* woman, the boys became of no interest whatsoever, other than they were like old friends. You know the song: 'Those wedding bells are breaking up that old gang of mine.' It didn't hit me until whatever age I was when I met Yoko, twenty-six. That was *it*. That old gang of mine was over the moment I met her. I didn't consciously know it at the time, but that's what was going on. As soon as I met her, that was the end of the boys. But it so happened the boys were well known and weren't just the local guys at the bar.

Yoko really woke me up to myself. She didn't fall in love with the Beatle, she didn't fall in love with my fame. She fell in love with me for myself, and through that brought out the best in me. She was the ultimate trip.[80]

Freedom is in the mind. It seems that as soon as a couple gets together, the man's supposed to go somewhere and work and the woman's supposed to be somewhere else, and I don't think that's very good for a relationship. It just so happens that's the way we all live. Maybe in the past they worked together or within sight of each other. She'd be digging the potatoes and he'd be cutting the hay or something, or they'd split for hunting, something like that. But I don't see why we should be apart, especially as we can work together and we have the same interests. It's not like I'm a mountain climber and she's an archaeologist. Our interests are the same, so that helps.

Nothing is more important than what goes on between two people, because it's two people that produce children, two people that fall in love. You don't generally fall in love with two people at once. I've never experienced it. Promiscuity is something else – it's for kids, really. I feel as though I went through it, and what's the point? It often isn't that satisfactory as an end product to living. It's like eating, you can't survive on it alone. You need something else.[70]

After Yoko and I met, I didn't realise I was in love with her. I was still thinking it was an artistic collaboration, as it were – producer and artist. We'd known each other for a couple of years. My ex-wife was away in Italy, and Yoko came to visit me and we took some acid. I was always shy with her, and she was shy, so instead of making love we went upstairs and made tapes. I had this room where I would write and make strange loops and things, like that for The Beatles' stuff. So we made a tape all night. She was doing her funny voices as I was pushing all different buttons on my tape recorder and getting sound effects. And then as the sun rose we made love, and that was *Two Virgins*. That was the first time.

*Two Virgins* happened by accident. I realised somebody else was as barmy as me – a wife with freaky sounds – and could equally enjoy non-dance music or non-pop music that was... they call it avant-garde.

That's the only word you can use for it, but I think a label like avant-garde defeats itself. You learnt to have avant-garde exhibitions. The very fact that avant-garde can have an exhibition defeats the purpose of avant-garde, because it's already formalised and ritualised. I didn't think anything of it other than variations on a theme of sound.[80]

JOHN:

WONSAPONATIME THERE WERE TWO BALLOONS CALLED JOCK AND YONO. THEY WERE STRICTLY IN LOVE-BOUND TO HAPPEN IN A MILLION YEARS. THEY WERE TOGETHER, MAN. UNFORTUNATIMETABLE THEY BOTH SEEMED TO HAVE PREVIOUS EXPERIENCE – WHICH KEPT CALLING THEM ONE WAY ORANOTHER (YOU KNOW HOWITIS). BUT THEY BATTLED ON AGAINST OVERWHELMING ODDITIES, INCLUDO SOME OF THEIR BEAST FRIENDS. BEING IN LOVE THEY CLOONG EVEN THE MORE TOGETHER, MAN – BUT SOME OF THE POISONESS-MONSTER OF OUTRATED BUSLODEDSHITHROWERS DID STICK SLIGHTLY AND THEY OCCASIONALLY HAD TO RESORT TO THE DRYCLEANERS. LUCKILY THIS DID NOT KILL THEM AND THEY WEREN'T BANNED FROM THE OLYMPIC GAMES. THEY LIVED HOPEFULLY EVER AFTER, AND WHO COULD BLAME THEM.[78]

DEREK TAYLOR: *Another morning in Apple (there was never a dull moment, and this was such a moment – not dull) and Jeremy Banks who worked with me said: 'There's something in your drawer – a mind-bending thing.' So I opened it up and there was a picture of John and Yoko with no clothes on.*

NEIL ASPINALL: *John had just given Jeremy a roll of film and said, 'Get that developed, please.' And when he got it back and saw the nude pictures he said: 'This is mind-blowing.' Everything was always 'mind-blowing' to Jeremy, but – just that one time – he was actually right. He couldn't believe it.*

JOHN: We were both a bit embarrassed when we peeled off for the picture, so I took it myself with a delayed-action shutter. The picture was to prove that we are not a couple of demented freaks, that we are not deformed in any way and that our minds are healthy. If we can make society accept these kind of things without offence, without sniggering, then we shall be achieving our purpose.[68]

What we did purposely is not have a pretty photograph; not have it lighted so as we looked sexy or good. There were a couple of other takes from that session where we looked rather nice, hid the little bits that aren't that beautiful; we looked good. We used the straightest, most unflattering picture just to show that we were human.[74]

PAUL: It wasn't a glamorous picture; it wasn't a nudie model with elastoplast and clear sellotape holding them up and stuff. It was the real thing: them baring it all to the world. But that was the whole idea with *Two Virgins*.

I know it was shocking, but I'm not sure whether us lot were too shocked by it – we just knew he'd have a bit of flak. Obviously, the minute the newspapers saw a shot like that, they were going to be on the phone. I knew John was inviting a lot of that. In the end, he'd invited a lot more than they wanted and they started to get busted and things. Quite an oppressive campaign started against them and it probably began with that cover. It's weird, isn't it? Our mothers and fathers all had to get naked to conceive us, and yet we're still very prudish about nudity, even in this day and age. But John and Yoko were looking at nudity as artists.

JOHN: We felt like two virgins because we were in love, just met, and we were trying to make something. And we thought to show everything. People are always looking at people like me, trying to see some secret: 'What do they do? Do they go to the bathroom? Do they eat?' So we just said, 'Here.'[75]

GEORGE: What I thought of the sleeve then was the same as I think now: it's just two not-very-nice-looking bodies, two flabby bodies naked. It's harmless, really – different strokes for different folks.

RINGO: The cover was the mind-blower – I remember to this day the moment when they came in and showed me. I don't really remember the music, I'd have to play it now. But he showed me the cover and I pointed to the *Times*: 'Oh, you've even got the *Times* in it...' as if he didn't have his dick hanging out.

I said, 'Ah, come on, John. You're doing all this stuff and it may be cool for you, but you know we all have to answer. It doesn't matter; whichever one of us does something, we *all* have to answer for it.' He said, 'Oh, Ringo, you only have to answer the phone.' I said, 'OK, fine,' because it was true. The press would be calling up, and just at that point I didn't want to be bothered – but in the end that's all I had to do: answer the phone. It was fine. Two or three people phoned and I said: 'See, he's got the *Times* on the cover.'

JOHN: George and Paul were a little shocked, that was weird. That really shocked me, the fact that they were prudish. You can't imagine – it was so uptight in those days. It's not that long ago, and people are uptight about nude bodies.[74] We didn't create nudity, we just put it out. Somebody else had been nude before.[72]

PAUL: I was slightly shocked but, seeing as I wrote a liner note for the sleeve, I obviously wasn't too uptight.

DEREK TAYLOR: *I said: 'Right. OK. Fine. Let's get on with things. Let's do something about this.' It was very interesting and exciting, and I thought that here was a monumental problem with which we could deal. Life there was such an 'action-reaction' situation that this was just one more thrilling thing.*

*And, of course, the Sunday papers were at us, and at this photograph. This filthy thing! 'Look at These Filthy People!' and there was a big circle over the naughty part and an arrow: 'This is where the naughty part would be if people like us were not so decent. We wouldn't dream of showing it to you – but aren't they awful!'*

*So I found something – I got a Bible. There's always something to hand, isn't there? And there was a bit in the book of Genesis which said: 'The man and his wife were naked and not ashamed,' or something like that, which I thought was suitable. John and Yoko were not married – but hey! This was life and... 'Here's this thing in the Bible – now what are you press going to do about it?'*

JOHN: It was insane! People got so upset about it – the fact that two people were naked.[80] I didn't think there'd be such a fuss. I guess the world thinks we're an ugly couple.[69]

NEIL ASPINALL: *At the time, I don't think the public liked Yoko very much – I don't know why, but they didn't seem to. It might have been because of the press, but I also think because of the avant-garde stuff. The public just didn't understand it, and I tend to find that if you don't understand something you're likely to be prejudiced against it.*

PAUL: The *Two Virgins* record itself I didn't find that interesting; the music wasn't shocking to me because I'd made a lot like that myself. I think John may have got some ideas from when I had a couple of Brennell tape recorders. I used to bounce sounds between them and multi-track to make crazy tapes for friends late at night. It was just ambient music.

I had a nice line in tape loops and crazy little classical things. I made a record for the guys called 'Unforgettable' after the Nat King Cole song; like a little radio show. I'd go down to the publishers and get a big 78 acetate made of it and send it round to the guys: 'Here's a little bit of music if you're feeling crazy.'

John asked me how I did it, so I showed him how to plug the machines up. John got two at his house in Weybridge, with exactly the same set-up, and I showed him how to use it all. If you take the superimposer out, you can multi-track it all and keep going endlessly – just bouncing it back and forth. You can make crazy records using relatively few tracks (as long as you don't need good-quality sound, because it loses quality each time).

GEORGE: I don't think I actually heard all of *Two Virgins*; just bits of it. I wasn't particularly into that kind of thing. That was his and her affair; their trip. They got involved with each other and were obviously into each other to such a degree that they thought everything they said or did was of world importance, and so they made it into records and films. (I was getting fed up with The Beatles by that time, let alone anything else around it. I was getting into all the other stuff, the Indian music.)

It was an Apple album, but Apple was distributed by EMI and they refused to handle it, so it was put out by Tetragrammaton in the USA.

JOHN: *Two Virgins* was a big fight. It was held up for nine months. Joseph Lockwood was a nice, nice guy; but he sat down on a big table at the top of EMI with John and Yoko and told me he will do everything he can to help us, because we explained what it meant and why we were doing it. And he got me to sign him one – he's got a signed edition of the very first one. Then, when we tried to put it out, he sent a personal note to everybody saying: 'Don't print it. Don't put it out.' So we couldn't get the cover printed anywhere.[80]

Actually, the first record that would have been out on Apple would have been *Two Virgins* if they hadn't held it up. They stalled and they said this, that and the other. Being naive in lots of ways, I had no idea I was going to get slagging from the immediate family. I thought maybe somebody out there will say something, but I was making a statement. It was as good as a song, it was better, you couldn't say it better – pictures speak louder than words. There it was: beautiful statement.[74]

…, is true to the best of my knowledge and belief and I make it knowing that if it is tendered in evidence I shall be liable to prosecution if I have wilfully stated in it anything which I know to be false or do not believe to be true.

This statement, consisting of 5 pages each signed by …

Dated the 22nd day of October 1968.

IN THE INNER LONDON AREA AND IN THE METROPOLITAN POLICE DISTRICT

MEMORANDUM of a CONVICTION entered in the REGISTER of the MARYLEBONE MAGISTRATES' COURT.

The 28th day of November, 1968.

| Name of defendant Age if known | Nature of offence or matter of complaint | Date of offence or matter of complaint | Plea or consent to order | Minute of Adjudication | Time allowed for payment and instalments |
|---|---|---|---|---|---|
| John Winston LENNON 28. Musician. | Having in his possession a dangerous drug to wit: a quantity of Cannabis Resin, without being duly authorised at … Square, W.1 on 18.10.68. -Con. to Reg.3. Dangerous Drugs (No.2) Regs. 1964 and Sec.13, Dangerous Drugs Act 1965. | 18.10.68. | EST. G. | £150. 20 guineas costs. (Signed) JOHN PHIPPS. Magistrate Adjudicating. | 7 … |

I certify the above extract to be a true copy.

Clerk of the said Magistrates' Court.

D.S. Pilcher told Lennon that unless he opened the front door it would be forced. Lennon still refused.

D.S. Pilcher then left me and I heard banging coming from the front door. Lennon moved away from the window shouting, "All right, I'll open it." I opened the window and entered the bedroom. Lennon said, "Oh well, you're in now."

he was a bit far away in this conversation in fact he only leaned down from the roof a hand … the paper.

I said to Lennon, "We are police officers and we have a warrant to search the premises for dangerous drugs. Open the window and let me in." Lennon leaned on the window preventing me from opening it and said, "I don't care who you are, you're not bloody well coming in here."

they/we – were all so exited they would never talk this gobble-de-gook.

(Signed) N. Pilcher. D/S …

RINGO: JOHN'S DRUG BUST WAS A REMINDER THAT A COP WAS LYING IN WAIT IF ANYONE HAD A PARTY – AND I'M AFRAID, IN THOSE DAYS, YOU COULD HAVE BUSTED ANY PARTY…

JOHN: I was got for possession. It wasn't on my body, but it was in the house. Possession means you could be a pusher. You can just see John Lennon pushing drugs for a living!

In the late Sixties there was a head-hunting cop (who was not very high up in the drug department in London – which was pretty new anyway, they had two dogs for the whole department). And he went round and bust every pop star he could get his hands on, and he got famous. Some of the pop stars had dope in their house and some of them didn't.[75]

GEORGE: John and Yoko were busted for cannabis in October, while they were staying at the flat they rented from Ringo. Jimi Hendrix rented it as well; it has a history, that flat. They were busted by a policeman named Sgt Pilcher who, as Derek would say, saw himself as Oliver Cromwell. He thought he was doing society a favour.

The Drug Squad must have had a list of people. It's easy to see it clearly now, because they went down the list. They busted Donovan first because he was easier. It wasn't difficult to attract their attention, and after they busted Donovan they worked their way up to The Rolling Stones and busted them, and then they thought they'd get The Beatles.

JOHN: We were lying in bed, feeling very clean and drugless, because we'd heard three weeks before that they were coming to get us – and we'd have been silly to have had drugs in the house. All of a sudden a woman comes to the front door, and rings the bell and says, 'I've got a message for you.' We said, 'Who is it? You're not the postman.' And she said, 'No, it's very personal,' and suddenly this woman starts pushing the door. She [Yoko] thinks it's the press or some fans, and we ran back in and hid. Neither of us was dressed, really; we just had vests on and our lower parts were showing.

We shut the door and I was saying, 'What is it? What is it? What is it?' I thought it was the Mafia or something. Then there was a big banging at the bedroom window, and a big super-policeman was there, growling and saying, 'Let me in, let me in!' And I said, 'You're not allowed in like this, are you?' I was so frightened. I said, 'Come round the front door. Just let me get dressed.' And he said, 'No, open the window, I'm going to fall off.'

There were some [police] at the front and some at the back. Yoko held the window while I got dressed – half-leaning out of the bathroom so they could see we weren't hiding anything. Then they started charging the door. I had a big dialogue with the policeman, saying, 'It's bad publicity if you come through the window.' And he was saying, 'Just open the window, you'll only make it worse for yourself.' I was saying, 'I want to see the warrant.' Another guy comes on the roof and they showed me this paper, and I pretended to read it – just to try and think what to do. Then I said, 'Call the lawyer, call the lawyer,' but [Yoko] called our office instead. And I was saying, 'No, not the office – the lawyer.'

Then there was a heave on the door, so I ran and opened it, and said, 'OK, OK, I'm clean anyway,' thinking I *was* clean. And he says, 'Ah-ha, got you for obstruction!' And I said, 'Oh, yeah,' because I felt confident that I had no drugs.

They all came in, lots of them and a woman. I said, 'Well, what happens now? Can I call the office? I've got an interview in two hours, can I tell them that I can't come?' And he said, 'No, you're not allowed to make a phone call… Can I use your phone?' Then our lawyer came.

STATEMENT OF WITNESS

Statement of MICHAEL ANSELL, M.A.

Age of Witness (if over 21 enter "over 21") Over 21

Occupation of Witness Senior Scientific Officer

Address The Metropolitan Police Forensic Sc… 2, Richbell Place, Holborn, W.C. 1.

Lab. ref: G/4757/68

On the 22nd October, 1968, I took po… the following sealed items which I have e…

| Item | Description | Result of Analysis |
|---|---|---|
| …M 1. | One binocular case containing binoculars and herbal mixture. | 12.43 grammes (191.8 grains) of Cannabis resin. |
| …S 1. | One tin containing herbal mixture. | Traces of Cannabis resin. |
| DS 2. | One envelope containing herbal mixture. | 1.77 grammes (27.3 grains) of Cannabis resin, |
| DS 3. | One cigarette case. | Traces of Cannabis resin. |
| DS 4. | One box containing a phial of brown tablets. | Three 'OMNOPON' tablets. Containing a total of 30milli-grammes ($\frac{1}{2}$ grain) Morphine. |

They [the police] brought some dogs. They couldn't find the dogs at first – and they kept ringing up, saying, 'Hello, Charlie, where are the dogs? We've been here half an hour.' And the dogs came.

I'd had all my stuff moved into the flat from my house, and I'd never looked at it. It had just been there for years. I'd ordered cameras and clothes – but my driver brought binoculars (which I didn't need in my little flat). And inside the binoculars was some hash from last year. Somewhere else in an envelope was another piece of hash. So that was it.[68]

NEIL ASPINALL: *I heard about it right away. John called me and said, 'Neil, think about all your worst paranoias – because they're here.' And I said, 'OK, I'll get somebody over there.' I asked Peter Brown to go. Peter had been Brian Epstein's personal assistant, but he was now working for Apple. He was looking after all their personal business, and I thought John being busted was quite personal. Peter organised legal advice and got the lawyers there; it was taken care of.*

JOHN: To cut a long story short, I'd just had everything moved from my other apartment – it was all over the place. So I thought, 'Well, maybe this is a bit of hash that was left over, and I'd forgotten all about it.' And I just copped a plea. He said, 'I won't get you for obstruction if you cop a plea.' And I thought, 'Oh, it's a hundred dollars or whatever, it's no skin off my nose,' little thinking it would reverberate. And he said, 'I'll let your missus go.'[75]

DEREK TAYLOR: *I thought people were out to get us. Being busted was a very serious thing then, and everyone was very frightened of it. It was even paranoia, if you like. It was the event we were all waiting for, all our lives; and for one of The Beatles to be busted was very, very serious because they were more or less used to being untouchable. They'd been going through Immigration without passports and living the life of Riley for donkey's years (two clichés there), and now things were going wrong. John's marriage was over, and now we've got drugs and we've got nudity. And it had been, I felt, manageable until 1968.*

*Neil told me about the call from John saying: 'Imagine your worst paranoia, because it's here.' And then he told me what had happened, and that the press knew.*

*The phone calls started to come in very quickly from Fleet Street – the* Evening Standard *and the Mail, the Mirror; all of them. I think Don Short rang and said, 'Oh, it's happened, has it? And I have another couple of dodgy ones: I think John's father is getting married, and we hear Yoko's pregnant.' So it was a case that nothing happened on its own. Everything was happening all the time, really; like the Royal Family's* annus horribilis.

*We believed in cannabis as a way of life. I was only concerned about the effects if anything unjust happened. I was very hot for injustice, having been brought up on Ealing comedies and all that; where the little man always won, and if you had a passion for something and you thought it was a good thing, then, in the end, stiff-necked people in suits and things would come round to your way of thinking.*

*Alas, it was not like that, and people kept clobbering us. I wasn't really worried about the bust, and we saw John as a martyr. Other people who'd been busted (like Donovan, and Mick, and Brian Jones) rang up with commiserations, and it was very much a gathering of the clans. Paul came into Apple that afternoon, John was there, and Ringo was phoned in Sardinia. Paul brought Ivan Vaughan with him (he who introduced John to Paul and Paul to John), and so it was very much everyone hanging in there with John.*

*So that was how I saw it, and by the end of 1968 I thought things were looking up. But I always felt things were looking up – I still do.*

PAUL: Being busted was something that we were all at risk of at that time – us and half of London; half of the world, in fact. That's what people were doing then instead of going out and getting crazy with drink – people were sitting at home until very late with wine and cannabis. We didn't really feel it was very wrong. I still believe alcohol is worse for you and has led to many more deaths – I've never heard of a cannabis-related death (although people won't like to hear that). So what happened to John and Yoko was shocking, and we felt sad for them. And it was a nuisance.

A lot of people were being busted around that time. In fact, it was put down to an actual officer – called something like 'Sgt Pilchard', I believe. He had it in for these drug-crazed hippies: 'I'll show them.' So he'd bust them on every occasion. OK, it *was* illegal – he had the right to do it, so you can't blame him. It was the idea of 'breaking the butterfly on the wheel' (that's what Rees-Mogg had said about the Stones in 1967). Most of us knew it wasn't that harmful. We weren't going round trying to make millions of converts, but we didn't believe all the rubbish spoken about it.

There are still people around who blame all our ills now on the Sixties, and I don't think that's right. They think we all went mad, and God and Country got forgotten. I don't think it was like that at all. I think you can go back to the last war to look for the beginning of those rumblings, when the soldiers got home and ditched Churchill. That was when I think the irreverence started to set in; I don't think it was anything to do with us.

GEORGE: They got John and Yoko, and later they busted me, too – and they chose Paul's wedding day to bust me on. Pilcher later emigrated to Australia, but then they extradited him and brought him back. He was charged with perjury and went to prison, but we still had trouble with our visas for years.

JOHN: It happened after I left, and he was caught in Australia, trying to escape (the English always run to Australia, thinking they're going to vanish there).[75]

GEORGE: It was certainly an Establishment plot against us. We were outspoken, and the Cromwell figures in the Establishment were trying to get their own back on us. This was the period when everything was going up and up and up and getting rosier, and suddenly it reached that point where it started to go down. Everything goes in a cycle, and once it starts going down and you get knocked to the ground, they start kicking you. What you have to realise with the press is that their whole thing is to build people up (and usually that's by putting somebody else down). They get people to be famous enough so they can make money out of them, and then they put them down. The Royal Family is the greatest case of that, but they did it with The Beatles too. It was only because The Beatles' popularity was so spread around the world and so many generations of people liked us that they couldn't put the nail in our coffin.

Brian Epstein had died, so they tried to say: 'OK, well, everything they've done since he died is crap,' meaning, for instance, *Magical Mystery Tour*. Then it was: 'Now they have gone mad – they've gone to India with some mystic.' It was the typical silly gossipy stuff that newspapers get into and that people love to attach themselves to. Then we started getting busted! John and Yoko were a great focal point for the negative 'let's beat them while they're down' attitude.

JOHN: I was frightened. I'm paranoiac, anyway – we both are, especially about people coming to the door. [But] it was better when it happened. It's been building up for years – thinking something would happen. Now, the fear has gone a bit. Now you know what it's like, it's a bit different. And it's not too bad; a £150 fine.

I think they should make some differentiation between hard and soft drugs. I think maybe they should have pot bars, if they're going to have alcohol. But I don't know – I'd sooner ban sugar.

I knew what Britain's Establishment were. I'd been around it a long time. It's just the same as anywhere else, only with a stiff upper lip. They don't show any happiness or sadness.[68]

It's strange when you hear people are snorting in the White House, after the misery they put a lot of people through, and the night they bust us in England. I have a record for life because the cop who bust me and Yoko was scalp-hunting and making a name for himself.

I've never denied having been involved with drugs. There was a question raised in the Houses of Parliament: 'Why do they need forty cops to arrest John and Yoko?' I mean, that thing was set up. The *Daily Mail* and the *Daily Express* were there before the cops came – he'd called the press. In fact, Don Short had told us 'they're coming to get you' three weeks before.[80] I guess they didn't like the way the image was looking. The Beatles thing was over. No reason to protect us for being soft and cuddly any more – so bust us! That's what happened.[71]

RINGO: *SGT PEPPER* DID ITS THING – IT WAS THE ALBUM OF THE DECADE, OF THE CENTURY MAYBE. IT WAS VERY INNOVATIVE WITH GREAT SONGS, IT WAS A REAL PLEASURE AND I'M GLAD I WAS ON IT, BUT THE 'WHITE' ALBUM ENDED UP A BETTER ALBUM FOR ME.

GEORGE: When we started, I don't think we thought about whether the 'White' album would do as well as *Sgt Pepper* – I don't think we ever really concerned ourselves with the previous record and how many it had sold. In the early Sixties, whoever had a hit single would try to make the next record sound as close to it as possible – but we always tried to make things different. Things were always different, anyway – in just a matter of months we'd changed in so many ways there was no chance of a new record ever being like the previous one.

After *Sgt Pepper*, the new album felt more like a band recording together. There were a lot of tracks where we just played live, and then there were a lot of tracks that we'd recorded and that would need finishing together. There was also a lot more individual stuff and, for the first time, people were accepting that it *was* individual. I remember having three studios operating at the same time: Paul was doing some overdubs in one, John was in another and I was recording some horns or something in a third. Maybe it was because EMI had set a release date and time was running out.

JOHN: All the stuff on the 'White' album was written in India when we were supposedly giving our money to Maharishi, which we never did. We got our mantra, we sat in the mountains eating lousy vegetarian food and writing all those songs.[80]

We wrote about thirty new songs between us. Paul must have done about a dozen. George says he's got six, and I wrote fifteen. And look what meditation did for Ringo – after all this time he wrote his first song.[68]

GEORGE MARTIN: *They came in with a whole welter of songs – I think there were over thirty, actually – and I was a bit overwhelmed by them, and yet underwhelmed at the same time because some of them weren't great.*

*For the first time I had to split myself three ways because at any one time we were recording in different studios. It became very fragmented, and that was where my assistant Chris Thomas did a lot of work (which made him into a very good producer).*

GEORGE: The experience of India and everything since *Sgt Pepper* was all embodied in the new album. Most of the songs that were written in Rishikesh were the result of what Maharishi had said.

When we came back, it became apparent that there were more songs than would make up a single album, and so the 'White' album became a double album. What else do you do when you've got so many songs and you want to get rid of them so that you can write more? There was a lot of ego in the band, and there were a lot of songs that maybe should have been elbowed or made into B sides. Having said that, there would just have been more bootlegs today because all of those that weren't put on the album would be out there.

JOHN: That [the 'White' album] was just saying: 'This is my song, we'll do it this way. That's your song, you do it that way.' It's pretty hard trying to fit three guys' music onto one album – that's why we did a double.[69]

After getting into electronics and heavy arrangements, I finally shook all that off and my songs on the double album were fairly simple and basic. It was a complete reversal from *Sgt Pepper*, and I preferred a lot of the music.[71]

GEORGE MARTIN: *During* Magical Mystery Tour *I became conscious that the freedom that we'd achieved in* Pepper *was getting a little bit over the top, and they weren't really exerting enough mental discipline in a lot of the recordings. They would have a basic idea and then they would have a jam session to end it, which sometimes didn't sound too good. I complained a little about their writing during the later 'White' album, but it was fairly small criticism.*

*I thought we should probably have made a very, very good single album rather than a double. But they insisted. I think it could have been made fantastically good if it had been compressed a bit and condensed. A lot of people I know think it's still the best album they made. I later learnt that by recording all those songs they were getting rid of their contract with EMI more quickly.*

RINGO: There was a lot of information on the double album, but I agree that we should have put it out as two separate albums: the 'White' and the 'Whiter' albums.

PAUL: People seem to think that everything we say and do and sing is a political statement, but it isn't. In the end it is always only a song. One or two of the tracks will make some people wonder what we are doing – but what we are doing is just singing songs.[68]

GEORGE: I wrote 'While My Guitar Gently Weeps' at my mother's house in Warrington (the spiritual home of George Formby). I was thinking about the Chinese *I Ching*, 'The Book of Changes'. In the West we think of coincidence as being something that just happens – it just happens that I am sitting here and the wind is blowing my hair, and so on. But the Eastern concept is that whatever happens is all meant to be, and that there's no such thing as coincidence – every little item that's going down has a purpose.

'While My Guitar Gently Weeps' was a simple study based on that theory. I decided to write a song based on the first thing I saw upon opening any book – as it would be relative to that moment, at *that* time. I picked up a book at random, opened it, saw 'gently weeps', then laid the book down again and started the song.

We tried to record it, but Paul and John were so used to just cranking out their tunes that it was very difficult at times to get serious and record one of mine. It wasn't happening. They weren't taking it seriously and I don't think they were even all playing on it, and so I went home that night thinking, 'Well, that's a shame,' because I knew the song was pretty good.

The next day I was driving into London with Eric Clapton, and I said, 'What are you doing today? Why don't you come to the studio and play on this song for me?' He said, 'Oh, no – I can't do that. Nobody's ever played on a Beatles' record and the others wouldn't like it.' I said 'Look, it's my song and I'd like you to play on it.'

So he came in. I said, 'Eric's going to play on this one,' and it was good because that then made everyone act better. Paul got on the piano and played a nice intro and they all took it more seriously. (It was a similar situation when Billy Preston came later to play on *Let It Be* and everybody was arguing. Just bringing a stranger in amongst us made everybody cool out.)

JOHN: 'Happiness Is A Warm Gun' was another one which was banned on the radio – they said it was about shooting up drugs. But they were advertising guns and I thought it was so crazy that I made a song out of it. It wasn't about 'H' at all. George Martin showed me the cover of a magazine that said: 'Happiness is a warm gun.' I thought it was a fantastic, insane thing to say. A warm gun means you've just shot something.[71]

I love it. I think it's a beautiful song. I like all the different things that are happening in it. I had put together three sections of different songs, it seemed to run through all the different kinds of rock music.[70]

PAUL: We'd had guest instrumentalists before – Brian Jones had played some crazy stuff on sax (for 'You Know My Name (Look Up The Number)'), and we'd used a flute and other instruments – but we'd never actually had someone other than George (or occasionally John or me) playing the guitar.

Eric showed up and he was very nice, very accommodating and humble and a good player. He got wound up and we all did it. It was good fun actually. His style fitted very well with the song and I think George was keen to have him play it – which was nice of George because he could have played it himself and then it would have been him on the big hit.

JOHN: We've just done two tracks. The second one is Ringo's first song. He composed it himself in a fit of lethargy.[68]

RINGO: I wrote 'Don't Pass Me By' when I was sitting round at home. I only play three chords on the guitar and three on the piano. I was fiddling with the piano – I just bang away – and then if a melody comes and some words, I just have to keep going. That's how it happened: I was just sitting at home alone and 'Don't Pass Me By' arrived. We played it with a country attitude. It was great to get my first song down, one that I had written. It was a very exciting time for me and everyone was really helpful, and recording that crazy violinist was a thrilling moment.

I also sang John's song 'Good Night'. I've just heard it for the first time in years and it's not bad at all, although I think I sound very nervous. It was something for me to do.

JOHN: ['Glass Onion'] That's me, just doing a throwaway song, à la 'Walrus', à la everything I've ever written. I threw the line in – 'the Walrus was Paul' – just to confuse everybody a bit more. It could have been: 'The fox terrier is Paul.' I mean, it's just a bit of poetry.[80] I was having a laugh because there'd been so much gobbledegook about *Pepper* – play it backwards and you stand on your head and all that.

At that time I was still in my love cloud with Yoko. I thought, 'Well, I'll just say something nice to Paul, that it's all right and you did a good job over these few years, holding us together.' He was trying to organise the group and all that, so I wanted to say something to him. I thought, 'Well, he can have it, I've got Yoko. And thank you, you can have the credit.'[70]

The line was put in partly because I was feeling guilty because I was with Yoko and I was leaving Paul. It's a very perverse way of saying to Paul: 'Here, have this crumb, this illusion, this stroke – because I'm leaving.'[80]

JOHN: I spent more time on 'Revolution 9' than I did on half the other songs I ever wrote.

The slow version of 'Revolution' on the album went on and on and on, and I took the fade-out part and just layered all this stuff over it. It has the basic rhythm of the original 'Revolution' going on with some twenty loops we put on; things from the archives of EMI. I was getting classical tapes, going upstairs and chopping it and making it backwards and things like that to get the sound effects.

There were about ten machines with people holding pencils on the loops – some only inches long and some a yard long. I fed them all in and mixed them live. I did a few mixes until I got one I liked. Yoko was there for the whole thing and she made decisions about which loops to use. It was somewhat under her influence, I suppose.[80]

'Revolution 9' was an unconscious picture of what I actually think will happen when it happens; just like a drawing of revolution. It was just abstract, *musique concrète*, loops, people screaming... I thought I was painting in sound a picture of revolution – but I made a mistake. The mistake was that it was *anti*-revolution.[70]

It's like an action painting. The 'number nine, number nine, number nine' was an engineer's voice. They have test tapes to see that the tapes are all right, and the voice was saying: 'This is number nine megacycles...' I just liked the way he said 'number nine' so I made a loop and brought it in whenever I felt like it.[74] It was just so funny, the voice saying 'number nine', it was like a joke, bringing number nine in it all the time, that's all it was. There are many symbolic things about it, but it just happened.[70]

In June 1952, I drew four guys playing football and number nine is the number on the guy's back, and that was pure coincidence. I was born on 9th October. I lived at 9 Newcastle Road. Nine seems to be my number so I've stuck with it, and it's the highest number in the universe; after that you go back to one.[74] It's just a number that follows me around (but numerologically, apparently I'm a number six or a three or something; but it's all part of nine).[80]

PAUL: 'Revolution 9' was quite similar to some stuff I'd been doing myself for fun. I didn't think that mine was suitable for release, but John always encouraged me.

**† Happiness is a Warm Gun**
*Lennon/McCartney*

She's not a girl who misses much
Do do do do do do do do
She's well acquainted with the touch of the velvet hand
Like a lizard on a window pane.

The man in the crowd with the multicoloured mirrors
On his hobnail boots
Lying with his eyes while his hands are busy
Working overtime
A soap impression of his wife which he ate
And donated to the National Trust.

I need a fix 'cause I'm going down
Down to the bits that I left uptown
I need a fix 'cause I'm going down
Mother Superior jump the gun
Mother Superior jump the gun
Mother Superior jump the gun
Mother Superior jump the gun.

Happiness is a warm gun
Happiness is a warm gun
When I hold you in my arms
And I feel my finger on your trigger
I know no one can do me no harm
Because happiness is a warm gun
—Yes it is.

Dirty old man

the junkie.

the gunman.

(satire

JOHN: I DON'T KNOW WHAT INFLUENCE 'REVOLUTION NO. 9' HAD ON THE TEENY-BOPPER FANS, BUT MOST OF THEM DIDN'T DIG IT; SO WHAT AM I SUPPOSED TO DO?[69]

2

Mr. George Harrison
3 Savile Row
London, W. 1

Dear George:

I am sending under separate cover those copies of the new U. S. Beatles album that are serially numbered from "A0000001 through A0000025" as personal souvenirs for you and selected friends. I have personally stolen number "A0000005," because I am a friend too. Besides, I love the music!

Sincerely,

PAUL: A nice thing about the album was the cover. I had a lot of friends in the art business, and with *Sgt Pepper* I had been involved with Robert Fraser. I knew a lot of artists through him, and one of his people at the time was Richard Hamilton.

I'd been to a couple of exhibitions and I liked Richard's work, so I rung him up and said: 'We've got a new album coming out. Would you be interested in doing the cover?' He said he would, so I asked everyone. They said 'yes' and then they let me get on with it, really. I used to go out to his house in Highgate and chat about it, and one day he said: 'OK. Get lots of snapshots: go back to all your baby photos, get photos of yourselves – any kind – and I'll make a collage.'

It was very exciting for me because I'm into art, and I could be his assistant for the week – liaising between the guys; getting the photographs and having them copied. Then I just sat round for the week watching him put the collage together. It's lovely just watching someone paint. The great thing at the end of it was that when he'd filled the whole collage with photos, his final move was to take pieces of white paper and place them strategically to give space through the whole thing, so that it wasn't just crammed with pictures. He explained that this was so the whole picture could breathe. You could see through the density, which was a great idea and gave me my education about negative space (which apparently is what it was called). I think I would have just left it as it was, because it looked great anyway; but if you look at that poster now, the white areas are very clever.

Then in the end he said: 'What are we going to do for the cover now that we've got the poster? What's the album called?' And he asked, 'Have you ever had an album called *The Beatles?*' I said 'no' and checked back because I wasn't sure. It had always been: *Beatles For Sale*, *Meet The Beatles*, *With The Beatles*. There had always been something similar, but never just *The Beatles*. So Richard said that was what we should call it, and everyone agreed.

Richard was very minimalist, and he wanted to have a completely white cover and emboss the word 'Beatles' on it. At that time he had a friend who always smudged things, like a bit of chocolate or whatever, so Richard wanted to put an 'apple smudge' on a bit of paper. That proved hard to do, so we said: 'Look, let's just leave it at the white cover.'

Then he had the idea to number each album, which I thought was brilliant for collectors. You'd have 000001, 000002, 000003, and so on. If you got, for example, 000200 then that would be an early copy – it was a great idea for sales. EMI weren't easy to persuade and they said they couldn't do it. I said: 'Look, if a milometer can turn over, you must be able to do that with every record that goes out.' And they found a way. I think they stopped at some point, so not all 'White' albums have the numbers on them. But it was a good idea and we got the first four. John, I think, got the first one. He shouted loudest!

RINGO: *I* got number one – because I'm lovely! John was actually the kindest and most loving overall, when he could be. And he wasn't quite as cynical as everyone expects. I got number one here and number four in America.

The Beatles LP numbering one to twenty should be shared between the four Beatles.

The Beatles LP numbering one to twenty should be shared between the four Beatles.

GEORGE MARTIN: *I can recall Yoko spending a lot of time with John in the studio whilst we were recording the 'White' album – so much, in fact, that when at one time she was actually ill, John would not let her be ill at home so she had a bed in the studio. While we recorded, there was Yoko lying in bed.*

*There was a huge bond between John and Yoko. There's no doubt about it: they were completely together mentally and I think that as that bond grew, so John lessened his bond with Paul and the others – which obviously caused problems. It was no longer the happy-go-lucky foursome – fivesome, with me – that it used to be.*

GEORGE: Yoko just moved in. Well, John moved in with Yoko – or she moved in with him – and from that point on they were never to be seen without each other (for the next few years at least). So she was suddenly in the band; she didn't start singing or playing, but she was there. Just as Neil and Mal were there, or George Martin was there, Yoko was there. She had a bed wheeled into the studio, so while we were all trying to make a record she would be in the bed, or under the piano on a mattress.

At first it was a novelty, but after a while it become apparent that she was always going to be there and it was very uncomfortable, because this was us at work and we were used to doing it in a certain way. Maybe it was just a habit that we'd got into, but there were just the four of us and George Martin. Occasionally people would come in and visit; Brian Epstein or the odd girlfriend or wife or whatever would come and go, but we never actually had somebody who was a stranger to all of us except John.

It was very odd, her sitting there all the time. It wasn't just that it was Yoko or that we were opposed to the idea of having a stranger sitting there; there was a definite vibe, and that's what bothered me. It was a weird vibe.

JOHN: Everybody seemed to be paranoid except for us two, who were in the glow of love. Everything is clear and open when you're in love. Everybody was tense around us: 'What is *she* doing here at the session?' All this madness is going on around us because we just happened to want to be together all the time.[80]

PAUL: Yoko was in the studio a lot. John and she had a very intense romance when they got together. She's a very strong woman, a very independent woman, and I think John always liked strong women. If you think about it, his Aunt Mimi was rather a strong woman and so was his mother, but Cynthia wasn't; and maybe that was why they divorced. Cynthia is a nice woman, but she was not able to dominate; whereas Yoko, I think, was.

She was a conceptual artist and John was very fascinated by her. She was into a lot of other topics. She would say things like: 'I do not know Beatles,' so it was like: 'Wow! Here is the one person who doesn't know about The Beatles.' That was very attractive to John.

JOHN: THE ONLY NAME YOKO KNEW BEFORE WAS RINGO, BECAUSE IT MEANS 'APPLE' IN JAPANESE.[71]

PAUL: She would say, 'Oh, I love guys in leather jackets,' so he'd get back into his leather and start acting like a teenage hoodlum again. It was a good excuse to get into all that stuff that he hadn't done for a long time, and I think she opened a lot of artistic avenues for him. The trouble, for us, was that it encroached on the framework that we'd had going for us.

NEIL ASPINALL: *This was the first album that I wasn't in the studio for. I was at Savile Row, taking care of the business and all the rest of it. I remember going over there once and John said to me, 'What are you doing here? You should be in the office.' Which felt a bit bad, you know. I didn't like being in the office; it wasn't my gig.*

*Yoko went everywhere with John; it wasn't just that she was in the studio all the time – it was that the two of them went everywhere together, so if he was in the studio, then she was.*

RINGO: Yoko being in the studio a lot was a new thing. It was all new. We're very Northern: the wives stayed at home and we went to work – we dug coal and they cooked dinner. It was one of those flat-cap attitudes which we were losing by then. I think if Maureen came to the studio five or six times that would be about it, and in all the years Pattie came several times at the most. I don't remember Cynthia coming much when she was married to John. It was just something that didn't happen. And suddenly we had Yoko in bed in the studio.

It created tension because most of the time the four of us were very close, and very possessive of each other in a way; we didn't like strangers coming in too much. And that's what Yoko was (not to John, but to the three of us). That was where *we* were together, and that's why we worked so well. We were all trying to be cool and not mention it, but inside we were all feeling it and talking in corners.

I used to ask John: 'What's this about, what's happening here? Yoko's at all the sessions!' He told me straight, 'Well, when you go home to Maureen and tell her how your day was, it takes you two lines: "Oh, we had a good day in the studio..." Well, *we* know exactly what's going on.' And that's how they started to live – every moment together. (That was something Barbara and I took up when we got married; we were absolutely moment by moment together for the first eight years of our marriage.) I was fine after that, and relaxed a lot around Yoko.

should be shared

PAUL: Now John had to have Yoko there. I can't blame him, they were intensely in love – in the first throes of the first passions – but it was fairly off-putting having her sitting on one of the amps. You wanted to say, 'Excuse me, love – can I turn the volume up?' We were always wondering how to say: 'Could you get off my amp?' without interfering with their relationship.

It was a very difficult time. I felt that when John finally left the group he did it to clear the decks for his relationship. Anything prior to that meant the decks weren't clear – he had all his Beatle baggage; all his having to relate to us. He just wanted to go off into the corner and look into Yoko's eyes for hours, saying to each other, 'It's going to be all right.' It was pretty freaky when we were trying to make a track.

Looking at it now you can be amused by it, and it was quite a laugh, really. But at the time, this was *us* and it was our careers. We were The Beatles, after all, and here was this girl... It was like we were her courtiers, and it was very embarrassing. The 'White' album was a very tense one to make.

JOHN: Paul was always gently coming up to Yoko and saying, 'Why don't you keep in the background a bit more?' I didn't know what was going on. It was going on behind my back.[72]

GEORGE: Maybe now if you talk to Yoko she may say she likes The Beatles or that she liked The Beatles. But she didn't really like us because she saw The Beatles as something that was between her and John. The vibe I picked up was that she was a wedge that was trying to drive itself deeper and deeper between him and us, and it actually happened.

It may be unfair to blame Yoko totally for any break-up because we'd all had enough by then, anyway. We were all going our own ways and she might have become the catalyst for speeding up that situation, whatever it was. I don't really regret any of that, but at that time I was definitely uncomfortable about her being there.

JOHN: If it is Yoko and Linda's fault for breaking up The Beatles, can they have the credit for all the great music that each of us have made individually? Linda and Yoko *never* had an argument ever. How can two women split up four strong men? It's impossible.[71]

Looking back, I understand there'd been four guys very close together, and the women that were with them, wives or girlfriends, had been the old-fashioned type of female that we all know and love. The one that was in the kitchen the whole time with the baby – she never came to the sessions even. You never saw the wives, only for openings and when they did their hair. And suddenly we were together all the time; in a corner mumbling and giggling. And there were Paul, George and Ringo saying, 'What the hell are they doing? What's happened to him?' And my attention completely went off them. Now it wasn't deliberate, it was just I was so involved and intrigued with what we were doing... And then we'd look round and see that we weren't being approved. But I understand how they felt, because if it had been Paul or George or Ringo that had fallen in love with somebody and got totally involved...[80]

I always preferred it to all the other albums, including *Pepper*, because I thought the music was better. The *Pepper* myth is bigger, but the music on the 'White' album is far superior.

I wrote a lot of good shit on that. I like all the stuff I did, and the other stuff as well. I like the whole album. I haven't heard it in a long time, but I know there's a lot of good songs on it.[72]

PAUL: I think it was a very good album. It stood up, but it wasn't a pleasant one to make. Then again, sometimes those things work for your art. The fact that it's got so much on it is one of the things that's cool about it. The songs are very varied. I think it's a fine album.

I don't remember the reaction. Now I release records and I watch to see who likes it and how it does. But with *The Beatles*, I can't ever remember scouring the charts to see what number it had come in at. I assume we hoped that people would like it. We just put it out and got on with life. A lot of our friends liked it and that was mainly what we were concerned with. If your mates liked it, the boutiques played it and it was played wherever you went – that was a sign of success for us.

I was in Scotland and I read in *Melody Maker* that Pete Townshend had said: 'We've just made the raunchiest, loudest, most ridiculous rock'n'roll record you've ever heard.' I never actually found out what track it was that The Who had made, but that got me going; just hearing him talk about it. So I said to the guys, 'I think we should do a song like that; something really wild.' And I wrote 'Helter Skelter'.

You can hear the voices cracking, and we played it so long and so often that by the end of it you can hear Ringo saying, 'I've got blisters on my fingers.' We just tried to get it louder: 'Can't we make the drums sound louder?' That was really all I wanted to do – to make a very loud, raunchy rock'n'roll record with The Beatles. And I think it's a pretty good one. (That's why I get annoyed when people say: 'You just do the ballads; you're the soppy one.' I say: 'Have you checked? Have you listened?' Not that I like justifying myself, but there is the other side of me.)

RINGO: 'Helter Skelter' was a track we did in total madness and hysterics in the studio. Sometimes you just had to shake out the jams, and with that song – Paul's bass line and my drums – Paul started screaming and shouting and made it up on the spot.

PAUL: Then it got over to America – the land of interpretive people. And as a DJ later would 'interpret' the fact that I had no shoes on the *Abbey Road* cover, Charles Manson interpreted that 'Helter Skelter' was something to do with the four horsemen of the Apocalypse. I still don't know what all that stuff is; it's from the Bible, 'Revelations' – I haven't read it so I wouldn't know. But he interpreted the whole thing – that we were the four horsemen, 'Helter Skelter' the song – and arrived at having to go out and kill everyone.

It was terrible. You can't associate yourself with a thing like that. Some guy in the States had done it – but I've no idea why. It was frightening, because you don't write songs for those reasons. Maybe some heavy metal groups do nowadays, but we certainly never did.

Bob Dylan thought that the line in 'I Want To Hold Your Hand' was 'I get high, I get high, I get high.' So there had been some funny little misinterpretations, but they were all harmless and just a bit of a laugh. Jake Riviera, Elvis Costello's manager, thought that 'living is easy with eyes closed' was 'living is easy with nice clothes'. But after all those little interpretations there was finally this horrific interpretation of it all. It all went wrong at that point, but it was nothing to do with us. What can you do?

JOHN: All that Manson stuff was built around George's song about pigs and Paul's song about an English fairground. It has nothing to do with anything, and least of all to do with *me*.[80]

He's barmy, he's like any other Beatle fan who reads mysticism into it. I mean, we used to have a laugh putting this, that or the other in, in a light-hearted way. Some intellectual would read us, some symbolic youth generation wants it, but we also took seriously some parts of the role. But, I don't know, what's 'Helter Skelter' got to do with knifing somebody?[70]

RINGO: It was upsetting. I mean, I knew Roman Polanski and Sharon Tate, and – God! – it was a rough time. It stopped everyone in their tracks because suddenly all this violence came out in the midst of all this love and peace and psychedelia. It was pretty miserable, actually, and everyone got really insecure – not just us, not just the rockers, but everyone in LA felt: 'Oh, God, it can happen to anybody.' Thank God they caught the bugger.

GEORGE: We had incredible things happening in our lives. We had wonderful clothes, psychedelic motor cars, houses; everything. All our songs were about 'All You Need Is Love', and 'Revolution', and so on. It was a 'turn on, tune in, drop out' mentality, and even nowadays a lot of people feel threatened. There is no flower-power revolution going on now, but people still feel threatened when they don't understand something, or if they feel that their lifestyle – the little rut that they've got in – is threatened by what you're saying. They will dismiss you or they'll think you're a crank, or even that you're crazy.

They've just about said everything by now, they've said how wonderful we are and how horrible we are, and they've been through up/down/up/down so many times that it doesn't make any difference. In some way we went beyond it all. We transcended the tabloids; they still have their field day now and again – still write their silly little things – but it doesn't really have any effect on us. Yet they don't like to hear something that's a deviation from that cosy little safe routine that people have for their lives.

Everybody was getting on the big Beatle bandwagon. The police and the promoters and the Lord Mayors – and murderers, too. The Beatles were topical and they were the main thing that was written about in the world, so everybody attached themselves to us, whether it was our fault or not. It *was* upsetting to be associated with something so sleazy as Charles Manson.

Another thing I found offensive was that Manson suddenly portrayed the long hair, beard and moustache kind of image, as well as that of a murderer. Up until then, the long hair and the beard were more to do with not having your hair cut and not having a shave – a case of just being a scruff or something.

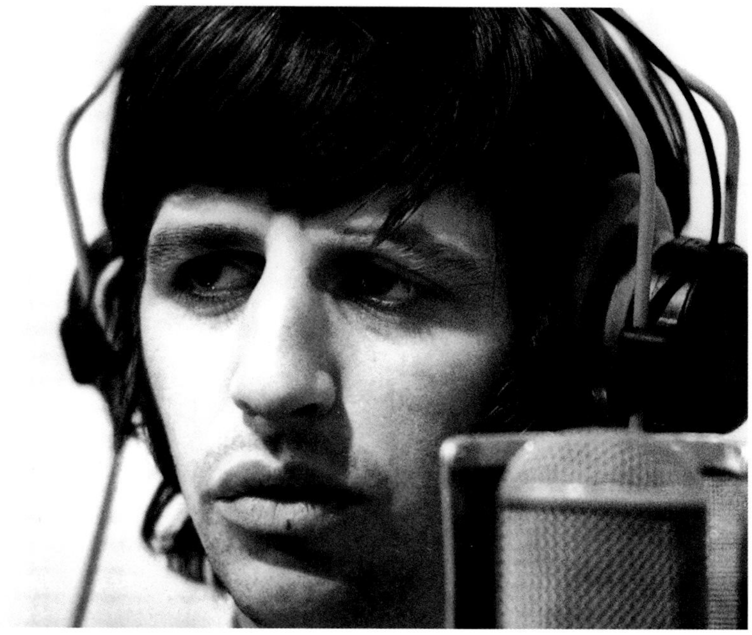

RINGO: While we were recording the 'White' album we ended up being more of a band again, and that's what I always love. I love being in a band. Of course, I must have had moments of turmoil, because I left the group for a while that summer.

I left because I felt two things: I felt I wasn't playing great, and I also felt that the other three were really happy and I was an outsider. I went to see John, who had been living in my apartment in Montagu Square with Yoko since he moved out of Kenwood. I said, 'I'm leaving the group because I'm not playing well and I feel unloved and out of it, and you three are really close.' And John said, 'I thought it was *you three*!'

So then I went over to Paul's and knocked on his door. I said the same thing: 'I'm leaving the band. I feel you three guys are really close and I'm out of it.' And Paul said, 'I thought it was *you three*!'

I didn't even bother going to George then. I said, 'I'm going on holiday.' I took the kids and we went to Sardinia.

GEORGE: I can't remember exactly why Ringo left. Suddenly one day somebody said, 'Oh, Ringo's gone on holiday.' Then we found out that he thought that the three of us all got on so well and he didn't. It was just one of those things. Everybody felt the same, we were all getting cheesed off. I felt: 'What's the point in me being around here? They all seem so cool and groovy and I just don't fit.' And I actually left on the next album.

PAUL: I think Ringo was always paranoid that he wasn't a great drummer because he never used to solo. He hated those guys who went on and on, incessantly banging while the band goes off and has a cup of tea or something. Until *Abbey Road*, there was never a drum solo in The Beatles' act, and consequently other drummers would say that although they liked his style, Ringo wasn't *technically* a very good drummer. It was a bit condescending and I think we let it go too far.

I think his feel and soul and the way he was rock solid with his tempo was a great attribute. I always say if you can leave a drummer and turn your back on him, then you're very lucky. You could just tell Ringo how it went and leave him – there was always this great noise and very steady tempo coming from behind you. Rock'n'roll is all about feel, really, and sound. So at that time we had to reassure him that we did think he was great.

That's what it's like in life. You go through life and you never stop and say: 'Hey, you know what? I think you're great.' You don't always tell your favourite drummer that he's your favourite. Ringo felt insecure and he left, so we told him, 'Look, man, you are the best drummer in the world for us.' (I still think that.) He said 'thank you', and I think he was pleased to hear it. We ordered millions of flowers and there was a big celebration to welcome him back to the studio.

JOHN: I love his drumming. Ringo is still one of the best drummers in rock.[72]

GEORGE MARTIN: *I think they were all feeling a little paranoid. When you have a rift between people – if you go to a party and the husband and wife have been having a row – there's a tension, an atmosphere. And you wonder whether you are making things worse by being there. I think that was the kind of situation we found with Ringo. He was probably feeling a little bit odd because of the mental strangeness with John and Yoko and Paul, and none of them having quite the buddiness they used to have. He might have said to himself, 'Am I the cause?'*

RINGO: I wrote 'Octopus's Garden' in Sardinia. Peter Sellers had lent us his yacht and we went out for the day. We told the captain we wanted fish and chips for lunch (because that's all we ever ate, being from Liverpool). And so when lunchtime came around we had the french fries, but then there was this other stuff on the plate. He said: 'Here's your fish and chips.' – 'Well, what's this?' – 'It's squid.' – 'We don't eat squid, where's the cod?' Anyway, we ate it for the first time and it was OK; a bit rubbery. It tasted like chicken.

I stayed out on deck with him and we talked about octopuses. He told me that they hang out in their caves and they go around the seabed finding shiny stones and tin cans and bottles to put in front of their cave like a garden. I thought this was fabulous, because at the time I just wanted to be under the sea too. A couple of tokes later with the guitar – and we had 'Octopus's Garden'!

I had a rest and the holiday was great. I knew we were all in a messed-up stage. It wasn't just me; the whole thing was going down. I had definitely left, I couldn't take it any more. There was no magic and the relationships were terrible. I'd come to a bad spot in life. It could have been paranoia, but I just didn't feel good – I felt like an outsider. But then I realised that we were *all* feeling like outsiders, and it just needed me to go around knocking to bring it to a head.

I got a telegram saying, 'You're the best rock'n'roll drummer in the world. Come on home, we love you.' And so I came back. We all needed that little shake-up. When I got back to the studio I found George had had it decked out with flowers – there were flowers everywhere. I felt good about myself again, we'd got through that little crisis and it was great. And then the 'White' album really took off – we all left the studio and went to a little room so there was no separation and lots of group activity going down.

George went to California to do some filming with Ravi Shankar in June, and Maureen and I went along with him. We were always going places with each other. If someone was going somewhere we'd go with them – we usually went in twos. Paul and I went to the Virgin Islands, John and I went to Trinidad. Every time we went on holiday it would be with one of the others. That's how close we were.

We got to Pebble Beach, where we were staying, and it was beautiful. We went to Esalen and saw what that was about: free love and fabulous ideas. Alan Watts and people like that were hanging out there. Then George went up to San Francisco. He even invited the Hell's Angels to come and stay with us – that's how much love was around.

GEORGE: Derek got a phone call one morning from Customs and Excise, saying: 'Is this right: we've got seventeen Harley Davidsons that you're going to pay the freight duty on?' I'd warned Apple about this because in New York I'd heard a guy saying: 'We may be coming over to England sometime, and we'll look you up.' I thought, 'That's all we need, isn't it?'

So this day arrived. The Hell's Angels came from San Francisco complete with their Harley Davidsons, checked in at Heathrow Airport and drove straight over to No. 3 Savile Row. I quickly put a memo out to everybody, saying: 'Watch out, don't let them take over. You have to keep doing what you're doing, but just be nice to them. And don't upset them because they could kill you.' It was a joke, but they *were* mean.

NEIL ASPINALL: *George had said: 'Oh, if you ever come to England, look us up,' or something. A couple of months later the motorbikes were outside Savile Row with these guys saying, 'Well, George said it was OK.' They ended up living at Apple and terrifying everybody.*

*We had the Hell's Angels' Christmas Party. I can remember that everybody was getting hungry, and then a huge turkey came in on a big tray with four people carrying it. It was about ten yards from the door to the table where they were going to put the turkey down, but it never made it.*

*The Hell's Angels just went 'woof', and everything disappeared: arms, legs, breast, everything. By the time it got to the table there was nothing there. They just ripped the turkey to pieces, trampling young children underfoot to get to it. I've never seen anything like it.*

RINGO: They proceeded to ruin the kids' party – and then we couldn't get rid of them. They wouldn't leave and we had bailiffs and everything to try to get them out. It was miserable and everyone was terrified, including the grown-ups. It was like the edgy Christmas party.

GEORGE: John and Yoko were dressed up as Father Christmas. I didn't go because I knew there was going to be trouble. I just heard that it was terrible and how everybody got beaten up.

NEIL ASPINALL: *They did get asked to leave Apple. I asked them, but they got into that hippy language: 'Well, you didn't invite us, so you can't ask us to leave…' In other words, as George had invited them, so George was going to have to ask them to go. I think George did it very well – I can't remember exactly what he said, but it was like: 'Yes/no – Yin/Yang – in/out – stay/go. You know – BUGGER OFF!' And they said, 'Well, if you put it that way, George, of course,' and left.*

DEREK TAYLOR: *George, in essence, had encouraged the Hell's Angels to come to Apple if they were ever in town. But many others came as well. A homeless family from California moved into Apple and did actually live in one of the offices – a mother and father and several children, with the San Francisco Hell's Angels weaving in and out.*

*Ken Kesey was in, borrowing a typewriter and tape recorder and doing poetry readings in my office in the morning. I would arrive and find the Hell's Angels sitting around on the floor doing those physical things they did – a lot of scratching and farting and generally being awful, and saying, 'Hey Ken, read some more, man.' They would assemble for the great man to speak to them in my working office: Billy Tumbleweed and Frisco Pete (who will be known to our American readers) and other men.*

# 1969-70

nineteen sixty-nine to nineteen seventy

CALL SHEET
No. Studio 1.
PRODUCTION NAME:- "APPLE RECORDS 1"
PROD. No.:- Apple Films Ltd.
STAFF CALL:- 8.30 a.m. on Stage 1.
CALL FOR DATE:- Thursday, 2nd January. 196
SETS OR LOCATIONS:- INT. RECORDING STUDIO.
ARTISTES
DRESSING ROOM No.
CHARACTER
TIME REQUIRED AT STUDIO
TIME REQUIRED ON SET
JOHN LENNON Apt.1 & 2. 10.00 a.m.
PAUL McCARTNEY " " 10.00 a.m.
GEORGE HARRISON " " 10.00 a.m.
RINGO STARR " " 10.00 a.m.
Props: 6 chairs and table required.
Canteen: a.m. and p.m. Tea Breaks for 24 people please.
Lunch: 1.00 - 2.00 p.m.
Sound Requirements: 2 Nagras
2 Neck Microphones
1 Rifle microphone
Camera Requirements: 2 Complete 16 m.m. B.L. outfits
Music and Equipment: As arranged with Mel Evans.
Unit: Producer Denis O'Dell
Lindsay-Hogg

PAUL: We started *Let It Be* in January 1969 at Twickenham Studios, under the working title *Get Back*. Michael Lindsay-Hogg was the director. The idea was that you'd see The Beatles rehearsing, jamming, getting their act together and then finally performing somewhere in a big end-of-show concert. We would show how the whole process worked. I remember I had an idea for the final scene which would be a massive tracking shot, forever and ever, and then we'd be in the concert.

The original idea was to go on an ocean liner and get away from the world; you would see us rehearsing and then you'd finally see the pay-off. But we ended up in Twickenham. I think it was a safer situation for the director and everybody. Nobody was that keen on going on an ocean liner anyway. It was getting a bit fraught between us at that point, because we'd been together a long time and cracks were beginning to appear.

GEORGE: I think the original idea was Paul's – to rehearse some new songs, pick a location and record the album of the songs in a concert. We would learn the tunes and record them without loads of overdubs: do a live album.

PAUL: I don't think we were consciously going for live feeling in those sessions. I'd say that's probably true, but I don't remember being conscious of trying to make it live. They were quite good sessions once we got into Apple Studios later on, and I remember sitting round quite enjoying the music. It was interesting music to play.

GEORGE MARTIN: *They were going through a revolutionary period at that time, and were trying to think of something new – and they wanted a new engineer. They have Geoff Emerick, so Glyn Johns came in. I guess basically they wanted a new producer, but they never actually said that to me. So I was still there.*

*At the same time, they did actually come up with a very good idea, which I thought was well worth working on. They wanted to write a complete album and rehearse it and then perform it in front of a large audience. A live album of new material. Most people who did a live album would be rehashing old stuff, but they thought: 'Let's have a completely new album that nobody has ever heard, and put it in front of an audience.'*

*It was a great idea, except that you couldn't have an open-air concert in England in February and there was no venue available that would take The Beatles and their crowds. So we then started thinking about staging it abroad; we thought about doing it in California, but that would have been too expensive. We thought of going to Marrakech and importing people – but that fell through. In the end, because there was so much vacillation, there was nowhere left at all. So they started rehearsing down in Twickenham Film Studios, and I went along with them.*

JOHN:
WHAT CAN WE DO IF WE CAN'T THINK OF ANY SORT OF GIMMICK? WELL, THE WORST THAT WE HAVE IS A DOCUMENTARY OF US MAKING AN LP, IF WE DON'T GET INTO A SHOW. ALL THE THINGS WE DO, THE WHOLE POINT OF IT IS COMMUNICATION. AND PUTTING IT ON TV IS COMMUNICATION, AND WE'VE GOT A CHANCE TO SMILE AT PEOPLE, LIKE 'ALL YOU NEED IS LOVE'. SO THAT'S MY INCENTIVE FOR DOING IT.[69]

*But there was a lot of dissension and lack of steering. Really, they were rudderless at this time. They didn't like each other too much and were fighting amongst themselves.*

JOHN: I wasn't consciously making any decisions. It was all sort of subconscious and I just made the records with The Beatles like one goes to one's job at nine in the morning. Paul or whoever would say, 'It's time to make a record.' I'd just go in and make a record, and not think too much about it. Always I've enjoyed the session if it was a good session. If we got our rocks off playing, it was fine. If it was a drag, it was a drag. But it had become a job.[80]

PAUL: I remember once, at a meeting to discuss *Let It Be*, John saying, 'Oh, I get it. He wants a job.' And I had said, 'I suppose that's right, yeah. I think we *should* work. It would be good.' They had all been quite happy to have the summer off, and I had felt we ought to do something.

As time went by, I'd talked them into *Let It Be*. Then we had terrible arguments – so we'd get the break-up of The Beatles on film instead of what we really wanted. It was probably a better story – a sad story, but there you are.

NEIL ASPINALL: *I'm not sure whether everybody was behind the idea of going to Twickenham. They'd decided to film whatever they were doing. It was the producer Denis O'Dell's idea that, if you were going to film it, you needed space for cameras. They had used Twickenham Film Studios before for* Help! *and* A Hard Day's Night, *so they ended up out there.*

*Twickenham was very cold in January, and a strange place to be making an album. It was like half recording and half filming. It didn't really feel right. Nobody was that comfortable out there. It was a big sound stage in a film studio – and they were working on portable equipment because it wasn't equipped as a recording studio. Trying to work creatively, with every single moment of what they were doing being filmed, was not ideal for making a record.*

PAUL: IN FACT WHAT HAPPENED WAS, WHEN WE GOT IN THERE, IT SHOWED HOW THE BREAK-UP OF A GROUP WORKS. WE DIDN'T REALISE THAT WE WERE ACTUALLY BREAKING UP AS IT WAS HAPPENING.

JOHN: It was hell making the film *Let It Be*. When it came out a lot of people complained about Yoko looking miserable in it. But even the biggest Beatle fan couldn't have sat through those six weeks of misery. It was the most miserable session on earth.[70]

GEORGE: I had spent the last few months of 1968 producing an album by Jackie Lomax and hanging out with Bob Dylan and The Band in Woodstock, having a great time. For me, to come back into the winter of discontent with The Beatles in Twickenham was very unhealthy and unhappy. But I can remember feeling quite optimistic about it. I thought, 'OK, it's the New Year and we have a new approach to recording.' I think the first couple of days were OK, but it was soon quite apparent that it was just the same as it had been when we were last in the studio, and it was going to be painful again. There was a lot of trivia and games being played.

As everybody knows, we never had much privacy – and now they were filming us rehearsing. One day there was a row going on between Paul and me. It's actually in the film: you can see where he's saying, 'Well, don't play this,' and I'm saying, 'I'll play whatever you want me to play, or I won't play at all if you don't want me to play. Whatever it is that will please you, I'll do it...'

They were filming us having a row. It never came to blows, but I thought, 'What's the point of this? I'm quite capable of being relatively happy on my own and I'm not able to be happy in this situation. I'm getting out of here.'

Everybody had gone through that. Ringo had left at one point. I know John wanted out. It was a very, very difficult, stressful time, and being filmed having a row as well was terrible. I got up and I thought, 'I'm not doing this any more. I'm out of here.' So I got my guitar and went home and that afternoon wrote 'Wah Wah'.

RINGO: George left because Paul and he were having a heated discussion. They weren't getting on that day and George decided to leave, but he didn't tell John or me or Paul. There'd been some tension going down in the morning, and arguments would go on anyway, so none of us realised until we went to lunch that George had gone home. When we came back he still wasn't there, so we started jamming violently. Paul was playing his bass into the amp and John was off, and I was playing some weird drumming that I hadn't done before. I don't play like that as a rule. Our reaction was really, really interesting at the time. And Yoko jumped in, of course; she was there.

PAUL: If I made a suggestion and it was something that, say, George didn't want to do, it could develop quite quickly into a mini-argument. In fact George walked out of the group. I'm not sure of the exact reason, but I think that they thought I was being too domineering.

It's easy for someone like me, who likes to get stuff done, to come on too strong. I get excited and I get too keen about something, and talk too fast – 'Oh, we could do that and we'd be there on Monday morning – Twickenham – we'll do it – it's great...' And then it got a bit difficult. I would say, 'It would be great if we could film The Beatles working. It would be fabulous.' And they'd be like, 'Well, are you sure you want to do it that way?' It was getting a very lukewarm reception – and I didn't quite realise how I was.

Looking back at the film now, I can see it could be easily construed as someone coming on a bit too heavy; particularly as I was just a member of the band and not a producer or director. For my part it was just enthusiasm, and I'd sit and talk with the director. But I think it led to a couple of barneys, and in one of them George said, 'Right. I'm not having this!' I think I was probably suggesting what he might play, which is always a tricky one in a band.

On 'Hey Jude', when we first sat down and I sang 'Hey Jude...', George went 'nanu nanu' on his guitar. I continued, 'Don't make it bad...' and he replied 'nanu nanu'. He was answering every line – and I said, 'Whoa! Wait a minute now. I don't think we want that. Maybe you'd come in with answering lines later. For now I think I should start it simply first.' He was going, 'Oh yeah, OK, fine, fine.' But it was getting a bit like that. He wasn't into what I was saying.

In a group it's democratic and he didn't have to listen to me, so I think he got pissed off with me coming on with ideas all the time. I think to his mind it was probably me trying to dominate. It wasn't what I was *trying* to do – but that was how it seemed.

This, for me, was eventually what was going to break The Beatles up. I started to feel it wasn't a good idea to *have* ideas, whereas in the past I'd always done that in total innocence, even though I was maybe riding roughshod.

I did want to insist that there shouldn't be an answering guitar phrase in 'Hey Jude' – and that was important to me – but of course if you tell a guitarist that, and he's not as keen on the idea as you are, it looks as if you're knocking him out of the picture. I think George felt that: it was like, 'Since when are you going to tell me what to play? I'm in The Beatles too.' So I can see his point of view.

But it burned me, and I then couldn't come up with ideas freely, so I started to have to think twice about anything I'd say – 'Wait a minute, is this going to be seen to be pushy?' – whereas in the past it had just been a case of, 'Well, the hell, this would be a good idea. Let's do this song called "Yesterday". It'll be all right.'

GEORGE: Personally I'd found that for the last couple of albums – probably since we stopped touring – the freedom to be able to play as a musician was being curtailed, mainly by Paul. There used to be a situation where we'd go in (as we did when we were kids), pick up our guitars, all learn the tune and chords and start talking about arrangements.

But there came a time, possibly around the time of *Sgt Pepper* (which was maybe why I didn't enjoy that so much), where Paul had fixed an idea in his brain as to how to record one of his songs. He wasn't open to anybody else's suggestions. John was always much more open when it came to how to record one of his songs.

With Paul, it was taken to the most ridiculous situations, where I'd open my guitar case and go to get my guitar out and he'd say, 'No, no, we're not doing that yet. We're gonna do a piano track with Ringo, and then we'll do that later.' It got so there was very little to do, other than sit round and hear him going, 'Fixing a hole...' with Ringo keeping the time. Then he'd overdub the bass and whatever else.

It became stifling, so that although this new album was supposed to break away from that type of recording (we were going back to playing live) it was still very much that kind of situation where he already had in his mind what he wanted. Paul wanted nobody to play on his songs until he decided how it should go. For me it was like: 'What am I doing here? This is painful!'

Then superimposed on top of that was Yoko, and there were negative vibes at that time. John and Yoko were out on a limb. I don't think he wanted much to be hanging out with us, and I think Yoko was pushing him out of the band, inasmuch as she didn't want him hanging out with us.

IT'S IMPORTANT TO STATE THAT A LOT OF WATER HAS GONE UNDER THE BRIDGE AND THAT, AS WE TALK NOW, EVERYBODY'S GOOD FRIENDS AND WE HAVE A BETTER UNDERSTANDING OF THE PAST. BUT TALKING ABOUT WHAT WAS HAPPENING AT THAT TIME, YOU CAN SEE IT WAS STRANGE.

RINGO: George was writing more. He wanted things to go his way. When we first started, they basically went John and Paul's way, because they were the writers. But George was finding his independence and he wouldn't be dominated as much by Paul – because in the end Paul wanted to point out the solo to George, who would say, 'Look, I'm a guitarist. I'll play the solo.' And he always did; he always played fine solos. It got a bit like, 'I wrote the song and I want it this way,' whereas before it was, 'I wrote the song – give me what you can.'

PAUL: After George went we had a meeting out at John's house, and I think John's first comment was, 'Let's get Eric in.' I said, 'No!' I think John was half joking. We thought, 'No, wait a minute. George has left and we can't have this – it isn't good enough.'

RINGO: We all went to visit George at his house and we told him we loved him, and it got sorted and then he came back.

JOHN: Paul had this idea that we were going to rehearse, more like Simon and Garfunkel, looking for perfection – and then make the album. And of course we're lazy fuckers and we've been playing for twenty years, for fuck's sake – we're grown men, we're not going to sit around rehearsing. And we couldn't get into it, and we put down a few tracks and nobody was in it at all.

It was just a dreadful, dreadful feeling and, being filmed all the time, I just wanted them to go away. We'd be there at eight in the morning and you couldn't make music at eight in the morning, or ten, or whatever it was, in a strange place with people filming you, and coloured lights.

It was another one like *Magical Mystery Tour*. In a nutshell, Paul wanted to – it was time for another Beatle movie or something – he wanted us to go on the road, or *do* something. And as usual George and I were going, 'Oh, we don't want to do it,' and all that. And he sort of set it up. There was all discussions about where to go and all that. I would just tag along, and I had Yoko by then, and I didn't even give a shit about nothing. And I was stoned all the time, too, on H, etc. I just didn't give a shit – nobody did. Like in the movie, when I got to do 'Across The Universe', Paul yawned and plays boogie, and I immediately say, 'Oh, does anybody want to do a fast one?' That's how I am. So year after year that begins to wear you down.[70]

PAUL: These things had been going down in *Let It Be*: George leaving because he felt he was being told what to do (I think that's why he left). Ringo had earlier left because he didn't think we liked him as a drummer. That wasn't as difficult to solve as maybe George's thing was, but at the same time John was looking to get out of the situation, and I think we were all really feeling that some cracks were appearing in the whole edifice.

JOHN: By the time The Beatles were at their peak we were cutting each other down to size. We were limiting our capacity to write and perform by having to fit it into some kind of format, and that's why it caused trouble.[71]

It's not that we didn't like each other. I've compared it to a marriage a million times, and I hope it's understandable for people that aren't married or in any relationship. It was a long relationship. It started many, many years before the American public or the English public knew us. Paul and I were together since he was fifteen and I was sixteen. It's a long, long time that the four of us have been together. And what happened was, through boredom and too much of everything – Epstein was dead, and people were bothering us with business – the whole pressure of it finally got to us. So, like people do when they're together, they start picking on each other. It was like, 'It's because of you – you got the tambourine wrong – that my whole life is a misery.' It became petty, but the manifestations were on each other because we were the only ones we had.

Maybe it was the camera of *Let It Be* – the idea that we were going to try and create something phoney. The camera went on and it almost happened in *Magical Mystery Tour*, but we'd managed to just pick a little magic out.

BY THE TIME WE GOT TO *LET IT BE* WE COULDN'T PLAY THE GAME ANY MORE. WE COULD SEE THROUGH EACH OTHER, AND THEREFORE WE FELT UNCOMFORTABLE, BECAUSE UP TILL THEN WE REALLY BELIEVED INTENSELY IN WHAT WE WERE DOING AND THE PRODUCT WE PUT OUT, AND EVERYTHING HAD TO BE JUST RIGHT. AND WE BELIEVED. SUDDENLY WE DIDN'T BELIEVE. IT'D COME TO A POINT WHERE IT WAS NO LONGER CREATING MAGIC.[76]

GEORGE MARTIN: *Paul was trying to keep things together by bossing people around because he's quite good at that, but John and George didn't like it at all.*

*John was being more difficult because he was always with Yoko, and he would turn up very late or not at all – and it got into very awkward circumstances. John was going through a very problematic period when we were making the record. He actually said to me: 'I don't want any of your production shit. We want this to be an honest album.' I said, 'What do you mean by an honest album?' He said, 'I don't want any editing. I don't want any over-dubbing. It's got to be like it is. We just record the song and that's it.' I answered, 'OK, if that's the way you want to do it, that's what we'll do.'*

*We would start a track and it wasn't quite right, and we would do it again… and again… and then I'd get to Take Nineteen: 'Well John, the bass wasn't as good as it was on Take Seventeen, but the voice was pretty good, so let's go on again.' Take Forty-Three: 'Well, yes…' So you go on forever, because it was never perfect – and it got very tedious.*

GEORGE: I was called to a meeting out in Elstead in Surrey, at Ringo's house that he bought from Peter Sellers. It was decided that it would be better if we got back together and finished the record. Twickenham Studios were very cold and not a very nice atmosphere, so we decided to abandon that and go to Savile Row into the recording studio.

NEIL ASPINALL: *By January 20th they decided to move to Savile Row. Alexis Mardas was building a studio there, although it wasn't finished. The control room and the console had wires everywhere, so they had to take the portable equipment in there. But the studio itself, the actual room to play in, was much nicer, much cosier and they were much more at home.*

RINGO: The days were long, and it could get boring, and Twickenham just wasn't really conducive to any great atmosphere. It was just a big barn. Then we moved to the new studios in the basement of Apple to carry on.

The facilities at Apple were great. It was so comfortable, and it was ours, like home. It was great to go to, and when we weren't working we could sit round the fire, which we'd had put in because we wanted it really cosy.

It was only at the playback we realised that we couldn't have the fire, because when we listened we heard 'crack, crack, crack.' We'd say, 'What the fuck is that?' and then we all worked out that it was the firewood crackling in the fire! We'd spent so long in studios that we wanted to be cosy, but it didn't work, of course. We had to put the fire out when we were recording.

Glyn Johns was working with us on the album and it didn't seem to work out, so we went back to George Martin.

GEORGE: I don't know why George Martin had not been involved at that time. Somebody had the idea of having Glyn Johns, maybe just for a change. It was definitely nothing personal.

Savile Row was a nice building before the builders got in there and turned it into Tesco's. I remember going round there when we were thinking of buying it, and the basement was fantastic. There was a huge fireplace and oak beams, and somebody said it was where Jack Hylton used to have his nightclub. We thought, 'This is great! We'll be down here writing and making records.'

By the time it had been made into a studio, it was covered all over, and made into a crappy place with polystyrene ceilings. The original culprit was Alex, who 'built' the sixteen-track studio with the sixteen speakers, which they had to rip out and redo. You only need two speakers for stereo sound. It was awful.

But even with the alterations, it was a better place to be.

GEORGE MARTIN: *Magic Alex said that EMI was no good, and he could build a much better studio. Well, he didn't, and when we recorded in Savile Row I had to equip it with EMI gear.*

*The Apple offices were pretty sparse at that time, clinical and groovy with white paint – a nice place to be – but the studios were hopeless, because they were just empty rooms. In fact Magic Alex, for all his technical expertise, had forgotten to put any holes in the wall between the studio and the control room, so we had to run the cable out through the door, and we had a nasty twitter in one corner that came from the air-conditioning which we had to switch off whenever we made a record. Apart from that, it was ideal!*

RINGO: I THINK EVERYONE WAS GETTING A LITTLE TIRED OF US BY THEN, BECAUSE WE WERE TAKING A LONG TIME AND THERE WERE MANY HEATED DISCUSSIONS GOING ON. ABOUT LIFE. ABOUT EVERYTHING.

PAUL: Facilities were OK at Apple because George Martin did what he'd done out at the Twickenham Studios: a bit of a 'lash-up', so it was good. The studio wasn't finished, but it was perfectly good technically.

DEREK TAYLOR: *There was a central heating boiler in the studio and it was not soundproofed. So somebody pointed this out: 'There's the central heating making a din,' and The Beatles said: 'We'll turn it off when we're in here. We'll just have quiet fires.' The rest of the building could go to hell – they were just ordinary people, little people. So it wasn't only in the press office that people were making wrong decisions.*

*Anyway, there was a studio of a sort – but in the end, when they made* Let It Be *down there, a portable recording system had to be brought in, so really it was like cooking with a primus stove on top of a big expensive gas cooker because the gas wasn't connected.*

*But all those albums followed! In that period, in the crazy Apple time, there was the 'White' album and the finishing of* Yellow Submarine, Let It Be *and* Abbey Road *– all made in the mad days.*

GEORGE: When I went with Eric Clapton to see Ray Charles play at the Festival Hall, before Ray came on there was a guy on stage playing the organ, dancing about and singing 'Double-O Soul'. I thought, 'That guy looks familiar,' but he seemed bigger than I remembered. After a while Ray came on and the band played for a few songs and then he reintroduced... Billy Preston! Ray said, 'Since I heard Billy play I don't play the organ any more – I leave it to him.' I thought, 'It's Billy!' Since we had last seen him in Hamburg in 1962, when he was just a little lad, he had grown to be six foot tall.

So I put a message out to find out if Billy was in town, and told him to come into Savile Row, which he did. He came in while we were down in the basement, running through 'Get Back', and I went up to reception and said, 'Come in and play on this because they're all acting strange.' He was all excited. I knew the others loved Billy anyway, and it was like a breath of fresh air.

It's interesting to see how nicely people behave when you bring a guest in, because they don't really want everybody to know that they're so bitchy. This happened back in the 'White' album when I brought Eric Clapton to play on 'While My Guitar Gently Weeps'. Suddenly everybody's on their best behaviour.

Billy came down and I said, 'Remember Billy? Here he is – he can play the piano.' He got on the electric piano, and straight away there was 100% improvement in the vibe in the room. Having this fifth person was just enough to cut the ice that we'd created among ourselves. Billy didn't know all the politics and the games that had been going on, so in his innocence he got stuck in and gave an extra little kick to the band. Everybody was happier to have somebody else playing and it made what we were doing more enjoyable. We all played better and that was a great session. It was more or less just as it is on the record.

RINGO: I don't think Billy Preston made us behave a bit better. I think we were working on a good track and that always excited us. His work was also a part of it, so suddenly – as always when you're working on something good – the bullshit went out of the window and we got back down to doing what we did really well.

'Get Back' was a good track. I felt, 'This is a kick-ass track.' 'Don't Let Me Down' also. They were two fine tracks. Quite simple and raw – back to basics. I'd done a hook to the track in 'Get Back' which sounded good and it's been copied since – by myself, in fact, in 'Back Off Boogaloo'. That's perfectly allowed by me!

PAUL: Billy was brilliant – a little young whizz-kid. We'd always got on very well with him. He showed up in London and we all said, 'Oh Bill! Great – let's have him play on a few things.' So he started sitting in on the sessions, because he was an old mate really.

It might have helped us all behave better with one another on the sessions. I think it also created problems, because as The Beatles we'd always just been four people in the band. We were very much a unit – the Four-Headed Monster, I've heard us referred to.

So when Billy came in, I think that though we *did* have to behave ourselves a bit – because it was like having a guest in the house, someone you put your best manners on for – there was a slight worry in the background also that maybe he was joining the group. That kind of thing *was* happening. So we couldn't tell whether it was a crack in the whole thing, or whether it was going to be good. It was a little bit puzzling.

But he played great and we all had a great time, so it worked out fine in the end.

GEORGE MARTIN: *Billy Preston was a great help and a very good keyboard guy, and his work on 'Get Back' alone justified him being there. He was an amiable fellow too, very nice and emollient. He helped to lubricate the friction that had been there.*

JOHN: 'Across The Universe' was first recorded at the end of the 'White' album. I couldn't get it on because we'd done so much material. It wasn't a very good recording. By the end of the double album we were really sick of recording. It was a shame because I liked the song.[71]

I was lying next to my first wife in bed and I was thinking. It started off as a negative song and she must have been going on and on about something. She'd gone to sleep and I kept hearing, 'Words are flowing out like endless streams...' I was a bit irritated and I went downstairs and it turned into a sort of cosmic song rather than, 'Why are you always mouthing off at me?'

But nobody was interested in doing it originally; everyone was sickened. The tune was good, but subliminally people don't want to work with it sometimes. I was so disappointed that it never went out as The Beatles. I gave it to The Wildlife Fund of Great Britain and it went out.[80]

And then I tried to do it again when we were making *Let It Be*, but anybody who saw the film saw what reaction I got with it when I tried to do it. Finally Phil Spector took the tape, and did a damn good job with it and made a fairly reasonable sound out of it, and then we released it again.[71]

The words are purely inspirational and were given to me – except for maybe one or two where I had to resolve a line or something like that. I don't own it; it came through like that.[80]

GEORGE: 'I Me Mine' is the ego problem. There are two 'I's: the little 'i' when people say, 'I am this'; and the big 'I' – i.e. Om, the complete, whole, universal consciousness that is void of duality and ego. There is nothing that isn't part of the complete whole. When the little 'i' merges into the big 'I' then you are really smiling!

After having LSD, I looked around and everything I could see was relative to my ego – like, 'That's *my* piece of paper,' and, 'That's *my* flannel,' or, 'Give it to *me*,' or, '*I* am.' It drove me crackers; I hated everything about my ego – it was a flash of everything false and impermanent which I disliked. But later I learnt from it: to realise that there *is* somebody else in here apart from old blabbermouth (that's what I felt like – I hadn't seen or heard or done anything in my life, and yet I hadn't stopped talking). 'Who am I?' became the order of the day.

Anyway that's what came out of it: 'I Me Mine'. The truth within us has to be realised: when you realise that everything else that you see and do and touch and smell isn't real, then you may know what reality *is*, and can answer the question 'Who am I?'

Allen Klein thought it was an Italian song – 'Cara Mia Mine'.

DEREK TAYLOR: *During the* Let It Be *sessions I went to the studio at Apple a couple of times for a few minutes and saw how happy that was. Billy Preston had then arrived in the session, and there was a very good atmosphere down there. It was quite fun – but it hadn't been fun at Twickenham, and reports had been coming back that there'd been endless talking about what they were going to do. Being of a suitably paranoid cast of mind by then, I assumed they'd been saying, 'What are we going to do about Derek and that bloody office?' So I was pretty anxious to be in denial about* Let It Be *– but glad when they came back to Apple, and were inside the building again. There was a two- or three-week period at the end of January when it was nice.*

I've got a feeling
I've got a feeling
A feeling deep inside - Oh yeah
I've got a feeling
A feeling I can't hide. Oh no.
1 Everybody had a hard year
Everybody had a good time
Everybody had a wet dream
Everybody saw the sunshine
Oh yeah Oh yeah.
TWO OF US (on our way home.)
1 Two of us riding nowhere
Spending someone's hard earned pay
You and me Sunday driving
Not arriving on our way back home
CHORUS
We're on our way home
... we're going home
2 Two of us sending postcards,
Writing letters on my wall
You and me burning matches
Lifting latches on our way home.
CHORUS.
MIDDLE You and I have
Longer than the road
That stretches out ahead.
3 Two of us wearing raincoats
Standing solo in the sun
You and me chasing paper, getting nowhe
On our way home

GEORGE: On the *Let It Be* project we were originally going to rehearse all the new songs and then make an album in a live show. That never really happened because the album became us in the studio. As we rehearsed the songs, they were recorded, and the film of us recording them was really a film of us *rehearsing*.

NEIL ASPINALL: *They were still talking about playing a concert on a boat, or in an amphitheatre in Greece, or maybe at the Roundhouse in London. There were lots of different ideas about where they might do a concert, and nothing was ever agreed.*

PAUL: We'd been looking for an end to the film, and it was a case of, 'How are we going to finish this in two weeks' time?' So it was suggested that we go up on the roof and do a concert there; then we could all go home. I'm not sure who suggested it. I could say it seems like one of my half-baked ideas, but I'm not sure.

RINGO: There was a plan to play live somewhere. We were wondering where we could go – 'Oh, the Palladium or the Sahara.' But we would have had to take all the stuff, so we decided, 'Let's get up on the roof.' We had Mal and Neil set the equipment up on the roof, and we did those tracks. I remember it was cold and windy and damp, but all the people looking out from offices were really enjoying it.

GEORGE: We went on the roof in order to resolve the live concert idea, because it was much simpler than going anywhere else; also nobody had ever done that, so it would be interesting to see what happened when we started playing up there. It was a nice little social study.

We set up a camera in the Apple reception area, behind a window so nobody could see it, and we filmed people coming in. The police and everybody came in saying, 'You can't do that! You've got to stop.'

PAUL: It was good fun, actually. We had to set the mikes up and get a show together. I remember seeing Vicki Wickham of *Ready, Steady, Go!* (there's a name to conjure with) on the opposite roof, for some reason, with the street between us. She and a couple of friends sat there, and then the secretaries from the lawyers' offices next door came out on *their* roof.

We decided to go through all the stuff we'd been rehearsing and record it. If we got a good take on it then that would be the recording; if not, we'd use one of the earlier takes that we'd done downstairs in the basement. It was really good fun because it was outdoors, which was unusual for us. We hadn't played outdoors for a long time.

It was a very strange location because there was no audience except for Vicki Wickham and a few others. So we were playing virtually to nothing – to the sky, which was quite nice. They filmed downstairs in the street – and there were a lot of city gents looking up: 'What's that noise?'

In the end it started to filter up from Mal (who would come creeping in, trying to keep out of camera range) that the police were complaining. We said, 'We're not stopping.' He said, 'The police are going to arrest you.' – 'Good end to the film. Let them do it. Great! That's an end: "BEATLES BUSTED ON ROOFTOP GIG".'

We kept going to the bitter end and, as I say, it was quite enjoyable. I had my little Hofner bass – very light, very enjoyable to play. In the end the policeman, Number 503 of the Greater Westminster Council, made his way round the back: 'You have to stop!' We said, 'Make him pull us off. This is a demo, man!'

I think they pulled the plug, and that was the end of the film.

RINGO: I always feel let down about the police. Someone in the neighbourhood called the police, and when they came up I was playing away and I thought, 'Oh great! I hope they drag me off.' I *wanted* the cops to drag me off – 'Get off those drums!' – because we were being filmed and it would have looked really great, kicking the cymbals and everything. Well, they didn't, of course; they just came bumbling in: 'You've got to turn that sound down.' It could have been fabulous.

GEORGE: We recorded four or five tunes and we might have played a lot more if they hadn't switched us off – but that was enough. The Rutles did a good version of that as well.

DEREK TAYLOR: *On January 30th, at the time of the concert on the roof, I remember I heard music upstairs. I'd been so very busy with the usual business, arriving at work to find things happening. I knew there was going to be something on the roof, but it was not my business. I had other things going on and I saw people outside in the street and heard the concert starting, and I thought it was wonderful to hear this music.*

*I didn't go on the roof because I was busy with the press. Fielding the calls. The phones started to ring off the hook because everyone in London, in no time, knew The Beatles were performing on the roof, and it was fabulous. It was the first good, big, positive story without any snags for months and months.*

*Admittedly they were being a 'nuisance' to some people, as the film shows, but by and large the calls were just from the press who were thrilled the boys were out playing music again. It was good – and it still is.*

NEIL ASPINALL: *I don't know who our neighbours were. I don't think we got on badly with them but I don't really think they liked the fans being around all the time. And some of them didn't like the concert on the roof. I wasn't there, though. I was in hospital having my tonsils out – so I missed the show!*

GEORGE MARTIN: *I was downstairs when they played on the roof, worrying like mad if I was going to end up in Savile Row police station for disturbing the peace.*

DEREK TAYLOR: *When they did the concert on the roof it opened up possibilities. That was the situation. Nobody had ever thought they would perform live, except that we kept saying things like, 'They may be doing another concert.' There was talk all through the back end of 1968 about doing ad hoc concerts, so after they'd done the concert on the roof everything was up in the air again. 'They may perform again,' we said – because it did go well.*

JOHN: We've finished it and the most finished number on it was 'Get Back'. We were doing this rehearsal for a show which we never finished, so we got fed up and put the rehearsal out. There's chatting and messing about and all sorts on it. And then we got halfway through another album so we stopped that, and we got tired and took a break. It'll be a single LP, but this one's got a book with it – a whole book of making the LP – and we also made a film of it at the same time, so we've got to get that together. We made a sort of documentary of us making the album. We've got sixty-eight hours of film there, so we've got to do a bit of work with it. All the traumas and the paranoia, all the different things that happen to you when you try and make a record.[69]

PAUL: THE BASIC THING IN MY MIND WAS THAT FOR ALL OUR SUCCESS THE BEATLES WERE ALWAYS A GREAT LITTLE BAND. NOTHING MORE, NOTHING LESS.

When we sat down to play, we played good – from the very beginning. From when we first got Ringo into the band, and before. But when we got Ringo into the band it really gelled. We'd never had too many of those times where it was not working – though like any other band we *did* have them.

So that was the main thing – live we were a great band. Forget about all your MBEs and recording careers and all this sort of stuff; it was really down to being a good band. I'd hoped that by playing like this in live performance, it would get us all to realise that maybe we didn't need all the highfalutin stuff. We could just keep playing and everything would sort itself out.

JOHN: The thing I miss most is just sitting down with a group and playing. With The Beatles it got less group-like. We stopped touring and we'd only get together for recordings, so therefore the recording session was the thing we almost rehearsed in as well. So all the playing was in the recording session. Sometimes it would be a drag – it's like an athlete: you really have to keep playing all the time to keep your hand in. And we'd be off for months and we'd suddenly come into the studio and be expected to be spot on again. It would take us a few days getting loosened up and playing together and so therefore The Beatles musically weren't as together in the last few years. Although we'd learnt a lot of technique where we could produce good records, musically we weren't as together as some of the earlier years and that's what we all missed.[72]

GEORGE MARTIN: *In the end, of course, a documentary was made – with warts and all – of the* Let It Be *album. Glyn Johns and I put the music together, and it was an honest album, which they wanted. But it lay fallow for a long time because nobody seemed to like the documentary that had been done, with all the mistakes. They were used to the polished production job – and I think it was because of this that it wasn't released.*

JOHN: The tape ended up like the bootleg version. We let Glyn Johns remix it – we didn't want to know. We just left it to him and said, 'Here, do it.' It's the first time since the first album that we didn't have anything to do with it. None of us could be bothered going in. Everybody was probably thinking, 'Well, I'm not going to work on it.' There was twenty-nine hours of tape. It was like a movie, just so much tape. Twenty takes of everything – because we were rehearsing and taking everything. Nobody could face looking at it.

I thought it would be good to go out – the shitty version – because it would break The Beatles. It would break the myth: 'That's us, with no trousers on and no glossy paint over the cover and no sort of hope. This is what we are like with our trousers off, so would you please end the game now.' But that didn't happen. We ended up doing *Abbey Road* quickly, and putting out something slick to preserve the myth.[70]

NEIL ASPINALL: *They waited for the film to be edited and graded and for a deal to be done with United Artists. The album* Let It Be *was the soundtrack to the movie – so it was really waiting for the movie. That's why it came out after* Abbey Road.

GEORGE MARTIN: Abbey Road *was a kind of afterthought – an encore, if you like.* Let It Be *was only released when it was because John had asked Phil Spector to work on it.*

GEORGE: I think that Phil Spector approached Allen Klein and was trying to get some work, or somehow he was hanging out with Klein – probably because he knew Klein was in with The Beatles. I think Klein suggested to us that we should get Phil Spector to come and listen to the tapes of *Let It Be*.

Phil Spector made the kind of records that I like: the wall-to-wall sound. I was a big fan of his, and we had spent some time with him in the early Sixties, when he was in London. So I was all for the idea of getting Phil involved. Also, he'd been through a bad patch and he'd given up making music, and I think he was trying to get back into it. I saw it as a way of helping him back on his feet.

RINGO: He's as mad as a hatter. The first time I met Phil, we were all on a plane going to New York and that's when we realized how crazy he was because he 'walked to America'. He was so nervous of flying he couldn't sit down, so we watched him walk up and down the length of the plane all the way.

Another time I spent with Phil was much later on when John and Yoko had an exhibition in Syracuse, New York State. A crowd of us were flying up there and we all started off in the bar. They called our flight, and as we walked to the plane Phil decided that this particular plane wasn't safe, so we all walked back to the bar. That was a good enough reason for us, and we got the next one. Phil was crazy with planes.

We like to say he's eccentric. He was pretty strange anyway, but he was a good guy – and when it came to music, he knew what he was doing.

JOHN: He really can play a control board. He just plays it. He can make any sound you like within seconds. His knowledge is incredible. I learnt a lot from him. Phil leaves you to present him with a picture you think you want, and then he'll take the best shot of it with his camera sort of thing. You present him with the stage set and he'll make sure you get a good picture out of it, a good sound. You get what you're making. The usual trouble is the person's interpreting all the time on the other side. Phil could have been on either side of the board. He's like one of the band, not like an A&R man. He likes the same old kind of rock crap that I like. When we did 'Instant Karma!' together he said, 'What do you want?' I said, '1950s – now.' And he did it.[70]

DEREK TAYLOR: *I met Phil Spector when he arrived around the time of* Let It Be. *I thought he was crackers – and I liked him. Phil was my kind of madman. I wouldn't want to go on holiday with him because he was too 'out there' even for me. I was basically the boy from West Kirby, who had a decent sober wife who had kept me from being Phil Spector or Allen Klein or any of those out-there men – but I felt at least that I could handle him.*

JOHN: The least you could call him is eccentric, and that's coming from somebody who's barmy.[75]

GEORGE: Paul has been quoted as saying that he didn't want Phil Spector involved, or didn't like him overdubbing orchestras on 'The Long And Winding Road' and other tracks. But I personally thought it was a really good idea.

PAUL: To me, it was really because *Let It Be* was the bare record that Glyn Johns had mixed – with no overdubs on it, no orchestras, no nothing. It was very, very simple. It was just a band, very live sounding – in a room or on a roof – and I really liked that. Maybe it was a bit tough to take. Maybe it wasn't that commercial, but anyway these were the kind of things that were starting to go wrong.

GEORGE MARTIN: *I didn't like Phil Spector's* Let It Be *at all. I'd always been a great admirer of him. I always thought his recordings were fantastic – and he actually created some great sounds. But what he did with* Let It Be *was to do all the things (and not so well) that we hadn't been allowed to do; and I kind of resented him for it, because to me it was tawdry. It was bringing The Beatles' records down a peg – that's what I thought. Making them sound like other people's records.*

PAUL: I heard the Spector version again recently, and it sounded terrible. I prefer the original sound that's shown on *Anthology 3*.

RINGO: I like what Phil did, actually. He put the music somewhere else and he was king of the 'wall of sound'. There's no point bringing him in if you're not going to like the way he does it – because that's what he does. His credentials are solid.

JOHN: He'd always wanted to work with The Beatles, and he was given the shittiest load of badly recorded shit with a lousy feeling to it ever, and he made something out of it. He did a great job.[70]

RINGO: In May 1970 *Let It Be* came out as the last album, though *Abbey Road* was, of course, the last to be recorded. It goes to show how quirky the world is – that the next to last album comes out as the last album, and the last album came out before it. But we split up after *Abbey Road* and weren't really thinking about splitting up on the one before. It's all very strange.

My cut of the movie would have been different. And I'm sure John's cut at the time would have been different – and Paul's cut. I thought there was a lot more interesting stuff than Michael Lindsay-Hogg put in.

JOHN: We haven't got half the money people think we have. We have enough to live on, but we can't let Apple go on like it is. We started off with loads of ideas of what we wanted to do – an umbrella for different activities. But like one or two Beatles things, it didn't work because we aren't practical and we weren't quick enough to realise that we need a businessman's brain to run the whole thing.

You can't offer facilities to poets and charities and film-makers unless you have money definitely coming in. It's been pie-in-the-sky from the start. We did it all wrong – Paul and me running to New York saying, 'We'll do this and encourage this and that.' It's got to be a business first; we realise that now. It needs a new broom and a lot of people there will have to go. It needs streamlining.

## IT DOESN'T NEED TO MAKE VAST PROFITS, BUT IF IT CARRIES ON LIKE THIS ALL OF US WILL BE BROKE IN THE NEXT SIX MONTHS.[69]

GEORGE: APPLE HAS, TO A CERTAIN EXTENT, BEEN A HAVEN FOR DROP-OUTS, BUT SOME OF OUR BEST FRIENDS ARE DROP-OUTS.[69]

RINGO: Apple wasn't being run; it was being run into the ground, really. We were all doing this, that and the other. I was in charge of Apple Films – after I did *Candy* in 1967 I thought I'd run it. So we were all running pieces of Apple, and we finally wanted some really heavy dude to put it all together. That was going to be Allen Klein's job.

JOHN: I got a note from an accountant saying, 'You're broke and if you go on it's going to all go, whatever you've got left.' He laid it out to all of us but I think I was the only one that read it. And then I announced it in the press and I said, 'We're going to be broke if they don't stop this game, this Apple business.'

But everyone wants to say, 'No, no, it's all wonderful.' Like the Royal Family: they're always pretending they never cry and they never go to the toilet, nothing ever happens to them. But they're just like anybody else – they cry and they go to the toilet.

I'm sure the others wanted it tightening up, but I don't think they were really aware of it. I mean, they could all tell. Sometimes George would go in and go crazy because of how many people were just lying around drunk there and living on the company. But you couldn't stop it. Somehow it needed a firm hand to stop it.[71]

NEIL ASPINALL: *The Beatles weren't businessmen, and trying to run shops and record companies and artists and publishing and buildings, as well as doing their own things, did become very chaotic. A lot of money was being spent without people really knowing what it was being spent on.*

*So it was a question of, 'Who is going to do it?' I was running it on the basis of, 'I'll do it until you find somebody who you want to do it.' I didn't want to do it myself.*

DEREK TAYLOR: *The Beatles had been looking for a 'leader' with some status in either the music business or the City. They were looking for someone who could get a grip of it. They were looking for 'the man' all the time.*

*One night John and I had some LSD down at my house – Neil was also there, and he'd had some too, I'm sure – and we came up with a wonderful ruse: we would go to the local bank manager in Weybridge and to the local solicitor and say, 'Listen, Apple is in a mess but we need a simple solution: a simple bank manager who is reliable and a simple solicitor who can see their way through all this mess.' This was the LSD solution.*

*It all died a death the next day. I still believe it would have been better than what actually happened, when we got into the hands of real 'money men' – but in the absence of the solicitor, the bank manager and all those other saviours...*

JOHN: It's easy after the fact – people are always saying about Apple and The Beatles' business: 'Why didn't you? Why didn't you?' *You* sit there with millions and millions of dollars floating around and try and work it out.[74]

GEORGE: To sort out Apple there were a number of people who were interviewed at the time. I remember the story about Dr Beeching, who shut down the railways of Britain – so they tried to get him to come and see if he could shut down The Beatles as well. But he didn't want the job so Klein got it instead.

DEREK TAYLOR: *I got a call one morning that Allen Klein thought I was in his way – that was why he was unable to reach The Beatles. He wanted to come and save them, and he believed that I was blocking his way for some reason. I thought, 'I'm not blocking his way – I never even think about him.' So a contact, Tony Calder, said: 'Well, if he puts a call through would you see that it gets through to Peter Brown?' and I said, 'Certainly, yes.'*

*So when he called and, sure enough, somehow his call was blocked, I removed the blockage, because my game was always removing blockages. I didn't believe in that 'who's in and who's out' thing. Unless people were actually known to be bad for Apple, I always made people available. I said: 'Look, he's got a bad reputation but have a look at him. You don't have to commit yourself.' So I told Peter Brown, 'Allen Klein is trying to reach you – take his call.' So he did, and then the boys (so-called) met him.*

NEIL ASPINALL: *Allen Klein was an American accountant/businessman/manager who was really the manager of The Rolling Stones. I know that John and Yoko met with him and decided that he would be a good manager for them.*

JOHN: Klein and Apple were bound to meet sooner or later. We were impressed by the way he handled the business deals for The Rolling Stones. Besides, he has some of the cleanest polo-necked sweaters I've ever seen. He's the only businessman I've met who isn't grey right through his eyes to his soul.[69]

RINGO: There was a whole lot of action going on at the time. Besides Allen Klein, there was John Eastman (Paul's brother-in-law) who was also looking to be the manager.

Anyway, we met with Allen Klein and we were convinced by him. Well, I was convinced by him, and John too. My impression of him when I first met him was: brash – 'I'll get it done, lads.' Lots of enthusiasm. A good guy, with a pleasant attitude about himself in a really gross New York way. So the decision was him or him – and I picked him. That was two of us – and George did the same.

PAUL: Eventually, after the show on the roof, it came down to a meeting. I was about to suggest to everyone that we might go back to doing even smaller gigs to really find our spirit again and get back to what we were. Then maybe from there we would have more big plans, if that's what we wanted.

But John and Yoko had had a meeting the night before with Allen Klein, and John reckoned Allen was going to be his manager. He sent the word round the business: 'As from now – Allen Klein is representing me.' When we asked him why, he said, 'Well, he's the only one Yoko liked.'

GEORGE: John came in and said, 'Well, I'm going to get Klein to manage me, and that's what's happening.' He asked us if we would like to meet him and give him a chance to talk to us – so Ringo and I went to talk to him.

After that, there was no alternative, really. There was nobody managing Apple. It was wasting away all this money, and nobody had any ability to be a business manager in our party. We needed somebody at that time.

Paul had met Linda and he wanted her brother, John Eastman, or her father, Lee Eastman, to become involved. We met Lee Eastman as well as Allen Klein, and I seem to remember saying, 'Let's get them both together' – Lee Eastman and Allen Klein – but I don't actually have any memory of them both in the same room. I remember meeting Lee and John Eastman in Claridge's.

RINGO: I liked Allen. He was a lot of fun, and he knew the record business. He knew records; he knew acts; he knew music. A lot of people we spoke to were trying to get in with the music crowd but didn't know anything about the music business.

GEORGE: I thought, 'Well, if that's the choice, I think I'll go with Klein, because John's with him and he seemed to talk pretty straight.' (However, years later, we formed a different opinion.) Because we were all from Liverpool we favoured people who were street people. Lee Eastman was more like a class-conscious type of person. As John was going with Klein, it was much easier if we went with him too.

27 Jan 69
29th January, 1969.
Dear Sir Joe,
I've asked Allen Klein to look after my things. Please give him any information he wants and full cooperation.
love,
Dick James Esq.
Dick James Music Ltd.
James House,
71 New Oxford Street,
London W.C.1.
MAY 5, 1969
Dear Dick,
This is to inform you that Alan Klein is also acting on our behalf, and request you to give him all information and co-operation concerning our business affairs.
Yours sincerely,
George Harrison
Richard Starkey
GENTLEMEN:
THIS LETTER WILL SERVE AS OFFICIAL NOTICE TO YOU THAT ALLEN KLEIN'S ABKCO INDUSTRIES, INC. HAS BEEN APPOINTED OUR EXCLUSIVE BUSINESS MANAGERS.
PLEASE, DIRECT ALL MATTERS RELATING TO OUR COMPANIES TO APPLE C/O ABKCO INDUSTRIES, INC. 1700 BROADWAY, NEW YORK, NEW YORK 10019.
VERY TRULY YOURS,
APPLE CORPS LTD. on behalf of THE BEATLES and THE BEATLE, APPLE GROUP OF COMPANIES
NO VISITORS ALLOWED IN THIS BUILDING FROM GROUND FLOOR UPWARDS WITHOUT THE CONSENT OF THE GENERAL FOREMAN
F.W. BARNARD LTD.
To be filed
EASTMAN & EASTMAN
ATTORNEYS
39 WEST 54TH STREET
NEW YORK, N.Y. 10019
July 8, 1969
Dear John, George, Paul and Ringo:
Before memories become too short I want to remind everybody that we could have settled the NEMS affair for very little. Klein killed my deal by claiming all sorts of improper acts of NEMS which his investigation would disclose and promising to get NEMS for you for nothing. We all know that no improper acts were found by Klein, if, in fact, Klein made an investigation at all.
Dear Harry,
I've asked Allen Klein to look after my things. Please give him any information he wants and full cooperation.
love,
Dear Clive,
I've asked Allen Klein to look after my things. Please give him any information he wants and full cooperation.
Dear Dick,
I've asked Allen Klein to look after my things. Please give him any information he wants and full cooperation.
love,

THE SHAMPOO FROM NEW YORK IS LEAVING VIA AEI TONIGHT. SEA BOARD WORLD AIRLINES FLIGHT 302. THE A E I NUMBER 501 4653.

I WILL CALL DR. BRONNER AND CHECK OUT HIS AIRWAYBILL INFO.

DOREEN

APPLE LONDON

NEIL ASPINALL: *I recall a meeting between Allen Klein, Lee Eastman and The Beatles that took place – I think it was at the Dorchester. There was a bust-up between Klein and Lee Eastman; they didn't like each other and they had an argument. Nothing was resolved.*

RINGO: John Eastman was involved in all the everyday meetings, but I don't have an impression of him coming in saying, 'Wow, lads! Let's go… '

Paul had different ideas from the rest of us about who we wanted to run Apple. We had great arguments with Paul. The three of us felt, 'Well, we have gone this way – why don't you?' I feel that he was tied because it was a family affair: if he hadn't been in the Eastman family – if John Eastman had been John 'Northman' – it could have been more easily sorted out. But it got really emotional, *because* it was a family matter.

NEIL ASPINALL: *Over a period of a few months they all worked things out and got some sort of one-page agreement together (before the formal contract that never appeared). The three of them signed – John, George and Ringo – but Paul didn't. I think the day that they signed it Paul just wanted more time. He didn't see what the rush was.*

PAUL: I think Allen had a very good way of persuading people. Basically, he used to say, 'What do you want?' and you'd say, 'Well, a lot of money…' – 'You got it!' Or, in Yoko's case, it was (I think) an exhibition; she wanted an art exhibition and she was having some difficulty maybe getting it on. I think Allen Klein said, 'OK, you got it. Exhibition? No problem!' So we all ended up paying for her Syracuse exhibition – a quarter each – and she wasn't even in the group. These were the kind of things Allen Klein was getting together, so he was very persuasive. He'd do anything anyone wanted – if he needed to influence that person.

I put forward Lee Eastman as a possible lawyer but they said, 'No, he'd be too biased for you and against us.' I could see that, so I asked him, 'If The Beatles wanted you to do this, would you do it?' And he said: 'Yeah, I might, you know.' So I then asked them before I asked Lee Eastman seriously, and they said, 'No way – he'd be too biased.' They were right – it was just as well he didn't do it, because it really would have got crazy with him in there.

So John was going with Klein, and George and Ringo said, 'OK, we're going with John.' I realised I was expected to go along with it, but I didn't think it was a good idea – simple as that, really. Actually I asked Mick Jagger when he came round, 'What do you think?' He said, 'Oh, he's all right if you like that kind of thing.' He didn't really warn us off him, so there it was – and that then was the three-to-one situation.

In The Beatles, if anyone didn't agree with a plan, it was always vetoed. It was very democratic that way, so the three-to-one situation was very awkward and as a result 'things' would happen.

I remember being at Olympic Studios one evening when I think we were supposed to be doing something on *Abbey Road*. We all showed up, ready to record, and Allen Klein showed up too. The other three said, 'You've got to sign a contract – he's got to take it to his board.' I said, 'It's Friday night. He doesn't work on a Saturday, and anyway Allen Klein is a law unto himself. He hasn't got a board he has to report to. Don't worry – we could easily do this on Monday. Let's do our session instead. You're not going to push me into this.'

They said, 'Oh, are you stalling? He wants 20%.' I said, 'Tell him he can have 15%.' They said: 'You're stalling.' I replied, 'No, I'm working for us; we're a big act.' I remember the exact words: 'We're a big act – The Beatles. He'll take 15%.' But for some strange reason (I think they were so intoxicated with him) they said, 'No, he's got to have 20%, and he's got to report to his board. You've got to sign now or never.' So I said, 'Right, that's it. I'm not signing now.'

There was a big argument and they all went, leaving me at the studio. Steve Miller happened to be around: 'Hi, how you doing? Is the studio free?' I said: 'Well, it looks like it is now, mate.' He said: 'Mind if I use it?' So I ended up drumming on a track of his that night. It was called 'My Dark Hour' – a good track actually. He and I made it alone. I had to do something, thrash something, to get it out of my system.

So those kinds of things started to happen, and that was the introduction of Klein – the three-to-one thing. He did get 20%.

DEREK TAYLOR: *Klein was supposed to be intimidating, but he didn't intimidate me because I felt he was like a lot of those heavy people: I felt he was vulnerable. I felt Frank Sinatra was very vulnerable when I met him too – I could see there was a side of Frank that really wanted to be liked. I felt there was a part of Klein that I could reach. Hard men are like that sometimes.*

*But if you were easily frightened – if you scared easily – he was a frightener. He had little eyes that were all over the place. Allen was from New Jersey, from another culture from us. We at Apple, who had been with The Beatles for a number of years, thought we could pretty well do anything. 'Hey, so he's got a hard reputation – we need his efficiency, and if there's anything awkward about him then we can contain that.'*

*He said to me: 'They say you're very wasteful, that you cost a lot of money because of all the drinking and the socialising – but you're not that expensive.' I said, 'I do know that. We don't go on big foreign trips or anything. It's mainly whisky, cigarettes and Kronenbourg lager.'*

*The Beatles (some of them) employed him pretty quickly. John said – after he and Yoko spent a night with him at the Dorchester – 'I'm going to give him everything.' They checked Donovan and Jagger and Mickie Most and others, who said: 'Well, maybe you wouldn't want to go on holiday with Allen, but he'll take care of you.'*

*So John and George and (I think) Ringo were happy fairly quickly. Paul was not happy for a very long time – never was – but he did sign something in the end, around the octagonal table. I think there was a photograph taken – one of those Terry Venables/Alan Sugar pictures.*

*I was in a very big bad lawsuit with Richard Branson at the time. Richard was then a very young man from* Student *magazine who was suing me for non-delivery of something John and Yoko had failed to deliver to me because they were having difficulties of some sort. In other words, I needed something they had and I had to give it to Branson and couldn't – and it was a £10,000 lawsuit.*

*John said, 'Oh, that lawsuit you've got with that fellow from* Student *– Allen's going to take care of everything. Everything's going to be OK. There is too much fear in this office – Klein will get rid of it all.' So, another Messiah was with us – and there was some relief, and some new fears.*

NEIL ASPINALL: *Allen Klein brought in his own people and fired a lot of people who were working at Apple. It didn't all take place in one day, but over a period of nine months. For example, he would rather have Les Perrin (who was a PR man with his own outside company who worked for lots of different people – he did PR for The Rolling Stones and other people in the music business) than Apple have its own press department. Ron Kass (Apple Records) went; Denis O'Dell (Apple Films) went after* Let It Be*; Peter Asher went, Tony Bramwell went, Jack Oliver went. It wasn't just slimming down – it was end of story.*

*Everything changed at Apple after he arrived. It was a completely different situation. First and foremost, Paul wasn't there. He totally disagreed with what was going on. But still, they went into the studios and recorded* Abbey Road *while Klein was around.*

MEMO

TO

Neil

OUR REFERENCE | YOUR REFERENCE

28th April 1969

I found some lost marijuana and mixed it with neppalese hashish, I then rolled a joint and smoked it and went into the garden and put up 50 yards of fencing and aquired a headache which took over the entire front half of my head. I took two codein and rolled another joint and smoked it. At that point Joan reminded me that you had called to find out what was happening. After giving the matter some thought I decided I didn't know what was happening., so I didn't call you.

I know you will understand.

Your friend.

**CONFIDENTIAL**

Dear Allen,

The financial position of Apple Electronics Ltd. is causing me considerable concern at present.

Via WU

RJH CXC

SYC234 LB123
L LLT069 SW INTL CNT PCG TDL LA CANADA CALIF 38/36 12 218A PST
LT THE BEATLES CARE APPLE CO
LONDON (ENGLAND)
HAVE INVENTED HYPERSOCAE DRIVE SUPER WAVE VARIATER TOPOLOGICAL BIOLOGICAL NUMBER THEORY MINIATURE POLARIZING LAZERS +NEW MAGNETIC METHOD+ DISNEY HISTORICAL SOCITY JUDEAN CLUB INTERNATIONAL
MICHAEL A WEINBERG PHONE 213-790-0636
213-790-0636.

CX APCORE TD/CX
THE BEATLES
C/O APPLE CORPS LTD.,
3, SAVILLE ROW W.1.

734-8232 10am-6.30pm Mons-Fris.

WESTERN UNION INTERNATIONAL INC.
21/22, GT. WINCHESTER ST., LONDON, E.C.2
TEL. 01-588 1234 TELEX. 22951

GEORGE: WHEN ALLEN KLEIN CAME TO APPLE IT WAS LIKE THAT SCENE IN *THE RUTLES* WHEN RON DECLINE COMES INTO RUTLE CORPS AND EVERYBODY JUMPS OUT OF THE WINDOW. HE FIRED PEOPLE – OR SOME PEOPLE RAN AWAY IN FRIGHT – AND THEN HE INSTALLED A BUNCH OF HIS OWN MEN, WHO THEN PROCEEDED TO CONTROL EVERYTHING IN THE MANNER HE WANTED.

Dear Costa,

As a result of recent discussions I have had with the Beatles it has been decided that the trading activities of Apple Electronics Ltd. should discontinue.

This means that the Company will no longer require your services and we would like you to accept this letter as formal notice of service and cheque representing one months fee.

c.c. Alexis Mardas
Neil Aspinall
Al Crotti

This is to confirm your instructions that all employees of Apple Electronics Ltd. are to have their employment terminated with effect from Friday 29th August, 1969, and that we are to pay each person the equivalent of one month's salary in lieu of notice as at that date.

DEREK TAYLOR: *Allen changed a lot at Apple. He was a very big presence when he was in town. He had an office right opposite mine, and it shows how crackers I was that I carried on as I was carrying on. I wouldn't do it now; I'd be far too nervous. But I was fuelled by the certainty that if I was still employed there then I had this other function: I was still representing, if you like, 'the old days'. I think there are still people out there who linger on after the mood's gone: the keepers of the mood.*

*Klein sacked a lot of people one terrible Friday when he said, 'I'm taking you out to lunch today.' I'd never had lunch with him. He said: 'Some guys and girls are getting... um... we're letting them go.' I think he had Peter Brown sack a long list of people who were surplus to Klein's requirements, and he said, 'Hey, you guys are lucky – usually I come in and fire everybody.' So those of us who remained must have convinced ourselves that we were doing it for the boys. But maybe we were just there because we hadn't been fired. We stayed.*

*In the office I had a light show machine with a projector on it and gels that went swirling round and round. It cost £150, I think. Allen Klein had been with The Rolling Stones and Donovan through the psychedelic time, and a light show was just part of something he understood but didn't understand: 'These guys do these kinds of things. I don't know what the hell they do it for but they do it. There's nothing to it, there's no money in it, but if he wants to do that and that's all he does – hey...' So I was allowed to carry on more or less 'as normal' for eighteen more months after Klein arrived.*

*Peter Asher, who was not fired, left anyway. He left also out of loyalty to Ron Kass (now, alas, dead), who was head of Apple Records and quite a big cheese around the building. Klein was after Ron Kass. He wanted him out because he was another American and another accountant with a high profile, and he was conspicuous. Peter Asher, who was a very important person at Apple, as head of A&R, said, 'I'm going with Ron,' and together they set up with MGM records and took James Taylor with them.*

*The atmosphere was not right after that – if it ever had been, really. It was a mad idea to believe you could save the world, but a lot of people were doing it at that time. They say that at the time of Christ there were a lot of Messiahs – not just Jesus – going round making speeches, and in the late Sixties there were many saviours, some malign and some benign. The Beatles were among the latter, but it got crazy, as it always does.*

JOHN: Allen was a human being, the same as Brian was a human being. It was the same thing with Brian in the early days: it was assessment. And I make a lot of mistakes character-wise – but now and then I make a good one.[70]

RINGO: Allen was great for me for the first couple of years, because all I wanted was to be looked after. I would get off the plane or the QE2 in New York and there'd be a guy there: a pretty stocky guy who would get me through, get me in a limo, give me a pack of money, get me a suite in a hotel – and that was it. That was cool for me; I was easily pleased. Just get me to the place on time!

What Allen proceeded to do when he arrived at Apple was get rid of anybody we knew, and put his own people in. I was losing control by then. I was getting out of Apple and out of my mind, so it started to go and I wasn't in charge at all.

PAUL: Allen Klein didn't manage to sort out Apple. The thing with Apple was that we were great creators, but nobody had half an idea about a budget, so we were spending more than we were earning. The idea was that he would be able to sort that out and give us an idea of where we were.

It got crazy because one of his first things he did was to go through all the filing cabinets that we'd never been through. We didn't even know they existed. (In fact, they lost half the files in one of the moves from Wigmore Street to Savile Row.) 'We're the creators, we're the artists, we're the producers' – we didn't have files. He found a ten-year contract of The Beatles that we didn't even know we'd signed. But for some deal somewhere we'd had to sign: 'Yes, we hereby link with each other for ten years.' (We'd always gone on trust before – we never actually signed something. We didn't think about it.) Klein found this in a drawer somewhere, so this is what they started to hold me to. I was definitely being held to the very letter of the law.

JOHN: We earned millions and millions, but I must tell you that The Beatles got very little of it. We've all got houses but we've managed to pay for them financially after all these years. And that only really happened since Klein came in – the so-called wolf. There's millions earned, but we never got it. There's lots of big companies in London with various names, and you just have to check them out and their connection with The Beatles and you see where the money's gone. And in America too.

Brian Epstein was a beautiful guy: he was an intuitive theatrical guy and he knew we had something and he presented us well. But he had lousy business advice. He was taken advantage of – we all were, Brian included – and none of us got it.

That's life. It's no big news that some artist or some kids in showbiz got robbed. It's the same old story. The attitude is: 'if they have money they won't work'. That's not true. If you give an artist money he's secure and he *can* work. My big worry always was, 'Am I going to be Mickey Rooney? I know we've earned it, but where's it gone? I've got to pay the tax some day. It's no good me saying, "I never got it." The books say it came to The Beatles, or something like that, and we're going to have to pay tax the rest of our lives.' That was my big worry. I just warn all the kids coming in the business: don't sign anything unless the lawyer's your brother. Keep it in the family.[71]

PAUL: What happened originally was that back in Liverpool John and I didn't know about song publishing. We literally thought that songs were in the air and everyone owned them. That's how we met our first publisher, Dick James. He said, 'Come in. Sit down. Is that what you think? Sit over here.' And that was the deal he did. To this day I'm virtually on that deal. So that meant we were pretty much sewn up from the word go.

In March 1969, when I was on my honeymoon and John was doing his bed-in, Dick James sold the songs – while we were out of town. When we got back to town, we said, 'Dick! You can't do that!' He said, 'You want a bet?' And he was quite right. It's just the way these things go. So it was sold, and it became merchandise then. It was then bought by Lew Grade, who used to control ATV. So that was how John and I lost the ownership of so many of our songs. And George, too – he lost some.

RINGO: In February I started filming *The Magic Christian* with Peter Sellers. I'd read the book (which was written by Terry Southern) and we got the film together by my knocking on Peter's door. I said to him, 'Let's make this movie.' So, as he was Peter Sellers, three phone calls later they put the money in and we were off.

The amazing thing with Peter was that, though we would work all day and go out and have dinner that night – and we would usually leave him laughing hysterically, because he was hilarious – the next morning we'd say, 'Hi Pete!' and we'd have to start again. There was no continuation. You had to make the friendship start again from nine o'clock every morning. We'd all be laughing at six o'clock at night, but the next morning it would be, 'Hi Pete!' then, 'Oh God!' – we'd have to knock the wall down again to say 'hello'. Sometimes we'd be asked to leave the set, because Peter Sellers was being Peter Sellers.

It was great to meet Terry Southern. He was in the next dressing room to me, so we became really good pals, and we'd write each other notes. The producers would come up to Terry and say, 'Terry, you'll never guess!' And he'd say, 'Well, what is it?' – 'We've got Yul Brynner.' So Terry would have to start typing in something for Yul Brynner. Then we'd be sitting there again, and they'd say, 'We've got Raquel Welch.' They would just call actors and actresses up, or if they were in town bring them to the movie, and poor Terry would have to write them in. It was a very strange movie to make, but it was a lot of fun. Terry would post the words under my door and then I'd be called in an hour and go down and do them.

It was a lot of fun with Peter; we had such great laughs – he was a really humorous person. I had some scenes with him which we couldn't do because we were in hysterics. One of us would open his mouth and we'd be gone. We had quite a few days of that.

Peter taught me a great lesson. There's a scene in the movie where I have all these lines but on the other side of the screen he just picked his nose. If you watch the film in the cinema, you see *everybody* shift from me right over to him. A thousand people think, 'Oh, he's picking his nose.' It was much more important than the speech I was saying – and so I never let anybody do that to me again in a movie. It was a good lesson. He would always say: 'It's your eyes, Ring. It's your eyes. They'll be two hundred feet big up there, you know.' He was a really cool guy, and we had a lot of fun.

John being involved with Yoko and me making a film shows as an absolute fact that we were going different places. I've mentioned it before: the energy for The Beatles was waning. We used to put in a thousand per cent, but now it was dwindling. Now it was like, 'Oh dear – do we *have* to turn up? Do we have to do those things again? I want to do this and John wants to do that and George wants to do something else…' We had families. The energy was dissipating because we had other things to do.

GEORGE: John wanted to go off and do his avant-garde or whatever it was, and I just wanted to be able to record some songs. Paul on the other hand wanted (I think) to keep playing live. As long as we were happy, I think Ringo would have been happy to have kept going. That's not to limit him, but I think the main thing for him was he felt that we were all getting on so well that he didn't fit.

NEIL ASPINALL: *The acrimony had started to come in as well in terms of Allen Klein and what was happening with the money. Paul really didn't want Allen representing him – so it was a slow process.*

JOHN: All of us are artists and we're nothing else, so we can't manage ourselves or look after ourselves in that way. It's a lot for four bigheads like The Beatles to stay together for such a long time, and in the early days there was the thing of making it big or breaking into America and we had a goal together. But when we reached about twenty-eight or twenty-nine it began to be: 'What's the goal? We've made it.' We were getting more talented. George began to write lots of songs, and you couldn't make an album – you were lucky to get a track on an album. Then we all started getting more interested in our own music and going different ways.[71]

Brookfields,
Cutmill Lane,
Elstead, Surrey.

May, 1969

To: Delegate Productions A.G.
Steinbockstrasse,
Chur,
Switzerland

"THE MAGIC CHRISTIAN"

I, RICHARD STARKEY HEREBY REQUEST AND DIRECT you to pay to Apple Films Limited at 3, Saville Row, London, W.1. or to their order all monies payable to me under Clause 5(a) and 6 of the Contract between us dated 24th February, 1969 relating to my services in connection with the above Film.

Richard Starkey

PAUL: We played to about 56,000 people at Shea Stadium. And after that you think to yourself, 'What more can you do?' The only thing you can do more is play to 57,000 people. So you start to realise that you've either got to keep trying to play to more and more people and be involved with bigger and bigger events or else just cool it down a bit. So that's what we're doing now, cooling it down and living a bit more normal lives.[69]

RINGO: John had probably really gone from the group by then – even in the mid-Sixties. Paul was the workaholic, or the Beatleaholic. Because John and I lived quite close to each other in Weybridge we'd be at his house or ours, and we'd be having a really lovely day, really smooth – and then the phone would ring and it would always be Paul saying, 'I think we should get back in the studio, lads. We gotta do this.' – 'Oh no, I don't want to. I want to be on holiday.' But Paul would kick us around and we'd go back in.

By the end of the Sixties, it was like, 'Oh well, what are we going in for? Who wants to?' The enthusiasm was just waning. Paul was still the person who was trying to whip everything together, as he is today. That's how he is.

229-5827. URGENT POP 4477 Carol

Dear Jack,
will you get in touch with Bob Gill, who is working for Dennis O'Dell on the "Magic Christian" and ask him to give you a print of the photo they are using for their advertising on the film.
When you get it, have a photo session fixed up with the IVEYS, and arrange them exactly as Ringo and Sellars are in the photo.
(Ringo is sitting on Sellars knee!)
So the Iveys will do it like this. Side by side.

Then ask Bob Gill if he will do the cover design EXACTLY like the film posters except for the replacement of Ringo + Sellars WITH the Iveys
So their advertising will be like this.

MAGIC CHRISTIAN
Ringo — Sellars

our cover will be like this.

MAGIC CHRISTIAN MUSIC BY THE IVEYS
Ivey Ivey Ivey

Just have the photo done – lettering to be decided later. Let me see it when it's ready to go to the printers

Thanks.
Paul.

RINGO:
IT WAS LIKE THE WIND-DOWN TO A DIVORCE. A DIVORCE USUALLY DOESN'T JUST HAPPEN SUDDENLY; THERE ARE MONTHS AND YEARS OF MISERY UNTIL YOU FINALLY SAY 'OH, LET'S END IT.'

RINGO: I think we expected Paul and Jane Asher to get married. They were lovers, they were together, and it seemed a natural thing to do. I don't know in the end what actually broke them up. We'll have to ask him about that, or ask her – that's probably more interesting!

PAUL: On March 12th 1969 I got married to Linda.

I had first met her a long time before that. We actually met in a late-night club I used to go to a lot in London, the Bag O'Nails. It was behind Liberty's. I used to go to a lot of those places, because we'd finish gigs and recording sessions about 11pm, and we'd be ready to have our evening off at about midnight when everything was closed, so we either had to go to cabaret places (originally I went to places like the Blue Angel and the Talk of the Town) or clubs and discos.

I liked the Bag O'Nails because, though it was not the most popular club, we could meet a lot of mates down there – music people like Pete Townshend, Zoot Money, Georgie Fame. So we could chat into the wee small hours and have a few drinks.

One night Linda showed up. She was in town photographing groups for a book called *Rock and Other Four Letter Words*. She'd been sent from America, and she'd just done a session with The Animals. They'd come over to the club: 'Let's go out and have a bevvie and a smoke.'

So she was sitting in an alcove near the band, which was Georgie Fame and the Blue Flames – with Speedy Acquaye on bongos. They were always a big favourite of mine. I saw her and thought, 'Hello...' When she was about to leave the club, I stood up and said, 'Hello, we haven't met' – which was a straight pull.

Then I said, 'We're going on to this next club called the Speakeasy. Do you want to come?' And if she'd said 'no' I wouldn't have ended up marrying her. She said, 'Yeah, all right.' So we went on to the Speakeasy, and it was the first time any of us had ever heard 'A Whiter Shade Of Pale'. We all thought it was Stevie Winwood. It turned out to be the group with a very strange name – Procol Harum.

That was the first time we ever met – and then we met on and off, because I would see her if I went to New York or if she was in London. There's a point, I think, in most people's lives when they start to think: 'If I'm thinking of getting married, if I'm thinking of getting serious – *now* is the time'. I was starting to have those sorts of thoughts, and I suppose I was thinking back over all the girls I'd known, and wondering who was the favourite to get serious with, and she was one who always came into my mind.

So I rang her up and asked her if she wanted to come over, and she came to London and we stayed together for a while and became an item. She'd been married before, so she wasn't keen to get married again. She was unsure but I persuaded her. I said, 'It'll be all right this time.' She was a bit 'once bitten twice shy' – but we eventually got married in Marylebone Registry Office.

I really don't remember whether or not I invited any of the band to the wedding. Why not? I'm a total bastard, I suppose – I don't know, really. Maybe it was because the group was breaking up. We were all pissed off with each other. We certainly weren't a gang any more. That was the thing. Once a group's broken up like that, that's it.

NEIL ASPINALL: *I didn't go to Paul and Linda's wedding, but they had lunch or tea afterwards at the Ritz, and I think it was just Paul, Linda, Mal, Suzy (my wife) and me. I don't remember anybody else being there.*

GEORGE: I'M A TIDY MAN. I KEEP MY SOCKS IN THE SOCK DRAWER AND STASH IN THE STASH BOX.[69]

GEORGE: They chose Paul's wedding day to come and do a raid on me, and to this day I'm still having difficulty with my visa to America because of this fella.

He came out to my house with about eight other policemen, a policewoman and a police dog, who happened to be called Yogi – because, I suppose, of the Beatle connection with Maharishi. They thought they'd have a bit of fun.

They took us off, fingerprinted us and we were busted. It was written in the papers like a fashion show: 'George was wearing a yellow suit and his wife Pattie had on…'

DEREK TAYLOR: *I was with George in the office when that call came through. It was the end of a long day at Apple. Pattie rang and said, 'They're here – the law is here,' and we knew what to do by then. We phoned Release's lawyer, Martin Polden. We had a routine: he came round to Apple, and we all went down by limousine to Esher, where the police were well ensconced by then – and I stood bail for George and Pattie. They went off to the police station. We were all extremely indignant because it was the day of Paul's wedding, a poor way to celebrate it. The police can be so nice.*

*George was calm about it. George is always calm – he sometimes gets a grump, but he's always calm – and he was extremely calm that night, and very, very indignant. He went into the house and looked around at all these men and one woman, and said something like, 'Birds have nests and animals have holes, but man hath nowhere to lay his head.' – 'Oh, really, sir? Sorry to tell you we have to…' and then into the police routine.*

*That's how calm and how cross he was, because, as he said, he kept his dope in the box where dope went, and his joss sticks went in the joss stick box. He was a man who ran an orderly late-Sixties household, with beautiful things and some nice stuff to smoke.*

*In my opinion he didn't have to be busted because he was doing nobody any harm. I still believe what they did was an intrusion into personal life.*

*I don't remember Paul's wedding much, as I wasn't at it. Paul and Linda dealt with it by being available and pleasant, and pictures were taken. It was a semi-public day, but it was a day where obviously the heat generated by these events spreads far beyond the event.*

*But it didn't give me any frenzy. It wasn't in my life, and also it was planned, it was known about. Often what we had to deal with at Apple was spontaneous and imposed on us, like nude album covers, Hell's Angels, busts and things like that, and they could be difficult.*

NEIL ASPINALL: *I was also in the office that evening when Pattie rang. George was saying to me, 'What should we do?' and I said, 'They'll just wreck the place, man. Where is it?' He replied, 'I've got a bit of hash in a box on the mantelpiece.' So he rang Pattie back and told her to tell them where it was – by which time the police already had a big chunk in their possession.*

I do hereby absolutely renounce and abandon the use of my former christian name of Winston and in lieu thereof do assume as from the date hereof the additional christian name of Ono

DEREK TAYLOR: *The next marriage was on March 20th: John married Yoko in Gibraltar.*

JOHN: We wanted to get married on a cross-channel ferry. That was the romantic part: when we went to Southampton and then we couldn't get on because she wasn't English and she couldn't get the day visa to go across. And they said, 'Anyway, you can't get married. The Captain's not allowed to do it any more.'

So we were in Paris and we were calling Peter Brown, and said, 'We want to get married. Where can we go?' And he called back and said, 'Gibraltar's the only place.' So – 'OK, let's go!' And we went there and it was beautiful. It's the Pillar of Hercules, and also symbolically they called it the End of the World at one period. There's some name besides Pillar of Hercules – but they thought the world outside was a mystery from there, so it was like the Gateway to the World. So we liked it in the symbolic sense, and the Rock foundation of our relationship.[80]

NEIL ASPINALL: *It's in the song 'The Ballad Of John And Yoko' that Peter Brown called to say, 'You can get married in Gibraltar.' They just chartered a plane, took off for Gibraltar and got married there. I think John had been drifting away from The Beatles for a while – since he got together with Yoko, really.*

JOHN: We both think alike, and we've both been alone. We both had these dreams, the same kind of dreams. I had this dream of this woman coming. I knew it wouldn't be someone buying the Beatle records. The way it was with Cyn was she got pregnant, we got married. We never had much to say to each other. But the vibrations didn't upset me because she was quiet and I was away all the time. I'd get fed up every now and then, and start thinking this 'Where Is She?' bit. I'd hope that The One would come. Everybody's got that 'thinking of The One'. The one what? Well, I suppose I was hoping for a woman who would give me what I got from a man intellectually. I wanted someone I could be myself with.[69]

PAUL: Yoko really became the central fact in John's life. I remember thinking of it being like army buddies. One of the songs we used to love in the past was 'Wedding Bells' – 'Those wedding bells are breaking up that old gang of mine…' – and the idea that you'd been army buddies, but one day you have to kiss the army goodbye, go and get married and act like normal people.

It was a bit like that for The Beatles; we always knew that day had to come. When John hooked up with Yoko so intensely, it was obvious that there could be no looking back. In the intensity of his love affair, that was the way he had to treat it. It was exciting him so much that he didn't really have much time for us. We were the past and she was the future. We were in the middle of that and we had to try to understand it.

DEREK TAYLOR: *Yoko had taken the place of everybody in John's life. Since they had met she was his life, and he was hers, and they were very co-dependent people. They had no life outside each other.*

JOHN: BUT NOW MY LIFE HAS CHANGED IN OH SO MANY WAYS… AWOP-BOP-ALOO-BOP-ABIM-BAM-BOOM.[69]

*I had been anxious when it was obvious I was going to have to deal with a broken marriage and press and all that kind of innuendo. I did have a word with John, though not in a pompous way: 'I'm prepared for what's coming. I just want you to know that what is coming is a lot of unpleasant stuff, about somebody breaking up a marriage, home-wrecking, that kind of stuff. This is what people and the press are saying, and you know how pompous and prurient they are,' and so on.*

*But once it had been established that they were a couple I was in on the thing. I was very fond of Cynthia, but this was it. So I was for it in the end, because he was besotted with Yoko and she was with him. They were quite an item.*

JOHN: The alienation started when I met Yoko, and people do not seem to like people getting a divorce. It's all right to do it quietly, but we can't do it quietly. So we fell in love and we married. A lot of people think that's a bit odd, but it happens all the time. And Yoko just happened to be Japanese, which didn't help much. So everybody had this impression that John's gone crazy – but all I did was fall in love, like a lot of people do who are already married, who had married somebody very young.

When Yoko and I got married, we got terrible racialist letters – you know, warning me that she would slit my throat. Those mainly came from army people living in Aldershot. Officers.[71]

RINGO: I think John and Yoko were trying to keep the wedding fairly quiet. That's why he went to Gibraltar.

GEORGE: I didn't know about John marrying Yoko in Gibraltar – I bought the record! I don't think he wanted anybody to know. He wanted it to be quiet and private.

JOHN: Yoko and I decided that we knew whatever we did was going to be in the papers. We decided to utilise the space we would occupy anyway, by getting married, with a commercial for peace.[75]

Now the bed-in was just to catch the attention of the press. The first bed-in was held in Amsterdam on our honeymoon. We sent out a card: 'Come to John and Yoko's honeymoon: a bed-in, Amsterdam Hotel.' You should have seen the faces on the reporters and the cameramen fighting their way through the door! Because whatever it is, is in people's minds – their minds were full of what they thought was going to happen. They fought their way in, and their faces dropped. There were we like two angels in bed, with flowers all around us, and peace and love on our heads. We were fully clothed; the bed was just an accessory. We were wearing pyjamas, but they don't look much different from day clothes – nothing showing.[72]

The press seemed to think we were going to make love in public because we made an album with us naked – so they seem to think anything goes. And, as I said, it might be a very good idea for peace, but I think I'd probably be the producer of that event rather than be actually in the event.[69]

We talked to the press. We met people from the Communist countries, people from the West – every country in the world. We gave the press eight hours of every day, every waking hour, to ask every question they wanted to about our position. People said, 'Well, what does this do for peace?' We thought, 'The other side has war on every day, not only on the news but on the old John Wayne movies and every damn movie you see: war, war, war, war, kill, kill, kill, kill.' We said, 'Let's get some peace, peace, peace, peace on the headlines, just for a change!' So we thought it highly amusing that a lot of the world's headlines on March 25th 1969 were 'HONEYMOON COUPLE IN BED'. Whoopee! Isn't that great news?[72]

We thought instead of just being 'John and Yoko Get Married', like 'Richard and Liz Get Married', [it should be] 'JOHN AND YOKO GET MARRIED AND HAVE A BED-IN FOR PEACE'. So we would sell our product, which we call 'peace'. And to sell a product you need a gimmick, and the gimmick we thought was 'bed'. And we thought 'bed' because bed was the easiest way of doing it, because we're lazy. It took us a long train of thought of how to get the maximum publicity for what we sincerely believed in, which was peace – and we were part of the peace movement.[75]

I think the only way to do it is Gandhi's way. And that's non-violent, passive, positive, or whatever he called it in those days.[69]

GEORGE: I liked the idea of their promoting peace – I was all for that. Right from the time we went to the dentist's dinner party I knew what John felt about things, and it was no surprise to me that he would want some peace, and the manner in which he did it wasn't really a surprise either. It was also fun for him because he could do it with Yoko, do it after his wedding, do it as his honeymoon/bed-in.

RINGO: I THOUGHT THE BED-IN FOR PEACE WAS GREAT. THEY WERE NOW THE AVANT-GARDE, DOING THAT FOR PEACE. THERE WAS A GREAT SCENE ON *THE DAVID FROST SHOW* WHEN THEY GOT IN THE BAG ON TV: 'JUST TALK TO US, NOT TO OUR IMAGE.'

JOHN: IN PARIS, THE VIETNAM PEACE TALKS HAVE GOT ABOUT AS FAR AS SORTING OUT THE SHAPE OF THE TABLE THEY ARE GOING TO SIT ROUND. THOSE TALKS HAVE BEEN GOING ON FOR MONTHS. IN ONE WEEK IN BED, WE ACHIEVED A LOT MORE. WHAT? A LITTLE OLD LADY FROM WIGAN OR HULL WROTE TO THE *DAILY MIRROR* ASKING IF THEY COULD PUT YOKO AND MYSELF ON THE FRONT PAGE MORE OFTEN. SHE SAID SHE HADN'T LAUGHED SO MUCH FOR AGES. THAT'S GREAT, THAT'S WHAT WE WANTED. I MEAN, IT'S A FUNNY WORLD WHEN TWO PEOPLE GOING TO BED ON THEIR HONEYMOON CAN MAKE THE FRONT PAGES IN ALL THE PAPERS FOR A WEEK. I WOULDN'T MIND DYING AS THE WORLD'S CLOWN. I'M NOT LOOKING FOR EPITAPHS.[69]

JOHN: We were asked to make a film for Austrian TV, which we did, called *Rape* – which wasn't a rape but it was called *Rape*. It was rape by camera, in fact. So when we went to Austria to show it, we did a press conference in a bag. And it was great, because all the press came in and they never saw us – we were both in a bag, and they interviewed the bag. They were saying, 'Is it really you?' and, 'What are you wearing?' and 'Will you sing a song?' They were saying, 'Why us? What is this?' and I said, 'It's total communication.' And they said, 'Why do you pick on us? We've never seen a Beatle!'

If everyone went in a bag for a job there'd be no prejudice: you'd have to judge people on their quality within. We call it total communication. It was a great press conference, and they all had a very serious conversation with a bag. The next day the headlines in Austria were – they'd show a bag with all the press men just talking to it.[71]

And [during] many of the openings in London where the white bag appeared in a big white Rolls Royce, actually John and Yoko were at home watching themselves being filmed, being shown on the nightly news. So put that in your bag and think about it.

Usually there was a serious intent behind it, because our feeling was there's nothing but 'MAN EATS BABY' on the news, or the *Daily Express* saying 'MORE BOMBS PLEASE', and our thing was: get some laughs on it.[75]

RINGO: 'The Ballad Of John And Yoko' only had Paul (of the other Beatles) on it but that was OK. 'Why Don't We Do It In The Road' was just Paul and me, and it went out as a Beatle track too. We had no problems with that. There's good drums on 'The Ballad Of John And Yoko', too.

JOHN: The follow-up to 'Get Back' is 'Ballad of John and Yoko'. It's something I wrote, and it's like an old-time ballad. It's just the story of us getting married, going to Paris, going to Amsterdam, all that. It's 'Johnny B. Paperback Writer'!

I don't regard it as a separate record scene... it's The Beatles' next single, simple as that. The story came out that only Paul and I were on the record, but I wouldn't have bothered publicising that. It doesn't mean anything; it just so happened that there were only us two there. George was abroad, and Ringo was on the film and he couldn't come that night. Because of that, it was a choice of either re-mixing or doing a new one – and you always go for doing a new one instead of fiddling about with an old one. So we did, and it turned out well.[69]

GEORGE: I didn't mind not being invited to the wedding, and I didn't mind not being on the record, because it was none of my business – 'The Ballad Of John And Yoko'. If it had been the 'The Ballad Of John, George And Yoko', then I would have been on it.

GEORGE MARTIN: *John and Yoko got better as they went along. Once they got down into their sensible period, so to speak, it was nice working with them. John would bring me a cassette of different things he had made, and say: 'Can you make something out of this?' I would try to do things for him because he wasn't terribly good technically.*

*I enjoyed working with John and Yoko on 'The Ballad Of John And Yoko'. It was just the two of them with Paul. When you think about it, in a funny kind of way it was the beginning of their own label, and their own way of recording. It was hardly a Beatle track – yet it was a Beatle track. It was a kind of thin end of the wedge, as far as they were concerned. John had already mentally left the group anyway, and I think that was just the beginning of it all.*

JOHN: 'The Ballad Of John And Yoko', by the way, was banned over here [in the USA]. So what they did was, because they don't like the word 'Christ' – unless you're wearing a white robe, you can't say 'Christ' here – they turned it round so it would go: 'Rrrrp, you know it ain't easy…'

DEREK TAYLOR: *There was also the bed-in in Montreal at the end of May. I went out on that as well – John and Yoko, the film crew, Yoko's daughter Kyoko, Derek, twenty-six pieces of luggage, and various white suits.*

*Joan and I went out on the QE2. It was arranged that we would travel with John and Yoko and Neil and Suzy – but, as the song says, 'Standing on the dock at Southampton…' John and Yoko weren't allowed on the QE2 because of visa trouble over the dope bust. (They flew to Montreal instead, via the Bahamas and Toronto.) Neil didn't go either, but Ringo and Peter Sellers and wives and others were elsewhere on this enormous liner on its second voyage. It was that kind of weirdness going on again. I telexed a long, long report on this adventure for* The Beatles Monthly, *by order of John.*

*The first destination for the bed-in had been Freeport in the Bahamas, where Allen Klein's nephew had spent his honeymoon in a horrible hotel with twin beds cemented to the floor with a big block of concrete between them painted white. John looked around and said, 'We can't do a bloody bed-in here. Let's go to Canada. That's the nearest place to America apart from the Bahamas.'*

*They had the bed-in for eight days. Hundreds of people came to the bedside. The questions were dealt with by John and Yoko in the full spirit of Apple, because they made themselves completely available to anybody on earth who wanted to come into the bedroom – provided they were not obviously carrying a blood-stained axe. People could come in and ask them questions. Maybe they came in thousands; it felt like it.*

*I was sort of controlling a big People Theatre. There is some footage of that time in which you see quite a packed room. Over a period of ten days you could process a great many people through a hotel suite, and they were doing broadcasts to the world on speaker-phones and hook-ups. It was before satellites.*

*My job was to be around day and night while they were in bed. They were able to rest between visits. They were able to lie down and get new pyjamas etc. A lot of us have had dreams about running our whole life from bed, and for ten days that was what they did.*

*They were having also to report – I think every few days – to the consul in Montreal, because they were only there on sufferance, and were in fact deported from Canada at the end of the bed-in because their appeal against not being allowed in had failed. They'd done the whole bed-in during an appeal period. As soon as the ten days were up, they were told to clear off. In fact they were put on the first plane out to Frankfurt – which is not where we were going; we were going to London. So that, again, is something people forget! Doing a bed-in and being deported when it was over.*

PAUL:
GEORGE MARTIN WAS ONCE TALKING TO US IN THE RECORDING STUDIO, AND HE CAME DOWN AND SAID, 'SOMEBODY WANTS TO SEE YOU.' WE SAID, 'WHO IS IT, THEN?' AND HE SAID, 'OH, IT'S SOME CRANK TALKING ABOUT PEACE.' HE WAS RIGHT: THERE WAS A CRANK TALKING ABOUT PEACE.
IF YOU TALK ABOUT PEACE YOU'RE A CRANK, AND YOU'RE PIGEONHOLED AND ASSOCIATED WITH VIETNAM AND SITTING DOWN IN TRAFALGAR SQUARE, AND EVERYBODY THINKS THEY KNOW WHAT YOU ARE THEN. AS *THEY* WERE, WHEN THEY WENT INTO THE BED-IN AND SAID: 'LOOK, THIS IS FOR PEACE.' IT WAS A GREAT WAY TO ATTRACT ATTENTION TO PEACE.

PAUL: If you watch some of the great footage in *Imagine* you see the cartoonist Al Capp. He comes into the bed-in and he's really bitter. He's a wicked old git, but John's brilliant with him. John really wants to deck him but you can see he controls himself. I think John behaved very well there, because the guy is actually slagging off Yoko – and that's one thing you don't do. You don't slag off someone's missus – that's tribal time, isn't it? I think John was very good. It was: 'Let's not sink to his level.'

DEREK TAYLOR: *By now it was quite clear there was a 'get The Beatles' type of thing going on. They were getting a terrifically mixed press. There was a lot of abuse and a lot of praise.*

*The American media tended to be more generous. There was a lot of 'alternative press' in those days. The* Village Voice, LA Free Press *and* Rolling Stone *were new then. But the day-to-day press in England – Fleet Street and so on – by and large thought John and Yoko were crackers. I knew they weren't and this was a good peace movement they ran. And 'Give Peace A Chance' was a great song.*

JOHN: I like 'Give Peace A Chance' for what it was. I couldn't say that was the best song as a song I'd ever written, but I'm always proud of it. I think one of the highest moments was hearing all those people in Washington, when the whole anti-war group were singing it. That was an emotional moment for me.[74]

I sort of cheated. The word 'masturbation' was in it, but I wrote in the lyric sheet – because I'd had enough of the bannings – I mean, I'd been banned so many times all over that I copped out and wrote 'mastication'. It was more important to get it out than be bothered by a word, 'masturbation'.[80]

DEREK TAYLOR: *By then we were embattled, and in the end John and Yoko did so much press and got involved with so many causes, from Black Power to trying to clear James Hanratty's name, that the press just got John and Yoko fatigue.*

JOHN: In Britain, the press treat us like children: 'We're not having that middle-aged Beatle lecturing us on peace, and philosophy isn't his forte.' As if politicians and journalists have some kind of super gift from God that gave them their wisdom.[69]

In Britain I'm the guy who got lucky and won the pools, and Yoko's the Hawaiian who married the guy who got lucky and won the pools. In America we're artists…[71]

DEREK TAYLOR: *I didn't think John was drifting away from the group, because they were still musically completely involved. It seemed to me that all that was happening could somehow co-exist – although it was not an easy year.*

*I don't think it was a very happy year; I'm extremely glad it is over. It got worse when Allen Klein arrived, and the atmosphere then wasn't as happy in the office.*

JOHN: REALLY, THERE'S NO DIFFERENCE BETWEEN WHAT WE'RE DOING NOW AND WHAT WE'VE ALWAYS DONE. THE IDEA OF PEACE HAS ALWAYS BEEN WITH US. YOU COULD SMELL IT IN THE EARLY BEATLE SONGS. IT'S LIKE THE BEATLES SINGING 'ALL YOU NEED IS LOVE' – I'M JUST SINGING 'ALL YOU NEED IS PEACE' NOW.'[69]

Via WUI

RJH

1969 MAY 22

CXC

20:42

SYC839 LU345 CXC 11

L OLC410 AD INTL OAKLAND CALIF 32 22 153P PDT

LT THE BEATLES CARE DEREK TAYLOR

3 SAVILLEROW LONDONWEST1(ENGLAND)

HELP BLUE MEANIES UPON US THEY HAVE CAPTURED OUR TEETER TOTTER PULLED UP OUR FLOWERS AND TORN DOWN OUR KITES LOVE

BESIEGED BERKELEY

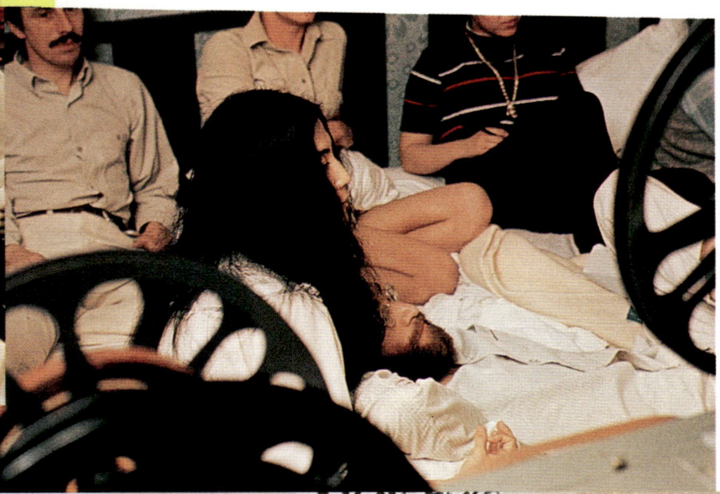

| | |
|---|---|
| May 16 | Ringo and family sailed on QE2 to America ... of "The Magic Christian"; then two weeks holiday in Bahamas. |
| May 22 | Ivor Novello award for "Hey Jude" which achieved highest c... British sales in 1968 although not released until August 1968. |
| May 24 | John and Yoko fly to Bahamas for a Peace "lie in". |
| May 25 | Change of plans for John and Yoko who flew to Montreal for Peace campaign instead. – not near enough to America |
| May 30 | SINGLE: THE BALLAD OF JOHN AND YOKO. |
| June 1 | George on holiday in Sardinia. |
| | Paul on holiday in South of France. |
| June 7 | John and Yoko return from Canada after Peace "lie in". + Movie |

World headlines!

Record + write Give Peace a chance!

55

Show picture with millions of People NOT 2

BATHROOM WINDOW.

(1) She came in through the bathroom window
Protected by a silver spoon
But now she sucks her thumb & wonders
By the banks of her own lagoon

CHORUS
Didn't anybody tell her?
" " see?
Sunday's on the phone to Monday,
Tuesday's on the phone to me.

(2) She said she'd always been a dancer
She worked at 15 clubs a day
And though she thought I knew the answer
I just knew what I could not say.

CHORUS.

(3) And so I quit the police department
And got myself a steady job
And though she tried her best to help me
She could steal but she could not rob.

CHORUS. and out.

Another Lennon + McCartney original.

GEORGE: The album *Get Back* (or *Let It Be*, as it became) was not released until May 1970 and became probably the most bootlegged record of all time. It was laying dormant and so we decided, 'Let's make a *good* album again.' We thought it was a good idea to get George Martin involved. We went back to Abbey Road and made the album.

RINGO: It felt comfortable being back at Abbey Road with George Martin. We felt at home. We knew George and George knew us. We knew the place: 'Here we are again, lads.'

PAUL: While we were in the studio, our engineer Geoff Emerick always used to smoke cigarettes called Everest, so the album was going to be called *Everest*. We never really liked that, but we couldn't think of anything else to call it. Then one day I said, 'I've got it!' – I don't know how I thought of it – '*Abbey Road*! It's the studio we're in, which is fabulous; and it sounds a bit like a monastery.'

RINGO: We went through weeks of all saying, 'Why don't we call it *Billy's Left Boot?*' and things like that. And then Paul just said, 'Why don't we call it *Abbey Road?*'[69]

GEORGE MARTIN: Let It Be *was such an unhappy record (even though there are some great songs on it) that I really believed that was the end of The Beatles, and I assumed that I would never work with them again. I thought, 'What a shame to end like this.' So I was quite surprised when Paul rang me up and said, 'We're going to make another record – would you like to produce it?'*

*My immediate answer was: 'Only if you let me produce it the way we used to.' He said, 'We will, we want to.' – 'John included?' – 'Yes, honestly.' So I said, 'Well, if you really want to, let's do it. Let's get together again.' It was a very happy record. I guess it was happy because everybody thought it was going to be the last.*

JOHN: Music is music. All these characters complain about us and Dylan not being progressive, but we're the ones that turned them on to the other stuff – so let them take our word for it. This is music, baby. When we feel like changing, fine. It's the same with this next album we're into. This will probably please the critics a bit more, because we got a bit tired of just strumming along forever. We got into production again.

We don't really write together any more. We haven't written together for two years – not really, just occasional bits. I do what I like, Paul does what he likes and George does what he likes – and Ringo. We just divide the album time between ourselves. As far as we're concerned, this album is more Beatley than the double album.[69]

NEIL ASPINALL: *I don't think I ever went to a session when they were recording* Abbey Road. *It didn't take them a long time – a couple of months. John was involved in a car-crash then as well, so he was away for a while.*

RINGO: After the *Let It Be* nightmare, *Abbey Road* turned out fine. The second side is brilliant. Out of the ashes of all that madness, that last section is for me one of the finest pieces we put together.

John and Paul had various bits, and so we recorded them and put them together. It actually points out that this is where it's at, that last portion. None of the songs were finished. A lot of work went into it, but they weren't writing together. John and Paul weren't even writing much on their own, really.

PAUL: I think it was my idea to put all the spare bits together, but I'm a bit wary of claiming these things. I'm happy for it to be everyone's idea. Anyway, in the end, we hit upon the idea of medleying them all and giving the second side a sort of operatic structure – which was great because it used ten or twelve unfinished songs in a good way.

JOHN: We always have tons of bits and pieces lying around. I've got stuff that I wrote around *Pepper*, because you lose interest in it a bit after you've had it for years. It was a good way of getting rid of bits of songs.

In fact, George and Ringo wrote bits of it as we did it, literally – in-between bits and breaks too. Paul would say, 'We've got twelve bars here – fill it in.' And we'd fill it in on the spot.[69]

PAUL: John had a bit called 'Polythene Pam' which was based on a girl he'd met a long time ago through the poet Royston Ellis, a friend of ours from Liverpool. We'd re-met him down South when we got out on tour, somewhere like Shrewsbury – he just showed up at the gig. John had gone out to dinner with him and back to his flat afterwards, and there was a girl there who apparently had polythene around her. He came back with all these tales about a girl who dressed in polythene: 'Shit! There was this chick and it was great...' and we thought, 'Oh, wow!' Eventually he wrote the song.

JOHN: 'Polythene Pam' was me remembering a little event with a woman in Jersey, and a man who was England's answer to Allen Ginsberg. She didn't wear jackboots and kilts, I elaborated. Perverted sex in a polythene bag. I was just looking for something to write about.[80]

PAUL: I had a couple of bits and pieces that weren't finished. They were songs that needed maybe a middle, or a second verse or an end.

I was playing the piano in Liverpool in my dad's house, and my step-sister Ruth's piano book was up on the stand. I was flicking through it and I came to 'Golden Slumbers'. I can't read music and I couldn't remember the old tune, so I just started playing my own tune to it. I liked the words so I kept them, and it fitted with another bit of song I had. I also had 'You Never Give Me Your Money'...

GEORGE: 'Funny paper' – that's what we get. We get bits of paper saying how much is earned and what this and that is, but we never actually get it in pounds, shillings and pence. We've all got a big house and a car and an office, but to actually get the money we've earned seems impossible.[69]

PAUL: We used to ask, 'Am I a millionaire yet?' and they used to say cryptic things like, 'On paper you are.' And we'd say, 'Well, what does that mean? Am I or aren't I? Are there more than a million of those green things in my bank yet?' and they'd say, 'Well, it's not actually in a bank. We think you are...' It was actually very difficult to get anything out of these people and the accountants never made you feel successful.

JOHN: My contribution is 'Polythene Pam', 'Sun King' and 'Mean Mr Mustard'. We juggled them about until it made vague sense. In 'Mean Mr Mustard', I said 'his sister Pam' – originally it was 'his sister Shirley' in the lyric. I changed it to 'Pam' to make it sound like it had something to do with it. They are only finished bits of crap that I wrote in India.

[On 'Sun King'] when we came to sing it, to make them different we started joking, saying *'cuando para mucho'*. We just made it up. Paul knew a few Spanish words from school, so we just strung any Spanish words that sounded vaguely like something. And of course we got *'chicka ferdi'* – that's a Liverpool expression; it doesn't mean anything, just like 'ha ha ha'. One we missed: we could have had *'para noia'*, but we forgot all about it. We used to call ourselves Los Para Noias.[69]

GEORGE:
A JOKE NAME FOR US WAS THE FLYING TRELINIS. THE MASKED ALBERTS WAS ONE OF JOHN'S FAVOURITE NAMES; A GOON SORT OF NAME. YOU COULD IMAGINE HUNDREDS OF ALBERTS.

PAUL: In 'The End' there were three guitar solos where John, George and I took a line each, which was something we'd never done before. And we finally persuaded Ringo to play a drum solo, which he'd never wanted to do. And it climaxed with, 'And in the end, the love you take is equal to the love you make...'

JOHN: A VERY COSMIC, PHILOSOPHICAL LINE.[80]

RINGO: I THINK IT SHOWS ON THE RECORD WHEN WE WERE EXCITED: THE TRACK'S EXCITING AND IT ALL COMES TOGETHER. IT DOESN'T MATTER WHAT WE GO THROUGH AS INDIVIDUALS ON THE BULLSHIT LEVEL; WHEN IT GETS TO THE MUSIC YOU CAN SEE THAT IT'S REALLY COOL, AND WE HAD ALL PUT IN ONE THOUSAND PER CENT.

RINGO: Solos have never interested me. That drum solo is still the only one I've done. There's the guitar section where the three of them take in the solos, and then they thought, 'We'll have a drum solo as well.' I was opposed to it: 'I don't want to do no bloody solo!' George Martin convinced me. As I was playing it, he counted it because we needed a time. It was the most ridiculous thing. I was going, 'Dum, dum – one, two, three, four…' and I had to come off at that strange place because it was thirteen bars long. Anyway, I did it, and it's out of the way. I'm pleased now that we've got one down.

(A sideline on *Abbey Road*, just a personal thing of mine: the drum sound on the record was the result of having new calf-heads. There's a lot of tom-tom work on that record. I got the new heads on the drum and I naturally used them a lot – they were so great. The magic of real records is that they *showed* tom-toms were so good. I don't believe that magic is there now, because there's so much more manipulation.)

GEORGE: During the album things got a bit more positive and, although it had some overdubs, we got to play the whole medley. We put them in order, played the backing track and recorded it all in one take, going from one arrangement to the next. We did actually perform more like musicians again.

Likewise with the vocal tracks: we had to rehearse a lot of harmonies and learn all the back-up parts. Some songs are good with just one voice and then harmonies coming in at different places and sometimes three-part work. It's just embellishment, really, and I suppose we made up parts where we thought it fitted because we were all trying to be singers then.

GEORGE MARTIN: *I tried with Paul to get back into the old* Pepper *way of creating something really worthwhile, and we put together the long side. John objected very much to what we did on the second side of* Abbey Road, *which was almost entirely Paul and I working together, with contribution from the others. John always was a Teddy boy. He was a rock'n'roller, and wanted a number of individual tracks. So we compromised. But even on the second side, John helped. He would come and put his little bit in, and have an idea for sewing a bit of music into the tapestry. Everybody worked frightfully well, and that's why I'm very fond of it.*

JOHN: We don't have conceptions. An album to me is a bunch of records that you can't have – I like singles myself. I think Paul has conceptions of albums, or attempts it, like he conceived the medley thing. I'm not interested in conceptions of albums. All I'm interested in is the sound. I like it to be whatever happens. I'm not interested in making the album into a show. For me, I'd just put fourteen rock songs on.[69]

'Come Together' changed at a session. We said, 'Let's slow it down. Let's do this to it, let's do that to it,' and it ends up however it comes out. I just said, 'Look, I've got no arrangement for you, but you know how I want it.' I think that's partly because we've played together a long time. So I said, 'Give me something funky,' and set up a beat, maybe, and they all just join in.[69]

PAUL: Some of my songs are based on personal experience, but my style is to veil it. A lot of them are made up, like 'Maxwell's Silver Hammer' which is the kind of song I like to write. It's just a silly story about all these people I'd never met. It's just like writing a play: you don't have to know the people, you just make them up.

I remember George once saying to me, 'I couldn't write songs like that.' He writes more from personal experience. John's style was to show the naked truth. If I was a painter, I'd probably mask things a little bit more than some people.

The song epitomizes the downfalls of life. Just when everything is going smoothly – Bang! Bang! – down comes Maxwell's silver hammer and ruins everything.

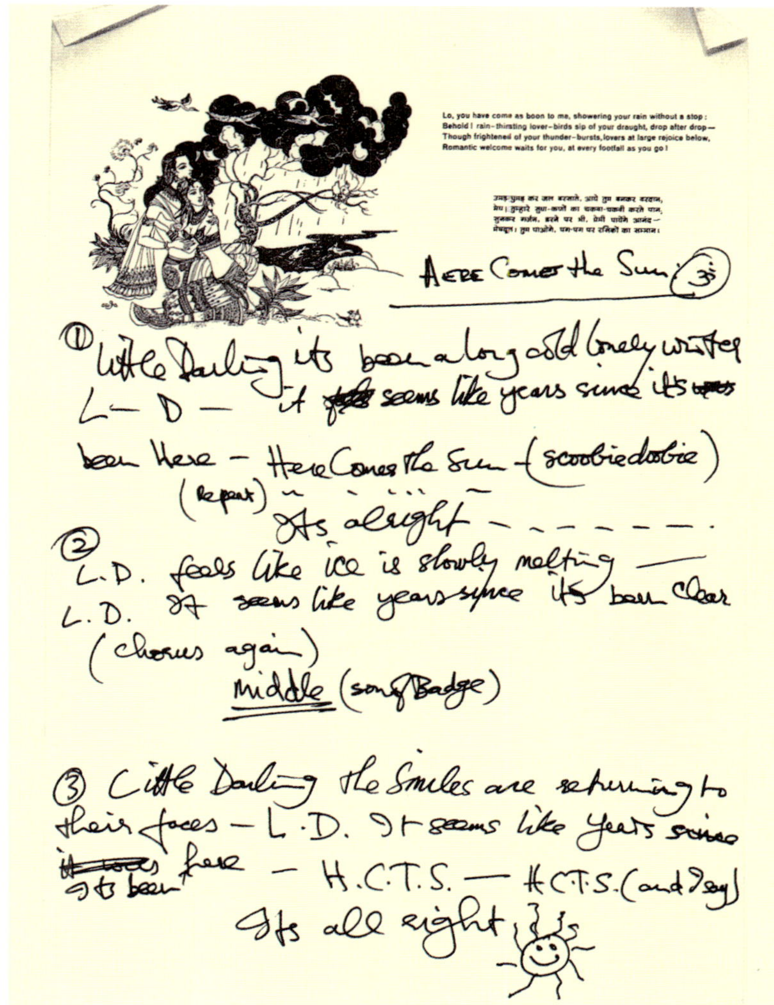


GEORGE: 'HERE COMES THE SUN' WAS WRITTEN AT THE TIME WHEN APPLE WAS GETTING LIKE SCHOOL, WHERE WE HAD TO GO AND BE BUSINESSMEN: 'SIGN THIS' AND 'SIGN THAT'. ANYWAY, IT SEEMS AS IF WINTER IN ENGLAND GOES ON FOREVER; BY THE TIME SPRING COMES YOU REALLY DESERVE IT. SO ONE DAY I DECIDED I WAS GOING TO SAG OFF APPLE AND I WENT OVER TO ERIC CLAPTON'S HOUSE. THE RELIEF OF NOT HAVING TO GO AND SEE ALL THOSE DOPEY ACCOUNTANTS WAS WONDERFUL, AND I WALKED AROUND THE GARDEN WITH ONE OF ERIC'S ACOUSTIC GUITARS AND WROTE 'HERE COMES THE SUN'.

JOHN: 'Come Together' is me, writing obscurely around an old Chuck Berry thing. I left the line in: 'Here comes old flat-top.' It is *nothing* like the Chuck Berry song, but they took me to court because I admitted the influence once years ago. I could have changed it to: 'Here comes old iron-face,' but the song remains independent of Chuck Berry or anybody else on earth.[80]

PAUL: John came in with an up-tempo song that sounded exactly like Chuck Berry's 'You Can't Catch Me', even down to the 'flat-top' lyric. I said, 'Let's slow it down with a swampy bass-and-drums vibe.' I came up with a bass line and it all flowed from there. Great record.

JOHN: The thing was created in the studio. It's gobbledegook. 'Come together' was an expression that Tim Leary had come up with for his attempt at being president or whatever, and he asked me to write him a campaign song. I tried and I tried, but I couldn't come up with one. But I came up with 'Come Together', which would have been no good to him – you couldn't have a campaign song like *that*.

Leary attacked me years later, saying I ripped him off. I didn't. It's just that it turned into 'Come Together'. What am I going to do, give it to *him?* It was a funky record – it's one of my favourite Beatle tracks (or one of my favourite Lennon tracks, let's say that). It's funky, it's bluesy and I'm singing it pretty well. I like the sound of the record.[80]

JOHN: It's a typical McCartney single, or whatever. He did quite a lot of work on it. I wasn't on 'Maxwell'. I was ill after the accident while they did most of that track and I believe he really ground George and Ringo into the ground recording it. We spent more money on that song than any of them on the whole album, I think.[59]

PAUL: They got annoyed because 'Maxwell's Silver Hammer' took three days to record. Big deal.

When we were recording 'Oh! Darling' I came into the studios early every day for a week to sing it by myself because at first my voice was too clear. I wanted it to sound as though I'd been performing it on stage all week.

JOHN: I always thought I could have done it better – it was more my style than his. He wrote it, so what the hell, he's going to sing it.[80] Whoever sings it is whoever's song it is. And if we sing together we usually both wrote it. 'Octopus's Garden' is Ringo's, and we all sing on it. That means we all helped with the arrangement or whatever. It's as simple as that.[69]

GEORGE MARTIN: *'Something' was George's first single, released in October. It was a great song, and frankly I was surprised that George had it in him. Super song.*

JOHN: I think that's about the best track on the album, actually.[69]

GEORGE: I had written 'Something' on the piano during the recording of the 'White' album. There was a period during that album when we were all in different studios doing different things trying to get it finished, and I used to take some time out. So I went into an empty studio and wrote 'Something'.

It has probably got a range of five notes, which fits most singers' needs best. When I wrote it, in my mind I heard Ray Charles singing it, and he did do it some years later. At the time I wasn't particularly thrilled that Frank Sinatra did 'Something'. I'm more thrilled now than I was then. I wasn't really into Frank – he was the generation before me. I was more interested when Smokey Robinson did it and when James Brown did it. But I'm very pleased now, whoever's done it. I realise that the sign of a good song is when it has lots of cover versions.

(I met Michael Jackson somewhere at the BBC. The fellow interviewing us made a comment about 'Something', and Michael said: 'Oh, you wrote that? I thought it was a Lennon/McCartney.')

PAUL: George's 'Something' was out of left field. It was about Pattie, and it appealed to me because it has a very beautiful melody and is a really structured song. I thought it was great. I think George thought my bass-playing was a little bit busy. Again, from my side, I was trying to contribute the best I could, but maybe it was his turn to tell me I was too busy. But that was fun; that went off well.

I thought it was George's greatest track – with 'Here Comes The Sun' and 'While My Guitar Gently Weeps'. They were possibly his best three. Until then he had only done one or two songs per album. I don't think he thought of himself very much as a songwriter, and John and I obviously would dominate – again, not really meaning to, but we were 'Lennon and McCartney'. So when an album comes up, Lennon and McCartney go and write some stuff – and maybe it wasn't easy for him to get into that wedge. But he finally came up with 'Something' and a couple of other songs that were great, and I think everyone was very pleased for him. There was no jealousy. In fact, I think Frank Sinatra used to introduce 'Something' as his favourite Lennon/McCartney song. Thanks Frank.

JOHN: Paul and I really carved up the empire between us, because we were the singers. George didn't even used to sing when we brought him into the group. He was a guitarist. And for the first few years he didn't sing on stage. We maybe let him do one number, like we would with Ringo: 'And here he is...' Paul and I did all the singing, all the writing. George never wrote a song till much later.

We couldn't exclude George. There was an embarrassing period where his songs weren't that good and nobody wanted to say anything, but we all worked on them – like we did on Ringo's. I mean, we put more work into those songs than we did on some of our stuff. So he just wasn't in the same league for a long time – that's not putting him down; he just hadn't had the practice as a writer that we'd had.[74]

RINGO: It was beautiful. George was blossoming as a songwriter. With 'Something' and 'While My Guitar Gently Weeps' – are you kidding me? Two of the finest love songs ever written, and they're really on a par with what John and Paul or anyone else of that time wrote. They're beautiful songs. It's interesting that George was coming to the fore and we were just breaking up.

GEORGE MARTIN: *I think the trouble with George was that he was never treated on the same level as having the same quality of songwriting, by anyone – by John, by Paul or by me. I'm as guilty in that respect. I was the guy who used to say: 'If he's got a song, we'll let him have it on the album' – very condescendingly. I know he must have felt really bad about that. Gradually he kept persevering, and his songs did get better – until eventually they got extremely good. 'Something' is a wonderful song – but we didn't give him credit for it, and we never really thought, 'He's going to be a great songwriter.'*

*The other problem was that he didn't have a collaborator. John always had Paul to bounce ideas off. Even if he didn't actually write the song with Paul, he was a kind of competitive mate. George was a loner and I'm afraid that was made the worse by the three of us. I'm sorry about that now.*

PAUL: We were holding it together. The music was OK and we were friends enough that, even though this undercurrent was going on, we still had a strong respect for each other even at the very worst points. It was getting fairly dodgy – but those weren't the worst times, funnily enough. We put together quite a nice album, and the only arguments were about things like me spending too long on a track: I spent three days on 'Maxwell's Silver Hammer'. I remember George saying, 'You've taken three days, it's only a song.' – 'Yeah, but I want to get it right. I've got some thoughts on this one.' It was early-days Moog work and it did take a bit of time. (Although nowadays three days is just for switching the machine on!)

JOHN: We used the Moog synthesizer on the end [of 'I Want You']. That machine can do all sounds and all ranges of sounds – so if you're a dog, you could hear a lot more. It's like a robot. George can work it a bit, but it would take you all your life to learn the variations on it. George has got one. He used it on the Billy Preston LP, and it also plays the solo in 'Because', and I think in 'Maxwell' it comes in too. It's here and there on the album.[69]

GEORGE: I first heard about the Moog synthesizer in America. I had to have mine made specially, because Mr Moog had only just invented it. It was enormous, with hundreds of jackplugs and two keyboards.

But it was one thing having one, and another trying to make it work. There wasn't an instruction manual, and even if there had been it would probably have been a couple of thousand pages long. I don't think even Mr Moog knew how to get music out of it; it was more of a technical thing. When you listen to the sounds on songs like 'Here Comes The Sun', it does do some good things, but they're all very kind of infant sounds.

PAUL: Again the feeling that I mustn't be dominating was plaguing me. I was trying to get a record made of my song the way I wanted it, but I didn't want to offend anyone, and it was getting very difficult. I remember backing off like mad and saying, 'OK.'

At some point I said, 'Look, would you guys tell me what to do?' Then they all went very quiet; we had a day of that, and I remember Ringo coming up and saying, 'No, go on. *You* tell *us*. Come on – produce us!' I was being asked to dominate – and yet I was starting to feel this was something I really mustn't do. It made working conditions pretty difficult and in the end it was getting to be less fun than it was worth.

GEORGE MARTIN: *John got disenchanted with record production. He didn't really approve of what I'd done or was doing. He didn't like 'messing about', as he called it, and he didn't like the pretentiousness, if you like. I could see his point. He wanted good, old-fashioned, plain solid rock: 'The hell with it – let's blast the living daylights out!' Or, if it was a soft ballad: 'Let's do it just the way it comes.' He wanted authenticity.*

JOHN: I personally can't be bothered with strings and things. I'd like to do it with the group, or with electronics. I can't be bothered going through that hassle with musicians – but Paul digs that; that's his scene. It was up to him where he went with the violins and what he did with them, and I think he wanted a straight kind of backing [on 'Golden Slumbers'] – nothing freaky.[69] That's what he was getting into on the back of *Abbey Road*. I never went in for that pop-opera stuff. I like three-minute records, like adverts.[71]

PAUL: WE NEVER GOT PAST EIGHT-TRACK. ALL OF THE BEATLES' WORK WAS ON TWO-TRACK, FOUR-TRACK OR EIGHT-TRACK. *SGT PEPPER* WAS FOUR-TRACK. BY *ABBEY ROAD* WE HAD GOT TO EIGHT-TRACK, AND WE THOUGHT IT WAS TOO MANY! WE THOUGHT IT WAS TOO BIG A LUXURY.

PAUL: The crossing was right outside, and we said, 'Let's just go out, get a photographer and walk out on the crossing. It'll be done in half an hour.' It was getting quite late and you always have to get the cover in ahead of the sound. So we got hold of the photographer Iain Macmillan, gave him half an hour and walked across the crossing.

It was a very hot day in August, and I had arrived wearing a suit and sandals. It was so hot that I kicked the sandals off and walked across barefoot for a few takes, and it happened that in the shot he used I had no shoes on, Sandie Shaw style. There's many a person who has gone barefoot, so it didn't seem any big deal for me at all.

But then I was rung one day by one of the blokes at the office, who said, 'Hey, there's a rumour started by a DJ in America that you're dead.' I said, 'You're kidding – just tell them I'm not.' He said, 'No, that won't do. You've got no shoes on on the cover: this is apparently a Mafia sign of death. And there's a car registration plate behind you which says "28 IF". Well, that means you'd be twenty-eight – *if* you'd have lived!' And I replied, 'Wait a minute – he's stretching it a bit here, isn't he?' He said, 'There's more. Ringo's wearing black: that means he's the undertaker…' and it went on like this. There were *all* these clues.

ATTN: DEREK TAYLOR

PAUL DEATH RUMORS STILL ABOUND IN NEW YORK. ALLEN KLEIN, PETER ASHER, AND LOVELY CHRIS ON CHANNEL 9 POST MCMORTEM LAST NIGHT VERUS LA AND CAMPUS HEAVIES. RESULT INDECISIVE DUE TO STIMULATING AND TIME CONSUMING DISCUSSION ON MERITS OF GROWING BLACK ROSES ESPECIALLY FOR PAUL.
JOHN'S MBE FURORE MADE ALL NEWSPAPERS/ TV NEWS BUT NO HEADLINED
THIS IS YOUR FRIENDLY NEW YORK INFORMATION CLEARING HOUSE

LOVE
JOHN K

JOHN: Paul walked barefoot across the road because Paul's idea of being different is to look almost straight, but just have his ear painted blue – something a little subtle. So Paul decided to be barefoot that day walking across the road. When you first glance at the album it looks like the four Beatles walking across fully dressed. That's his little gimmick. I didn't even notice until I got the album. I didn't notice on the day that he was barefoot. We were just wishing the photographer would hurry up. Too many people were hanging around. 'It's going to spoil the shot. Let's get out of here. We're meant to be recording, not posing for Beatle pictures' – that's what we were thinking. And I was muttering, 'Come on, hurry up now, keep in step.'

RINGO: A DJ put all those signs together: Paul with no shoes (that's the easy one) and the Volkswagen Beetle. Then there was *Magical Mystery Tour*, where we three had red roses and he had a black one. It was just madness, but if you looked at it all you could come to that conclusion. There was no way we could *prove* he was alive. We said, 'Well, how can we prove this rumour isn't true? Let's take a photo!' But, of course, they would say, 'That's just his stand-in in the photo.'

It was silly, really, and it didn't worry us. It was part of rock'n'roll. It kept the madness going: we had an album out, and it was in every newspaper and on the TV. It was big doings.

PAUL: IT WAS A BIT WEIRD MEETING PEOPLE SHORTLY AFTER THAT, BECAUSE THEY'D BE LOOKING AT THE BACK OF MY EARS, LOOKING A BIT THROUGH ME. AND IT WAS WEIRD DOING THE 'I REALLY *AM* HIM' STUFF.

APPLE LONDON

8881290 ELEC D
13.11.69

DEREK TAYLOR
GERMAN JOURNALISTS HAVE PICKED UP RUMOUR FROM STATES THAT PAUL MC CARTNEY IS DEAD . INQUIRIES COME IN DAILY AND IN ORDER TO END THESE WOULD APPRECIATE CONFIRMATION THAT SUCH RUMOURS ARE FALSE .
REGARDS = PRESS DEPT. ELECTROLA ++

APPLE LONDON

8881290 ELEC D

Maarweg 149
B-5 Cologne – BRAUNFELD
German.

JOHN: Paul McCartney couldn't die without the world knowing it. The same as he couldn't get married without the world knowing it. It's impossible – he can't go on holiday without the world knowing it. It's just insanity – but it's a great plug for *Abbey Road*.[69]

DEREK TAYLOR: *I dealt with that just as a matter of routine – it was the typical old nonsense that we had to deal with. There were thousands of calls along those lines. (The rumour is still roaming around. There are books on it, and there's a man making a living lecturing on it.) In the end I conceded that it may be true. That's usually the way I deal with those rumours: 'Maybe he is dead – I don't know, do I?'*

*(That's what happened at the Monterey Pop Festival. The rumour got round that all The Beatles were there. I just said, 'OK. I think three of them are, but they're in disguise – and we don't know which three.' The logic was: if there are three of them here, and you only think so, and they're in disguise – how do you know? 'Ah, that's another story. Now, if you'd asked that earlier...' Red smoke fills the air and the mind clouds over. So it's now: 'Are they here?' – 'No, they're not really.' It was a joke. Once you throw in the towel, it's OK.)*

*So you say he's dead. Now the doubter says, 'Well, that's very like him – the same mouth, the same eyes!' Then he's alive all of a sudden. People are perverse. So we can move on to the next subject.*

PAUL: In the end I said, 'Well, we'd better play it for all it's worth. It's publicity, isn't it? This guy is going mad about our new album and doesn't care what he's saying, so tell them, as Mark Twain said: "Rumours of my death are greatly exaggerated." There's nothing more I can do.'

But that was *Abbey Road*. We had the cover, we had the title, we had all the music, and it came out before *Let It Be* (which was being screwed for disc by our friend). *Let It Be* was actually the last release, but *Abbey Road* was the last recording.

I think it worked out OK as an album. I think John thought in the end it was a bit slick – but I don't think it was bad for that. That's just structure. I don't think it really looks slick now.

JOHN: I'll tell you honestly: I don't remember it, because *Abbey Road*, for me – as always with all the albums – I like some of the tracks and I don't like other tracks. That's always been the same: I've never been a knocked-out Beatle fan by any of our albums. I like some of the work we do, and some of it I don't. *Abbey Road* was a competent album. I don't think it was anything more than that or anything less.[70]

GEORGE MARTIN: *Nobody knew for sure that it was going to be the last album – but everybody felt it was. The Beatles had gone through so much and for such a long time. They'd been incarcerated with each other for nearly a decade, and I was surprised that they had lasted as long as they did. I wasn't at all surprised that they'd split up because they all wanted to lead their own lives – and I did, too. It was a release for me as well.*

GEORGE: I didn't know at the time that it was the last Beatle record that we would make, but it felt as if we were reaching the end of the line.

I can't honestly say what I felt after that record was finished. I remember liking the record and enjoying it, but I don't recall thinking that was it because there was so much going on all the time. When you pick out all the 'Beatle days' and 'Beatle moments' or records, there were long gaps in between. If we had a day off from The Beatles, we'd be doing something else – or if we had a year off, or (as it's been now) twenty-five years off. There were plenty of other activities to fill the gaps. I was certainly not missing being in the band.

DEREK TAYLOR: *On 22nd August, The Beatles all turned up at Tittenhurst Park, John's new house in Ascot (which Ringo later bought from him), for what turned out to be their last set of photos taken together.*

RINGO: IT WAS JUST A PHOTO SESSION. I WASN'T THERE THINKING, 'OK, THIS IS THE LAST PHOTO SESSION.'

PAUL: LINDA SHOT SOME 16mm FOOTAGE ON MY CAMERA. THAT TURNED OUT TO BE THE LAST FILM TAKEN.

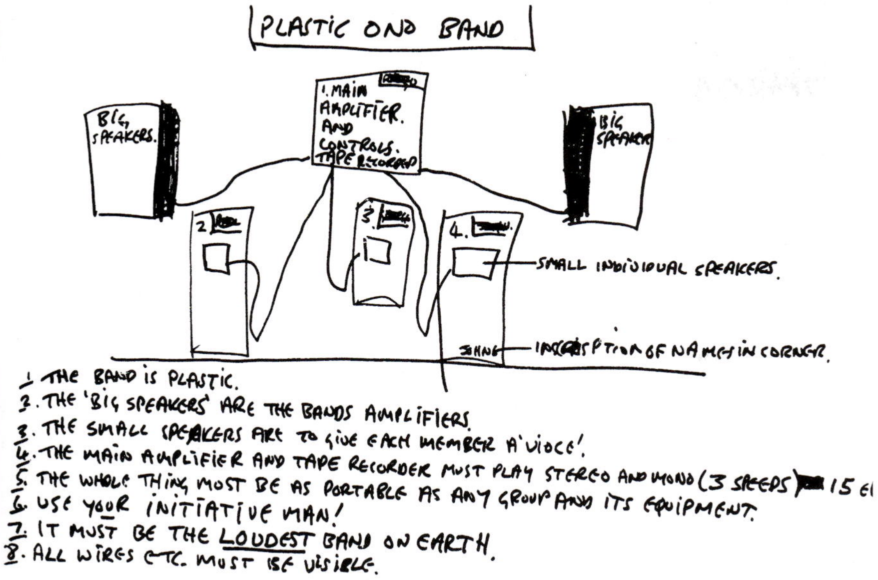


JOHN: The Plastic Ono Band's going to be pretty flexible – because it's plastic. The Beatles playing live is a different matter – we've got that great thing to live up to, it's a harder gig – but just for me and Yoko to go out we can get away with anything.

We got this phone call on a Friday night that there was a rock'n'roll revival show in Toronto with a 100,000 audience, or whatever it was, and that Chuck was going to be there and Jerry Lee and all the great rockers that were still living, and Bo Diddley, and supposedly The Doors were top of the bill. They were inviting us as king and queen to preside over it, not play – but I didn't hear that bit. I said, 'Just give me time to get a band together,' and we went the next morning.

It was very, very quick. We didn't have a band then – we didn't even have a group that had played with us for more than half a minute. I called Eric and I got Klaus, and we got Alan White and they said, 'OK.' There was no big palaver – it wasn't like this set-format show that I'd been doing with The Beatles where you go on and do the same numbers – 'I Want To Hold Your Head' – and the show lasts twenty minutes and nobody's listening, they're just screaming and the amps are as big as a peanut and it's more a spectacular rather than rock'n'roll.[69]

JOHN:
THE ONLY TIME WE TOOK DRUGS WAS WHEN WE WERE WITHOUT HOPE, AND THE ONLY WAY WE GOT OUT OF IT WAS WITH HOPE, AND IF WE CAN SUSTAIN THE HOPE THEN WE DON'T NEED LIQUOR, DRUGS OR ANYTHING. BUT IF WE LOSE HOPE WHAT CAN YOU DO?

GEORGE: When the Plastic Ono Band went to Toronto in September John actually asked me to be in the band, but I didn't do it. I didn't really want to be in an avant-garde band, and I knew that was what it was going to be.

He said he'd get Klaus Voormann, and Alan White as the drummer. During the last few years of The Beatles we were all producing other records anyway, so we had a nucleus of friends in the studios: drummers and bass players and other musicians. So it was relatively simple to knock together a band. He asked me if I'd play guitar, and then he got Eric Clapton to go – they just rehearsed on the plane over there.

DEREK TAYLOR: *John played* Live Peace in Toronto *and I didn't believe that it would mean the end of anything. In fact, it didn't, did it? I was very committed to John and Yoko things, and I thought the Peace Campaign was very well done.*

JOHN: The buzz was incredible. I never felt so good in my life. Everybody was with us and leaping up and down doing the peace sign, because they knew most of the numbers anyway, and we did a number called 'Cold Turkey' we'd never done before and they dug it like mad.

I offered 'Cold Turkey' to The Beatles, but they weren't ready to record a single, so I did it as Plastic Ono. (I don't care what it goes out as, as long as it goes out.)[69] It was self-explanatory: the result of experiencing cold turkey – withdrawal from heroin. It was an *anti*-drug song, if anything. But, of course, it was banned again all over American radio, so it never got off the ground. They were thinking I was promoting it [heroin].[80]

RINGO: After the Plastic Ono Band's debut in Toronto, we had a meeting in Savile Row where John finally brought it to its head. He said: 'Well, that's it, lads. Let's end it.' And we all said 'yes'. And though I said 'yes' because it *was* ending (and you can't keep it together anyway, if this is what the attitude is) I don't know if *I* would have said, 'End it.' I probably would have lingered another couple of years.

But when we all met in the office, we knew it was good. It wasn't sulky and we weren't really fighting. It was like a thought came into the room, and everyone said what they said. John didn't think we should *leave*, just that we should break it up. It was not: 'I'm leaving, you're leaving.' It was: 'Well, that's it! I've had enough. I want to do this…'

If that had happened in 1965, or 1967 even, it would have been a mighty shock. Now it was just 'let's get the divorce over with', really. And John was always the most forward when it came to nailing anything.

JOHN: I knew before we went to Toronto. I told Allen I was leaving, I told Eric Clapton and Klaus that I was leaving and that I'd like to probably use them as a group. I hadn't decided how to do it – to have a permanent new group or what? (Later on I thought, 'Fuck, I'm not going to get stuck with another set of people, *whoever* they are.') So I announced it to myself and to the people around me on the way to Toronto. Allen came with me, and I told Allen it was over. When I got back there were a few meetings and Allen had said, 'Well, cool it, cool it,' because there was a lot to do business-wise, and it would not have been suitable at the time.

Then we were discussing something in the office with Paul, and Paul said something or other, to do something, and I kept saying 'no, no, no' to everything he said. So it came to a point I had to say something, of course. Paul said, 'What do you mean?' I said, 'I mean the group is over. I'm leaving!'[70]

PAUL: I'd said: 'I think we should go back to little gigs – I really think we're a great little band. We should find our basic roots, and then who knows what will happen? We may want to fold after that, or we may really think we've still got it.' John looked at me in the eye and said: 'Well, I think you're daft. I wasn't going to tell you till we signed the Capitol deal' – Klein was trying to get us to sign a new deal with the record company – 'but I'm leaving the group!' We paled visibly and our jaws slackened a bit.

I must admit we'd known it was coming at some point because of his intense involvement with Yoko. John needed to give space to his and Yoko's thing. Someone like John would want to end The Beatles period and start the Yoko period; and he wouldn't like either to interfere with the other. But what wasn't too clever was this idea of: 'I wasn't going to tell you till after we signed the new contract.' Good old John – he had to blurt it out. And that was it. There's not a lot you can say to, 'I'm leaving the group,' from a key member.

I didn't really know what to say. We had to react to him doing it; he had control of the situation. I remember him saying, 'It's weird this, telling you I'm leaving the group, but in a way it's very exciting.' It was like when he told Cynthia he was getting a divorce. He was quite buoyed up by it, so we couldn't really do anything: 'You mean *leaving*? So that's the group, then…' It was later, as the fact set in, that it got really upsetting.

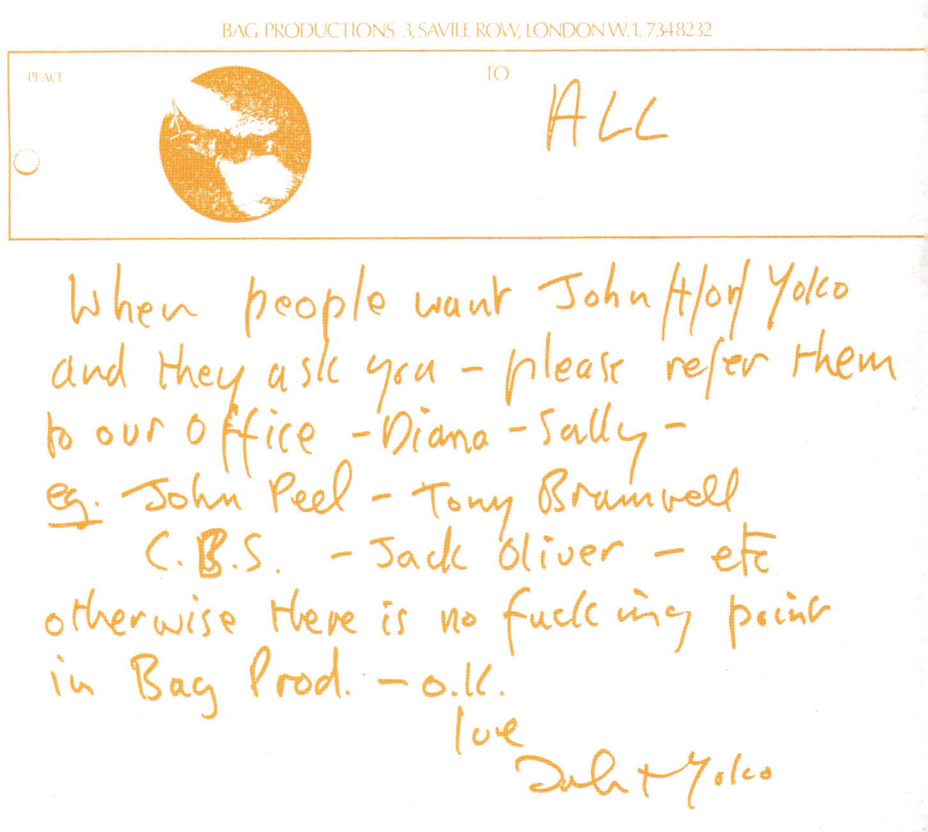
BAG PRODUCTIONS 3, SAVILE ROW, LONDON W.1. 734 8232
PEACE TO ALL
When people want John &/or Yoko and they ask you – please refer them to our Office – Diana – Sally –
eg. John Peel – Tony Bramwell
C.B.S. – Jack Oliver – etc
otherwise there is no fucking point in Bag Prod. – o.k.
love
John + Yoko

GEORGE: I don't remember about John saying he wanted to break up The Beatles. I don't remember where I heard it. *Everybody* had tried to leave, so it was nothing new. Everybody was leaving for years.

The Beatles had started out being something that gave us a vehicle to be able to do so much when we were younger, but it had now got to a point where it was stifling us. There was too much restriction. It had to self-destruct, and I wasn't feeling bad about anybody wanting to leave, because I wanted out myself. I could see a much better time ahead being by myself, away from the band. It had ceased to be fun and it was time to get out of it. It was like a straitjacket.

NEIL ASPINALL: *It was a sad thing that there was now talk of breaking up. We'd all been together for a number of years going through the most incredible series of situations and successes and everything else, and for that to be over meant there was a certain amount of sadness and apprehension. It was a bit scary for everybody.*

*The split was a slow process. For a start, Paul's not signing with Allen Klein didn't mean The Beatles had split up because they then made* Abbey Road. *And John was working more and more with Yoko rather than with The Beatles, but he still made* Abbey Road *with the others. So there wasn't one moment in time; it was gradual, and then they just weren't together any more after* Abbey Road – *I couldn't see them actually going into a studio and working together again.*

RINGO: There was the story I told about leaving during the 'White' album because I'd thought they were really close and they'd thought the other three were. It was just craziness. With George leaving, we didn't know what was going to happen. But I don't think it actually ended till it did, till the meeting in the office in Savile Row when we said, 'That's it.'

We'd kept it together for the sake of *Abbey Road*. But, you know, it had gone already then. And then it was really a case of although it had ended, your brain couldn't assimilate it. Your body was still living this life, and then you went on doing your own thing.

JOHN: I started the band. I disbanded it. It's as simple as that.

My life with The Beatles had become a trap. A tape loop. I had made previous short excursions on my own, writing books, helping convert them into a play. I'd even made a movie without the others, but I had made the movie more in reaction to the fact that The Beatles had decided to stop touring than with real independence in mind – although even then my eye was on freedom.

When I finally had the guts to tell the other three that I, quote, wanted a divorce, unquote, they knew it was for real – unlike Ringo and George's previous threats to leave. I must say I felt guilty for springing it on them at such short notice. After all, I had Yoko, they only had each other. I was guilty enough to give McCartney credit as a co-writer on my first independent single ['Give Peace A Chance'] instead of giving it to Yoko, who had actually co-authored it.[78]

RINGO: We didn't go public about the break-up immediately. Allen Klein had this thing: 'Split up, boys, if you want to – but don't tell anybody.'

People didn't want us to break up, but I don't think that was too much of a pressure. We felt: 'We've done this so long, so we keep doing it.' That was why we kept on and on a lot of days, even with all the craziness – it really *worked*. But instead of working every day, it worked, say, two days a month. There were still good days because we were still really close friends, and then it would split off again into some madness.

JOHN: Paul and Allen said they were glad that I wasn't going to announce it; like I was going to make an event out of it.

RINGO: It was a relief once we finally said we would split up. (I think that was as much a relief as 'Strawberry Fields'/'Penny Lane' not making Number One; *that* was a huge relief.) I just wandered off home, I believe, and I don't know what happened after that. I sat in the garden for a while wondering what the hell to do with my life. After you've said it's over and go home, you think: 'Oh, God – that's it, then. Now what do you do?' It was quite a dramatic period for me – or *traumatic*, actually.

GEORGE: My feeling when we went our separate ways was to enjoy the space that it gave me, the space to be able to think at my own speed and to have some musicians in the studio who would accompany me on *my* songs. It sounds strange, because most people would like to be in The Beatles, or at that time it looked like such a great thing to be in. And it *was*. But it was also a great thing to get out of – just as when you grow up and leave home and spread your wings.

There was a feeling that it was a big step to decide to leave the group, but at the same time there was so much pressure that the downside was much bigger than the upside. The upside was that The Beatles were so famous and it was a cosy rut to be in. But it was so negative at that point that I would have given anything to get out.

We always thought the idea would be to have a bit of space to do some solo recordings and then just see what happened. But, also, my life had taken on a whole other dimension. Being in a little pop band, which was The Beatles, was very limiting. I wanted to go to the Himalayas and do that, and hang out and play with other people. I had lots of outside friends – as did the other Beatles.

PAUL: I felt, 'Well, this will be the start of a new phase now. The Beatles won't be recording together again, so do I leave the music business and not work again? I'm too passionate about it.' Even now I couldn't do that easily. It's just a bug I've got. I knew I had to carry on in some form or other.

I spent a lot of time up in Scotland where I have a farm. I normally go for holidays, but I began what was to be a whole year up there, just trying to figure out what I was going to do, and that was probably when it was most upsetting. I really got the feeling of being redundant. People say, 'But you still had your money, it wasn't exactly redundancy. It's not like being a miner who's laid off.' But to me it was. Because it wasn't about money, it was about self-worth. I just suddenly felt I wasn't worth anything if I wasn't in The Beatles.

It was a pretty good job to have lost – The Beatles. My whole life since I'd been seventeen had been wrapped up in it; so it was quite a shock. I took to my bed, didn't bother shaving much, did a lot of drinking: 'What's it matter?' you know. You hear about guys who've been made redundant doing that. Just staying in a lot, not wanting to go out, not wanting to socialise. So I lost the plot there for a little while – for about a year, actually – but luckily Linda's very sensible and she said, 'Look, you're OK. It's just the shock of The Beatles and all of that.' I was thinking: 'Well, can I ever write and sing again? What does anyone want with an out of work bass-player?' It hit me pretty hard.

After a while I thought: 'Jesus! I had better really try to get it together here,' and that took the form of making a record, the simplest way. I had a recording machine, without a desk or anything, and made a real home-grown record; working on my own, thinking of getting a new band – although, obviously, The Beatles was a tough act to follow.

RINGO: In November I started recording tracks for my *Sentimental Journey* solo album. That was me wondering what to do when it was all over. I got an idea to record an album of songs that I had been brought up with.

There was a pub on the album cover. My family used to go to that pub and all my mum's friends and the family would come back to our place, and at the parties everybody sang those songs. They were my first musical influences, so for want of a better idea I thought I'd do that. None of the others worked on it, but I still had George Martin so I didn't feel completely alone.

NEIL ASPINALL: *Ringo and George Martin put* Sentimental Journey *together. We got a list of songs that Ringo wanted to sing, in a key that he could sing them in, and a list of arrangers that he really liked. I rang the arrangers and asked: 'Which of these songs would you like to produce? Just go into a studio with whatever musicians you want – and please send us the tapes.' On to which Ringo overdubbed his voice.*

*It could have got a bit difficult when there was only one tune left and you were ringing a producer. He could ask: 'Why don't I have a choice when everybody else did?' But we had fifteen or sixteen songs and we only used twelve, so they always had a choice somewhere along the line.*

*That's how that album came together. It was quite an enjoyable thing to be involved with. It was a bit laid back; but it was the way to do it.*

GEORGE: In December I was working with the Delaney and Bonnie band with Billy Preston. I'd heard about Delaney and Bonnie, and I'd seen them playing in the Valley in Los Angeles. They were a great band, and I tried to sign them to Apple Records; but when Peter Asher went over to sign them he fell asleep at the audition, so they decided to go with Atlantic Records.

I went to see them at the Albert Hall and thought they were such a fun band it would be nice to play with them. Most times I go to concerts and think, 'I'm glad I'm not in the band,' but in this case I thought it was fantastic.

After the Albert Hall they played at the Speakeasy, and I suppose we had a few drinks and before I knew what was happening their bus arrived at my house the next morning and I was with them. I got a guitar, got on the bus and we did a tour of Europe.

It was really good because I don't think many people knew I was there. The people were coming to see Delaney and Bonnie, or they knew Eric Clapton was in the band. I was just along for the ride, really; I was at the back and didn't have to be anything, and it was really nice. Even being at the back of The Beatles, it was still like being right at the front; we could never hide behind a couple of horn players.

PAUL: For about three or four months, George, Ringo and I rang each other to ask: 'Well, is this it then?' It wasn't that the record company had dumped us. It was still a case of: we might get back together again. Nobody quite knew if it was just one of John's little flings, and that maybe he was going to feel the pinch in a week's time and say, 'I was only kidding.' I think John did kind of leave the door open. He'd said: 'I'm *pretty much* leaving the group, but...'

So we held on to that thread for a few months, and then eventually we realised, 'Oh well, we're not in the band any more. That's it. It's definitely over.'

I started thinking, 'Well, if that's the case, I had better get myself together. I can't just let John control the situation and dump us as if we're the jilted girlfriends.' I was recording the album *McCartney*, and round about then I said, 'Isn't it about time we told people?' Everybody said, 'No, no – don't tell anyone we're breaking up,' but I felt we should. I don't know why they didn't want to say anything. I think Klein had a lot to do with it.

GEORGE: The Beatles had become an institution that nobody on the outside really wanted to split. Except the press, because the press want *anything* that will be a headline. They don't care whether it's good or bad, as long as it's worthy of a headline, so the press tend to try to nudge things along – particularly in negative directions if they think they're on to something. The public all over the world may have wanted more Beatle records, but the British press could sense it was all over.

I think Paul was already making a solo album in his house. John was going off to do his Plastic Ono thing, and it was very obvious it was finished, but nobody said, 'Well, that's it – we'll never get together again.' If the newspapers asked us, we were still saying, 'Who knows? Sure, we're still together.'

PAUL: Things had got bad by that point and I was still trying to phone, trying still to communicate and keep the doors open. But the difficulties lasted, really, for the twenty years that it took to sort The Beatles out.

I'd fallen out with the other three at once over the Klein thing. I didn't want him representing me in any way. They had persuaded me that we had to give Klein 20%. The only way they could was that they said, 'OK, he'll have 20% on any increases he gets us. If Capitol are giving us *that* much on royalties and he gets *this* much, then he'll have 20% of the difference.'

So it was three against one. Never mind three against one – it was me against the world! It was me against three hundred million as far as I was concerned. The way I saw it, I had to save The Beatles' fortune. All we'd ever earned was in that company – and I wasn't about to see it go.

JOHN: I always remember the film with those British people who wrote those silly operas, Gilbert and Sullivan. I remember watching the film with Robert Morley in and thinking, 'We'll never get to that.' And we did, which really upset me. I really never thought we'd be so stupid, like splitting and arguing. But we were naive enough to let people come between us and that's what happened. But it was happening anyway. I don't mean Yoko, I mean businessmen. It's like when people decide to get a divorce: quite often you decide amicably, but then when you get your lawyers and they say, 'Don't talk to the other party unless there's a lawyer present,' that's when the drift really starts happening.

It's really lawyers that make divorces nasty. If there was a nice ceremony like getting married for divorce it would be much better. Even divorce of business partners. But it always gets nasty because you're never allowed to speak your own mind. You have to talk in double Dutch, you have to spend all your time with a lawyer, you get frustrated and you end up saying and doing things you wouldn't do under normal circumstances.[71]

RINGO: In the end we did get rid of Allen Klein. It cost us a small fortune – but it's one of those things that we found all through life: two people sign a contract and *I* know exactly what it means and *you* know exactly what it means, but when we come to split up magically it means something else entirely to one of you.

GEORGE: John phoned me one morning in January and said, 'I've written this tune and I'm going to record it tonight and have it pressed up and out tomorrow – that's the whole point: "Instant Karma!", you know.' So I was in. I said, 'OK, I'll see you in town.' I was in town with Phil Spector and I said to Phil, 'Why don't you come to the session?'

There were just four people: John played piano, I played acoustic guitar, there was Klaus Voormann on bass and Alan White on drums. We recorded the song and brought it out that week, mixed – instantly – by Phil Spector.

JOHN: We have so many songs, and we've got to get them out some way or other. It's nicer to do them yourself, actually. I prefer doing my own songs than giving them to somebody else – half of them, it's the only way we make it happen.[69]

NEIL ASPINALL: *Phil Spector was involved with Allen Klein on some business level or another, and was brought in to remix* Let It Be. *I have no idea whose idea it was for him to get involved. It might have been Klein's, with John and George going along with it.*

GEORGE MARTIN: *That made me very angry – and it made Paul even angrier, because neither he nor I knew about it till it had been done. It happened behind our backs because it was done when Allen Klein was running John. He'd organised Phil Spector and I think George and Ringo had gone along with it. They'd actually made an arrangement with EMI and said, 'This is going to be our record.'*

*EMI came to me and said, 'You made this record originally but we can't have your name on it.' I asked them why not and they said: 'Well, you didn't produce the final thing.' I said, 'I produced the original and what you should do is have a credit saying: "Produced by George Martin, over-produced by Phil Spector".' They didn't think that was a good idea.*

JOHN: If anybody listens to the bootleg version, which was the version which was pre-Spector, and listens to the version Spector did, they would shut up – if you really want to know the difference. The tapes were so lousy and so bad none of us would go near them to touch them. They'd been lying around for six months. None of us could face remixing them; it was terrifying. But Spector did a fantastic job.[71]

PAUL: Allen Klein decided – possibly having consulted the others, but certainly not me – that *Let It Be* would be re-produced for disc by Phil Spector.

So now we were getting a 're-producer' instead of just a producer, and he added on all sorts of stuff – singing ladies on 'The Long And Winding Road' – backing that I perhaps wouldn't have put on. I mean, I don't think it made it the worst record ever, but the fact that now people were putting stuff on our records that certainly one of us didn't know about was wrong. I'm not sure whether the others knew about it. It was just, 'Oh, get it finished up. Go on – do whatever you want.' We were all getting fed up.

DEREK TAYLOR: *I know that Paul was very cross about 'The Long And Winding Road' being interfered with. I took the view that nobody should have ever interfered with their music. That was to me – I don't want to say shocking – but wrong, certainly. And if you were a McCartney seeing your work being altered… I can imagine the outrage!*

PAUL: I had now made the *McCartney* record, my first album after The Beatles, and we had a release schedule on it; but then the others started buggering that around, saying, 'You can't release the *McCartney* album when you want to. We're releasing *Let It Be* – and Ringo's solo record.'

I rang Neil who was running Apple and I said, 'Wait a minute – we've decided my release date!' I had an understanding: I'd marked my release date on the calendar. I'd stuck to it religiously, but they'd moved it anyway.

14th April, 1970.

A. Klein, Esq.,
Apple Corps Limited,
3 Savile Row,
LONDON, W.1.

Dear Sir,

In future no one will be allowed to add to or subtract from a recording of one of my songs without my permission.

I had considered orchestrating "The Long and Winding Road" but I decided against it. I therefore want it altered to these specifications:-

1. Strings, horns, voices and all added noises to be reduced in volume.
2. Vocal and Beatle instrumentation to be brought up in volume.
3. Harp to be removed completely at the end of the song and original piano notes to be substituted.
4. Don't ever do it again.

Signed

PAUL MCCARTNEY

c.c. Phil Spector
John Eastman

From my point of view I was getting done in. All the decisions were now three against one. And that's not the easiest position if you're the one: anything I wanted to do they could just say, 'No.' And it was just to be awkward, I thought.

Ringo came to see me. He was sent, I believe – being mild mannered, the nice guy – by the others, because of the dispute. So Ringo arrived at the house, and I must say I gave him a bit of verbal. I said: 'You guys are just messing me around.' He said: 'No, well, on behalf of the board and on behalf of The Beatles and so and so, we think you should do this,' etc. And I was just fed up with that. It was the only time I ever told anyone to GET OUT! It was fairly hostile. But things had got like that by this time. It hadn't actually come to blows, but it was near enough.

Unfortunately it was Ringo. I mean, he was probably the least to blame of any of them, but he was the fall guy who got sent round to ask me to change the date – and he probably thought: 'Well, Paul will do it,' but he met a different character, because now I was definitely boycotting Apple.

RINGO: It was just two guys pouting and being silly.

We had our solo albums to bring out, and I said, 'Mine's ready and I want to bring it out.' Paul's wasn't quite ready – but he had a calendar with the date (I've forgotten the day now) marked in yellow saying, 'That's my day – I'm bringing my record out then.' I don't know what happened – he probably did.

PAUL: I got so fed up with all this I said, 'OK, I want to get off the label.' Apple Records was a lovely dream, but I thought, 'Now this is really trashy and I want to get off.' I remember George on the phone saying to me, 'You'll stay on this fucking label! Hare Krishna!' and he hung up – and I went, 'Oh, dear me. This is really getting hairy.'

I didn't show Apple anything of *McCartney* or the cover or anything until I'd finished it all. I did it all myself, and just gave it to them for release. It was a very difficult position for me.

NEIL ASPINALL: *Paul's album came out before* Let It Be, *and the statement, of course, came with it. I can't really speak for how it was received by the people in Apple – I can't remember who was still in Apple at the time. As to why the dream of Apple hadn't worked – maybe it hadn't worked because it was a dream.*

PAUL: I didn't leave the Beatles. The Beatles have left The Beatles, but no one wants to be the one to say the party's over.[70]

DEREK TAYLOR: *For the release of Paul's solo album we did a questionnaire in the press office, a general issue thing: 'Will you ever appear with The Beatles? Do you believe in this? What are your plans?' etc. I thought he very generously answered – in an uptight way, but nevertheless answered – the questions, more or less ruling out reunion or working with The Beatles: 'And I'm now working with Linda and this is the way I want it to be…' That was a very unhappy time. That was the pits.*

PAUL: I didn't want to do any interviews at the time because I knew the first thing they'd ask about was The Beatles and all that stuff and I didn't really want that. I didn't want to face the press, and I said so.

Derek at the office said, 'We *should* do something.' I said, 'I'll tell you what – you do a questionnaire of anything you think the press would want to know and I'll try and answer honestly, and we'll stick that in with the press copies of the record.' He did and one of the questions was: 'Have The Beatles virtually broken up?' I answered, 'Yeah – we won't play together again.' (This was four or five months after we'd actually decided that, so I felt it wasn't exactly a scoop.)

I felt the group finished the minute John said, 'I'm leaving.' We'd all (except John) had goes at trying to keep the group together and failed. So it wasn't any longer a case of trying to keep it together; it was now whether we tell the world or not, and I thought, 'Well, if we are going to go our own separate ways it'll only work against us if they all still think we're in The Beatles.' So I said, 'There's been a clean break. Let's just admit it. Let's just tell the world now. Isn't it time?' John was a bit annoyed with me because I think he wanted to be the one to tell anyone – or *not* tell them.

RINGO: There was always the possibility that we could have carried on. We weren't sitting in the studio making *Abbey Road* saying, 'OK this is it: last record, last track, last take.'

But Paul put his solo record out and made the statement that said that The Beatles were finished. (If you look back through the Beatle history Paul has always made the statements: They're On Drugs; They're Breaking Up; They're Finished.) I think because it was said by one of The Beatles people understood it was over.

March 31

Dear Paul,
We thought a lot about yours and the Beatles L.P.s – and decided its stupid for Apple to put out two big Albums within 7 days of each other (also there's Ringo's and Hey Jude).
– So we sent a letter to E.M.I. telling them to hold your release date til June 4th (there's a big Apple – Capitol convention in Hawaii then)
– We thought you'd come round when you realized that the Beatles album was coming out on April 24th
– we're sorry it turned out like this –
– its nothing personal,
love John
and George
Hare Krishna.
A Mantra a Day Keeps MAYA' Away

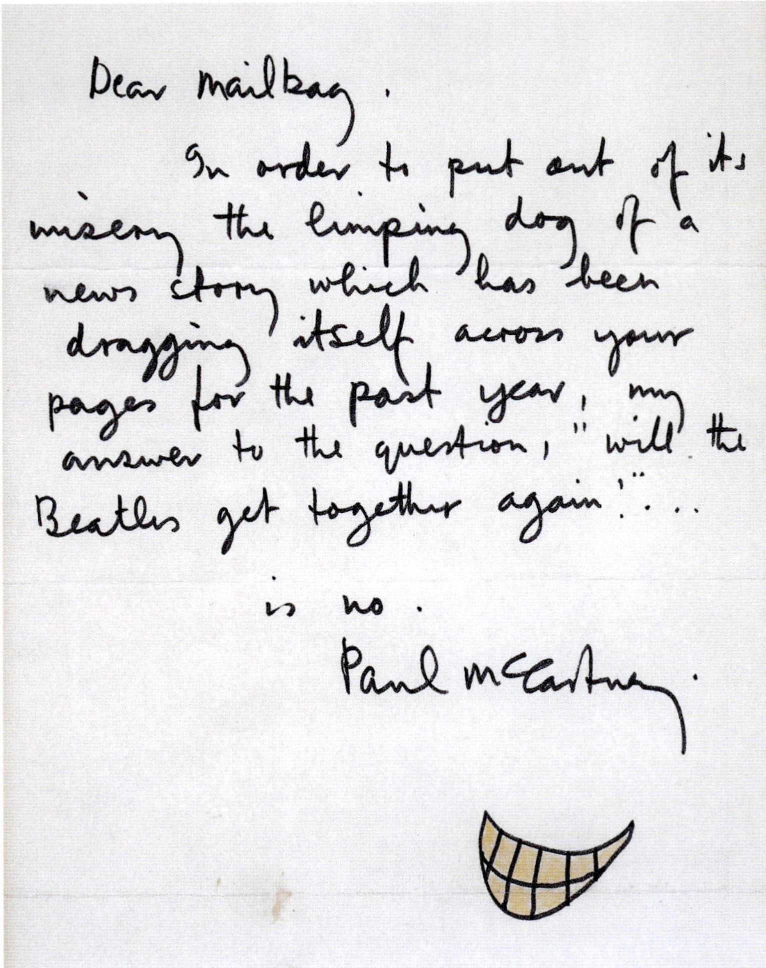

Dear mailbag.

In order to put out of it's misery the limping dog of a news story which has been dragging itself across your pages for the past year, my answer to the question, "will the Beatles get together again"... is no.

Paul McCartney.

PAUL: The world reaction was like 'THE BEATLES HAVE BROKEN UP – IT'S OFFICIAL' – we'd known it for months. So that was that, really. I think it was the press who misunderstood. The record had come with this weird explanation on a questionnaire of what I was doing. It was actually only for them. I think a few people thought it was some weird move of me to get publicity, but it was really to avoid having to do the press.

GEORGE: Paul has a way of using stuff. I mean, even now, if he is going to do a tour he'll conveniently tell the press that we're all getting back together again or something. It's just his way, really. It's something that over the years may have kind of annoyed us, but I think after all these years we're used to it. But in that period everybody was getting pissed off at each other for *everything*.

With his album, I think what he was trying to do was just grab a bit of the momentum of the time, and while everybody else was just accepting the fact that we'd split he was the one to use that for his own benefit: 'Oh, my album's coming out. And, incidentally, The Beatles have split up, you know.'

He had that press release, but everybody else had already left the band. That was what pissed John off at the time. It was, 'Hey, I've already left and it's as if he's invented it!'

PAUL: The others all saw me as the one who issued the statements, as if it was to my advantage (but I got caught with the LSD thing, and all I did on the break-up was, unlike them, to tell the truth). Years later, when the *Anthology* was coming together, I was asked in a press conference if we were getting back together. It was going to be true, so I said 'yeah', nothing more.

DEREK TAYLOR: *Reaction to Paul's statement was worldwide. Hot news. I'm a bit vague as to whether there was an actual announcement: 'The Beatles have broken up' at that time. I did put out a statement, one of those very circular statements that actually says nothing: 'John, Paul, George and Ringo are still John, Paul, George and Ringo; the world keeps spinning and when that stops that will be the time to worry. See you again.' Something like that. But there was worldwide reaction, and genuine dismay.*

*I absolutely did believe – as millions of others did – that the friendship The Beatles had for each other was a lifesaver for all of us. I believed that if these people were happy with each other and could get together and could be seen about the place, no matter what else was going on, life was worth living. But we expected too much of them.*

JOHN: They all have this wonderful dream of how it was, and it'll never be like that because it never was like everybody thinks it was. It was wonderful and it's over. And so dear friends you'll just have to carry on. The Dream Is Over.

GEORGE: I realise The Beatles did fill a space in the Sixties and all the people The Beatles meant something to have grown up. It's like with anything: you grow up with it and you get attached. That's one of the problems in our lives, becoming attached to things. And it's appreciated that people still like them, but the problem comes when they want to live in the past and want to hold on to something and are afraid to change.

JOHN: Everything's fun off and on, so I suppose it could have gone on being fun off and on or it could have got worse. It's just that you grow up. We don't want to be the Crazy Gang or The Marx Brothers being dragged on stage playing 'She Loves You' when we've got asthma and tuberculosis and when we're fifty.[71]

GEORGE: I think our splitting up was for the same reason, really, as for any individual. It was that we all needed more space and The Beatles had become a small place. Although it was an international hit recording band, it was still a very small place. When we talk about The Beatles, when it touches on our individual lives we can't really get into that much depth, because the perimeters of The Beatles were defined and our lives spilt over into other areas. We all had to get out. It was a pigeon-hole for us. We were bigger than The Beatles. I think we were, the four of us individually, bigger than it was.

It was too much stress, as well. We had taken on such a lot of stress from 1963, although at first we didn't realise it. It was just something which crept up on us. The pressure from our touring and the time schedule. When you look back at how many records we made and how many tours we did, you can't imagine that these days.

JOHN: We're all individuals. And in The Beatles we grew out of it. The bag was too small. I can't impose far-out films or far-out music on George and Paul if they don't want to do it. Vice versa, Paul can't impose on me whatever he likes, especially when there's no common goal any more. We have to live our own lives separately. We've grown up now, we've left school. We never left school – we went straight into showbiz.[71]

One has oneself in the beginning, and it's a constant process of society and parents and family trying to make you lose yourself: 'Don't cry. Don't show any emotion,' that kind of jazz. And that goes on all your life. I remember at sixteen I still had *myself* – from sixteen to twenty-nine is when it got lost. The struggle to mature, to be a man, to take responsibility... although we were in a cocoon of super-life we still had to go through the basic maturing that any teenager goes through (whether it's alone in a room or alone in a big office). Probably thirty is the age you should be just about waking up and realising that you're in control of yourself.

GEORGE MARTIN: *The split arose from many contributory things, mainly that each of the boys wanted to live his own life and had never been able to. They'd always been having to consider the group; so they were always a prisoner of that – and I think they eventually got fed up with it.*

*They wanted to live life like other people, where your wife is more important than your working partner. As Yoko came along, as eventually Linda came along, they were more important to John and Paul than John and Paul were to each other, and the same went for the other boys too.*

RINGO: Yoko's taken a lot of shit, her and Linda; but The Beatles' break-up wasn't their fault. It was just that suddenly we were all thirty and married and changed. We couldn't carry on that life any more.

JOHN: I was married from before The Beatles left Liverpool; that never made any difference. Cyn didn't have a career like Yoko does, but Pattie had a career – that never upset it. Maureen is a fantastic artist in her own right as well, apart from bringing up that tribe of Ringo's. She also is an artist, and it is nothing to do with wives.

The Beatles were disintegrating slowly after Brian Epstein died, it was slow death and it was happening. It's evident in *Let It Be*, although Linda and Yoko were evident then, but they weren't when we started it. It was evident in India when George and I stayed there and Paul and Ringo left. It was evident on the 'White' album. It's just natural. It's not a great disaster. People keep talking about it as if it's the end of the

earth. It's only a rock group that split up. It's nothing important. You have all the old records there if you want to reminisce. You have all this great music.[71]

RINGO: You don't turn the key and hear, 'OK, you're not a Beatle any more.' Because out there, to this day, that's all I am. You know what I'm saying? It's not like you could just slam the door and it's all over: you're back to being Richard Starkey, 10 Admiral Grove, Liverpool 8. It just carried on; we each carried on being one.

GEORGE: The Beatles were all of those things that happened. It's a matter of learning that up and down are the same thing. Everything keeps changing, and there's always a balance, and whatever happens is what you cause yourself. The moral of the story is that if you accept the high points you're going to have to go through the lows.

For The Beatles, our lives were a very heightened version of that: of how to learn about love and hate, and up and down, and good and bad, and loss and gain. It was a hyper-version of what everybody else was going through. So, basically, it's all good. Whatever happened is good as long as we've learnt something. It's only bad if we didn't learn: 'Who am I? Where am I going? Where have I come from?'

PAUL: No matter how much we split, we're still very linked. We're the only four people who've seen the whole Beatlemania bit from the inside out, so we're tied forever, whatever happens.

JOHN: The Beatles is over, but John, Paul, George and Ringo... God knows what relationship they'll have in the future. I don't know. I still love those guys! Because they'll always be those people who were that part of my life.[80]

PAUL: The Beatles felt like it was forever, but actually it was only ten years. It felt like twenty, the amount we packed into those ten years – all the music, all the different looks, even: the beards, the moustaches, the clean shavens, the little Cardin jackets, all that. It seemed like a long, long time. But I loved it.

JOHN: We were together much longer than the public knew us. It wasn't just from '64. I was twenty-four in '64 and I'd been playing with Paul since I was fifteen, and George about a year later. So it's a long time we spent together, in the most extraordinary circumstances, from lousy rooms to great rooms.[75]

It takes a lot to live with four people over and over for years and years, which is what we did. We'd called each other every name under the sun. We'd got to blows. We'd been through the whole damn show. We knew where we were at, we still do – we've been through the mill together for more than ten years. We've been through our therapy together many times.[74]

GEORGE: There was a close bond between us through all those years.

The Beatles can't ever really split up, because as we said at the time we did split up, it doesn't really make any difference. The music is there, the films are all there. Whatever we did is still there and always will be. What is there is there – it wasn't that important. It's like Henry VIII or Hitler or any of these historical figures they're always going to be showing documentaries about: their name will be written about forever and no doubt The Beatles' will be too. But my life didn't begin with The Beatles and it didn't end with The Beatles. It was just like going to school. I went to Dovedale, then I went to Liverpool Institute and then I went to The Beatles University for a bit and then I got out of university and now I'm having the rest of my life off.

The bottom line is, as John said, it was only a little rock'n'roll band. It did a lot and it meant a lot to a lot of people but, you know, it didn't really matter *that* much.

RINGO: I think that's too simple. For me it was a *really great* rock'n'roll band and we made a lot of good music which is still here today. But I know what John and George mean – we *were* just a little band from Liverpool. What always amazed me was that people like De Gaulle and Khrushchev and all these world leaders were shouting at us. I could never understand that.

I feel now, on reflection, that we could have used our power a lot more for good. Not for politics, but just to be more helpful. We could have been some bigger force. It's an observation, not a regret – regrets are useless. We could have been stronger for a lot more causes if we'd pulled it together.

JOHN: I don't regret anything I've done, really, except for maybe hurting other people. I wouldn't have missed any of it.[71]

GEORGE: I suppose in the mid-Sixties when the hippy stuff was starting we had a lot influence, but I don't think we actually had much power. (For instance, we didn't have enough power to stop some crazed Oliver Cromwell coming round to bust us all.)

Looking back, we'd probably change everything that we did, right from day one. But it'll do the way it was; you can't change things.

We *would* have changed things. We would have had more control if we'd known what we know now. But we did pretty good considering we were just four Liverpool lads. We did not do badly coping. I think that was the main thing we did – cope. A lot of other people who had less stress didn't cope as well. People would have one hit and be in strait-jackets and mental institutions. We just went on and on.

We were put under the heaviest pressure. I don't think anybody had had as much pressure as The Beatles; maybe in some way Elvis, but it was not quite as intense as with us. Part of the pressure of the time was the mania that was going on, plus the drugs and the police, and then the politics – everywhere we went there was political upheaval and riots.

JOHN: When I look back on it, it's vaguely astounding, the fact that I was in it. We always called it 'the eye of the hurricane'. It was calmer right in the middle than on the peripheries.[74]

GEORGE: It was a very one-sided love affair. The people gave their money and they gave their screams, but The Beatles gave their nervous systems, which is a much more difficult thing to give.

In some way we helped calm the places we went to, or we focused the energy on a positive energy, but for ourselves we were in the eye of the hurricane, weren't we? Everybody saw the *effect* of The Beatles, but nobody really ever worried about us as individuals, or thought, 'I wonder how the boys are coping with it all?' (People always called us the boys or The Beatles, more often than not failing to realise that The Beatles was four people. Four individuals.)

I got experience from it all, all the knowledge you gain by being famous and by dealing with all the situations, all the people, and the battering we received from the fans and the press and all that. It was an immeasurable amount of experience.

It was quite an astounding experience to have, but at the same time if we weren't in The Beatles we would have been in something else, not necessarily another rock'n'roll band. Karma is: what you sow, you reap. Like John said in 'All You Need Is Love': 'There's nowhere you can be that isn't where you're meant to be,' because you yourself have carved out your own destiny by your previous actions. I always had a feeling that *something* was going to happen, right from when I was at school – which is why I didn't get involved too much with schoolwork. It didn't really signal the end of my life that I didn't get any GCEs.

PAUL: The best times? For me it has to be split into segments: so the early days would be the pure joy of meeting showbiz stars – that star-struck element, the wonder of showbiz. In fact, I can still remember the others taking the mickey once, because I was really quite taken by meeting the Duke of Edinburgh. They'd all gone: '*What?!*' – 'Well, he is the Duke of Edinburgh after all.' I was convinced about all that at the time. So that would be the first phase. Then it was getting our first hit. We made Number Seventeen in the *NME* chart and I remember wanting to wind the window down – I was going past a little place called the Grafton in Liverpool – and I wanted to shout, 'We're Number Seventeen – wey-hey!' The thrill of our first chart position, and then our first Number One, all of that was pretty incredible. Then as we got together as a group... There were millions of great times. Too many to actually go over, so I'm picking out bits. Like in the back of the Austin Princess in the early days of cannabis indulgence – we used to have some very hysterical moments. About what I know not, but it was very, very funny.

Another wonderful thing was the joy of writing with John. John was a great talent. He was great to be around, very quick-witted and a very lovely soul. He could be a right bastard as well, unfortunately. But all in all, deep down, and having said that, he was a great person to know. He was a very charismatic guy. I was a bit of a John fan. I think we all were. And I think we had a mutual admiration going on there. When we started to bitch at each other I had quite a heavy period of self doubt. I'd be thinking, 'Uh oh, John was the great one, I was just stringing along.' But then I'd have to think to myself: 'Wait a minute, he wasn't a mug. He wouldn't work with me all that time if it didn't mean something to him.' One of the nicest little moments I remember from those years was when John had said he liked 'Here, There And Everywhere' better than any of his songs at the time – there were those silly little things.

RINGO: I was a big fan of John's. I always felt he had the biggest heart, and he wasn't the cynic that people thought. He had the biggest heart and he was the fastest. He was in and out. While we were still getting in he was out and on to the next round.

JOHN: All my friends were The Beatles, anyway. There was The Beatles and about three other fellas that I was really close with.

PAUL: It helped that we were like a gang together. Mick Jagger called us the Four-Headed Monster because we went everywhere together, dressed similarly. We'd all have black polo-neck sweaters and dark suits and the same haircut, so we did look a bit like a four-headed monster.

RINGO: There were lots of high points: one time when we played a gig in Glasgow – there was this *communication* going on, with the band and with the audience. That would have been 1963 or '64. There were some dates we did, some gigs when it was magical, and there were some gigs in the studio – some playing and some non-playing.

All the albums have great moments. There was so much good music. I was always (and still am to this day) really interested and excited about being in a band, and what a band does.

GEORGE: In the big picture it doesn't really matter if we never made a record or we never sang a song. That isn't important. At death, you're going to be needing some spiritual guidance and some kind of inner knowledge that extends beyond the boundaries of the physical world. On that basis I would say that it doesn't matter whether you're the king of a country or you're the Sultan of Brunei or you're a fabulous Beatle; it's what's inside that counts. Some of the best songs that I know are the ones I haven't written yet and it doesn't even matter if I don't ever write them, because it's only small potatoes compared with the big picture.

The 'White' album had some great music. I liked the musician situation, not everything else around it. *Sgt Pepper* is my least favourite, though it has some amazing stuff on it – it was great for (mainly) John and Paul to create all those sounds and get the violins in and instruments like that, because they were their songs; and when it came out it was *the* album. I don't know why I like it least – something to do with where my head was, or what was happening.

But, for me, *Revolver* – God! Some great stuff. Also, *Abbey Road*, the second side. And 'Yer Blues' on the 'White' album, you can't top it. It was the four of us. That is what I'm saying: it was really because the four of us were in a box, a room about eight by eight, with no separation. It was this group that was *together*; it was like grunge rock of the Sixties, really – grunge blues.

JOHN: In spite of all things, The Beatles really could play music together, if they're not uptight. And if I get a thing going, Ringo knows where to go, just like that, and he does well. We've played together so long that it fits. The thing that I sometimes miss is being able just to blink or make a certain noise and to know they'll all know where we are going on an ad lib thing.[70]

RINGO: I felt with us four it was magical and it was telepathy. When we were working in the studio sometimes it was just... it's indescribable, really. Although there were four of us, there was one of us; all of our hearts were beating at the same time. But the moment you think, 'Oh, aren't I playing well!' then you turn into shit.

JOHN: Anyway, I saw the life of Gauguin on TV, and it struck me that he'd died in such a pitiful way (VD, for which the 'cure' was mercury), with a foot broken and twisted from a drunken brawl after returning home for his first 'successful' opening in Paris.

He had gone to Tahiti to escape his own strait-jacket: working at a bank. A wife and children, one whom he was particularly fond of, a daughter to whom he had been dedicating a personal journal he kept whilst living in the South Pacific, explaining why he had left his family. When he returned to Tahiti, he received a letter from home telling him his daughter had died! What a price to pay to 'go down in history'. He finally finished his large 'masterwork', and died, the point being that, OK, he was a good painter, but the world could manage quite well without one scrap of his 'genius'. I believe the 'masterwork' was destroyed by fire after his death. The other point being, had he had access to so-called mysticism... fasting... meditation... and other disciplines (as in disciple), he could have reached the 'same space'. Hard work, I grant you, but easier than killing yourself and those around you.[78]

GEORGE: That was the great thing about John and what I got from him, from all those years. (And don't forget we all had different relationships with John. You can't just expect that all four of us felt or understood the same thing, or got the same relationship from one another. It's the story of diversity or multiplicity that many different relationships went on. John and I on a one-to-one basis had a very different relationship than I think he had with Ringo or he had with Paul.) He saw that we are not just in the material world; he saw beyond death, that this life is just a little play that is going on. And he understood that. You wouldn't claim something like Gauguin neglected his family for art, or dying for your painting is stupid – why bother? – unless you have a feeling that there *is* something bigger in life. A painting of a sunset cannot compare to the real sunset. Art (like music) is an insignificant attempt at reproducing what God does every moment.

Having gone through that LSD period with John, right from the first day we ever took it, I understood him and I believe our thoughts were much more in line with each other.

RINGO: I didn't find the answer. I think that would be really arrogant: 'Yes, I've got the answer!' I found *my* answer somewhere along the line. I thank God that I went through the Sixties, the Seventies and the Eighties to get where I am today, to feel comfortable with my spirituality.

No growth without pain is always the question and the answer. There is a lot of banging your head against the wall when you could be actually walking through the door. But that's what we all are – little human beings. God saved my life, I've always felt blessed. But there have been times I've got crazier and crazier and forgot about that blessing.

NEIL ASPINALL: *My happiest memories of being with the band were some of the laughs that we had backstage and in dressing rooms – when nobody else was around and we were swapping jokes together. No big deal, really. It was those little personal things that are my favourite moments and still are today. We did all enjoy one another's company and we always had a laugh. That was one of the big things right the way through everything, even today – we enjoy a laugh.*

RINGO: They became the closest friends I'd ever had. I was an only child and suddenly I felt as though I'd got three brothers. We really looked out for each other and we had many laughs together. In the old days we'd have the hugest hotel suites, the whole floor of a hotel, and the four of us would end up in the bathroom, just to be with each other. Because there were always pressures. Someone always wanted something: an interview, a hello, an autograph, to be seen with us, to speak to my dog, whatever.

SO THE FOUR OF US WERE REALLY CLOSE.
I LOVED IT. I LOVED THOSE GUYS.

We took care of each other and we were the only ones who had that experience of being Beatles. No one else knows what that's like. Even today, when the three of us get together, Paul and George are the only two who look at me like I am – not with the view: he's that and a Beatle. Everyone else does that; even our friends do that, there's always that underlying current.

In the way that the astronauts who went to the moon shared that unique experience together, it's absolutely true of The Beatles. We three are now the only people who can sit and understand each other and understand it.

I actually met a man who went to the moon and I asked him, 'When did the Earth stop being like we know it and get round like a planet?' And he said, 'Oh, I was too busy to notice.' I couldn't believe it! That was the big question – he was maybe the twelfth guy to be up there who could have noticed the point at which it became round, and didn't. I was shocked. But the Beatles were busy too, up there: though we were changing things, we were doing it and not looking around us. We were *it*, so we weren't looking for *it*. We were wearing collarless suits and suddenly the whole world was wearing them – we bought them in Cecil Gee's, it's not like we invented them. And we wore colourful clothes, and because we did it allowed a lot of other people to do the same.

PAUL: I think we gave some sort of freedom to the world. I meet a lot of people now who say The Beatles freed them up. If you think about it, the world was slightly more of an upper-class place till The Beatles came along. Regional actors had to have also a very good Shakespearean voice; and then it started to be enough just to have your own accent, your own truth. I think we set free a lot of people who were blinkered, who were perhaps starting to live life along their parents' authoritarian lines.

Whenever I'd get asked by a journalist, 'Have you studied anything?' – I studied a bit of literature, nothing much – I'd say, 'Oh yeah, Shakespeare,' and I'd always quote: 'To thine own self be true.' I think that was very apt with The Beatles. We always were *very* true to ourselves – and I think that the brutal honesty The Beatles had was important. So sticking to our own guns and really saying what we thought in some way gave some other people in the world the idea that they too could be truthful and get away with it, and in fact it was a good thing.

JOHN: The youth have hope because it's their future that they're hopeful about and if they're depressed about their own future, well, then we are in a bad state. And we keep hope alive by keeping it alive amongst ourselves and I have great hope for the future.

I think The Beatles *were* a kind of religion and that Paul epitomised The Beatles and the kind of things that were a hero image more than the rest of us, in a way. He was more popular with the kids, girls and things like that.

I think the Sixties was a great decade. I think the great gatherings of youth in America and in the Isle of Wight might have just been a pop concert to some people, but they were a lot more than that. They were the youth getting together and forming a new church, as it were, and saying, 'We believe in God, we believe in hope and truth and here we are, 20,000 or 200,000 of us, all together in peace.'[70]

GEORGE: The Beatles somehow reached more people, more nationalities, more parts that other bands couldn't reach. (If you listen to the music that's going on now, all the good stuff is stolen from The Beatles. Most of the good licks and riffs or ideas and titles. The Beatles have been plundered for thirty years.)

I think we gave hope to the Beatle fans. We gave them a positive feeling that there was a sunny day ahead and that there was a good time to be had and that you are your own person and that the government doesn't own you. There were those kind of messages in a lot of our songs.

PAUL: I do these songs still: 'Let It Be' and the like. And to actually see young kids crying over the spirit in the song, I'm very proud of that. It could have gone another way. I say to people, 'Hey, if The Beatles were really bad, we could have played Hitler's game. We could have got kids to do anything, such was our power.'

RINGO: I do get emotional when I think back about those times. My make-up is emotional. I'm an emotional human being. I'm very sensitive and it took me till I was forty-eight to realise that was the problem!

We were honest with each other and we were honest about the music. The music was positive. It was positive in love. They did write – we all wrote – about other things, but the basic Beatles message was Love.

RINGO: THERE WERE SOME REALLY LOVING, CARING MOMENTS BETWEEN FOUR PEOPLE: A HOTEL ROOM HERE AND THERE – A REALLY AMAZING CLOSENESS. JUST FOUR GUYS WHO REALLY LOVED EACH OTHER. IT WAS PRETTY SENSATIONAL.

GEORGE: I'D LIKE TO THINK THAT THE OLD BEATLE FANS HAVE GROWN UP AND THEY'VE GOT MARRIED AND THEY'VE ALL GOT KIDS AND THEY'RE ALL MORE RESPONSIBLE, BUT THEY STILL HAVE A SPACE IN THEIR HEARTS FOR US.

PAUL: I'M REALLY GLAD THAT MOST OF THE SONGS DEALT WITH LOVE, PEACE, UNDERSTANDING. THERE'S HARDLY ANY ONE OF THEM THAT SAYS: 'GO ON, KIDS, TELL THEM ALL TO SOD OFF. LEAVE YOUR PARENTS.' IT'S ALL VERY 'ALL YOU NEED IS LOVE' OR JOHN'S 'GIVE PEACE A CHANCE'. THERE WAS A GOOD SPIRIT BEHIND IT ALL, WHICH I'M VERY PROUD OF. ANYWAY… IT WERE A GRAND THING, THE BEATLES.

JOHN: WHEN I WAS A BEATLE, I THOUGHT WE WERE THE BEST GROUP IN THE GODDAMN WORLD. AND BELIEVING THAT WAS WHAT MADE US WHAT WE WERE![80] I'VE GROWN UP. I DON'T BELIEVE IN FATHER FIGURES ANY MORE, LIKE GOD, KENNEDY OR HITLER. I'M NO LONGER SEARCHING FOR A GURU. I'M NO LONGER SEARCHING FOR ANYTHING. THERE IS NO SEARCH. THERE'S NO WAY TO GO. THERE'S NOTHING. THIS IS IT. WE'LL PROBABLY CARRY ON WRITING MUSIC FOREVER.[67]

# SELECTED CAPTIONS

2: The Beatles in *A Hard Day's Night*.
5: The Beatles in April 1969.

## 1960-1962

41: (upper) Marlon Brando in *The Wild One*; (lower) Billy Fury and, right, John Lennon; (document) letter by Paul McCartney.
42-44: Auditioning for Larry Parnes, May 1960.
45: The Beatles' tour bus en route to Hamburg.
46: (bottom) Taken by John at Arnhem Cemetery: (l-r) Allan Williams, Beryl Williams, Lord Woodbine, Stuart Sutcliffe, Paul, George, Pete Best.
46-47: Photograph from George's collection.
48: (top two and middle right) Supplied by George; George's written note is from the reverse of the print pictured top left; the *Film Foto Pressedienst* logo is from the reverse of the original framed polaroid print.
49: Rory Storm and the Hurricanes, from Ringo's private collection (Ringo first left).
51: The Reeperbahn (top) and Grosse Freiheit (upper middle); George's handwritten set list (middle left); (bottom) Beatles on ship in Hamburg harbour, from George's private collection, with George's note (lower middle) from the reverse of the print.
52: (bottom left) Astrid Kirchherr.
57: (background) Illustration by Paul and Michael McCartney.
58-59: On the roof of the Top Ten Club, from George's collection. John is standing on the chimney on page 58.
59: (top) Paul's letter to Bob Wooler.
62: (bottom right) The cover of John's *Daily Howl* book, which he put together while at school.
64: John on the trip to Paris with Paul.
68: Poster from Paul's collection.
70: All photographs except bottom are from George's private collection.
71: The main image is from Ringo's collection.
72: Rehearsing at the Cavern.
73: (top left) John and Cynthia, newly married; in the background is their marriage certificate; photograph of Ringo with beard is from his private collection.
74-76, 78: Documents from Paul's private collection. The photographs on page 75 show the session at EMI Abbey Road Studios, 4th September 1962. George still has a black eye from the Cavern.

## 1963

82: Sessions at the BBC.
85: (top two pictures) Neil Aspinall is at the wheel of both the van and the car.
86: (main picture) Mal Evans; (bottom left) Mal is the one wearing glasses.
87: Eating with The Beatles (bottom centre) is Neil Aspinall, who is also pictured bottom right; the documents are from Paul's collection.
89: (upper centre) Paul's handwritten song list.
90-91 and 92 (left): At Abbey Road Studios with George Martin.
94: Paul supplied the poster, George the Roy Orbison document.
97: (top) George and John in the studio with Dick James; (middle) Dick James, George Martin and Brian Epstein; (bottom left) Neil and George in Bournemouth, August 1963.
99: On holiday in Tenerife, pictures courtesy of Ringo (middle left), Klaus Voormann (the two in colour) and George (all others). Also pictured are Astrid Kirchherr (top left and bottom right) and Klaus (bottom left).
100: All colour photographs supplied by Ringo; documents from Paul.
101: With Johnny Gustafson, bass-player with The Big Three, and Mick Jagger.
103: (drawing) From Paul's schoolbook; playing the London Palladium on 13th October 1963 (upper left) and 12th January 1964 (bottom right).
105: (top left) The Beatles meet Princess Margaret; (bottom left) Marlene Dietrich.
105-106: Documents from Paul's private collection.
107 (bottom right) With George Martin (left) and Brian Epstein (behind).
109: At a party at the Park Lane, London, home of John Bloom, then a successful washing-machine tycoon, 9th November 1963.

## 1964

112: (top right) John holds up a fan letter addressed to 'The Beatles, France' which has reached him at the George V Hotel, Paris; (middle) Brigitte Bardot.
114: (bottom) Bob Dylan.
115: (top) Paul's song lyric for 'I Want To Hold Your Hand'; (bottom left) in front of the Eiffel Tower; (right) with Brian Epstein.
118-119: *The Ed Sullivan Show*, February 1964; 119 (left) With Ed Sullivan; (right) Brian, Neil and John.
122: Miami Beach, February 1964.
124-125: At Abbey Road Studios recording *A Hard Day's Night*.
126: George at Marylebone Station, London, during the filming of *A Hard Day's Night*, April 1964.
127: Further shots of cast and crew including, in the third row, director Dick Lester (pictured on the left in the first image), and George with future wife Pattie Boyd and other actresses from the film (second image).
129: (bottom right) Dick Lester with the band.
131: (bottom left) Watching the rushes of *A Hard Day's Night*; (main picture) delivery of the prints to the Beacon Theatre, New York City.
134: (bottom) John, guest of honour at the bookshop Foyle's literary lunch held at The Dorchester, 23rd April 1964.
135-137: John, Cynthia, George and Pattie in Tahiti holiday photographs. Except for the one of Cynthia and Pattie in the middle of page 137, these are from George's collection.
140: Arriving in the rain in Sydney, Australia; Jimmy Nicol is on the right in both photographs.
141 (all), 142-143 (main picture) and 143 (bottom right): Tour photographs by George.
144: (top) The Beatles (John and Cynthia arm in arm) at the première of *A Hard Day's Night*, London Pavilion, Piccadilly Circus, 6th July 1964.
145: (top) John receiving the Variety Club of Great Britain's silver heart-shaped 'Show Business Personalities of 1963' Award, presented at London's Dorchester Hotel by the leader of the Labour Party, Harold Wilson (pictured left), 19th March 1964 – the occasion when John made his 'Purple Hearts' joke.
150: (lower right) Jayne Mansfield.
152: Derek Taylor is pictured with (main picture) George and (top right) Paul.
153: Derek addressing the crowd.
157: With Fats Domino.
159: Shown bottom middle are Brian and George Martin in a sequence of photos from the recording of *Beatles For Sale*.
161: (bottom) With George Martin.

## 1965

164-174: With the cast and crew on the set of *Help!* 165 (top) with Eleanor Bron, who plays Ahme in the film; 170 (top row, first picture) Eleanor Bron; (second picture) John with Dick Lester and Mal Evans; (third picture) Eleanor Bron with Dick Lester; (second row, first picture) Paul and Neil; (fourth row, second picture) Paul and Mal; (fifth row, first picture) John and George in disguise; (third picture) Neil and Mal; (sixth row, first picture) Leo McKern, who plays Clang in the film; 174: John's song lyric for 'Help!'
175: Paul's song lyric for 'Yesterday'.
176: (bottom left) Drawing by John; (bottom right) George beside his swimming pool mosaic, featuring John's illustration.
181: (top) George's MBE medal.
183: (bottom) Paul and George wore their MBE medals for the *Sgt Pepper* album cover photo session.
186-189: Performing at Shea Stadium, New York.
192: (letter) Memo from Brian Epstein to his personal assistant Wendy Hanson regarding The Beatles meeting Elvis Presley.
194: Paul and George with (centre) George Martin.
197: (background) John's lyric for 'In My Life'.
199: (bottom) Neil and Paul with a fan.

## 1966

206: (top left) Letter from George Harrison to Derek Taylor.
207: Includes George's song lyric for 'Taxman', and cheques from Paul and George to the Inland Revenue.
208: Gravestones of Eleanor Rigby and John McKenzie in the cemetery of St Peter's Parish Church, Woolton, Liverpool.
209: (middle left) George Martin with Paul, George and John; George with tamboura, the Indian drone instrument.
210: Robert Freeman's original design for the *Revolver* sleeve.
213-214: Making the promotional films for 'Paperback Writer'/'Rain' at Chiswick House and Abbey Road Studios, London; in the colour picture on 213 Paul is examining slides of the 'Butcher' cover photographs.
215: (top) Europe's smallest press photographer is lifted up to photograph The Beatles; (bottom) a Beatles fan in Tokyo, 1966.
216-219: Photographs from the 1966 tour of Japan and the Philippines; on 217 the two colour images feature Paul with Brian; below them are pictured Mal and Neil; bottom left is Brian; featured on 218 are (inset middle right) Imelda Marcos, and (background) John's handwritten verdict on the tour.
221: (letter) John's annotated reply to a 1971 letter from Peter Brown of Apple, on the tax controversy in the Philippines.
222: (top left) Letter from George Harrison to Derek Taylor; colour photographs supplied by George.
223: (bottom right) Letter from Brian to Maureen Cleave.
228: The Beatles at Candlestick Park, San Francisco, 29th August 1966, the last concert of their last tour.
230-232: John on the set of *How I Won The War* in Almeria, Spain.
233 and 234 (top): George's photographs from India, 1966, featuring him learning sitar with Ravi Shankar, and at the beach with Kamala Chakravarty and Ravi's student Shambhu Das.
235: (background) 'Ceiling Painting' from *Unfinished Paintings and Objects* by Yoko Ono, as exhibited at Indica Gallery, London, November 1966; (bottom right) illustration by John.

## 1967

239-240: Filming the promotional footage for 'Strawberry Fields Forever' and 'Penny Lane' in Knole Park, Sevenoaks, January-February 1967.
243-247: Recording *Sgt Pepper* at Abbey Road Studios; also pictured are (244 third row, first picture) George Martin with Paul; (245 top right) Mal, Paul and Neil; (245 fifth row, first picture) George and Paul laughing with George Martin; (245 bottom row, first picture) Neil.
248-253: The photography session for the *Sgt Pepper* cover.
249: (upper middle right) Neil and Paul with Michael Cooper, the cover photographer; Cooper's son Adam is also pictured with Paul and George in the main image; (bottom) the drumskin, today in Paul's private collection, was an alternative design to that pictured on the album cover.
252: (bottom left) One of the cardboard cut-outs included with the *Sgt Pepper* album.
253: (bottom right) At the press party to launch the album, which was held at Brian's London residence, 19th May 1967.
254: Message of peace and goodwill from The Beatles to the Monterey Pop Festival.
256-257: The *Our World* live broadcast of 'All You Need Is Love'.
258: Alexis Mardas, Pattie and George at London Heathrow Airport about to depart for Greece, 20th July 1967.
259: (top) George and Pattie in Golden Gate Park, San Francisco; (bottom) George on guitar with Alexis Mardas, Pattie and (centre of picture, facing George) Derek Taylor, and too many other friends besides.
264-267: Photographs of Brian Epstein, including (lower right on 264) the television presenter Richard Dimbleby announcing Brian's death.
269: (photographs) Various designs proposed for Apple's logo.
271-277: Making *Magical Mystery Tour*: the recruiting sergeant with Paul on 273 is played by Victor Spinetti; on 276 John is shovelling spaghetti for Aunt Jessie (Jessie Robins) in his dream sequence; and on 277 George is at the striptease show.
278: (top photographs) The promotional film for 'Hello, Goodbye'; (background) Paul's song lyric for the song; (bottom) Ringo filming *Candy*.

## 1968

281-286: The Beatles in Rishikesh in early 1968. The pictures on 282 and the two on the left on 283 are George's; on the right on 283 John is in the helicopter with the Maharishi; Mike Love is pictured with George (bottom right on 283) and again at bottom left on 284, this time with John (left) and Donovan; the handwriting and drawing on 284 is Paul's list of songs written in Rishikesh, plus a drawing of Mal Evans, taken from Paul's notebook, which is itself featured on 285 (lower middle); top right on 285 is Mia Farrow.
287: John and Paul at the press conference in New York to launch Apple, May 1968.
288: (top left) Apple advertisement for musicians to send their tapes to the new label; Paul's original sketch for it is at bottom right.
289: (top left) Paul with Mary Hopkin; (right) Drawing by John picturing Derek's office at Apple.
291: Alexis Mardas and documents relating to Apple Electronics.
292-293: (illustrations) Animation from the film *Yellow Submarine*.
294-295: On 28th July 1968, The Beatles undertook a full day of photo sessions at locations around London, including (four portrait shots on 294) Wapping, (294 bottom right) Thomson House Studio, and (all others) St Pancras Gardens; (294 top left) yearbook with John's annotated verdict on the day, from Paul's private collection.
297: John and Julian.
298: Filming 'Hey Jude' at Twickenham Film Studios; David Frost is pictured at bottom right.
299: During the filming of the 'Revolution' promo.
300: John and Yoko in the cover image from *Two Virgins*.
303: (middle left) Drawing by Paul; annotations to documents are by John.
304: Illustration by John.
305-311: The making of the 'White' album; documents featured include George's lyric for 'While My Guitar Gently Weeps' (in the background on 306), and annotations by John to printed lyrics for 'Happiness Is A Warm Gun' (on the left on 307).

## 1969-70

314-317: Recording and filming *Let It Be* at Twickenham Film Studios, January 1969.
318-321: The *Let It Be* sessions at Apple Studios, late January; Billy Preston is pictured on 319 (top left); the lyrics on 320 are John's 'I've Got A Feeling' and Paul's 'Two Of Us'.
322: The concert on the roof at Apple on 30th January.
323: (top) Original sleeve designs proposed for the *Let It Be* album (originally titled *Get Back*), the cover image taken at EMI House in exactly the same location as that of their first UK album *Please Please Me* (see page 93); the unsigned memo (bottom right) is addressed to Paul.
325: The front door of Apple, 3 Savile Row.
328: (top) Peter Sellers in *The Magic Christian*.
329: (top) Ringo and Peter Sellers in *The Magic Christian*; (illustrations) Paul's sketched ideas for the soundtrack album design.
330: (main picture) Linda and Paul on their wedding day with Heather; (bottom right) Mal, Linda and Paul in the back of the car.
332: Illustrations are by John; the document is the official declaration by John of his change of name from John Winston Lennon to John Ono Lennon, signed 22nd April 1969.
334: The Beatles with Yoko Ono.
335: John and Yoko's bed-in, Montreal, May 1969; annotations on yearbook by John.
336-339: Recording *Abbey Road* at Abbey Road Studios; on 336 is Paul's lyric for 'She Came In Through The Bathroom Window'; the document on 338 is the police list of John's possessions held for him following his car accident on 1st July 1969; on 339 is George's lyric for 'Here Comes The Sun'.
341-343: Photo session outside Abbey Road Studios for the *Abbey Road* album cover; illustrations on 341 are Paul's sketches for the session.
347: (top left) Illustration by John.
350: (top left) John with The Plastic Ono Band performing 'Instant Karma' at BBC TV Centre, 11th February 1970, for the programme *Top Of The Pops*.
351: Paul and Heather, photographed by Linda.
353: The final photo session, at Tittenhurst Park.
355: The Beatles in 1963.
357: The Beatles at the beginning of 1966.

# ACKNOWLEDGEMENTS

*Genesis Publications would like to thank the following whose kind assistance was invaluable in compiling this book:*
Neil Aspinall, Jeremy, Aaron, Brian and Cathy at Apple, all at Apple Productions, Michael Shulman and Eric Young at Archive Photos, Geoff Baker, Johnny 'Guitar' Byrne, Maureen Cleave, David Costa and all at Wherefore Art?, Andy Davis, Joe Dolce, Susanne Eder, Ruth Edge at EMI Archives, Kai-Uwe Franz, Giuseppe and Nicola Gilardi, Tetsuo Hamada, Hugh Hefner, Paul Higgens, Trevor Hobley, Jools Holland, David Hughes at EMI, Shelagh Jones and all at MPL, Astrid Kirchherr, Allan Kozinn, Arthur Kretchmer, Ulf Krüger, Diana LeCore, Mark Lewisohn, Virginia Lohle, Ian MacCarthy, Michael McCartney, Stephen Maycock, Karla Merrifield, Elliot Mintz, Robbie Montgomery, Pete Nash, Zoe Norfolk at Linda's Photo Library, Staffan Olander, Alan Ould, Michael Phillips, Pete Shotton, Greg Swan, Derek Taylor, Sue Weiner, Jann Wenner, Kay Williams, Joan Woodgate.

# PHOTOGRAPHIC CREDITS

*The following copyright holders kindly provided photographs and/or other illustrative material for the book:*

Paul McCartney, Linda McCartney, Michael McCartney, George Harrison, The Harrison Family, Ringo Starr, The Starkey Family, Yoko Ono Lennon, Lennon Archive, Apple Corps Ltd.

Gene Anthony, Archive Photos, Glenn A. Baker Archives, Barnaby's, The Bluecoat Press, Jane Bown, Leslie Bryce/Beat Publications Ltd, Johnny 'Guitar' Byrne, Camera Press, Capitol Records Inc., CBS News, Christie's, Maureen Cleave, Commonwealth Films, Andy Davis, EMI Records, Express Newspapers, Curt Gunther, Steve Hale, Hulton Getty, K&K Hamburg, Leslie Kearney, Astrid Kirchherr, Richard Lester, London Features International, Iain Macmillan, Gered Mankowitz, Jim Marshall, Mirror Syndication International, Popperfoto, Redferns, Reuters Television, Rex Features Ltd, Geoff Rhind, Charles Roberts, Cheniston Roland, Max Scheler, Walter Shenson Films, Sotheby's, Subafilms Ltd, Derek Taylor, Tom Wilkes.

*Works owned by Apple Corps Ltd that are used in this book include photographs taken by the following:*
Michael Cooper, Robert Freeman, Monte Fresco, Stephen Goldblatt, Dezo Hoffmann, Peter Kaye, John Kelly, Angus McBean, Bruce McBroom, Richard Matthews, Ethan Russell, Terence Spencer, Robert Whitaker.

# TEXT SOURCES

The John Lennon narrative has been compiled from a great many individual sources. The following have all granted their material to be reproduced in *The Beatles Anthology*—

Apple Corps Ltd; Archbuild Ltd; Beat Publications Ltd; Jerry G. Bishop; CAPITAL RADIO, LONDON; *The Daily Mail*; *The Daily Mirror*; Daphne Productions; Hunter Davies; EVENING STANDARD / SOLO; IPC Magazines; KSAN Radio; INA—INSTITUT NATIONAL DE L'AUDIOVISUEL; ITN; Larry Kane; *The Liverpool Echo*; Miller Freeman Entertainment; Elliot Mintz; Annie Nightingale; Paul Drew Enterprises; PolyGram Television International; *The Sunday Times*; Westwood One, Inc; WNEW-FM; WPLJ-FM.

Extracts from *Skywriting By Word Of Mouth*, written by John Lennon, appear courtesy of Jonathan Cape and Yoko Ono Lennon.

Extracts from Stuart Sutcliffe's letters appear by kind permission of Pauline Sutcliffe.

Extracts from JOHN LENNON—FOR THE RECORD by Peter McCabe. Copyright © 1984 by Peter McCabe and Robert Schonfeld. Used by permission of Bantam Books, a division of Bantam Doubleday Dell Publishing Group, Inc.

THE MIKE DOUGLAS SHOW excerpts courtesy of EYEMARK Entertainment.

Excerpts from The Tonight Show and The Tomorrow Show © courtesy of National Broadcasting Company, Inc. All Rights Reserved.

*New York Times* excerpts copyright © 1966 by The New York Times Company. Reprinted by permission.

Quotes taken from 'John Lennon In His Own Words' by Miles used by permission of Omnibus Press.

A Cellarful of Noise, written by Brian Epstein, published by Souvenir Press.

Extracts from the following programmes reproduced by kind permission of the BBC: 24 Hours; The Andy Peebles Show; Beatles Abroad; The Charlie Gillett Show; Lennon & McCartney Songbook; The Mersey Sound; The Michael Parkinson Show; The Old Grey Whistle Test; BBC Overseas; Pop Profile; The Kenny Everett Show; Where It's At; Release; Saturday Club; Scene and Heard; Tonight; Transcription Service; World of Books.

Excerpts from LENNON REMEMBERS reproduced by kind permission of Jann Wenner and Rolling Stone.

# SONG CREDITS

I WANT TO HOLD YOUR HAND
Written by Lennon/McCartney
Copyright © 1963 Sony/ATV Music Publishing
All Rights Reserved Used by Permission

HELP!
Written by Lennon/McCartney
Copyright © 1965 Sony/ATV Songs LLC. (Renewed) All rights administered by Sony/ATV Music Publishing, 8 Music Square West, Nashville, TN 37203
All Rights Reserved Used by Permission

IN MY LIFE
Written by Lennon/McCartney
Copyright © 1965 Sony/ATV Songs LLC. (Renewed) All rights administered by Sony/ATV Music Publishing, 8 Music Square West, Nashville, TN 37203
All Rights Reserved Used by Permission

YESTERDAY
Written by Lennon/McCartney
Copyright © 1965 Sony/ATV Songs LLC. (Renewed) All rights administered by Sony/ATV Music Publishing, 8 Music Square West, Nashville, TN 37203
All Rights Reserved Used by Permission

TAXMAN
Written by George Harrison
Copyright © 1966 Sony/ATV Songs LLC. (Renewed) All rights administered by Sony/ATV Music Publishing, 8 Music Square West, Nashville, TN 37203
All Rights Reserved
Used by Permission

HELLO, GOODBYE
Written by Lennon/McCartney
Copyright © 1967 Sony/ATV Songs LLC. (Renewed) All rights administered by Sony/ATV Music Publishing, 8 Music Square West, Nashville, TN 37203
All Rights Reserved
Used by Permission

LUCY IN THE SKY WITH DIAMONDS
Written by Lennon/McCartney
Copyright © 1967 Sony/ATV Songs LLC. (Renewed) All rights administered by Sony/ATV Music Publishing, 8 Music Square West, Nashville, TN 37203
All Rights Reserved
Used by Permission

WHEN I'M 64
Written by Lennon/McCartney
Copyright © 1967 Sony/ATV Songs LLC. (Renewed) All rights administered by Sony/ATV Music Publishing, 8 Music Square West, Nashville, TN 37203
All Rights Reserved
Used by Permission

HAPPINESS IS A WARM GUN
Written by Lennon/McCartney
Copyright © 1968 Sony/ATV Songs LLC. (Renewed) All rights administered by Sony/ATV Music Publishing, 8 Music Square West, Nashville, TN 37203
All Rights Reserved
Used by Permission

HEY, JUDE
Written by Lennon/McCartney
Copyright © 1968 Sony/ATV Songs LLC. (Renewed) All rights administered by Sony/ATV Music Publishing, 8 Music Square West, Nashville, TN 37203
All Rights Reserved
Used by Permission

SHE CAME IN THROUGH THE BATHROOM WINDOW
Written by Lennon/McCartney
Copyright © 1969 Sony/ATV Songs LLC. (Renewed) All rights administered by Sony/ATV Music Publishing, 8 Music Square West, Nashville, TN 37203
All Rights Reserved
Used by Permission

TWO OF US
Written by Lennon/McCartney
Copyright © 1969 Sony/ATV Songs LLC. (Renewed) All rights administered by Sony/ATV Music Publishing, 8 Music Square West, Nashville, TN 37203
All Rights Reserved
Used by Permission

I'VE GOT A FEELING
Written by Lennon/McCartney
Copyright © 1970 Sony/ATV Songs LLC. (Renewed) All rights administered by Sony/ATV Music Publishing, 8 Music Square West, Nashville, TN 37203
All Rights Reserved
Used by Permission

# INDEX TO ALBUMS & SONG TITLES

# INDEX